PLACE IN RETURN BOX
to remove this checkout from your record.
TO AVOID FINES return on or before date due.

DATE DUE	DATE DUE	DATE DUE

1/98   c:/CIRC/DateDue.p65-p.14

FDB

FDB

COMPILED BY

Lakshmi Dias Bandaranaike

Published in Sri Lanka 1994
by Lakshmi Dias Bandaranaike

© Copyright Lakshmi Dias Bandaranaike

Designed by
Ananda Harischandra

Printed & Bound by
Aitken Spence Printing (Pvt) Ltd.
Colombo 2, Sri Lanka

ISBN 955-95743-0-2

This book is essentially a wife's tribute to a husband whom she loved and admired as a unique friend and companion.

We shared many triumphs and experienced hurtful turbulence, injustice and ingratitude.

But most of all we lived to enjoy and remember the simple joys of our marriage.

Lakshmi Dias Bandaranaike

Contents

Acknowledgements

FDB is a labour of love by friends and associates of Felix Dias Bandaranaike in which they have recorded their impressions and recollections of him. These represent a wide range of experiences reflecting different relationships which include the observations of friends and relatives, accounts of his Ministerial activities in the various portfolios which he held, by officials who worked closely with him and general assessments of his remarkable and many-faceted career which spanned a period of 17 years and had a decisive impact on the life of the nation. As eye-witness accounts which are based on first-hand knowledge and experience they are both authentic and authoritative. They are intended to serve as a testament to the achievements of a man who was a giant in his lifetime. The outstanding feature of his Ministerial career was the number and crucial importance of the portfolios he was called upon to handle, at times concurrently with his Deputy Ministership of Defence and External Affairs as the only continuity. He was a veritable *tour de force* who made an indelible impression in his several spheres of activity resulting in a record of achievement which is unequalled.

All the contributions embodied in this book were made voluntarily and freely by the writers concerned as their individual tributes to Felix Dias Bandaranaike. Their names are indicated with the Chapter headings and there is no need to enumerate them here, besides saying that they are all public servants, writers and other persons who have distinguished themselves in the public life of our country. I am indeed moved by their ready co-operation in this project and the time and energy they have contributed to realise it. To them I wish to extend my sincerest thanks and appreciation for their labour of love to honour the memory of a leader whom they held in the highest esteem. I also wish to place on record my appreciation of the services rendered by all those associated with the publication of this work. Their ready co-operation and promptness have enabled me to ensure its publication on schedule.

Apart from the contributors and publishers there are also a large number of persons who helped in various ways in carrying out this project. I refer to those who provided me with valuable source material whether as documents or relating their personal experiences of Mr Bandaranaike which have been incorporated and enriched it. There was besides valuable advice and suggestions which I received from various quarters which I acknowledge with gratitude. This book therefore represents the combined efforts of writers, friends, well-wishers who acting in regular consultation with me made it possible, thereby realising what was for me a cherished dream of paying my own tribute to my husband.

I must however make special mention of Haris Hulugalle, a close friend of Felix and our university contemporary who assisted me from the very genesis of this compilation. Haris who has stood by Felix in good times and in bad was a source of inspiration and encouragement in this undertaking. Without his perceptive comments and advice this book would have taken longer to publish.

I must also mention with appreciation the many ways in which Elmo de J. Seneviratne, one of the officials who accompanied Felix on several missions to the Middle-East in 1974 and 1975; helped to collect relevant material before it was sent for publication.

Finally I should like to thank Victor Gunewardena for the assistance he so readily gave me during the final stages in the preparation of this book.

But above all I would like to thank my cousin, Reggie Wijesekera, retired Director of Aitken Spence Printing (Pvt) Ltd., for all the co-operation and technical advice he gave me in attending to this arduous task.

Lakshmi Dias Bandaranaike

Felix Dias Bandaranaike caricatured by Wijesoma, 1972.

Introduction

Felix Dias Bandaranaike

Felix Dias Bandaranaike is dead and his funeral obsequies have taken place on his own wishes without fanfare or flourish. The end was not typical of the man, for the ebullient touch and the theatrical flourish were so much an intrinsic part of his public personality. But then Felix Dias Bandaranaike died in limbo, without public office and even civic rights, and the obsequies on his death were appropriate for a man who in political exile had increasingly turned to his own inner vision of things and his own peculiar faith.

Felix Reginald Dias Bandaranaike will defy assessment by students of politics and history for some time because if ever there was a politician who aroused controversy and passionate feeling it was Felix Dias Bandaranaike. There was little doubt that his was among the pivotal influences within both the SLFP and its Government during the 1960-77 era. This influence was sources both in his family connections with the then Prime Minister Mrs Sirima Bandaranaike as well as in his own undoubted brilliance which he brought into the many vital portfolios which he adorned. He was the chief spokesman and strategist of the SLFP, the iron figure on whom the Party and the Government fell back in their moments of crisis, activist and ideologue – in short the quintessential politician.

Felix Dias Bandaranaike belonged to a different time and milieu – the milieu which produced the SLFP's own founder in fact – but when he was so suddenly hurled into politics on the death of Mr S. W. R. D. Bandaranaike he adjusted himself to the vastly different times with characteristic aplomb.

The pipe-smoking Felix Dias Bandaranaike relished electioneering in Dompe once riding a bicycle much to the glee of newspapers. His was a spirit bubbling over with wit and repartee, revelling in the wisecrack and the back-handed gambit – the eternal Puck who could smile even in the face of withering defeat.

But there was also another Felix Dias Bandaranaike – the politician and administrator who was impatient with the ingrained habits of the inherited system, who did not suffer fools gladly and whose patrician ways at the height of power could easily deteriorate into arrogance.

As a SLFP politician he belonged to the party's right-of-centre track and was the favourite whipping-boy of the Left once it had tottered from the coalition pedestal, but as the reforms which he introduced into the Administrative Service as Minister of Public Administration and into the Judicial System as Minister of Justice show he was acutely sensitive of the need for change in the administration and the judicial service.

Felix Dias Bandaranaike, then, was among the most brilliant of Sri Lanka's home grown politicians. He had no benefit of a foreign education but, both in intellectual standing and ability to hold his own on his feet, he was the equal of any politician both, Sri Lanka and foreign.

He was neither a product of the London School of Economics or Oxford or Cambridge – those nurseries of so many post-independence politicians of newly emergent Third World countries.

His was an intellect and wit honed in essentially indigenous conditions, but he made an art of mental agility until this became his most striking hallmark. The apotheosis of his public career was the role he played as Chairman of the Non-Aligned Foreign Ministers' Meeting which preceded the Non-Aligned Summit of 1976 in Sri Lanka.

If that was the hour of his glory he died under different skies but overlaying the personality of the eternal Puck was the nature of an introvert which would have helped him to reconcile himself to the sudden transformation difficult though it would have been.

Patriot

1O DOWNING STREET

THE PRIME MINISTER

25 July, 1985

My dear Mrs. Bandaranaike,

    I was very sorry indeed to hear of your husband's
death and send you my deepest sympathy. I knew him because
we were lawyers as well as politicians and I had the greatest
respect for him. He gave most distinguished service to his
country; and his loss will be felt no less keenly among his
many friends in Britain.

Yours sincerely

Margaret Thatcher

Mrs. Lakshmi Dias Bandaranaike.

Excerpts from the FDB Memorial Lecture by Mrs Sirimavo R. Dias Bandaranaike

ON
"SRI LANKA AND NON-ALIGNMENT"
AT THE BANDARANAIKE MEMORIAL INTERNATIONAL CONFERENCE HALL, COLOMBO, 5TH NOVEMBER 1987

I am greatly honoured by the invitation extended to me by the Felix Dias Bandaranaike Memorial Trust to deliver this lecture on "Sri Lanka and Non-Alignment" and I wish to thank the Trust Committee for their kind invitation.

This lecture is more than a formal academic occasion. For me it means a memorial tribute, in the first place, to a distinguished Sri Lankan who stood with me and by me in the exciting, turbulent and often dangerous arena of politics for almost a quarter century – a close associate and an exceptionally able aide.

Felix Dias Bandaranaike was a remarkably gifted man. He had a fine scholastic record at school, University and Law College. He was a born orator and a debater, resourceful and sharp in argument, and blessed with a cutting wit and an impish sense of humour. His opponents in Parliament, all of them older and more experienced, recognised a formidable foe.

Felix Dias Bandaranaike was a brilliant lawyer, his initial choice as a career. However, unlike other members of his immediate family, who won renown in the field of Law, as Judge or Scholar, Felix chose the path of politics, a profession which allowed him wider and more direct access to the people, and therefore ampler opportunities to serve them. He joined the Sri Lanka Freedom Party and entered Parliament in 1960.

From that very first year I recognised his intellectual calibre, his boundless capacity for work and his total dedication to the democratic socialist ideals, principles and programmes of our party. While his intellectual commitment to those ideals never wavered, I was soon to discover that he shared with the founder of our party, Mr. S.W. R. D. Bandaranaike, a passion and a flair for International Affairs, a subject which gave them both a special intellectual excitement.

As you know the late Mr Felix Dias Bandaranaike was a Minister in my cabinet in both Governments I headed after the general elections in 1960 and 1970. He was one of the brightest and ablest Ministers I appointed. At various times he held some of the most important portfolios in my cabinet and despite his relative youth distinguished himself in all of them....

...The late Mr Felix Dias Bandaranaike, as a member of my Government played an important role in helping me to formulate and implement the country's foreign policy on the basis of these principles and considerations. His untimely death has robbed us all of the services of a remarkable politician when such services are most needed in these troubled times.

Reminiscences

John de Saram

Lakshmi has asked me to write a few words in remembrance of Felix for inclusion in these recollections of Felix recorded, by some of those who were closely associated with Felix at various stages in his much too short a life.

I was among those who were privileged to know Felix in the earlier years.

The wonderful years when one is neither too young nor too old; when there is still exuberance to feeling and thought; a lightness of step; a vibrancy to relationships; when friendships made are often of a closeness that survives the passage of time.

These years, for us, encompassed, I would say, the years between the Lower Sixth of the Royal College and our first few years at the Bar at Hulftsdorp.

We went our different ways thereafter. He, as we all know, to great national and international distinction and, as we all know, to great unjustifiable tragedy.

Yet our paths would cross from time to time. The feelings of personal friendship would endure.

I feel greatly privileged, and feel the more so as I now, composing this recollection, look back in twilight years through mists of times gone by, to have known Felix, and Lakshmi, in those early years: at the time they first got to know each other and when Felix first told me Lakshmi was the girl he would marry as we were both riding our bicycles back from the Royal College up Deal Place in Colombo; later when we were all undergraduates in the Law Faculty of the University; and later still when I was Felix's bestman at their marriage.

It was Lakshmi, of course, it seemed to all of us who knew both Felix and Lakshmi then, who gave Felix the deep affection, the care, the intellectual companionship, and above all the understanding; which he, reared as he was in a tradition of almost Victorian formality, seemed to require so vitally if he were to live as fully as his extraordinarily superior intelligence required that he should.

From when I first met him in the corridors of Royal till when, more than a quarter century later, I last said good-bye, shortly after the injustices against him in his final years, it was that extraordinary personality of Felix's that was so impressive. It was certainly of no common or garden variety.

The clarity and quickness of mind, the precision and sharpness of language, the analysis, the retort, the flashes of humour, the impatience with pretence, the loyalty to friends and I would think often to a fault, the vast energy of intellect, the great moral and physical courage. And then, also, surprisingly, some might say in a personality of such forcefulness, the kindness, warmth and gentleness, especially to the young, which endeared him to all who were privileged to know him closely.

There was in him, one might say, an extraordinary confluence of many qualities, an amalgamation of traits, a crystallisation of a personality of leadership. And of this there were so many instances.

One still lingers in memories of those who were there; Sir Ivor Jennings, the brilliant constitutional lawyer and first Vice-Chancellor of what was then the University of Ceylon presiding over the Board of Examiners conducting the "awesome" oral interviews of candidates for admission to the University, and inquiring jestingly of the 18-year-old Felix whose father, like his grand-uncle, was a judge of the Supreme Court: "And I suppose entering the Faculty of Law; you would expect in time to become a Judge of the Supreme Court," and receiving the immediate response in corresponding jest: "On the contrary, Sir, I think I would rather be the Vice-Chancellor of a University examining candidates for admission."

Looking back now through the mists of past times I still think of Felix as one of the most impressive people I have known. I am grateful for the privilege of having known him in those more carefree times in the nineteen forties and fifties in Colombo.

As someone once said, we are in this life like travellers on voyages; our various paths crossing and recrossing from time to time and allowing some of us to continue on the same path for a while; and, as the more spiritual amongst us may say, indeed travellers on endless journeys through eternity and with our paths crossing and recrossing from time to time in years to come.

If that is so I feel privileged to have travelled with Felix for a while and look forward to when our paths hopefully will cross once again.

To Lakshmi who has, with such profound love and profound sadness, put together this volume of recollections, I would like to say in closing how grateful I am to her for having asked me to record my own personal note of recollection of Felix in the earlier years.

Part I
The Human Story

CHAPTER I

My Husband, Felix

To compile a book about your own husband is no easy task because it would not and could not be as dispassionate as it should be. Married life – the joys, sorrows, trials and burdens are intertwined with one's own emotions and attitudes, some of them preconceived, and some conditioned by the environment in which we moved. Nevertheless, I have attempted to put down the events in some kind of order so that the reader can see a connection between the various incidents, some highlighted, some underplayed, some barely stated in a factual sort of way which constituted the life of a man who was an idealist in every sense of the word, a man who fought for what he thought was the right even though the whole world may have opposed him. In this he made himself vulnerable because he did not realise that he was enveloped in a scheming political ring where the characters were willing to sacrifice him for their own advantage. It is a sad commentary on the rewards of human loyalty, selflessly given with no strings attached.

Felix's Schooldays

Felix spent his kindergarten years at Trinity College, Kandy, as his father was District Judge of the district.

Later he entered Ladies College, Colombo. At his first interview with the Principal of Ladies College (an English lady) he was asked to relate a Bible story and he promptly related the story about the woman with an issue of blood. Felix recalled that she showed astonishment at a five-year-old possessing such knowledge. When asked how he learnt this particular story, he remembered informing her that this was just one of the many Bible stories his mother had taught him.

To Felix, attending a girls school and specially the one his sister Christine attended as well, was definitely below his dignity. He did have cause to be uncomfortable at school. Since Felix was a well-built boy, he said many a time the big girls teased him, using the word "fatso." His mother, who was convinced that Felix should learn all the social graces sent him for dancing classes to Mrs Timmy Ingleton and to Miss Marjorie Sample. I remember

1

Mrs Kelaart, an excellent seamstress known very well to the family, often going into raptures over how well Felix looked in a pumpkin costume made by her for a concert.

Felix had vivid recollections of afternoons spent on tiny mats provided by the school and that he never liked staying near mats that had been watered by his classmates. He recalled often sharing a drink of orange with the present principal of Ladies College (Mrs Sirancee Goonewardene). Among the humorous episodes retold by him about his school life, was the mock marriage ceremony he was forced into with Sheila Oliver, another classmate at Ladies College.

Although boys were permitted to study up to the 5th Standard at Ladies College, his father was summoned one day to the school and advised to send his podgy son to a boys school. It was felt that he would be more at home with boys of his own age, and so he was admitted to the leading boys school in Colombo, Royal College, which was the old school of his father and brother Dr. R. W. M. Dias (later of Magdalene College Cambridge). Felix was in his element at Royal College because here he could be on par with his classmates. Moreover he had learnt that girls are not always made of sugar and spice and all that's nice!

He loved his mother very dearly. He recalled that when he went home with a huge black bruise on his face after a fight, she gently treated it by placing a patch of raw meat over the area. (The home remedy at the time!)

The Royal-Thomian cricket match was, I believe, an event to give vent to pent-up feelings. I remember at Ladies College it was customary to watch the Royalists invade the school premises on the Royal-Thomian match days. Once the dare-devil Felix opened the gates and entered the premises on the pretext of borrowing a pencil from his sister Christine. Of course, the three days of match fever at the Oval or the SSC ended with glorious nights when one got totally sozzled meeting with friends. And on such occasions Felix had no alternative but to creep up the stairs on all fours. However, for Felix his mother would be there at the top of the stairs, ready to receive her son with a tender touch and forgiving eyes.

His father was on the contrary very strict. Felix recounted the times his father entertained his foreign friends, Freemasons or fellow colleagues in the legal profession. Christine and Felix were made to have their dinner upstairs, not to be seen or heard on these occasions. They used to wait patiently for the pudding (or rather for whatever was left of it) after the dinner.

During the war when there were air raids over Colombo by the Japanese, the Royalists were forbidden to leave their school premises. Felix recounted an incident, where he scooted off to a theatre with some friends. The moment they entered the premises, the air raid siren had sounded. Unfortunately for

Felix a photographer had taken a picture of them huddled together. This appeared in the newspapers the next day. Not only was he punished at school but he had to bear the extreme anger of his father. Of course, his mother was there to console him and advise him not to repeat it.

Then there was the time he and his classmates had painted in a multitude of colours the statue of Sir Solomon Dias Bandaranaike which had been erected in the vicinity of his school. They did get caned for this by their form teacher. Felix was once caught riding a bicycle without a light one evening and when the case came up before Magistrate Ramachandran the name Perera was called. The learned Magistrate, who obviously knew that Felix was no "Perera" and aware of what pranks youngsters are up to, warned and discharged Felix.

Felix maintained that he was a mediocre student. He said many a teacher knew him to be a bookworm. He had three good friends – John de Saram, David Chanmugam and Eustace Fonseka – Although there were others like Roger Modder and Lakshman Perera, who according to Felix ate a fried cockroach cooked on a bunsen burner for a tall sum of Rs. 10! Later in life when Eustace was losing his eyesight Felix was visibly moved and helped him with whatever means he could to enable Eustace to go abroad for treatment.

Felix was in the Boy Scout movement. He did know to tie the bottle knot and do a few useful things boy scouts were expected to know. Except for this, I don't think he was very practical. At Royal he preferred to grow papaws rather than take part in sports. Perhaps this was an early sign of his being Minister of Agriculture later on! He claimed that on a tennis court he could not keep pace with the speed of a tennis ball!

My parents and I regularly attended the Royal College prize-giving in order to see my brother N. O. J. Jayasundera take away his prizes. My first recollection of Felix was on such a day. Felix the podgy boy who carried away many prizes each year was a treat to watch. He once extended his left hand to Governor Sir Andrew Caldecott, the chief guest, much to the amusement of the other students. It later transpired that this was in consequence of a bet taken with his friends!

Initially Felix offered science subjects for his O'Levels. This was in protest against his father's demands that he study Arts, after which he could offer law at the University and continue the legal traditions of the family. However, after completing one year, he relented and offered Arts subjects for his University Entrance. He felt that he had not covered adequately the prescribed reading for the subject English at the A'Levels. Therefore he fell back on his knowledge of the Bible to help him to fill in the necessary literary allusions, and passed with flying colours.

When he won the Turnour Prize at Royal College he got the opportunity to buy a typewriter. This he treasured. His one-finger typewriting continued into later life on an electric typewriter. Many an hour was spent hammering away, putting down his thoughts, hopes and aspirations into the articles he wrote.

Incidents from his early years

There are other incidents he related to us. These were sometimes about him and sometimes about his family. Some were hilarious and some were touching. All these recreate a picture of his early years.

Felix used to visit his relations with his mother. His favourite place was the home of his mother's brother, Bertie Dias Abeysinghe who was a much-loved Proctor at the Hulftsdorp Court complex. Felix could not initially understand why Uncle Bertie loved fish-head curry especially with the eyes of the fish ogling at him! Ultimately he came to the conclusion that tastes differ. Another incident at one of the birthday celebrations of Uncle Bertie used to bring back memories to Felix. The party had been preceded by a prayer meeting where a young clergyman had assiduously prayed for Bertie and asked God to grant Bertie intelligence. This evoked such a bout of laughter from Felix, his sister Christine and the young people present that they were forced to run to the rear verandah to control themselves.

He was often taken by his mother to visit her sister, Aunt Norah, wife of Dr. A. C. Seneviratne, a most affectionate uncle. Felix thought her three children were pampered too much for each was given daily a delicious packet of biscuits from the famous store Elephant House. Of course Felix himself was a great patroniser of the high tea organised by his mother and this consisted of delicious Green Cabin chocolate cake, ham sandwiches and other mouth-watering goodies.

Felix was not without his impishness. When a treasure hunt was organised at a party at his home, one link to finding the treasure was to bring an ayah. Felix was heard to have remarked with perfect equanimity that to find an ayah was no problem in a particular doctor's house, knowing the penchant that good pupil of Hippocrates had for members of the opposite sex!

At Felix's home – Number 3 "Granta" – named after a river in Cambridge – November 5th Guy Fawkes Day was always celebrated by his father as it was Felix's birthday. Even after we got married I have happy memories of stuffing a Guy Fawkes together with Felix's good friend and fellow lawyer H. D. Perera. For the eyes, we used jets that could be lit with fire crackers which made such a wonderful bonfire. Naturally, every friend who visited on this day each year recalled the story of how Guy Fawkes blew up the British Parliament!

There was a great attachment between Felix and his sister Christine who was two and a half years older than he. They had both been groomed by their father to say the correct thing at the correct time and observe all the social graces. Felix recounted an interesting *faux pas* he made on an occasion when Proctor of Puttalam was invited to dinner and Felix had honestly mistaken the worthy gentleman's "talappawa" (or headgear in English) for that worn by the manservant in their home and had innocently bade him to bring a tumbler of iced water! For this he was unceremoniously whacked on his bottom by his father and packed off to bed. No amount of explaining, that it was a *bona fíde* mistake on his part was able to vindicate young Felix in his father's eyes.

On one occasion, Felix's mum had asked his Aunt Evie if she could find a "cookie" for their home. In Ceylon parlance, "cookie" referred to a female cook to help out in the kitchen. Felix was totally unaware of his mother's request and on answering the phone one day found himself being told by his aunt Evie that she had a "nice cookie" to which the delighted Felix had replied in no uncertain terms that he loved cookies, and this to the utter embarrassment of his dear aunt who had reprimanded him by saying "chee, chee, what a bad boy you are!"

Felix often related the story of the juicy mango which he had been eating at the top of the stairs until he was caught redhanded by his mother. Being thoroughly flustered he missed his step and rolled down the stairs. Thanks to his obesity he did not suffer any injury.

On another occasion Felix had manoeuvred his Baby Austin car up and down, around Lipton Circus to the tune of "Mexican Merry-Go-Round" much to the delight of its occupants.

There were also the stories of the fox terrier that Felix owned. On several occasions when Felix had no cash he would sell his dog to Christine his sister. When his financial position improved he would buy his dog back. "Blackie" a perfectly white dog which Felix owned would bear a grieving countenance when his master was sad and would be all jumpy when his master was happy. I will never forget how Felix would go to church on Sundays wearing a short-sleeved shirt. He would explain to me that he did not wear a jacket to church because there were people like Manickkam, a fellow parishioner and friend, who could not afford a jacket.

University days – 1948-51 LLB

During Felix's University days the winner of the Oratorical Contest was compelled to stand the others to a good treat at Green Cabin. This was the most famous and interesting haunt during that time for any University student. The award was only Rs. 10/- but the feed at the Green Cabin was Rs. 50/- ! This was the sort of fun that prevailed.

Once, I remember when I was at Peradeniya in the Law Faculty, Felix and I paid a visit to the home of the peon of the Law library. He graciously offered us two plain teas. Felix not only gulped his own but relished mine too. He was never finicky about moving with the not-so-well-off whatever their station in life was.

At University Felix knocked around with friends on his bicycle. He also prided himself that he never accompanied his father, then a Supreme Court Judge, to Queen's House ever for any formal occasion. Queen's House was the residence of the Governor-General. He was perhaps the rebel in the family, who refused to be sent abroad for his studies and was proud to be a product of the Ceylon University and the Ceylon Law College, although he later ended up as a Barrister of the Inner Temple like his father and grandfather. I also recollect Felix contesting the Union Presidency at the University. Although he secured most of the girls' votes he still failed to win. He lost to K. Shinya on two occasions: once in Oratory and the other time when he got a Second Upper in his LLB and Shinya got a first the next year. Felix took defeat admirably. He did not harbour hard feelings because he considered defeat a part of the game in life. Later, when Shinya was ailing and his eyesight deteriorating, Felix always made it a point to visit him and console him. He took Malcolm Perera, a former Judge turned preacher, to minister to him. Of course, Ferdi Wijewickreme, another lawyer and mutual friend, could not have been a better source of consolation to Shinya in his last days, when he had completely lost his sight.

Justice Soertsz and Felix's father who were both colleagues on the bench had their differences and there was no love lost between the two. Felix mentioned that if the opportunity arose whenever Justice Soertsz was lecturing to them (after retirement) on some legal matter he would not fail to have a dig at old RFD. On one occasion Justice Soertsz wanted to advance his lecture by half an hour. Felix replied promptly "Suits" and pat came the rejoinder from Justice Soertsz: "chip of the old blockhead!" The rift between them stemmed perhaps from his grandfather's remark, made in a facetious manner, that "this is the rock on which the Soertsz split", referring to the divorce case between Justice Soertsz's daughter who was married to J. C. W. Rock. Then, there was retired Justice H. W. Tambiah's characteristic method of introducing his own book "Landlord and Tenant" to his students: they were unfailingly advised to turn to a particular page and see what the learned author had to say!

Felix was in the Ceylon Law College from 1951-1952 and apprenticed under Dr. Tambiah, a personal friend of the family. He passed out as an advocate in 1953 and had a wide practice, and became a Barrister-at-Law of the Inner Temple, London, in 1958.

Felix the Lawyer

Felix passed out as a lawyer in 1953 and we got married on Armistice Day, November 11th 1953, at St. Michael's Church, Colombo 3 with the Bishop of Colombo, the Rt. Revd. Rollo Graham Campbell, officiating. Though born with the proverbial silver spoon in his mouth he did not rest on family titles but worked extremely hard to establish himself. He achieved what he sought sooner than he expected and had to make arrangements to expand the small house he had built on his father's property to accommodate his growing clientele. In the law courts he did not hesitate to move freely with his clients. In many a provincial court, be it in Kandy, Galle, Matara, Tangalle, Jaffna or Kurunegala he would argue with all the strength at his command on behalf of his clients. I will never forget the times we would motor to Jaffna in the night for bus company cases with Ivan Dassanaike, later a UNP MP., Hambantota was equally interesting. Talking about Jaffna, Felix used to relate the story of a learned Queen's Counsel who used to go up to Jaffna with his junior not infrequently. The Q.C. instructed his junior to arrange for a young damsel with whom he could while away the time. The junior was quite up to it and he made the request from the Rest House keeper "The learned advocate requests that "two sweets" be arranged!"

One day after motoring for a long distance we stopped at the Rest House only to discover that the two rooms available had been occupied by another lawyer and his family. Of course, we had no alternative but to sleep on the Rest House verandah on camp cots. I always maintained that I democratised Felix and made him get used to the rough and tumble of life – eating corned beef sautéd with chillie and onions and oven-hot garlic bread. But I think I was wrong – the seeds of democratic socialism were ingrained in Felix from his young days.

Felix recollected quite clearly his stay in Chilaw when his father was District Judge. The DJ's bungalow was a fine building adjacent to the sea beach. He would spend the evenings playing on the sands and enjoying the vast expanse of the sea and everything it afforded – the breeze, the waves breaking on the shore. It was great fun.

Felix's privileged background did not deter him in any way of thinking and feeling for the poor litigant. When he passed out as a lawyer and came to Hulftsdorp, people remarked since he was well-off that he need not practise to earn money. But he still persevered in his profession.

It is with a great deal of amusement that I recall an incident at the Chilaw courts during this period. Felix had hurriedly boarded his van (which was really a milk delivery van) in Colombo, forgetting to take his black jacket. On learning of his plight, Mrs Muthurajah, wife of the District Judge, unhesitatingly took out her husband's best black jacket (which was neatly packed with moth balls) and gladly gave it to Felix as the Muthurajah's were family friends. From the moment Felix started addressing the court the Honourable Judge became very restive and seemed to notice something vaguely familiar in Felix's attire. During the adjournment he sent word for Felix. To his surprise he found that Felix had been addressing his Honour in his Honour's own jacket!

The next time Felix went to Chilaw, the judge invited him to share the purple yam jelly made by his wife. Felix remarked that he liked it and the result was his getting dollops of it on his plate. He had to consume it all because mother had taught him when he was young, that it was rude not to eat everything that was served to him as a guest!

The bungalow of the District Judge Hatton had a small lake in front where Felix and Kimen (Akkimen abbreviated to Kimen referring to his elder sister) used to sail their paper boats. It was by a strange coincidence in 1968 when Felix had gone for a case to the Hatton courts, he insisted on viewing the lake from the DJ's bungalow. Proctor Selladurai whom he dearly liked and Mrs Selladurai who would make him delicious sweetmeats, were with him. It was at that moment when viewing the lake, Felix later understood, that his beloved sister Christine was found unconscious in her home at Piliyandala. Felix would later remark that if there were some telepathic communication between his sister and himself, it manifested itself that day.

I must at this point include some incidents that Felix related to me about his father and uncles in the legal profession. Felix would recall how, on one occasion, his father displayed a high sense of justice and strong character by conceding that he had made a mistake and by apologising in open court for an error he had made on the bench the previous day.

Felix would good-humouredly say that the Bandaranaikes, as a clan, were "not all there." He related two very amusing stories. One was about an uncle who was functioning as a magistrate and suddenly discovered that he was the accused in a case before himself! He therefore decided to come down from the bench, get into the box and plead guilty, then take the judge's seat to pronounce sentence and thereafter go to the court office and pay his fine! He thus performed the functions of accused and judge! The other was about a cousin who was also a lawyer, appearing before his uncle, Felix's father. At one point, when his cousin had felt that the judge's remarks were completely irrelevant, he emphatically blurted out, "No, no, Uncle Bunny, you've got it all wrong"!

I should like to quote from an article by Amita Abeysekera reported in "The Island" of 1st July 1985 that I feel describes Felix the lawyer well.

Felix Reginald Dias Bandaranaike, was one of the most controversial politicians of our time but it is too early to assess the impact he had on the events of the last two and a half decades. But he did have an impact on them, and in the days to come political analysts will no doubt attempt to tell us what they were.

Today I shall only relate a story told me by a very respected District Judge (now retired.) about Felix the Lawyer.

"If Felix did not dissipate his talents and his time in politics," said the D.J., "He would have easily been a second H. V. Perera. His intellectual brilliance was awesome, and with his incisive mind and astonishing grasp of the law, no goal in the legal profession was beyond his reach. In court, Felix Dias Bandaranaike was always calm, unruffled, and well-mannered. He was courteous and respectful to the judges, his opposing counsel, and the witnesses. He did not bully and rage and harass and make a spectacle of himself. And he was, above all, scrupulously honest.

"He appeared many times before me," continued the ex-DJ, "and he never failed to impress me with his courtly manners and his extraordinary knowledge of the law. Once, in a civil case, he proceeded to demolish very effectively the arguments put forward by the other side, making rings round his opposing counsel. He presented his case so well, that before he had quite finished, I had decided to give judgement in his client's favour. It was obvious to everybody that Felix's arguments were irrefutable. Concluding his address to court, Felix paused: "Your honour, before entering judgement, may I humbly request your honour to refer to NLR No: such and such, in the case of ABC v. XYZ."

"Puzzled, I went to my chambers and sent for a copy of the NLR he had mentioned, and turned to the case he had quoted. And discovered to my consternation that Felix's client had no case in law, and that judgement should be entered in favour of his opponent!"

That was the kind of great gentleman Felix the Lawyer was. He had done his best by his client; indeed, more than his best. But his unswerving professional integrity would not permit him to allow a miscarriage of justice.

Lincoln the Lawyer

When Abraham Lincoln was practising as a lawyer, a man came to him one day with a case which he wanted Lincoln to take. Lincoln listened to him for a considerable time with undivided attention, and said thoughtfully, "Well, you have a pretty good case in technical law, but a pretty bad one in equity and justice. You will have to get some other fellow to win this case for you. I couldn't do it. All the time, while standing talking to the Jury, I would be thinking. "Lincoln, you are a liar!" I believe I would forget myself and say it aloud!"

Talking about the law, Felix never forgot one of his earlier cases when he appeared before District Judge, L. W. de Silva, in a seduction case Felix, appearing for the woman was leading her evidence to prove the seduction but was coming against a blank wall. She was not co-operative in her answers. The judge, L. W. de Silva, remarked in his rather heavy manner of speech: "Mr Dias is it your position that this can be done only in the rear seat of a car."

I personally witnessed this incident when a client brought his fees in a wad of Rs. 2/- notes. Felix was very sympathetic and told his client not to bother about any fees at all. There were innumerable occasions similar to this which were not openly displayed for exhibition but remained an integral part of his character.

Another interesting episode was Felix's visit to England to become a barrister, under a reciprocal arrangement between the countries' legal professions. There were five of us; Lakshman Kadiragamar, the present Foreign Minister in the People's Alliance Government, Ivon Perera, Maurice Perera, Felix's kinsmen, Felix and myself who were called to the Inner Temple. I squashed his idea of buying a Mercedes Benz by pointing out that at 27 if he were to buy a Mercedes that at 50 it would have to be a Rolls Royce! Of course we all knew that Felix was a very keen car enthusiast. His cars ranged from Baby Austins, Mayflowers, Austin Princesses, a Mercedes Benz and ended with a Baby Austin once again. How Felix enjoyed the trip of six weeks all over Europe. I was a hopeless navigator but it was a wonderful experience. We would assemble on special evenings in London with his lawyer friends and enjoy a typical rice and curry which was cooked in the flat occupied by Ivon Perera, at Lancaster Gate. Felix was no great shakes as a cook no Cordon Bleu! So he was asked to keep the conversation going whilst the others made tasty rice and curried chicken with plenty of "Bisto". It was really a life without any problems.

During the war when his father was serving as a volunteer officer, he would salute his senior officer C. Thiagalingam, QC. On the same day Thiagalingam addressing court would address Felix's father as "Your Lordship" – his junior volunteer officer. Both Felix and I were fond of Thiagalingam and we used to spend many an evening with him and his dear wife Mahes. When Thiagalingam died his son rang Felix and wanted him to be a pall-bearer as that was his father's wish.

Felix would recount how his father was not appointed Chief Justice because he did not bow down to any improper requests from the government of the day! Felix would say the "old man" had no regrets for the stand he took even though it cost him the rightly deserved post of Chief Justice.

Felix's grandfather, apart from being a cousin of Sir Solomon Dias Bandaranaike, was also his good friend. When Felix was a child his father had recounted stories of the two gentlemen going to the horse races together. He had said they were both keen punters who also enjoyed a ride on horseback on the Galle Face Green.

In 1951 Sir Solomon's son S. W. R. D. Bandaranaike (or SWRD as he was known – by many) broke away from the UNP and formed his own party, the Sri Lanka Freedom Party. Felix recollected SWRD visiting 'Granta' to request Felix's father to take up the post of Minister of Justice in a government he hoped to form in 1952. It never happened, but little would SWRD have thought that his wife Sirima would, years later, form a government in which RFD's son Felix would become a Minister of Justice! Felix was a little boy in shorts when SWRD brought his young bride to his Uncle Bunny's home. Felix would recall how happy his family were to meet the newly-weds.

I recollect very clearly SWRD, when he was Prime Minister, coming over to our little home with A. P. Jayasuriya for consultations in Seelananda Thera's case in Badulla. Our servant Kiri Mudiyanse would be thrilled to make coffee for the Prime Minister. Once later on, this servant, perhaps in a moment of extreme enthusiasm, even scaled the walls of Temple Trees (the Prime Minister's official residence) in an effort to see the Prime Minister in his official surroundings. He was arrested by the Police and hauled up in court. Felix had to appear on his behalf and secure his release.

In November 1953, soon after our marriage, we motored to Nuwara Eliya to thank SWRD's wife Sirima for being an attesting witness at our wedding. During this visit I remember SWRD advising Felix to contest a seat some time. Felix replied, "Uncle Sonny, your branch of the family had the money for education and politics but our branch exhausted theirs trying to educate their children abroad at Cambridge. Nevertheless I will think about it in the future."

SWRD was assassinated on September 26th 1959 and Parliament was dissolved by the caretaker Prime Minister W. Dahanayake. Mrs Sirima Bandaranaike soon afterwards sent Barnes Ratwatte, her brother and later Supreme Court Judge, and James Obeyesekere to request Felix to contest the other half of the old Attanagalla seat which her late husband had represented as a Member of Parliament until his untimely death. I was astounded because I never really believed that Felix would enter politics. He had a good practice at the bar in Ceylon and had just returned after being called as a Barrister at the Inner Temple. It was a difficult decision for this 29-year-old to make but Felix was a quixotic character who enjoyed trying new things. Felix was able to accept Mrs Bandaranaike's offer since by that time the laws were changed to limit expenses on elections to a fixed amount.

The year 1960 was a watershed in Felix's life. Mrs Bandaranaike though not a candidate herself spearheaded the campaign from her residence in Horagolla. Her sister-in-law Mrs Alex de Alwis whose country residence was in Weke in the Dompe electorate was also actively engaged in promoting her nephew Felix for the Dompe seat. Aunty Alex was such a lovable person. At the same time she was never short of naughty stories which she related in such an amusing manner. I remember the first speech that was written for Felix in Sinhala. Felix preferred to tear up the paper in the presence of his audience saying that he would address them in the home grown Sinhala that he knew and this drew a round of applause for its spontaneity. He seemed to be set for victory and he did win Dompe with a large majority.

Felix the Political Strategist,Troubleshooter and Think Tank of the Sri Lanka Freedom Party (SLFP)

These words were used by some to describe Felix's role in the SLFP from as early as 1959 when he was requested by Mrs. Sirima Bandaranaike to draft the SLFP manifesto. He was assisted by his kinsman James Obeyesekere. Whilst he sat working away on his typewriter, he was planning the whole operation of winning an election like a commander planning his attack.

S. W. R. D. Bandaranaike the Prime Minister had been assassinated. Normally, after such a cruel assassination of a leader, the SLFP government could have won a tremendous sympathy vote. Unfortunately the caretaker government of Wijayananda Dahanayake started dismissing Ministers in stages. This did not help to consolidate the SLFP.

The SLFP had a new leader in Mrs. Sirima Bandaranaike. She was not going to contest a seat. She intended to operate from the Senate. Legal opinion had to be obtained both from eminent Queen's Counsel in Sri Lanka and from legal eagles abroad regarding the constitutionality of this position. (See S. A. de Smith's opinion).

Felix complained that the manifesto he had prepared was spirited away from Rosmead Place (where Mrs. Bandaranaike resided) by one of the people who attended the meeting to discuss the draft manifesto and the next day the United National Party (UNP) published a manifesto which had a startling resemblance to one prepared by him for the SLFP. Felix painstakingly went through the material again and rewrote the manifesto from a different slant to the earlier one. I remember the document being drafted on the night of December 31st 1959 on the balcony of our house, amidst innumerable cups of black coffee.

The manifesto had been excellent – it had promised democratic socialism. However, in the face of the actions of Dahanayake's caretaker government the SLFP could not hold its position in March 1960 as the majority party. Moreover, Dahanayake had meanwhile formed his own party, the Lanka Prajathantravadi Pakshaya (LPP). The SLFP had been close enough to win but not sufficiently strong to beat the UNP which was able to form a minority government. The SLFP had to formulate a strategy to collect the other parties within its fold to defeat the UNP. It was imperative that the minority UNP government of Dudley Senanayake in March 1960 be brought down if the SLFP meant serious business. In fact, the SLFP would have to rise as a phoenix from its ashes.

S. J. V. Chelvanayakam, the leader of the Federal Party, met Felix at our home, then at 101, Galle Road, Kollupitiya. Felix convinced him that, on behalf of the SLFP, he would unilaterally make certain changes on matters of language and implement some other demands put forward by them. This was not a pact. A speech by Chelvanayakam, which was reported later in the year in the Hansard, confirmed this position taken by the SLFP. Chelvanayakam and his party voted with the SLFP on the UNP Throne Speech and helped to defeat the UNP Government.

C. P. de Silva, who had led the SLFP at the March election as the most senior Minister in the previous Mahajana Eksath Peramuna Government, was then called by Sir Oliver Goonetilleke, the Governor-General to Queen's House in March 1960. That morning CP got cold feet and so he came over to our house and having partaken of a breakfast of hoppers and a cup of tea, he insisted on Felix accompanying him to Queen's House – but Sir Oliver was wise to it and very tactfully asked Felix to be in the lounge and took CP into another room. Sir Oliver was not satisfied that CP could form a government, and instead ordered a dissolution of Parliament. Felix always thought that this was due to caste reasons. The no-contest pact drawn up and designed at 101, Galle Road, Kollupitiya, with the Lanka Sama Samaja Party (LSSP) and the Communist Party (CP) helped in consolidating the SLFP front and in July 1960, the SLFP formed a government with Mrs Sirima Bandaranaike as the Prime Minister but with her seat in the Senate.

A. P. Jayasuriya who had been a strong supporter of the slain S. W. R. D. Bandaranaike and one of his Ministers in the MEP Government continued to be a source of strength to Mrs Sirima Bandaranaike at every stage. Mrs Bandaranaike together with Felix started a systematic campaign for the collection of funds. It was forcefully conveyed to the country that new blood had been injected into the party in the form of SWRD's youthful and adventurous widow who was determined to uphold the ideals of her late husband. She was supported by Felix the young and able lawyer who was a close relation of SWRD's, James Obeyesekere, another close relation who was experienced in campaigning from as early as 1952, C. P. de Silva, a former civil servant and experienced politician, Maithripala Senanayeke, Minister in the MEP government, T. B. Tennekoon, Ratne Deshapriya Senanayake (another Senanayake a good orator though not from the same clan as Dudley Senanayake but rather the SLFP candidate to oppose Dudley at Dedigama), and R. S. Perera whose homespun speeches had a terrific appeal with the masses – they all contributed to a very successful campaign at the July elections in 1960.

Philip Gunawardena who was from the Mahajana Eksath Peramuna (MEP) just could not understand how the SLFP was gaining strength daily in their campaign. Philip Gunawardena thought that his association with S. W. R. D. Bandaranaike in the MEP would make him the choice of the people. Somehow, the grass under his feet appeared to be cut even without his knowledge although at many a meeting of his, an advance squad would go around announcing that Philip Gunawardena the future Prime Minister was on his way! The left parties, keen on ousting the UNP Government, accused them of being capitalist, merely protecting capitalist mercantile interests.

"No portfolios for the Reds" was Felix's assurance to the people at the meetings he addressed for the July 1960 elections. He was unafraid of letting the people know the exact relationship of the SLFP with the left parties. This was the strength of Felix's political acumen. Years later when asked about the famous bank strike of 1972, Felix said "I have nothing to do with it. I am only watching it. Nice to see men who led strikes, trying to break a strike."

Felix recollects quite clearly how he had sent his Triumph Renown with lots of red rosettes for Colvin R. de Silva when he contested the Dehiwala seat on an earlier occasion. His father had an enormous regard for Colvin's ability as a lawyer.

During the July 1960 campaign I heard C. P. de Silva tell Felix that if the SLFP won Felix should be Finance Minister. And so it happened. In addition he became the Parliamentary Secretary to the Minister of Defence and External Affairs. Mrs Bandaranaike was in the Senate and Felix was responsible to Parliament on foreign policy and defence, of the SLFP.

When they had to talk seriously with the Federalists and the TULF, they did so boldly without mincing words. When the TULF opened post offices – the government had housed them at Panagoda and gave them Galle Face Hotel Food.

Minister of Finance – 1960
(Parliamentary Secretary – Defence)

Felix became the Minister of Finance in July 1960. The Korean War boom had brought in a tremendous amount of foreign exchange. Unfortunately, in the earlier regime it had been greatly reduced by an unrestricted issue of foreign exchange for travel abroad etc. All this was money that could have been usefully deployed for the development of agriculture and production of goods by imports of necessary machinery.

In these circumstances Felix as the Finance Minister had to make an important and quick decision to conserve the country's foreign exchange. He introduced a drastic restriction on imports in order that the scarce foreign exchange would be available for the import of essential commodities like rice and sugar. This was a courageous decision. It was a difficult task for Felix, a relatively young man to muster the support of his Cabinet colleagues to agree with his decision. However, with the backing of his Prime Minister he was able to make it a reality. S. F. Amerasinghe and thereafter Shirley Amerasinghe were his Permanent Secretaries.

His decision naturally upset big businesses. I remember Cyril Gardiner (an important businessman and hotelier) telling Felix that if the free import of cars was to be curbed, businessmen would have no option but to put up their shutters. Felix assuaged his fears, replying that the innate capabilities of our local mechanics (baases as they are called) would keep our vehicles on the roads. Furthermore, Felix held the view that there were sufficient vehicles in the country to serve the people's needs. He also said that with entrepreneurs like Cyril, the car business would never fail.

V. A. Kandiah of the Federal Party often came to meet Felix at the Ministry of Finance. Once, over a cup of tea he said, "Felix, we as a Party have to take up these extreme positions – but that does not mean that your people as a Party can concede all our demands." Felix was always very receptive to anything told to him by the Federal Party and he always tried to understand their point of view although he could not agree with them on all their demands.

I remember quite clearly being severely insulted at Cargills (the store widely patronised by Colombo society's elite). Nevertheless, I could quite understand their thinking. They were accustomed to a certain standard of living and resented the restriction on imports of some food items like apples and grapes. However, because of the curbs on imports, there was an upsurge of the local industry as well as agriculture. The quality could have been improved but import restrictions were a major catalyst in developing the concept of entrepreneurship in the economic and industrial fields. We produced our own jams and jelly which were as good as any previously

imported brand. Felix gave every encouragement to the company producing
Goldi meat products at Mattakkuliya, one of the very early entrepreneurs.
Maithripala Senanayeke's facetiously termed "Seeni Bola Industries"
(meaning very small and loosely run concerns) nevertheless produced sweets
which were in great demand. I remember Ena de Silva coming to the Finance
Ministry to request that a thousand yards of material be issued for her batik
industry and Felix readily agreed and it must be said that Ena has been one of
the earlist producers of extremely high quality batiks as is evident in the long
banners in the lobby of the Hotel Oberoi.

Felix presented his budget on July 26, 1962 and resigned on August 25th
1962 after withdrawing a budgetary proposal to reduce the rice ration by half
a measure. He was the first Minister to resign after a budget proposal was
withdrawn. He joked over his own departure. At this time the film "Singer
not the Song" was running at a Colombo cinema. Felix raised a hearty laugh
when he said that in his case both the singer and his song had been
eliminated. He said he was not going to increase the price of rice, but was
only going to reduce the ration by half a measure. Felix's own Parliamentary
Secretary George Rajapakse described the proposal as "a gross betrayal of
the people." Among one of the few MP's who supported the Minister of
Finance was the MP for Kurunegala Jaya Pathirana later Judge of the
Supreme Court, called him "an honourable and honest man who had the
stamp of honesty." He said "whatever we may say now regarding the policy
of the Minister of Finance, when the history of this country comes to be
written, it will endorse that the decision made by the Minister of Finance
today as correct" said Pathirana.

Felix said that he would not come back even to plant grass but on
November 5th he was back again as Minister without Portfolio and in early
1963 became the Minister of Agriculture, Food and Co-operatives. He, with
the assistance of Dr. Terence Seneviratne, an international expert on
agriculture reorganised the entire system of agriculture by encouraging the
maximum use of fertilizer for paddy production, introducing new varieties of
seed paddy, new planting material for the cultivation of potatoes, onions and
other subsidiary food crops; and the cultivation of mushrooms, apples, and
strawberries in the Nuwara Eliya district. All the state farms which were
working unprofjtably were taken in hand and completely reorganised to be
profitable ventures. When the UNP government came into power in 1965
Mr M. D. Banda, the new Minister of Agriculture paid a warm compliment
to Felix commending him on the work done by Felix and said that he sees no
reason to deviate from it.

In co-operatives too Felix gave responsibility to the young officers to
make their own decisions and to clean up the administration paying emphasis

to the basic needs of people, so that the Co-operative Wholesale Establishment could be a ready source of supply for them. Ratna Deshapriya Senanayake, the chairman gave all the support to Felix to crack down on the crooks and racketeers. Felix, set up a separate market survey division in the ministry headed by M. R. P. Salgadoe who had come from the world bank on a temporary assignment. Salgadoe kept a tab on world food prices, and when the prices of foodstuffs were low especially dried chillies ordered large quantities to be stored in the new CWE godowns which were constructed at Welisara. This enabled the government to supply the CWE outlets goods at reasonable prices when there was a scarcity of such goods.

Felix on the Socialist Approach and Nationalisation of Banks

Felix in his budget speech of 1960-1961 (page 2) said "we believe that wealth entails not merely the right to enjoy material comforts and privileges, but also the obligation to use such wealth for national development and the welfare of the community. We believe that the right to employment, a fair wage and decent working conditions also entail the obligation to work hard, loyally and honestly, for the good of the country." He expressed the view that a National Planning Dept. which would consist of a group of economic advisers, would work in close co-ordination with the Ministries in implementing the "Ten Year Plan" formulated during the period of office of the late Prime Minister. He said "To get on with the job, we need, foremen not architects, and with proper technical advice we are confident that the structure we build will run little risk of being jerry-built."

He went to say "In order to arrest this continuous decline in our external assets we introduced certain measures (a) by the increase of the import duty on various commodities barring those which are in use by the mass of the people so as to ensure that the cost of living is not affected.

"The second line of action was to increase the rate of interest at which commercial banks could borrow from the Central Bank, on the pledge of government securities. Of course, the lending rate to commercial banks from the Central Bank was much less for food, fertilisers, textiles and cotton yarn; and the export of commercial crops was at a lower rate of interest.

"A third line of action is the restriction of credit to hire purchase companies for financing the purchase of non-essential commodities from importing firms."

He went on to say "One of the highlights of policy set out in the Sri Lanka Freedom Party manifesto was the controlled introduction of foreign capital to give an impetus to the progress of our economic development." He also elaborated "when the terms on which foreign investment is allowed in any particular enterprise or undertaking have been settled, they should be set out under the hand of the Minister of Finance and tabled in the House in the usual way. All safeguards necessary for the investment of foreign capital in any particular undertaking could be provided in such documents and no better assurance of security can be given."

He also went on to say: "In order to encourage the private sector to participate in Industrial Development and in keeping under the Government Policy, provision has been made for completing the establishment of the Industrial Venture and the Government participation along with the private capital in the establishment of small-scale and medium-scale consumer industries."

He further said "I have referred already to Ceylon's dependence on foreign trade. It is essential therefore that our ports which are the channels through which the trade is conducted should be improved and developed." Referring to the scheme of national development he went on to say "This will involve the active encouragement of the Rural Development Movement as an instrument for generating self-help and also as an agency for increasing the participation of the people in the process of economic development."

He said that in order that the manpower requirements of economic development could be met, emphasis is being given to the teaching of science and to courses in practical education.

"We have tried to adjust the irregularities of our society. We have tried by various measures to introduce the social changes that were called forth by the revolution of 1956. We have tried to give voice and substance to the needs of the majority of the people of this country to whom the name SWRD Bandaranaike signifies an amelioration of their social conditions."

In the 1961-1962 budget he said "The socialism to which we aspire is not doctrinaire or revolutionary. It is based on the will of the people and may I tell the Hon. Minister for Avisawella that Dompe is proud to give our political philosophy a "local habitation and a name." He pointed out the role of the private sector.

"Our Government has defined the area in which it would leave private enterprise free to operate and in which it would create the conditions of successful operation. In addition to the exemptions and inducements contained in our taxation laws, the recent restrictions, and even more the bans on imports of several items have created an opening that never existed before for profitable investment in numerous manufacturing industries. He goes on to say "The depletion of our external reserves is the price we have had to pay for maintaining stability in the domestic price level in Ceylon. It was not until the present Government came into power that special measures were taken to deal with the problem of our declining external assets. The measures were both of a fiscal and monetary nature and included increases in import duties, quantitative restrictions and even bans on imports designed to curtail demand and arrest the drain on foreign exchange as well as to increase Government revenue.

He went on to say "The Bank of Ceylon, was established to fill a vacuum in the banking structure of the country. There was no institution backed by local capital to which Ceylonese business could confidently turn for assistance for the promotion of advancement of Ceylonese enterprise." He said: "The Government proposes, in accordance with its policy of socialism, to nationalise the Bank of Ceylon."

In 1938 the State Council discussed the establishment of a state bank to provide credit facilities to the Ceylonese engaged in commerce and trade. After the Bank of Ceylon was opened it was found that about sixty-five percent of the loans were given to foreign companies and business interest mainly British and Indian. The Ceylonese businessmen were called upon to provide securities to obtain credit facilities. The securities demanded were so high that few Ceylonese could comply with this requirement.

S. W. R. D. Bandaranaike participating in the above debate in the State Council quoted from the report of the Ceylon Banking Commission chaired by Sir Sorabji Pochkanawalla as reported in "Expanding Horizons, Bank of Ceylon first 50 yrs." at page 44.

"The history of Ceylon records the exploitation of its commerce by the Portuguese, the Dutch, and the British, and the Indians for over 100 years.

The House will observe these words.

Even at present its entire trade is being run by foreigners, with foreign capital, foreign labour and foreign brains. The non-Ceylonese element has kept a stronghold on the business, trade and industries of the country, and few opportunities have been allowed to the average Ceylonese to engage in trade and industries either by Government or by business firms."

The Coup – 1962 – My Impressions

Felix and I were invited for the wedding of the daughter of C. C. Dissanayaka, who was a Deputy Inspector-General of Police, whose brother Neal was married to my first cousin Ena de Alwis. Therefore, as a matter of courtesy, I urged Felix to attend the wedding. Little did we guess that within a week of the wedding, C. C. Dissanayaka together with certain other police officers, army personnel and civilians were to stage an organised coup to topple the legally-constituted government of Mrs Sirima Bandaranaike.

On the evening of January 27th 1962, Felix was sleeping after a very busy day at Malwana, in his electorate. He had also kept up the whole of the previous night inquiring into a bribery charge against a clerk in his office. Felix, in his characteristically meticulous fashion had wanted the charge

Commander Rajan Kadirgamar was also seen on the verandah of Temple Trees vociferously contending that he could handle any coup. I believe this coup to topple the Government was the first of its kind in Sri Lanka's history. Temple Trees, with its green lawns and large shady trees, the venue for receptions or after lunch or dinner chitchats, for exhibitions of the pet baby elephant drinking enormous quantities of milk, was also the place where the coup suspects were questioned interminably to find out the truth.

Finally the code names given to each exercise in the plan were deciphered and the whole pattern of the operation came to light. This was after endlessly confronting one suspect with the statement of another. It was amazing how tiredness and fatigue were forgotten when engaged in an exercise of such nature and dimensions. It was a very tired Felix who presented the White Paper to Parliament after days of such interrogations, containing a detailed account of the steps taken by the Government to abort the coup.

Later it was discovered that plans had been made to incarcerate Felix. A police officer who was instructed to arrest Felix did not know that the coup had failed. He was subsequently arrested by the police, when found marking time in the vicinity of Mahanuge Gardens until the pre-arranged moment to carry out his instructions. Photographs of Felix, together with lists of the arrests to be made if the coup was a success were gathered by the coup suspects and dumped into the Beira Lake according to information at that time.

The coup suspects were convicted but later acquitted by the Privy Council on a legal point. It is interesting to note that some of these very people were given high positions in the private sector in 1965 with the change of government.

Felix, the Law and Conciliation

I remember Felix studying his law of Fidei Commissum from T. Nadarajah's book from cover to cover before his final examination and consequently he did extremely well, but vowing one day or another that he would help to wipe out the law of fidei commissum because it had been an encumbrance on property ownership. He got this opportunity when he became Minister of Justice. Testamentary cases also took so long and it was always felt that lawyers made a packet on these by delaying their conclusion and – so Felix was most anxious to correct this procedure and have quick finality to such proceedings. The Public Trustee was given added responsibility in dealing with these matters. Felix was definitely a man ahead of his time and even though he was roundly condemned by certain sections of the bar – most of the provisions of the Administration of Justice Law are still there in some form or another. What was the thinking behind the AJL? (Administration of

Justice Law) Briefly it was to enable the client to get speedy justice without being in a stranglehold of interminable procedures.

With the schools takeover in 1961, the schools all over the country, some of which were in a shoddy condition and had no amenities for science or in fact even for normal arts studies benefited beyond all recognition. That goes to the eternal credit of the SLFP. But Felix was not involved in the decision. He assumed responsibility as a member of the Cabinet and it was as a conciliator between the Catholic Church and the Government that Felix played a major role. I will never forget the heads of the churches assembling in our upstair sitting room at No. 1 Mahanuge Gardens. The Catholic Church with a message from Cardinal Valerian Gracias, Archbishop of Bombay, who overlooked this region, and the Minister of Justice and Fisheries Sam P. C. Fernando and Felix both on behalf of the Government did their best to sort out problems – the differences that seemed unbridgeable. The argument of the Roman Catholic Church was "we can manage our own schools without your assistance" – but there had to be conformity, all the schools except the ones that opted to be private had to be taken over – so a Roman Catholic Army General H. W. G. Wijeyekoon maintained, and I remember this very well – I quote: 'Sir, I am a Catholic but my duty to the Government comes first, I will take the armoured cars along the streets of Colombo because we have to keep the peace for the whole country.' So it was a difficult decision even for Felix Bandaranaike, the Parliamentary Secretary who himself was a committed Christian.

The SLFP Government of Mrs Bandaranaike did much from the point of housing and settlement. Housing schemes were begun where the plot and the material were given and it was good seeing small villages having their own housing schemes. The small banks extended credit facilities – branches of the People's Bank started by T. B. Ilangaratne and the Bank of Ceylon started springing up in the remote areas. Incidentally, it was Felix who nationalised the Bank of Ceylon by the Finance Act 1961 and appointed H. V. Perera QC as its first Chairman. In 1961 it was a courageous decision to make and the Bank of Ceylon has now turned out to be one of the most powerful of the banking concerns in Sri Lanka. Housing, health, and the provision of the basic necessities for everyday living at affordable prices for the poor man was the primary emphasis of the SLFP Government. With the cut in imports, rural folk got organised in various crafts using their own particular skills and we found various locally turned out articles on the market.

The decentralised budget in 1971 was the brain-child of Felix as Minister of Public Administration and even though Dr. N. M. Perera resisted it at the start, he later saw the enormous benefits of it and wholeheartedly supported it. Large allocations began to be made for each electorate and the electorate decided how it would use the moneys. In other words, the priorities were decided by them. Soon construction work sprang up, and each electorate became a hive of activity with the development councils headed by assistant government agents assisting them. Felix always maintained that if this idea of the decentralised budget had been worked out even more fully, this ethnic problem which grew into outsized proportions would never have occurred.

Felix was exceptionally good at selecting the correct official for a job. Lionel Fernando who was and is known for his administrative ability and his public relations was the Divisional Revenue Officer at Dompe and he did a wonderful job. M. Rajendra, Baku Mahadeva, H. S. Wanasinghe, Princie Siriwardane, Rajah Gomez, Francis Pietersz were some of the officials he selected to work with him and they were officials who had the courage to challenge Felix.

Dompe – A Brief Survey

True Felix accepted a pocket borough in 1960 – one half of SWRD's seat after the delimitation – but he became a political personality in his own right in Dompe and was truly loved by his people who increased his majority at each successive election until 1970 when he won with the largest number of votes.

Felix's spell at Dompe as MP from 1960-1977 were eventful years for Dompe, which like all other electorates had in 1956 seen a new light. Rural people who for so long had been subjugated in every way, now began to see economic development. The dusty roads which joined the main Dompe-Attanagalla road began to be macadamised. Schools started springing up in every area. After the schools takeover the Government was in a position to make equitable distribution of the education vote and not just confine it to the big schools in Colombo. Schools began to get a new look. Science education began in the more remote schools and this became a phenomenon all over Sri Lanka.

I recollect quite clearly what criminal areas places like Mitirigala in the Dompe electorate were. After the setting up of police stations and the strict maintenance of law and order, the crime rate in Dompe dropped significantly. In 1960 I started sewing societies on a co-operative basis. They undertook many contracts and found employment for large numbers of rural girls. Their earnings helped to release mortgaged paddy fields and houses. The building co-operatives manned by the people of the area undertook the construction of more than three wards and the kitchen of the Dompe hospital. People began to have a sense of participation in what they did. In all these endeavours it was the leadership given by the MP that counted. The young people rallied round and gave ideas on how they could improve their electorate. This resulted in the building of the Hanwella bridge by the Dompe-Hanwella engineers themselves. Therefore large numbers of people were able to come across from the Hanwella area and go to Kandy via Dompe and Attanagalla. What really thrilled Dompe was that it was one of its students who designed the bridge and not a foreign expert. A statue of S. W. R. D. Bandaranaike was also unveiled at Dompe near the hospital.

After long negotiations, the Pugoda Textile Mill was to be constructed with the assistance of the People's Republic of China. Unfortunately, when the UNP came to power the whole scheme was abandoned. However, in 1970, after the SLFP was back in the saddle the mill was built and hundreds of youth from all over the country were given employment. The plans for the development of the Pugoda Town were laid. Flood control, a major problem was looked into. Dompe which was only known for its ayahs, and its song "Dompe Ayah" soon became the talking point in Sri Lanka. I still recall the Tarala Buddhist monk Devananda Thera – organising a co-operative to grow manioc and other crops, on an extent of 100 acres of government land. As a result a large sum of money was collected for the development of the area. Once rural credit was made available, people began to improve their paddy fields, and grow subsidiary crops in a more organised way.

The silver thread that ran through Dompe for the 17 years that Felix was MP, was the leadership qualities he displayed which really took the young people by storm. Just before the 1970 elections Felix organised the bicycle pelapaliya (bicycle procession) and all the young boys joined him on bicycles and covered the entire electorate. It was a great day because on the roadside stood the people with booths ready with food and drink to entertain the cyclists, who rode with their candidate from one end of the electorate to another.

Felix's schedule for visiting Dompe after victory was tiring but he enjoyed it. I had to rush to Dompe at 3 a.m. to look for him during the so-called victory tour. He had no qualms in travelling in a grey van which Dompe called the "kiri van". He did not bother about what people had to say of him. Felix got to know Dompe as individuals and not as merely voters. So they were prepared to carry him on their shoulders in victory. When one of his supporters was stabbed by another and brought to the General Hospital he did not spare any pains trying to get the best of doctors to look after him and he spent many hours in the ward of the voter. He knew hundreds of people in Dompe by their name.

The insurrection of 1971 brought to the forefront youth of particular communities who felt they had been downtrodden. Their leader was Rohana Wijeweera. They felt the need to fight for social justice in the way of equitable distribution of land. Actually when we read the police reports at Temple Trees about the activities of the insurgents, it became clear that they as a body had started their planning in the late 1960's. This was during the UNP regime but the government of the day especially the higher echelons of the Police had not paid much heed to these reports. These youths, it appears, voted for the SLFP to come to power hoping that their demands would be satisfied promptly. However, even the SLFP really took to reading earnestly the police reports was when the first police station was attacked. There were exercise books in which the insurgents had expressed their feelings about being self-sufficient without exporting any of the major crops. They did not want to have any international connections with the World Bank or IMF. This domestic policy could never really work, but that was their credo.

I shall never forget how a few of us, Nissanka Wijeyeratne, Nihal Jayawickreme, Gamini Wikramanayake, Felix and I spent hours examining these reports. Quick action was called for since the insurgents had a very detailed plan on how they were going to attack Colombo and what were the houses they intended razing to the ground. Our house was one and another was the house of the Leader of the Opposition J. R. Jayewardene. This plan was discovered in the precincts of the army camp at Panagoda.

By attacking one police station ahead of the scheduled date they bungled their whole plan and the Government was in a stronger position to resist their attack when it actually came. Felix with the consent of the PM got the two entrances to Colombo blocked at the main Colombo bridges, CTB buses were put across to block the entry of the insurgents, who had already attacked the Mahara police station. Then again it was blocked at Havelock Road near the bridge to prevent hordes invading Colombo from Maharagama. A small boy who decided to disclose the whole plot was brought to Rosmead Place. I remember well how the PM, Felix and the Army Commander extracted the details of the plot and plan of the insurgents. Felix had the uncanny knack of knowing when to take immediate action on any issue or bide his time on another and this was a great help. In fact he knew how to put all the incidents in focus. Because of Sri Lanka's unwavering stand on Non-Alignment Mrs Bandaranaike was assisted in the quelling of the insurgency by many countries including India and Pakistan. The emergency was declared on the advice of Jingle Dissanayaka, the Acting Permanent Secretary, who acted on the advice of John Attygalle, the I.G.P. This was necessary because of the fear of the insurgents regrouping and coming forward again. They had caused enough havoc to people and their property. On their initial attack innocent people were slaughtered by them and so the Government had to take quick action against them and thousands of youth were taken into custody. It is a fact that insurgents died – no doubt in the flower of their youth and the leaders of the opposition parties loved to get political mileage from it. Felix always had the knack of seeing the opposite point of view – that of the insurgents and how they would react to government pressure. Mrs Bandaranaike asked them to lay down their arms and decided to give them an amnesty. When the emergency was required to be extended, it was done so without reservations not to keep oneself in power but for the greater good of the people. The acute tension caused by the insurgency did hamper the Government politically, economically and in every way, but the Government kept a close tab on their activities and Wijeweera together with the rest were soon behind bars. The UNP Government released Rohana Wijeweera in 1977. The group that processed the applications for amnesties really worked hard and did an excellent job. The insurgents had to be gradually rehabilitated. This was done with all the political finesse the SLFP was capable of. It is strange that Felix who helped to crush the insurgency appeared for Wijeweera after his release, in a case with Prins Gunasekara, Attorney-at-Law. Loku Athula Nimalasiri Jayasinghe was found a job at the Galle Face Hotel through Cyril Gardiner's good offices and is now a Deputy Minister of the PA (People's Alliance) Government of Mrs Chandrika Kumaratunga Bandaranaike.

Benefits of Reduction of Imports

Felix felt that excessive consumerism would inevitably break down the fabric of our country – because for economic survival we have to work together as a group, be it Sinhalese or Tamil, Burgher or Muslim. In 1970-1977 there was no idle land in Jaffna. Everyone was busy growing onions, chillies, potatoes, cauliflower or any grain which would thrive on Jaffna soil. All these products were sent South to be consumed by their Sinhala brethren. The Jaffna man's pockets were full, it was indeed a green revolution in Jaffna. All this was confirmed at the Government Agents' Conferences from 1970 onwards and which were held annually. Millions of rupees which were going to the farmers outside Sri Lanka began to go into the pockets of the cultivators in Jaffna. At that time there was no clamour to get into the clerical service and the Jaffna cultivator was quite happy in his own environment. In late 1976 and early 1977 we had a group of twenty-five young people from Jaffna coming to Dompe for two weeks and Dompe reciprocated in the same way. There was total rapport between the two communities even though they did not know their respective languages.

Felix and Conferences abroad

Felix enjoyed conferences because it gave him the opportunity of putting his country's case before the countries represented. The major difference between his approach as Finance Minister and later approaches was that on

down till the operation was successfully completed. We were also shown when going to the Kremlin Museum, a particular gate called the Madam Frutzova Gate which had a rather spicy tale behind it, involving political high-ups. As a non-aligned nation, we were not committed to any bloc and so we were entertained with all the warmth and hospitality of the members of the Government of the Soviet Union and we had really happy memories of our trip which were not only recorded as a photograph album but also as a film reel. Shirley Amerasinghe was Felix's Permanent Secretary and he was an invaluable asset to Felix on this trip – he being the older and more experienced man. Dr. Malalasekera had established an excellent rapport with his host country – he was always that whether in England as our High Commissioner, whether in the United Nations as our Permanent Representative or in Moscow as our Ambassador. I always attributed a lot of his success to his charming wife Lylie whom I really liked.

At the UN Dr. Malalasekera had booked us in at the Waldorf Astoria but after one night, we moved out to a less expensive hotel because the finances of the Ceylon Government would not permit us such luxury.

Ceylon and the Sino-Indian Conflict – The Border Dispute, 1962

One of the greatest successes of Mrs Bandaranaike's foreign policy was the skilful manner in which we were able to maintain the most cordial relations with our great neighbour India whilst maintaining an equally cordial and warm relationship with China which had come into conflict with India in 1962 over the MacMohan Line defining the Sino-Indian border.

Mrs Bandaranaike saw the danger of the emerging differences between these two Asian giants and the dangerous consequences for peace in Asia if prompt steps were not taken to prevent or limit an armed conflict between them.

She outlined her views to Felix who worked out the strategy with the Foreign Ministry officials to summon to Colombo the non-aligned leaders in Asia and Africa to promote a ceasefire within days of the armed conflict.

At this conference in Colombo Mrs Bandaranaike was mandated to convey personally the views of these leaders to Pandit Nehru and Prime Minister Chou-En-Lai urging them to cease hostilities and solve the dispute through bilateral negotiations.

Felix and I accompanied Mrs Bandaranaike to Delhi and Peking. The world press went to town on a remark made by Mrs Bandaranaike at the official banquet given in her honour by Prime Minister Chou-En-Lai on which occasion she referred to the industrialised countries as "the rapacious west." Many thought that Felix was responsible for this whereas the fact is that we arrived in Peking on a bitterly cold evening about an hour before the banquet. Our envoy in Peking the late A. B. Perera had prepared a statement which was hurriedly given to her minutes before she was called upon to speak.

Apart from this episode our mission was a success and we had the opportunity of being received by Chairman Mao and were also taken to the historic Great Wall and the beautiful cities of Hanchow and the industrial centers in Shanghai and Canton. The Foreign Minister Marshall Chen-yi was an interesting conversationalist who spoke of the Long March. Premier Chou-En-Lai entertained us to a special lunch cooked by him in our presence and he explained that all the dishes were entirely vegetarian although the appearance and aroma appeared to be decidedly non-vegetarian. We enjoyed the meal heartily, to his delight. He was amused when we asked him where he learnt his cooking whether in China, France, or the States?

Indo-Ceylon Relations and the Sirima-Shastri Pact, 1964

While the keystone of Sri Lanka's foreign policy was the adherence to the principles of non-alignment, the core of this in hindsight appears to be quite distinctly the very close and cordial friendship between the Bandaranaike family and the Nehru family, which was so clearly manifest in the relations between the two countries whenever the Bandaranaikes were in office.

Nevertheless there was the problem of the stateless residents of Indian origin which was an irritant in our bilateral relationships which did not in any way sour our relationships. When Ceylon became independent in February 1948 the indigenous Ceylonese automatically became citizens of Ceylon. There was however a category of residents in Ceylon mainly of Indian origin brought to Ceylon by the British to work on the coffee plantations and later in the tea plantations. All of them came from "British India" but with independence "British India" was divided into the Union of India and Pakistan.

Ceylon had adopted legislation in 1948 to define those who were entitled to Ceylon citizenship. This law did not cover all those who had been normally resident in Ceylon. It clearly defined citizens as those whose fathers and grandfathers were born in Ceylon as citizens by descent. To consider the grant of citizenship to others who had been resident in Ceylon for a long period, another Act called the Indian and Pakistani Registration Act was adopted in 1949. But not all residents in this category applied for registration. Discussions with India were not fruitful. The Indians took up the position that prior to Independence all were British subjects and if those of Indian origin were not given Ceylon citizenship, then they were "stateless." It was open to them to apply for citizenship according to the provisions in the Indian constitution.

I remember our visit in October 1964 to New Delhi. Felix told me that before her departure Mrs Bandaranaike discussed with Dudley Senanayake, Leader of the Opposition how she proposed to negotiate a settlement in Delhi with regard to the repatriation of the Indians working in the tea plantations. In fact she invited Mr Senanayake to join her delegation as two other cabinet ministers T. B. Illangaratne and Felix were also accompanying him.

Mr Senanayake had declined the invitation. After the preliminary round of talks, Mrs Bandaranaike phoned Mr Senanayake in Colombo to brief him on the progress of the talks so that any agreement reached would also have the support of the Opposition.

Mrs Bandaranaike realised that the real issue was to agree on specific numbers who would get citizenship of Ceylon or of India. She did not wish to keep this issue unresolved for a further period of time because these so-called stateless citizens were in fact in Sri Lanka and could always be a political factor.

"In their search for a solution to the problem the two Prime Ministers agreed to a fresh approach to the problem. They reached agreement to the effect that out of 975,000 persons of Indian origin Ceylon will accept as Ceylon citizens 300,000 and India 525,000 persons. The status of the remaining 150,000 persons of Indian origin in Ceylon was left for determination at a subsequent meeting of the Prime Ministers in Ceylon at an early date. It was agreed that the repatriation should be spread over 15 years and the two processes should keep pace with each other."

When the UNP Government assumed office in March 1965, the Sirima-Shastri Pact was not implemented in the spirit in which the agreement was entered into. It is generally believed that S. Thondaman, leader of the C.W.C. was responsible for this. Thondaman was a Minister of the UNP government from 1965-1960. He is of Indian origin and represents the interests of Indian plantation workers who are members of the Ceylon Workers Congress under his leadership.

Our social engagements were quite interesting. We viewed a Son and Lumiere show at the Red Fort in old Delhi where the subject was woven around King Aurangzebe. We went for a really good dance performance of the age-old epic of Rama and Sita. Although a visit to the Taj Mahal was arranged Mrs Bandaranaike was more keen to get the terms of the pact sorted out as thoroughly and expeditiously as possible and so we left that for a later occasion. I remember Mrs Bandaranaike making this point clear to Prime Minister Shastri at the Ashok Hotel just prior to an official dinner given in her honour by the Indian Premier, a really sincere and simple leader.

Commonwealth Conferences – Bahamas

At the conference in the Bahamas in 1968, when the UNP was in power and Felix was in the Opposition, Shirley Corea, the then Speaker, led the delegation. So many interesting things happened. Every evening Shirley used to insist on the members of the delegation coming over for drinks to his room. There Dr. N. M. Perera who made rather capitalist-oriented speeches when abroad – because after all he was addressing the very capitalist group at these conferences, was at his best. Dr. N. M. Perera even though he disagreed with Felix politically on many matters, was a very kind-hearted person. During my eye operations in England he as Finance Minister gave me all the assistance by releasing the foreign exchange that I wanted. Vivienne Goonewardene came with a bunch of orchids to see me before I left for my eye operation in London and I was really touched. There was Festus Perera of the United National Party and of course Sam Wijesinha, the then Secretary-General of Parliament, always amiable and always willing to oblige anyone.

Shirley Corea had to make a speech the following day and Sam was greatly perturbed that no preparation had been made towards it, and so in his affable manner asked Felix whether he would oblige by preparing one for Shirley. To produce speeches was no great problem for Felix who was adept at hammering away on his typewriter (which incidentally he carried with him on his trips to whatever part of the globe he went) and he produced a very good UNP speech for Shirley. Shirley spoke of the lack of co-operation on the part of the SLFP (Felix being a SLFP top runger in the opposition) and defended the policies of the UNP. The papers were slipped under Shirley's door by Sam Wijesinha and the next day Shirley was roundly applauded for his most interesting and thought-provoking speech, Shirley being quite unaware who the author was! Those were good days when being in opposing parties whose policies were dramatically opposed so to speak – still enabled Members of Parliament to enjoy without rancour each other's company.

I remember quite clearly in the early 1960 elections and even in 1965 and 1970 elections there was so much good feeling between the UNP candidate at Dompe and Felix that the UNP candidate never hesitated to partake of the sandwiches and coffee, generous portions of which I used to organise during the night of the count.

It was in the Bahamas that Felix really got to know Mrs Margaret Thatcher who was then a Member of Parliament of Her Majesty's Opposition. There was some misunderstanding over a statement made by a member of one of the delegations from a Commonwealth country in Africa and Felix was assigned the difficult task of talking things over with Margaret Thatcher at a working lunch where Sam Wijesinha was also present. Felix had to convince Margaret Thatcher that the pointed remarks made by this member should not be taken too seriously and that Britain's role in the Commonwealth was even at that time very useful and important.

It was interesting watching the Prime Minister of the Bahamas dance with the waitresses after the official dinner to the delegates to the tune of a hot calypso. Prime Minister Pindling really knew how to move with Bahamians and was therefore able to hold power. Mrs Pindling with her brown complexion and beautifully chiselled features was a very interesting woman to talk to as she entertained the wives of the delegates including Pakistan President Ayub Khan's daughter at the very expensive and elegant Cafe Martinique.

The Bahamian Government was determined to take the delegates to the more important islands in the Bahamas. The Members of Parliament were to be taken to Eluthera and the wives of the delegates to the Virgin Islands. Owing to some mix-up the men were taken to the Virgin Islands and this was the cause for a lot of ribald laughter among the male delegates. The wives were met by a group of Elutheran islanders who quite unself-consciously recited their little pieces on the assumption that they were addressing the men with no change in the gender, much to the amusement of us all. We had a heavy day's programme because we had to make hastily improvised speeches in response to the welcome speeches at each point of the receptions organised to entertain the MPs. We planted saplings, hugged kids and we were sure we came up to the standards of the MPs. Whilst we were busily engaged in all these, the MPs had rather an easy programme which had really been laid on for us. Felix had heard that there was a Sri Lankan who had come on a contract to do agriculture and when he called on him the latter insisted that he have lunch with him. By some mistake Felix missed the plane and when I questioned the others who returned without him I was told by them that Felix was last seen swimming in the Bahamian waters with them. I really got frantic because I knew that Felix was no swimmer – but my fears were allayed in a matter of half an hour when Felix rolled into the hotel. He said that an American millionaire who has his own private plane brought him back. This was confirmed when we received as a gift – a big first aid box from the Johnson and Johnson company he owned.

How the waiters balanced about ten glasses on a tray and brought them around waving their torsos is a picture I shall always remember. Sam never forgot to order the delicious crepe suzette laced with rum for the Sri Lankan delegation who seemed to have a great liking for this dessert.

We were all waiting for the cars to come to the porch of the hotel to be taken to a night club at the Bahamas – this was part of the programme laid on by the conference authorities. There were the British, the Canadians, the

Indians with their headgear (this did not prevent them from dancing quite happily with the beautiful Bahamian ladies) and the delegates from the South Sea Islands. One of the delegates from Fiji – a very stout gentleman who wore a cloth wrapped round his shorts was waiting for a taxi to be taken to the night club. The taximan refused point-blank to take him when he said "Man, you have got no pants on." There was laughter.

The Belgrade Non-Aligned Summit Conference, 1961

In foreign affairs during both SLFP governments 1960-1965 and in 1970-1977 the SLFP played a major role in the Non-Aligned Movement. There was the Belgrade Conference in Yugoslavia where SWRD's policy of Non-Alignment was upheld in every respect. I myself was present with Felix and I can never forget the momentous speech when Mrs Bandaranaike declared as a woman and a mother her horror of nuclear weapons. I remember quite clearly the thunderous applause she received. The attitude of a poor Third World country, yet so independent in her outlook, was greatly appreciated by all.

The highlight of this conference from my point of view was that Mrs Bandaranaike seated next to the Swaziland delegate was surprised that the leader had only chains round his enormous chest and no upper garments. At one stage she nervously remarked to N. Q. Dias in Sinhala that she was reminded of the story of Angulimala.

We visited the underground caves of Posteina I believe used by President Tito for purposes of attack during the war, from which caves hung stalactites and stalagmites.

President and Madam Tito who were personal friends of Mrs Bandaranaike arranged a trip to Zagreb where a dinner was given in her honour which was also attended by the King and Queen of Nepal.

We were also taken to the Brioni islands where we in a horse-carriage enjoyed its scenic beauty – the plethora of anthuriums against the backdrop of verdant pasture and spreading trees.

The Non-Aligned Afro-Asian Summit in Cairo, 1964

The independence of Sri Lanka as a country with a distinct attitude, without bowing or cowing down to outside political pressure be it from the West or the East was much respected by the founder members of the Non-Aligned group. Here, too, Felix was not without his humour. He, referring to her earlier remarks in Belgrade that she spoke as a mother, said that at Cairo she should speak as a "Mummy." I remember very clearly, the visit paid by King Hussein on Mrs Bandaranaike at the Nile Hilton, and after very valuable discussions prior to the actual conference His Majesty was pleasantly surprised that there was a Christian Minister amongst Mrs Bandaranaike's delegation, and very promptly offered my husband and myself a trip to Jordan. It was very interesting going to view the grape orchards, also dipping our feet in the Dead sea and getting our feet encrusted in the salt and brine, whilst conscious of the impact of the "Dead Sea Scrolls" on Christianity. A formal lunch was given to the President of Mali, to which we were also invited. The black smooth chiselled face of the President in his flowing national gown, and the beautiful French that emerged from his lips have left a permanent impression on me of a great leader wanting to do his best for his people.

We had the opportunity of seeing the historical olive tree in the Garden of Olives which is so preciously guarded and which has come down from Christ's time. The protocol officer who accompanied us gave me an olive which I treasure.

Invitations by a Head of State were welcome and even though we were relieved of the burden of paying for our tickets and accommodation, we nevertheless were really financially depleted by the time we paid all the numerous tips – for the motor cycle escorts, etc. which we frantically said we did not want, but were still thrust on us.

Amman is a beautiful city and so is Jerusalem because the whole area looked so picturesque with its beautiful vineyards and its lovely little houses dotted around on the hillsides. We recalled with interest a hymn we had sung when we were children when we viewed the walls of Jerusalem –

"There is a green hill far away,
Outside the city wall
Where the Dear Lord was crucified
Who died to save us all."

As we climbed the steps that led to Pilate's office a certain excitement entered us, a kind of thrill that Jesus too had traversed this same route 2,000 years ago – when he boldly claimed to Pilate that he was the "King of the Jews." It is sad that this area has been commercialised by vendors displaying all kinds of wares.

Bethlehem was really beautiful, decorated with beautiful lamps of the Armenian Church but the actual area seemed to have retained its ancient simplicity. Lazarus' tomb was equally impressive. I went down and made a close inspection of it. Now there is a church built around it.

The Non-Aligned Conference in Zambia, 1971

Lusaka was the venue of the Non-Aligned Conference. The foreign dignitaries were housed in the Mulungishi village where there were a number of cottages constructed for the purpose. The houses were very well equipped but for security reasons the food was brought from outside from a central kitchen. A trip was arranged to Livingstone for the PM to see the Victoria Falls, which are on the border between Zimbabwe (Rhodesia) and South Africa. We went in small Cessna planes and were able to see the scenery at close quarters because the pilot was quite obliging and dived down for our benefit. The Falls were really gorgeous and this was the highlight of our trip. President Kenneth Kaunda tends to be rather emotional and during provocative speeches he becomes very lachrymose to the point of pulling out his handkerchief from his arm band to dry his eyes.

Both the President and the Tanzanian President Julius Nyerere are committed Christians and would quote from the Psalms to strengthen their arguments. On our way to Zambia, we stopped at Nairobi and a trip was arranged for Mrs Bandaranaike to go on a small safari to view the wildlife there. At the Kafui Park, she missed seeing the elephants. So she got up very early next morning and did a second trip and saw many elephants. Felix good-humouredly remarked that Mrs Bandaranaike was so keen to see elephants in Africa but wanted to liquidate the UNP elephants in Sri Lanka.

The Parliamentary Conference in Malawi, 1972

We were at the dinner of President H. Kamuzu Banda called HELP – His Excellency the Life President. (I sometimes wonder whether we brought the know-how of how to do this to Sri Lanka.) Hastings Banda makes interminably long speeches at his formal dinners that most of the delegates imbibed with the Bacchus brew tended to nod off and fall asleep. The tables were arranged in a rather unusual fashion, the husbands ranged on one side of the table and the wives opposite them. Incidentally the invitation card is addressed to the MP with an empty space for the name of the wife or the mistress as it so happens. Having seen the President with his glamorous lady-in-waiting half his age beside him, Felix, when asked by an innocuous questioner who I was, replied that I was his lady-in-waiting!

Sam arranged a trip outside the city for the Sri Lankan delegates but on this occasion Dr. Colvin R. de Silva, Sam, Felix and I set out for Mozambique. At the border Colvin being de Silva and Felix and I being Dias Bandaranaikes had no problem and the Portuguese virtually slapped Colvin and Felix on their backs as being one of them.

We were much impressed with the low-grown tea plantations resembling the tea in the Galle area but what amazed us were the adobe houses made of wattle and daub that the natives lived in. They were like half moons raised in the centre with a tiny door and a very tiny window, ochre in colour somewhat like the ochre of our wattle and daub houses. There did not appear to be any light and air in them. The Portuguese Fort was similar in appearance to the Fort area in Galle, but it had pictures of a De Azevedo or similar Portuguese character engraved on the side facing the entrance. The giant prawns flown into the market from the coast had been fried in spice by our host, a young Tamil gentleman who had come over as a tea taster in charge of the tea factory. We were told that the machinery had been manufactured by Walker & Greig specially to take in low-country teas. We were so hungry that we really enjoyed the home-cooked curry and rice whilst our host entertained us with Sri Lanka tapes with both Tamil and Sinhala music. Sri Lankan hospitality was showered on us and we were gifted with beautiful shirts with African prints and other mementos. We urged our young host to get a nice Tamil girl to be his wife as soon as possible.

At Malawi too Felix had the opportunity of meeting Mrs Margaret Thatcher and exchanging views on commonwealth matters. Swaran Singh, then Foreign Minister of India, who died recently, was a clever and astute man and yet so warm and friendly. We had occasion to meet him at several International Conferences.

The Non-Aligned Conference in Algiers, 1973

The key figure at this conference was President Boumedienne and his Foreign Minister Bouteflika, who spoke excellent French, and who commanded the respect of all the OPEC countries. I was very keen to hear President Fidel Castro of Cuba and President Idi Amin of Uganda speak as they were very much in evidence and mobbed by the foreign correspondents. Algiers was flooded with succulent mandarins, very edible olives, and pistachios. We really enjoyed the latter. Anura Bandaranaike accompanied the Prime Minister and made some useful suggestions with regard to Ceylon's approach at the conference.

Trip to Middle-East

In 1974 when Felix led a delegation to the Middle-East I accompanied him as his Private Secretary. The officials who went along with him were Dr. Lal Jayawardana, Dr. Austin Fernando and Elmo Seneviratne. For reasons of economy we always travelled economy class. Since our delegation was aware that no liquor was permitted in some of the countries in the Middle-East and to fortify themselves against a very hard-working Minister they had found it handy to carry an Air Lanka case containing the forbidden pre-dinner aperitif. At the Kuwait airport one of the officials who carried the Air Lanka case whilst standing behind a Kuwait passenger in a black kabaya (dress worn by women in the Middle-East) found to his horror that the contents of his bag were dripping badly. When the lady looked back peering through her face veil, thoroughly embarrassed, the official smiled sweetly and hurriedly left the queue leaving the bag.

In Kuwait, Felix had arranged a discussion in his room at 2 p.m. with his officials prior to the main discussion with the Kuwait Minister the next day. One of the officials with my connivance introduced a note supposed to come from a foreign tourist inviting one of the learned doctors in our delegation to a tryst with her beside the swimming pool at 3 p.m. When the meeting began the officials engaged in lengthy discussions but when it was almost 3 p.m. the recipient of the invitation was restive and impatient to get away and asked to be excused. But after a while he came back looking very downcast. Later on that night at dinner the whole story was out and we had a good laugh.

The Middle-East countries do not in any way tolerate dishonesty and anyone who is on the wrong side of the law is dealt with quite severely and may even lose his hand if found guilty of theft. The sending of maids to Kuwait was discussed but the SLFP Government fell and the next Government took over the exercise.

Trip to Iran

Felix paid two visits to Iran. The first was to explore the possibilities of negotiating a loan and inviting the Iranian Government's co-operation in setting up joint ventures in Sri Lanka. This visit was so successful that the Iranian Government invited Prime Minister Sirimavo Bandaranaike who was also the Minister of Planning, Defence and External Affairs to visit Iran for discussions and to finalise a programme of economic co-operation between the two countries. The question of establishing a diplomatic mission in Teheran was also considered.

Accepting the invitation Mrs Bandaranaike left for Iran with Felix and the other officials who had accompanied him earlier. Mrs Bandaranaike thought it appropriate to take a gift of a Sri Lankan baby elephant for the Teheran Zoo. The Princess Farah Diba was so happy about it and wanted a formal presentation on the Palace ground. The baby elephant was caparisoned with a beautiful batik and drank enormous quantities of milk given by the keeper. The lunch that followed was so sumptuous and so elegant. The Princess was knowledgeable about Sri Lanka and often referred to the book Island-Ceylon by Roloff Beny.

We were taken to inspect a carpet-weaving centre in Teheran and we found that some of the more intricately-woven and beautiful carpets had been hand-woven by women who had grown old in the industry because some of the carpets took over fifteen years to be completed. The carpets at Isfahan had such a thick pile and were equally beautiful.

We were invited to dinner by a Wijewardena, a Sri Lankan who had married an Iranian lady. He held a high position in the Iranian Civil Air Line as he was an Aeronautical Engineer. He informed us that the Shah occasionally travelled incognito in the city to gauge his popularity among his people. Perhaps the Shah had some intuitive perception of what was in store for him and his government, even though the U.S.A. itself seemed to have been taken unawares when it happened.

We were amazed at the Shah's knowledge of world affairs particularly of the United States of America, which regarded him as the bastion of peace and security in the Middle-East where the monarchy in Iraq had been overthrown.

The Cabinet headed by Prime Minister Hoveda consisted mainly of technocrats trained in the United States who were thought to be an ideal team to develop Iran fast with the millions of petro dollars that flowed to those countries as a result of OPEC (Organisation of Petroleum Exporting Countries).

When the Khomeni Government took over, the Shah fled the country but his Prime Minister and Cabinet were liquidated along with a number of high officials.

Trip to Saudi Arabia

Our visit to Saudi Arabia was equally interesting. We went to Riyadh and Jeddah. Felix met the Minister for Petroleum Products Sheikh Amani, and a key figure in the OPEC countries and asked for financial assistance to help us to tide over the problems in the oil crisis which had its beginning in October 1973 – when Sri Lanka had to pay very high prices for oil.

Another remarkable thing I noticed was that no interest is charged for any loan given by the Middle-East countries because it violates the tenets of religion of Islam. Felix acquainted himself with the Islamic law and studied the Koran before he embarked on his trips to the Middle-East and this proved to be of immense use to him to set the tone for his negotiations.

Felix the Man – The Human Face

Felix was young but he had the stamp of his father as if he belonged to the same vintage. It was said that Felix had a proud and imperious and sometimes arrogant manner which irritated his colleagues but he moved comfortably with his voters. To me, he was "my only friend" warm, loving and so kind and considerate, never rushing to conclusions.

Felix's was six feet tall and stately with a deep voice, double chin and had a very imposing personality. It was said that if he entered a room even with a host of people one could feel his presence and all eyes naturally turned towards him. Felix's weakness was that he could not suffer fools gladly, especially when his officials came unprepared for conferences. He was an excellent teacher who also displayed the same administrative ability which his father possessed when he reorganised the district court; a quality he inherited from his father. At the same time he mixed so well with the homespun Dompe voters to whose level he came down so easily. In 1960 when he was campaigning in Dompe – the voters wanted to try out how down-to-earth he was. They insisted on giving him toddy (distilled from the coconut palm) and he drank with the best of them.

I remember when one of his supporters, Kamala, a staunch Buddhist was taken ill with breast cancer, Felix spent hours at the Cancer Hospital, Maharagama studying the case, questioning the doctors, especially the surgeon, Dr. Tony Gabriel and doing everything possible by way of treatment for this lady. When Bishop Chu Ban It came from Singapore Felix made her come with her husband to the Cathedral and made the clergy pray for her to give her the moral courage to carry on and not be resigned to her fate. To this day when she comes home she has never forgotten the peace of mind she got at that solemn scene at the Cathedral, and the fact that she has outlived her former MP.

There was a supporter of his, a Jayawardene from Mandawala, whom he liked very much. When his wife suddenly for no apparent reason lost her mental balance, Felix had no hesitation in spending hours and hours with the family at Malcolm Perera's healing services.

The electorate was well looked after. Anyone who had six fingers – promptly had one out, those with goitres were taken to his own doctor for advice and Dr. O. R. Medonza always gave medical advice so readily. Dr. P. R. Anthonis helped a Dompe patient and understood his problems of finances. The generous doctors would readily waive their fees.

Felix was a Sirima loyalist and he never wavered from this position right to the end. Even in defeat when he was put under a lot of pressure by the SLFP he did not fail in his loyalty to his leader at a time when Maithripala Senanayeke and Anura Bandaranaike moved away from her. Felix joined with Chandrika, Sri Lanka's present President, and Vijaya Kumaratunga her husband and organised a fantastic come-back for Mrs Bandaranaike by getting key representatives on the party from all over Sri Lanka to collect at a huge meeting at Nittambuwa to express their solidarity with her. This made Vijaya remark at later meetings of his that the SLFP never really appreciated

Felix as a loyal lieutenant to his leader. When Vijaya was detained in custody by the UNP Government on a charge that he was a Naxalite, Felix visited him several times and presented him with the famous Chuck Colsen book "Born Again", written whilst Colsen was in prison.

Felix was a man who was never on the defensive. His political thinking was nationalist and socialist and so he went bravely into the political field with tenacity and courage. Felix was a towering front-runner whose shoulders were broad enough to handle the most difficult of situations – be it a coup, insurrection, bank strike – Ceylon Transport Board strike, what have you.

When the SLFP government imposed an islandwide curfew, as the need arose banned all opposition meetings and sealed the Independent Newspapers group the following obituary appeared in a national daily.

O'CRACY. – The death occurred under tragic circumstances of D. E. M. O'CRACY, beloved husband of T. Ruth, loving father of L. I. Bertie, brother of Faith, Hope and Justitia. Interred on Saturday, 20th inst. – Araliya Medura, Panagiyawatte, Anduruwala.

Felix's response in Parliament was reported in the newspapers as follows:

O'CRACY STILL ALIVE AND KICKING

Mr Felix Dias Bandaranaike yesterday demonstrated that he was as good a hand at defusing explosive parliamentary situations as he is at tossing (verbal) grenades into Assembly debates.

After Dr. Dahanayake had been carried out by a posse of Police, Mr Bandaranaike took the floor last evening to make a brief speech that Dr. Colvin R. de Silva was to later describe as "brilliant."

Using a master raconteur's talent for telling a good story, Mr Bandaranaike punned a beautiful yarn about an Irishman from Limmerick, Mr O'Cracy, who'd sunk roots here in Sri Lanka.

"Within the banter, Mr Bandaranaike had a lot of telling points: that Mr O'Cracy had been a very close friend of Mr S. W. R. D. Bandaranaike (in fact, it was SWRD who had introduced Felix to the Irishman), that he had a couple of narrow shaves in 1962 and 1971 but survived these ordeals, and that in spite of the obituary notice published in the local press the gentleman was alive and kicking.

And that concluded, Felix went for the O'Cracy family, T. Ruth, L. I. Berty and the lot.

It showed him as a man – who when attacked responded with humour, wit and grace.

Felix did not borrow a leaf from anyone else's book. He was a pragmatic socialist with compassion for the poor and an earnest desire to improve their lot. He gave his fullest support to the Free Trade Zone proposal which Dr. Seevali Ratwatte put up, but at that time the Communist Party in Sri Lanka did not want to accept the proposal even though in the Soviet Union there were multinational companies like Coca Cola, etc.

Felix had a fantastic memory. He could remember details of a conversation he had with the PM years afterwards and she would not hesitate to draw on his memory whenever the situation arose. Even as a young child he spent many a Saturday morning reading voraciously at Cave & Company so many books that suited his fancy, but ultimately buying one with his saved-up pocket money just before the shop closed. There wasn't a Wodehouse or an Erle Stanley Gardiner or a Dickens, or a Walter Scott that Felix had not read. He enjoyed reading, and he never missed his reading in the night before he went to bed. In such a moment it was impossible to disturb him because if you did he would give rather random and disconnected answers because he had not fully understood the word pictures of the writer which recreated for him a new world in which he moved, a world of laughter and fun, mystery, and sorrow and despair. Reading had disciplined his mind at a very early age and Felix when he spoke, spoke seriously and meant every word he said so that there was no hypocrisy which marred his thoughts. All the little bookshops along McCallum Road were not spared and so from week to week he would renew his stocks. How he enjoyed reading his favourite Wodehouse books to our daughter Christine when she was a young child. He introduced her to the mysteries of the world of books and she has become like Felix a voracious reader. Even at a party she would quietly detach herself from the rest of her friends, get into a corner and start reading. She has now got an honours degree in Economics and is reading for her Master's at Toronto University. Felix was waiting for this day but fate decreed otherwise.

I am told that Felix's grandmother was presented in the Royal Court of His Majesty in 1904. From the time I married Felix he used to mention that she was an excellent cook and that she was a specialist at making ginger chocolates which were beautifully glazed. She also made marzipan and various sweets such as fudge and bola fiados which recipes came down from Portuguese and Dutch times. During Christmas or for that matter at any time Breudhers were special favourites with the Bandaranaikes, and so were the cheeses of all makes. Felix's father's brother, Sammy Dias Bandaranaike, inherited this culinary expertise and we used to enjoy his dinners, and the beautiful hand-done marzipans. I remember Felix tucking into goat cheese both in Norway and East Berlin where the cold platter with a variety of cheeses was very popular at supper. 'Gova kaldu' was the famous Bandaranaike dish consisting of stringhoppers – soup with ham and tender cabbage and chicken curry, and buttered eggs and seeni sambol, which Felix enjoyed. It was made on festive occasions.

Felix started smoking cigarettes whilst he was young and at Royal College and had received many a punishment from the Royal College Principal Bradby for disobeying school rules. He even led a strike at Royal College. Later on he took to the pipe, and unlike his grandfather Felix who was a cigar smoker, Felix stuck to his pipe. He had a tidy collection of at least fifty pipes. He learnt the art of selecting the best brand of tobacco, rolling it on his palm, seasoning his tobacco by mixing different varieties and adding a little sherry to improve the flavour.

Dudley Senanayake, the former Prime Minister, was also a pipe smoker and I have seen on many an occasion Felix sending gifts to Dudley Senanayake of pipes and tobacco after a trip of his abroad. Dudley Senanayake too used to reciprocate in the same manner. Felix mentioned to me that about two weeks prior to Dudley Senanayake's death, he called Felix into his room in Parliament and told him that even though they are on opposite sides of the political spectrum, Felix should continue in politics for the good of his country.

An interesting incident that happened in the 1965-1970 Parliament is difficult to forget. Dudley Senanayake was extolling the virtues of Gal Oya and the work done by the United National Party on the Gal Oya Valley to make it very productive. Dudley talked about the Green Revolution in the valley. Felix with his puckish sense of humour, with a straight face asked Dudley from the Opposition benches "How green was your valley." Dudley got very upset and sought to come across shouting "I'll teach you how green was my valley." Friendly MPs intervened and separated them as it often happens when feelings run high between Government and members of the Opposition. Within minutes of the incident the tea bells rang and I had to convey an urgent message to Felix and would you believe it I found him seated at a table in the restaurant with Dudley Senanayake tucking into a tremendous amount of eats like levariya, kavun, vadai, cakes and other sweetmeats. In those days political rivalries were not taken into people's private lives and many an MP fought an Opposition MP in a straight clean argument and there were no hidden grudges for which one would bide one's time to crush the other.

Felix like his great grandfather James d'Alwis, was also ahead of his time. His imposition of the cut in the rice ration in the Budget of 1962 to save much, needed foreign exchange could not be understood by his fellow party people, some of whom quite naturally had not the foggiest notion of what foreign exchange meant. Therefore they ganged up to get his proposal knocked on the head, even though it was a Cabinet decision. Shirley

Felix and Lakshmi
University Days.

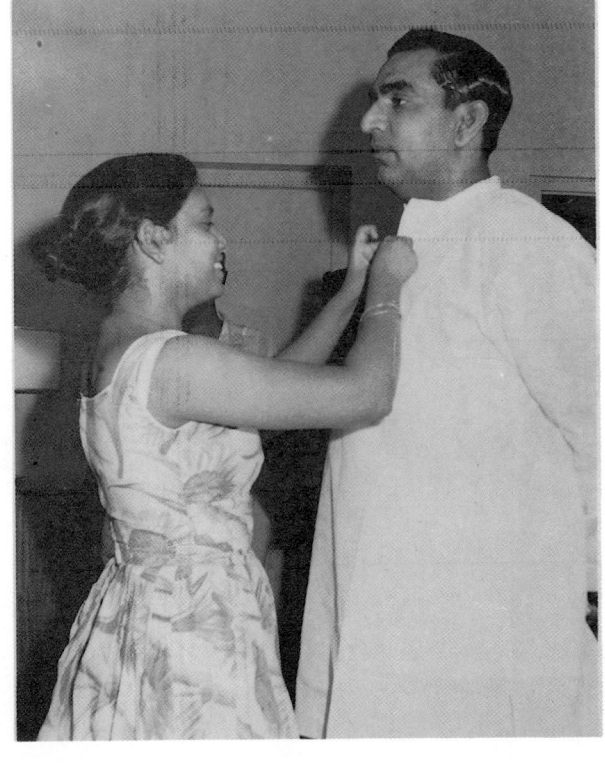

Felix in National Costume.

Felix's father Dr. R. F. Dias
Bandaranaike.

Felix's
mother Fred

Felix and his Godmother
Ursula Bloom (Mrs Gower Robinson).

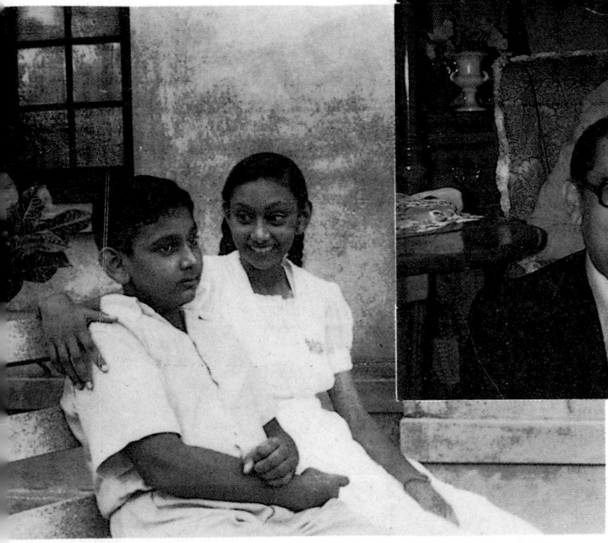

Felix with his sister Christine.

In happier
times Felix
and his sister
Christine.

Felix in Jaffna with
Justice
H. W. Tambiah,
Sri Kantha, GA.,
P. B. G. Kalugalle,
Maitripala
Senanayeke,
M. Sivasithamparam,
and others.

Felix with his
lawyer friend
H. D. Perera,
D. A. P.
Suriyapperuma and
other supporters in
Dompe.

Felix with JVP
Leader Rohana
Wijeweera and
Prince Gunasekera
outside the
Court-house.

Felix with Dudley Senanayake, former Prime Minister.

Felix at Commonwealth Parliamentary Conference with Lord Home, British Foreign Secretary and Robin Vanderfelt, Secretary-General.

Felix with C. P. de Silva.
Mini Non-Aligned Summit Colombo, 1962.

Felix with Mrs Bandaranaike and
Maitripala Senanayeke.

Felix welcomed in Jaffna.

Amerasinghe, his Permanent Secretary, was most disappointed. Felix was forced to withdraw his proposal and in accordance with Cabinet convention resigned his portfolio. Never had any Minister prior to 1962 or afterwards resigned his portfolio in a similar situation.

Felix in Finance – 1975

Differences in opinion began to emerge between Mrs Bandaranaike and the LSSP and for reasons best known to Mrs Bandaranaike, the LSSP was asked to leave the Government.

With the exit of Dr. N. M. Perera, Felix was offered the portfolio of Finance in late 1975, when he had gone for the Non-Aligned Foreign Ministers' Conference in Georgetown capital of Guyana. Georgetown was familiar ground for Sonny Ramphal, earlier Foreign Minister of Guyana and later Secretary-General of the Commonwealth Secretariat in London whom Felix got to know very well. Shirley Amerasinghe was the chief official of the team. Felix was present at the unveiling ceremony of the busts of President Tito of Yugoslavia, Prime Minister Nehru and President Nasser. Mr T. B. Ilangaratne had declined to become Finance Minister in place of Dr. N. M. Perera – knowing well that treading on one's friend's corns is dangerous, but Felix had no choice because the Prime Minister rang him up again in Washington where he had gone for the World Bank Meeting and asked him to accept the post. My advice was not always taken and so Felix was sworn in as Finance Minister in Washington before Neville Kanakaratne our Ambassador with a fanfare of trumpets, kiribath and kokis.

On his return to Sri Lanka Felix's Deputy Minister Neale de Alwis who had been a Samasajist earlier advised Felix to get people loyal to him to the Ministry. Therefore cleaning the decks of a Left Ministry set-up, to a SLFP set-up, was a difficult task during the course of a government. Dr. Lal Jayawardana helped Felix with the budget which was due in a very short time. To present a budget was no easy task even though one thinks one can cope with such a situation. The war was on, the ousted left party, the LSSP, actively encouraged by the Opposition, were determined to crush the Government. If the SLFP had an election at the end of five years without reckoning the five years from the 1972 Constitution, as suggested by Dr. Colvin R. de Silva the situation would have been immensely better for the SLFP.

Dr. N. M. Perera had given Felix the nickname "Satan" and kept on hammering Felix right through from 1975-1977. Perhaps Felix paid the price for helping to keep the Government of Mrs Bandaranaike from 1960-1965 and from 1970-1977 going, by following the genuine middle path policies of the late Prime Minister S. W. R. D. Bandaranaike. They may have called him Satan – but Satan is very often the evil tempter who tries to keep a person from the straight and narrow way – but it is this "Satan" Felix who did not swerve to the right or left but acted so fast and so swiftly to protect his Prime Minister and her government in the1962 coup and the insurrection in 1971. A no-confidence motion sponsored by the UNP and the LSSP was brought against Felix. He put forward such an excellent defence that ultimately no vote was taken and it all fizzled out. What Felix felt was the best decision at that time was to call a general election and not to persevere with a depleted cabinet. But other factors such as the on-coming Non-Aligned Conference to be held in Colombo in September 1976 was very much on the horizon – especially after such a hard fought battle at Georgetown at the Non-Aligned Foreign Ministers' Conference to have the next Non-Aligned Conference of Heads of States in Colombo. It seemed a pity not to have the Conference with Colombo as its venue. Even after the victory at the Tissamaharama by-election in 1976 the party could easily have gone to the polls, and perhaps not got a runaway victory – but would not have fared so badly as in 1977. Even in defeat, the United Front Government left a Sri Lanka which could be freely traversed from South to North and from West to East. Unfortunately it is not so now because the LTTE is in full control of the North and their permission is necessary to leave the province or enter it.

Human beings, ordinary persons do get tired of the same government and the same faces after a considerable period of time, and the hacked age-old saying "familiarity breeds contempt" is not without its point. As I said earlier, Felix spoke of a "little bit of totalitarianism" when governing and he was at the receiving end of innumerable attacks but thinking aloud sometimes helps to formulate one's thoughts. I do not think he was referring to the totalitarianism of a dictatorship where every independent thought is not allowed to raise its head, but firm discipline without which it is impossible to carry out any task for the good of the people.

A Journey into Spirituality

Born to Anglican parents, who were meticulously on time at St. Michael's and All Angels, Polwatte, every Sunday, religious disciplines were instilled into Felix from a very early age. The distinction between right and wrong was made very clear to Felix by his father and there was no question of shades of right and wrong. Groomed in such a tradition, there was also bound to be a protest at some stage. Although he carried the silver cross on festival days in his church, engaged in Christian activities at Christmas time, Felix always felt that the organised church with all its rituals which he respected in no uncertain terms, was not sufficient to satisfy the spiritual needs of a person and give him the necessary spiritual strength to carry on.

In his 1960 campaign in Dompe he clearly indicated to the would-be voters that religion to him was something very personal and he did not come to them with the intention of building churches in Dompe, nor did he come there to destroy the Buddhist temples. In short, he was not going to be a hypocrite. It was so succinctly put that from the very inception the people accepted him, and appreciated the position he took up so much so that in 1970 they gave him the biggest majority in Sri Lanka even though it was a 99% Buddhist electorate. But the ways of human beings are very unpredictable and so this same electorate voted him out of power in 1977.

In the midst of a Presidential Commission of Inquiry against him Felix always found the time to intensify his religious reading and begin to get a much more comprehensive understanding of the position of the individual in relation to his God and his creator. From this point on he read intensively and started correspondence courses with various religious institutions in America. After all the slating he received at the hands of the late Bunty de Zoysa at the Presidential Commission he never lost his faith. In fact his faith grew stronger. He was also very keen to bring together the various religious groups in Sri Lanka and many a time he would organise a tea party at home and invite the leaders of such groups for discussions. He called himself a "grasshopper Christian" because he felt a great urge to go to the various groups and join in their worship. So it was not uncommon to see Felix seated on the floor of Malcolm Perera's house religiously every Saturday afternoon, taking part in his service or on a Thursday at Vimala Ellalasingam's house singing choruses, or at Pastor Lloyd Perera's at the Gospel Tabernacle.

At the Dutch Reformed Church he enjoyed hearing from Pastor Neville Koch the implications of various truths of the Bible whilst following a TAFTEE (The Association for Theological Education by Extension) course, or from Pastor Duleep Fernando of the Methodist Church – learning the finer points of the Epistle to the Romans. After being literally crushed and humiliated by a scourge of enemies around him, his faith in God grew stronger and he yearned to learn the Bible in much greater depth than he knew and so in 1983 at the instance of Pastor Don Rubesh he decided to go to Portland, Oregon and join the Multnomah School of the Bible on the West Coast of USA and do a degree course in Christianity.

Felix integrated beautifully into the school's programme with lectures on all aspects of the Bible and its relationship to past, present and future. He had lecturers like Dr. Kovisto, Dr. Donald Blake, Dean of Multnomah Graduate School, Mr David Needham, Dr. Willard Aldrich and Professor John Mitchell who took great pains to instil the finer aspects of biblical doctrine into the minds of their students. Apologetics was Felix's favourite subject. It was in effect an exhaustive study of the arguments for the existence of a God, of creation, of the values and tenets of Christian doctrine and a training in the technique of how to present an argument for Christianity, what can Christians say to agnostics, to natural scientists or to Buddhists or Hindus? Felix was able to identify himself with the students or even with the Cambodian community to whom he taught English on Saturdays as part of his Christian ministry, and this was a great achievement for a man coming from a Third World country whose cultural values and background were so different from the U.S.A.

Felix was 51 then but his class-mates were young students. He treated them so well that many a time they would drop by at our house in the evenings and ask Felix to help them over their work. Felix always maintained that he was really born to be a teacher and so he enjoyed helping them.

Simultaneous with his attendance at Multnomah he was in touch with the Haggai Institute based in Singapore – an organisation sponsored mainly by rich American millionaires for purposes of training Third World leaders to go out and spread the good news.

During his course at Portland he got leave from the school and went to Georgia for a special conference organised by the Haggai Institute. Georgia had a large black community and he was most impressed how God's Word was being communicated there and how positive was the reaction of those who heard it. After the termination of his course at Multnomah, he attended a conference at San Francisco where our daughter Christine and I too had the opportunity of going. It was really for the purpose of collecting funds from Christian millionaires by explaining to them the work that was being done in Singapore. Needless to say being an able speaker he together with another delegate, I believe a Supreme Court Judge of Singapore, managed to persuade the audience to make very generous contributions towards the cause.

Felix registered for a post-graduate course at the Orange Law School, USA run by Professor Montgomery specially concentrating on apologetics, but he was taken ill on his return to Sri Lanka on a short holiday and was unable to make it.

Last Days

Dr. Oliver Medonza, during the harrowing period after 1977 told me that it would have been better to put a pistol to Felix's head rather than for him to go through all the mental agony of appearing before Commissions. "You must not fail in your task to obtain a CAT Scanner for Sri Lanka" said the ailing Felix to me so that the mistakes made in my case may not happen to any other person in Sri Lanka.

"Has your husband been under great stress?" Dr. Goldstraw asked me at the London University Hospital. My quick response was that I did not think any man in Sri Lanka had been put under more stress in recent times, under more mental torture with Presidential Commissions and with films like "Sagarayak Meda" attacking him than Felix. Addressing a meeting some time after the deprivation of his civic rights, Felix remarked: 'Although I have been deprived of my civic rights in Sri Lanka I am assured of them in the New Jerusalem.'

"I have filed action against the State Film Corporation for showing "Sagarayak Meda" and I know I will succeed" said Felix. "Gamini Fonseka is not worth suing, he is only a paid actor. After all, haven't I succeeded in two cases during my political career of 17 years and both against Lake House, the latter on defamation."

Felix died on June 26th 1985 of a lung cancer. I did not take long to form the Felix Dias Bandaranaike Memorial Trust and all the members of the newly-constituted trust went all-out on our collection campaign to reach our target of Rs. 16 million. There was newspaper publicity calling for public donations and the response was very good. All the moneys went into the Government National Health Development Fund. There were contributions ranging from Rs. 1 lakh to even small sums of Rs. 10/- because even the poor began to realise how important a piece of medical equipment this was. It was really touching to see Felix's everfaithful servant Lucy contributing her savings to the FRDB Trust. Very soon everyone in Sri Lanka began to know what Computerised Axial Tomography (CAT) was. A Sri Lankan lady who had become an American citizen came over on one of her usual trips to Sri Lanka and in a moment of generosity came over to my house where we were at one of our trust meetings and on her own promised in the presence of all our trustees to donate this equipment to Sri Lanka as she said she had done in the States to a hospital there, and as a token of her good faith issued a cheque for 25,000 dollars, which was handed to the appropriate authority. The publicity given to her over Rupavahini and the local newspapers was so great that all the donors who promised us, especially the big mercantile establishments which started competing with one another in their offers did on this piece of information forget their promises. Even in the case of a dead man I wonder whether politics had its part to play. I do not know, but unfortunately the whole campaign of ours was aborted when the lady did not fulfil her promise. The trust did not give up hope and we forged ahead in our collection campaign. The services of such an instrument which helps in the early detection of cancer and also of other illnesses cannot be underestimated.

When Mrs Sunethra Ranasinghe was Minister of Health in the last UNP Government she arranged for a CAT scanner to be installed in the Neurology Department of the General Hospital in Colombo headed by Dr. J. B. Pieris who together with Dr. George Fernando took a great interest in this project. The FRDB Trust which had a collection of nearly a million rupees contributed the moneys towards this and I had the good fortune of being a party to the opening of the ward with the CAT scanner which had a plaque in memory of Felix. I got two swans intertwined on the plaque and in my speech that day remarked that in any concern dealing with health there should be no politics and that all parties should co-operate in whatever development work we do for our country.

How does one explain the defeat in 1977?

Felix maintained that half our problems in Sri Lanka today are due to the fact that we are not good listeners. Have we given heed and listened to the people's voice, their feelings, and frustrations or have we unilaterally pushed ahead a programme which we thought was good for the people materially. Is that all, that a human being wants, is that all that a young man, a young university student wants? True, his parents may be in a position to give him fair housing and clothes, but surely the spiritual needs of the young person whatever his religion, should be looked after. A young person's aesthetic sense, his innovative spirit, his demands, his frustration and his inadequacies have all to be considered and given their due place. The value system of the new generation has to be understood and not overlooked – their idiosyncrasies have to be put up with. Their anxieties with regard to their aged parents in a distant home far away have to be understood. Some intimate counselling is required to enable them to feel that they are not alone.

In 1970, Felix came in with all the enthusiasm of the youth with the largest majority because they felt that he understood them. The "bicycle pelapaliya" provided them with tremendous fun and togetherness. But what happened as the years wore on, with all the problems of government he didn't have sufficient time to spend with his people, not sufficient time to confer with the Buddhist clergy as in 1965-1970, not enough time to plan for the psychological feelings of his young voters and so the estrangement set in which ultimately made him lose his seat.

Perhaps it was Felix's uncompromising nature and adherence to principles in politics that was partly responsible for his defeat. Also, Felix was a man ahead of his time. His reforms were both radical and rapid, causing thereby many enemies among those who were reluctant to change.

Part II
Assessment of the Man – Personal Insights

CHAPTER II

Measuring Felix and
the Bandaranaikes

Haris Hulugalle

Sri Lanka had an identity of its own for the better part of 2000 years, which was preserved by great men of the past who had both strong Sinhala and Tamil connections. Containing this contention which in recent times has erupted into savagery unknown since the middle European war, nearly 50 years ago, required men as extraordinary as Vijayabahu the Great 1000 years ago who held and finally repelled continuing Tamil invasions to secure to this day its unique and indigenous Sinhala culture. Significantly, Vijayabahu was of Tamil origin. It is therefore not fanciful to judge our contemporary leaders in the context of our earlier history and the great men of that time.

How did Felix measure? How well did he hold the line? Would our history have been different, had he not been struck down before his time.

Felix had the bearing of an aristocrat, the intellect of a Brahmin and the compassion of a practising Anglican, qualities which had placed him above any of his contemporaries in Politics, Law or Society. What then went wrong? Why did he allow the slide not only of himself and the Party but, the country itself.

Was he too big for a puny people? Or did he himself allow his great qualities to inflate themselves into his own destruction? We would do well therefore, to study his antecedents, his upbringing, his performance as a politician and above all his own ideas of his country and his world, as expressed in his speeches and writing.

There are a few Sinhala families who can trace their genealogy with great accuracy before the registration of Christian births, deaths, and marriages, after the European arrival. Claims of lineage before that are oral. Myth, most of all embellishes accomplishment among most families. Another curious feature among the Sinhalese was their endogamy to preserve property, but even more to secure themselves against conniving rivals for favour at Court.

Continuing Tamil invasions, compelled Kings to move their capital and often replace their ruling courtiers with new families who had more influence and strength to protect the King in the territories into which he moved. The ruling families of the Kurunegala Kingdom, had replaced those of Yapahuwa or Polonnaruwa and they in turn were replaced, according to Sinhala chronicles by families with new names, when the Court was moved to Kotte, or to a new principality established in Kandy. It was therefore not unusual for the European invaders to create a new native elite and re-educate them in their own culture, to be more faithful to them than to their own Kings.

The Bandaranaike family emerged, according to their own accounts, from an interpreter to the British army invading Kandy and from middle class Kandyan origins (a scribe called Sirimalhamy from Kurunegala is often mentioned). The family embellishes its account with a Tamil ancestor called Nilaperumal. They recognised the strength of the Europeans, admired their life style, shed their own heritage, and went to extremes to emulate them. They became interpreters of Governors, and Government Agents acquiring titles by being firmly on the side of their British Rulers. Bertolacci, an early British Civil servant, describes their likes, "they know to perfection, the art of insinuating themselves into the good opinion and favour of their Superiors...this art is accounted as a necessary part of their education."

At first, they had few of the qualities of the traditional Sinhala Buddhist aristocracy, to whom birth was more important than wealth. There is no record of an eight year old Madduma Bandara, bravely advancing to his execution. In fact, the new ruling class in the Low country, was often abject in their attitude to the European ruler, to secure for themselves place, privilege and wealth in a manner where the highest among them was not unknown for acquisitive instincts which overrode his loyalties.

In an excellent book on their family called "Relative Merits", Felix's cousin Yasmine Gooneratne, reproduces an extract of an account of the "self-help" as she calls it, of one of her craftier forebears from Galle. "Governor Vander Graaf, who was by all acknowledged to bear a superior character among those who have ruled Ceylon, was most grossly deceived by his first Mudaliyar, Abesinga. This man was carrying on a false correspondence between the Governor and the Pilima Talao, first adigar of Kandy, in whose name Abesinga was fabricating letters addressed to the Governor. During this correspondence, on matters of great weight, which were naturally, never brought into conclusion, many presents were interchanged on both sides. Those from the Governor were, as customary always the most costly. When the expectation of Vander Graaf was raised to the highest waiting to the conclusion of a very favourable treaty, Abesinga happened to die and to the great surprise and mortification of the Governor, the whole of his correspondence with the Candian Minister was found in Abesinga's desk, and the presents in his chest."

But the Bandaranaike family soon acquired by marriage, patrician virtues which the older Sinhala aristocracy lacked. There was a sudden flowering of a remarkable succession of scholars. James d'Alwis was outstanding as the first Sinhala scholar, to make comparative studies of Eastern and Western thought and make a brilliant assessment of the Sinhala language and trace its origins to its earliest "Aryan roots." Sir Harry Dias was erudite as a Judge of the Supreme Court, when other Sinhalese could not aspire to be more than clerks in Kachcheries. His brother Canon Dias translated the book of Common Prayer into Sinhala. The Canon's son Felix Dias and his grandson, R. F. Dias, Felix's father, were both Judges, the latter of the Supreme Court. In another branch of the family, Sir Paul Peiris was a distinguished scholar at Cambridge, to be succeeded in similar intellectual attainments by his son, and grandson, Siran Deraniyagala, who is the most knowledgeable Archaeologist to still serve this country.

SWRD

Those of us who were not too enamoured with European rule may discount the public service of this family, in the 19th and 20 century, but, we cannot grudge them praise for the Sinhala revival, which enabled the indigenous culture to withstand, in recent times, fresh onslaughts from South India.

S. W. R. D. Bandaranaike was the well spring of this revival, which was augmented by Felix himself in Education, Justice and Foreign Policy.

Though one does not have to worship departed ancestors, forebears to condition lives by transmitting a heritage which is ultimately reflected in the virtues, attainments and vices of an individual, the Bandaranaike clan, used every device to rise from their interpreter ancestor, to the highest title of Maha Mudaliyar in the British times and secure most other positions of prominence. There were threats from other emerging communities like the Salagamas, who themselves had once been Maha Mudaliyars, they were even overcome on the occasional social scramble, as when Karawe Mudaliyars were given precedence in entertaining the Queen Empress' son, but they always closed ranks, even to the extent of playing Tennis at an exclusive family club, called the 'Nomads,' thus preserving their influence even to this day.

Felix's mother was known to be a gentle and kindly woman who embodies the vestigial virtues of their Sinhalese ancestors before they acquired British colonial attitudes. His father on the other hand, was disowned if not disliked by his peers and had few friends, outside his close kin. In the most charitable assessment of him by his own eldest son Mickey, which is repeated by Yasmine Gooneratne, in her book, "my dislike and resentment of so many things he did distorts a proper appreciation of a good and worthy man underneath, the unstinting length to which he went in educating us, his fine example of integrity, standard and tradition, but I did not like him bullying Freda; or Christine or people beneath him of his overweening esteem of the worth of Dias bandies. My mother, once wrote in one of her letters that his two great faults were selfishness and temper, to that I would add his impetuous jumping to conclusions to him $2 + 2 = 22$, and no one could correct him, he as District Judge of Kandy, of Colombo, Supreme Court Judge knew better. Freda, Christine and I were terrified of him not so much Felix because by the time he grew up pater had lost his fire. Freda, I am told, looked forward to his going off on circuit. Do you wonder why I was so anxious to leave for England in 1939? Never once did I feel homesick or want to go back ever. Home was happier when he was not there." Bred by a martinet and a gentle woman Felix was a bit of both, but even more, he was his own man, an educated man, and a good husband, influenced considerably by a wife of distinguished stock, who had a blind faith in the goodness of God but was questioning about the depravity of man.

When Felix first went to school at Ladies College, he was stepping out into unfamiliar territory, peopled by strangers, perhaps, a step below his own grand and exclusive family. He appears to have had fun and recalled being fascinated by the likes of a fulsome Parsi girl, who was then blossoming into puberty.

The family mould is most often modified by life at school. Trinity was next. As a day scholar, from the privileged household of his father, the District Judge of Kandy, he may not have had the best of Trinity, but he did come to know, for the first time, children of a very varied social and ethnic background.

If Trinity College Kandy, his first boys school, had character, Royal had intellect. For more than a hundred years before Felix was admitted, it was a school which the cleverest boys of every community attended, to produce by itself more distinguished Supreme Court Judges, Physicians, Surgeons, Lawyers, Engineers, Architects and Academics than all the other schools in Ceylon combined. Felix was one of those clever boys but his school career is not particularly distinguished. In the Arts stream there were no pace-setters to spur him to capacity. But he sailed his exams, exploiting the freedom to play truant at will, outside the confines of his strict home. He smoked and played cards against the rules. He openly espoused the cause of the revolutionary left. He gave inspired speeches to spellbound colleagues, when the new Ceylon government of land-owners first began to suppress labour, and entered the University of Ceylon in 1948, unscathed and more mature.

As a student Felix was versatile. There were some contemporaries who may have excelled, as specialists in mathematics or the Sciences, and others who had special talents in the Arts, in English Literature, History. Most of these students followed straight and narrow paths into universities, the Civil Service or the Professions. Felix's genius was that he could apply his mind to any subject at will. He could be as curious about Euclid as of Shakespeare's sonnets. Jewish history fascinated him as much as osmosis in chemistry. He continued these attitudes throughout his life and one of his hobbies even as a Minister, was to study the elements of motor mechanism with a vintage baby Austin in which he had once given J. R. Jayewardene a ride home from Parliament. His sophistication in other spheres of activity did not prevent him from a childlike enjoyment of popular music. His favourite songs had titles like, "I am a lonely child' and 'My baby loves loving.' In fact, once the adolescent in Felix took him to a record counter where he inquired of a shocked sales girl whether she had the 'Urge,' meaning of course a recording of a song called 'Urge.'

In early life he offered science for his O/Levels, rebelling against the legal tradition of his family, but he relented when he reached his A/Levels and offered Arts subjects with which he was not too familiar, except in the exposure he had to the Bible, the Classics and English as in an upper class family of his day. He did not merely master these subjects within one year but was awarded a Scholarship as an outstanding student, a reward from which he could not derive any benefit because of his father's relative affluence. At his scholarship interview he was asked by the Vice Chancellor how he had planned his career after passing out. His precocious reply was that he would continue at the University until he became the Vice Chancellor. Jennings was not impressed but the scholarship was nonetheless awarded, Felix's residual reward being Rs. 8/- per month which he never failed to collect and 'blow' fivefold on his friends in the University tuckshop on savouries and tea.

The faculty which he joined in Ceylon, in preference to the ancestral habit of acquiring prestige by a presence at Oxbridge Universities, had scholars who were at par with any offered by foreign Universities. They included Sir Ivor Jennings, later Vice Chancellor of Cambridge, Sir Francis Soertsz, retired Chief Justice, Professor Nadaraja, an international authority and H. W. Thambiah, later to be a Judge of the Supreme Court. Felix enjoyed his first year at the Faculty, more than most, because of some stimulating experiences with Sir Francis Soertsz, who had been a colleague on the Bench of Felix's father, Justice R. F. Dias. Their only common characteristic was an abrasive wit which they would often use against each other. Perhaps, Justice Dias finally won the day when, in conversation he paid compliments to a Bench comprising of Soertsz, Koch, Rose, names of three well-known Judges at the time. Soertsz could not restrain himself unfairly from exercising his caustic wit at lectures to which of course, his young student could not retort. However, Felix had his turn at a mock trial, staged on the occasion of a dance, organised by the Law Faculty, when he impersonated his father down to his least mannerism. There were lighter moments with others in the Faculty. There was an occasion when a Senior Lecturer, Ahlip came into the hall without his usual composure, profusely apologising "I am sorry, I am late, I am sorry, I am late, my wife has just had twins." The comment remembered to his day and often repeated by Felix was "this is the danger of repeating yourself."

Unique

As a student Felix had a unique method of study. He first took his textbooks, read them from cover to cover and rewrote them in a condensed form. This gave him a mental imprint onto which he was easily able to interpolate cases from the Law Reports and the opinion of learned Jurists. However, all his talent, his heritage, and remarkable memory failed him in his finals. He did not get his First class. The Faculty was very surprised, but some of his tutors put about a story that he had not spent enough time at the University library and this about a young man whose house had the finest legal library in the land, inherited from generations of Judges. Nevertheless, the University gave him a good grounding in the law and inspired many of his reforms as a Minister, a few years later in life. He was fascinated by the subjects of Fidei Commissum. He saw how, tying the ownership of land, from generation to generation, retarded agricultural development in the long term. His revision of Civil Procedure, accelerating testamentary proceedings, speeding the issue of Summons, all contributed to alleviating the appalling tribulations of the poor litigants, who were his concern. But he did not go far enough, and even in this day and time, cases can be dragged on in Sri Lanka, for 10, 15 or even 20 years, by various devices to enrich the profession and impoverish society, to whom much of this Law is losing its relevance.

Felix was not without political ambition from an early age. He once tried to raise the Royal College rabble in protest against Police action, when a Trade Unionist called Kandasamy was shot dead while marching in a procession which had been banned. Even then he showed his brilliance as an orator but misjudged his audience, who came mostly from affluent families, committed to maintaining the existing order. He did not fare any better at the University, when he was beaten in elections for a student body by a Tamil in a constituency of mainly Sinhala students.

This was before the two communities acquired a conviction of separate identities within a common culture. For a while his political inclinations remained dormant, despite a heritage of radicalism. It was his ancestor the great James d' Alwis, Oriental Scholar and Legislative Councillor, who first expressed opinions which were egalitarian at a time when there were no voters to please and which were to find a final expression one hundred years later in the political philosophy of his other remarkable descendant, S. W. R. D. Bandaranaike, the most radical Sri Lankan Prime Minister of them all.

As long ago as the mid 19th century, when caste was inflexible and one needed 7 generations of family descent designated by the appellations of *Appa, Mutta, Mimutta, Natta, Panatta,* or *Kirikitta,* to be a noble, James d' Alwis a blue blood himself, decried the system as having, "a very baneful effect on society. But it may be traced," he said, "to the exclusive social privileges arrogantly claimed by a few families, whose numbers may be counted on one's fingers." To the unreflecting mind indeed, this social distinction presented a formidable barrier against elevation of the masses in the social scale, the greatest and highest duty of every free state, and the happiest and noblest privilege of every philanthropist and patriot. If James d'Alwis had his own way, he has said in his Memoirs that he would have pursued the amalgamation of different castes. His ambition was achieved in the 20th century, when class rather than caste distinction had more relevance, by his descendants, S. W. R. D. Bandaranaike and Felix himself, who broke these class barriers.

Felix's academic career was conducted at the Law College a year after leaving University. He was called to the Bar and commenced a modest practice which took him to most Courts in the island, often accompanied by his newly wedded wife, who had passed out as a lawyer a year after he did. By marriage to his wife Lakshmi Jayasundera, Felix established kinship with a family which included Sir Arthur Ranasinghe and E. J. Samarawickrema, K.C., a man whom H. A. J. Hulugalle in one of his books has called "the keeper of the conscience of the national movement" and "one who had perhaps the greatest influence on the political leaders of his time." This family also included C. L. Wickremasinghe, a distinguished senior civil servant of his time, who was the father of that much compassionate of clerics the Bishop Lakshman.

In those years, mid century, the Ceylonese lived in a society which had seen few changes, especially in the maritime provinces, for several hundred years. There had been a prelude to coming events in the 19th century with the growth of a new class with extraordinary wealth even by international standards, from outside the predominant Govigama caste. This coincided with the rise of the Bandaranaikes who now had to contend with those whom they considered a lesser caste for Royal Victorian patronage and titles. The British readily accommodated these new aspirations because there were similar changes in their own order at home, where the landed aristocrats were rapidly losing ground to middle class mandarins and working class voters. In Ceylon, they balanced the contending forces with an almost equal distribution of Knighthoods, much to the displeasure of the Bandaranaikes, who though they were not ancient land-owners had by now acquired the life style, the manners and affectation of the English aristocracy. These English influences began to pervade and perhaps pervert our society even more.

Assassination

The assassination of Solomon Bandaranaike changed Felix's conventional attitudes because it did not require him to enter the arena by compromising any of his beliefs or inhibitions. The wave of sympathy which was to sweep Mrs Bandaranaike, with Felix as her guide, allowed him to retain his Anglican faith, his roast beef and his pyjamas.

When the Prime Minister S. W. R. D. Bandaranaike was assassinated in his house by a Buddhist monk, the Governor-General summoned W. Dahanayake to replace him. Dahanayake had considerable experience in Parliament and even in the State Council in British times before independence. He was however not a good choice. Divisions quickly arose within the Cabinet followed by dismissals, recriminations and rumour of his own complicity in the tumultuous political events of the time.

The Prime Minister decided to go to the polls after detaching himself from the SLFP and appointing a caretaker cabinet entirely of his own choice. The SLFP countered swiftly, bringing in new blood for the battle, under the leadership of C. P. de Silva, who had once been one of the mandarins of Civil Service but did not quite have the physical disposition for turbulent politics in uncertain times. Felix contested the family seat of Dompe with which he was not very familiar, while his kinsman James Obeyesekere succeeded to the seat of the assassinated Prime Minister. For well over a century these territories had been the core of Bandaranaike influence and its peasantry were not merely proud of being associated with their grandeur and benevolent patronage in imperial times, but even more, impressed by the manner in which the head of the family had accommodated their new aspirations for a more equal society after independence. While in the latter days of Empire, Sir Solomon Dias Bandaranaike had presented a final flourish of patrician glory, his son SWRD the future Prime Minister, had presented himself in an image of humility as a servant of the people. He had stepped down from their pedestal to be among them. The impact on the electorate though diminished remains to this day, even after the motor car has replaced the bullock, jet aircraft, the steam-ships and the fax machine, the postman.

Felix, who could speak little Sinhalese and had hardly any contact with the common people except in the courts, won a pocket Bandaranaike borough, which he was to nurse for the rest of his political career until his final fall in 1977 both from Office and Parliament. The UNP had the largest number of seats in the House and its leader Dudley Senanayake was asked to form a Government. The balance of power was held by the Federal Party which was the Tamil monolith at the time. It was Felix's skill exercised in the privacy of his house at No. 101, Galle Road, Colombo 3, which convinced the Tamils to support the SLFP in defeating the Government. There was no secret pact as many thought at the time, but an agreement between two gentlemen, Felix and Chelvanayakam who were both from the Anglican Christian community. Chelvanayakam was to say publicly a short while later that "the position taken by the SLFP was that they would not enter into any agreement with us and that they were not asking for our support on the basis of any agreement...if they were called upon to form a Government they would make a policy statement covering among others the issues in which the Federal Party was interested and it would then be open to our Party to support the SLFP Government or vote against it according to our view of that policy statement."

Felix's next important task after the defeat of the UNP Government was to forge an electoral alliance with the Marxist Parties in the elections which were called in June 1960. While he was aware of the need for an United Front to take on the powerful financial and territorial interest of the UNP, he was not unaware of the desperate interests which the Marxists had in acquiring positions of influence from which to infiltrate the administration. He then proceeded to impose an electoral agreement so favourable to the SLFP, that it ultimately led to the destruction of the Marxist parties and the political exile of their leaders until Dr. N. M. Perera became Finance Minister in 1964. Felix's own tragedy was that the ultimate beneficiary of his skill was the UNP who far from showing any gratitude proceeded to destroy him after their victory in 1977.

At the time Felix as the Secretary of the SLFP and Leslie Gunawardena as Secretary of the LSSP, signed a statement and an electoral agreement on 17th May 1960. The statement announced that "The Sri Lanka Freedom Party in order to form an independent and stable government with an absolute majority in Parliament and the LSSP have entered into the following electoral agreement for purposes of the forthcoming General Election. This agreement, which will eliminate contests between these two parties in all seats was signed this morning. The agreement is an electoral agreement only and does not signify a change of principles or policy on the part of either Party."

SLFP

Felix's next important task was to prepare the SLFP manifesto on which he had begun work the year before. While tapping it out on his own typewriter he acquired an overview on the entire strategy of government, when his Party was elected. Another early contribution was to secure a seat for Mrs Bandaranaike in the Senate. Though Leader of the Party, she was not quite ready to engage in the tedium of electioneering at constituency level. Felix then consulted his brother, Michael, who was a Cambridge Don, whether it was possible under the Ceylon Constitution for the Prime Minister to sit in the Senate which was an Upper House with restricted powers rather than in the House of Representatives, which was a popularly elected body. Since the Legislature was a Queen with both Houses, Michael's opinion was that the Prime Minister or for that matter any minister could be from the Senate. This was bolstered by S. A. Smith's opinion which was sent by Felix's brother Michael.

Difficult

In the new Government, Felix held the portfolio of Finance the most difficult Ministry in an impoverished country and while the Prime Minister retained Defence and External Affairs. Felix was her deputy. The triumphant young leadership of the country represented by Mrs Bandaranaike and Felix was extremely well received by the Commonwealth Prime Ministers, who were far fewer in number than today, because, Britain still had an Empire. The North South divide or, more to the point, the division of the planet's spoils between the whiteman and the coloured was not as blatant as today and international relations outside the communist bloc were altogether more accommodating. The withdrawal of rich nations to islands of affluence in Europe and America in oceans of misery, had only just begun. Such meetings of Commonwealth leaders therefore had considerable relevance to us, and Felix's remarkable eloquence, his wit, his easy flow of conversation and physical presence made him an outstanding figure among the Foreign Ministers assembled in London from all parts of the world. The fact that we were non-aligned was not found offensive among the leaders, the majority of whom were committed to contending Power blocs. There was also an empathy among the upper classes internationally, from which most of the leaders were drawn, which is absent in today's more democratic society.

In his first year in Office while Felix lit the usually dreary foreign conferences in London with his wit and eloquence, the country he represented was however in the minor league in world affairs. His impact was felt far more in his own patch at home. There was a time, when there was a strong possibility that the country would choose, even by democratic election, a Marxist regime to administer it. The consequences as we now see, 40 years later, in Eastern Europe as little short of disaster could well have meant a total collapse of our society. We did not even have the skills and economic resources which are now enabling the Europeans to survive. Our fate would have been the plight of Ethiopia, Sudan or Cambodia where millions have died of starvation with the collapse of social order. S. W. R. D. Bandaranaike averted the disaster. He offered a sedative to the demented emotions of a deprived and desperate people, an alternative to the exploitation by a privileged class which had repressed, humiliated and enslaved them for centuries with a cultural bondage, sanctioned by traditional religious beliefs. He had little time to consolidate his own ideology before he was assassinated and it was left to Felix to exorcise the myths and demons of Marxism which were still very much a part of the new folk religion.

Confidence

Felix was only 29, but he had the supreme confidence and even arrogance of his class, fortified by his formidable intellect. Writing later in a newspaper group which was hostile to Felix and his Party, a Sri Lankan journalist, described Felix's attitude as "down with the politics of survival up with the national cause do what you think is the right thing and to hell with electoral reactions." Felix did not hide his disdain of Marxist theory in our cultural context and proclaimed his antagonism from public platforms. The response of his protagonists was muted because they were engaged in infiltrating the administration aided by some of the most senior SLFP Ministers out of either political expediency or genuine conviction. The leader of the LSSP, Dr. N. M. Perera, though he supported the Government in Parliament called Felix's financial management of the country, "The economics of Bedlam." In an article reproduced in the Times of Ceylon, he stated, "what is at stake in the Economics of Bedlam is not merely the fate of this government. If that was so, it were a small matter. What is at stake is the undermining of the progressive forces of the country. It involves a resurgence of reaction, herein lies the tragedy of the present situation."

The foremost intellectual of this Marxist Party Hector Abhayawardhane conceded defeat to Felix when he admitted that there was "nothing false in Felix Dias Bandaranaike's assertion, that the SLFP had never accepted Marxist policies, that if the Marxist Parties had joined the coalition with the SLFP it must mean a repudiation of their past and acceptance of the late S. W. R. D. Bandaranaike's politics of the middle path. However, their apologies were that "in the midst of a hard-fought political battle, however, what matters is not literal truth. Anything that is said or done...is important only from its implications for the cause of the battle and the fortunes of either side." And within his own ranks, Felix had Hugh Fernando the Deputy Speaker promising a full Marxist state within five months and T. B. Ilangaratne, Minister of Trade, saying "capitalism will be smashed wherever it may be found."

Capitalism of course, took to its heels and Felix was left with the unpopular task of trying to stop this flight by imposing exchange and immigration controls. There was just no other alternative, in the panic of that time, with the country, still teetering on the edge of Marxism and sustained only by the weight of Felix's magnificent courage and extraordinary energy.

Felix in Parliament, Foreign Affairs

Felix was as the Junior Minister of Foreign Affairs the chief spokesman for the government in the Lower House when Mrs Bandaranaike the Prime Minister who also held the portfolio of foreign Affairs was in the Senate. His perspective was global though his main preoccupation was with the Indian subcontinent and our stateless citizens. He had more faith in the United Nations than most in its ability to maintain some sort of order in the lop-sided world. In a speech on 5th October 1960 in Parliament he said 'we accept the fact that Dag Hammarskjold has made mistakes...but we do accept the *bona fídes* of his conduct...and think it a matter of tragic significance if the institutions...were to be discarded merely because mistakes have been made by persons holding office.'

The Indian Problem

Felix had an early insight into the core of the Indian problem. Analysing the granting of citizenship to people of Indian descent he made the following observations in a speech of 15th November 1960: 'The problems in our country are of a physical nature and not of a legal nature...these people have been with us for many years, one can understand it from a human angle....merely giving the status of...citizenship to a certain number of people is not the solution. The question is, is there going to be a factual, physical, migration or not...We hope in the very near future to open negotiations on this question and indeed to do so on an all-Party basis. These observations preceded the serious discussions and negotiations which were conducted in India where even Dudley Senanayake, the Leader of the Opposition was consulted, leading to the conclusion of the Sirima-Shastri paot. Felix was proved correct in his assessment that the problem was physical and not just legal because a considerable residue of those expected to migrate to India remained behind to be granted Citizenship in later years despite formal undertakings by India to receive them back.

The Sri Lankan Tamils

He perceived the Sri Lankan Tamil problem in a different but equally accurate manner. In a speech in Parliament in April 1961 he said, 'so long as there was a slightest vestige of the question becoming a language problem pure and simple, there was a chance of it being solved on the basis of a language problem. Indeed the Federal party misled their supporters at every turn by regarding this as a language problem and nothing else....the demand of Chelvanayakam and his Party is not a demand within the framework of the Official Language Act...it amounts to nothing more than a demand for the setting up of a separate state...once that problem is clear no government can possibly do anything else but resort to use its authority and power...it becomes a question of Law and order.

Felix's economic theory was precisely defined when he introduced the Budget of the SLFP as Finance Minister on 15th September 1960 'we believe that economic development will be experienced when all levels of the people...are willing to pay the price and make the sacrifice that progress demands.'

He believed that wealth entails not merely the right to enjoy material comforts but also the obligation to use such wealth for...the welfare of the community. He did not exclude the working class either at a time when most politicians proclaimed their rights but neglected to spell out their duties. In his budget speech he said 'we believe the right to employment, fair wages, and decent working conditions also entail the obligation to work hard loyally and honestly.' Felix felt that these obligations were not respected because people had become cynical due to corruption and inefficiency at high levels, a problem which was to become endemic in later years.

Apart from his objections to foreign investment in areas which could be competently secured by local enterprise and the State sector, his programme for agricultural, industrial and social development is reflected in his Budget, and is hardly different from the Manifesto of the SLFP in 1994.

The Land Tax which he introduced on January 19th 1961 showed his awareness of the need for wealth creation in economic development rather than controls and restrictive practices. His decision to introduce the Tax was not punitive action against land-owners but a method of inducing them to increase the productivity of their land to offset taxation. He said 'the imposition of the tax should be an incentive to development of undeveloped land...land which is being developed under the rehabilitation programme of the government will be exempt.' Few land-owners recognised the significance of this Act and were to pay the penalty about 12 years later when the Land Reform Bill was introduced after the insurrection of 1971 restricting their holding to 50 acres.

It would appear too trite to describe Felix as an orator. He had prescience, an accomplished style of delivery and a remarkable facility of expression equal to or excelling any Parliamentarian in the English speaking world. His genius was his prescience which became evident in his very first maiden speech in Parliament in April 1960.

Marxist dogma was discredited in the '90s and there is considerable rethinking of free market policies with the USA demanding regulation on its terms in Japan and Japan doggedly holding out on its own form of State intervention. In his maiden speech Felix emphasised 25 years ago that the government of a country did not depend on divergences between capitalism (open market) and Marxism (State regulation). He saw deeper into the pressing questions which would have to be considered by any government. He went on to say 'we think that the real questions are what interests do you represent...how are you going to resolve the different conflicts which arise in the business of government. What interests are going to be subordinated to which and under what circumstances.' 25 years later in its issue of June 11th 1994, advocating a new start for socialism, the Economist states that 'socialism must continue to define itself less in terms of needs and more in terms of priorities...it would then be far more likely to change society as it wants to for the better.'

Another obsession among governments throughout the world has been their inability to control inflation which has raised the cost of living to unbearable levels. The consequence of this has been a reduction of savings and low surpluses which are required for investment in development. What is worrying world statesmen today was alarming Felix 25 years ago. 'The true criminal...responsible for introducing deficit budgeting into the finances of this country is the Hon. Leader of the House (J. R. Jayewardene). If the Hon. Leader of the House…is declaring that it is the policy of his government to reduce the price of rice then indeed the finances must be forthcoming from somewhere. We have grave doubts as to whether the country will not come under some other control.' For electioneering, the economy was being scorched in 1960 as it is being torched in 1994 and it was Felix's unfortunate responsibility to control the collapse when he became Minister of Finance shortly afterwards.

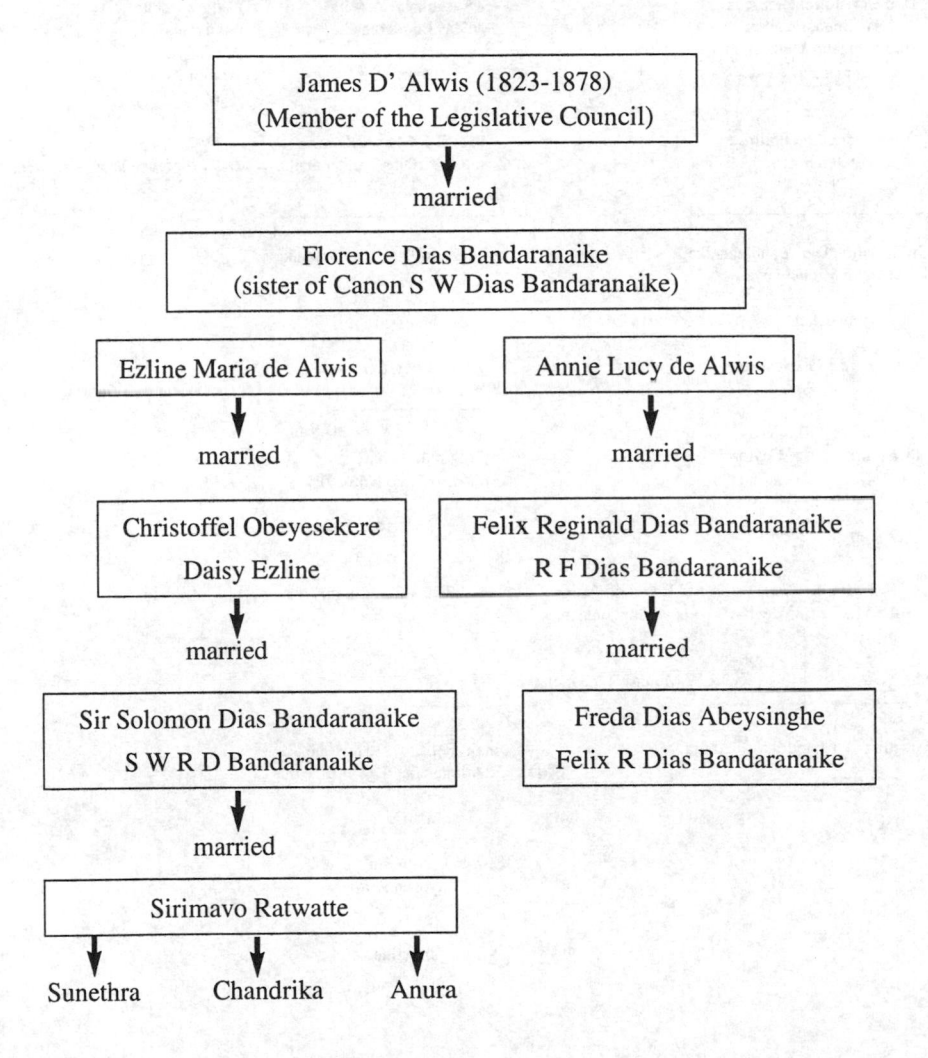

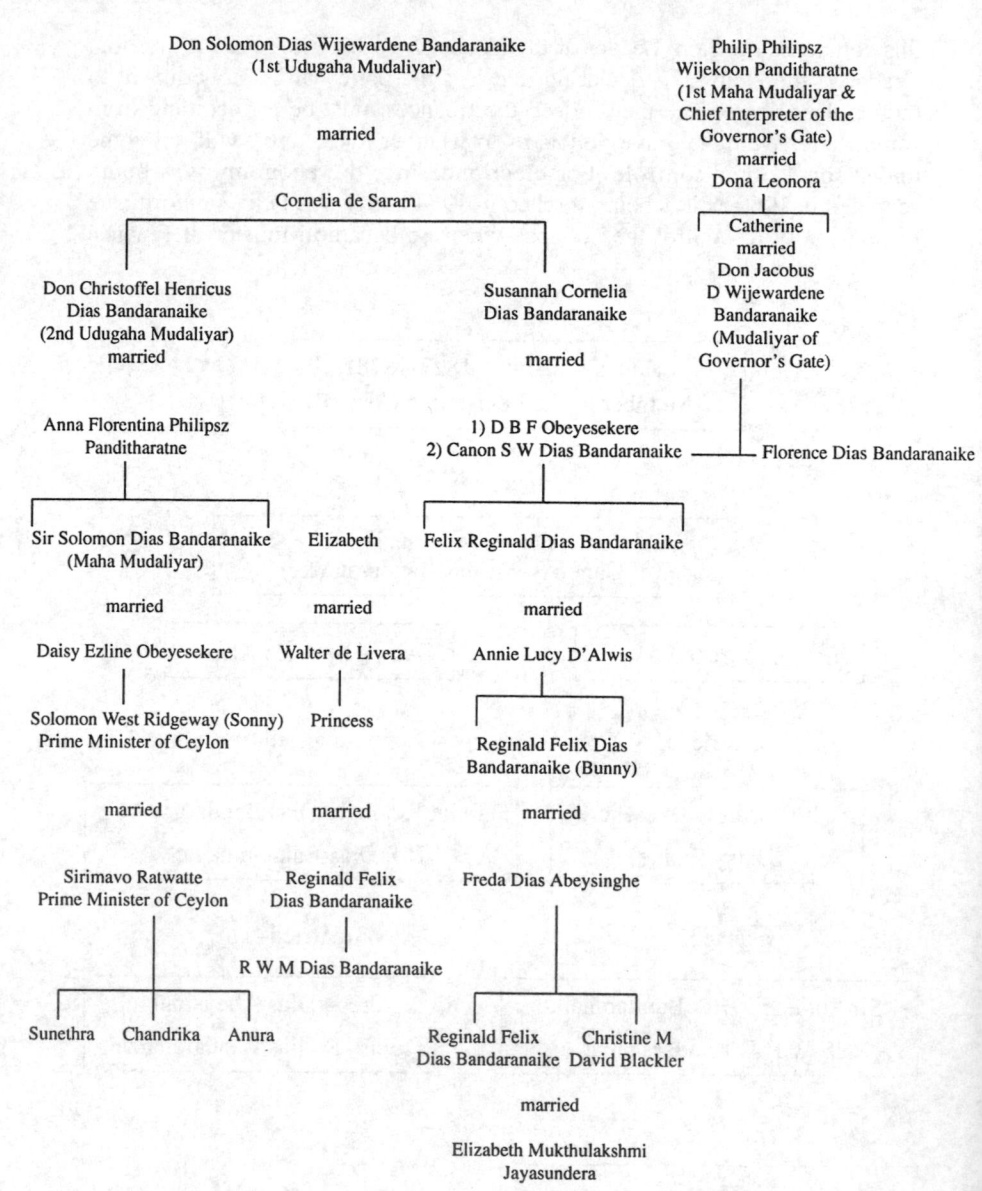

Don Solomon Dias Wijewardene Bandaranaike
(1st Udugaha Mudaliyar)

married

Cornelia de Saram

Philip Philipsz
Wijekoon Panditharatne
(1st Maha Mudaliyar &
Chief Interpreter of the
Governor's Gate)
married
Dona Leonora

Don Christoffel Henricus
Dias Bandaranaike
(2nd Udugaha Mudaliyar)
married

Susannah Cornelia
Dias Bandaranaike

married

Catherine
married
Don Jacobus
D Wijewardene
Bandaranaike
(Mudaliyar of
Governor's Gate)

Anna Florentina Philipsz
Panditharatne

1) D B F Obeyesekere
2) Canon S W Dias Bandaranaike —— Florence Dias Bandaranaike

Sir Solomon Dias Bandaranaike
(Maha Mudaliyar)

Elizabeth

Felix Reginald Dias Bandaranaike

married

married

married

Daisy Ezline Obeyesekere

Walter de Livera

Annie Lucy D'Alwis

Solomon West Ridgeway (Sonny)
Prime Minister of Ceylon

Princess

Reginald Felix Dias
Bandaranaike (Bunny)

married

married

married

Sirimavo Ratwatte
Prime Minister of Ceylon

Reginald Felix
Dias Bandaranaike

Freda Dias Abeysinghe

R W M Dias Bandaranaike

Sunethra   Chandrika   Anura

Reginald Felix   Christine M
Dias Bandaranaike David Blackler

married

Elizabeth Mukthulakshmi
Jayasundera

Christine

CHAPTER III

Cousin Felix

Christine Wickramasinghe

The family physician stood at the top of the staircase at "Granta" and
announced to the anxious relatives assembled below: "Mrs Dias has just
given birth to a fine baby boy weighing a little over thirteen pounds." "Good
Lord!" exclaimed our grandfather. "A Mighty Atom!" That was how Felix
Reginald Dias Bandaranaike (Jnr.) joined the family at 1st lane, Colpetty
(now Mahanuge Gardens).

His parents were delighted. Large family units were still popular in the
'30s. His stepbrother Mickey and his sister Christine looked forward to even
happier times than they already enjoyed while the cousins down the lane
were always thrilled to welcome another kid into their midst, a symbol of
endless possibilities.

Reginald Felix (Bunny), Felix's father, had him christened Felix Reginald
after grandfather, hoping that the grandson would take after his paternal
grandfather in some respects, notably a predisposition for the law and a
generous portion of wit and intelligence. Interested observers might discern to
what extent these wishes were fulfilled.

Young Felix spent a happy childhood, his father's restrictive rules being
greatly tempered by his mother's milder regime. His birthdays were
celebrated every November 5th with a grand 'Guy Fawkes' party. His father
was a loyal British subject (with certain reservations regarding intermarriage
and joining their armed Forces). He was an authority on British History so
we looked forward to this annual event with its lavish display of fireworks
culminating in the burning of a guy. This often upset the women servants in
the neighbourhood as they refused to believe it was only an effigy of a
British Traitor four centuries ago.

At an early age, Felix's instinct for the humorous became evident. Auntie
Freda's bouncing, bonny baby showed no lack of bounce literally or
metaphorically. He could take the hardest knocks and come up smiling.
When Christine and he were being driven home from school in their Baby
Austin the car door flew open as they rounded the bend from Turret Road

69

into Galle Road and podgy Felix rolled out on to the road. They decided not to mention the fact at home fearing that the driver might lose his job. But on second thoughts the man decided to tell the mistress about it. She was most concerned and wanted to send for the doctor. Felix cheerfully dismissed her fears saying: "I stopped for a roll at Perera & Sons."

Felix exploited his sense of humour to his advantage as well as amusement. His father, the strict disciplinarian, was never the target of his jokes but his mother suffered occasionally. A teacher by profession she controlled her children with gentle restraints. However, even those irked Felix at times. He got up one morning pretending to be possessed by the spirit of a dead ancestor. "Freda!" he intoned in sepulchral tones. "Give your youngsters plenty of bacon, not cod liver oil." Again "Stop sending Felix to dancing classes" or "Sack his Maths and Sinhalese tutors" and "It's perfectly safe for him to ride his bicycle on the roads or drive the car." Our aunt was frantic not knowing what to make of these utterances. On medical advice she kept him from school until Felix, at the pleading of Christine (who found it difficult to sustain her role in the act), gave up the pretence. He manoeuvred the demetamorphosis so artistically that his mother never solved the mystery.

Females, both young and old, were popular objects of his teasing. There were the relatives at "The Rosary," his mother's home, where the "Granta" children were sent on regular visits and where they received much spoiling from a bevy of old ladies complete with lavender, lace, muslin jackets and Victorian skirts. On one occasion the old dears came for dinner to "Granta." Felix's mother's cook was one who had been passed on to them by a retiring English judge. This man was a master of English cuisine. He used to get his mistress to leave menus on the table at formal dinner parties. Alice Auntie, a delicate spinster grand-aunt, who was seated next to Felix, inquired from him about the first item on the menu. "That's Mock Turtle Soup," explained Felix. "Oh!" said Aunt Alice. "And where does your mother get the turtles from?" "Ah those," said Felix. "We get plenty of them in our back garden, crawling up from the Beira Lake." Alice Auntie put down her spoon and sent away the rest of the soup untasted and most of the meal that followed. When Felix's mother questioned him later as to whether anything had upset the old lady he disclaimed all knowledge, his face the picture of innocence.

Then there was the nurse who sponged Felix when he was recovering from appendicectomy. She sponged him down to the navel and then adroitly continued from his knees downwards. "Why don't you do the whole of me? After all I'm only a little boy," he simpered coyly and she had to comply.

Felix was a lovable rascal and masterminded many a fun-filled escapade. This suited his brother, sister and cousins who acknowledged his organising ability while keeping a wary eye on him in case his ego exceeded its bounds.

Happily for Felix and his siblings their father was a dedicated Freemason. He would disappear to the Masonic Temple for several hours of an evening every month. That was the time his children would be their natural selves.

They would drag out a big black box from under a bed in the Visitors' Room. Pandora's Box, we called it. The cousins (excepting the nursery group) were rarely left out of the goings-on at "Granta." Our aunt was persuaded to go visiting on such occasions but she must have had an inkling of the conspiracies.

The box contained books, letters, diaries, newspaper cuttings, photographs and objects considered "forbidden fruit" for youthful consumption. Avidly we pored over this material ranging from facts of life to unpublicised activities of staid and pious members of earlier generations, their romances, feuds and lapses; we learned about our British, German, Italian and West Indian connections and heaps more that was beautiful, exciting, sad and sometimes downright foolish. I think we benefited from what we learned. Felix too. It was a lesson about life that went deeper than anything we acquired from school or parents.

Then followed a feast of another kind, a delicious meal consisting of goodies such as masalavadai, godambs, Buhari Chicken, seeni sambol, pawkies, cream buns and ice-cream. We really enjoyed those evenings although not always around Pandora's Box.

Admittedly Felix possessed an IQ above the average, bordering possibly on the precocious. But he was unsnubbable, countering all critics with his disarming chuckle and twinkling eye. One had to allow for the fact that he was the product of three generations of men of the law, religion and letters on his father's and mother's sides, not to speak of the access he had to the libraries of his father and grandfather. Literature, law books, encyclopaedias were always available. What is surprising is that friends and relations continued to tolerate him considering the way his otherwise undemonstrative father loved to show off Felix.

In wartime, for instance, the skies were constantly being ripped through by Allied planes flying over Colombo. "Felix," ordered his father, "what is the name of that plane that just flew overhead?" "Hurricane," replied Felix promptly. "How can you tell?" we used to ask. Felix could describe the identifying marks which, on checking, were found to be perfectly correct. He could tell a Spitfire from a Hurricane or an American B2 Bomber from a Reconnaissance plane, and he was only twelve.

He knew most of the answers be they to Grandfather's trickiest Crossword clues or to cousins preparing for a Radio Quiz. Irritating? sometimes. But he was merely being helpful.

He was no good at Sports unlike his brother. He loved reading; the Holy Bible, Charles Dickens, Sir Walter Scott, Conan Doyle and Oscar Wilde amongst his favourites. The works of Dickens were popular with the family for two reasons: one being that Sir Henry Fielding Dickens (Charles's son) had been Grandpapa's tutor at Cambridge and had visited his pupil and family in Ceylon with his wife; also, because Uncle Bunny used to read "A Christmas Carol" to his children every Christmas Eve in order to keep them out of the way of their mother, preparing to play Mother Santa at night.

Christmas was a particularly happy time for Felix and his family. It had a lot to do with gift-giving, eating, drinking, carol singing, concerts and the like and centred round our grandfather. Felix Dias (Snr.) had a puckish sense of humour not unlike his grandson's but a trifle more wicked. He knew most persons by a nickname of his coinage. At New Year he would sometimes take his grandsons to visit relations' houses where unattached young ladies were on show for eligible bachelors while their mothers vied with each other for praise of their culinary skills. This was part of family tradition and Felix was never bored by tradition. Though not even an eligible bachelor at the time he used to amuse himself by chatting up the girls or pulling funny faces at them and sending them into whales of giggles. In either case they failed to impress the bachelors. The two Felix's chuckled for days over the comic situations they had encountered.

It was difficult to tell which was the real Felix. The humorist, the serious student of law and religion, the genial companion or the politician. We often wondered uneasily. Were his politics also another act? No. He had to sacrifice too much to do it for his own amusement. But his natural love of teasing appeared even in Parliament when he used it to embarrass his foes as during the "Baring of M.P's Assets" Bill.

Was he a despot and a dictator? In the Family he was the peace-maker, dealing with the toughest old ladies and the knottiest legal problems with satisfaction to all and malice to none.

Did he deserve the titles "Super Brat," "Mighty Atom," or did he become too big for his boots? History can make its own judgement. With us it was he who kept alive our childhood bonds, becoming a child again every Christmas, waiting for the carol-singers on Christmas Eve, having the family round his own Christmas table and playing Father Christmas to those who shared his life from infancy – the old, their children, the domestic Staff and the disabled.

Yes, there were some things which Felix took seriously like his loyalty to his Faith, his Family, his friends and his ideals.

CHAPTER IV

Felix Dias Bandaranaike – Lawyer and Legislator

A. C. Alles

Had Felix Dias Bandaranaike chosen to follow the footsteps of his distinguished forefathers and concluded his legal career as a Judge of the Supreme Court he would surely have joined that galaxy of great judges who have made a lasting contribution to the administration of justice in Sri Lanka. His ancestors were born and bred in the law and even today his elder brother Michael carries on the traditions of the Dias family far from the shores of our country. Had Felix decided to concentrate on his legal career at the Bar he would have reached great heights and the glittering prizes at the Bar would have been his for the asking. From his University days he had been a keen student of the law and graduated from the Colombo University and was called to the Ceylon Bar. Subsequently on one of his trips to England he and his wife were both called to the English bar and qualified as barristers-at-law.

Felix appeared before me at the Kandy Assizes on several occasions in cases from Kandy and Kurunegala and I was able to assess his qualities as a practising lawyer in the original courts. He was a model advocate, studied his brief with care, ascertained its strength and weaknesses and applied the law when necessary. He made a deep study of the facts and displayed those great qualities of learning, advocacy and the intimate knowledge of human nature which is the hallmark of every successful advocate. Courtesy to the bench, tolerance to his opponent and terse but fair in his cross-examination of the prosecution witnesses he had adapted himself admirably to become a successful criminal lawyer. He was one of those excellent defence lawyers who never failed to put his client into the witness-stand when such defences as provocation and the right of private defence were raised since no doubt he correctly felt that in such cases the most competent person to testify would be the person provoked or the person who claims that he acted in the exercise of the right of private defence.

Felix has not appeared before me in the Appeal Court but with his talents, his devotion to his work and fluent advocacy he would have been as successful as a pleader before the appellate tribunal as he was at the Assize Court. As a friend and close admirer of his forensic ability, I tried to persuade him to give up politics and concentrate on the law where his roots lay and where his talents would have richly earned for him undoubted success, but by then he had tasted the vagaries of the political world and decided to forsake his first love and personal advancement to serve the needs of his motherland. To Felix's strong sense of justice it was a challenge. Having experienced the confusion, corruption, incompetence and greed in which politicians dabbled he was determined to do his bit in cleansing the Augean stables in the interests of the nation.

There are several aspects in Felix's political career which have been referred to by various writers and some of his critics but I propose to deal with only that aspect of his political career which is closely connected with the administration of justice. There is one important episode in this sphere which will always be remembered with gratitude by the peoples of Sri Lanka – the prominent part played by him in unravelling the attempted coup of 1962. He tackled a most dangerous situation with considerable skill, almost lone-handed, and saved our country from what might have been a blood-bath similar to those which plagued some South American countries and recently some nations of the African continent. If the coup succeeded it might have been the precursor of future coups which would have shaken the pillars of democracy in Sri Lanka for generations.

In October, 1961 Felix, as Parliamentary Secretary to the Minister of Defence and External Affairs, gave an order to the Armed Services to be prepared to meet the possibility of a series of strikes promoted by Leftist and Trade Union leaders. In November and December, 1961 there were a series of strikes in essential undertakings – the Transport Board, Bank employees and Oil companies. Strikes continued in January 1962 affecting workers in the public and private sector of transport, industry and commerce. A general strike probably accompanied by violence was expected by the end of January, 1962. A critical state of affairs was imminent and the Armed Services and Police had been alerted to ensure the maintenance of essential services and supplies. In Parliament leftist leaders like Dr. N. M. Perera sought this opportunity to suggest that Felix Dias Bandaranaike was making arrangements with the Armed Services to seize power and become a dictator. It was his plan, they said, to arrest Opposition leaders and also some Government Ministers and stage a coup. *[Vide Queen vs. Liyanage 67 NLR at p. 202].* The allegation against Felix was stated by Sansoni J. to have been made by Dr. N. M. Perera, Pieter Keuneman and W. Dahanayake. [Vide

Hansard (13.4.61) and 9.1.62 and 12.1.62]. Unfortunately there was a hook provided by Felix himself to support this allegation when in one of his speeches he stated "that a little bit of totalitarianism might be of benefit to the country." The dangers pregnant in the critical state of the country at the time was referred to in Liyanage's case (67 N.L.R. 193) when it stated –

'The conditions existing and contemplated in January, 1962, including the imposition of censorship, the full mobilisation of the services on security and civil duties and the public concern was such as in other countries had in fact given rise to attempts, whether successful or not, to overthrow democratically elected Governments and to establish some form of unconstitutional rule' (ibid p. 203)

In this volatile state of affairs some top-ranking police and security officers conceived the ambitious step of staging a coup and overthrow the democratically constituted government of Sri Lanka on the pretext that Felix Dias Bandaranaike was trying to seize power, arrest opposition leaders and some ministers to prevent the communists from gaining control. Their ostensible objective was to avoid a catastrophe and ensure that the country would be saved. They decided that once the disaster was averted that civil administration on democratic lines would be restored. The police and security services involved planned the coup for the night of January 27, 1962. Were the leaders genulne in their motives or did they contemplate seizing power themselves and bringing the country under military rule similar to the fate that befell many another country which experimented on this kind of strategy? Would there not be opposition by those loyal to the Government and in the case of a confrontation would there not have been violence and loss of life? It was a most dangerous and quixotic plan that had to be promptly nipped in the bud. Felix was unaware of those machinations and sinister plans. On the 26th he had a full night's work in the Ministry of Finance and only returned home in the morning. After a hasty breakfast he had to rush off to Malwana and only returned at 2.30 p.m. and then able to snatch a few hours of sleep when he was awakened by the visit of Salman who had come to meet him urgently and give information of the proposed coup arranged for that night.

Meanwhile the plan had been disclosed to P. de S. Kularatne by the Senanayake brothers (Stanley Senanayake, Superintendent of Police and his brother Lionel Senanayake, Asistant Superintendent of Police) and Kularatne realising the seriousness of the situation contacted the Inspector-General of Police, Abeykoon who was at that time participating in a game of bridge at the Orient Club. The only action Abeykoon took was to attempt to contact S. A. Dissanayake of the Criminal Investigation Department and request him to telephone him at the Orient Club. The Order of the Court in Liyanage's case has passed serious strictures on Abeykoon for his seeming indifference and the lackadaisical manner in which he dealt with a matter which seriously affected the security of the State. It was in this background that the Cabinet of Ministers including Felix was hastily summoned to Temple Trees to deal with the situation. The Cabinet decided to take over the investigation and appointed Felix as chief interrogator. With his legal knowledge he was the only member of the Cabinet who could effectively deal with a difficult situation. It was an arduous and highly responsible task. Here were top-ranking police and security officers accused of planning a coup and an Inspector-General of Police who gave him no assistance and the entire responsibility of unravelling the plot fell on Felix's shoulders. The Order of the Court in Liyanage's case refers to the important and responsible task undertaken by him to save the country from a catastrophe when it stated –

'We can appreciate the anxiety of those who were trying to ascertain the facts quickly from Senanayake, for they had to decide what action should be taken. This, we think, was the reason for dispensing with manual recording at that stage and for relying solely on the tape-recorder. The situation in which the authorities at Temple Trees found themselves was without precedent. Bandaranaike said that from the time he arrived at Temple Trees until midnight they were mainly taking measures to ensure the safety of the State rather than to investigate the alleged offence. A decision was taken about midnight that the Cabinet should have overall direction and control of the entire investigation, while he was to carry on the interrogation on behalf of the Ministers some of whom attended the interrogation of the witnesses. Investigations went on almost continuously till February 2nd. Although the Police also played a part, it is apparent that Mr Bandaranaike largely controlled the course of the inquiries. There was no legal basis for much that was done, including the arrest of the 4th defendant and Johnpulle that night. But in time of extreme emergency the State may be compelled by necessity to disregard for a time the ordinary safeguards of liberty in defence of liberty itself, and to substitute for the careful and deliberate procedure of the law a machinery more drastic and speedy in order to cope with the imminent danger' – *Provincial Administration v. Hanniball (1942 A.D. 1 at P. 14).*

The observations of the Court reveal the imminent danger to the State which called for swift action. Police officers like Tyrell Gunatileke were present to record the statements of the suspects but the entire burden of investigating the plot against the Government rested on the shoulders of Felix who performed a magnificent job in unravelling a dangerous plot which sought to overthrow the democratically constituted Government of Sri Lanka. The account of the Coup case is now past history and it was only three years later on April 6, 1965 that the Order of the Court at the Trial-at-Bar was delivered by Chief Justice Sansoni with whom were associated H. N. G. Fernando and L. B. de Silva JJ. finding eleven of the twenty four suspects arraigned before it guilty on the serious charges of conspiracy to overthrow the Government. A considerable part of the incriminatory evidence against the suspects was the result of Felix's investigations. Felix surely deserves the plaudits of the entire country for having saved it from a national catastrophe.

No Minister of Justice before or after Felix Dias Bandaranaike has contributed so much to reforms in the administration of justice as Felix Dias Bandaranaike. It was his object to revolutionise the administration of justice to meet the needs of the people. As a strong-willed Minister there was determination of purpose in the measures he considered necessary and would brook no opposition from any quarter. His endeavours to streamline the administration of justice met with stiff opposition from vested interests. He was responsible for the fusion of the two branches of the Legal Profession and established the single category of Attorneys-at-Law. Lawyers were up in arms at what they considered to be some of his autocratic reforms. Of course, there is an inherent weakness in the attitude of persons of Felix's calibre. Being men of strong will they could not tolerate knaves and fools and also ignored mature advice once they had set their heart on a particular purpose. Perhaps it was Felix's little bit of totalitarianism that prompted him to act in this fashion.

But those human frailties were completely overshadowed by the progressive pieces of legislation which were promulgated during the SLFP Government. The Conciliation Boards Act of 1958 was a great boon to the poor litigant. Minor disputes, both civil and criminal, could be adjusted under this law without the necessity of retaining lawyers and embarking on expensive litigation. This law was repealed by the subsequent Government but it has again been reintroduced under the UNP Government with a different nomenclature called the Mediation Boards Act but containing practically the same provisions that existed under the repealed law. In abolishing the troublesome and litigious concept of Fideicommissa Felix got rid of a legal headache, which tied property for generations and prevented it from being used for productive purposes, but he was fair to the heirs of such property when he included a clause enabling the fiduciary to nominate the beneficiary who had been designated by the testator to inherit the property according to his wishes, provided this was done within a prescribed period. Critics have urged that the law abolishing Fideicommissa in 1972 be reintroduced to provide for the children in a salutary manner. This is an unnecessary step as there is other legislation like the Law of Trusts which can be suitably adjusted with certain modifications to meet the situation as it has been done in England. The same critic who wanted this antiquated law reintroduced maintained that the abolition was a device created by Felix Dias

Bandaranaike to recover taxes by the sale of properties belonging to fiduciaries to fill the coffers of the Government – a reckless statement without any data to support it.

But the most progressive piece of legislation introduced by Felix was the Administration of Justice Law in the year of 1973. This law was intended to achieve the following objectives –

(a) Simplicity and uniformity in procedure;
(b) Fairness in Administration;
(c) the elimination of unjustifiable expense and delay; and
(d) the just determination of every judicial proceeding.

This law revolutionised the administration of justice in the country and considerably assisted in alleviating the great hardships which the litigant, especially from the rural areas, underwent to obtain expeditious solutions to his legal problems. It would perhaps be no exaggeration to state that had this law been fully implemented up to date the present chaotic state of the law and perpetual complaint of the law's delays would have been considerably minimised. A brief reference to some of the measures contained in the law would illustrate this aspect. The law practically obviated the necessity of long drawn-out inquiries in cases of grave crime. The investigation notes of the police were forwarded to the Director of Public Prosecutions who functioned under the Attorney-General and after examining all the material the Director would decide whether there was a *prima facie* case against an accused or whether further investigations were necessary or whether the material was sufficient to forward an indictment to the High Court. All the notes of investigation were available to the defence and defence lawyers were entitled to make their submissions to the DPP for a discharge of the accused and present applications for bail. The appointment of a Director of Public Prosecutions is a step adopted in all progressive countries for the expeditious disposal of criminal cases.

Adoption of this procedure enabled the inquiries to be completed expeditiously, avoided needless and lengthy cross-examination by defence counsel, curtailed the time of the Magistrates and enabled litigants without retaining lawyers at the non-summary inquiries to retain competent counsel to defend the prisoner at the trial. This procedure would have eliminated unjustifiable delay and expense and considerably assisted the poor litigant. Testamentary actions which took a great deal of the time of the District Judge were brought under control when the new law directed the transfer of the administrative machinery in these actions to the Public Trustee who would appoint a probate officer to the various courts to deal with such matters leaving the Court free to only deal with disputed legal matters including inquiries into disputed wills. Summons were permitted to be sent by registered post and assisted in eliminating the malpractices employed by dishonest Fiscal's officers in the personal service of summons. The UNP Government of 1977 however repealed this salutary piece of legislation and brought back the antiquated procedure and the rot has continued today with greater force to make the administration of justice in this country a scandal.

No account of Felix's remarkable career as a lawyer and politician would be complete without some reference to the Presidential Commission of Inquiry No. 7 of 1978 introduced by the UNP Government after it had come into power to report on various allegations of corruption and abuse of power by Felix Dias Bandaranaike during his tenure of office as a Minister of the previous Government. As a result of his revolutionary reforms in the law he had incurred the hostility of several members in the opposite camp who were determined to have his alleged misdeeds investigated by a Presidential Commission. The Commission consisted of two judges of the Supreme Court, Weeraratne and Sharvananda, JJ. and a member of the minor judiciary K. C. E. de Alwis. Justice Weeraratne was appointed Chairman of the Commission. The prosecuting counsel was A. C. de Zoysa, a leading lawyer of the governing party assisted by some members of the Attorney-General's Department while Felix was represented by President's Counsel H. L. de Silva assisted by his juniors. The fact that leading counsel for the prosecution was not a member of the prosecuting department at the time but only a member of the unofficial bar is perhaps indicative of the intention of the ruling party to make every possible effort to bring home the charges to the respondent. The prosecution witnesses were tendered for cross-examination but were not cross-examined by respondent's counsel and the only evidence led in Court was that of the respondent. The inquiry lasted 20 days and was concluded on December 31, 1979. There were 15 allegations against Felix, one of corruption and the others of abuse of power. He was found guilty by the Commission on the charge of corruption and on three allegations of abuse of power. Since this article is only confined to Felix's activities in the sphere of justice and not in any other capacity, observations will only be confined to his culpability in regard to the allegations of abuse of power. The most serious allegation of which he was found guilty was his alleged interference with a criminal case in which a political rival G. M. Premachandra was charged with murder. The Commission held, "that he was motivated by political considerations to get Premachandra re-remanded in order to undermine the election campaign of the UNP in the Mawathagama electorate and thereby promote the campaign of his party" and further, "by directing the DPP to make a decision to indict Premachandra he had pressurised the DPP and thereby interfered with the judicial process and was guilty of abuse of power." According to Government sources the entire incident centred around the release on bail of Premachandra which the Prime Minister and Felix thought unsatisfactory since this action would lead to a spate of applications for release resulting in the Government losing control of law and order. On the other hand the prosecuting authorities, the Director of Public Prosecutions and the Attorney-General considered the evidence inadequate on the charge of murder and wanted the indictment against Premachandra deferred, while Felix insisted that it should be forwarded and so directed Abeysuriya, the Director of Public Prosecutions. Although the Attorney-General had decided to have the order of the Magistrate releasing Premachandra on bail, revised by the Supreme Court, Felix took the position that this would result in unnecessary delay and wanted an indictment forwarded which according to Abeysuriya was justified on the evidence. Premachandra's case came up for trial before Justice Soza who was then High Court Judge while Premachandra continued to be on bail and he was acquitted at the trial. Felix did not interfere with the judicial process of which the commission found him guilty. He only made an abortive attempt to pressurise a public servant to perform the official act of filing an indictment when real pressure was necessary since the indictment was justified. The whole incident savours of a storm in a tea-cup with no substance to support it. Abuse of power in the case of a political figure is a very illusory term. In the course of a politician's career he or she must necessarily wield power and the line of demarcation between the use and abuse of power is extremely thin. No doubt to gain political advantage, a politician in the interests of his party, may tend to cross the dividing line to the detriment of his opponent. But this can hardly be characterized as an abuse of power. If there are serious lapses on the part of the Government or an individual Minister and there is gross violation of the Rule of Law, the normal course would be a vote of no confidence or perhaps a motion of impeachment which would compel the Government to resign. Without in any way attempting to detract from the findings of the Commission in this instance, it must be appreciated that a powerful politician is likely to trespass on the bounds of propriety to achieve a political advantage. This was in fact what Felix sought to achieve in Premachandra's case when he sought to have him remanded on the charge of murder – a non-bailable offfence – and persuading a public officer to file an indictment as expeditiously as possible in spite of the protests of the prosecuting authorities.

The other two allegations of abuse of power on which Felix was found guilty by the Commission was in connection with the appointment of his brother-in-law G. B. Wikramanayake as a Secretary to the Ministry of

Finance, and the other that he directed his Ministry officials to investigate an election offence alleged to have been committed by his political rival J. R. Jayewardene contrary to normal practice.

In the former case it was Felix's position that when he succeeded Dr. N. M. Perera as Minister of Finance he found that the Ministry was packed with Sama Samajists and Sama Samaja sympathisers and being unable to rely on them appointed Wikramanayake in whom he could have confidence as a Secretary to the Ministry to handle the day-to-day administration. It was his position that he could not devote time for the day-to-day administration of his Ministry because he was busy with the preparation of the budget. This is a plausible reason and although he may not have followed the proper procedure according to governmental regulations the necessities of the situation required him to appoint a trusted officer.

In regard to the second allegation Felix was obviously trying to gain a political advantage, a procedure adopted by all politicians in the course of a bitterly contested election in regard to several matters affecting the election.

It would hardly be urged on the facts of these two allegations that there was an abuse of power. There may have been a wrong use of power as a result of rising enthusiasm and an excess of zeal but it is extremely doubtful that such conduct could be characterised as an abuse of power. Felix's actions in these instances are hardly comparable with much more examples where leading politicians have abused their powers to gain political advantage.

It is ironic that Felix who was the brain-child of the Administration of Justice Law should find himself charged with violating its provisions. But on a dispassionate view of the facts it could hardly be urged that there was any breach on his part.

Many harsh things have been said about Felix's conduct as a politician. It was even suggested that he interfered with the judiciary. I have been a judge of the Supreme Court for 10 years since 1964 and during my tenure of office never experienced any interference with my judicial duties, nor do I think that any of my colleagues experienced such interference. If there was any such lapse on the part of the Minister one would have expected such an allegation to be brought against him before the Presidential Commission.

A politician's life is constantly one of turmoil and confrontation which has to be faced boldly. There were lapses in Felix's political career due to his strong personality but his important contributions to the administration of justice in our country during the period in which he dominated the Sri Lankan scenario will be appreciated by knowledgeable and grateful Sri Lankans in the years to come.

CHAPTER V

Felix in Parliament and at Parliamentary Conferences

Sam Wijesinha

The Legislative Council of Ceylon was established by Letters Patent of March 19, 1933, its first meeting being held on May 22, 1834. There were nine Official and six Unofficial Members, three to represent the Europeans and one each to represent the Sinhalese, the Tamils and the Burghers. From the inception the representatives of the Sinhalese and the Tamils tended to be from two well-known family groups. The Tamils were mainly the descendants of one of the first Unofficial Members, Mudaliyar S. Edirimanesingam. They included Sir Muttu Coomaraswamy and his three nephews Ponnambalam Coomaraswamy, Sir Ponnambalam Ramanathan, K.C., and the Official Member, Sir Ponnambalam Arunachalam.

One of the earliest Sinhalese Members was J. G. Philipsz Panditaratne succeeded by his sister's two sons J. C. Dias Bandaranaike and H. Dias Bandaranaike the two younger brothers of Rev. S. W. Dias Bandaranaike who later became a Canon of the Anglican Church, Colonial Chaplain and Vicar of All Saints' Church, Hulftsdorp. J. C. Dias Bandaranaike was enrolled a Proctor in 1839 and was a Member of the Legislative Council till 1861. He was succeeded by H. Dias Bandaranaike who was not only the first Sinhalese to be called to the Bar in England but also the first such to be appointed a Judge of the Supreme Court (1879) and also to be knighted. Sir Harry Dias Bandaranaike was succeeded in the Legislative Council by Philipsz Panditaratne's grand nephew, Advocate James D' Alwis in 1864. He was not only an outstanding Legislator but also a great Oriental Scholar whose contributions to the development of our language and literature alone earned him a place in our recent history. Another of James D' Alwis' relatives, Albert L. D' Alwis was also an Unofficial Member of the Legislative Council.

Meanwhile, in the 1840's Susannah Cornelia, Rev. S. W. Dias Bandaranaike's cousin, married D. B. Ferdinandus Obeyesekere, Mudaliyar of Talpe Pattu in the then distant Galle District. After two sons, James Peter and Christoffel were born, the young Mudaliyar died. The widow left the ancestral home at Kataluwa and came back to her father's Udugaha Walawwa in Colombo. Thereafter the widowed mother of the two Obeyesekere boys married her cousin, the Rev. S. W. Dias Bandaranaike. To them were born two boys and two girls. The younger of the two boys Felix Reginald Dias Bandaranaike was also called to the Bar in England and retired in 1920 whilst on the Supreme Court Bench. His son was Justice R. F. Dias Bandaranaike our Felix's father. Incidentally the two step-brothers Christoffel Obeyesekere and Felix Reginald Dias Bandaranaike married the two younger daughters of James D'Alwis. The elder brother James Peter Obeyesekere was a Member of the Legislative Council for a short time and after his untimely death his younger brother Christoffel Obeyesekere became a Member of the Legislative Council and continued till 1916. He was knighted in 1911. Felix Reginald Dias Bandaranaike's elder brother William Chapman who was also a Proctor was the grandfather of Justice Tissa Dias Bandaranaike of the Supreme Court which has taken over the functions of the Privy Council since 1972.

Susannah Cornelia (Dias Bandaranaike's) brother C. H. Dias Bandaranaike married Anna Philipsz Panditaratne and their only son was Sir Solomon Dias Bandaranaike who married the eldest daughter of his cousin Sir Christoffel Obeyesekere. Their only son was S. W. R. D. Bandaranaike. Our present President Chandrika Dias Bandaranaike Kumaratunga, the daughter of Mr and Mrs S. W. R. D. Bandaranaike who were both Prime Ministers of this country, is the proud heir to this illustrious heritage.

I have dealt with these matters in detail to indicate that our Felix has had four generations of Supreme Court Judges and several generations of Legislators in our country. Once, when Felix was Minister of Agriculture etc. he was speaking in the House on Animal Husbandry. He referred to the Australian cows imported thirty years earlier by D. S. Senanayake and went on to say that each of them gave forty bottles of milk a day at that time. But thirty years later at Ambewela and Bopatalawa each gave only four bottles a day. "You know why Mr Speaker?" he asked. Leaning forward from the Ministerial front row, he looked to his right at Mrs Sirimavo Bandaranaike the Prime Minister, and with his usual impish glint in his eyes and a straight face he said "Those cows, like the Bandaranaikes, are in-bred." He never missed a chance to have a good crack – even at his own family.

The Attanagalla electorate was literally a "pocket borough" represented in the Legislature by S. W. R. D. Bandaranaike from the inception of our adult franchise in 1931 for over twenty eight years continuously through five elections till his death in 1959. The Legislature was expanded from 95 elected members to 151 in 1960. Dompe was a new electorate carved out of the old Attanagalla seat. The ablest and the youngest member of the "Clan" who could be put forward for Dompe with confidence was Felix and Felix certainly won Dompe with majorities increasing progressively from over 12,000 going up to over 22,000 in the four elections held from March 1960 to May 1970 and after 17 years was defeated in July 1977 by 2400 votes. I suppose after 17 years, even men of Felix's calibre of the old order had to change yielding place to the new. Today 17 seems a prophetic number !

With his party in office in August 1960 Felix was appointed Minister of Finance in Mrs Bandaranaike's first Government. He plunged into his duties with the competence of an experienced veteran. He was ready to learn and was outstanding in debate. His almost flawless oratory and remarkable memory enabled him to silence critics with good-humoured defiance. He had a devastating ability to marshall his facts lucidly and precisely with order and method. Although he never spoke to a text, he was most resourceful on his feet. He entered the Houses of Parliament like a fish to water – just as he did eight years earlier entering the Courts of Law.

At the opening of the Commonwealth Parliamentary Conference in 1973 in London by the Queen, Felix as the Vice-President of the C.P.A. expressed the gratitude of the Association to Her Majesty and to His Royal Highness proposing a vote of thanks. The delegates sitting with the Queen on the dais had to be in morning dress or national dress. Fred Daly, Minister and Leader of the House in Australia and Felix Minister of Justice etc. did not want to be seen in morning dress. Lakshmi had to make do what she thought was a national dress for her husband and to get it ready overnight. Felix, rather doubtful of her sartorial efforts, was holding his waist firmly with his left hand whilst speaking the next morning in the presence of the Queen and the vast gathering of notables in Westminster Hall. With only his right hand to occasionally emphasize a point, he made a courageous speech that brought out a spontaneous ovation from the vast concourse gathered before the Queen. E. L. Bradby, Principal of Royal College in Felix's time was an overjoyed member of the audience who greeted Felix with tears of joy.

Joining a discussion on Racial Harmony at a Parliamentary Conference in the Bahamas he said referring to Immigration *"The truth of the matter is that the people who are going are not always the people who ought to go. Sometimes the standard of living for performing certain relatively menial tasks abroad is somewhat better than the corresponding pay for Ceylonese at home, and the basic reason seems to me to be economic more than anything else. I do not think the United Kingdom should really complain about immigration. See how much their country has been enriched by the waves of immigrants. They are learning to play cricket from the West Indies. They are learning music from the calypso beat of the Mighty Sparrow of Jamaica and Lord Kitchener of Trinidad and Tobago. I think Britain would have been much poorer if they did not have curry, calypso, and cricket. Think what would happen if London Transport was not serviced by the West Indies. When there is a cricket match at Lords, london Transport nearly comes to a grinding halt. Take the nursing services, the only white people are usually Irish nurses. The rest of them come from the underdeveloped countries of the Commonwealth. What we are looking at is not a racial problem, it is a question of survival and maintenance of living standards. The only way you can stop this wave of immigration is not by legislation and creating bitterness. Living standards must rise in the rest of the Commonwealth, and the need to migrate to other more developed countries must be eliminated.*

At a Conference in Malaysia in 1971 speaking to Parliamentary Democracy he said *"Countries become independent, then we imagine that we are our own masters, we form political parties; political manifestoes and tell the people, "We have a solution to the problems of this country, we can do something for you." In practice in the context of the modern international society, a country of primary producers with limited resources lacks the necessary capacities. We are unable to do anything practical about our economic situation in order to fulfil the promises and to satisfy the aspirations of the people. Let the other fellow, fighting the elections against you, come into power, he is no better either; he cannot do much unless there is a growing realization that parliamentary democracy itself becomes a cherished ideal. something worth protecting, something worth fighting for, something worthy of protection in its own right. However much we follow the forms of parliamentary democracy – rival candidates coming forward with rival sets of promises, hopes, aspirations for the future, let it be nationalization, let it be private enterprise, it makes no difference – if the net result is that the life of the people and the country remain unaltered substantially. Then you will find that the seeds of revolutionary movements, of insurections, and dissatisfactions will become manifest sooner or later. The unrest will not present itself in the shape and form of overthrowing a particular Government which is unpopular. It will become a challenge to Parliamentary democracy in itself. It will become the very rationale for saying that this system is no good; we are not making progress this way, Parliamentary democracy is, by its very nature, a slow system. It is slow so far as economic growth is concerned. We talk and debate and argue about the rights and wrongs of every little thing. I think that, that sort of democracy is making people impatient."*

Speaking on World Security at a Parliamentary Conference in 1968 he said *"If we are honest and sincere with ourselves in talking of a right of self-determination, of practising parliamentary democracy with all the attributes identified with the Commonwealth, recognition of national sovereignty, the unifying influence of a Monarchy, the need to recognize the rule of law, the independence of the judiciary, it seems to me that when we are talking of communism and capitalism, we should all recognize the right of people in their own minds to be communists if they want to. Just as much as we recognize the right of the other fellow to have his point of view, it seems to us that is wrong to start with the assumption that these two groups, communist and capitalist to be in conflict which necessarily has to lead to war or military intervention. Indeed, sometimes we become extremely aggressive in defence of freedom, and that I think constitutes the greatest danger to world peace in our present times."*

At a discussion referring to Parliamentary Government and a remark that the Mass Media are ahead of Parliament is expressing their opinions on current controversies that help to form public opinion, Felix said *"In underdeveloped countries the problem is really in the reverse. Very often the newspapers are not really an expression of public opinion, but vehicles for the expression of editorial opinions of individuals in a few newspaper groups representing monopoly capital. They sometimes like to impose their views upon an unsuspecting public, as being views representing public opinion. There is only one remedy that I can think of, and that is, to keep the electorate under constant review and ensure that the people who are elected are really and truly not allowed to become remote from the people."*

He had a good reply to Senator Grosart of Canada at another Parliamentary Conference where Pollution Control was discussed when he said:

> *"If you visit American City*
> *You will find it very pretty.*
> *Of just one thing you must beware,*
> *Do not drink the water and do not breathe the air ! "*

Speaking on the problems of minorities, particularly of the Tamils in Sri Lanka at the C.P.A. Conference of 1974 in Colombo he said *"We are prepared to go to all the corners of our country to talk to them in their own language if we can and try to persuade them. You would imagine that minority problems here are very difficult ones, but I know of no other country in the world where a majority had made it possible for the minority to achieve unheard of economic wealth and to become the most prosperous people in our country through the policies being followed consciously and deliberately by the majority. I should like to urge that even in our own little land dialogue and discussion are fundamental and essential to good relations. Recently I had the privilege of visiting the Northern Province. I tried to speak to the people there in my own faulty Tamil, trying to make contact and to express our point of view. All I can say is that we stretch the hand of friendship and invite our friends the Tamils to do the same – to come down South and talk to us. It does not matter if they do not know our language. They can talk to us in English or in Tamil. We are prepared to listen. We say that once the dialogue is established, as it can be established – we cannot afford to talk of dialogue in international terms unless we are prepared to do precisely that in our own problems can be resolved."*

In Malaysia in 1971 Felix wrapped up three sessions of the 17th C.P.A. Conference on "The Commonwealth and Problems of World Security" where around 45 delegates intervened. He did this without a note referring to the substance of every worthwhile contribution and concluded *"I think the best feature of our discussions so far has been the avoidance of double standards; that we, speaking as Parliamentarians, have spoken freely and frankly. We have expressed strong views sometimes, emotional views sometimes, and sometimes views which may not have met complete agreement and accord around the room, but we have all spoken with sincerity from the bottom of our hearts. If the little bit of what we said has struck a responsive chord in the hearts and minds of some other Members of Parliament in a more distant and remote area of the Commonwealth, I think we have served our purpose as a Commonwealth Parliamentary Association."* The Chairman Hon. F. E. Walker, MP of Canada, thanking the distinguished delegate from Sri Lanka added "The attention you received should be gratifying to you. Your masterly summing up has added enlightenment to us all."

It was always a source of pride and elation to be with him at an International Conference. Felix Dias Bandaranaike was an outstanding "character" who stood out anywhere and was pre-eminent always. He took decisions without fear, it is a pity he could not be of service to his country in his more mature years.

CHAPTER VI

Foreign Affairs and Diplomacy

Vernon Mendis

Of the several Ministerial positions which Felix Dias Bandaranaike held in the course of his illustrious career as a Cabinet Minister in the successive Governments of Mrs Sirimavo Bandaranaike from 1960 to 1965 and 1970 to 1977, the one which was closest to his heart one would think was Foreign Affairs. This was as Parliamentary Secretary in the Ministry of Defence and External Affairs which was a lesser position but one necessitated by the circumstance that the Prime Minister under the Constitution was the Minister of Foreign Affairs. Whether he would have enjoyed being Foreign Minister alone it is difficult to say considering the larger than life range of his extraordinary capacity. Perhaps he may have felt underused the foreign policy issues of Sri Lanka though important being relatively small. However it can be said that whatever other portfolios he held at any given time they never affected or diverted from his outstanding role in foreign affairs. This was in fact the only position which he held unchanged in both governments thereby giving continuity to the administration of Foreign Affairs. Indeed as Mrs Sirimavo Bandaranaike acknowledged in her Felix Dias Bandaranaike Memorial, lecture 1987 "whatever portfolios Felix Bandaranaike held, I always relied on his advice in the implementation of the SLFP's foreign policy." From this statement it could be inferred that without prejudice to the Prime Minister's own remarkable intuitive sense and charisma in this field, the foreign policy of the successive administrations were to a large extent moulded and conceptualised by him and on occasions also implemented. It was a harmonious relationship of perfect understanding and mutual trust based on the Prime Minister's appreciation of Felix Bandaranaike's singular faculties.

Educational & Family Background

No one who knew Felix Bandaranaike could deny that he was uniquely endowed to deal with foreign affairs. He had a dominating personality being tall, well-built, with a commanding almost imperious presence, perfect poise and an air of easy self-confidence. His greatest gift, however was his oratorical powers where with his baritone-like voice, choice diction, analytical skills and effortless delivery he could captivate an audience. Though forbidding in appearance he had an outgoing temperament with an impish sense of humour, a ready wit, and an essentially amiable nature which won him many friends and made him very good company. This was an incongruous streak where despite his heavy build and scholarly face which made him look remote he could be quite a prankster as his schoolboy antics revealed. Felix Bandaranaike had other attributes which equipped him for the leadership role in Sri Lanka. He came of patrician stock which had been in the forefront of the political and social life of the country and these circumstances apart from his inborn talents were a natural passport to leadership. He was closely connected to the famous S. W. R. D. Bandaranaike who conceivably was a source of inspiration to him at least in their common zest for foreign affairs while his father was a legendary figure on the bench who had a reputation which his son would acquire for a combination of impish humour and stern justice. He inherited a legacy therefore not only of belonging to the ruling class but also of national leadership, professional eminence and intellectual achievement from his forebears.

It is pertinent to consider how such a background of ancestry and intellectual heritage could have contributed to mould a role in foreign policy. Felix Bandaranaike it should be said at the outset represented a plebian administration committed to a People's government which was the battle cry that installed S. W. R. D. Bandaranaike in power. This meant that his rise to power cannot be attributed to any overt class or birth factor. Yet one cannot discount the appeal of his name as one which had been associated with the heights of power in colonial British times. Diplomacy is referred to as a sport of kings and associated with royalty and hence it could have come naturally to a bearer of such a name. At the same time one must concede that Felix Bandaranaike's principal and transparent qualification for a role in diplomacy was undoubtedly his exceptional intellectual calibre.

As a student at Royal College he was an intellectual prodigy with a voracious appetite for reading and also food in which respect coupled with his penchant for japes he was a bit of a Billy Bunter. He won the coveted Turner prize from the proceeds of which he purchased a typewriter on which he feverishly hammered out articles and other memoranda foreshadowing his later prowess where as Minister he typed out his own speeches and drafts of official documents. He entered the University of Ceylon with a scholarship and chose to read law no doubt in the family tradition. Passing out as a lawyer he soon acquired a legendary reputation for his prowess at the bar and the stage seemed set for him to become one of the legal giants of the land. Fate decided otherwise when in 1960 he embarked on a political career where he became no less a giant than he would have been in the legal field. This lightning ascent to eminence when he became the youngest Finance Minister in the Commonwealth was an ample demonstration of his remarkable intellectual powers which enabled him to excel in the field of diplomacy and foreign affairs.

Leadership Qualities

These powers comprised a range of skills which included a phenomenal memory, encyclopaedic knowledge, an analytical mind which penetrated the heart of a problem, quick grasp of issues, lucid and logical exposition, choice diction, felicitous and faultless presentation. These may sound at first sight like a checklist of the ideal attributes required of a statesman but those who knew Felix Bandaranaike and saw him at work would testify that these attributes found living expression in him. Their relevancy to diplomacy and the conduct of foreign relations would be self-evident depending on one's understanding of these vocations.

Diplomacy as commonly understood is the art of conducting inter-state relations at a bilateral and multilateral level and a knowledge and study of the issues involved which are the content of such relations. This means a familiarity with the technical and structural aspects such as procedures, forms and institutions and the major bilateral and multilateral issues in the international scene at any given time. For an individual country diplomacy is the medium for the preservation and promotion of its vital interests through its relations with other countries and international society as expressed through the United Nations and multilateral organisations.

The substance of practical diplomacy is representation of one's country abroad in the widest sense of the term which calls for a veritable armoury of skills such as communication, formulation and exposition, negotiation and debating, mastery of language, spokesmanship, alertness and quick reflexes combined with personability and personal charisma. As a corollary they should be accompanied on the domestic side by a decision-making process in the administration based on critical assessment of available intelligence and other information gathered from various sources as well as the machinery of the implementation of such decisions through the Ministry of External Affairs and its network.

Diplomatic Skills

Needless to say Felix Dias Bandaranaike's abundance of abilities encompassed all these skills and enabled him to carry out these responsibilities with a Gulliver-like ease. There is no doubt that he bestrode the relatively small world of foreign affairs in Sri Lanka like a Colossus. Although his actual contacts with the Foreign Ministry were limited to *ad hoc* conferences with its officials and occasions when urgent matters were on hand, he was remarkably well informed on any situation however technical and more than a match for the professionals.

Professional officers were inspired, intimidated and exhausted by his command of their subject and he lost no opportunity to inculcate the standards required of them as career officers on which he showed an appreciation which senior exponents of the profession would have envied. He was a tireless indefatigable worker imbued with an overwhelming zest which bore him onward and it was normal for him to hold conferences at 1 a.m. with one Ministry and follow up with another at 3 a.m., revealing at the same time his versatility in switching from one subject to another. At no time during his crowded Ministerial career was his responsibility confined to a single Ministry but covered others as well. His infinite capacity for desk-work whether drafting, spelling out instructions or directing policy was matched by his nimbleness on the floor whether of Parliament or International Assemblies where he could deliver weighty pronouncements and speeches with effortless ease to the astonishment of those around.

His crowning achievement in this regard was his reply to Her Majesty Queen Elizabeth II of Britain at a Commonwealth Parliamentary Conference in London which is still talked about for its sensational character. All these achievements he took in his stride as his outgoing personality excelled in such opportunities. When it came to hard bargaining at the conference table he had no difficulty switching from the mellifluous orator to the persuasive advocate arguing his case with the matchless forensic skills which had earned for him an awesome reputation at the Sri Lanka bar. Yet he was no volcanic Krishna Menon cold and remote but won the respect and regard of his colleagues by his knack for couching his words so as not to cause offence and even deliver rebuffs or rebukes with a graciousness without antagonising those affected.

In the cut and thrust of Parliamentary debates or international conferences he bore himself with dignity in the highest traditions of statesmanship. His interventions were marked by an innate rationality, an analytical approach which reduced issues to essentials, an appeal to logic and commonsense which could not fail to impress and even defuse emotionally charged situations. When the battles were done he was equally adroit in the cocktail lounge or at dinners mixing easily with his colleagues and even amusing them with his fund of good humour, ready wit and even naughty stories. Such were the ample talents which Felix Dias Bandaranaike placed at the disposal of the Government throughout a period of 12 years as the principal adviser and spokesman on foreign affairs. There was a natural element of delicacy in being such a spokesman when the Foreign Minister was the Prime Minister but as the latter has testified there were never any cross purposes in the relationship as the Prime Minister had the fullest confidence and relied on him. Bandaranaike's role was essentially to conceptualise foreign policy and oversee its implementation while taking charge of special tasks.

Evolution of Foreign Policy

Bandaranaike's stewardship of Foreign Affairs spread over a number of areas and it would be convenient to deal with them separately. These were his broad vision of foreign policy and how he saw Sri Lanka's role and its application and manifestations in different areas which were mainly the Commonwealth, Non-Alignment, the United Nations, *ad hoc* initiatives, Economic and Financial issues. Together they will afford a panoramic view of the country's foreign relations and diplomacy in terms of its several initiatives during that period.

Felix Dias Bandaranaike came into the diplomatic scene at a crucial moment in the evolution of the foreign policy of Sri Lanka. It was the period of uncertainty which followed the demise of the great S. W. R. D. Bandaranaike when the future of the policies which he had enunciated and so zealously espoused seemed to be in question as much as the likely directions of the country's foreign policy. This policy was described by him as dynamic neutralism which in his own words was "not the kind of neutralism of just remaining on a side, of sitting on the fence, trying to get what you can from here and there. It is not so. It is something much more positive in my view. "Dynamic neutralism in that sense amounted to a positive commitment to promote peaceful settlement of international disputes, to arrest polarisation which was the primary source of tension by refraining from joining power blocs and spreading goodwill and understanding between nations," so that in the course of time perhaps the world will find some stable state of society that will banish this ever constant and ever present danger of war." This marked a repudiation of the policy of alignment of the past through defence pacts and even a disbanding of the regionalism of the Colombo Powers which in any case was falling apart at that time.

S. W. R. D. Bandaranaike no doubt with memories of the League of Nations in mind pinned his faith on the United Nations as the only hope for world peace and the champion particularly of the small nations. He felt therefore that it was incumbent on the latter to identify themselves to the utmost with the UN and help towards a realisation of its ideals. His vision for Sri Lanka was that it should be an Asian Switzerland because as he once stated "I feel that the geographical situation of our country does give it a special position in South-East Asia which is analogous to the position occupied by a country like Switzerland."

In the lifetime of Bandaranaike, dynamic neutralism had the misfortune to suffer two setbacks in the Suez invasion of 1956 and the Hungarian uprising of that year which it was unable to cope with adequately except for the show of solidarity of the Colombo Powers. These experiences shook its credibility and on his demise therefore there was a void which had to be filled as regards Sri Lanka's foreign policy either through a reformulation or new paths. The caretaker interlude when Sri Lanka created a stir by its accreditation of an Ambassador to Tel Aviv underlined this need.

This was the challenge which faced the new Government of Mrs Sirimavo Bandaranaike when she assumed office in 1960 as the world's first woman Prime Minister. As the Government was pledged to follow the policies of the late Prime Minister it inherited to that extent the legacy of dynamic neutralism. The question at issue was to reformulate it in a shape which would enable it to respond more effectively than it had done in the past to international events. S. W. R. D. Bandaranaike was committed to a world view of universality for the realisation of which he regarded the United Nations as the ideal and even sole instrument. However the recent experiences had revealed certain limitations and there seemed to be a clear need for alternative approaches. S. W. R. D. Bandaranaike had referred on occasions to the need for an appropriate form by which the small countries would act as a buffer. Actually the real limitations of the credo of dynamic neutralism was that it was an unstructured concept which lacked any tangible institutional expression. Its inability to act effectively was understandable.

The history of foreign policy has repeatedly demonstrated the inadequacy of ideas and concepts alone to produce an impact unless supported by firm logistics. The history of Non-Alignment would in the future provide ample demonstrations of this fact. This problem would no doubt have been perceived by the new administration and engaged its attention. However a solution was already in the making in the initiatives of the tripartite Brioni combination of President Tito, Prime Minister Nehru and President Nasser to create the new vision of Non-Alignment for the Third World. At this time there were two movements competing for ascendancy which were the idea of a second Bandung asserting Afro-Asian solidarity and liberation, and Non-Alignment which combined the latter with the dynamic neutralism and universality of S. W. R. D. Bandaranaike and Nehru, and as it turned out it was Non-Alignment which prevailed and became the new Crusade of the Third World. It was natural that with the pioneer role of S. W. R. D. Bandaranaike as an exponent of dynamic neutralism and the close association which had grown between Sri Lanka and India under him and now under Mrs Sirimavo Bandaranaike, Sri Lanka became automatically one of the founding fathers of Non-Alignment.

Thus Non-Alignment became the keynote of the foreign policy of the new administration which would shape its attitude on its external relations and developments in the international scene. The latter at this time was dominated by the Cold war which witnessed an intensification at this juncture over the Berlin crisis followed by that of the Cuban missiles despite talk of a detente on the basis of peaceful co-existence. The United Nations was facing a crisis in the Belgian Congo in which the Secretary-General had been a victim and there were strong moves to restructure the Organisation and replace the Secretary-General by a troika. The threat of nuclear war which had been raised by the explosion of a nuclear bomb by the Soviet Union on the eve of the Belgrade Non-Algined Summit of 1961 was partly defused by the Partial Test Ban Treaty of 1963 and there was some sense of relief.

Within the Asian region Sri Lanka was concerned over the establishment of the US naval base in Diego Garcia with its implications for the security of the region with the possibility of rival fleets entering the Indian Ocean in a state of military confrontation. Of course, the shattering event of this period was the Sino-Indian border conflict which took the world by surprise and was a turning-point in the diplomacy of the region. It occasioned a memorable diplomatic initiative by Sri Lanka. In the bilateral sphere the focus at this time was on Sri Lanka's relations with India over the so-called Indo-Ceylon problem which led to the landmark Sirima-Shastri pact of 1964. It can be said of the first administration of Mrs Sirimavo Bandaranaike that it gained distinction and recognition in the eyes of the world for its clear-cut enunciation of policy and adherence to it and acts of adroit statesmanship.

1964 Statement on Foreign Policy

As the principal adviser on foreign affairs in his capacity of Parliamentary Secretary for the subject Felix Dias Bandaranaike can justifiably claim some credit for this achievement. A fair assessment can be made of his contribution in this regard from a statement which he made in Parliament in 1964 on the foreign policy of the Government. Although this is an official statement as distinct from a personal testament it affords an unrivalled picture of his ideas and perceptions of foreign affairs during that period.

The foundations of Sri Lanka's foreign policy he states is twofold namely Non-Alignment and universality meaning friendship with all nations. These can be divided into 4 categories which are territorial associations or regional groups, non-territorial associations between diverse states based on adherence to principles like Non-Alignment or even military blocs like NATO, the United Nations and the Commonwealth. He speaks at some length on the Commonwealth referring to the conferences which he had attended and his experiences of them from a diplomatic point of view.

His conclusion about the role of the Commonwealth is significant and is to the effect that "Our experience shows that the Commonwealth becomes a convenient organisation or an Association which can be built to become whatever we want it to become." He brushes aside the fear of the Commonwealth becoming an instrument of British imperialism or that membership in it would detract from our independence or damage our national interests. This statement gains added significance if one recalls that a few years before, after abrogation of the Defence pact with the UK there was talk of even leaving the Commonwealth. It shows a growing realisation of the value of membership in the Commonwealth for Sri Lanka from a diplomatic viewpoint.

This statement covered a number of issues affecting Sri Lanka's foreign policy at that time and therefore provides a useful insight to the Government's thinking on these matters. On the situation in South-East Asia he referred to two matters. The first was US intervention in Vietnam which he deplored as cold war tactics contrary to the terms of the Geneva agreement. He considered it indefensible that the lives and property of citizens of small countries in South-East Asia should be forfeited in these circumstances and stated that far from being indifferent the Government was making its own contribution through the councils of the world.

The second was Sri Lanka's attitude on the prevailing confrontation between Malaysia and Indonesia over the decision of Malaysia to allow foreign bases on her territory and conflicts between them in Borneo. The position of the government was that both Indonesia and Malaysia were good friends of Sri Lanka and it was not for the latter to advise them besides hoping that harmony would be restored in the interests of the peoples of the archipelago working together for a common purpose. On the question of representation by unrecognised countries which posed a problem to Sri Lanka at that time he said it was unfortunate for countries to be divided in this way but without being indifferent to the situation altogether, the Government has taken the lesser course of accepting Consuls-General though some countries had objected and threatened suspension of aid.

The Partial Nuclear Test Ban Treaty to which Sri Lanka acceded was hailed at that time as a significant breakthrough towards disarmament. Sri Lanka supported it because whatever the limitations and the continuing desire of the big powers for nuclear weapons, this was at least a forward step to disarmament which could conceivably lead to complete and total disarmament which was the goal of Non-Alignment. In this connection he made a statement which is of monumental significance to the effect that "our front-line of defence so far as this country is concerned must be our friendship with other countries and other nations. It must be our diplomacy. That is our front-line of defence." This statement ably sums up what one would consider is the essence of the foreign policy required for a country like Sri Lanka. The Colombo mini Non-Aligned Summit of 1962 and its outcome known as the Colombo Proposals aroused much interest and brought credit to Sri Lanka which had taken the initiative to convene the conference. Felix Dias Bandaranaike played a decisive role in it and his comments on it are of interest. His view was that the Colombo Proposals have served their purpose not only in consolidating the ceasefire but also in preventing an recurrence of the conflict. They had thereby created a setting which should be conducive to a settlement of the larger questions by negotiations between the parties concerned. He further mentioned that the Sri Lanka Prime Minister had not concluded her initiatives and was proposing to use her good offices further to bring about a complete peace and restore normalcy in relations between the two countries.

The subject of South Africa and of Africa in general had been a focus of Non-Alignment in the context of the liberation struggle and decolonisation to restore dignity and independence to downtrodden peoples. He affirmed that it was the policy of the Government to seek to eliminate racial discrimination in the form of Apartheid which was akin to Fascism. As regards the question of Sri Lanka's trade with South Africa on which criticism had been levelled, the position was that the real need was for collective action on the part of the entire international community. He did not think that the action of a single country could have any impact and hence the efforts of the government would be directed to bring about a satisfactory imposition of an effective embargo. He also felt that not voting for the expulsion of South Africa at international gatherings which had invited criticism was not the best way calculated to influence the policies of South Africa.

Finally he clarified the position regarding the obligations incurred by Sri Lanka under its Defence Agreements with the United Kingdom. His view was that the enabling Agreement which should have accompanied these Agreements had not been effected and to that extent there was no real binding agreement. He further pointed out that there was no contravention of

Hon. James D'Alwis,
Felix's great-Grandfather.

Canon S. W. Dias Bandaranaike,
Felix's great-Grandfather.

Felix in the Finance Ministry.

Budget Day 1961.

Felix at Finance Ministers' Conference in Ghana, 1961.

Felix at Finance Ministers' Conference in London, 1961.

During the visit to the Chairman of the Council (Soviet) of Ministers of the USSR with N.
Khruschev and officials of the USSR, 19

Mrs Bandaranaike
with Duncan
Sandys –
Commonwealth
Heads of State
Conference, 1961.

Mrs Bandaranaike at Buckingham Palace.

Felix with Mayor Willy Brandt, West Germany, presenting Bell of the City of Berlin.

During the visit to the First Deputy Chairman of the Council (Soviet) of Ministers of the USSR, A. N. Kosigin.

Felix addressing the UN General Assembly, 1961.

Visit of His
Holiness Pope
Paul VI to
Sri Lanka,
December 4th
1971.

Felix at the UN with Foreign Minister Krishna Menon and
Foreign Minister Golda Meir, Israel, 1961.

Felix with President Boumedienne at the Algiers Non-Aligned Summit Conference, 1973.

Prime Minister Pierre
Trudeau of Canada.

Felix in the Middle-East.

Felix with Indian Prime Minister Shri Morarji Desai and A. B. Vajpai, Foreign Minister, India.

Felix in Washington after taking his oaths as Finance Minister before Ambassador
Neville Kanakaratne, 1975.

Felix with S. B. Chavan,
Foreign Minister of India,
1977.

Heads of State Non-Aligned Conference in Colombo, 1976.

Commonwealth Heads of Government Meeting, London, June, 1977. Felix deputises for the PM.

Her Majesty Queen Elizabeth II are (left to right) *Front Row:* HE Ngwazi Dr. H. Kamuzu Banda (President, Malawi) HE Shri Morarji R. Desai (Prime
ister, India) The Rt. Hon Malcolm Fraser (Prime Minister, Australia) The Hon. Michael Manley (Prime Minister, Jamaica) His Beatitude Archbishop Makarios
resident, Cyprus) The Rt. Hon. James Callaghan (Prime Minister, Britain) HE Dr. Kenneth D. Kaunda (President, Zambia) HE Major General Ziaur Rahman
dent, Bangladesh) The Rt. Hon. R. D. Muldoon (Prime Minister, New Zealand) Brigadier Shehu Yaradua (Chief of Staff, Supreme Headquarters, Nigeria).
d Row: The Rt. Hon. Michael T. Somare (Prime Minister, Papua New Guinea) HE Dr. Siaka P. Stevens (President, Sierra Leone) Dr. The Rt. Hon Sir
oosagur Ramgoolam (Prime Minister, Mauritius) The Rt. Hon. J. M. G. M. Adams (Prime Minister, Barbados) The Rt. Hon Sir Eric Gairy (Prime Minister,
da) The Hon Aboud Jumbe (Vice-President, Tanzania) Lieutenant-General F. W. K. Akuffo (Chief of Defence Staff, Ghana) The Rt. Hon Lynden O. Pindling
e Minister, Bahamas) HRH Prince Fatafehi Tu'ipelehake (Prime Minister, Tonga).

Back Row: The Hon. Tupuola Efi (Prime Minister,
Western Samoa) The Hon. Datuk Hussein Bin Onn
(Prime Minister, Malaysia) The Rt. Hon. Ratu Sir
Kamisese Mara (Prime Minister, Fiji) The Hon
Dr. Leabua Jonathan (Prime Minister, Lesotho) The
Hon Daniel Arap Moi (Vice-President, Kenya) The
Hon. Lee Kuan Yew (Prime Minister, Singapore)
The Hon. Felix R. D. Bandaranaike (Minister of
Finance, Sri Lanka) The Hon. F. R. Wills (Minister
of Foreign Affairs, Guyana) HE The Rt. Hon.
Colonel Maphevu Dlamini (Prime Minister,
Swaziland) Senator The Hon. John Donaldson
(Minister of External Affairs, Trinidad and Tobago)
HE Alhaji Sir Dawda Kairaba Jawara (President,
The Gambia) HE Sir Seretse Khama (President,
Botswana) The Rt. Hon. Pierre E. Trudeau (Prime
Minister, Canada).

Elizabeth R

at the Non-Aligned Foreign Ministers' Conference, Sri Lanka, 1976.

Felix outside the Buddhist Vihare at Los Angeles.

B. Mahadeva, Professor G. L. Peiris, Minister of Justice, R. W. M. Dias, Percy Colin-Thomé and Dr. Gamani Corea.

Felix after Graduation in Theology with Christine, Hiran Wikramanayake and Lakshmi,
Multnomah School of the Bible, 1984.

Felix with Dr. Willard and Mildred Aldrich in Portland Oregon, USA, 1984.

These are the Judges of the Supreme Court and the High Court and officials who took part in the ceremonial opening of the Courts in Sri Lanka on the introduction of the Administration of Justice Law (1973).

In the picture seated left to right are:

Mr Justice Sharvananda, Mr Justice Vythialingam, Mr Justice Ismail, Mr Justice Wijesundera, Mr Justice Sirimane, Mr Justice Wimalaratne, Mr Justice Walgampaya, Mr Justice Thamotheram, Mr Justice Samerawickrame, Mr R. S. Wanasundera, Acting Attorney-General, Mr Ratnasiri Wickramanayake, Deputy Minister of Justice, Mr Victor Tennekoon, Chief Justice, The President of Sri Lanka, Mr William Gopallawa, Mr Felix R. Dias Bandaranaike, Minister of Justice, Mr Nihal Jayawickrama, Secretary to the Ministry of Justice, Mr Justice Alles, Mr Justice Wijayatilake, Mr Justice Deheragoda, Mr Justice Pathirana, Mr Justice Rajaratnam, Mr Justice Udalagama, Mr Justice Perera, Mr Justice Weeraratne, Mr Justice Tittawella, Mr Justice Walpita.

Standing: (Left to Right) Mr S. Y. B. M. P. B. Herat, Additional Registrar, Mr B. S. C. Ratwatte, Public Trustee and High Court Judges, Mr Justin S. Abeywardene (Ratnapura), Mr I. G. N. de Jacolyn Seneviratne (Kalutara), Mr K. A. P. Ranasinghe (Badulla), Mr T. J. Rajaratnam (Jaffna), Mr C. N. de S. J. Goonewardena (Galle), Mr J. R. M. Perera (Matara), Mr M. M. Abdul Cader (Kurunegala), Mr E. F. de Zilva (Kandy), Mr J. F. A. Soza (Avissawella), Mr P. Colin-Thomé (Colombo), Mr H. A. G. de Silva (Gampaha), Mr L. H. de Alwis (Batticaloa), Mr K. D. O. S. M. Seneviratne (Negombo), Mr N. Devendra (Anuradhapura), Mr D. E. Dharmasekera (Kegalle), Mr A. A. de Silva (Chilaw), Mr O. M. de Alwis, Legal Draftsman, Mr L. Wickremasinghe, Registrar.

Felix's Memorial Service.

Left to Right: Delia Perera, Revd. Theodore Perera, Revd. Lionel Pieris, Roshini Perera, Susan Wikramaratne, Mrs S. Bandaranaike, Lakshmi

sovereignty under these Agreements which obliged either side to help each other. The proof of this was that these Agreements did not prevent Sri Lanka from opposing British action in the Suez or denying the use of Sri Lanka ports by aircraft and vessels. His conclusion was that "this agreement to agree in future does not in any way tie down or limit the sovereignty of this Government to determine its own future, its own defence policy and what is most important of all to exercise independent judgement with regard to the rights and wrongs of any particular international situation and to express the will of this country without any fetters and limitations."

From this general survey of Sri Lanka's foreign relations as expounded by Felix Dias Bandaranaike in his capacity as Parliamentary Secretary for that subject, we should now turn to his role in the principal areas of Sri Lanka's diplomatic activities. The most conspicuous of them was the Commonwealth which was in fact a parental connection inherited from our colonial past under Britain but which had now become an integral part of Sri Lanka's relations as an independent state with Britain. At the outset this was a very close relationship to which Sri Lanka's Prime Minister at the time of independence attached great importance. This relationship was to some extent sealed by its Defence Pact with the UK in 1948.

Commonwealth Conferences

After the abrogation of the latter in 1957 it seemed as if this link had been weakened but it was reaffirmed by the new administration as witnessed by its active participation in Commonwealth conferences of Heads of States and Governments. The Sri Lanka Prime Minister regularly attended all these meetings and made significant contributions. Felix Dias Bandaranaike invariably accompanied the Prime Minister as principal adviser but he also contributed in his own right to Commonwealth activities through his membership in the Commonwealth Parliamentary Association and attended several of its conferences. His statements on these occasions afford an insight into his thinking on foreign policy in relation to the issues of those times and on the Commonwealth.

It is clear that he enjoyed these occasions and the opportunities they afforded for him to meet his counterparts and colleagues socially and discuss matters of common interest with them in a frank and friendly spirit. The atmosphere of these Commonwealth Parliamentary conferences was ideally suited to his temperament and background as an inborn democrat who revelled in Parliamentary democracy with its freedom of expression and the cut and thrust of debate which would be field day for his forensic skills. He pointedly referred to this at the Kuala Lumpur conference of 1971 when he stated that "We in the Commonwealth Parliamentary Association stand for parliamentary democracy. We may not think it is the best form of government in the world but nobody has yet devised a more satisfactory form." Elsewhere in the same speech he said "I think the best feature of our discussions so far has been the avoidance of double standards; that we speaking as Parliamentarians have spoken freely and frankly. We have expressed strong views sometimes, emotional views sometimes and sometimes views which may not have met complete agreement and accord round the room; but we have all spoken with sincerity from the bottom of our hearts."

The main agenda at these meetings was a discussion of developments in the international scene in so far as they affected member countries in the course of which representatives expressed their standpoints on these subjects. Unlike in UN organisations or other multilateral bodies their aim was not to arrive at any substantive conclusions but instead to voice their opinions freely. In his statement at the Kuala Lumpur conference Bandaranaike summed it up admirably when referring to the debate he said "It gave us all an opportunity as Parliamentarians who are accustomed to debating in our own countries to hear the opinions of Commonwealth Parliamentarians from other parts of the world and to learn the thoughts and feelings which inspire your own Parliament when they sit discussing foreign affairs and other related questions in your own countries. I think there is this positive gain from these discussions. As members of Parliament we have been given the opportunity to be able to find out how each of us thinks and works in our own Parliaments, the kind of reasoning which prevails, the emotionally charged feelings that we have on certain subjects and of course we are all talking in the context of our own national interests." These meetings were therefore attempts to promote understanding on international issues at a Parliamentary level in the Commonwealth and create thereby a sense of fellow feeling and tolerance.

Felix Bandaranaike participated in a number of these conferences which included those of Nassau (1968), Ottawa (1971), Kuala Lumpur (1971), Malawi (1972), Colombo (1973) and London (1974). These were equally convivial and social occasions when delegates struck up friendships and disported themselves partaking of the diversions available in such esoteric and salubrious surroundings as those of the Bahamas and Kuala Lumpur. At the business sessions matters which engaged the attention of the world at those times were discussed by delegates and in all the meetings which he attended Felix Dias Bandaranaike made notable contributions.

In the course of a debate on the subject of "South-East Asia and the Indian Ocean; Security and Neutrality" he clarified Sri Lanka's proposal which was first tabled at the Singapore Commonwealth Heads of State conference, to ensure peace and security in this region through the creation of a peace zone which will be free of foreign bases or armed activities of foreign navies. He referred to the so-called communication base in Diego Garcia which was established without any prior consultation and could be a source of tension. He thought that there was general agreement on the need for keeping the Indian Ocean as an area of peace and security.

In this connection the question of British arms sales to South Africa which had been raised at the Singapore conference was discussed. Many countries had objected to it fearing that the arms would be used for repression. He pointed out that a study group of 8 members had been appointed to investigate this subject but the committee in which Sri Lanka was a member never met. As regards the larger question of Apartheid and the South African government itself the ethics of having a dialogue with it were debated, African countries holding the view that countries should outlaw it and desist from dealing with it. Bandaranaike appreciated this position but felt that the most effective weapon was an economic boycott provided that all concerned including the most economically powerful countries co-operated unlike in Rhodesia where sanctions had failed for lack of support. An interesting debate arose on the subject of the causes for coups and one delegate attributed them to economic reasons and another to leaders being out of touch. Bandaranaike's position was that the economic factor was the root cause in that in his own words "if the life of the people and the country remains unaltered substantially, then you will find that the seeds of revolutionary movements, of insurrections and dissatisfactions will become manifest sooner or later." It will become he thought a challenge to Parliamentary democracy itself.

His conclusion was that the responsibility for the preservation of democracy lies not only on those practising it but on those better and more fortunately placed and therefore "that we all have the responsibility for its preservation." At the Malawi conference he spoke again on the Indian Ocean peace zone in reply to delegates who had endorsed the idea but felt that it was not practical. His reply was that it was in the wider interest of the big powers to co-operate as a step which will not only promote the well-being of the region but contribute further to international peace and security as a whole.

At Nassau, Bandaranaike replied to a comment by a delegate that the biggest problem of the time was the ideological dispute between Capitalism and Communism where the latter represented a negation of democracy. His answer was that it was up to the country concerned to choose its own form of government, to decide its own affairs and in this connection he questioned the basis of US intervention in Vietnam which he felt had the right to whatever government it wanted. He deplored the bombings of several months which had destroyed thousands of Vietnamese and also Commonwealth youth. Sri Lanka for its part was concerned about the Buddhists in that country who had been oppressed by the Diem regime and had sponsored a UN commission to look into the situation.

At the Colombo conference he returned to the subject of the Peace zone in the Indian Ocean which had been discussed at other conferences to reply to comments about its impracticality. He was critical of the attitude of some delegates in dismissing it as pure idealism which he thought was a negative approach to problems of international peace and security where in his view a broad-minded approach instead of a purely Cold war attitude was needed which took into account the public opinion of countries.

The crowning achievement of Felix Dias Bandaranaike's participation at Commonwealth Parliamentary Association conferences was by common claim his brilliant almost impromptu address of welcome and thanks to Her Majesty Elizabeth II for declaring open the 19th Commonwealth Parliamentary conference. Apart from being superb natural oratory for its effortless ease of expression and delivery it also embodied some noteworthy thoughts on the value of the Commonwealth and the Parliamentary Associations under its aegis. These were that "Every member of Parliament who has had the opportunity of attending CPA conferences will I am sure support me in saying that the friendships made with overseas colleagues have proved invaluable to him and that he has returned home to the service of his own Parliament with his experience and knowledge of Parliamentary practice enriched by participation in CPA activities" and "the people of Sri Lanka have never wavered in their commitment to the due processes of law within the framework of Parliamentary democracy." In participating in these conferences of the Commonwealth Parliamentary Association, Felix Dias Bandaranaike was on his own, speaking in his own right and being himself. It brought out his oratorical and forensic skills and his profound insights into world affairs and earned him recognition as one of the outstanding statesmen in the Commonwealth of that time.

Pursuit of Non-Alignment

The keynote of the foreign policy of the successive administrations of Madame Sirimavo Bandaranaike was the pursuit of Non-Alignment. This has been defined by her in a recent statement in the following terms: "The pursuit of a genuinely independent foreign policy in a world dominated by power blocs and complicated by superpower conflicts and tensions is the essence of Non-Alignment. In practice it entails equally or more importantly relations with other states especially in our neighbourhood, founded on trust and goodwill, mutual respect or equality and sovereignty and a common appreciation of national interests of each country. It is only on the basis of such mutual confidence between Governments that problems can be equitably resolved."

In her address to the first Non-Aligned Summit held in Belgrade in 1961, she stated by way of explaining the objectives of Non-Alignment that "we are gathered here in the firm belief that the positive policy of non-alignment with power blocs followed by each of our several countries and that our common dedication to the cause of peace and peaceful co-existence gives us the right to raise our voices in common decisions and declarations in a world divided into power blocs and moving rapidly towards the brink of a nuclear war." In a statement to the Senate in 1964 she spelt out further details on this subject and refuted the notion that it was an isolationist attitude of evading responsibility and washing our hands off matters. Instead she affirmed that it was the means by which Sri Lanka would after an independent evaluation of a situation throw its moral weight and use the Councils of the world for the purpose.

Indeed as she pointed out it was incumbent on Ceylon, vitally necessary in fact for her as a part of the international community to play a role and it will not be fulfilling its responsibilities if it refuses to express its attitude on particular international questions and seek to help in resolving them at the United Nations or by participation in regional conferences. These ideas were re-echoed by Felix Dias Bandaranaike in an article which he wrote at the time of the Colombo Non-Aligned Summit of 1976 where he stated that the Non-Aligned impulse arose from a desire of countries like Sri Lanka, India, UAR, Yugoslavia to seek their destiny through an independent course, steering clear of the major power blocs and determined to fight for peaceful co-existence within the framework of a just international order, independent of great power conflicts and rivalries which characterised the '50s and the '60s. These countries therefore decided that it would be desirable for them to explore areas of agreement among themselves in the light of their own independent foreign policies so that within the framework of the United Nations and its Charter they could formulate principles which would give a new meaning and purpose to international politics.

The movement began with only 25 countries attending the first Belgrade Summit of 1961 but it has since grown beyond the widest imagination of those who launched it to become a force to be reckoned with which not even the great power veto in the Security Council can stifle.

Non-Alignment had its roots in two earlier ideas which were the Afro-Asian solidarity of Bandung and the dynamic neutralism of S. W. R. D.

Bandaranaike. Bandung was an emotional driving force among these countries while dynamic neutralism conceived of these countries acting as a buffer between rival blocs in the Cold war confrontation in the interests of international peace and relaxation of tension such as could trigger off a nuclear war which seemed an imminent danger in the light of the Berlin crisis. The Non-Alignment movement represented the convergence of these two streams. The members were at pains to disavow any character as a third force or bloc or any desire to be one. That would have been counter-productive and exacerbated the very tension they wished to defuse. They were instead a community of like-minded countries wedded to common principles which were in accordance with the United Nations Charter.

Therefore, in lieu of forming a bloc or membership in one, Non-Alignment was based on adherence to a number of principles which were first enunciated as the criteria on which countries were invited to the first Non-Aligned Summit of Belgrade. These principles to which Felix Dias Bandaranaike referred in his article and which are embodied in the joint communique of the Preparatory meeting for the first Belgrade Summit held in Cairo in June, 1961, were as follows:

1. The country should have adopted an independent policy based on the co-existence of States with different political and social systems and on non-alignment or should be showing a trend in favour of such a policy.

2. The country concerned should be consistently supporting the movements for national independence.

3. Non-membership in a multilateral military alliance concluded in the context of great power conflicts.

4. If a country has a bilateral military agreement with a great power or is a member of a regional defence pact, the agreement or pact should not be one deliberately concluded in the context of great power conflicts.

5. If it has conceded military bases to a foreign power the concession should not have been made in the context of Great power conflicts.

As the mainstay of the Foreign policy of the successive governments of Madame Bandaranaike, it became a major preoccupation of Felix Dias Bandaranaike as the principal adviser. Indeed as she acknowledged in her Memorial Lecture on Felix Dias Bandaranaike "Equally importantly I chose Felix Dias Bandaranaike as my Deputy Minister of Defence and Foreign Affairs since the constitution itself determined that the Prime Minister should hold these portfolios. From that time on whatever portfolios Felix Dias Bandaranaike held, I always relied on his advice in the implementation of the Sri Lanka Freedom party's foreign policy. Indeed the late Felix Dias Bandaranaike represented me at all of the Non-Aligned Foreign Ministers Conferences and I know he was held in high respect and regard by those participating. At these conferences on the many special missions I entrusted to him he proved to be an exceptional negotiator."

These two periods, namely from 1960-65 and 1970-77 marked the high tide of the Non-Aligned movement and witnessed its peak achievements in all of which Bandaranaike played a central role. Sri Lanka in fact was associated with the initiatives which led to the formation of the movement and was in its forefront since then culminating in its becoming the first Asian venue of a Non-Aligned Summit. It also made original contributions towards enabling the movement to play a positive role in accordance with its ideals and objectives. Needless to say the driving force in all these activities was Bandaranaike who played a many-sided role in these initiatives, in planning, directing, guiding them almost under his personal supervision with in many instances impressive results which added to the prestige of Non-Alignment and Sri Lanka.

We may proceed to consider some of the landmarks in Sri Lanka's role in the Non-Aligned movement which by implication would represent the personal contributions of Felix Dias Bandaranaike in his official capacity. From the outset the process of giving shape to the movement involved intricate negotiations leading to the preparatory conference held in Cairo in June, 1961, where thorny questions such as agenda, criteria for invitations were resolved for the Belgrade Summit and Sri Lanka was associated with these preliminary activities.

The Belgrade Summit though marred by the Soviet nuclear bomb explosion successfully launched the movement and caught the imagination of the world. The major issue at this meeting was Disarmament which was really highlighted by the nuclear explosion and Mrs Bandaranaike's statement in the course of her address that she spoke "not only as a representative of my country but also as a woman and mother who can understand the thoughts and feelings of those millions of women, the mothers of the world who are deeply concerned with the preservation of the human race" went to the heart and made a profound impression. Thus inaugurated it became the endeavour of the Government to give expression to it in any possible way.

Sino-Indian Conflict, 1962

One of the most dramatic steps which it took in this direction was the holding of the Mini Non-Aligned Summit of December, 1962, in Colombo to consider what action if any could be taken over the outbreak of the Sino-Indian border conflict. Six Non-aligned countries participated, namely Sri Lanka, Egypt, Cambodia, Burma, Indonesia and Ghana and they were represented by the Sri Lanka Prime Minister as Convenor and Host and

Foreign Minister Aly Sabry of Egypt, Chairman Ne Win of Burma, King
Norodom Sihanouk of Cambodia, Foreign Minister Subandrio of Indonesia
and Justice Minister Offori Atta of Ghana. Considering the short time within
which this conference was convened, it was indeed a rare achievement which
speaks highly for the sense of solidarity shown by the participating countries
in responding so readily and for the organisational efficiency of Sri Lanka in
arranging it.

Preparations for the conference involved receiving delegations from China
and India to present their positions and finalisation of the agenda and
arrangements through telegraphic communications. More remarkable than
the act of organising it was the success of the conference in achieving
tangible results. These were in the form of agreed proposals to consolidate
the ceasefire and prepare the way for negotiated solutions between them
which were to be communicated to the latter. In her opening statement
Mrs Bandaranaike said that "I feel confident that this Conference of six Afro-
Asian Non-Aligned countries will also make a useful contribution towards
keeping alive non-alignment as a significant influence for world peace." In
her closing statement she summed up the achievement of the conference as
one of preventing a serious compromising of non-alignment and Afro-Asian
solidarity and showing that these policies are still a living force and are
capable of contributing something worthwhile to the maintenance of peace in
our region and perhaps in the wider world.

The sequel to this conference was the personal mission which
Mrs Bandaranaike undertook to formally communicate these proposals to the
two Governments concerned. She was received with great cordiality and
affection and hailed as a peacemaker for which she thus received
international recognition.

The part played by Felix Dias Bandaranaike in this momentous event is
implicit in the heavy responsibilities which it imposed and which he had to
discharge. Its success therefore redounds to his credit. He was at the helm of
the preparatory arrangements, planning and steering them at every stage. In
the proceedings itself he was the principal negotiator for Sri Lanka and the
formulation of the proposals owes not a little to his skill and acumen.

In the folow-up stage he accompanied the Prime Minister on both the
missions to India and to China counselling her in the sensitive negotiations
which accompanied discussion of the proposals with the two Governments.
As is well known they were readily accepted by the Prime Minister of India
and China welcomed it as a basis for negotiation. Whatever the immediate
response that fact remains that there was no recurrence of conflict ever since
and this speaks for itself on the decisive and lasting impact of the conference.
This Colombo Mini Non-Aligned Summit as it is called was certainly a star

diplomatic performance of Sri Lanka for which Bandaranaike as one of its architects deserves praise.

Sri Lanka undertook a similar task though on a much larger physical scale when it was the host of the Preparatory meeting in March, 1964, for the second Non-Aligned Summit which was due to be held. 23 countries participated at this Preparatory conference, and it lasted 5 days. Its decisions included fixing the date and venue of the next Summit which was to be the first week of October, 1964 and Cairo respectively. It also recommended a draft agenda for adoption by the Summit. Bandaranaike accompanied the Prime Minister at the Cairo Summit as the Deputy leader of the delegation. In the sequence of Non-Aligned Summits the distinctive place of the Cairo Summit was for its focus on the Middle-East and Africa. This was understandable being on Afro-Arab soil at a time when the African continent was in the throes of the liberation struggle and the Arab world of the Middle-Eastern crisis.

Indian Ocean Peace Zone

As far as Sri Lanka was concerned this Summit was notable for the recommendation in its Declaration for the denuclearisation of Africa in accordance with the Declaration to the same effect adopted by the African states. In fact, the Cairo Summit went further in recommending the creation of denuclearised zones in other parts of the world and in the oceans of the world. This was a decision of particular interest to Sri Lanka as the Prime Minister stated in her address in view of its decision to restrict the proliferation of nuclear weapons into the Indian Ocean and to close its ports and airfields to ships and aircraft which either carry nuclear weapons or are equipped for nuclear warfare. On the strength of this the Prime Minister urged the Cairo conference to adopt a resolution to declare as a nuclear free zone not only the continent of Africa but also the waters of the Indian and South Atlantic Oceans and that all Non-Aligned countries should take action to close their ports and airfields to vessels with nucelar arms or capacity or also prohibit overflights of craft thus equipped.

This proposal foreshadowed the initiative for which Sri Lanka became famous later in its proposal for a Peace zone in the Indian Ocean. This was first tabled by the Prime Minister at the Non-Aligned Summit in Lusaka. This had two aims which were the elimination of great power rivalry within the region which was a threat to our security and reciprocal obligations on the part of the regional states to behave in a manner that does not prejudice the peace and safety of fellow members in the region. This proposal in fact was presented by the Prime Minister to the United Nations General

Assembly of 1971 and adopted by it. It was referred by the UN to an *ad hoc* committee for implementation.

This has not made much headway since then but what is notable was the initiative itself as a manifestation of Sri Lanka's adherence to Non-Alignment and its desire to genuinely advance those principles. The formulation of a proposal of this kind with its technical and legal implications called for skilful drafting and strategy which once again engaged the unique abilities of Bandaranaike. He himself had occasion at several venues to be a spokesman for this proposal. While the inspiration and the impetus came from the Prime Minister reflecting her preoccupation with threats to the region particularly in the light of the establishment of the base at Diego Garcia, it was Bandaranaike's expert handling of it and negotiations that enabled it to go as far as it did.

Colombo Summit, August, 1976

Sri Lanka's most spectacular achievement in its career of Non-Alignment was the Colombo Summit of August, 1976, when it was the host to representatives of 85 states of whom 41 were Heads of States. It was the first Non-Aligned Summit to be held in an Asian country and this itself was no small feat in view of the larger and powerful countries which were interested. This Summit has been acclaimed as one of the best of its kind for its immaculate and near perfect organisational arrrangements which were a glowing tribute to the exemplary standards of its public and security services who together handled the tremendous logistical responsibilities with perfect co-ordination and unison. Equally in the history of Non-Aligned Summits it was a landmark for its original and innovative record.

At the preceding Lusaka and Algiers Summits the theme of economic advancement came to the forefront with the adoption of the document known as "A declaration of Non-Alignment and Economic progress" which was the curtain-raiser for another momentous stride in the "Declaration for the establishment of a new International Economic order," of the Algiers Summit. These steps opened a new chapter in the development of the policy perspectives of Non-Alignment in that they focussed on the need for accelerating the economic advancement of the member states as a consummation of their political liberation.

The timing of the Colombo Summit was ideally suited for this purpose because it coincided with the ascendancy of the OPEC countries and their ability to challenge the developed world with the weapon of oil prices. This was also an opportunity for them to divert part of this oil riches towards financing development programmes of member countries. In point of fact the

Colombo Summit launched positive initiatives towards this end with its adoption as part of its Economic Declaration of a comprehensive scheme designated as "Action programme for Economic Co-operation" which spelt out specific plans for concerted action in a number of crucial areas such as Raw Materials, Trade, Monetary and Financial Co-operation, Industrialisation, Food and Agriculture, Transport, Technical Co-operation and Consultancy Services, Scientific and Technological development, Employment and Human Resources Development, Private Foreign Investment, Nucelar Energy. There is no doubt that this multi-faceted plan which embraced every conceivable sector of development represented a new dimension in Non-Alignment which to that extent made the Colombo Summit the threshold of a new era.

Alongside the organisational tasks the conduct of the proceeding was the responsibility of the host country which as in other such events was borne by Felix Dias Bandaranaike. As Supreme G.O.C. of the operation he supervised every detail of it for weeks from before its commencement through rounds of conferences at his residence lasting till the small hours of the morning and on-the-spot checks at the BMICH where the conference was being held. In the conference itself, he had the specific role of Chairman of the conference of Foreign Ministers which preceded the Summit conference.

In his address of welcome he referred to the Summit as a jubilee marking the 15th anniversary of the movement since its inception. He affirmed the desire of the Government to ensure the success of this Summit in keeping with its historic place in the movement. The Colombo Summit of 1976 was the last great triumph of the SLFP Government which had been an architect of Non-Alignment in the latter, as it fell from power in the following year. There have been Summits since then but also a perceptible decline in the movement due to an ideological rift, hostilities between member states, a lack of purpose and a weakening of solidarity. Essentially it reflected a void in its leadership after the passing away of the giants such as President Tito, President Nasser and Prime Minister Nehru who had inspired the movement and then sustained it. At the moment it is not clear whether Non-Alignment has a future and if it has what shape it will assume even though ironically the need for such a movement is never more urgent than now.

FDB at the UN

Like the Commonwealth the United Nations was the other great multilateral body in the world with the difference that it was representative of the global international community of independent states and was truly a World Parliament. In 1961 Felix Dias Bandaranaike addressed the General Assembly of the United Nations and this was no doubt an occasion after his own heart as it gave an opportunity to display his eloquence and incisive analytical powers and knowledge of the world situation before the official bar of the world. His statement was a masterly survey of the prevailing international situation in the course of which he expressed the views of the Government of Sri Lanka and of the Non-Aligned community in general on the leading events of that time. These included a wide range of subjects such as the Cold war, Non-Aligned policies, Nuclear Testing, Restructuring of the UN, Economic problems of the Third World and Disarmament.

Speaking of the Cold war he regarded this as a grave threat to peace and a source of tension because of the obsessive preoccupation of the superpowers with their own political and economic ideologies to a point which will not prevent them from resorting to the use of force in defence of what they cherish. Sri Lanka could not accept that premise because of its belief that the United Nations has developed the concept of peaceful co-existence which should enable them to find a *modus vivendi* to live together peacefully. This Cold war has prompted the big powers to interfere in the affairs of other countries resulting in subversion but most of the countries in Asia, Africa and Latin America resolutely oppose such pressures because their earnest desire is to be left alone to work out their own destiny and forms of social, economic and political life in accordance with their own domestic forces.

In the circumstances he concluded that the basic principles the great powers should follow should be non-intervention and non-interference in internal affairs. Referring to the suggestion made by a Foreign Secretary of a Western country about double standards in that some of the governments which have membership are not representative of the wishes of the people he pointed out that this was a dangerous assumption on which to proceed as it had deprived the People's Republic of China of membership and could lead to questioning of the credentials of countries in a way which would undermine the Charter.

The sudden death of Dag Hammerskjold had caused a kind of constitutional crisis in the UN over the appointment of a successor because the Soviet Union had taken the opportunity to propose the Troika arrangement of 3 instead of one. Sri Lanka he said had categorically opposed this proposal which it thought would deprive the UN of the capacity for effective executive action. He deplored a proposal which was in the air to appoint a distinguished person from a member country to function as the Secretary-General pending formal appointment. He dismissed this as an idea too fantastic for serious consideration. Nor did he favour action by a majority vote of the Assembly where the Security Council is paralysed by a veto which he thought would have dangerous consequences and would be the first step to the disintegration of the entire Organisation. The Security Council was so constituted so as to ensure decisions in a spirit of conciliation and compromise which he thought was the only basis on which the Organisation could operate. If it was felt that the Charter needed revision it was for the Assembly to consider ways and means of improving it.

On disarmament he affirmed that what was sought was general and complete disarmament such as would enable all nations large or small to find security and resolve differences by peaceful means instead of a transient balance of power arrangement. He welcomed initiatives undertaken by the superpowers to explore possibilities as regards a basis for such negotiations. He hoped at the same time that this would not be undertaken in a spirit of a radical break with past concepts such as nuclear deterrent, massive retaliation, limited wars and positions of strength without utilising it to play for time or seek concessions. He did not think that the question of control was an insuperable obstacle.

He submitted in fact a proposal of the Sri Lanka Prime Minister that representatives of Non-Aligned countries should be invited to participate in these negotiations and to that end suggested that the Ten-nation committee on Disarmament should be expanded to include a number of Non-Aligned states. He further called for an immediate cessation of underground and atmospheric nuclear tests in view of the tensions they have caused, the damage to the environment and the health of mankind. He did not think that it was necessary to wait for a treaty to effect such a moratorium.

The dramatic expansion in the membership of the United Nations in his view called for a corresponding restructuring of that body. This was needed not only to make it more representative of the world and in particular Asia and Africa but also to enable it to carry out its tasks more effectively. Such changes were called for in the Security Council and the Economic and Social Council which are noticeably under-representative. A parallel change should also be effected in the Secretariat to make it more representative of the African and Asian countries proportionately.

As Finance Minister in addition to his responsibilities in foreign affairs, he thought it appropriate to speak on the economic problems of the developing countries. The recent past had been marked by a decline in the terms of trade and external finance had not increased and fell far short of requirements. His conclusion which remains valid up to now was that "there is a very grave need for urgent consideration by the Assembly of some form of automatic access to reserves and some form of insurance against commodity price fluctuations." He concluded with a stirring appeal to the big powers in particular not to forget the principles that inspired them at San Francisco inasmuch as the real challenge is not to the developing countries which are victims of events but to the big powers to whom the rest of the world look forward to constructive and positive action.

Ad hoc Missions USSR, Indo-Ceylon Talks, World Bank & IMF Meetings

Felix Dias Bandaranaike's Ministerial career was interspersed with a number of *ad hoc* missions either on his own or accompanying the Prime Minister and also combined with his office as Finance Minister. One such solo mission was to Moscow in his capacity as Finance Minister to discuss trade matters but it was notable for the very cordial reception accorded to him as the first Minister of the Government to visit the Soviet Union. A reception was given in his honour at the Kremlin by no less than the great Krushchev himself then at the height of his power. Characteristically he was a hit on this occasion in replying to the toast in his honour in Russian.

There was a similar fulsome public reception for him at the Moscow House by the USSR-Ceylon Friendship Society where in the presence of a distinguished gathering of Soviet political leaders, Scholars, Scientists he was received with utmost cordiality. In his reply to the address of welcome he again spoke a portion of it in Russian which was highly appreciated. In the course of that visit he toured several parts of the country and it is interesting that on his train journey to Leningrad by the Soviet Union's man of destiny Gorbachev then the Finance Minister accompanied by his very sophisticated wife who in her taste for fashions foreshadowed the social revolution in that country in the future.

A key mission on which he accompanied the Prime Minister as an adviser was for the Indo-Ceylon talks in New Delhi in October, 1964, which led to the historic breakthrough of the Sirima-Shastri pact. This was the outcome of protracted negotiations going back for decades during which relations between the two countries had been strained. This was a great diplomatic achievement which was the result of skilful negotiation and persistence by Sri Lanka and a positive and constructive response by India which opened a new chapter in Indo-Ceylon relations. Likewise he accompanied the Prime Minister to several conferences of Commonwealth Heads of States/Governments as the Deputy leader of the delegation and participated at these conferences where he distinguished himself for his drafting skills.

OPEC Countries

One of Bandaranaike's *alter egos* during his many-sided career was that of Finance Minister in both the administrations. In this capacity he attended meetings of the IMF of 1961 and 1975. In his statement at the 1971 meeting he spoke on the declining terms of trade of primary commodity countries which should he felt engage the attention of the Fund. He referred to a statement in the annual report of the Executive Directors that the "strength and wealth of the industrial countries should be used not only to give economic aid to the countries with lower per capita incomes but also to absorb more readily the growing diversity of their products," and called upon the Fund to play a more positive role in giving its assistance to the underdeveloped countries. Speaking of balance of payment problems he said that the development programmes of developing countries which have as their objective a continuous improvement in the living and social standards of the people cannot be implemented if industrial countries follow a stop go policy and hence continuous funding is required.

As the newly appointed Governor to the Fund in 1971 he drew its attention to Sri Lanka's predicament as a result of the rise in oil prices which while it was welcome to the developing world as a whole in giving it leverage yet it put Sri Lanka in the category of the most seriously affected countries. Urgent help was therefore required from the Fund and the Bank but in rendering assistance he felt that some thought should be given to their approaches and image as an attitude of being an arbiter would not be helpful. He thought that these bodies should attempt to do some public relations about their policies and image in these countries. He expressed his appreciation of the assistance rendered during the last three years and specially thanked McNamara of the Bank and Witteveen of the Fund for their initiatives. He attended the annual meeting of the Bank and Fund held in Manila in 1976 and his statement dealt with the suggestions made by the Fund that the developing countries should make adjustments as regards their oil deficits rather than seek external financing. He pointed out that this can only be achieved through measures of import liberalisation by the developed countries. The prevailing situation was a negative one where developing countries have no assured access to export markets while they are in effect denied reasonable access to Fund resources through the conditionalities insisted upon. As a solution he suggested a fresh issue of SDRs which he thought could breathe new life to a proposal which was endorsed by the Colombo Non-Aligned Summit that with a view to establishing a New International Economic order the credit agencies should think in terms of the need to bring reserve currencies under control with a view towards establishing a countervailing currency not controlled by any one country but by the international community of nations.

A special assignment which demonstrated Bandaranaike's remarkable versatility and ability to move with ease from one subject to another was his mission to a number of Middle-Eastern countries to negotiate for aid in the context of the rise in oil prices which had seriously affected Sri Lanka. It was typical of his mature and realistic diplomatic acumen that he viewed this not as a mission to solicit aid on the usual grounds of fellow feeling, Non-Aligned sentiment and support for the Arab cause but instead as an opportunity to explore a basis for meaningful and mutually benefical economic co-operation with them. As the object of the mission was to obtain loans he surmised that their response would depend on Sri Lanka's proven ability to repay them. Sri Lanka's exports to those countries were limited to tea but he thought that the development of other export lines of goods in demand in these countries would provide an answer. The mission could be an opportunity to obtain inputs for the establishment of such industries and the conclusion of buy-back arrangements as a means of repaying the loans. With his usual professional thoroughness he prepared himself for the task by obtaining and studying detailed reports from the Ministries concerned on the openings available and planned his strategy accordingly.

In undertaking this mission Bandaranaike had the advantage of being known and respected by the leaders and key personalities of these countries whom he had met at Non-Aligned meetings and worked together with them. His designation Special Envoy of the Prime Minister who was held in very high esteem in these countries further enhanced his image. Prior to leaving he informed them in advance and this prior intimation which was necessary as there were only two Sri Lankan missions (Cairo, Baghdad) facilitated his mission. The mission was a discovery to him in that it revealed great opportunities for Sri Lanka in the way of openings for employment in their development projects which were employing labour from several Asian countries and also for skilled professionals such as nurses, teachers, engineers and accountants. Countries like Kuwait which had employed Sri Lankans expressed satisfaction with their services. The loan negotiations were a success but the follow-up of economic collaboration was left for negotiation later by the Ministries concerned. Besides at that time the Sri Lankan government had as yet not spelt out its policies on foreign investment.

Missions of this kind were an object lesson in Bandaranaike's working methods and approaches. Just as back home he maintained a relentless work schedule of working from early in the morning till midnight but he allowed himself and the staff regular breaks when he would mix with them freely sharing jokes and banter in his inimitable way. Officials found him a pleasure to work with because of his readiness in a truly democractic spirit to listen to their points of view. Though outwardly he had a forbidding air he was gentleness itself and endeared himself to those around. His reputation as a workaholic is well known in that he typed his own drafts and notes and faithfully reported back to the Prime Minister on his return.

Commonwealth Parliamentary Association

With his powers of lucid exposition, imperturbability and ability to field question whether in Parliament or elsewhere, he excelled as a spokesman. On many occasions he answered queries on a multitude of matters and in foreign affairs he was adroit at press conferences. One such conference was in Ottawa in 1971 held at the Parliamentary Press gallery in Ottawa on the occasion of his visit to attend the Commonwealth Parliamentary Association meeting. The subject-matter and the timing lent it significance because it was not long after the 1971 JVP insurrection and the outside world was anxious to have an authentic account of it. In the course of the conference he gave a masterly survey of the overall situation in the country in respect of the major problems facing it and Government policy on them. He referred to the aims of the government and the progress made in realising them. He made special mention of the economic policies of the government in view of reports in the world press that it was Communist or left wing. While admitting that it was not a traditional capitalist economy he pointed out that the Government welcomes foreign investment and provides better terms than many other countries. On foreign policy he highlighted its attitude of non-alignment which some have castigated as being anti-West which is a falsehood in that Sri Lanka has close ties with the Commonwealth and the international community. The proof of the success of Non-Alignment was the support which it received in 1971 to combat the insurgency. He spoke appreciatively of relations between Canada and Sri Lanka and the close rapports of the Sri Lankan government with Prime Minister Trudeau who had visited Sri Lanka and he himself had accompanied Prime Minister Trudeau on that occasion. Canada was an exceptionally good friend of Sri Lanka and had given it much aid without strings. Some of the questions he had to answer were about foreign involvement in the insurgency and whether it had affected the tourist trade.

Felix Dias Bandaranaike died alas far too young at an age when others were starting their political career. Some may think that he had already attained the peak of his career but in the process he had shown promise and talent to indicate that there were no heights which were unattainable for him. In foreign affairs he had shown outstanding statesmanship and in the political field he had been a giant. One cannot do better than conclude with the soulful tribute, one of many from all parts of the House, paid to him by Anura Bandaranaike another rising star in the vote of condolence passed in Parliament after his death. The concluding para of his statement was that "His memory will live not for years but for decades and with the passage of time when historians and his associates can distance themselves away from the events which are far too close to them and wipe away the cobwebs, even his most fervent opponent will admit that he bestrode the political stage of Sri Lanka more as a colossus than as a politician."

CHAPTER VII

F.D.B. and Public Administration

B. Mahadeva & H. S. Wanasinghe

Throughout his career in politics, Felix R. Dias Bandaranaike evinced a keen interest in the efficiency and effectiveness of the country's public administration system. Whatever his specific sectoral responsibility was, whether Agriculture, Co-operatives and Food, or Finance or Justice or Public Administration, Home Affairs and Local Government itself, he recognised that the efficiency of the delivery of public goods and services, the ensuring of justice and fair play for the citizen, the furtherance of economic development all depended on the quality of the administrative system.

Mr. Felix R. D. Bandaranaike's political career spanned a period of Sri Lankan history wherein the role of the State was dominant both in the economy and the society. In this context, the importance of the efficiency of the public administration system was self-evident to him and he sought to mount a multi-faceted attack on removing its deficiencies and on improving its performance.

He was of the view that, at every level, the public service should strive to attract the best human resources which were available in the country and that this should be done in as objective a manner as possible. He was equally concerned that the process of inducting recruits to the public service, particularly at the middle levels, should be less time-consuming. It was this objective which led him, in 1970, to replace the existing system of recruitment to clerical grades which was based on cumbersome and time-consuming examination procedures with a new system based on the allocation of points for the candidates' performance at their G.C.E. (O. Level and A. Level) examinations. In implementing the new system, he brought in the use of computers (at that time, very little known in Sri Lanka) for the management of the data bases. This not only speeded up the hitherto tardy process of recruitment but also introduced the critical elements of transparency and objectivity which enhanced the public credibility of the process. For as long as the system was maintained, it provided the public service with competent cadres who, to-date, are acknowledged as being far superior in quality to most who were recruited thereafter through politically biased methods.

If there was one thing that was anathema to Felix R. D. Bandaranaike, it was corruption in public life. During his periods of office as a Minister, he waged a relentless war against such corruption – a fact which became clearly evident during his term as the Minister in charge of the subjects of Agriculture, Food and of Co-operatives. During this period he devoted considerable time to personally leading raids and investigations into irregularities in major food stores, and pursued the resultant enquiries with vigour and drive. Many are the occasions which one vividly recalls of such raids and investigations in which one participated with him and the command of operational detail which he displayed therein.

Food Ministry officials who worked closely with him when he was Minister of Agriculture, Food and Co-operatives recall how scrupulously Felix avoided any interference with tender procedures in the Ministry. It was a period during which the import and distribution of all the country's major foodstuffs – rice, flour, sugar, dhal and many other commodities – were State monopolies. Food tenders were the largest business transactions handled by the Government. Not once did Felix ever attempt to influence the decisions of a Ministry Tender Board or even to seek information relating to the award of a tender. It is sad that, tender processes have since been highly politicised and that the number of serious allegations of irregularities in the award of tenders, has risen sharply in recent years.

Through his own example and efforts, Felix R. D. Bandaranaike succeeded in conveying a message to the senior management rungs of the departments and corporations under his Ministry of the critical importance of fighting corruption and the need, on their part, to exercise vigilance as well as to continuously review operational systems and processes in order to effectively combat corruption on a sustained basis. The lessons that he drew from the experiences of the sectoral ministries, particularly of the Ministry of Agriculture, Food and Co-operatives, he brought into his exercise of reform of the public service as a whole as Minister of Public Administration, Home Affairs and Local Government during the period 1970 to 1974.

Another area of public service improvement which received Felix R. D. Bandaranaike's attention was that of training of cadres at all levels. He provided his fullest support to the Academy of Administrative Studies (now the Sri Lanka Institute of Development Administration) in its efforts at providing systematised training to all grades of the public service both in Colombo as well as in the Provinces. He was keenly interested in the content of the different training programmes and never failed to closely question the relevance of the programmes to the rapidly changing demands of the environment of development management. These approaches, for the first time in Sri Lanka, contributed to a move away from the classical concept of public administration and to a recognition of its critical role in the management of the country's development.

It was during his period as the Minister in charge of public administration that a systemic plan of overseas training for the managerial grades of the public service was launched and external technical assistance was pro-actively sought for implementing the plan. Under this system it was possible to provide for advanced overseas training to be integrated into the career plans of individual managers in the public service. Within a few years it was possible to provide the senior rungs of the public service with a critical mass of relevantly trained cadres who could significantly contribute to the tasks of development management. It is indeed a pity that these efforts were not maintained in the subsequent years and that the system so carefully planned and introduced fell into disarray and that even those trained were not effectively deployed for tasks for which they were trained.

A further area of public administration which interested Felix R. D. Bandaranaike was that of the effective management of the Combined Services of the government which played a critical role in the administrative system in that, at every level of the administrative structure, they staffed the key positions. The absence of a logical system of posting and transfers, training, career advancement etc. had contributed not only to inefficiency but also to much discontentment.

Through the Directorate of Combined Services of the Department of Public Administration, steps were taken to systematise the transfers and postings in these Services. The postings were linked to the training undergone by the respective individuals, the training itself being linked to the aptitudes shown by them. For the first time in the history of the Services at the managerial level, detailed records were introduced for each member of the Service bringing together data on qualifications, work experience, special aptitudes displayed, special assignments undertaken as well as training undergone both in Sri Lanka and overseas. These records provided a useful management tool for effective use of the human resources within each Service.

This innovation also, unfortunately, was one that, over time, fell by the wayside. The result was that the maintenance of such personal records was progressively abandoned and career planning came to be a thing of the past. Training of managerial grades became *ad hoc* and unstructured. Postings within these grades took on a 'hit and miss' character more, in the nature of responses to individual and trade union pressures and to political preferences, rather than a matching of job demands and competence. The net outcome was a continuing downward trend in performance of public sector organisations with the inevitable negative impact on development management.

Two other aspects of the administrative system which attracted Felix R. D. Bandaranaike's attention were the continuous review of organisational relevance and the improvement of public administration systems and procedures. He was quick to recognise the degree to which the traditional organisation structures of departments and agencies had failed to keep in step with the changing demands on them by the emerging compulsions of the country's development process. He was shocked at the tardiness of the decision-making processes caused by cumbersome work systems and procedures and the tremendous inconvenience caused thereby to the citizens who needed to transact business with government departments and agencies. He recognised how this situation was a major contributor to the level of bribery and corruption which prevailed in the interface between the public and the bureaucracies.

Hence, he provided every encouragement to the Directorate-General of Public Administration to carry out systematic reviews of organisational structures and of work systems and procedures and to institute the changes and adjustments which were necessary to enhance the effectiveness of administrative responses to citizens' demands. With his customary vigour, he overrode the inevitable resistance of the vested interests and put his full weight and authority behind the reform effort. This helped, in no small measure, to implement and to stabilise the changes.

An important contribution which Felix R. D. Bandaranaike made towards improving the public administration system in Sri Lanka, was the preparation and publication of a detailed and comprehensive "Establishments Code" which set out in a single volume all the rules and regulations relating to the governance of the Public Service in Sri Lanka. Prior to the publication of this Code, the rules and regulations governing the Public Service were contained in a host of Financial Regulations and Treasury circulars, which were frequently amended on an *ad hoc* basis. These amendments were often made in ink on the printed Financial Regulations, or little printed correction slips were untidily pasted on the pages of the Financial Regulations. Most Government Departments did not even have complete sets of the Financial Regulations and Treasury Circulars and all the amendments made to them.

This made the administration of the Public Service extremely difficult. The publication of the Establishment Code removed these difficulties. The Code was printed and bound in loose-leaf form, so that if any Section of the Code needed change, the entire page on which it appeared could be easily removed and a fresh page substituted. Unfortunately, the Establishment Code was not regularly revised and updated by Bandaranaike's successors, so that its full benefits were not reaped by the Public Sector.

Felix R. D. Bandaranaike was the first to head a separate ministry exclusively concerned with public administration. The government which came into office in 1970 was the first to recognise the need to address public administration issues on their own merits rather than as a subordinate component of finance issues – which had been the case in the entire post-independence period. This, perhaps, was an outcome of a recognition of the critical role which public administration, in its own rights, played in strengthening development management.

The constitution of a separate ministry responsible for the inter-related subjects of Public Administration, Local Government and Home Affairs, which constituted the three constituents of governance, enabled Felix R. D. Bandaranaike to bring, for the first time in Sri Lanka, a co-ordinated approach to administrative reform, change and management. Much of his success in enhancing the effectiveness of public administration can be attributed to this co-ordinated approach which he brought to bear on the task. Through this he was able to appreciate the inter-linkages between the different facets of administrative reform – for example, between organisational restructuring and training, between training and systems modifications, between career development and effective personnel utilisation etc.

His instrument for this co-ordinated management was the Directorate-General of Public Administration which combined within itself responsibility for public personnel management, administrative systems and procedures, training and career development, superannuation and other related functions. The creation of this overarching institution made it possible, for the first time in the country's history, to adopt a holistic and independent approach to the task of administrative improvement.

Felix R. D. Bandaranaike's contribution to administrative development in Sri Lanka has to be understood in the context of the overt as well as covert resistance which ran counter to reform efforts of the time. He recognised the importance of administrative reform if the development management system was to deliver the services and goods which the public had been led to and had a right to expect. He also recognised, all too clearly, the consequences of the failure to live up to such public expectations, in terms of societal instability. He identified the eradication of corruption, the achieving of organisational effectiveness and of systemic relevance as well as the citizen-bureaucracy interface as major administrative reform goals to be achieved. He went about the task of achieving these goals with a remarkable single-mindedness, contemptuous of the obstacles placed in his path and using his remarkable capacity for cutting through the webs of irrelevancies which those vested interests in the status quo attempted to weave around his efforts.

One of his great achievements was the manner in which he galvanised and mobilised the co-operative support of the many public officials who were germane to achieving the goals which he had set. For the first time in the country's administrative history he created a cohesive 'reform team.' His leadership held the team together and inspired it towards concerted purposeful action.

One looks back on this period with a feeling of nostalgia and a sense of gratitude that one was able to be a participant of what, in essence, was Sri Lanka's first serious attempt at administrative reform and capacity improvement. It was Felix R. D. Bandaranaike's single-minded commitment and effective leadership which provided the reform exercise with its richness. It was, in a sense, unfortunate that his leadership was interrupted by the vicissitude of politics, first with his having to move on to other tasks and, then, with a change of government. Even with several later attempts at revival, the process remains in suspended animation waiting for someone with vision and leadership to reactivate it.

The best tribute that can be paid to Felix R. D. Bandaranaike is to reactivate the process which he launched with the same dedication and vision which he provided at the start.

foreign investment and quoted with approval Nobel Prize winner Gunnar Myrdal's recommendation of 1958:

> "Ceylon should in the long run attempt to avoid the creation of foreign enclaves in the field of industry. For this purpose it would be desirable for Ceylon to work out a new institutional framework which would guide the inflow of private foreign investment. From this point of view the "management contract" was advocated. Such a contract would represent an agreement between the Government of Ceylon and foreign firms. The foreign firms could undertake to set up the factory, bear the management risks of profit and loss and provide the necessary technicians. The Government of Ceylon, for its part, would permit the remittances of profit and capital and secure facilities for the training of Ceylonese personnel. After a specified period of say 15 to 20 years the enterprise would be taken over by the Ceylon Government or its nominees in the public or private sector on terms whose basis is clearly specified in advance. The Government should work out in some detail a model contract on these lines with assistance of experienced corporation lawyers."

However, the Government's term ended not long after this speech and the Government was defeated at the General Election in 1977. It was left to the UNP Government which followed to implement this idea by opening the doors to Foreign Investment.

There is no question but that he approved of Gunnar Myrdal's recommendation because of the experience he acquired in 1975 when he visited a number of OPEC countries in the Middle East – Iran, Iraq, Kuwait and Egypt – some of them more than once, as the Special Envoy of Prime Minister Sirimavo Bandaranaike. Projects in these countries were precisely as recommended for Ceylon in 1958, with the vital difference that these countries had the petro-dollars to pay for the projects, get the latest technology and when necessary send their nationals abroad for further studies.

Felix Dias Bandaranaike was the Minister of Finance from 1960-63. On his resignation on the rice issue as mentioned earlier T. B. Illangaratne took over as Minister of Finance in 1963 followed by Dr. N. M. Perera in 1964. In the United Front Government of 1970 Dr. N. M. Perera became Finance Minister and held the Portfolio till 1975 when he and his party left the Government, whilst Felix was abroad in June '75 attending a special session of the General Assembly. The Prime Minister Mrs Bandaranaike asked him to proceed to Washington to take his oaths as Finance Minister before Ambassador Neville Kanakaratne.

Felix Dias Bandaranaike realised that some of the budget proposals since 1970 had placed severe hardships on the middle classes (e.g. the rates of taxation ranged from 15% to 65%). He granted them relief by raising the exemption limit for liability to income tax from Rs. 6,000 to Rs. 9,000 per annum. He abolished the aggregation of the wife's employment income with that of her husband up to certain limits. He reduced the level of taxation from 65% to a maximum marginal rate of 50%. He also abolished compulsory savings and the ceiling on incomes which stood at Rs. 2,000 per month. In regard to the last measure he said that three years experience of that ceiling (1972-75) showed that it did not curtail luxury consumption; on the contrary it had the effect of damaging incentives and of encouraging people to live on their capital, leaving no domestic savings for investment.

It is a fact that the United Front Government represented a wide spectrum of political opinion ranging from the parties right of centre to the extreme left. The ceiling on the private ownership of land and houses, and on incomes, the expenditure tax and several other taxes e.g. Sri Tax on Motor Cars and even on essential food items, also on tobacco and liquor and on kerosene, diesel and petrol had the cumulative effects of discouraging investment both local and foreign, imposing hardships on all sections of society and of alienating the commerce and business circles from co-operating with the Government.

Indeed, these were designed to eliminate privileges and the disparities between the living standards of the middle and low income groups. It would appear that some of these measures e.g. ceiling on land, houses and incomes were a panic reaction to the youth insurrection of 1971. The fourfold increase in the price of imported oil in 1973 delivered a devastating blow to the economy. The international economic environment was unfavourable. The oil crisis of 1973 was followed by steep increases in the price of fertiliser and consequentially to reduction in the output of tea, rubber, coconut and locally-produced food and other agricultural products.

1973-75 were crisis years. Increases in the price of fuel had a chain reaction on the prices of fertiliser, grains and food products, which Sri Lanka had to import to maintain the existing level of the rations.

The Finance Minister Dr. N. M. Perera also had to provide for grants and loans to the Public Sector Corporations most of which were inefficiently run. From 1970/75 there was a rapid increase in the number of Corporations set up and the workforce increased from 22,997 in 1970 to 55,026 in 1975. What these figures show is that the United Front Government increased the workforce though most Corporations incurred financial losses which were met by grants and loans from the Consolidated Fund. From a political angle it was preferable to subsidise the Corporations than to reduce the workforce.

By 1977 the shortcomings of the policies of the United Front Government were seen to impose hardships on all sectors of the population not just the well-to-do and privileged minority. More significant, the economy was stagnant due to lack of local resources for development and an atmosphere of uncertainty as to the country's goals. The political complexion of the United Front Government was hardly one which would attract foreign investment or participation in economic development. Its policy was to depend on local resources, grants and project loans mainly from socialist countries.

Felix Dias Bandaranaike was aware that the administration in general and the State Corporations in particular needed a complete overhaul. In regard to the General Administrative Service, he took several measures to make it efficient having instituted several innovative steps in regard to recruitment, training of cadres, specialization in different areas and branches of administration whilst improving career prospects. These are examined and evaluated in the chapter entitled "FRDB and Public Administration." He probably had to leave the Corporations out of this Reform Scheme because Corporations came under different Cabinet Ministers who preferred to run these perhaps according to their particular wishes.

In 1977 when the Elections were held the country was ready to vote for a different set of policies and Felix Dias Bandaranaike was blamed quite unfairly for the SLFP defeat. In accordance with the principle of collective responsibility of the Cabinet he did not in his lifetime try to distinguish between his policies and those of the others who served as Finance Ministers in the SLFP Government of 1960-65 and the United Front Giovernment of 1970-77.

Economists and political analysts will continue to debate whether Felix Dias Bandaranaike and his colleagues could have adopted other policies more acceptable which would have averted their electoral debacle in 1977. The fact remains however that their commitment to socialism, different interpretation of socialism and its goals and means of achieving them rather led to situations where consensus in speech and action were absent. Such situations inevitably develop in coalition Governments. Felix Dias Bandaranaike was held responsible for the defeat simply because he happened to be Minister of Finance when the Elections were held. In politics it is normal to point to a scapegoat in defeat and a hero in victory!

Let it be said that when Felix Dias Bandaranaike was in sole charge of a Ministry, e.g. Justice, Home Affairs, Public Administration and Local Government, he was able to achieve what he set out to do. In the case of Finance, however, in both administrations 1960-65 and 1970-77, there were three other Finance Ministers as well and praise or blame had to be shared.

CHAPTER IX

F.D.B. – Planning Secretariat

P. H. Siriwardena

The formation of a new Government by the SLFP In 1960 gave F.D.B. the first opportunity to divert his energy and talents to the political field. His role in the new Government as the Minister of Finance and the Deputy Minister of Foreign Affairs was indeed a very important one to which he had to acclimatise himself in different ways.

My association with F.D.B. began in 1947 when I was lecturing to the University entrance students at Royal College in a subject newly introduced Economics and Government. He joined this group after switching completely from the science stream which he had pursued upto that time. Despite his late entry he was able within a few weeks to keep pace with the other students and within a few months became one of the best students of the class. His ability to grasp the new subject was clearly demonstrated in his tutorials and later entered the University on a scholarship.

After he became Minister of Finance he was assigned the subject of Planning and Development which was under the Prime Minister and in his capacity as Deputy Minister of Foreign Affairs he became the *'de facto'* Minister of Planning. In reorganising the Planning Secretariat which serviced the National Planning Council established by the former Prime Minister S. W. R. D. Bandaranaike one of the main objects was to make the Planning Organisation direct its activities, a practically oriented service unit, geared to carry out the new priorities in economic policy. To effect this transformation he appointed a Director to the National Planning Department which was responsible for formulating and implementing the overall economic program. The primary consideration he had in view was to evolve a clear-cut down-to-earth Economic Plan which would enable the government to fulfil the needs and requirements of the people in the shortest possible time. With this end in view the Department set out to formulate a program of Economic Development on the basis of the priorities that were decided upon. That marked the beginning of the short-term three national Budgets of 1961-1962.

F.D.B's association with the National Plan and the policies he formulated as Minister of Finance were very closely linked. F.D.B. was quick to grasp and understand the Finance and Economic policy so vital for the creation of a realistic and practical work program to suit the country's needs. For the purposes of discussing economic and financial policies he had a team of three advisors – the Secretary to the Ministry of Finance, the Governor of the Central Bank and the Director of National Planning.

Within a short time F.D.B. was quite conversant with the theories underlying economic and financial policy and participated in the conferences with great ease and understanding.

Very often he intervened appropriately and brought to bear a sense of humour which greatly enlivened the lengthy and sometimes abstract discussions. Soon he became very knowledgeable of the system and was able to give clear-cut and decisive instruction in matters relating to the formulation of the budget and the National Plan. The short-term Implementation Plan itself was tailored to providing the country with rapidly yielding results.

Another aspect of F.D.B. was his ability to participate fully in the work that was being done. The short-term Implementation Plan was a "Crash Program" and had to be completed within a short space of time to run concurrently with the budget. He involved himself fully with the work that was being done and as the work progressed particularly during the final stages he visited the Planning Office every night and kept on late looking into the various aspects of the National Plan. This enabled the Planning Department to work zealously and also provided much encouragement to the officers who were able to sort out with the Minister various problems which otherwise could have hindered the smooth progress of the work in hand. Soon he established a close rapport with the working team and this spurred the team to give of their best and deliver the Three-Year Implementation Program in time.

In his discussions of the budget he was associating himself very closely at all stages and was always ready to provide answers on issues that were politically sensitive. Wherever he disagreed he never insisted on his point of view until every aspect of the matter had been considered. On many instances he even welcomed the opposite view so long as reasonable arguments were adduced in its favour. He always encouraged participants at a discussion to put forward views that were even opposed to his own thinking, and a final decision was always taken in the way of a consensus and agreement by all. Wherever he imposed his own point of view and these – related to questions which were politically sensitive – he did so taking full responsibility for his decision.

CHAPTER X

The Imposition of Civic Disability

H. L. De Silva, PC

Among the numerous acts ot misgovernment alleged against the UNP administration that took office after the General Election of 1977 perhaps the most infamous of them all was the deprivation of the civic rights of the former Prime Minister, Mrs Sirimavo Bandaranaike and her Cabinet Minister Felix Dias Bandaranaike who held various important portfolios from time to time and wielded much power and influence in the two Administrations under her. Presumably, not content with having routed the SLFP at the General Election of 1977 when the UNP secured a five-sixths majority in Parliament, it was sought from the commencement to neutralise the influence of key political figures – these two in particular and thus prevent any challenge to the hegemony of the UNP for the next seven years. The supreme irony in this whole exercise was that the Government of the day violated every norm of democracy in its professed object of safeguarding democracy. In this act of political victimisation they involved both the Legislature and the Judiciary and compromised the integrity of both institutions in that process. In this brief note I have sought to explain the grave violations of legal rights and fair procedure that were committed by the Special Presidential Commission that recommended the imposition of civic disability after a finding of guilt on certain of charges made against them.

There were fifteen "allegations" made against him. They were deliberately not described as "charges" because not only would fuller particulars have had to be given, it would have been necessary to indicate whether any particular allegation amounted to "abuse of power", "misuse of power", "corruption", "political victimisation" or any "fraudulent act" and whether they were committed "in relation to any court or tribunal or any public body or in relation to the administration of any law or the administration of justice" and if so in relation to which of these institutions. Section 9 of Act No. 4 of 1978 empowered the Special Presidential Commission to recommend to the President that any person found guilty of these acts be made subject to civic disability. Despite a long argument on behalf of the Respondent addressed to the Commission that these particulars were necessary for a proper conduct of the defence, the Commission refused this request and the accused person did not know throughout the inquiry how these acts if established would be construed by the Commission.

The Commission after investigation of the facts must have surely satisfied itself that those selected by it for inquiry fell within the offences specified in section 9 referred to above. If so, why did it decline to inform the accused of the particular offence constituted by any act or omission? Yet this information was deliberately withheld till its judgement was published in the report finding him guilty of four out of the fifteen allegations made. Incidentally this extraordinary procedure reminds one of a story related by the comedian Groucho Marx of how he went down a village street and found to his amazement evidence on a wall showing that a man had scored a bull's eye each time he had fired a shot. So he remarked to a bystander pointing to the wall that the village must be very proud of this brilliant marksman. Oh that, the man drily replied, is the work of the village idiot. The silly man had first fired the shots and then drawn the bull's eye round them!

Out of the fifteen allegations made the Commission arrived at a finding of guilt only in respect of four. It described one as "corruption" and each of the other three as acts of "abuse of power." None of these terms were statutorily defined in the Special Presidential Commissions Act nor in the provision of the Constitution – Article 81 which empowered Parliament to pass the resolution imposing civic disability and expulsion from Parliament. Indeed strangely enough the Constitution itself made no mention of these specific offences but referred to the power given to the Special Presidential Commission by the said Act. What is even more surprising was that even in its Report the commission did not venture to define what constituted "corruption" or "abuse of power" for the purpose of their findings. Nor do the words in relation to section 9 explain with clarity what was the nature of the nexus that had to be established between the act or omission (which was designated abuse of power or corruption) and the institutions referred to in section 9.

Let us consider the very first allegation. Briefly it was that he enjoyed rights or benefits of a contract made by him for the supply of eggs to the Marketing Department and milk to the National Milk Board. The contracts in question had been in existence from about April, 1967 (when he was a Member of Parliament in opposition) through May, 1970 (when he became a member of the Government) and continued up to July '77 when the UNP came to power. The "specific question" says the Commission Report (pg. 7) is "whether it could be inferred from the evidence placed before (it) that there was a disqualifying contract" between Bandaranaike and the two public bodies aforementioned. At pg. 15 of the Report the Commission found that he held disqualifying contracts with two "public bodies," viz., the Milk Board and the Marketing Department during the period 28th May, 1970 to 23rd July, 1972 when he was an elected M.P. Nowhere in the Special Presidential Commission's Act or in the warrant issued to them, was the Commission empowered to find whether an M.P. had become disqualified as an M.P. or from sitting and voting in Parliament while enjoying the benefits of such a contract.

It is passing strange how a vigilant opposition failed for seven long years from 1970 to 1977 to raise the question in Parliament, or before the Courts, whether a Minister of the Government who was the *bête noire* of the opposition was disqualified from sitting in Parliament and therefore holding office on this ground, if indeed there existed such disqualifying circumstances under the Constitution. It served no purpose for the Commission to stop with such a finding. They had to hang this finding on one or other of the kind of acts specified in section 9. It was patently clear that being an M.P. while being subject to a disqualification could not on any reasonable view come within any of the specified acts. The ordinary meaning of the term corruption connotes receiving an illegal gratification oneself or giving an illegal gratification to another as defined in the Bribery Act. There was not a scintilla of evidence to even suggest such a situation.

The Commission had therefore to look for an interpretation with wider coverage. At this juncture the Commission embarked on what appears to be a tortuous process of reasoning, straining statutory language beyond permissible limits to bring the Respondent within its net. The line of argument was somewhat as follows: First, the Commission sought refuge in Webster's unabridged English dictionary in order to find an appropriate meaning for the word "corruption" and picked on as its meaning – "the act of vitiating integrity." From here they argued that the word "takes within its sweep every situation involving loss of integrity." They did not seek to define the Word "integrity" which ordinarily means the quality of being honest and upright in character and embraces every form of human conduct and is not confined to financial dealings.

The Commission then gleaned from the election cases cited in the Report that by holding such disqualifying contracts he "threw open the gates" for this type of wrongdoing – that is, providing opportunities (for others) to get illegitimate favours and on the other hand implied that he himself obtained favours in return for which he compromised his own freedom and independence as an M.P. The Commission has overlooked the fact that on the Constitutional doctrine of collective responsibility, as a Cabinet Minister, he could not have criticised his own Government in Parliament and could not have functioned as an independent M.P. By reason of this labyrinthine process of reasoning on the part of the Commission, a great injustice was done to Felix Dias Bandaranaike in finding, on these facts, that he was guilty of corruption. Indeed when one reads of the astronomical heights to which corruption has risen during the last decade, the allegation made against him appears to be a mere peccadillo for which the deprivation of civic rights – a punishment that was grossly disproportionate was itself an act of political victimisation by the UNP Government.

There were three allegations which the Commission held were an abuse of power. They were Allegation No. 5 which related to the appointment of G. B. Wikramanayake as a Secretary to the Ministry of Finance, while there was a Secretary in office, which enabled him to exercise control over the Gem Corporation while also being a gem-dealer. Allegation No. 8 which related to certain directions given to the Director of Public Prosecutions concerning the arrest and indictment of G. M. Premachandra, and organiser of the UNP. Allegation No. 10 related to a direction to the Police, contrary to normal practice, to investigate a complaint of an election offence committed by J. R. Jayewardene, the UNP candidate for the Colombo South election.

In respect of these allegations the Commission was not prepared to accept the personal explanations for his conduct which were given by Felix. Under the Constitution the exercise of executive power by a Minister is a matter in respect of which he is answerable and responsible to Parliament and the ultimate sanction is a vote of censure in Parliament. It is only if in consequence of such acts individual rights are violated that such acts are subject to judicial review through the various prerogative Writs. This was the first time when such acts and decisions were retrospectively made a ground for the deprivation of civic rights which as far as a political career is concerned is the equivalent of capital punishment!

When Felix along with Mrs Sirimavo Bandaranaike sought to challenge the findings and recommendations of the Commission through Writs of Certiorari, Parliament scuttled the proceedings before the Supreme Court by passing the resolution imposing civic disability on them both. Having done this the Attorney-General and Counsel for the Commission objected to the continuance of the hearing relying on the preclusive clause in Article 81 (3) of the Constitution which declared that the Speaker's Certificate that the resolution had been passed to be conclusive for all purposes and that it shall not be questioned in any Court. This objection was upheld and thus became the final act of political victimisation.

CHAPTER XI

A Special Presidential Commission of Inquiry Law

National Committee for Democratic Action in Sri Lanka

A Political Assessment of the Government's Aims and Objectives

Background

Sri Lanka has a distinguished record of having maintained democratic institutions the hard way. Despite the assassination of a Prime Minister, an attempt at a Coup d'etat by military and police personnel, and an armed insurgency, democratic traditions have flourished. Now it seems, however, that the nation stands at the crossroads. It may even be that the country is about to follow a different course.

The United National Party Government elected to power in 1977, by an unprecedented five-sixths majority, campaigned upon its firm and total commitment to democracy, paying lip-service to all the traditional catchwords, like the "rule of law," the "independence of the judiciary," and "constitutionality." But once elected, the Government's major preoccupation became the ensuring of its own continuance in office at any cost, and by means of devices and techniques, which to say the least of it, were blatantly political.

Judges of the highest Courts, presumably because they were "inconvenient", had their periods of office summarily terminated, in breach of the constitutional guarantees upon they were appointed. The independence of Members of Parliament, too, has been effectively eroded, by constitutional provisions that a Member who is sacked from his Party loses his seat. The Party that so sacks a Member, has the right to nominate a successor, without submitting to the test of public opinion at a by-election; Crossovers by Members of Parliament have been so regulated, as to ensure "One-way Traffic" only – from the Opposition to the Government, and not *vice versa;*

Decisions of the Constitutional Court, pronouncing against the constitutionality of draft Bills submitted to Parliament, have been brushed aside. Such Bills have often been enacted with a two-thirds majority, without Members of Parliament even being given the time or opportunity, to study what the Constitutional Court has said in its judgements. Legitimate trade union action has been severely curtailed. Laws of the former Government which had been denounced "draconian" at the hustings, have found their way back in other forms into the Statute Book. Parliament has even assumed judicial powers, to sit in judgment upon and to inflict punishments for breaches of Parliamentary privilege. One need hardly emphasize that the existence of such a legal provision, must inevitably and effectively inhibit, the freedom of speech and expression against the Government.

More ominous than all of this, are the attempts being made to destroy political opposition, particularly by the elimination of political opponents. In the past, no Government sought to sit in judgment upon the actions or decisions of its predecessors by means of *ex post facto* legislation, that could have the effect of liquidating political foes. But it would seem that this is exactly the exercise upon which the present Government is engaged.

Two Commissions of Inquiry were appointed under the Commissions of Inquiry Act, upon alleged acts of maladminstration and misconduct in the area of Local Government. As was the case with the Shah Commission in India, no sanctions or consequences attached to the findings of Commissions appointed under the Commissions of Inquiry Act. The Government of Sri Lanka, unlike the then Government of India, was not inclined to use the findings of fact in the Commission Reports, to institute criminal or civil proceedings under the ordinary law of the land, against the persons named. Such a procedure would have been unexceptionable, and it was probably not followed, only because no criminal or civil liabilities were established. Instead, the Government proceeded to impose "civic disabilities" by legislation upon persons against whom certain findings had been made in the Commission Reports. And this was done, notwithstanding that some of these persons had not even been heard by the Commissions in their own defence; and also notwithstanding that the Constitutional Court had declared the draft legislation imposing "civic disabilities" to be unconstitutional.

Notices issued by the Supreme Court for the issue of Writs of Certiorari against the Commissions, did not deter the Government or Parliament from its determination to impose "civic disabilities." The legal battle over these Writs is still in progress. The Court of Appeal has given the Opposition a first round victory, but the Commissioners have taken the matter to the Supreme Court in appeal.

The Special Presidential Commissions of Inquiry Law

It is probable that after this experience with the two Commissions of Inquiry on Local Government, the Government realized that the Commissions of Inquiry Act was an unsatisfactory tool, from their point of view, for the destruction of their political enemies. They began to look around therefore, for a better alternative, and one which would be so designed as to have "teeth." Such an alternative was found in the "Special Presidential Commissions of Inquiry Law." Apart from section 9, this Law consists of the combination of the Commissions of Inquiry Act and the Criminal Justice Commissions Act of the former Government, which after being denounced as "draconian," had been repealed by the Government.

Section 9, which provides the "teeth," says that when a Special Presidential Commission of Inquiry finds that "public officer" (who for the first time has been defined to include Ministers and Judges) has committed (a) an abuse or misuse of power, (b) fraud, (c) corruption, or (d) political victimization, in relation to the administration of any law, of the Courts, of Justice, or of any Department or Institution of the Government; the Special Presidential Commission of Inquiry is required to make a recommendation as to whether or not such "public officer" should or should not be subjected to the imposition of civic disabilities, for a period that could extend to seven years. After the Commission Report to the President is gazetted, Parliament has to decide whether or not to impose "civic disabilities" as recommended, by a resolution that has to be passed by a two-thirds majority; as was done in the case of the former Secretary to the Ministry of Justice, Nihal Jayawickrema. Such civic disabilities include not merely disabilities of voting at Parliamentary elections or contesting Parliamentary seats; but also disabilities of holding office as a Judge, a Public Servant, or Corporation Official.

The purpose of this Law, is therefore, obviously not intended to deal with alleged wrongdoing by Members of the former Government. If that was the objective, there would have been no need for any Special Presidential Commissions of Inquiry. Without any difficulty whatsoever, the principles, procedures and punishments available under the ordinary law, could have been invoked. The true purpose of the Government is essentially different. It is to punish Members and Officials of the former Government, whose conduct did not and does not amount to the transgression of any law, upon a recommendation which itself is based upon pronouncement that conduct is *ex post facto* declared to fall within one or other of the four undefined categories of liability under section 9 of the Law.

An illustration will help to make this clear. In the Second Interim Report of the Special Presidential Commission of Inquiry, Nihal Jayawickrema has been found guilty of an abuse of power, for sitting in Court upon a ceremonial occasion at the "Inner Bar," in defiance of the former Chief Justice, Victor Tennekoon. And this is one of the findings upon which the Commission had recommended the imposition of civic disabilities. Tennekoon, who was called as witness to testify against Jayawickrema, stated categorically, that while he deplored Jayawickrema's conduct, he certainly did not think that it amounted to an abuse of power. Tennekoon is obviously quite right on this point, for Jayawickrema's conduct is manifestly not in relation to the administration of any law, of the Courts, of Justice, or of any Department or Institution of Government, by him as Secretary to the Ministry of Justice.

Ex Post Facto Nature of the Law

When the Special Presidential Commissions of Inquiry Law was introduced and debated in Parliament, it is uncertain whether the full implications of the law, were clearly understood by the public, or even perhaps, by all Members of Parliament. Some may have thought that what was intended was a normal type of judicial inquiry, because of the emphasis placed upon the fact that the Commissioners were to be serving Judges, not below the rank of District Judge. It may even have been assumed (quite wrongly,) that the Commissions would be examining the conduct of persons within a known and recognised frame of law – as was done for instance in the Bribery Commissions, e.g. the Thalgodapitiya Commission.

At all events, the Sri Lanka Freedom Party Members of Parliament voted in favour of the law. But within a very short time, particularly when it became apparent, from the procedures that were being followed, that there was a grave danger that the Law had not been designed to ensure fair trial procedures in accordance with known recognised judicial norms, Mrs Sirimavo Bandaranaike, M.P. for Attanagalla, and Leader of the Sri Lanka Freedom Party, moved for a Writ of Prohibition before the Court of Appeal, against the Special Presidential Commission of Inquiry. The Attorney-General himself appeared for the Commission, but after a full argument, the Court of Appeal allowed the Writ.

The principal ground of the decision in Mrs Bandaranaike's favour was that the legislation should not be interpreted to be *ex post facto,* as the language of the statute did not reflect such an intention. The Government, however, reacted swiftly, by amending the legislation so as to make it quite clear beyond any doubt that that was what Parliament had intended namely *ex post facto* legislation. In other words, the objective of the Government was to eliminate their political opponents, by having their conduct pronounced to be reprehensible and worthy of punishment after the event, although at the time it was not merely lawful conduct, but political conduct for which no politician could have been answerable to any authority other than Parliament or the People.

The Shah Commission and the Indian Experience Compared

In India, the political stance of the Janatha Government of Shri Morarji Desai though committed strongly to the cause of capitalism and of big business interests, was not really in the nature of a last-ditch fight against Mrs Gandhi's socialism. It was rather in the nature of a struggle against Mrs Gandhi's alleged authoritarian rule and inroads made into democratic liberties during the Emergency. Indeed, the Janatha Party was no more than loosely knit coalition, whose only motivation was a common opposition to Mrs Gandhi, and a common fear of her re-emergence as a political force, as happened in fact, at the 1980 General Elections.

In Sri Lanka on the other hand, the United National Party was ideologically a capitalist party, committed to a free economy, to private enterprise and the elimination of all forms of controls and subsidies. Their determination to prevent the re-emergence of Mrs Bandaranaike and of the Sri Lanka Freedom Party goes far beyond the matter of personal apprehensions – it is based upon a real class interest. For, Mrs Bandaranaike and her Party are still very much the alternative Government in the minds of the people. And this is true, particularly in the inflationary situation forced upon the country to suit the dictates of the International Monetary Fund.

The Shah Commission in India, appointed under the Indian equivalent of the Commissions of Inquiry Act, was not intended to be a direct means to end Mrs Gandhi's political career. It was more in the nature of a propaganda exercise, to harass her, the material upon which she and her son Sanjay could be prosecuted upon criminal charge after criminal charge – regardless of what the ultimate outcome of those charges might be.

The Sri Lanka experience, though it has striking parallels to its Indian counterpart, shows that the Government strategy in Sri Lanka has been different. It is directed towards ensuring the continuance in office of the United National Party Government at any cost, and for that reason, demands the elimination of Mrs Bandaranaike and her Party from the political scene. The principal elements or strands of that strategy can be identified and summarized in this way:-

1. To divide the leftist parties from the Sri Lanka Freedom Party, particularly by playing upon the vanities of individual leftist leaders.

2. To keep the Sri Lanka Freedom Party divided against itself, by spreading false propaganda and particularly that there are internal struggles

for leadership within the Party; and to isolate from the Party those personalities who are hated and feared both by the Right as well as by the Left, and to cast as far as possible, on these personalities, responsibility for the 1977 election defeat.

3. To keep the leading persons in the Sri Lanka Freedom Party in a state of fear and uncertainty as to what the future may hold, with the Special Presidential Commissions of Inquiry Law, constituting an ever-present spectre. The eventual aim of this strategy would be to pressure individual members of the Party to defect to the United National Party; if not to force the Party leadership to compromise its political position in one way or another – perhaps even to the point of being pressured to join in a "National Government" under J. R. Jayewardene.

Commission Procedures

The Special Presidential Commissions of Inquiry Law leaves the Commissions very much in control of their own procedure. The guiding principle is that "natural justice" and its observance, are the essential safeguards. The Commission now functioning, however, has adopted procedures which differ from the procedures followed in the past by Commissions of Inquiry under the Commissions of Inquiry Act, and it is worth noting what the differences are:

1. The Commission has delegated its function of selecting the "allegations" for inquiry, as well as the selection of the evidentiary material in support of the allegations to a Special Prosecutor appointed by the State. The Commissioners have explained that they did so, in order to be free from prejudice. But, is that what Parliament intended? Surely, Parliament could not have intended that a Special Prosecutor who is the nominee of the President and his Government, should present selected material to a Commission appointed by the President, for that Commission to report upon that material to that self-same President? The position becomes even more incongruous, when the "allegations" relate to J. R. Jayewardene who has expressed his views strongly upon these self-same matters while in Parliament. To put it at its very lowest, His Excellency the President should realize that this could be construed to be a violation of a basic principle of natural justice, that justice should not only be done, but must be seen to be done. Another unfortunate consequence of this same procedure whereby the Commission has delegated the formulation of "allegations" to the Special Prosecutor, in the first instance, is that evidence has been placed before the Commission upon matters upon which the Commissioners, (or some of them) had personal knowledge or personal views. On these matters the Commission eventually declined to come to any findings. But does that suffice to

eliminate the danger of prejudice? For, however hard a tribunal may try to erase elements of prejudice from their minds consciously and deliberately, there is always the danger that an element of prejudice would unwittingly or inadvertently creep into the minds of the tribunal.

2. Unlike in the procedures followed by previous Commissions of Inquiry, when after a preliminary examination of the available material, all the persons thought to be "concerned" or "implicated" are noticed at one and the same time to appear together with their lawyers, for one enquiry; the present Commission has instead proceeded with its inquiries against each of the persons thought to be concerned or implicated, separately. This inevitably leads to the Commission arriving at findings affecting persons who are not before the Commission, as yet, though they may eventually come before the Commission – at a time when they have not afforded an opportunity of being heard. The former Minister of Justice, and a former Judge of the Supreme Court have already through respective lawyers, protested to the Commission, about some of the findings affecting them in the Report on the Nihal Jayawickrema Inquiry, upon matters on which they had not been heard.

3. In the past, the preliminary investigations by Commissions of Inquiry were conducted by the Commissioners in their chambers, "behind the scenes," so as to avoid prejudice to those who might eventually be noticed. The present Commission, however permitted the "Special Prosecutor" to make an Opening Address, which far from being a statement of the matters that the Prosecutor expected to be able to prove by evidence of witnesses, proved to be no more than a political speech of the views and opinions held by the Government of the conduct of its political foes, who were intended to be brought up eventually before the Commission. To make matters worse, the Commission permitted edited excerpts of the Special Prosecutor's Address to be broadcast over the State Radio, several times each day. The prejudicial effect of this procedure upon the persons to be noticed would be incalculable.

4. Witnesses were examined *ex parte*, very often upon impressions, without being shown the contemporaneous documents. Former Chief Justice, Victor Tennekoon was constrained to say that certain items of his evidence were wrong, for just that reason.

5. Though many prejudicial matters were raised in the Special Prosecutor's Address and in the evidence of witnesses, against personalities of the former Government, the present Commission has not given the persons concerned, even after they are noticed, an opportunity to reply to all of this. Instead, they have been confined to those matters upon which the Commission has presented "allegations."

6. According to the procedure followed by the present Commission, not only has the Commission made no attempt to define the concepts in section

9, it has also made no attempt to give the parties noticed, information as to which of the concepts in section 9, any particular allegation relates.

All these points of procedure mark a departure from past practice, which prejudice those "on trial" before the Commission, and which have the effect of denying natural justice to them.

The Arena of Controversy

If the objective of the Government was to establish by means of a judicial Commission of Inquiry, whether or not its political foes have transgressed, it is surely a matter of fundamental importance that the Government must scrupulously avoid descending into the arena of controversy. But that is exactly what the Government has done, and is continuing to do.

Soon after the Commission had commenced its public sittings in August 1978, J. R. Jayewardene invited the people at a political rally at the Sugathadasa Stadium; to listen over the radio to A. C. de Zoysa's Opening Address, in order to learn about the misdeeds of the former Government.

At the time of Nihal Jayawickrema's civic disabilities being considered, the Hon. Prime Minister is reported to have declared that it was the whales and "big fish" they were after – the ones who formulated policy – and not "small fry" like Jayawickrema. J. R. Jayewardene went further when he addressed the Railwaymen's Union. He declared that Jayawickrema deserved to lose his civic rights for having ordered the arrest of Athulathmudali – in fact, he should, according to Jayewardene, consider himself fortunate for not being sent to jail.

Is it not straining the bounds of credulity to expect a Commission appointed by the President to be deaf to, or unaware of the expression of such views by the President or the Prime Minister? Is it realistic to imagine that a Commission could avoid being influenced even subconsciously, by the views of the President, particularly when he identifies himself with his Special Prosecutor's Opening Address? Especially, when it is to that self-same President that the Commission has to report its findings.

The Salmon Commission

Justice Salmon was appointed in England some years ago to head a Commission of Inquiry to examine the working of the English equivalent of the Commissions of Inquiry Act. The principles that he laid down were not only embodied in the Royal Commission Report; he also cited them in the Cohen lecture at the Hebrew University in Israel, as follows:-

"That the tribunal should be nominated by the head of the judiciary, so as to avoid any appearance of political bias; because the enquiries ordered 'most often have highly charged political overtones.'"

"Secondly, that the investigation work, that is carrying out inquiries, interviewing potential witnesses, should be undertaken by officials, free from party political influence."

"Thirdly, that the Tribunal should be represented by independent counsel, with no close association with any political party."

That everyone of these principles has been ignored or observed in the breach by the Government of Sri Lanka is more than apparent. And the only answer that has been given by the Government, is to make a weak pun, by calling every reference to "Salmon" as no more than a "Red Herring!"

Conclusion

The President once declared that the Special Presidential Commissions of Inquiry Law was intended to cleanse public life, including those in his own Party, where necessary. The President has already found it necessary to ask one of his own Members of Parliament to resign his seat. No action, however, has been taken publicly to explain even to his own voters, for what fault he was asked to resign. The President has also stated recently that 90% of the complaints received against those in his Party and Government, are false complaints.

With the passing of time, it seems that glosses have already had to be overwritten on the lofty principles of "Justice and righteousness" which were to be the foundation of the President's vision of the new society. Double standards seem to be the order of the day. A great deal of time and effort is spent by Presidential Commissions of Inquiry to examine with meticulous care and attention, the smallest matters concerning the former Government. If it were to result in personalities of the former Government being recommended for the imposition of civic disabilities, the Government may feel that they have got what they want. It is not the purpose of this study to examine the cases of any individuals. But the course that the Government is now following is fraught with dangers, even if the Government takes comfort from the thought that a future Government may not be able to command a two-thirds majority under proportional representation to deprive their political foes of civic rights! But, while every Government can treat every political action of its predecessor as an "abuse of power," it will surely erode the very foundation of our democratic system.

CHAPTER XII

Felix

J. P. Obeyesekere

It is an acknowledged fact that Felix Dias Bandaranaike is a hitherto unmatched colossus in the political field of Sri Lanka. When his biography comes to be written it is imperative that his activities in this capacity be traced accurately from the very inception.

To know how and why he came to deviate from his chosen profession as a lawyer it is necessary to understand the circumstances that led to his sacrificing a chosen career at the Bar for a far less predictable profession as a politician.

For this purpose the only single person who can recount in detail as to how this came about is myself (J. P. Obeyesekere), and on what I have to say hinges the beginning of his onward political march.

It all happened after the demise of Prime Minister S. W. R. D. Bandaranaike, and Mrs Bandaranaike was in deep mourning. Very soon afterwards when a General Election was announced for 1960 it was found that a delimitation of electorates had taken place. What was until then the Attanagalla electorate was divided into two, for the first time, namely, Attanagalla and Dompe. Understandably Mrs Bandaranaike did not wish to enter the political field at this juncture, and so it was that she requested me to contest the Attanagalla seat, to which I agreed. The question then arose as to a suitable candidate for Dompe. She was inundated with a flood of requests from Mr Bandaranaike's staunch supporters of that area, the large majority of whom did not match up to the required standards as far as voter-acceptance was concerned. It was a precarious situation which lasted for quite sometime, until suddenly one night a thought came to me that there was a young man (Felix Dias Bandaranaike) who might be the answer to our problem. I suggested it to Mrs Bandaranaike who was quite taken up with the idea and requested me to sound him on such a proposal.

Without delay I paid Felix a visit and told him of the situation and how we were very keen that he should come forward to represent Dompe. He was quite taken aback at the suggestion, whereupon he and I had quite a discussion during which he admitted that he was on the bottom rung of a ladder, as a lawyer. He was Colombo born and bred, knew not anything about speaking to gatherings in Sinhala, or for that matter mixing with rural folk generally, and why was I suggesting that he should give up the Bar in order to step out into the unknown. He in turn asked me as to why I was continuing in politics. It was then that I told him I personally felt that people like ourselves owe it to the country to come forward and serve the people to the best of our ability, and as I was already in politics in a mild way as a Village Committee member I found it to be a very rewarding service to the nation It was a sacrifice I was prepared to make. This I believe struck a chord in his mind. We parted, with Felix wanting me to contact him in a few days time when he would think over the proposal together with his wife Lakshmi. The few days went past and I called over again for *a final word*. It did not take long for Felix to say *"Yes James, I am willing to make the sacrifice."* His very words to me.

And so it was that I took Felix along to meet Mrs Bandaranaike. There was a Christmas Party to be held for St. Mary's Church, Veyangoda, at the Malwatte residence of Mr & Mrs Vernon Perera and both of us drove to Horagolla via the Christmas Party. That was to be the beginning of an historic and meteoric political exercise which, alas, ended as a "sacrifice" for which he was prepared, when he decided to take the plunge *that first day, long ago.*

Justice P. Ramanathan

Mr Felix Dias Bandaranaike was one of the distinguished and able Ministers of Justice of Sri Lanka. The law reforms introduced by him in the areas of Civil and Criminal procedure had far-reaching effects of a very salutary nature on our legal system. They were designed to ensure an effective, proper and speedy justice system. He also introduced significant changes in the structure of our courts. The High Courts which were established during his tenure of office remain up to date.

The unification of the legal profession brought about by the abolition of the distinction between Advocates and Proctors was another notable achievement of Mr Felix Dias Bandaranaike. It was a change which had significant beneficial effects on the less affluent litigants who appear before our courts. Successive governments have accepted, and adhered to, many of the reforms introduced by him.

Stanley de Alwis

Felix Reginald Dias Bandaranaike is a name that will go down into the history of our country through the dim mists of time as a name you could conjure with. The man behind the name was a six-footer with matchless personality and a giant brain. Listening to him at an election meeting or in Parliament there was that inescapable feeling that none could compare with his brilliance. In the courtroom one could only listen spellbound to the magic of his oratory and the clear, lucid trend of thought which expressed his arguments.

Behind this imposing facade was a man who was child-like and lovable. A man who cherished the simple things in life and blessed the Almighty God, his Creator, for what he was. One day at my home the smells of cooking came from the kitchen and Felix walked into the kitchen. My wife explained to him that she was making a few parcels of food to be distributed among beggars. She was doing this in memory of her mother whose death anniversary it was. Felix appreciating the smells of the cooking paused for a while and said, "I wish I was a beggar."

When Felix was a Minister he used to come to my place cycling and the two of us would go for long rides. Soon it became apparent to me that we were drawing curious crowds and I told Felix that if anyone wanted to bump him off he had only to drive into the two of us who were riding abreast. It was only then that he realized the risk and we put an end to cycling. Once at Wilpattu we drove to where a herd of elephants was bathing. There were about 20 to 30 in the pool but I noticed a huge beast covered partially by the trees keeping watch. Soon as we passed he came and gave chase. All those in the jeep were very alarmed and shouted out to me, the driver, told me that the elephant was gaining on us but Felix remained clam and unruffled. I was watching the elephant's performance and after a minute or two drove away.

Felix had many friends among ordinary people, and in the evenings he would pick me up and visit one or another of them. There was a Buddhist

Priest he visited, and once, the priest had given Felix some medicine when he was ill and this had put him to right. When Felix good-humouredly ragged the priest about his cures, that worthy pointed out to a drawing-room suite in the hall and said it was Felix who had gifted it to him. The priest was fast losing his eyesight as a result of cataracts in both eyes. Felix pleaded with him to enter Macarthy Nursing Home and stand a Cataract operation under a prominent Surgeon. Felix promised that all expenses would be borne by him in full.

When he was dying of Cancer he did not complain but carried on cheerfully. The daughter of a Supreme Court Judge of India had come with a friend to see Felix who was ill. She was surprised to see him so full of life and never a complaint did he make of his illness but kept her enthralled with anecdotes of his visits to India specially to Indira Gandhi. When she left she turned to me and said, "What a man."

There are may incidents in Felix's life especially during the period when he was ill which disclosed his indomitable courage. My close association with him during the heyday and during the time of his defeat and illness compels me to say of him, "He was a man."

Cyril Gardiner

A Classical wag once remarked that Felix has been described in the writings of the Roman Poet Lucretius. *'Felix qui potuit, rerum cognoscere causas.'* Liberally translated Happy is the man (Felix) who had the ability to discern – quintessentially.

Once I had to meet him to discuss a rather 'common or garden' problem of the ban on the import of cars. I remember how quick he was to appreciate the impending loss not to the entrepreneur but to the large band of employees whose benefits would be diluted by such a ban. His initial stern aspect melted away very quickly and he beamed out suggestions to temper the ill-winds.

On another occasion he had heard that I was invited by the DFCC Chairman and some other DFCC Directors to join the Board of the Development Finance Corporation of Ceylon (DFCC). He generously agreed, without any contact with me whatsoever, that the shareholders should decide. Fortunately I obtained unanimous support of the shareholders. I served on the DFCC Board for a period of eight years which is the maximum period allowed by the DFCC Act.

After Felix passed away his wife Lakshmi asked me to help her fulfil one of Felix's dying wishes. A CT Scanner was a crying need in Sri Lanka. Felix wanted to assist the poor who could not afford to go abroad like the rich. I was honoured when she asked me to be one of the Trustees.

I must also recall another facet of this man of credit and renown – one orientated in opposition to the oft remembered rapier thrust of winged words of an intellectual touche. And that is his tenderness in the company of children. I have seen him at their birthday parties – he laughs, he sings, he dances. A ministering archangel, he.

Yes, elements tough and elements tender were so well mixed in him that the world could stand and acclaim –

That was a gentle MAN

CHAPTER XIII

Queen's Speech & Reply by FDB

Speech by Her Majesty the Queen at the opening of the 19th Commonwealth Parliamentary Conference

As Head of the Commonwealth it gives me much pleasure to welcome all gathered here today, in Westminster Hall, to take part in the 19th Commonwealth Parliamentary Conference. I hope all of you who have come from overseas will enjoy your visit to this country and that your discussions will be valuable and interesting.

The Commonwealth Parliamentary Association is one of the many organizations which give the Commonwealth its abiding strength and vitality. Your particular part, which is of great value, is to promote contacts between Parliamentarians from all parts of the Commonwealth. In your conferences, and in your many other activities, you make it possible for information and experience to be shared, and by so doing, increase understanding of the problems which face us all.

It is perhaps in this way that the Commonwealth functions most effectively. As a free association of peoples coming from "the six continents and the five oceans," transcending all barriers of race, religion, and culture, the Commonwealth is, of course, of great significance simply because it exists. It is all the more remarkable as its members remain in it because they are drawn together by common interests and not because of any sense of compulsion or obligation.

One of the main sources of strength of the Commonwealth is the informality and freedom from restriction with which it conducts its business.

But just because there are no "rules and regulations" we sometimes think of it as a nebulous idea. There is a danger that we may forget the practical contacts, the bridges of communication, the exchange of ideas, the help and friendship that are being promoted day by day in innumerable ways by organizations such as yours. It is in these that the Commonwealth has a special value.

This process is going on at all levels. It was only a few weeks ago that I returned from Ottawa where the Commonwealth Heads of Government met

value of Commonwealth connections. Parliamentary traditions have taken firm root in Sri Lanka and this is proved by the fact that governments have changed five times by peaceful elections in twenty years. Faced with the challenges of coups d'etat, conspiracies and insurrections, the people of Sri Lanka have never wavered in their commitment to the due processes of law within the framework of a Parliamentary Democracy.

We look forward to welcoming the Delegates of all Commonwealth Parliaments to our country next year. And the Conference programme which we have in hand will enable them to see something of our ancient civilization, our beautiful scenery, while also seeing at first hand our attempts to cope with some of the economic problems besetting developing countries like ours at this time.

I should like to express to you Honourable Prime Minister of the United Kingdom and to other Commonwealth Prime Ministers and Heads of Government who met in Ottawa recently, the thanks of the CPA for including in the text of the communique of that Conference a kind reference to the value in usefulness of the work of the CPA upon a proposal made by my Prime Minister, Mrs Bandaranaike. I should also like to thank you Sir Alec, as our President, and the Members of the U.K. Branch for the kind hospitality extended to all Delegates to this Conference. The programme that has been arranged for Delegates as well as their wives has been most thoughtful and I am sure will be most enjoyable.

Finally, knowing of Your Majesty's deep and abiding interest in the Commonwealth as shown by the many visits you have made at different times to almost all Commonwealth countries, including my own, on behalf of the Parliamentarians gathered here may I again express to you and Your Royal Highness our warmest thanks for your presence here and our sincere acknowledgement of your role as the Head of the Commonwealth.

Reception

A fanfare by the State Trumpeters heralded the entry of Her Majesty and His Royal Highness into Westminster Hall where they were received by the Lord Chancellor, Rt. Hon. Lord Hailsham of St. Marylebone, the Speaker of the House of Commons, Rt. Hon. Selwyn Lloyd, the Prime Minister, Rt. Hon. Edward Heath, MBE, MP, the President of the Commonwealth Parliamentary Association, Rt. Hon. Sir Alec Douglas-Home, the Vice-President of the Association, Mr. F. R. D. Bandaranaike, and the Deputy Chairman of the United Kingdom Branch of the Association, Sir Bernard Braine

Her Majesty and His Royal Highness were conducted to their places on the lower platform, and the assembled company was seated. The President of the Association then invited Her Majesty to declare the Conference open.

Following the speeches of the President, Her Majesty, the Prime Minister and the Vice-President, a fanfare of trumpets was sounded and the National Anthem played. The Queen and the Duke of Edinburgh then proceeded down the central aisle of the Hall to the North Door, escorted by the Lord Great Chamberlain and the Minister for Housing and Construction, and accompanied by the Prime Minister, the President of the Association, the Lord Chancellor, the Speaker of the House of Commons, the Vice-President of the Association and the Deputy Chairman of the United Kingdom Branch. A fanfare of trumpets was sounded as Her Majesty left the Hall.

The Opening Ceremony was followed by a Reception, given by the General Council of the Association, at the Whitehall Banqueting House, at which Her Majesty and His Royal Highness graciously consented to be present. Following the introduction of Members of the General Council, Her Majesty, escorted by the Prime Minister and the Secretary-General, and his Royal Highness, escorted by the Foreign and Commonwealth Secretary and the Deputy Secretary-General, Mr. Ian Grey, then circulated among the other guests.

CHAPTER XIV

Selected Speeches by FDB

GENERAL ASSEMBLY – SIXTEENTH SESSION PLENARY MEETINGS, 1961

Mr BANDARANAIKE (Ceylon): First and foremost, I should like to extend to Mr. Slim the cordial congratulations of the Government and people of Ceylon upon his unanimous election to the office of President of the General Assembly at its sixteenth session.

There is no single country in the world today that looks forward to the prospect of war without dismay. A worldwide referendum is not needed to establish that the millions of people in all countries do not want war.

We meet at a time of crisis, when there is a great danger of the whole world being laid waste by the ravages of nuclear war, and the whole future of the United Nations is at stake. The ultimate nature of the weapons available to the great Powers of the world is a compelling reason for the General Asembly at its sixteenth session to find practical ways and means to give effect to the ideals and objectives which prompted the formation of the United Nations at San Francisco. It is imperative to put an end to cold war concepts and to the arms race now in progress if mankind is to survive.

Year by year these same questions have arisen before the United Nations General Assembly, but our collective thinking has not resulted in the production of any conclusive answer. From time to time the United Nations has made a useful contribution towards the reduction of tensions and has thereby avoided the danger of an immediate outbreak of hostilities. The stage has been reached, I think, today where we all agree that this is not enough. Countries all over the world are convinced that they cannot live with the cold war any longer. The time has come when it is worth taking a calculated risk to find permanent and general solutions as the only alternative to the appalling risks which are built-in features of the world in which we live.

The United Nations was founded with a sense of determination and purpose. The ideals for which the United Nations stand are enshrined in the Charter and must continue to inspire our thinking on all international problems. The spirit of idealism in the Charter has not, however, always found expression in the realities of the current international situation. We must recognize, in particular, that national policies of the great Powers are not controlled and directed by principles of idealism alone. It is in the nature of international politics that national policies must take account of national interests, and sometimes there is a clash of competitive and conflicting interests. It would be unreal for us to believe that such conflicts of interests can be resolved by an appeal to principles alone. It would be equally unreal, I submit, and indeed positively dangerous to permit these conflicts to remain unresolved.

We believe that there is a very genuine desire on the part of the peoples of the United States of America and of the Soviet Union to maintain world peace. We are convinced that neither of these great countries wants war, in spite of the number of cold-war speeches that we have heard in the Assembly during this session. But that does not mean, of course, that either of the great Powers would contemplate for a moment the possibility of negotiating settlements from a position of weakness or at any price. Of course not.

The will for peace, though genuine, would not prevent either of the two great Powers from resorting to the use of force in defence of what they cherish and seek to preserve as vital for the well-being of their citizens. In the realities of the situation, the fact remains that the actions of one great Power, even if prompted by motives of defence and self-preservation, are open to interpretation by the other that there is an intention to have an aggression made upon it.

Each of the great Powers today follows its own way of life and the political ideology to which it is committed, and with good reason. For the people of the United States of America, a society conditioned by private enterprise has spelt prosperity and progress and a high standard of living. For the people of the Soviet Union, likewise, a society conditioned by the public ownership of productive enterprise has meant a very high rate of growth and industrial expansion. The essential premise on which the cold war has been built is that these two ideologies of the great Powers must seek extra-territorial victories and that each requires an armoury of inter-continental missiles aimed permanently at the other to preserve its own security.

As a non-aligned country, we just cannot accept that premise. Both in the United Nations and elsewhere the concept of peaceful co-existence has developed as a means to weaken the logic underlying this assumption and to establish a *modus vivendi* to keep the peace. In our view, it would be an over-simplification for either of the great Powers to say of the other, "We are standing by the United Nations and the principles of the Charter, while you are not." Recriminations of that sort will not lead to positive results. So long as each of the great Powers regards its way of life as a kind of religion to be propagated or defended outside its territories with zeal and fanaticism, peaceful co-existence becomes reduced to a phrase that lacks meaning.

The cold war conflicts of the present day reflect implicitly the tendencies of the great Powers to carry their differences into areas that reject the idea of the cold war in all its forms. Self-determination is one of the governing principles of the United Nations, and if it is to be a reality and not just an ideal, it is essential that the great Powers should refrain from interfering with the processes by which each nation and people choose the kind of Government and the kind of economic arrangements that they like to have.

The battle for the minds of the uncommitted world has taken various new forms and has produced curious results. It has sometimes meant intervention – I am sorry to have to say it, but it has – in the internal affairs of those countries. There has been political subversion and attempts to influence forms of government, economic and social systems in one way or another and, in extreme instances, there have been attempts to intervene directly by military action. The examples of the Congo and of Laos reflect the degree of disruption which has been brought into the lives of those nations with further accentuation of world tensions.

Most of the countries in Asia, Africa and Latin America want to be free from cold war pressures. We would like to be left to work out our own destiny and our own forms of social, economic and political life according to the action and interaction of our own internal domestic forces.

The reason for this attitude is not just a wish to be left in splendid isolation or to be removed from current world events. No, we want to be in a position to make a direct contribution to the cause of world peace and to the building up of a world order for international security. We think this can only be ensured if the peoples of Asia, Africa and Latin America can be insulated from external ideological pressures and cold war tensions. These areas of the world do not want to be the cause of any accentuation of world conflict nor to become the battleground for it.

It seems to me, therefore, that an ideological truce covering Asia, Africa and Latin America is vital. The basic principle in the relations of the great Powers to these countries must be non-intervention and non-interference in internal affairs. For instance, military assistance to countries which need it for their internal security purposes should be given only through the United Nations. The widening ideological conflict makes it all the more imperative to implement the Declaration on the granting of independence to colonial countries and peoples [resolution 1514 (XV)] formulated during the last session.

When actual arrangements are being made for the transfer of power to dependent countries, it is essential that metropolitan States should be placed under the obligation not to involve colonial territories in cold-war arrangements by, for example, the retention of military bases.

We do appreciate that the success or failure of one ideology or another is a matter of paramount concern to one or other of the great Powers. But it must be realized, and the great Powers must act in the realization, that the conflict must take peaceful forms. If any country, by virtue of purely indigenous development, were to choose one ideological form of government in preference to another, the choice must rest with that country; and it is a ohoioe whioh muot be reepected and with which all nations must learn to live.

One thing that has struck me very sharply, as a newcomer to General Assembly sessions, has been the tendency, which very often arises in this chamber, for delegations representing countries already enmeshed in the cold war to express attitudes and to take up positions based on the rather unrealistic line that there is no other possible attitude except their own. We have seen examples of that in the course of some of the speeches which have preceded my assumption of the rostrum.

Let us take the case of some of the propositions put forward by the representative of the United Kingdom, the Foreign Secretary, who spoke a moment ago. For instance, he quite rightly pointed out that the resumption of nuclear tests cannot be regarded by anybody – not by the non-aligned nations or by anybody else – as a step forward or as a step in the right direction. It is so obviously not in the right direction that I do not think much purpose is served by hammering home the point. The assumption that the non-aligned nations have, either out of a sense of fear or out of a sense of politeness, or out of a sense of anything else, refrained from making comments, is simply untrue. The non-aligned countries have, each of them, expressed their point of view very clearly and forcibly indeed; and, speaking for the Government of my country, I can only state that I was in Belgrade before I came here, with my Prime Minister, and in the course of her statement my Prime Minister did deplore the resumption of nuclear tests by the soviet Union, just as we deplore the resumption of nuclear tests by the United States. It is a retrograde step.

But consider the reasoning that follows that. It is suggested that, inasmuch as these nuclear tests must have taken many months to prepare, there is an element of bad faith underlying the resumption of nuclear tests by the Government of the Soviet Union because, while negotiations were going on, the implicit assumption is that preparations must have been made.

I do not think that I know sufficient about what it takes to prepare for nuclear tests to express any opinion in regard to that. But supposing it does take many months to prepare for nuclear tests, then does it now follow that when the United States Government resumes nuclear tests in answer to the act of the Soviet Government, it too must have been preparing for many months? Can you have it only one way? In other words, is it fair to take an argument on the basis of bad faith and to present it in that way even though we do deplore the act of both the great countries concerned in the resumption of nuclear tests?

Then, again, the Foreign Secretary made the point – which I think is perfectly valid – that it will not do merely to satisfy yourselves by inspection in any scheme of disarmament that – shall we say? – 500 aircraft are going to be destroyed in a bonfire when you do not know the production lines and the assembly lines of the great countries that may or may not be preparing for war. There is a great deal of force in that and one can certainly appreciate it; but one must also appreciate, I think, that there is the opposite point of view. And the opposite point of view is that a lot depends upon the number of aircraft that are going to be thrown away and the number of weapons that are going to be placed on this bonfire. What would be the position, for instance, if the number were increased from 500 to – shall we say – 10,000? Would it not significantly affect the argument? And supposing one does not even take figures in a relative sense. Let us carry the case one step further and suppose that there is an outbreak of war; does not the destruction of even those 500 aircraft mark a step forward and a step forward in the right direction? Those are matters that one cannot view in isolation.

I do agree that disarmament without controlled stages is a futile concept and a concept which cannot be accepted on mere statements of principle. But there is the point of view that a scheme of controls must not become a system of espionage; and so long as there is force in that argument, it will not do for either of the countries engaged in this conflict to adopt self-righteous tones or self-righteous attitudes and to refuse to face the realities that exist and on which a compromise must be found if the world is to move forward towards peace and prosperity in a real sense.

The Foreign Secretary again made the point that the sanctity of treaties must be respected if the United Nations is to mean anything. He is quite right. If treaties are going to be treated as scraps of paper, of course the world can have no security and we are all left in a state – a very parlous state – balanced between peace and war and wondering what the future is going to bring to us all. But, the Foreign Secretary says, our contract in regard to Germany has not run out – a contract made at a time when the victorious Powers, in a spirit of friendliness, sought to do what they thought at that time was the best possible thing to heal the ravages of war. It was not intended that a peace treaty should be signed until a reunified, demilitarized Germany could be established – no doubt with the consent and will of all the victorious Powers who had succeeded in the course of the conflicts of the Second World War.

One has to be realistic about these things. Is there any likelihood of the contract running out in the present situation? Is there any immediate prospect of a reunified Germany? Is there any likelihood that one can contemplate a situation in which the great Powers, who fought the Second World War to ultimate victory and the unconditional surrender of Hitlerite Germany, will now agree to the setting up of a united Germany in the existing context? Supposing it never happens, the contract will never run out. And once left with the reality that the existing situation will continue, that contract will have to remain merely because it is a contract.

We prefer to look at things not from the point of view of the Soviet Union; no, there are no two codes of behaviour in regard to the arguments which we present. We do not accept the philosophy of communism. We seek to move towards socialism according to our own indigenous form that it has taken in our country. But it would be completely unrealistic to suggest that countries such as ours, which are non-aligned, are either being bullied or are being compelled to take lines which we do not want to take, or are adopting a set of double standards – one set of standards for the countries of the West and a different set of standards for communist countries which are here present in the assembly.

The suggestion was made again by the United Kingdom Foreign Secretary, that one cannot have double standards with regard to countries, shall we say, of the British Empire and countries of what was described as the Russian Empire. There is implicit in that statement an assumption that existing governments in countries in different parts of the world are not really representative of their peoples. There is the assumption that there is not a communist country in the world which wants communism. There is the assumption that, inasmuch as one-party government does imply a greater degree of government controls, a degree of freedom is lacking.

We do not know enough to be able to test the correctness or incorrectness of that assumption. It may be that there are countries of which that can be said, but if we adopt it as a general principle, then we must go on the basis that the Government of the Soviet Union does not represent the will and desire of the peoples of that great country. We would have to build on the assumption that there is in force a regime that does not command the respect and confidence of its people. How realistic is that? Are we really to believe that the people of the Soviet Union, from 1917 to 1961, did not want the kind of government that they had established for themselves? Are we to assume that governments cannot command confidence merely because there have been no elections in the immediate past, or merely because a space of time has elapsed?

In other words, if we start on that kind of assumption we shall get into extremely deep water. Indeed, the Assembly has already got into very deep water by adopting that kind of argument. Is it not precisely on that assumption that the great People's Republic of China has been excluded from the Assembly? Is it not on that argument that we assume that a country whose form of government has been in existence for the last decade is incapable of determining its own destiny, and that the true peoples of China still want the restoration of a regime which territorially has been now diminished to Taiwan?

In the face of realities one must not make assumptions of entering into debates which presuppose such a premise which none of us, as independent sovereign States, can possibly accept on the floor of the Assembly. If we start making assumptions of that sort and saying that such and such a representative in this chamber does not really represent the people of his country, and that he has no business to be here, then of course we find that underlying that assumption there would be willingness to accept the fact that the principles of the Charter were going to be undermined by the adoption of that very same argument.

There is a matter of great importance which has arisen in the course of the last few days, particularly since the sad and tragic death of the late Secretary-General, Mr Hammarskjold. We in our country have had compelling reason sometimes to disagree with some of the decisions made by the late Secretary-General, particularly with regard to the conduct of the situation in the Congo last year, and, as a member of the Security Council, we have expressed our views fairly and frankly in the only spirit in which one is capable of expressing one's views in an Assembly of this type, where one seeks to influence positively the thinking of nations. But that does not mean that we have no confidence in Mr Hammarskjold or in the institution. When the issue was raised of our attitude with regard to the proposal formulated by the Government of the Soviet Union in relation to the creation of a "troika," which would require the amendment of the United Nations Charter, the Government of Ceylon expressed the view categorically – and it sees no reason to change it now – that it does not stand for any principle of a "troika." We see in the principle of a "troika" a grave danger – a danger that the United Nations may lose its capacity for effective executive action, and executive action we must have if the United Nations General Assembly and its other institutions are to become a true vehicle to establish a world order and international peace.

With that firm conviction in mind we have expressed our view. By that view we stand to date, and we would earnestly appeal to the Government of the Soviet Union to consider the question, within the realities of such divisions as exist in the world today, of making a choice of a person capable of interpreting correctly the collective views of the Assembly and of giving executive force to the decisions which we make here.

The realities are there. There is no doubt that the world is divided. The argument has been presented on the floor of the assembly that the world is divided into two groups of nations – nations which want to preserve the United Nations and its Charter, and nations which want to destroy the United Nations and its Charter. The analysis does not seem to us to be quite so simple. It is not a question of saying, "We want to establish the Charter, while you do not." Both sides say just that. The truth of the matter is that there are three groups of nations. There is a group of nations that stand by the ideologies of the Western world – the free world, as it is sometimes called; there is a group of nations that stand solidly behind the ideology of communism; but there is a very significant group, a group of persons who constitute – although it is sometimes disregarded – the rest of the world, and we represent in that sense a small constituent element of that third group, the rest of the world. The rest of the world does not get together and establish itself as a bloc or say to itself, "We have a group of principles which we formulate and which we adopt on every occasion." We do not exist according to a code of rules; we exist merely because there are countries which are not concerned with these great Power conflicts and which wish to be left alone and to stand aside without involvement, and that is where we belong.

It is not sufficient for any country to say, "We stand by the United Nations Charter, the other side does not" and, by implication, to suggest, "Here, then, is a group of neutrals who also stand by the United Nations Charter, and therefore we are on their side." It just is not as simple as that. On every particular constructive qustion that arises for the decision of the Assembly we are compelled to take a position. We cannot stand aside and say that we are going to behave like the ostrich to which the United Kingdom Foreign Secretary referred a moment ago. We are vulnerable, and we know it. But, being vulnerable, we are not afraid to speak our mind, to take our head out of the sand, unlike the proverbial ostrich, and to face the realities.

During the last few days there has been a certain amount of discussion in the lobbies of the United Nations General Assembly to which, I must confess, I did not pay any particular attention. I did not pay any particular attention to it because, as the representative of a country which is a member of the Security Council, I found that what was being discussed was a proposition which I did not think would ever see the light of day or emerge in the form of any concrete resolution. I did not intend to refer to it here at all, but in view of something that was said by the United Kingdom Foreign Secretary I think that it is clearly my duty to make a statement with regard to it.

Owing to a fear that there will be a deadlock with regard to the finding of an executive arm to carry out the resolutions of this international body, because of the difficulty that the Security Council might become deadlocked over the proposition put forward by the representative of the Soviet Union for a "troika" and the equally firm decision on the part of other countries not to yield to it but to maintain a single person as Secretary-General – a view which I personally accept on behalf of the Government of Ceylon – there is a proposal now being talked about in a rather shadowy form with regard to the presentation of a draft resolution to the General Assembly whereby it would consider the appointment of some distinguished person, I suppose from one of the countries represented in the Assembly, who would function as a temporary Secretary-General, an interim officer, pending the resolution of the permanent dispute, a person who would be determined by the force of a majority vote.

I thought the suggestion was so fantastic that I did not even give it any serious consideration earlier. But, with regard to the statement by the Foreign Secretary of great Britain, that where the Security Council is paralysed by the possibility of vetoes, it then becomes necessary for us to consider action by the General Assembly according to the wishes of the majority of the world – I consider that an extremely dangerous statement, though uttered no doubt in perfect good faith and without perhaps a realization of some of the dangerous consequences it can entail for the whole of the Assembly. We are here, all of us, whether we believe it or not, to carry out the principles of the Charter. Now, the Charter did not provide for decisions by a majority rule. There are some things in regard to which the Assembly, however significant it is as an international body, is incapable of deciding by a majority rule. Visualize to yourselves that if all the representatives assembled here in this conference room were to get together and say, "We will determine the pattern of life for the United States of America and the Soviet Union to follow." Supposing all of us vote on this – barring, of course, the representatives of the Soviet Union and of the United States. Is it suggested that the Governments of the Soviet Union and the United States should be bound by that majority decision? If one accepts a principle of that sort, then one has got to go the whole way and accept it as a general principle of subordinating one's own decisions to resolutions determined by majority rule. To start with, there is the weakness that we are not completely represented here. The most significant omission perhaps is still the People's Republic of China. And so long as that stands we cannot set ourselves up in that way. Besides, in the Assembly we all stand as independent countries, whatever our size may be. We have only 10 million people, but we still count for one vote in the Assembly. I would still hesitate to take decisions which could influence the life of the people of the United States of America or of the Soviet Union, based on majorities here.

The proof of the matter is this; the Charter contemplated decisions to be taken by the Security Council in a spirit of compromise and co-operation. And that spirit of compromise and co-operation must be established between the United States and the Soviet Union if our decisions are really to mean anything. If we are not going to do that, and if we are going to look at this thing as a deadlock, a situation into which we have been forced where one country or the other is going to say, "We cannot solve the problem in the Security Council, therefore, let us take a decision based on majority votes" – all I can say is, that would be the first step towards the disintegration of the entire Organization and all that it stands for. The country which puts forward a proposal of that kind will be responsible for destroying the principles set forth in the United Nations Charter under cover of seeking to find a practical solution to a very real problem that is there.

I do agree that the principle of the "troika" cannot be accepted. There is a very large body of opinion, I believe, represented in this hall which cannot agree with that point of view submitted by the Soviet Union. It certainly does not go to show that the non-aligned nations are adopting two codes of behaviour. But may I say this: the fact that they are opposed to a "troika," the fact that we realize that there is a need for some person to replace the late Mr Hammarskjold, that cannot mean that we are going to decide these things on a majority vote, on a railroaded decision taken before the Assembly, mainly because the majority of us are opposed to an idea set up by the Soviet Union.

The argument against the point of view I hold seems to be this: the Government of the Soviet Union, by presenting the argument of the "troika" has in effect negated the principles of the Charter by making impossible the election of a single person as Secretary-General. That is the argument. Therefore, if the Government of the Soviet Union is going against the principles of the Charter, we have to find a solution outside the principles of the Charter. In other words, we are getting back to the age-old argument: at some time somebody else does wrong, let us do wrong too. But I do not agree that the point of view expressed by the Government of the Soviet Union necessarily amounts to a rejection of the principles of the Charter.

The Government of the Soviet Union as it sees things within the realities of the existing situation takes the line – I think quite wrongly – that the Charter requires amendments, that the Charter requires change, at any rate in regard to the Constitution of the office of the Secretary-General. Now, they may be right or they be wrong, but it must surely be open to any one of us in the Assembly to consider ways and means of improving the institutions of the Assembly as we think best. The best we can do is to put forward a proposal. Whether the proposal is going to find acceptance or not is a matter that must be decided by the entire body.

At the moment it does not seem to me that the "troika" proposal of the Soviet Union meets with any general acceptance. But here is the point: one cannot regard a suggestion made for amendment, prejudge it and decide that it is a clear attempt to sabotage the Organization itself. If you make that assumption and start with a position that you are going to meet with the veto even before a proposal is submitted, if you start with an assumption that one cannot arrive at a satisfactory settlement among the great Powers, then the United Nations has reached a very sorry stage indeed. In these circumstances I do submit that it would be completely wrong and contrary to the principles of the Charter to take the argument: "The Charter is silent in regard to acting appointments or temporary appointments. Let us create a procedure and let us use the technique of majority decisions before this Assembly to achieve that object." I do submit for the earnest consideration of a number of small countries like my own, the seriousness and the implications that any such proposal will have if it is seriously presented in the Assembly at any time.

The late Mr Hammarskjold himself expressed a point of view once that the United Nations exists for the protection of the small nations. If the United Nations is to serve a useful purpose within that context and to serve the small countries of this world well, it is surely a matter of great importance that merely because there is a need to find some replacement for the late Mr Hammarskjold, we should not allow that sanctity of the institutions established in the Charter, which we respect, to be set aside and brought to nought by the result of hasty thought.

The late Mr Hammerskjold has now been dead, unfortunately, for some days, and yet we are here – the Assembly is functioning, the work of the United Nations has not been paralysed yet. We are able to carry on, at least during these few days. Does it matter if this question is given a little further carefully considered thought? In other words, should we not endeavour to recall to our mind the lofty principles that inspired the United Nations in its thinking in San Francisco sixteen years ago – the principles of compromise, of trying to find solutions between the great Powers. That surely must be the standard which we must adopt in regard to our thinking.

The question of the Republic of the Congo (Leopoldville) always comes up. I think, in the course of any discussion in regard to the General Assembly and its plenary sessions these days. One cannot avoid it. The situation in the Congo is there and it must be faced. We, in Ceylon, were one of the countries that were responsible for setting up the United Nations Command in the Congo. And having set up that command, we cannot help but feel a sense of disappointment in regard to the subsequent phases of that operation. The United Nations Forces there today have certainly not covered themselves with glory – and it is not their fault.

We are not proud that the forces of the United Nations, the forces of independent, neutral countries, which were deliberately sent to the Congo to preserve the objectives of the United Nations, to maintain peace and the territorial integrity of the Congo, have been held up for ransom by a lone jet fighter which, according to all reports, is piloted either by a Belgian pilot of SABENA Airlines or by someone from Northern Rhodesia. We are not proud of that fact. We are not proud of the fact that Mr Hammarskjold had to fly at night, when he was seeking to arrive at some settlement in furtherance of the objectives of the United Nations. We are not proud of the fact that Mr Hammarskjold had to have a number of airfields alerted because he could not have any definite plans about where he was going to land. These are not matters of which we can be proud.

We are glad to see the determination of the great Powers to support the operations of the United Nations. We are indeed glad to hear the Foreign Secretary of the United Kingdom expressing that view in no uncertain terms. I do not know whether or not it is true, but we did hear some time ago that a little difficulty had arisen in regard to the refuelling and landing rights of an aircraft from Ethiopia – it was, I believe, a figher aircraft which was on its way to the Congo through Uganda. We are glad that the declaration of the United Kingdom Foreign Secretary has reassured us that all co-operation will be given to United Nations soldiers in the Congo in order that they may achieve their objectives and carry out the tasks which have been assigned to them by the United Nations.

Many complex problems arise out of cold war tensions. To my mind, the important thing now is to get rid of them. It is most necessary that the great Powers should resolve that they are not going to make this a world forum in which to wage their battles extraterritorially.

Cold war tensions are most sharply reflected in the city of Berlin, where the situation has almost reached the breaking point. When one makes an assessment on Berlin, it is not sufficient to think only in terms of legal rights and technicalities arising from agreements concluded among the victorious Powers at the end of the last war. The situation has changed a good deal since then, and existing realities cannot be ignored. One of these realities happens to be the existence of two Germanies today, whether we like it or not. Equally we have to bear in mind that no solution in regard to Berlin can be accepted which does not accord with the wishes of the people of West Berlin to retain their way of life. I agree with the Foreign Secretary of the United Kingdom that it is a most dangerous thing to express any views at all when negotiations are about to start on any subject under the sun. We do not wish to place any obstructions in the path of negotiations. We welcome the spirit in which the recent negotiations have been viewed by the great Powers. We think that their attitudes have been far more realistic that in the past. I shall therefore refrain from making any further comments on this subject and shall merely express the hope that the negotiations undertaken will meet with success and lead ultimately to an overall settlement of the problem of Germany.

Then, there is the question of disarmament. The hopes which we had that the Ten-Nation Committee would reach some affirmative decisions on disarmament have been disappointed. But it is heartening to feel that the great Powers do realize the need to persevere, for on the success of negotiations on disarmament depend all hopes of world peace. However much we may keep ideological conflicts within bounds and seek to minimize tensions in given areas of the world, world peace will remain insecure as long as the world is possessed of weapons and the armaments race continues.

Our consistent view has been that there should be general and complete disarmament, and that the objective of negotiations should be to achieve an agreement on general and complete disarmament. This is a radical and not a pragmatic or partial concept. The compelling argument for it is not just the negative fear of a future war, with all that it means for mankind, but the positive and affirmative need for a secure world basis for peace for the evolving international community of States. It is no more our purpose, on the old theory of the balance of power, to provide for the security of one group of Powers as against another. What we urgently require is an international order of security for our international community of States, an order which would enable all nations, large or small, to find security and resolve differences by peaceful means.

Disarmament is a compelling issue for all of us; it is not the concern of only the great Powers and of militarily significant states. As I have said before, disarmament must proceed side by side and step by step with the construction of a world order which would provide for security in a disarmed world. We, the small nations, have an abiding concern in the construction of this order and want to be associated from outset with its formulation.

We are very happy indeed that the Governments of the United States and the Soviet Union have been able to agree on the general principles which are to form the basis of negotiations on disarmament [see A/4879]. We are particularly happy that the agreement was reached in consonance with the concept of general and complete disarmament, and that in this the great Powers have heeded the General Assembly's resolution [1378 (XIV)] on this subject and the desire of peoples everywhere to be freed forever from the dread prospect of war and conflict.

But – and there is a "but" – we feel that these objectives will be realized only if the nations which reached that agreement are firmly and irrevocably committed to giving up cold war thinking. If one embarks on negotiations with the attitude that, if one makes a concession or tries to understand the other side's point of view, one is yielding territory or giving ground, then of course there can be no ultimate solution. If, on the other hand, these countries are prepared for a radical break with the suicidal conceptions of nuclear deterrents, massive retaliation, limited wars and positions of strength, an agreement on general and complete disarmament should not be an impossible achievement. The question of control should not prove to be an insuperable obstacle either, notwithstanding the undoubted complexity of the numerous problems connected with the setting up of credible control and supervisory organization; the latter must not be allowed to become a final difficulty.

My Government, however, has grave doubts, fears and anxieties. We feel that this mutual adjustment has still not been made, that the cold war is still a lingering presence and that the negotiations which are shortly to begin will be dogged by the recurrent fate of many such negotiations in the past. We have had negotiations before, followed by breakdown and mutual recrimination. This has happened too often. It cannot happen again. We cannot afford to let it happen. We must therefore take precautions to prevent it from happening.

My Prime Minister has asked me to suggest to the Assembly that future negotiations between the great Powers should be joined by representatives of non-aligned countries. Non-aligned countries do repressent a significant point of view, although perhaps they lack the cohesion of a bloc of countries committed to a particular ideology. Fundamentally what we, the non-aligned countries, have in common is that we are outside the cold war and want to remain outside. The non-aligned countries reject the contradictions and assumptions of the cold war. They are committed by their very policies to an unfettered exercise of judgement on the basic issues which confront the world within the framework of the realities. This should not be unacceptable to either side, since the non-aligned countries are pre-eminently in a position to exercise a salutary influence on the course of negotiations. We should therefore propose that the Ten-Nation Committee on Disarmament be expanded to include a number of non-aligned States. We do not really think that the enlargement of that Committee should be on a population or geographical basis. The only merit in such a proposal would be the purely formal one of increasing the representation on the Committee. We, the non-aligned nations, want to be able to affect the argument, and this can be done effectively only by associating non-aligned countries with the ten nations.

It is our firm conviction that atmospheric and underground nuclear tests should be immediately abandoned. We appreciate the fact that nuclear testing cannot be viewed in isolation from the many interrelated and complicating factors which are causing world tension, but the tests must cease, if only because they cause international tension, prejudice the health of mankind and affect even the kindliness of our human environment. Such a situation cannot be allowed to continue, and no cold-war argument, however inevitable the situation may appear within the framework of that war, can justify its continuance. We do not think that a treaty on nuclear tests is of immediate importance. For three years man has been able to live free from these menacing blasts on the basis of a voluntary moratorium. Do we really need to wait for a treaty? It may even turn out to be unnecessary if there is agreement on total disarmament; but what we do need meanwhile is a moratorium. This must be immediately restored.

Recently we have often heard expressed the theory that colonialism has ceased to be a real problem as more and more dependent territories have advanced to the stage of independence. We are happy to be reassured by the British Foreign Secretary that the United Kingdom is taking positive steps – steps which we know from our own experience it has always taken where colonial territories have been concerned – to that end: that it is even prepared voluntarily to place before the General Assembly the details of those positive processes.

We welcome the fact that Sierra Leone, a former British territory, has risen to its full stature and become a member of the Commonwealth. However, the theory that, because the percentage of people living under colonialism has continued to shrink, colonialism is no longer a real problem, is simply not true. Mr Hammarskjold's death, in itself, is proof that colonialism is still not dead. Indeed, it has a knack of taking new shapes and forms in the face of evolving realities. Implementation of the resolution [1514 (XV)] containing the Declaration on the granting of independence to colonial countries and peoples, which the General Assembly adopted with not a single dissentient vote at its last session, is a matter of urgency. I would invite Members to look at the recent happenings in Angola, the new developments in the Congo, the continuing bloodshed in Algeria and the peculiar problem of South West Africa. To take just one example, Angola: the whole world knows that the metropolitan State is waging a war of extermination, without precedent in recent times, in that country. The resolutions of the United Nations have been treated with contempt. In the face of this intransigence, this cynical and calculated indifference to world opinion, it is in our view a matter directly concerning the organization that Portugal should not be permitted to continue its wilful policies in Angola with impunity.

Other countries have suggested that nations such as South Africa and Portugal, which follow such policies, should be excluded from membership of the Assembly. I cannot accept that view as correct, or regard it as a positive step in the light of present international thinking. We are not here as members of a common club – people with one way of thinking and no other. We are not here to act as a kind of superior body, a holy alliance, an "elite" which alone is capable of enlightened thinking. That is not the position: we do disagree with one another. We do have differences of policy. It is surely no solution to say that because we disapprove radically of a policy followed by a country such as Portugal or South Africa, we should exclude it from membership of this community of nations. What would happen if we carried that argument to its logical conclusion? We might reach a position in which the policies followed by any one of us might not find general acceptance. To take an absurd example, the United States might actually disapprove of the policies followed by the Soviet Union, or *vice versa*! One would not suggest that those two great countries should leave the Assembly as a result. We are here in a spirit of compromise and understanding. We must seek other means of making world opinion felt by the Governments and peoples of Portugal and South Africa.

I have already spoken of the situation in the Congo and should like now to deal briefly with one or two aspects of the position in Katanga. Ceylon was one of the nations which offered support to the Government of Mr Lumumba. It was also one of the many nations to ask the United Nations to give effective support to the lawful Prime Minister's desire to restore law and order and maintain the territorial integrity and unity of the Congolese Republic. When the Prime Minister, Mr Lumumba, died, the people of my country were deeply shocked. We deplored what had happened, and had no difficulty in identifying the forces responsible for the crime. Following Mr Lumumba's death, our Government took up the position that it could not recognize any other person as Head of the Congolese Government unless the National Parliament, under the "Loi fondamentale," validated such appointment. In our view, the Congo has today a Government with parliamentary backing and we are prepared to give it all possible support in helping it maintain law and order, and the unity and integrity of the Congolese Republic. Its Government has asked for the support of the United Nations in achieving these objectives, and it is our task to see that the resolutions of the Security Council are fully implemented.

There is strong evidence that insidious forces still remain in Katanga province – forces which would do everything in their power to resist the implementation of the Security Council resolutions. A ceasefire agreement has been concluded, but my Government does not consider it of any significance unless it leads to such implementation. The territorial integrity of the Congo must be maintained. The dissidence in Katanga must be eliminated and the provincial government of Katanga brought within the framework of the Congolese Constitution.

countries that the losses we sustain in the falling prices, the change of the terms of trade, are in excess of the benefits which we have received from foreign aid.

There is therefore an urgent need for United Nations financial agencies, either existing or proposed, to find a process to help offset the unavoidable balance of payment crisis of the underdeveloped countries in so far as they stem from development programmes, commodity price fluctuations and short-term capital outflows. There is a very grave need for urgent consideration by the Assembly of some form of automatic access to reserves and some form of insurance against commodity price fluctuations.

Before I conclude, I should like once again to appeal to the rest of the world, if not to the great Powers: let us not try to enter into recriminations and into argument. Let us avoid making the mistake of analysing the arguments, or trying to say who is right and who is wrong. Let us not try to enter into arguments on this question.

For example, we heard a few moments ago from the Foreign Secretary of the United Kingdom that, as things appear to his Government, there is an overt declaration on the part of communist countries that they mean to subvert Governments from outside and that they mean to go on with that process in furtherance of their ideology. But we must also be realistic and look at the other side of the picture if we are going to enter into that kind of argument. We like to imagine, for example, that there is no crusade against communism. But the facts of history are there. One cannot expect the Russians to forget, for instance, that in 1917 their country was actually invaded, that battles were fought on their territory against communism, that they have been hemmed in from time to time, that attempts have been made to contain their own particular ideology, so that they might themselves perhaps have a very real feeling of fear that they are going to be the victims of aggressions. We sincerely hope that that is not going to happen, and we sincerely hope that they are not going to subvert any other countries which do not want to be subverted. The argument goes both ways.

We do not want to enter into this pattern of argument. We do not wish to divide ourselves into groups trying to find alignments. We stand with the rest of the world and we think it is a complete mistake to try to enter into arguments for or against, to try to arrive at solutions in that way. That is not the answer. Recriminations will get us nowhere. It is no good trying to pretend that the fault is entirely on the other side, that one particular country has distinguished itself by its clean record in foreign affairs. We in the non-aligned nations, certainly we in Ceylon, do not propose to enter into that argument, and we shall maintain our independence and strive for what we believe to be the true principles set forth in the Charter. We are not going to enter into arguments as to who is the best defender of the Charter, whether it is the countries of the Western world or of the communist world. We want the Charter to exist and we want both those great groups of countries to stay clear of our affairs and of the affairs of the rest of the world. They should let the rest of the world develop in peace towards the form of government, the forms of social and economic development, that our countries require.

I find that it is ten minutes to two, and I must thank all my colleagues who have had the patience to forgo some part of their luncheon interval to give thought to some of the considerations that the Government of Ceylon would like to present for careful consideration in this forthcoming session. We urge all Governments to act with a realization that whatever decisions the Assembly makes now are probably going to affect the future course of world events to such an extent that we must take the right decisions here and now. There is no postponing the issue. There is no question of avoiding an issue. It has to be faced, and it has to be faced correctly.

In conclusion, may I appeal once again to the great Powers of the world, and particularly the United States of America and the Soviet Union: do not forget the principles that inspired you in San Francisco, when you were concerned with arriving at compromise solutions and co-operating with one another for the peace of the world. We need that co-operation now. The real challenge is not so much a challenge to countries like ours, which cannot affect events, which are merely the victims of events. The challenge faces you, and we, the rest of the world, look up to you and look forward to constructive and positive action on the part of the two Governments.

STATEMENT ON THE ABORTIVE COUP D'ETAT OF 27TH JANUARY, 1962

Information

At about noon on Saturday, the 27th of January, Mr S. A. Dissanayake, D.I.G., C.I.D., received information which led him to suspect that there was a danger of a coup d'etat by certain police and army officers to overthrow the Government after midnight on the same day. He decided to verify his suspicions, before reporting anything to the I.G.P., Mr M. W. F. Abeykoon, and the Prime Minister. The D.I.G., C.I.D. alerted his men and took necessary action immediately.

Meanwhile, at about 5.15 p.m., the I.G.P., when he was at the Orient Club, also received information of the coup planned for that night. He then telephoned S.P. Colombo and asked him to see him immediately at the Orient

Club. S.P. Colombo saw the I.G.P. at the Orient Club and spoke to him. The I.G.P. then got down the D.I.G., C.I.D. to the Club, and the D.I.G., C.I.D. told the I.G.P. that he too had received information of the planned coup, and that he expected to have proofs of his suspicions very soon. The I.G.P. asked the D.I.G., C.I.D. to let him know as soon as the proofs were ready, so that both of them could go at once to the Prime Minister, and lay the proofs before her.

At about 7.00 p.m., Mr Bandaranaike, the Minister of Finance, received information of the planned coup. He contacted the I.G.P. immediately and got him down to his house, and asked the I.G.P. to get the D.I.G., C.I.D. and for both of them to go at once to the Prime Minister, to apprise her of the situation. Mr Bandaranaike remained at his house to ascertain more facts from his informant who was with him at the time. On receiving a call from the I.G.P., Mr Bandaranaike went to Temple Trees.

Action

At about 8.30 p.m., the I.G.P., the D.I.G., C.I.D. and Mr Bandaranaike met the Prime Minister at Temple Trees, and informed her of what each of them had heard of the planned coup. From the information then available, it appeared that the coup had been planned for the overthrow of the Government at about midnight, that Mr. C. C. Dissanayake, D.I.G. Range I was one of the principal suspects, that the plan involved the arrest of Ministers, and some leftist leaders, and that Army Officers were also in the plot.

After a discussion, the Prime Minister gave orders that the Police Depot at Bambalapitiya should be immediately sealed off, so that no vehicles, arms, ammunition or men could be taken from the Depot for any purpose that night. She also directed that the room at Police Headquarters from which radio or radio-teletype messages could be sent to all stations, should be sealed off, so that unauthorised messages could not be despatched. She also asked the I.G.P. to issue a general directive to all police stations, that no orders of an unusual or non-routine character, should be carried out by any Police Officer unless expressly authorised by the I.G.P. himself.

The Prime Minister then ordered the Service Commanders to report immediately to Temple Trees. The first to be sent for and to arrive was Commodore Kadirgamar, Acting Captain of the Navy. Upon his arrival, he was told the facts so far as they were known, and arrangements were immediately made to have some Internal Security Platoons of Navy personnel standing by for the further protection and defence of Temple Trees, should the need arise. All the service Commanders, Major-General

Wijekoon, Air Vice Marshall Barker, and Commodore Kadirgamar, informed the Prime Minister that they were completely unaware of the coup. They were asked to stand by at Temple Trees to give every assistance to foil the coup.

A number of S.P's and A.S.P.'s in Colombo Division and in the Western Province, who were believed to have received certain instructions from Mr C. C. Dissanayake, D.I.G. Range I, in connection with the coup, were asked to come to Temple Trees.

The Prime Minister also telephoned the Minister of Justice and the Minister of Agriculture, Lands, Irrigation and Power, who were the only other Ministers in Colombo. The Minister of Justice had earlier been presiding at a public dinner, and the Minister of Agriculture, Lands, Irrigation and Power had been at a Pirith Ceremony at his house. They both arrived soon afterwards.

After a discussion with the Ministers present, as well as the I.G.P. and the Service Commanders, it was decided to order the arrests of Mr C. C. Dissanayake, D.I.G. Range I, and of Mr B. Johnpillai, A.S.P. (Traffic). A party consisting of police officers, with a detail of service personnel to assist them, set out to effect each arrest. The Prime Minister also directed that Mr Stanley Senanayake, S.P. Colombo should be found and brought to Temple Trees. Before a party could set out to look for Mr Stanley Senanayake, however, he came to Temple Trees with his father-in-law, Mr P. de S. Kularatne, M.P.

The First Arrests

Mr C. C. Dissanayake, D.I.G. Range I, was arrested in his house, soon after midnight. While he was being arrested, a very senior police officer arrived there, dressed in uniform and driving his car. The officers making the arrest, asked him to come to Temple Trees with them. This police officer was then seen throwing something away into the bushes in the garden. It was found that what he had thrown away was a leather pouch containing live ammunition for a revolver. Mr Dissanayake was taken to Welikade Jail, and detained there by the party making the arrest, while the other police officer was brought to Temple Trees.

Mr B. Johnpillai, A.S.P. (Traffic), was not at his house when the party making the arrest called there. His house was searched, and a box of 9 mm ammunition for a Luger pistol was found on a table, as well as a telegram. He was later arrested at his house at about 4.00 a.m. and detained at Welikade Jail.

Investigation

Because of the importance of the coup, and the urgent need to take into detention all persons concerned in the coup, so as to prevent any further attempt being made to overthrow the Government, it was decided that the Cabinet should have overall direction and control of the investigation, and that the investigation should be made with all speed. The I.G.P. and the D.I.G., C.I.D. welcomed this decision, particularly because the principal suspects at the early stages were senior Police Officers, and one of them was the brother of the D.I.G., C.I.D.

Most of the important witnesses were questioned at Temple Trees, by Mr Bandaranaike, Parliamentary Secretary for Defence and External Affairs. As many Ministers of the Government as found it possible to do so, were present. The I.G.P., the D.I.G., C.I.D., Mr Attygalle, S.P., C.I.D. and other C.I.D. officers were also present. Each witness was questioned by Mr Bandaranaike, thereafter by the other Ministers present, and also by the I.G.P., the D.I.G., C.I.D. and the other officers of the C.I.D. The proceedings were recorded on a tape-recorder, and the statements of the witnesses were also taken down by C.I.D. officers, read over and signed by them.

Two witnesses asked for legal assistance, and their requests were allowed, but they decided to make their statements without such help. Several witnesses said that they would rather not answer certain questions, and they were not compelled to do so, although their refusal to answer particular questions was recorded. When military officers were being questioned, the Army Commander or his Chief of Staff was present, and on one or two occasions when those witnesses desired to confer privately with the Army Commander they were allowed to do so.

Besides the questioning of the important witnesses, a great deal of work has also been done by C.I.D. officers in the checking and verification of statements, and the finding of corroborative material.

As the investigation proceeded round the clock, and the story of the plot unfolded, other persons who had participated in the coup were arrested and detained. Mr Royce de Mel, former Captain of the Navy, against whom a detention order has been issued, has so far successfully evaded arrest and detention. The names of the persons arrested and detained have been announced from day to day, and the full list is as follows:-

1. Mr C. C. Dissanayake, D.I.G., Range I
2. Mr B. Johnpillai, A.S.P., Traffic
3. Mr L. C. S. Jirasinghe, A.S.P., Colombo West
4. Col. Maurice de Mel, Commandant of the Volunteer Force
5. Col. F. C. de Saram, Deputy Commandant of the Volunteer Force

6. Mr Sidney de Zoysa, former D.I.G.
7. Lt. Col. B. R. Jesudasan, C.O. Volunteer Signals
8. Lt. Col. W. Abraham, C.O. 3rd Field Regiment of Artillery
9. Major B. I. Loyola of the 3rd Field Regiment of Artillery
10. Major W. G. White of the 3rd Field Regiment of Artillery
11. Major L. P. Joseph of the Armoured Corps
12. Lt. Col. J. H. V. de Alwis, C.O. Volunteer Engineers
13. Captain J. A. R. Felix, Staff Officer, C.V.F. Headquarters
14. Mr V. E. Perera, S.P., S.P. West
15. Mr D. J. F. D. Liyanage, Deputy Director of Land Development
16. Mr T. V. Wijesinghe, A.S.P. (P.A. to D.I.G. Range I)
17. Lt. Col. Noel Mathysz, C.O., C.E.M.E.
18. Captain D. E. Weerasinghe of the 3rd Field Regiment.
19. Captain A. J. B. Anghie of the 3rd Field Regiment
20. Mr David Thambyah, S.P., S.P. East
21. Mr Collin Vandendriesen, A.S.P., Depot
22. Captain N. S. Jayakody of the 3rd Field Regiment
23. Mr Anura de Silva
24. Mr W. E. C. Jebanesan, S.P., Crimes Colombo
25. Mr W. D. O. Siri Chandra, Sub-Inspector of Police, Police Training School
26. Mr R. E. Kitto, former S.P.
27. Mr Lionel Goonetilleke, former A.S.P.
28. Major V. J. H. Gunasekera of the 2nd L.A.A. Volunteers
29. Mr Ossie Corea

The investigations are not yet concluded, and will be completed as soon as possible. Nevertheless, the Government has decided that in the public interest, it is essential that the details of the coup, so far as they have been revealed by the present investigations, should be disclosed.

The Plan of the Coup

It does seem a strange coincidence that the coup d'etat was planned to take place on the night of 27th January, 1962 on which day the Honourable the Prime Minister was to be at Kataragama. Planning had gone on for quite some time by a very few at the top and the security precautions of the "need to know" were strictly observed. The detailed plans were revealed less than 48 hours from "H" hour.

Colonel Maurice de Mel and Colonel F. C. de Saram were in charge of army arrangements for the coup, while Mr Sidney de Zoysa and Mr C. C. Dissanayake were in charge of police arrangements. Mr Royce de Mel was also associated in the detailed planning of the coup, and it seems that the co-ordination of army and police operations was undertaken by Mr Sidney de Zoysa.

Ministers of the Government, the Permanent Secretary for Defence and External Affairs, the Inspector-General of Police, the Deputy Inspector-General in charge of the Criminal Investigation Department, the Superintendent of Police of the Criminal Investigation Department, and some leftist leaders were among the persons to be arrested at some time after midnight. The Acting Captain of the Navy was also down to be arrested, while the other Service Commanders were to be restrained, and prevented from leaving their houses that night after a certain hour.

The persons arrested in Colombo were to be taken to Army Headquarters and imprisoned in the Ammunition Magazine, which is a reinforced concrete structure, partially underground. Those arrested outside Colombo were to be taken to the Headquarters Police Station of the area pending further instructions.

Soon after midnight, Police Cars equipped with Radio and Loud Hailers were to be sent out to announce an immediate curfew in the City of Colombo.

The Central Telegraph Office at Colombo Fort, as well as the other telephone exchanges in Colombo were to be put out of action. The offices of the newspaper buildings, Police Headquarters, the office of the Criminal Investigation Department and other key points were to be taken over. Tanks and armoured cars were to be stationed at certain points to ensure the success of the operation. Troops from Panagoda were to be prevented from reaching Colombo that night, at any cost. Army vehicles, fitted with radio transmitting and receiving equipment were to be stationed at several places, including the two Kelani bridges and the Kirillapone bridge. Armed police motor cyclists were to be at Torrington Square from about 11 p.m. that night. A special direct telephone line had been laid the previous day, from Lower Lake Road to Echelon Square, for use by army personnel. It was also intended to withdraw the Armoured Cars from Temple Trees.

The house of Colonel Richard Udugama at Lunawa was to be kept under surveillance, in case he returned there from Jaffna. Steps had also been taken to see to it that Colonel D. S. Attygalle, the Commanding Officer of the Armoured Corps would not be available at the time of the coup.

Preparations had also been made to ensure that all officers and men, both from the Army and the Police, who were to go out on the night of the 27th for the coup, should be fully armed, 378 rounds of ammunition for Stirling, Lancaster and Sten machine guns had been unlawfully issued from the Police Training School and handed over to a Police Officer taking part in the coup, on the morning of the 27th. 3 Stirling machine guns were drawn from the Police Depot by another Police Officer taking part, with instructions that no record should be made of the fact. 12 Stirling machine guns were drawn by the Commanding Officer of an Army Unit, who participated in the coup, also on the morning of the date of the coup, and these guns were returned by him the following Monday, after the coup had failed. Records show that the following arms and the following quantities of ammunition were available to Army Units on the 27th:-

Army Unit	Arms		Ammunition	
2(V) L.A.A. Regt. C.A. ..	Bren Guns ..	6	.22..	1,229
	Stirling Guns ..	4	.38..	380
	Sten Guns ..	13	.303..	15,000
	.303 Rifles ..	370	9mm..	2,951
	.38 Pistols ..	30		
	.22 Rifles ..	4		
2 (V) Fd. Pl. Regt. C.E. ..	Bren Guns ..	16	.22..	1,002
	Stirling Guns ..	14	.38..	608
	Sten Guns ..	28	.303..	9,220
	.303 Rifles ..	315	9mm..	3,824
	.38 Pistols ..	20		
3rd Field Regt. C.A. ..	Bren Guns ..	10	.22..	3,825
	Stirling Guns ..	6	.38..	176
	Sten Guns ..	36	.303..	11.249
	.303 Rifles ..	477	9mm..	9,320
	.38 Pistols ..	20		
2 (V) C.S.C. ..	Bren Guns ..	2	.38..	66
	Sten Guns ..	19	.303..	4,301
	.303 Rifles ..	154	9mm..	1,120
	.38 Pistols ..	11		
	.22 Rifles ..	2		

Ladders for the purpose of scaling balconies were also obtained from the Training School and kept in readiness for the coup.

Investigations have so far revealed the identity of the Police and Army Officers to whom certain tasks had been assigned by the Coup leaders for the night of the 27th of January. The persons who were expected to make the arrests of Mr F. R. D. Bandaranaike, Mr M. W. F. Abeykoon, Mr S. A. Dissanayake, Mr John Attygalle and Commodore R. Kadirgamar are known. So also, the names of the persons who were to restrain Major-General Wijekoon and Air Vice-Marshall Barker in their respective houses, are known. The names of the men from the Detective Agency run by Mr Sidney de Zoysa, all of whom are retired Police Officers, to whom were assigned the tasks of watching the houses of some of the persons to be arrested and of noting the people who entered and left those premises, are known. The names of the persons to whom were assigned the task of immobilising the telephone exchanges, of taking over the newspaper buildings, and of making certain deployments are known. The names of the officers of the Army and Police to whom were assigned the task of identifying and admitting to Army Headquarters, the police parties and prisoners brought there for incarceration in the Ammunition Magazine and the name of the officer, whose function it was to seal off the office of the C.I.D. are known.

The Object of the Coup

The whole purpose of the Coup was undoubtedly to overthrow the Government on the night of the 27th of January. Investigations have not so far, however, revealed the whole of the plot. Mr C. C. Dissanayake had told one of his subordinates on the morning of the 27th and on the previous day, that a large organisation was behind the move to overthrow the Government, that certain political leaders were in the know of it, and that persons even higher than that were in it. He had also told two of his officers who participated in the coup, that after they made the arrest assigned to them and taken their prisoner to Army Headquarters, they should thereafter report to Queen's House, and that they would "make no mistake as to whom they should report." A Police Officer whose statement was recorded said that he had been told by one of the leaders of the Coup that Sir John Kotelawala and Mr Dudley Senanayake were in the know of the plan to overthrow the Government. In fact 3 officers said so.

Mr Sidney de Zoysa told some of the officers to whom he assigned tasks in connection with the coup, that he, Mr C. C. Dissanayake, Mr. Royce de Mel and a number of army officers had planned the Coup to overthrow the Government and to take over with the Governor-General as head. He said that Mr C. C. Dissanayake and himself, both in uniform, would go into Police Headquarters and take over, and later on in the night, he and some Army officers would go into Queen's House. His plan as put to these officers, contemplated the forcible dissolution of Parliament, and the suspension of the Constitution "by getting the Governor-General to sign on the dotted line."

Colonel Maurice de Mel, speaking to one of the officers who was to participate in the Coup, about four days prior to the 27th of January, said that orders for the Coup were being given "from the top." The officer to whom Colonel de Mel was speaking, understood by this, that the orders for the Coup had come from Queen's House.

On the morning of the 27th of January, Colonel F. C. de Saram, put it to another military officer who participated in the Coup, that orders has been received "from the highest level" and asked the officer whether he would be willing to help. Earlier, on the night of the 26th, Colonel de Saram outlined the plan for the Coup to three officers who were to take part in it. He said that the plan was not actuated by selfish motives, but by patriotic motives, and that in the first instance, a military dictatorship would have to be set up, to be replaced soon afterwards by a Government consisting of "selected people", whose names he did not disclose.

When questioned on the afternoon of Sunday, the 28th of January in the course of the investigation, Colonel de Saram decided "to take the rap" for the whole affair. He claimed that he alone was responsible for the attempted Coup, and that everyone else who had played any part in it, had done so on his orders. According to Colonel de Saram the plan for the Coup, besides the arrest of leftists, envisaged only the arrest of Mr F. R. D. Bandaranaike and Mr N. Q. Dias, because in his view, they were the only persons 'who could give lawful and effective orders to the Service Commanders, so as to frustrate the Coup; and possibly Mr S. A. Dissanayake, whom he thought was "potentially dangerous." After Mr F. R. D. Bandaranaike and Mr N. Q. Dias had been imprisoned in the Ammunition Magazine at Army Headquarters, he intended to go at once to Queen's House, and to "co-erce" the Governor-General to take over the Government. The Governor-General he emphasised had nothing to do with the Coup. He admitted that a military dictatorship would not work for any length of time, and that the whole of his scheme depended upon the Governor-General. He said he had taken no steps to ascertain the views of the Governor-General in advance, although he realised that the whole of his plan depended upon the Governor-General. He admitted also that he had no clear plan as to what he should do, if the Governor-General did not act as he had hoped.

There were several questions to which Colonel de Saram declined to give an answer in the course of investigation.

The Governor-General has been informed of the fact that his name has been mentioned in the course of the investigation, and he has volunteered to submit himself to interrogation and investigation like any other citizen, and enquiries are now proceeding accordingly.

The Events of the Coup

Four or five days prior to the 27th of January, Mr C. C. Dissanayake, D.I.G., Range I, gave instructions to one of his officers that the men in the stations under his charge should be rehearsed in their "take post" orders and that he should hold sten-gun practices. Police officers also worked out a plan to seal off the entrances and exits from Colombo city so as to prevent vehicles within the area from moving out of it. This exercise was practised on the 16th of January, 1962, and was labelled "Operation Runaway."

On the 26th of January in the evening, Mr C. C. Dissanayake also instructed that a conference of many gazetted officers be called for the following evening at 6 p.m. at the office of the S.P. Colombo.

On the 27th morning, Mr C. C. Dissanayake met various gazetted officers of his Range, as well as others at his office and gave them certain instructions. He told two of them that there was a plan to take over the Government some time after midnight that day, and that they were being assigned the task of arresting the Navy Commander, Mr Rajan Kadirgamar, to whom was assigned the code name "Commo." This task had to be performed after the Navy Commander had retired to bed, for which the code was "After Commo had roosted." They were required to report at specified times on the movements of the Navy Commander and to have in readiness Police parties of certain strengths to effect the arrests at the proper time. They were told that the code name for the whole operation was "Holdfast," and when the arrest was made, the Navy Commander was to be taken to Army Headquarters, and that they should thereafter report to Queen's House. The password for admission to Army Headquaters that night was to be "Yathura." One of these officers was also required to send 15 armed motor cyclists to Torrington Square to be near the tar barrels by about 11 p.m. He was also required to have a covered lorry standing by. Later on, Mr Dissanayake saw a very Senior Police Officer at his office, and instructed him to contact a certain Army Officer and to arrange for both of them to be at the entrance to Army Headquarters by about midnight. His function was in cases of doubt to identify the Police Officers who would bring in prisoners to Army Headquarters that night. Mr Douglas Liyanage, C.C.S., Deputy Director of Land Development, also visited Mr C. C. Dissanayake in his office that morning. Mr Dissanayake also met the Gazetted Police Officers of Western Province (Central). He told them that an operation would be launched that night for the arrest of "Leftists," "Troublemakers" and "disruptive elements," and mentioned certain names of persons to be arrested by them. On that occasion, he also said that the house of Col. Richard Udugama should be kept under surveillance. He also met some outstation Police Officers that morning.

At 6 p.m. on the evening of Saturday the 27th, the Gazetted Officers of Colombo Division assembled at the office of the S.P. Colombo. Two other Gazetted Officers were also present, although not within Range I, on special instructions from Mr C. C. Dissanayake. Mr C. C. Dissanayake came to the conference a little late and dismissed the assembled officers in batches. He made some remarks about one of his senior officers having been tracked down by C.I.D. Inspectors. Two of the last officers to be dismissed were told by Mr C. C. Dissanayake that they would be required to take armed police parties of specified strength from the Depot and to prevent the Army Commander, Major General Wijekoon, and Air Vice-Marshall Barker from leaving their residence after 12.15 a.m. Another officer was detailed to surround the C.I.D. from about the same time.

Mr Dissanayake had also ordered one of his officers to be the duty officer at Police Headquarters on the 27th of January from 9 p.m. onwards instead of Mr V. T. Dickman, A.S.P., C.I.D.

After the conference at the office of the S.P. Colombo was over, Mr C.C. Dissanayake met several officers participating in the Coup from time to time either at his own house or at the house of Mr B. Johnpillai A.S.P. (Traffic) who lived next door. While at the house of Mr Johnpillai, Mr C. C. Dissanayake received a telephone call from Mr Sidney de Zoysa. Mr C. C. Dissanayake also took a senior Police Officer with him that night to a house at Wellawatte where he met the following persons:-

1. Mr Royce de Mel,
2. Col. F. C. de Saram,
3. Mr Sidney de Zoysa, and
4. Col. Maurice de Mel.

Late in the night Mr C. C. Dissanayake left his house for a while and on his return he instructed his subordinates that the whole plan was off.

There is a great deal of material to show that in many of the Police Stations under the authority of the officers to whom Mr C. C. Dissanayake had given instructions, everything was in readiness to carry into immediate effect the execution of the Coup on receiving a message. For instance, at Mirihane Police Station, men were standing by on duty from 11 p.m. onwards on 27.1.62 till the following morning. Then again, at Kohuwela, the Sub-Inspector was on stand-by duty at the station with 7 men till morning. At the Mount Lavinia Police station, an Inspector was ordered to check on the movements of a certain Government M.P. and the tanks of all Police vehicles were filled with petrol and required to stand by at 11 p.m. In many other stations parties of men were on stand-by duty until shortly after midnight. At Homagama District, in 6 of the 7 stations, Police parties on stand-by were armed and ready for special duty. In several Colombo Division Police

Stations special instructions were issued to the officers in charge to have large bodies of men armed and ready to go out that night.

In fact shortly before midnight several senior police officers moved to their posts in order to carry out the assignments given to them by Mr C. C. Dissanayake.

On 29th January, on instructions of D.I.G., C.I.D., the office of Mr C. C. Dissanayake, D.I.G. Range I, was searched and it was found that the waste paper basket had been emptied that morning. C.I.D. Officers were able to recover the contents of the waste paper basket from the incinerator where they had been deposited. Some of the documents in the writing of Mr C. C. Dissanayake afford ample corroboration of the abortive Coup d'etat. In these documents, there is reference to the protective custody of Ministers and a proposed curfew.

Apart from the Police Officers who received their instructions in relation to the Coup given by Mr C. C. Dissanayake, there were other Police Officers who participated in this affair on instructions received from Mr Sidney de Zoysa, retired Deputy I.G.P., now employed by the Times of Ceylon as Circulation Manager. He was also running a private detective agency. On 23rd January, Mr Sidney de Zoysa applied for leave from Mr Felix Goonewardene of the Times of Ceylon Ltd., for 5 days on "urgent private business." On the 25th afternoon he was travelling down South in his car accompanied by his wife, when he called at the Police Training School, and left a message with an officer that he would be calling that night at a certain house in the Training School, and that he would like to meet him and two other officers while he was there. Mr Sidney de Zoysa called that night at the Training School and while he was there, he saw these Police officers. He called upon these officers to assist him by making available the ladders, arms, ammunition and men from the Police Training School for the Coup, and he called for the active participation of two of them, whom he detailed to make certain arrests. He threatened these officers that if they breathed a word of the plot, they would be killed. While Mr de Zoysa was at the house in the Training School, he put through four telephone calls to certain senior outstation Police officers. He spoke on the telephone to one of them and said that he would meet him on the following day.

Acting on his instructions, these officers in the Training School sent ladders and ammunition to Colombo on 27th January, but they did not send arms or men. On the 26th, two of these officers saw Mr Sidney de Zoysa twice in Colombo, at Mr de Zoysa's flat near the Empire Theatre, and were instructed to come the following night armed and ready with a party of men to take part in the Coup. One of them was given some letters forged in his presence, for delivery, and a document which was to be shown to

Mr V. E. Perera, S.P., Southern Province (West), and to Mr David Thambyah, S.P., Southern Province (East). One of the letters was addressed to Mr V. E. Perera, S.P., Southern Province (West). That officer was asked to go down that very night and to meet Mr V. E. Perera and Mr David Thambyah. He did so after returning to the Police Training School and having his dinner. One of the things that Mr V. E. Perera had to attend to on the night of 27th January was the arrest of Mr Neale de Alwis, M.P. for Baddegama. Mr David Thambyah had to arrest the Honourable Minister for Local Government and Housing and some others. In the course of that trip, the officer also made arrangements for other Police Officers and men to be sent from the Southern Province to the Police Training School to accompany him to Colombo for the Coup the following day.

On the 26th morning Mr Sidney de Zoysa travelled up-country by car and met a senior police officer by appointment. He made inquiries from him about a certain person, and he also inquired whether Col. Roy Jayatilleke was at Diyatalawa or on leave. On the 27th morning Mr Sidney de Zoysa called a conference of his men employed at the Detective Agency, all of whom were retired Police Officers. At that meeting no instructions were given, but the employees of the Agency were required to meet again at the office at about 8 p.m. When the Detective Agency employees met that night, four of them were given assignments to watch the houses of four of the persons to be arrested that night. Mr Sidney de Zoysa went from his house to Sakvithi Lane, Thimbirigasyaya and left certain police officers in the company of Mr Berry Jackson, Mr Sidney de Zoysa's brother-in-law and another person. He said that he would call back for them when it was time for action. The other officers who had come from down South were left in a neighbouring house close by. Mr Sidney de Zoysa also went to the Police Officers' Mess at Brownrigg Road where he met some officers including Mr B. Johnpillai from whom he made inquiries regarding the whereabouts of Mr C. C. Dissanayake. On being told, he promised to ring up Mr C. C. Dissanayake at the house of Mr Johnpillai in a short while. Mr Sidney de Zoysa said that he was concerned to know whether the plan would have to be called off in consequence of the C.I.D. having discovered their plans. He was particularly concerned because he said that he would have to inform the Army Officers. Later on the same night Mr Sidney de Zoysa and Mr Berry Jackson picked up all the employees of the Detective Agency who had been posted to watch the several houses of the persons to be arrested presumably after the plan was called off. In pursuance of the instructions to Mr V. E. Perera, S.P., West, Mr Neal de Alwis, M.P. for Baddegama was in fact arrested on the night of 27th January, by an armed police party and was taken to the Galle Police Station.

did most of the talking which was quite informal. The officers taking part were informed that the Coup was "on." It was remarked that Mr Sidney de Zoysa had gone round the Provinces to harness police support, and also that the D.I.G., C.I.D. and Mr Attygalle seemed to have got wise to the plan. The meeting did not last very long and there was no briefing. All the officers were in civil clothes excepting one or two. Col. de Saram asked everybody to rendezvous on the beach at the end of Kinross Avenue by about 8.30 p.m. Shortly after 8.30 p.m. these same officers, with the exception of Mr Royce de Mel, met at Kinross Avenue as directed. Col. de Saram and Col. de Mel briefed the officers on their assigned tasks in connection with the Coup. The code name for the operation was given as "Hold Fast" and every officer was asked to await a signal by that name. "H" hour at which the operation was timed was to be notified to the officers taking part with five hours added to the proper time. The password was given as "Yathura". From "H" hour onwards, the officers taking part in the Coup were expected to report back to Queen's House. Every officer was asked to remain at his unit location because it was not intended that the operation should be put into effect until the persons to be arrested had retired to bed. All officers excepting one or two attended this meeting in civil clothes, but they were required to be in uniform for the actual Coup itself. The officers dispersed after the meeting and went back to their units and awaited a signal. They were later informed that the operation was off.

In certain Regiments stand-by Platoons were ready in case a signal was received from Col. de Saram or Col. de Mel, to go ahead with the Coup.

The Government Attitude to the Coup

The Government takes a very serious view of the abortive Coup d'etat on 27th January, 1962. It is a comforting thought that most of the regular units of the Army were unaffected by the spirit of disloyalty that manifested itself among certain officers who have been involved. In the Police too it is fortunate that a large number of loyal officers remain who are capable of giving valuable services to the Government at this critical time. It is particularly satisfying that the majority of the rank and file both in the army and in the police remain completely loyal to the Government and to their country.

The opportunity must not, however, be lost to effect complete and radical reforms in the Police Service, in the Armed Services, and indeed in the Public Services, which this inquiry had revealed to be essential to the nation. Many Army Officers and Police Officers who participated in the Coup have bitterly regretted their action and one Army Officer has committed suicide in consequence of his participation. It is also essential that deterrent punishment of a severe character must be imposed upon all those who are guilty of this attempt to inflict violence and bloodshed on innocent people throughout the country for the pursuit of reactionary aims and objectives. The investigation must proceed to its logical end and the people of this country may rest assured that the Government will do its duty by them.

STATEMENT TO PARLIAMENT IN 1964 ON THE FOREIGN POLICY OF THE GOVERNMENT

The Parliamentary Secretary to the Minister of Defence and External Affairs, Mr Felix R. Dias Bandaranaike, made an announcement on August 19th about the foreign policy of the Ceylon Government when the votes of the Ministry of Defence and External Affairs were taken up in the House during the Committee Stage of the Budget Debate.

Mr. Bandaranaike said:

"Our Government has built its foreign policy basically – I am not referring to questions which directly involve Ceylon in relation to any foreign country, I am referring to general questions as between foreign countries and the attitude of the Ceylon Government – on two foundation stones. One is the policy of non-alignment, and the second is friendship towards all nations. Those two principles may seem right and may seem simple to formulate in that way. But, if we examine them more closely, what does it really mean? It means that Ceylon appreciates her position as a small country...We appreciate that we cannot live in isolation and seek to solve major international questions like a minnow Government among the sharks. We accept the fact of our smallness, and accepting it, what does it mean? We have with us a number of forums, international forums, international associations, international groupings of nations through which we try to express our views, to influence international public opinion, and use our authority and influence, however small it may be, consistently and in a manner which will bring respect for our country and help preserve peace and order throughout the world, and help in the elimination of tensions, war-like propensities, so that we, as an underdeveloped nation, along with others, will be free to grow in a peaceful context in this world. Particularly speaking, these are the associations through which we work. There are the territorial associations, groupings, particularly of the Afro-Asian countries, associations which, I think, started off in a sense with the first Bandung Conference, although I cannot say that we are proud of the contributions which we made at that time ...

Non-Alignment

"Then there is the second grouping which is built on the principle of non-alignment, a group which is not territorial by its nature, not associated geographically, but consists of a group of countries which accept the theory of non-involvement in power blocs, in military alliances like the SEATO, NATO, the Warsaw Pact or any other group of countries, and whose basic principle is to stand for what is right and non-involvement in power blocs or the big groupings of countries. That is the basic principle, and on that have grown an association of countries which accept and adhere to the principle of non-alignment.

"Then, thirdly, there is the forum of the United Nations Assembly, in which, no doubt, we act particularly in association with the Afro-Asian countries, on a geographical grouping, and also in association with the non-aligned countries, and seek to make the impression of our views felt in association with those countries.

"Fourthly, there is an organization or grouping of countries which cuts across all of us at the moment. It is not possible to tie it down either to a geographical grouping or to a principle of acceptance of any definite idea and that is the idea of the Commonwealth. The Commonwealth undoubtedly has undergone a change. I myself had the privilege of attending the Commonwealth Conference from time to time. I had the privilege of attending the Prime Ministers' Conference in 1961 and the Finance Ministers' Conference in 1961 as well as in 1960. At this conference it was clear that the Commonwealth is no longer the organization – if ever it was – in which a few dominant partners of the Commonwealth are in a position to lay down the law and earn implicit obedience or acceptance of their leadership from the small group of countries which have newly emerged to independence. In the old days there used to be the tradition when the Commonwealth communiques were drafted by Great Britain; if there was any sentence which was objected to by anybody that sentence was simply dropped. The result was that the communique drafted in respect of the Commonwealth grew shorter and shorter and became more and more generally phrased until finally, reading this communique, one would begin to realize that the general genius of British diplomacy was to avoid controversy and state their things in the simplest form having avoided all difficulties. See what contrast was there in the Conference of Commonwealth Prime Ministers held in 1964. A very long and detailed communique was issued. I did not have the privilege of attending this conference. In that conference it became equally clear that the drafting proposals or the drafting elements behind the conference have certainly moved away from the British tradition. A great deal of detail has been included, including subjects such as the sharp controversy of Southern Rhodesia; a great deal has been said, and very bluntly, in a language which approximates much closer to the real thinking of the newly developing nations which are now coming forward in the Commonwealth. I do not know how one could really say that the Commonwealth tie becomes an instrument of imperialism. It might have been so sometime ago. I admit that there are countries with military alliances with the West within the Commonwealth, that there are non-aligned countries in the Commonwealth, and that there are countries which have not declared their policies in the Commonwealth in one way or other. Can this organization by its very nature be an instrument of British imperialism for the purpose of continuing colonial subjection within the nations of the Commonwealth? Now our experience shows that the movement is quite in the reverse direction and that the Commonwealth becomes a convenient organization or an association which can be built to become whatever we want it to become. I do not think it is correct any longer to assert that the Commonwealth, that this tie, becomes a bond, a fetter or a chain by which we are tied to any particular thought ...

Practical Case

"Then let us take a practical case. During the recent Commonwealth Prime Ministers' Conference there were some countries which I thought tried to ensure if possible some degree of support for Malaysia in her problems that exist with Indonesia. The problem is there. I will explain it on behalf of the Government of Ceylon in a moment. In the course of the communique some degree of sympathy and support was expressed towards the Government of Malaysia in relation to these problems. Has it in any way prevented the Commonwealth from expressing their views? No, for the reason I said a moment ago. One decision referred to by the Hon. Members of the Opposition during the course of this Debate has been that the Government of Ceylon has been able to adopt the attitude of stating that we will not permit Ceylon ports or Ceylon airports to be used for the transport of strategic war materials to either side by their respective friends or friendly countries for the purposes of continuing or increasing the dangers of actual conflict arising out of the problems in that area. I am not now discussing the actual problems of this confrontation but merely pointing out that the Commonwealth Association has in no way limited the capacity of Ceylon to decide for herself. This Association becomes a useful forum for us to meet a group of countries whose only common ground is that at one time they had the misfortunes of being under British domination as colonies and now have the privilege of emerging into nationhood by a gradual process and remaining on reasonably good terms with their former conquerors. In that situation, I must state that the British Commonwealth Association is something which is capable of becoming a dangerous thing only if that tie is made into a means of continuing colonial subjection or economic colonialism, if I may use that term, which it is not. Ceylon is certainly alive to the need to preserve that independence and not to permit the Commonwealth tie to be so abused. I do not think any Hon. Member of this House can say that the Government of Ceylon lacks the independence or the stature or the capacity to think for itself and to express clear views, although in particular instances we may disagree. I do not think anyone can seriously assert that the continuance of the Commonwealth Association has done any damage to our national interests.

"Questions were raised in regard to Ceylon's attitude to various problems in South-East Asia. Hon. Members have asked questions in regard to our attitude to the problems of North Vietnam. If I may say so, our attitude to the problem can be very clearly stated. So far as the Government of Ceylon is concerned, we deplore the division of Vietnam into two parts, North and South. We deplore the circumstances of cold war tactics and the conflicts in the emergence of South-East Asia from colonialism that led to a division in this way. We appreciate that the group of countries that decided this question at their meeting at Geneva ruled – I do not know whether the word "ruled" is correct – that there should be no foreign forces in Vietnam. And, I must say, the Government of Ceylon does not consider the North Vietnamese to be foreigners in Vietnam. The only foreign forces of which we are aware are the forces of the U.S.A. and the forces of the U.S.A. have been present in South-East Asia contrary to the terms of the Geneva Agreement, which, I believe, the American Government refused to ratify at the time. I entirely agree with the Hon. Member for Bulathsinhala that it is a futile exercise for us to engage in argument about who is the aggressor and who is not the aggressor in North Vietnam.

Foreign Warships

Speaking about foreign warships in international waters, Mr Bandaranaike said:

"I do not know about the technicalities or where you draw the lines across the waters for the purpose of defining territorial waters. But I do not see that the presence of American warships in the Gulf of Tonkin could possibly be conducive to peace in South-East Asia. We deplore the actions of the American Government in relation to North Vietnam, and those are certainly actions which can easily be construed as constituting aggression against the people of a free country, which ought to be free and will be free of military influence from outside in terms of the Geneva Agreement.

"You ask us why we have made no denouncement on this matter. It is precisely because this matter was to be taken up in the United Nations Councils, if possible to be settled in some way. As it was to be taken up at international conferences, I do not know if a private denouncement by any individual country, unilaterally made, could really produce much effect upon this matter. One point of view which has been urged, upon which we can hardly comment, is that recent American actions in Vietnam are inspired or influenced by domestic considerations of policy pertaining to the United States Presidential elections which are now in the offing. It may be so, it may not be so. I do not wish to express an opinion in regard to the internal affairs of another country.

"I must say this. It does seem to us, on behalf of the Government, completely indefensible that the lives and property of the citizens of small countries in South-East Asia should have to be forfeit, or be the penalty, in the struggles that might take place in a perfectly democratic way to determine the future of a big power in the world. Therefore, if in this matter one imagines that the Ceylon Government has no attitude, that it stands aside unconcerned, that it has not moved in this matter, all I can assure you is that we have sought to do more than make plain denouncements. We have sought to make a practical contribution in the councils of the world by using our influences in what we believed to be the right direction, which I am sure all sections of this Honourable House would agree are the right directions as far as this particular question is concerned.

"The question of Ceylon's attitude towards Malaysia in relation to the confrontation with Indonesia at this time has nothing to do with non-alignment. It is covered really, if I may say so, by the second link of the foundation principle I referred to, which is friendship with all nations. We as a country have recognised Malaysia. Indonesia has been recognised by us for a very long time since she achieved independence, and both countries are our friends. They are countries which have diplomatic exchanges with us.

"It is true that Malaysia has decided, rightly or wrongly, in pursuance of her policies, to continue to permit foreign bases on her land. But for that reason alone it will be very difficult for us to do anything beyond exercising pure persuasions, such as they might be, on other countries, against the wisdom of this course of having foreign bases upon one's own soil. We say that it would be completely wrong for us to seek to regard a friendly country as an enemy or to seek to distinguish between our friends because one friend has chosen in pursuance of their own independent policy to permit foreign bases on their soil. In that situation it becomes extremely difficult for us to say to our friends, "Look! You are wrong.""

Friendly Terms

"We think the whole situation is rather unfortunate. As far as the Government of Ceylon is concerned, we would like to see Malaysia and Indonesia on friendly terms once again. We would like to see peoples with ethnic connections in South-East Asia, in the Eastern Archipelago, working together for a common purpose. We would like to see the problems of actual conflict, which seem to threaten particularly parts of North Borneo, coming to an end and a peaceful settlement evolved. We are glad to see that there have been many, efforts made in this direction, particularly by the President of the Philippines who has been acting as a friend for both sides in this matter.

"We do not want to take sides in these matters. We are sympathetic towards Indonesia as a friend. We are sympathetic towards Malaysia as a friend. We agree with Indonesia that it is an unfortunate thing to have foreign bases on one's territory. We disagree with Malaysia that it is a good thing to have foreign bases. But as for this question of Malaysia having foreign bases on her own territory, it surely is a question for Malaysia and not for us.

"In the circumstances I do not think it is fair for the Hon. Second Member for Colombo Central to seek to pillory the foreign policy of this Government by trying to say, "Surely it is carrying non-alignment to absurd limits," or to try to bring non-alignment into this question. It is not non-alignment. It is purely and simply our policy of friendship with all countries.

"Let us see the application of this principle. When the Hon. Prime Minister received a request on behalf of Indonesia for certain military transport planes to be used for military services in Indonesia – that is the basis on which the application was made – when the application was made by the Government of the Soviet Union to fly the planes purchased by the Indonesian Air Force across Pakistan through Karachi and across Ceylon through Katunayake to Medan, and from there to Indonesia, after careful consideration the matter was brought up by the Prime Minister to the Government and it was decided that it would be better to avoid this request because we did not think it a good thing to help either side to receive their military supplies through the territory of Ceylon.

Military Supplies

"The situation is of such a character that the dividing line between a state of war and a state of confrontation can wear extremely thin. Therefore the Ceylon Government adopted the position of saying that we are not going to permit military supplies from any source to proceed through our country, or our country to be made use of to take military supplies or resources, either to

Malaysia or to Indonesia as the case may be or such supplies to be transported over the territory of Ceylon.

"Having explained the position, may I pass on to the next point which is Ceylon's attitude towards various countries which we have been blamed for failing to recognise? I refer to East Germany, North Korea, Algeria and North Vietnam ... Algeria was mentioned by somebody and I wish to take it up right away. It is not correct to say that we have not recognized Algeria; we have in fact recognized Algeria.

"With regard to North Korea, East Germany and North Vietnam, at the moment, I believe we have Consul-General relations with these countries. The principle underlying our policy with regard to this question has been as I have stated before on different occasions also, that we as a country still feel that it is a very unfortunate thing that these countries which were nations and were entitled to nationhood have unfortunately been split in halves as a result of conflicts between power blocs. We, as a Government and as a country, hope to see these countries re-united some day. But the realities of the situation have to be accepted. Therefore, rather than have nothing to do with either side and pretending to ourselves that these countries are not divided, we have adopted the practical course of according to them Consul-General status falling short of complete diplomatic exchanges.

"Our attitude, I admit, is somewhat illogical as far as Germany is concerned. We have admitted that all the time. The reason for that is that prior to our Government coming into office, West Germany was actually accorded diplomatic status by the UNP Government and diplomatic exchanges had already been made before our Government came into office in 1956. In consequence of that, we have not been in a position to apply the same uniform policy that we have applied to the divided countries I referred to. To that extent there is an incongruity in the degree of recognition accorded to West Germany as against the other divided countries of the world to which we have applied this principle quite uniformly and without exception.

"I must refer to one fact in relation to the Consul-General status we have with East Germany. Hon. Members should know and are entitled to know that for a long time some countries objected very strongly – particularly West Germany – to any degree of recognition being accorded to East Germany. We move slowly in these matters.....First of all we established trade relationships; later on we have moved to Consul-General relationship with which the East German Government have expressed themselves as being quite satisfied for the time, and in respect of this matter, I should like to inform Hon. Members of this House that the Ceylon Government took this step notwithstanding the pressures exerted on us by other countries, and it finally concluded with a declaration by the West German Government, the Federal Republic of Germany, that foreign aid for Ceylon would be completely suspended and withdrawn in future, consequent upon our action. I should like to inform Hon. Members that we have proceeded to take this step in the full realization of the consequences that were threatened to us and other consequences which we are likely to face. But I must state for the information of Hon. Members of this House that we have never deviated from what we believe to be correct and proper, as a result of pressures and threats ...

Test Ban Treaty

"On the Partial Nuclear Test Ban Treaty, our attitude is very simple. I stated it last year too. We appreciate that the advance made by the treaty is extremely limited. We appreciate that there are lots of things in regard to which the treaty is incomplete – the possibility of nuclear stockpile is still there, the danger of an outbreak of war is not totally eliminated – and we appreciate the fact that there are smaller countries today like ours who do not have nuclear weapons and who, if they accede to the treaty, will never have nuclear weapons. But all I can state is that every country that wants nuclear weapons, as far as we know, always seems to want them for the purpose of defence, to repel possible aggression, and it is the very danger of their possession, with that objective, that constitutes in itself the threat of war in the future. The United States of America does not claim that she wants nuclear weapons for aggressive purposes; she wants them to defend herself against the possibility of aggression. The Soviet Union does not want nuclear weapons for aggressive purposes; she wants them for the purposes of defence. The People's Republic of China wants nuclear weapons, although she does not have any, for what? Not for aggression; she wants them to defend herself. And every country which wants nuclear weapons wants them with that objective.

"But surely if we want to move forward in regard to disarmament, we want to move towards total and complete disarmament, we have ultimately got to accept one fact: whatever the suspicions, threats, which make countries refuse to accept the *bona fides* of one another, the very motives for which we want nuclear weapons have got to cease to exist. In that way, as far as our country is concerned, we do not hope at any stage to break our Budget to increase our military expenditure by even aspiring for a fraction of a nuclear missile.

"The important question is this. Our front-line of defence, so far as this country is concerned, must be our friendship with other countries and other nations. It must be our diplomacy. That is our front-line of defence. And if we do not accept that position we will also fall into the grave error of the wiser and the larger countries which seem to be spending a very large percentage of their budgets each year on military expenditures. We are proud that our total military budget, our defence budget, including the police force, comes to something like 2 1/2 per cent of our total expenditure – an achievement indeed, as far as our country is concerned. In this matter, at least, we are in a position to set an example to much larger countries than ours ...

Colombo Proposals

"As far as the Colombo Conference Proposals are concerned, I should like to give this House a very short history of what is happening now, of the current situation. I am not going to get involved in arguments about the particular sectors, about the Colombo Proposals, about their merits and demerits who is to blame for the fighting, and who is not to blame.....we will try on behalf of the Government of Ceylon to try to ensure the acceptance of the Colombo Proposals and bring about a final peace settlement by negotiation between the Governments of India and China. In this matter I am glad to inform Hon. Members of the House that the last two statements made by Prime Minister Nehru in the Lok Sabha have certainly shown a somewhat different approach and a willingness towards accepting a slightly modified or slightly softer approach to the whole question.

"In the recent discussion the Prime Minister had with Prime Minister Chou-En-Lai when he was here in Ceylon, the question was discussed and in the course of those discussions various possibilities towards further approaches in this matter were considered and discussed. I think perhaps it is fair to say that the most important question on which the two sides can meet and discuss matters round a table would be the establishment of the basic principles of what they are to discuss. At the time the Colombo Proposals were being formulated as long ago as December, 1962, and January, 1963, the problem was one of consolidating a ceasefire. The ceasefire is now well and truly consolidated not by the effect of the Colombo Proposals directly but because subsequent to the withdrawals the tension has eased. The Colombo Proposals have prevented an immediate outbreak of conflict again. To that extent, they have made a contribution and what remains is the ultimate negotiation of a boundary and, if both sides are agreeable to that, I rather think that it is possible that the Government of China may agree to remove the one last obstacle standing in the way, namely, the withdrawal of the seven posts in the controversial demilitarized sector on the Ladakh side. And I think the Indian Government might be agreeable to settling larger questions than the consolidation of a ceasefire and towards agreeing to meet to settle the final alignment of the boundary on definite principles. I know the

Prime Minister has been making approaches to both sides on this matter. I can assure Hon. Members of this House that she has not finished with this question. She proposes to use her good offices in an endeavour to bring about complete peace in this part of Asia and to ensure that the traditional friendship that has existed for many years between the peoples of China and the peoples of India will be restored once again to normalcy in spite of all the differences that may exist today.

Seventh Fleet

"In regard to the Seventh Fleet, we have already stated our attitude I think it is well known. I do not think it would be correct to say that our attitude is one of stewing in our own righteousness for the reason that the very idea of nuclear free zones being constituted is an idea put forward many times by many people, from the Rapacki Plan of Poland downwards, and the Government of Ceylon certainly proposes at the forthcoming international conferences to place this question in the forefront of the agenda and try to make an attempt to achieve something practical in this regard.

"Hon. Members may also be pleased to know that according to the latest information, the recent African Nations Conference has also approved a similar proposal in regard to the entire continent of Africa, namely, to denuclify, if I may use the term, the entire continent of Africa and perhaps to extend the same concept to the southern half of the Atlantic Ocean.

"I do not propose to deal with the problems of the Voice of America and the Asia Foundation which the Hon. Second Member for Colombo Central this time only mentioned in passing. But I do propose to talk for a few moments on our attitude to South Africa and apartheid since this has been mentioned many times. On this question our attitude to the freedom struggle of the people of Africa has been very clearly stated more than once.

"We deplore racial discrimination in Africa. We deplore the oppression by the South African Government. Indeed it is one of the few governments in modern times which can really and truly be called a dictatorship of the worst and most virulent form, corresponding to fascism in Europe during the Second World War. The people of that country are certainly receiving every practical assistance from all countries which cherish freedom in their onward struggle towards complete emancipation.

South Africa

"The criticism was levelled about our trading with South Africa. We were asked 'Why are you trading with it? Why are you selling tea to them? Why are you importing goods from them?' These questions were raised. And the

Hon. Appointed Member had a further question: "Why are you refraining from voting at some international conferences when the expulsion of South Africa on racial policies is being considered?

"I should like to briefly state the position of the Government of Ceylon on these three matters. The United Nations is considering a number of resolutions towards the theory of trade embargoes being directed at South Africa as a means of enforcing our collective views on apartheid and racial policies of South Africa. The general policy has been the stepping up of the need for collective action in such a way as to make it impossible for South Africa to proceed in her policies, for instance, that strategic materials and military assistance be denied to her. In other words, it is absolutely necessary that the embargoes must be absolutely effective. The imposition of embargoes by countries that have no significant trade as a gesture is not really going to add very much to it. There are a number of countries which have proposed it, some of which have no trade at all with South Africa. But the general principle adopted at the United Nations General Assembly was the need for collective action, and towards that collective action, Ceylon will certainly participate regardless of losses or gains either in respect of tea or imports, if and when such action is taken collectively. But we maintain that it is completely incorrect and wrong for us as a small country to seek to bring South Africa to her knees on racial policy by individual unilateral action which, at most, can be considered gesturewise. We shall express a point of view with all the force at our command, but certainly not in order to make gestures which are ineffective, not in order to make a gesture for the sake of making a gesture. The Ceylon Government will certainly exercise all its authority and power and force in order to bring about a satisfactory imposition of an effective embargo. An embargo, in order to make it an effective embargo, must be applied in respect of goods like oil and armaments by denying them to the Government of South Africa in its move towards oppression.

"In regard to the foreign conferences, the Ceylon Government has never taken the view that the expulsion of South Africa from the councils of the world will constitute an effective measure to bring sense and realism into the minds of the South African Government. It has not been our view that by excluding a country which follows wrong policy, you can influence the thinking of its Government by that means. You may not associate with that country in any association or grouping, territorial or otherwise or in any other form, you may not associate with that country that you do not agree with, but I do not think that excluding her from the councils of the world, U.N. organizations and so on, is going to make the position different.

Indian question

"So far as the Indian question is concerned, I should like to inform Hon. Members of this House that the Hon. Prime Minister proposes to visit India on her way back from the Conference of Non-Aligned Nations in Cairo round about October, and she will be taking up these questions for discussion with Mr Shastri, the Prime Minister of India.

"The Hon. First Member for Colombo South referred to the Defence Agreements. There is a very full statement in the Hansard of the 11th July, 1956, Volume 25, No. 2, column 225 to 234, made by the late Hon. S. W. R. D. Bandaranaike when he was Prime Minister in relation to the takeover of the bases and on the whole question of the Defence Agreements. I do not propose to read it because the statement is too long, but I propose to state very briefly the attitude he took then, which is also the attitude of our Government on the Defence Agreements.

These Defence Agreements were worded substantially in this way:

'The Government of the United Kingdom to base such Naval and Air forces and maintain such land forces as may be requested for the purposes mentioned in (a) as may be mutually agreed to.

The Government of Ceylon will grant to the Government of the United Kingdom all the necessary facilities for objects mentioned in Article 1 as may be mutually agreed to.

The two Governments to establish such administrative machinery as they may agree to, to co-ordinate their defence requirements.'

"In other words, this is an agreement to agree. In other words, it is an agreement between the Government of the United Kingdom and ourselves entered into in 1947, that both parties shall have the power to help each other militarily as may be mutually agreed to, that is, in future. It is really an enabling agreement in that way. And the late Prime Minister in examining this document said, 'As an enabling agreement I have tried hard to find out what further agreements were made between the United National Party Government at that time and the British Government in pursuance of this enabling agreement.' He said further, 'I have been trying to find out under what authority Katunayake and Trincomalee had been handed over to the British and to the British administration.' He said again, 'I can find no authority for it, I can find no such agreement in existence. There is an agreement by which Britain and Ceylon can agree, but have they in point of fact agreed or not?' And the conclusion he came to was that there was no agreement ...

"So far as the Ceylon Government is concerned, the existence of an agreement of this type, an agreement to agree, surely does not contravene the sovereignty of this country or its capacity to determine its own attitude on any international question independent of this agreement. Consider for a moment, are we committed to fight side by side with Britain in any war in which Britain happens to get entangled? No. Is Britain obliged automatically to come to our rescue and to fight for us in any war in which we might become entangled? No. It must depend upon the mutual agreement at the time and there are many occasions on which, subsequent to this agreement, we have taken an independent attitude. Take the Suez question, for instance. Great Britain's attitude on Suez was certainly not in any way condoned or accepted by this Government notwithstanding the existence of this agreement. This agreement has not prevented the Government of Ceylon from exercising its rights, for example, even to the extent of denying to military aircraft and vessels the right of using Ceylon ports.

"In other words, this agreement to agree in future does not in any way tie down or limit the sovereignty of this Government to determine its own future, its own defence policy, its own foreign policy and – what is most important of all – to exercise independent judgement with regard to the rights and wrongs of any particular international situation and to express the will of this country without any fetters or limitations.

"I should like to thank Hon. Members for the kind and patient hearing that they have given me in regard to all these questions."

FOURTEENTH COMMONWEALTH PARLIAMENTARY CONFERENCE – NASSAU, BAHAMAS, NOVEMBER 1968
F. R. Dias Bandaranaike, MP

Ceylon

Mr Chairman, fellow Delegates, as a new boy it gives me great pleasure to have the opportunity to address the Delegates of the Commonwealth Parliamentary Conference. I am particularly grateful to senator McIntyre for having recognized the excellence of Ceylon Tea. I hope he enjoyed the cup of tea as much as the other beverages he enjoyed with his daughter on the occasion of the cocktail party.

Mr Chairman, we have been talking of many things. I was particularly impressed by the request of my good friend on my right, Dr. De Souza, that we should all speak frankly. In this spirit of frankness, I was much taken up with the remarks of Mr Goodhew, of the United Kingdom delegation, that the particular questions we are looking at are really not so important, because, in his view, it seems to us that he was confronted with the bigger ideological question of a dispute between communism on the one side, which he associates with a lack of freedom, dictatorship, and all that goes with it, and, against that, the practice of parliamentary democracy as we know it in the Commonwealth, associated with the right of a free choice between sometimes equally unpleasant alternatives in Houses of Commons or Houses of Representatives.

Now, Mr Chairman, if we are honest and sincere with ourselves in talking of a right of self-determination, of practising parliamentary democracy with all the attributes with Senator Connolly in his opening remarks identified with the Commonwealth recognition of national sovereignty, the unifying influence of a monarchy, the need to recognize, as we all do, the rule of law, the independence of the judiciary, certain common institutions, no doubt varying in content from country to country, it seems to me that when we are talking of communism and capitalism, as Mr Goodhew did a minute ago, we should all recognize the right of people in their own minds to be communists if they want to.

Now, once we start from that point of view, we in Ceylon have a different approach than perhaps to merely express a different point of view by saying that communism is a bad or a good thing, that we do not like it. Frankly I am not a communist; never have been.

Our Governments in Ceylon have changed not by coups d'etat but by free elections more than once in the course of the last 20 years. We have not had a communist Government yet, but we do have Representatives of the people who are communists; not very many. I am proud to say that our Clause 24 Council Member on the CPA, Dr. Perera, who has served this Association with distinction, is a Trotskyite present within this very Assembly; and after you have seen him I think you will agree that he is not really dangerous in any sense to any of you.

Now, Mr Chairman, I would like to tell you this; just as much as we recognize the right of the other fellow to have his point of view, it seems to us that it is wrong to start with the assumption that these two groups in the world, communist and (shall I use the word?) capitalist, not with any overtones of insult but merely as a description, may I say, that these two groups do not seem to us to be in conflict which necessarily has to lead to war or military intervention?

I grant that Vietnam is not a country of the Commonwealth, but should not the people of Vietnam have the right to decide their own affairs just as much as anybody else? Now, it is quite understandable and I do appreciate the juridical basis of the intervention in Vietnam on the part of our friends in the United States of America when they say they were invited there to protect a Government, a Government which felt it was under threat from a communist group in the North. After the Geneva accords, it would be nice to think that the Americans were there by invitation, and I think they were in the first place. But it seems that their hosts have disappeared so many times that one cannot help wondering by what right the guests remain thereafter. It may be that the guests themselves had a hand in changing their hosts around. One does not know. But if this is the argument, one begins to wonder who it is that these people are fighting. Are the Chinese crossing the border, the 700 million communists indoctrinated in China, indoctrinated in the thoughts of Mao Tse-tung contained in the little red book? Are these the thoughts which are fighting American bombers in Vietnam?

We all welcome the action of President Johnson; may be he had good reasons for picking the time for the bombing halt. One does not know. Perhaps it might help. It might not. We shall know on 4th November, but meanwhile if they are calling a halt to the bombing now, and we all welcome it in this Assembly, I do not think anyone stands against the bombing halt.

I would like to ask this: was it necessary to have the bombing all these months, all these years? Could it not have been called off sooner? Was it necessary for so many people to have laid down their lives and died? Young people, not merely the young people in the United States, not to mention the thousands in Vietnam, not even the young people of Australia and New Zealand, members of our own Commonwealth. I appreciate very much the reasons given by the distinguished Delegates, Mr Cramer, and Mr Allen of New Zealand, as to the reasons for the intervention by Australia and New Zealand. Fair enough; but if it is left to the people of Vietnam one can understand that there would be a difference if there were a military intervention by a foreign communist power seeking to impose communism upon people who did not want it. But that to us does not seem to be the question at all.

Indeed, when we talk of the recognition of democracy by the people of South Vietnam, we in Ceylon have had occasion once or twice to be somewhat concerned about the way they treat their own Buddhists in Vietnam.

In 1963 we in Ceylon sponsored a commission from the United Nations to visit South Vietnam and to look into the conditions of oppression which existed there under the Diem regime, one of the hosts of the United States. While the commission was there looking into questions – I do not know whether your representative on the commission had anything to do with it – we found that the host changed once again. Diem ceased to exist along with his influential lady, Madame Nhu.

Now, Mr. Chairman, take the question of Czechoslovakia, which we have been talking about. Here, it seems to me that we seem again to be getting mixed up in cold war politics of another sort. I myself recognize the national sovereignty of any country, whether it is communist or not, to look after its own affairs without foreign interference; and Czechoslovakia has every right to go liberal if it wants to without any interference from the Soviet Union or any other Warsaw Pact country, and we in Ceylon have unequivocally condemned the interference in Czechoslovakia as completely unjustified.

I do think we should all look at the facts of the people of Czechoslovakia. They are still communists, they have not ceased to be communists, they have not become good democrats merely because of the military intervention of the Soviet Union. It should also be noted that the people of Czechoslovakia – their Government still exists under Mr Dubcek – have not invited any assistance from anywhere; may be after the experience of Vietnam they feel it is dangerous to invite guests, but the fact remains that the people of Czechoslovakia still remain communists. They have got their differences, they maintain their national sovereignty and integrity, and they are determined to fight their own battles as far as one can see without giving in an inch; and we are proud of them for that.

Let us all remember that in 1938 when the people of Czechoslovakia had a similar problem, being threatened by fascist Germany at that time, they called for assistance from France and Great Britain and they were offered assistance by the people of the Soviet Union, who even volunteered to cross the national boundaries of Poland in order to come to their assistance.

Now it does seem rather strange that the same spokesmen in the U.K. who sold Czechoslovakia down the river in 1938 are now so concerned about the liberal tendencies being completely stamped upon by the Soviet Union. I see the identical spokesman whom I think functioned as Private Secretary to Mr Neville Chamberlain at Munich being now the leading spokesman for foreign affairs of the Conservative Party of the United Kingdom. Now, I do not object; these are the rights of all of us. One must accept that national questions ultimately determine foreign policy, and certainly in any given question the degree of intervention, the attitude one takes, are all governed by national considerations.

I think the United States is developing very good signs in recognizing now that it is now always possible to be the self-appointed policeman, guarding the rights of the "free world." Sometimes if the free world is left to be naughty entirely on its own it is not quite as naughty as all that, and does not constitute a threat to security at all. Indeed, if the Government of the United States had backed a different man, both in Korea and North Vietnam, at the appropriate times, it may be that the whole of world history for the last 20 years might have been different. It is unfortunate that when picking friends one sometimes does make mistakes; but if one does, perhaps the best thing is not to get involved in a confrontation costing many lives, taking many years to resolve, and ultimately being forced to make a virtue out of a withdrawal and disengage militarily.

If one follows the argument to its logical conclusion, if the war in Vietnam is a necessary war in the defence of freedom for the newly emerging peoples of South-East Asia, as presented by Mr Cramer, then surely we must not stop the bombing, we must continue with the war because of what might happen to the people of South-East Asia in consequence of the disengagement. It would be a major disaster; we might all go communist; we might be infiltrated by the 700 million in China; they might overrun us: So, therefore, if that argument is to be really a meaningful one, should we not stand firmly against the bombing halt and insist on maintaining the freedom we have in Southern Asia?

It is almost really as ludicrous as the argument of logistics in Rhodesia. That has already been adequately dealt with by my colleagues in Africa and I do not propose to dwell on it except to say that they have our firm support. Last time when the UN intervened in the Congo, India sent a very substantial contingent. Ceylon contributed nine soldiers and a military cook. I am afraid our defence budget is one of the smallest in the world, and I do not know how much we can contribute to help you to resolve the problems of Rhodesia; but we shall certainly be willing to try. At least our moral support is with you completely, and we do not believe, as does the distinguished delegate from Lesotho, that Ian Smith should be allowed to continue his own little ways, behaving as he pleases in the face of world opinion.

I myself may not be an African, but I do recognize that, in accordance with the principles enunciated by Senator Connolly, people must indeed be free to make their decisions, to take their decisions in their own countries and stand by them; and certainly it is one thing to wage war against aggression if the Soviet Union decided to go on the rampage or the peoples of the Republic of China decide to go on the rampage. But we see no evidence of this. Indeed sometimes we become extremely aggressive in defence of freedom, and that I think constitutes the greatest danger to world peace in our present times. Thank you.

SUMMARY PROCEEDINGS – ANNUAL MEETING 1961 – IMF
Statement by the Governor for Ceylon
Felix R. Dias Bandaranaike

First of all, I should like to extend my thanks to the Managing Director, his Deputy, and his energetic staff, and to the Board of Executive Directors for the efficient conduct of the business of the fund and for the co-operation extended to Ceylon whenever that co-operation was sought.

In introducing the Annual Report, Mr Jacobsson has referred to the pressures on the two main currencies of international trade, the dollar and the pound sterling. The major cause for concern has been the ever-increasing gap in the growth rate between the developed countries and the underdeveloped countries. This, no doubt, is a problem that must be tackled on many fronts. We saw three years ago that action could be taken to provide a further backing to the reserves available to each member by increasing the resources of the International Monetary Fund. This has been a very useful step for the members as a whole to maintain and expand their trade, but the key problem remains as before, as revealed by the 1961 Report of the Fund, presented to us at this meeting, in its discussion on the position of the primary producing countries, as well as some of the more advanced countries. The export trade of the primary producing countries was helped by the boom in industrial countries, but the fact remains that their current account position has deteriorated – a deterioration by a quantum that exceeded the inflow of capital and economic aid. This, no doubt, is going to be the key problem of this quarter of the second half of this century, and upon its solution will depend the prosperity and happiness of a large part of the world.

We believe the Fund's Executive Board, with the able guidance of Mr Jacobsson, the Managing Director, will work out some practical precedures and changes in the coming months to meet the present situation, the circumstances and origin of which also happen to be debated by economists. These changes may be important, may be useful, and may even be timely to improve the world's trade, and we will all, I hope, share in that expansion of the world's trade; but what is of significance is that recently international organizations, including the Fund, have begun to heed the special balance of payments problems of underdeveloped countries.

The facts are clear that the terms of trade of primary producers *vis-a-vis* industrial countries have deteriorated; the uneven tempo in the expansion of the economies of industrial countries, and the steps they have been obliged to adopt to meet this over the last ten years, added to the quota of troubles of the primary producers and minimized even the aid that has been given; and further planned economic development with any degree of reliance on a substantial export surplus has become hazardous. In this situation, we welcome the statement of the Executive Directors in their Annual Report, which is as follows: "In particular, the primary producing countries ask the industrial countries not to seek solutions for the problems of their farmers, miners, or industrial producers, by means of policies that transfer the weight of adjustment onto the economically weaker producers in the other countries. The strength and wealth of the industrial countries should be used not only to give economic aid to the countries with lower per capita incomes, but also to absorb more readily the growing diversity of their products."

While welcoming such a statement, it would be natural for the primary producing countries to expect that consideration be given to a more positive role by the Fund in the matter of giving its assistance to the underdeveloped countries where the reserves problem has to be contended with in any scheme of worthwhile development.

Today, the peoples of the world will not stay quietly just watching their unused resources while the countries around them, particularly those with planned economies, go racing past to achieve levels of growth unheard of before.

We welcome the suggestions made by our Managing Director to increase the resources of the Fund by close consultation with the countries that are able to release such resources, and certainly there are such countries today. But even so, the question still remains whether, with the low quotas of the less developed countries that need assistance and with the strict Fund policies on each segment of the quota to be drawn after the initial gold tranche, there is very great hope for rapid economic development for the small countries.

It is a highly debatable theory, whether the mere improvement of the economies of the industrialized countries, with or without the assistance of Fund drawings, is bound to lead to the employment of the large unutilized resources of the less developed countries and the consequent increase in their trade. We can only hope it will, but there certainly seems to be no assurance from past experience that this will happen. Since the Fund management appears to put its faith on this happening, i.e., the simultaneous development of trade or assistance for development of trade in the less developed countries, let us hope that the Fund will through its "consultations" and other procedures secure through the industrially advanced countries a degree of expansion that will stimulate the trade and payments position of the less developed countries.

It is often said here that a country must mobilize its own resources in looking for assistance from outside. We have raised taxes on many sources and have extended the tax net wider and wider; we frequently mop up all savings available by the issue of public loans, which, I must say, have always been well supported by institutional and other investors, and we have taken other measures in the field of credit and consumption; but the assistance we get from external sources is just a mere fraction of our requirements to maintain a steady and expanding rate of economic growth.

I think a few words on the balance of payments problems of the underdeveloped countries deserve to be said in this gathering. It is clear, of course, that the development programs of underdeveloped countries now are not disjointed, haphazard adventures. They stem from planning of one type or another and have as their base the social and political philosophy of the mass of the enfranchised people who return the members of their choice to Parliament. Thus, the programs of these countries are varied, but the objective is clear, namely, a continuous improvement in the social and living standards of the people. Such an achievement is not possible on the type of "stop-go" policy which industrial countries have been in the past compelled by circumstances to follow. It is also not possible for those economies to live and prosper in isolation. While the causes of balance of payments deficits in underdeveloped countries are many, one stands out prominently, namely, the shortage of external development finance and the compelling tendency to proceed continuously with development programs even at the risk of inflation.

Now we all know the Fund does not like this, but the remedy is also partly with the Fund, namely, consideration on a broad front of policies to meet the problem of inadequacy of reserves of all countries, whether industrial or primary producing countries.

As you will have seen from the Fund Report, from the many speeches of the representatives of the industrially advanced countries, and from the not so few speeches of those from the less advanced countries, all of us, including the Fund, have problems; but there is no reason why with proper co-operation, which is the *sine qua non* of this international institution, these problems could not at least be alleviated, if not even solved, to the material satisfaction of all concerned.

SUMMARY PROCEEDINGS – ANNUAL MEETING 1975 – IMF
Statement by the Governor of the Fund and Bank for Sri Lanka
Felix R. Dias Bandaranaike

I have, I believe, the unusual distinction of being appointed to function as a Governor of this august body only after the commencement of the World Bank and International Monetary Fund meetings this year. And to the extent that I am approximately one day old. I am perhaps the youngest of the Governors present here. And I claim your indulgence, therefore, if I do not read from a prepared text, but speak to you instead on the international monetary situation as I see it, using the language of politics rather than the language of economics, which I think would perhaps be more relevant to the purposes for which we are gathered here today.

I am a new boy in one sense, but I did have the privilege of addressing this same august assembly as long ago as 1961 in my capacity as Minister of Finance of Sri Lanka at that time also. That was in Vienna …

The changes that I see are perhaps typified in regard to approach and attitude.

In those days, every country was essentially preoccupied with its own national interests, with questions of its own sovereignty and trying to see what we could get for ourselves, with preserving our own national interests – our own objectives, and with making certain that we were able to get the best we could for ourselves, to develop but, at the same time, without too much consideration and care perhaps to how we affected others.

Today that has changed very substantially.

In all the speeches I have been listening to over the last few days, it has become very apparent that today there is a fundamental change of mood, of attitude. There is today emerging the will to co-operate among nations, not on the basis of self-interest, not on the basis of saying "I don't care what happens elsewhere, I am only interested in our own personal future, our own currency, our own stability, and our own future." We are now concerned with generating a genuine will to co-operate.

This is manifest today in the speeches which we have heard – encouraging speeches – from some of the developed countries.

I was present in New York when Mr Moynihan read the speech of Dr. Kissinger at the United Nations General Assembly Special Session. I have also read through carefully the statement of Secretary Simon.

As far as I can see, there is much in that that contains what could be new initiatives, new initiatives of great value, which certainly shows that there is much that can be done if there is indeed the will to do it.

Now, I am not saying that I am in a position to make a comment straightaway in regard to our attitude to those initiatives. We cannot. Not merely because I am a new boy, but for other reasons.

The first reason would be that many of those things leave questions in our minds to which we really cannot see the answers straightaway.

I am not saying that the formulation is inaccurate or wrong. It is merely that the questions themselves would depend upon the actual concrete proposals that emerge when the detailed proposals are placed before the governing bodies of the Fund and of the Bank. And until that is done, this question still remains.

But in a perfect spirit of co-operation, we, as a developing country, would be quite prepared to go into these questions, to raise those questions ourselves, to await the answers with considerable interest, hopeful that the new approach and the new attitude will pay off.

Now, how did all this happen? Why did this change of attitude take place?

We in the developing world see it directly as the effort of the Third World countries, the developing countries, in a spirit of disenchantment, to take control of their own economies in the hope of being able to solve our problems. It was spearheaded by the OPEC countries in 1973 when they took control of their own resources and put up the prices of oil. It has resulted in bringing dramatically to the attention of the whole world the desperate needs of developing countries who can no longer be satisfied with statements made in UNCTAD or the United Nations or in other international forums, seeking solace, seeking solutions, when none are forthcoming over the years.

Now, Sri Lanka is in a difficult situation here. We happen to be one of the worst affected countries in consequence of the oil price increase. In economic terms, it has affected very badly indeed our own development programs and plans for the future. Many of these things had to be shelved. We are desperately short of finance for these very purposes. And yet we had to think carefully about what we were going to do in regard to the attitude we were going to express on these questions.

I believe, by the classic definition. We are one of the most seriously affected nations in this category.

We take the view that while it has hurt us in a literal sense. The OPEC countries have nevertheless achieved a great deal for the whole of the Third World by focusing attention upon a basic fact of international existence – the interdependence between countries. And we see in the present will to co-operate a logical extension of many things which we have fought for and sought to achieve in the non-aligned world, to which we belong, in the Third World, in the United Nations and its related agencies, and we see in this great hope for the future. And we are very glad indeed to find particularly the distinguished representatives of France and the United States making responses which could mark a new beginning and a fresh start.

A fresh beginning is important, indeed, for the reason that there have been many mistakes in the past which we ourselves have got to admit – mistakes on our part, as individual nations. We in Sri Lanka are not without our quota of mistakes. We have indeed made mistakes. But then so have many others. The developing countries have made mistakes in not perhaps being as responsive and appreciative that mere protection of one's own interests is not always the way to a prosperous world, the way to create an international economic order which is meaningful, purposive, for the good of humanity, and indeed for everybody.

I think everybody now has come to realize that our futures are interlinked in a manner in which it is not possible for anybody to look at it in any other way.

Now, in this situation I think the most practical approach to it is to forget the mistakes of the past, not to engage in recriminations, not say, "Well, perhaps if the other country had not made this mistake we wouldn't be in this situation today," or to start arguments in regard to who was right or who was wrong.

And when I talk of mistakes, I do not only refer to mistakes of individual nations. I also refer to mistakes of the international institutions themselves. I think the World Bank and the International Monetary Fund are also not without their quota of mistakes in the past. And perhaps a fresh look, a new beginning, with a will to co-operate could mark the real victory of what started in Bretton Woods.

Now, I myself would like to add a few words in regard to the World Bank and the International Monetary Fund as we see it.

I think most of our countries from time to time receive missions which come to examine economic progress in our nations, how we are faring, what is being done, the policy lines being followed, how creditworthy we are, to make assessments of the progress, our gross national products, things of that sort, all of which are very relevant to the future.

I wonder how often it happens that the World Bank and the International Monetary Fund stop for a moment to give thought to how these institutions appear to the people in the developing countries themselves. It is not really what the World Bank thinks of us alone that matters. And here I am not referring to governments and ministers, the elite with whom they deal. I am talking of the people, the ordinary people in the countries with which these institutions deal, and what kind of a reaction and feeling does it really generate?

As far as the ordinary people in the countries like Sri Lanka are concerned, the World Bank and International Monetary Fund are names that they have heard. They have never seen these places. They don't know the men who work in them. They may not even know their names. They know of those institutions. May be they consider them a cornucopia with plenty of money, in whatever currencies, capable of giving assistance.

But in real terms the image is something like this.

Whenever unpopular decisions have to be taken, difficult decisions have to be taken, very often decisions have to be taken to correct economic imbalances and set right the economies of particular countries – very often they see the decisions are taken in times of difficulty, in times when living conditions are tough, not through anybody's fault, in times of drought, in times of near starvation, in times of famine, in times of rapid price increases, in times of galloping inflation. And yet action has to be taken to correct these things. Nobody denies it. It has got to be done.

But when they consider that as the price of help, the World Bank becomes the arbiter, or the Fund becomes the arbiter of policies which are not always easy to follow. And they do not regard it as something which does anything more than add to their immediate burdens, without realizing the advantages of what is in store for them. There could be difficulties in evaluation and working out practical ways and means. But these things have to be done. And, let's face it, the developing countries are not interested in following incorrect or unrealistic policies. No country is. It is only the following of correct policies that can ultimately lead to prosperity and to the development of countries. And if this is to happen, I think I would be right in saying that ministers and governors in all our developing countries are anxious to develop our countries by our own efforts, to take the correct action, to do what has to be done in the interests not only of our own countries but of self-interest.

We want it for ourselves. We believe that it is only by following correct policies that we can really make our countries go. And for that purpose, we want to do it. Not because we are in a difficult situation and have to seek temporary accommodations or assistance. We want to set our economies right. And that is fundamental to the exercise.

Sometimes, for circumstances totally beyond our own control, we are not in a position to do it. But even when this happens, it is most unfortunate if these international institutions earn the reputation of being institutions which unrealistically do not take into account the prevailing circumstances in the kind of conditions which are imposed in particular situations. And this I think is one of the things where these institutions might perhaps consider a public relations job with the peoples of the world – not merely with finance ministers and governors – but in presenting the kind of image which could perhaps give the World Bank and the International Monetary Fund a new role, a new perspective, and a new image.

May I give an illustration of the kind of thing I am thinking about.

Now, we all happen to know that in the matter of food production the United States easily leads the world today. It is the most efficient and economic producer of food, having exportable surpluses in large quantities, merely through good techniques, correct inputs, and utilization of capital resources to that purpose. Supposing the World Bank or the International Monetary Fund were able to think of ways and means of functioning as a catalyst to make sure that some of these resources could be diverted to the lands in the Third World. The lands are there. The fertility is there. The labour capacity is there. And the capacity to produce food is there. Perhaps the many millions throughout the world need not go hungry.

In Sri Lanka, we have a tradition of having changed governments five times by peaceful elections since independence, which is about 27 years old. In the last 20 years we have changed governments five times. And without any trauma, in perfectly constitutional forms and manner. And we would like to think that in this framework we have got to live and move, and we cannot think of a better system which we would like to adopt. We like to take control of our own resources, not for any ideological reasons, but only for the reasons that we believe that the national resources of a country will have to be used for the betterment of, and to create social justice and a better life for, our people.

We seek the assistance and understanding of all countries throughout the world. And we are heartened and encouraged by the will to co-operate which we can see around us at this meeting.

I should like to close with particular referene to the last three years. I think we, in Sri Lanka, as indeed many other delegations around this hall, must surely be extremely grateful to the initiatives that Mr McNamara, on behalf of the Bank, has taken during the last three years, and Mr Witteveen in the Fund more recently, particularly in regard to the oil facility.

There has been a far greater realization of what we can achieve in co-operation with one another. And perhaps we are now at the point at which everything that we have worked for over the last few years can now reach fruition. And let us hope that in a spirit of goodwill these things can and will happen.

In conclusion, I should like to thank you once again for having listened to me patiently, though I haven't made a traditional speech in the way I should have done. And I should like to say that when we move forward in Sri Lanka, we hope to do so in co-operation, not merely with the international institutions in which we participate, but in co-operation with every single country in the world and taking account of every single person's problems.

The Indo-Ceylon Talks

At the invitation of the Prime Minister of India, Shri Lal Bahadur Shastri, the Ceylon Premier, Mrs Sirimavo Bandaranaike, visited India from October 22nd to 29th, to discuss the question of persons of Indian origin in Ceylon. She was assisted at the talks by Mr T. B. Illangaratne, Minister of Internal and External Trade and Supply; Mr Felix R. Dias Bandaranaike, Minister of Agriculture, Food and Fisheries and Parliamentary Secretary to the Minister of Defence and External Affairs; Mr H. S. Amerasinghe, High Commissioner for Ceylon in India Mr N. Q. Dias, Permanent Secretary, Ministry of Defence and External Affairs; and other officials.

Mrs Bandaranaike was given a ceremonial send-off at Palam Airport at the conclusion of her eight-day visit to New Delhi. The Indian Prime Minister, Shri Lal Bahadur Shastri, the Indian Minister of External Affairs, Sardar Swaran Singh, and a large number of diplomats and officials were present at the airport.

The Ceylon Prime Minister took the salute and reviewed an inter-services guard of honour. The national anthems of the two countries were played.

Before she emplaned from New Delhi, Mrs Bandaranaike, in a statement to the Press, said that she was happy that after 25 years of effort the two countries had reached a settlement on the Indo-Ceylon problem.

She said: "Although there is still a small area which is not covered by our settlement, I have every confidence that a satisfactory solution will be reached even in regard to that residue and within a very short time.

"We succeeded in effecting a settlement on this occasion because there was a fresh approach to the question. I am most grateful to the Indian Prime Minister, Mr Lal Bahadur Shastri, for the spirit of understanding which contributed significantly to a settlement.

"I wish to express my profound thanks to the Prime Minister and to those Ministers of the Government of India and officials of the Government of India who assisted him in the negotiations for the successful result that has been obtained.

"I deeply appreciate the warm hospitality extended to the members of my party and myself by the Government of India."

Mr Lal Bahadur Shastri said: I am happy that we have arrived at this settlement. It is good both for Ceylon and India. This will further strengthen our bonds of unity. I am indeed thankful to the Prime Minister of Ceylon who decided to come here in order to resolve this outstanding problem between the two countries.

"Although our discussions were long and protracted, we have ultimately come to a satisfactory solution of their problem. I would once again like to thank the Prime Minister of Ceylon and her colleagues."

Joint Communique

At the conclusion of their talks in New Delhi, the Prime Minister of India and Ceylon issued the following joint communique on October 30, 1964:-

"At the invitation of the Prime Minister of India, Shri Lal Bahadur Shastri, the Prime Minister of Ceylon, Her Excellency Mrs Sirimavo Bandaranaike, visited Delhi from the 22nd to the 29th October, 1964. The Prime Minister of Ceylon was accompanied by His Excellency Mr T. B. Illangaratne, Minister of Internal and External Trade and Supply, His excellency Mr Felix Dias Bandaranaike, Minister of Agriculture, Food and Fisheries and Parliamentary Secretary to the Minister of Defence and External Affairs, Mr N. Q. Dias, Permanent Secretary to the Ministry of Defence and External Affairs and other officials of the Government of Ceylon.

"The Prime Minister of Ceylon assisted by His Excellency Mr T. B. Illangaratne, His Excellency Mr Felix Dias Bandaranaike, the High Commissioner for Ceylon in India, His Excellency Mr H. S. Amerasinghe and Mr N. Q. Dias, and other officials of the Government of Ceylon, and the

Prime Minister of India assisted by the Minister of External Affairs, Sardar Swaran Singh, the Minister of Works in the Government of Madras, Shri V. Ramaiah, the Commonwealth Secretary, Shri C. S. Jha, the High Commissioner for India in Ceylon, His Excellency Shri B. K. Kapur, and other officials, held discussions on the outstanding issues relating to the problem of persons of Indian origin in Ceylon.

"The talks were frank and friendly and were held in an atmosphere of mutual understanding. The discussions were characterised by a sincere desire on the part of both Prime Ministers to arrive at a mutually satisfactory, equitable and honourable settlement of the problem, without prejudice to their respective earlier positions.

"In their search for a solution to the problem the two Prime Ministers agreed to a fresh approach to the problem. They reached agreement to the effect that out of 975,000 persons, Ceylon will accept as Ceylon citizens 300,000 and India 525,000 persons. The status of the remaining 150,000 persons of Indian origin in Ceylon was left for determination at a subsequent meeting of the Prime Ministers in Ceylon at an early date. It was agreed that the admission to Ceylon citizenship of the 300,000 persons and the repatriation of the 525,000 persons should be spread over a period of 15 years and that the two processes should keep pace with each other. The text of the Agreement in the form of exchange of letters between the two Prime Ministers is being released separately.

STATEMENT BY THE GOVERNOR OF THE FUND AND BANK FOR SRI LANKA, 1976
Felix R. Dias Bandaranaike

First of all, I should like to take this opportunity to thank the President, the Governor, and the people of the Republic of the Philippines for the warm and generous hospitality extended to all of us and for the excellent arrangements made for the success of this Annual Meeting of the Fund and the Bank. As spokesman for the Group of 77, His Excellency, President Marcos, in presenting the Manila Declaration to UNCTAD IV in Nairobi this year, proposed the adoption of a new economic order embodying universal principles of justice, fair sharing, mutual understanding and co-operation, the protection of the weak, and freedom from the domination of the strong. It is therefore particularly appropriate. I feel, that we should be meeting here, in Manila, to take important positions concerning the Fund and the Bank. I should also like to welcome to our midst our newest members, the Comoros and Vietnam. It is also a matter of singular pleasure for us that we shall be able to welcome very shortly Seychelles, who are present here as observers, and we also look forward in the near future perhaps to the People's Republic of China taking its rightful place as a member of this family of nations in the Fund and the Bank.

The context for our discussion has been set by the addresses we have listened to from Dr. Witteveen and Mr McNamara, whose reports have been objective and sensitive to the problems and the harsh realities of the poorer developing countries like my own.

Dr. Witteveen made the point that, in the immediate aftermath of the oil crisis, it was imperative that payments imbalances should be financed for developing and developed countries alike, in order to prevent the downturn in world economic activity that might have otherwise occurred. Developed countries have, in his view, by and large succeeded in adjusting to a higher import price level in a purely arithmetical sense, with the result that the counterpart of the surplus of oil exporting countries has now turned out to be the deficit of non-oil developing countries. Dr. Witteveen has contended further that the time has come for non-oil developing countries to attempt a process of more rapid adjustment because the continued financing of their deficits could hamper the process of demand management and the control of inflation by developed countries, which is rightly seen as an imperative necessity, if the conditions necessary for steady investment and growth in the world economy are to be established. Dr. Witteveen added that policies aimed at stimulating growth and employment cannot succeed in the long term unless inflation is controlled. In the hard choice between controlling inflation and stimulating growth, the former must take priority. He has recognized at the same time that the process of inflation control in developed countries proceeding simultaneously with more rapid adjustment by developing country economies can cause a slowing down of world economic growth and has prescribed rightly that developed countries should, as an offset to this, undertake a reduction in their barriers to the exports of the developing countries. I myself, would add, indeed, that exchange rate adjustment by developing countries would be stultified unless such export access is available.

No one – least of all the developing countries, committed as they are to a process of collective self-reliance can be said to be owed a living over the longer haul. Development must always be the responsibility of individual countries themselves and they must accept the necessary adjustment disciplines. However, developing countries, for more than a decade, have called for the dismantling of the trade barriers that affect their exports. It would be politically naive to think that such dismantling would be accepted, let alone implemented, in a reasonably short space of time. Moreover, the type of barriers that face the developing countries' exports nowadays are mainly quantitative in character and are more difficult to dismantle. They continue to block the effectiveness of exchange rate changes as a mechanism for balance of payments adjustment through export promotion. If developed countries pursue demand management policies as suggested, in the interest of controlling domestic inflation, at the same time denying export access to developing countries, while the latter are compelled to adjust by means of exchange rate changes, it is virtually certain that world economic activity will slow down, and present pace of recovery from the recession will be halted. If Dr. Witteveen's argument calling upon developing countries to adjust to their oil deficits, rather than to seek financing for them, were to be accepted, then it is imperative that there should be a prior commitment on the part of developed countries to implement immediately and in short order, measures of import liberalization. It is only after this becomes an accomplished fact that orderly adjustment measures taken by developing countries can hope to succeed.

There is a second reason for my cautious attitude toward asking developing countries to adjust in the manner demanded by traditional Fund disciplines. In the case of a developed country, where production capacities are sufficiently diversified to allow a change in relative prices to switch production from domestic consumer needs to exports, exchange rate changes would have a ready impact in correcting payment imbalances. On the other hand, in the case of developing countries, whose economies are relatively more rigid, exchange rate changes take considerably more time to promote investment in new production capacities of the right kind – a case of the lag which the U.S. Secretary of the Treasury, Mr Simon, described as a politician's nightmare.

It was in recognition of these structural differences between developed and developing economies that the IMF instituted the extended Fund facility which sought to provide greater support than is normal from the Fund – and for a longer period – on condition that the recipient country undertakes to implement a sequence of appropriate policies. The fact that only two countries have so far felt able to draw on this facility testifies to its present emptiness, and the Group of 24 has already gone on record as saying that the facility is likely to remain so, unless conditionalities are considerably diminished. The facility has to take account not only of the time-lag between investment in export-oriented industry and the resulting output, but also the complex political realities of developing countries in relation to the timing of corrective actions. The Jamaica communique makes it clear that the "domestic, social and political policies" of developed countries are to be taken account of by the Fund when it comes to surveillance of exchange rate systems; and this happens also when it comes to the mobilization of bilateral facilities and safety nets outside the Fund to support key countries in balance of payments difficulty. No such realism is built into the international institutional framework for dealing with the deficits of developing countries. It is therefore not surprising that developing countries seek to escape the rigors of Fund conditionality by seeking to borrow from commercial and Eurocurrency markets. This would further aggravate the problem of controlling the expansion of international liquidity. The number of countries, however, that have the capacity to borrow in this manner are indeed few.

It is imperative for the Fund to take a more realistic view of the working of the adjustment process of the developing countries by providing developing countries with reasonable access to Fund resources if it is to bring the expansion of global liquidity under IMF control. I am saying this because the practical way for developing countries to accomplish their transition from adjustment to development would be through intelligent recourse to the extended Fund facility. Otherwise, the gains of absolute – and therefore premature – adjustment through the IMF may be bought at the cost of the absolute impoverishment of the poor in developing countries, against which the Bank has very correctly set its face. The bridging finance for the transition from adjustment to development through whatever channels it is provided, be it through the IMF Trust Fund and other facilities or the Fifth IDA Replenishment or increases in the capital stock of the Bank, there must necessarily be better official aid performance from rich countries which have hitherto failed to measure up to expectations.

Developing countries thus have no guarantee of assured access to export markets so as to make exchange rate adjustments worthwhile or feasible. In addition, they are denied, in effect, reasonable access to Fund resources, through the kind of conditionalities now insisted upon, as in the case of the extended Fund facility.

Views are divided today on whether or not world liquidity is adequate. Those who argue that it is excessive – and this argument finds clear support in the prevalence of inflation in developed countries – would be inclined to resist the creation of SDRs. On the other hand, there are those who would argue that there is evidence in today's world economy of reserve stringency, particularly affecting developing countries, to which attention was drawn in Chairman Imady's speech.

Moreover, there is no sense whatever in talking of a system based on SDRs as a principal reserve asset without keeping the SDR alive by continuity in its creation.

A practical way of reconciling these divergent points of view would be to seek an allocation of SDRs where the amounts are not substantial in relation to global liquidity, but are not insubstantial in relation to existing Fund facilities, on a basis where their distribution is weighted much more heavily in favour of developing countries. I would, therefore, endorse the 50 per cent share of additional SDR creation suggested by Mr Imady for developing countries, so that, given the adverse effect of any tightening of Fund conditionality and in the absence of unrestricted access to developed country markets of developing country products, the momentum of world economic activity can be maintained. It is not that one is seeking to undermine the acceptance of adjustment disciplines under Fund auspices. It is simply that, in the absence of a fresh issue of SDRs in the face of the other political realities of the present situation, developing countries will be compelled to adjust in a manner which would result in world economic activity and their own development settling down at a lower level.

The opportunity of making a fresh issue of SDRs, which the situation I have outlined presents, could, in my view, be availed of to breathe life into a concept that surfaced and was indeed endorsed by the non-aligned summit in Colombo. The non-aligned countries being determined to establish a New International Economic Order within the framework of the United Nations, the IMF, and the Bank, thought in terms of the imperative need to bring reserve currencies under control with a view toward eventually establishing a countervailing currency not controlled by any one country but by the international community of nations. The SDR, if it were shorn of the limitations presently affecting its use as a genuine international currency, could serve as such a countervailing currency.

The opportunity of fresh allocations of SDRs at this time could be availed of to give the SDR more of the character of a currency by abandoning the reconstitution provisions, which the Committee of Twenty had already agreed. It seems to me that the ideas put forward by the Governor for Greece, Mr Zolotas, for a multicurrency reserve system could constitute a valuable interim step toward the concept of a countervailing currency or a fully improved SDR.

The recent Colombo summit conference of the non-aligned nations reaffirmed the Manila Declaration and the Heads of States of 86 non-aligned nations formulated their decisions as follows:

The reform of the international monetary system should incorporate a built-in mechanism to promote the flow of real resources from developed to developing countries and necessary measures to maintain the real value of currency reserves of the developing countries. These objectives involve concerted action by the developing countries within the IMF, the Bank and the United Nations system and elsewhere to restructure the present system of monetary and financial arrangements which will *inter alia* provide for a process of balance of payments adjustment and financing that will remove the inequities involved in the present system, reallocate and create international liquidity in ways which will mobilize resources for development, stabilize exchange rates, remove the dominant role of national currencies in international reserves, ensure parity in decision-making as between developed and developing countries and prevent the domination of any single country over decision-making, so that the system becomes more responsive to the needs of developing countries.

I am taking this opportunity to make available to the Governments, the Economic Declaration and Program of Action decided upon at the Colombo summit.

THE RECENT EVENTS IN CEYLON, 1971
The Hon. Felix R. Dias Bandaranaike
(Minister of Public Administration, Local Government and Home Affairs)

The following is the text of a Press Conference handled by the Hon. Felix R. Dias Bandaranaike at the Parliamentary Press Gallery, Ottawa, Canada, on May 31st, 1971. Mr. Bandaranaike was in Ottawa for the Executive Committee Meeting of the Commonwealth Parliamentary Association:-

I came to Canada for the Executive Committee Meeting of the Commonwealth Parliamentary Association. I happen to be the elected regional representative for two years, representing the region of Southern Asia which really means the Commonwealth Parliamentary Association Branches of India, Pakistan and Ceylon. This is really a preparatory meeting for the main conference which is being held in Kuala Lumpur in September this year.

This is the first time I had a chance to visit Canada and I was naturally very pleased to take the opportunity to come here. I also thought it would be helpful if at this time one of our Ministers had a chance to wander around a bit to set right some of the wrong impressions that have been gaining ground in the world, particularly in some of the leading newspapers in London, in some of the papers in the United States of America, some of the impressions I think which have been gathered even in Canada relating to recent events in Ceylon, and, if I did get a chance, to set the record straight. I thought I would take the opportunity to do so. I am very glad to take the opportunity to talk to the Press Club here in Ottawa for that very reason.

Landslide Victory

General Elections were held last in May, 1970, and the party to which I belong, which is the Sri Lanka Freedom Party, in association with two junior partners in the coalition so to speak, the Lanka Sama Samaja Party and the

Communist Party of Ceylon, each of which has got a small number of seats in the Coalition, won a landslide victory. We won approximately 120 seats out of a total of 151. The party to which I belong, Mrs Bandaranaike's party, which is the major partner in the Coalition, won 98 seats. The Sama Samaja Party which is a left-wing Trotskyite party (that is what they claim to be) won about 15 seats and the Communist Party of Ceylon won about 4 or 5 seats. That is more or less the breakdown. We defeated the previous government which held approximately 90 seats in Parliament for the period 1965-1970.

We have a strong healthy democratic tradition in Ceylon by which governments have been changing periodically since independence. Over the last 20 years, we have changed governments five times through peaceful elections and, in the Commonwealth we are probably one of the developing countries which have taken very kindly to democracy and established a very strong healthy democratic tradition. Democracy, of course, has its good points as well as its weaknesses in a developing country. One of the weaknesses is that while you throw everything open to discussion and debate, publish white papers and sessional papers and practically throw open for discussion every single item of reform for public discussion, sounding out opinions everywhere, it is essentially a slow process with letters to the editor being written by everybody who has got an interest in writing these things.

It is, as I said, a slow process and sometimes young people tend to get impatient with this process. I think it happens in every country in the world and Ceylon is no exception to it. We have a high level of literacy in our own languages, of course; in English too we have a relatively high level of literarcy – about 8-12 per cent, in different areas – and many of the young people feel that, notwithstanding changes of government by democratic procedure, the whole process is not moving fast enough or effectively enough to give the people the kind of radical reforms which they feel are necessary.

Now, in the political spectrum in Ceylon, probably Mrs Bandaranaike's party is rated as being a "left-wing" party, but actually it is slightly left of centre and would really, in international terms, qualify I think as a Liberal Democratic Party more than anything else. It would be difficult to classify it as being a Communist party or a left-wing party in the sense in which you would use the term right here in Canada. Many of the reforms which are envisaged are essential reforms. Land reform, as you can well imagine, is an important item in countries like ours. Then again the same sort of controversies which prevail right here in Canada also become important in Ceylon, because of decisions, the hard political decisions between, shall I say, the containment of inflation on the one side and problems of unemployment on the other. This is a difficult nut for any government to crack and decisions have got to be taken according to the political realities which governments are called upon to face. In my own view, in Ceylon there is very little alternative to adopting a policy of controlled inflation, risking that to tackle the pressing problem of unemployment.

Unfortunately, there are considerations which do not apply in Canada which do apply to us, which is the need to conform to standards laid down by international bankers and credit agencies which determine for us the level of inflation which they consider permissible. There is a very hard restraint imposed upon us by world institutions particularly like the World Bank. This leads to the position that, even where Ceylon is in a position to help herself, where we have the materials, the capacities, the wherewithal to go in for a programme of employment in a worthwhile kind of way, for example in regard to communications, housing and infrastructures of one form or another, international agencies fix the limits for us and say "no, you shall not if you want to qualify for international finance." We are not all that self-sufficient that we can do without international finance, but the problem of allowing unemployment to prevail in a country is pretty much the same as in yours, because when you have unemployment you have to fall back on some level of subsidisation. You do it in a direct sense in the form of national assistance; whether it be $80 or $100 in the form of unemployment relief or dole if you like. We give it in the form of food subsidies. We have no direct national assistance, but we subsidise food and we subsidise other services like health and education.

Whole Picture

Some people say that we are running a level of social services which we cannot afford, but actually that is not the whole picture. The picture is that we would be quite happy to cut subsidies if we were free to develop our own economy using rupee finance and using local materials, while we contain the level of imports. That we can do, but this is a debate which we have been having with international agencies over a long time and no government has really succeeded very far in beating this problem.

Our government has done a great deal in regard to unemployment but not sufficient in my personal opinion. We started out with approximately 12,000 graduates who were unemployed in May, 1970, soon after the election. Of them, approximately 9,600 have already been given employment before April this year by the new government. Between 1960 and 1964, when Mrs Bandaranaike was previously in power, we did not have a single unemployed graduate in Ceylon. The unemployment level really rose during the time of the last government and there again it is not their fault. Although

I say it, we did criticize them for it while we were in the opposition, but that I suppose is politics in Ceylon as well as anywhere else. The truth of the matter is that they were stuck with the need to contain inflation according to the requirements of international agencies and that is precisely how it happened. This problem is I suppose the ultimate basis of where our difficulties begin and end – one is the impatience with democracy, and the second is the need for our people to progress and to develop a level of economic activity necessary to meet our problems commensurate with our problems and to find a way of doing it without at the same time disqualifying ourselves for international assistance abroad.

No Strings Attached

International assistance, apart from these multilateral agencies, comes to us in many forms. It comes to us from Canada. Canada is not the biggest aid-giver as far as Ceylon is concerned. It ranks quite low down in the list of aid-givers, but I must say that the people of Ceylon are extremely grateful to the people of Canada, and this has been expressed not only by one Government, but by successive Governments over the years. I have seen this happen periodically and it is perfectly true because Canada is one of the few countries from whom aid is received with absolutely no strings attached. There has been no arm twisting in the United Nations or elsewhere; no requests for support for any particular policy line; she has always left Ceylon free to take her own decisions and the feeling has always grown in Ceylon – although you may not be aware of it here – that in you, in Canada, we have a very disinterested friend.

The policies of the Ceylon Government are sometimes characterised in the world press as being Communist or left-wing. This is highly arguable. I do not really see it in quite that way though I do agree that we are not a traditional capitalist economy, but that is because we cannot afford to be. The capital resources of Ceylon in the present form largely consist of what the British invested in Ceylon, between the years 1830 to 1850. They opened up tea plantations and made their investments at about a shilling an acre at that time. They have drawn the profits and dividends off this for the last 100 years or so and they have probably taken back about 400 times or 500 times the value of their investments over the years. Nobody grumbles; nobody complains; that is fair enough, but it is a question whether we can afford to let them realise the appreciated investment now and carry it away without reducing the country to a level of bankruptcy, and therefore we have been forced in Ceylon to draw a distinction between the investments that were made before 1948 and the investments that were made after 1948.

As far as investments made after 1948 are concerned, we probably give better conditions to foreign investors than many of the countries I know around the world. They get tax holidays for very long periods; many of my friends in Canada have been asking me "Can you really afford it?" But we do, as an incentive, allow these things. They have virtual guarantees against nationalisation, they have been offered treaty terms, Acts of Parliament, all manner of things, to ensure the security which naturally a foreign investor would like to have: international credit guarantees through banking systems, all that is there, but the answer is, we are always told that the climate of investment in Ceylon is all wrong and for no other reason than that we are not prepared to allow the pre-zero British investment running back to the mid-19th century, by way of free repatriation terms. We just cannot afford it. We did allow free repatriation terms from 1948 to 1957 and our experience was that practically all the investment that came in was more than offset by a total draw off of double the amount, which went into the investments of competitors in the tea industry in East Africa. We could not allow our capital and our know-how reserves to be drawn in this manner. No country in the world can afford that and this is the argument on which we are always told that Ceylon is not a very good place for investment and not favourable for private enterprise, but that is not, if I may say so, factually true.

The next matter I should like to mention in this regard is that very often the solutions which we adopt are basically pragmatic. It is difficult to classify it, but you will find Ceylon taking decisions ultimately based on her own self-interest and nothing else. In many respects you will find licences and charters given to foreign industrialists and enterprises to come and establish the kind of enterprises which we find useful. On the other hand there may be refusals to produce commodities which involve very little more than creating captive markets or monopolies for particular people in consumer goods which we may not happen to need. Against that, whenever particular monoplies, and this applies just as much to Ceylonese enterprises as to foreign enterprises, become dangerous from the point of view of the economy, we do not have anti-trust laws, we do not have any special legislation of that kind, but we do take *ad hoc* decisions to deal with them in that way. For example, the only bank that has ever been nationalised in Ceylon was nationalised by me as Minister of Finance in 1961. That was the Bank of Ceylon, but British banks still operate and are still continuing today, though naturally the volume of business they control is probably in the aggregate less than 20 per cent of the total volume of business in Ceylon. The nationalised banks – there are two of them, one was set up by the Government directly and the other was nationalised from private ownership-control, I would say 80 per cent of the total volume of banking business in Ceylon.

Foreign Policy

A third matter that I would like to mention is our foreign policy. Since 1956, when Mr S. W. R. D. Bandaranaike was first elected as Prime Minister of our country, our policy has been one of total non-alignment in world affairs. Non-alignment is sometimes misunderstood in international affairs. Some people in the West tend to regard non-alignment as a feeble excuse for being anti-West, but that is not strictly speaking true. We have maintained our contacts and friendship with all countries and I would particularly refer to the Commonwealth. We may have our own problems, but we speak the same language and we have always found it far easier to deal with our friends in the Commonwealth, whatever our differences, than probably with any other country in the world. Our contacts with the United States of America are excellent and have remained so over the years whatever differences we may have had, but we do not feel that we have been called upon to make a choice between one or the other and we have always felt that our line of defence as a little country lies not in treaties with big powers on one side or the other, but in total and genuine friendship with all sides. I see that Canada seems to be moving, I would not say towards non-alignment but towards multiple-alignments nowadays, and so it seems that may be the policy line which we are adopting is not after all that far different from lines of thinking which seem to be gaining vogue in other parts of the world. We established diplomatic relations with China as long ago as 1957. I think you are now in the process of exchanging your first Ambassadors; and I think each of the Ambassadors is on his way now to his respective destination.

We think that the best proof of the success of non-alignment was found in the recent insurgency we had in Ceylon, where we found the Russians, the Americans, the Chinese, the Indians and Pakistanis, whatever their differences may be among themselves, expressing total solidarity and support for the Government of Ceylon against the insurgents. The insurgents may have been led to believe by their local leaders that they would be supported by either China or Russia, or may be by both of them, on the basis of being ultra left-wing people. The last example we had was when the Chinese solidly came forward, expressing solidarity and support for Mrs Bandaranaike against what Mr Chou En-lai in a message described as ultra-left reactionary insurgents, and backing it up with a loan of Rs. 150 million in convertible foreign exchange repayable over a term of years to be negotiated, which could be as long as Ceylon finds it convenient for repayment purposes.

Commercial Purchase

The Russians have given us equipment for which we have paid. We found it was the cheapest; we have not asked for any Russian pilots nor have we given them any bases. It is merely a commercial purchase of a relatively small amount of equipment. I think it consisted of 5 MIG aircraft, 12 armoured troop carriers and a small quantity of hand grenades and some 2" and 3" mortars. Some people may be wondering why we wanted MIGs at all to fight the insurgents. Well it is quite true we cannot use them to fight terrorists, but it is our coastal deterrent. We cannot afford to have a flotilla of destroyers patrolling the seas around the island. It is more expensive and frankly what we wanted were a few jet fighter bombers, not of any modern quality. The MIG 23 is the latest one. We got MIG 17s and 5 of them were sufficient for our purpose; we did not require a whole squadron. These 5 fighter bombers are things to which our pilots have been able to convert within 48 hours of training. When it came to helicopters, we could have bought them from France or from the U.S.A. or from Britain, but we preferred the Bell Jet Ranger which is the American version merely because our pilots are used to it and will not have to convert at all.

When the insurgent movement happened, we were caught completely off guard. We have been turning swords into ploughshares with a vengeance and our jet provost squadron had been turned into tractors!. For purposes of agricultural development the last Government had decided to cut back on defence. The result was that in the first week we were in a situation where it became rather doubtful as to who was going to run out of ammunition first, the insurgents or the Ceylon Government. I am glad to say that the Commonwealth, particularly the U.K., made arrangements for an immediate shipment of small arms and ammunition from Singapore to Ceylon and that helped very considerably to solve the immediate problems. They also helped to negotiate the purchase of the Bell Jet Rangers from the United States for us and helped us to get the necessary equipment for them.

The actual strength and size of the insurgent movement has been estimated variously in the world press – some as low as 1,500 and some as high as 100,000. The truth is that there were between 5,000 and 7,500 insurgents in the totality as at April, 1971. It is difficult to give exact figures but that is an approximate estimate. Of them, I think it is true to say that they have probably lost about 500-600 in casualties, and approximately 5,000 have surrendered on Mrs Bandaranaike's surrender call under amnesty. The numbers who surrendered have certainly exceeded our expectations, with the result that we have lots of problems in regard to the provision of necessary sanitary facilities and the like to provide for the clearing camps in which they are now. Universities are being used as temporary accommodation pending final rehabilitation plans. That should take place in the next one and a half months and I am in charge of that.

The total numbers remaining now are probably anything between 1,000 and 1,500 in the jungles and in the forests and, rather than unleashing an offensive to destroy these people, we have decided to play it a little more cautiously and wait for lack of supplies and monsoon rains to discourage them a little further. May be they will give up the unequal struggle and come back to sanity and decide to join the mainstream of the country's development, once they realise that their leaders have misled them into the belief that political support was coming from elsewhere.

Basic Economic Problem

Of course, a military solution is not what Mrs Bandaranaike or her Government requires. We quite realise that this particular movement is merely symptomatic of a basic dissatisfaction with a basic economic problem that requires a solution which is that the young people, when they go to school, must feel that there is a life ahead of them, a future to look forward to. So long as they are not quite certain of this, they will wonder where all this is going to lead, unless there are expanded employment opportunities, a resurgent economic situation, new activities, new building programmes, new constructions, new towns, and new cities coming up. What they are looking for is what President Roosevelt did in the United States in 1926, what Hitler and Mussolini did in Gerrmany and Italy, what Stalin did with his first 6-year plan in 1935 in Russia. It is basically the same thing. In economic terms it makes sense whether it happened in the United States or in Russia. It was the decision to risk a measure of inflation, to develop the country and to move ahead. It made sense then and it makes sense to us now. It is not a problem where we can say, in the next few months we expect to be out of the woods. It may be all right for you, I hope it will be, I hope things will turn out well. In Ceylon it will be difficult to think of any alternative to this and so long as the present situation continues, we are stuck with the subsidies and we are stuck with the level of economic life, standards of living, which we happen to have now.

We look forward to better times and think it can be achieved through the democratic process. We do not think it is necessary to throw it away and to embark on situations leading to military dictatorships or to abandon traditions which we consider valuable. The Communist and left-wing parties associated with our Coalition are basically democratic parties; they have come into power by election and not by any other process. They have abandoned the paths of revolution when they joined in coalition with us on a common programme and at the moment they are probably somewhat embarrassed by the fact that they are probably the only left-wing parties in the world who have been at the receiving end of a revolution!. The truth of the matter is that while the programmes envisaged are radical in form and content and substance, it is certainly not a Communist programme leading to a Communist situation. Probably the only other country in the world which has a parallel situation in this part of the world would be the government of Chile, but I do not know sufficient about the programmes there or conditions there. Certainly in agriculture and agrarian reforms, the conditions are not parallel to what exists in Chile, because our need is to maximise our production and to ensure that available land is used to the maximum for the best advantage of everyone and this is something which has to be achieved through a land reform which is not simply a question of saying, "Take it away from the landlords and give it to the tenants." We have already done that in regard to some lands as long ago as 1958 and 1959 but the present situation is one which does call for urgent action and we propose to do something about it.

Quite Normal

Well, I have tried to give you a very brief statement of what the recent events in Ceylon have all been about, but I can assure you that life is quite normal, and tea, rubber and coconut exports have not been interrupted at all, which is important for us, because we have got to live off them. They are our principal sources of foreign exchange. We keep on producing more and more and selling more and more and getting lower and lower prices, as the years go by. The more we produce, the poorer we get.

In Canada, we have had good trading contacts, but our tea still sells through London, and Canada buys from Ceylon the best tea in the world, but only after it gets mixed up with other teas which are not quite so good. When Prime Minister Trudeau visited us early this year and I had the privilege of looking after him in Ceylon during the four days of his stay, we made the practical suggestion to him that it might be a good idea for both our countries if Canada considered buying tea directly from Ceylon and your main private sector food organisations might find it worthwhile. The Canadian housewife would get a cup of tea at a lower price and we in Ceylon could get a slightly higher price if both sides decide to bypass Mincing Lane. It looks as though something is going to happen on those lines. At least we all hope so. The Government of Canada is most responsive and, at this particular time, the Government of Canada has also been very helpful to us in saying that they would like to make a contribution in practical terms to help us with the reconstruction efforts that will be necessary to set right the damage done by the insurrectionists over the last couple of months. Mr Trudeau has already communicated with Mrs Bandaranaike on this subject and Mrs Bandaranaike has gratefully accepted Mr Trudeau's offer on behalf of your country.

I must tell you that all the stories which you have been reading in the papers, the horror stories, are totally false. There are said to have been things like the My Lai massacres going on in Ceylon, which are most unfortunate from our point of view because such things never happened at all. I do not know how it is that a few reporters who had come from Singapore and who had gathered in the Galle Face Hotel, Colombo who had never left Colombo owing to curfew restrictions – I do not know whom they met or whom they discussed matters with – could come up with stories of thousands of bodies floating down the rivers almost like Canadian log jams. These stories are totally false. Stories of people being crucified to trees – there has not been one such instance. All we can say is that we have investigated the few alleged charges and found them to be totally false. There may be others I do not know, but if we do come across any, I can assure you that the law will follow its normal course.

Of course, there have been acts of violence on the part of the terrorists on innocent people supposed to be co-operating with Government Security Forces. These stories never seem to have hit the world press – of people, civilians, being cut to pieces, of being burnt in kerosene, but we are not trying to find fault or apportion blame or trying to find fault with the other side. All we are trying to say is that these things do happen but in Ceylon we are a very democratic people. In 1962 we had a military coup run by army and the police officers against the government and we are probably the only country in the world that dealt with a military and police coup not by putting people against walls and shooting them but by bringing them to democratic trial under the ordinary law and dealing with them under the rule of law.

Discussion

Q: *Mr Bandaranaike, I wonder if you could tell us just what portion of the aid is tied up with the question of inflationary financing?*

A: The position is that the International Monetary Fund is very very strict – in regard to standby credits or inflationary financing. Standby credits are usually required whenever a country finds its balance of payments position running into problems because its commodity prices have dropped a bit in world markets and it is trying to find temporary accommodation to survive. Usually very very hard conditions are imposed and we are asked to cut back subsidies first while allowing no degree of inflation to offset it.

Secondly, in the International Bank for Reconstruction and Development, a lot of good ideas have seen the light in the years between 1960 and 1970, one of which was the creation of the International Development Association and the International Finance Corporation, both of which are supposed to help in giving soft loans for infrastructural work – the I.D.A. rate I believe is 1/2 per cent. For some strange reason which we have never been able to understand, Ceylon does not apparently qualify for any International

Development Association assistance. Although it is made readily available in some countries in South America, in some parts of Europe and in one or two countries in Africa with far less stringent conditions, the argument we always meet is that the level of subsidies and social service assistance given by the Government to its people is far too high. Our answer is that none of our people wants social service assistance. We do not want to live on a dole but we do want the opportunities to have economic activities under our own power. That is the second point.

The third is in regard to World Bank assistance. The levels of assistance have always been as generous as the donor countries can afford to make it. We have a consortium of countries. They met in Paris in April and they made a contribution which is slightly larger than it was last year and we are very grateful for it, but the eternal problem is that every World Bank team that comes out to Ceylon to investigate the economy and to examine the facts periodically – any banker must have the right to ascertain facts himself about any debtor – always comes back with the position that with our level of economic activity we cannot afford the subsidies which we are running, which of course is true. Subsidies are not good economics either in a socialist or capitalist country. It does not sound good economics. We grant that, but at the same time people must live. They are not given a chance to be employed in the absence of a certain degree of inflation and you are told nothing is possible. The actual degree of inflation which has been permitted is very very small indeed. It amounts to approximately 0.5 per cent of the total budget.

Q: *Would it mean in other words, Mr Bandaranaike, that if you go over 0.5 per cent, you would not qualify for World Bank assistance?*

A: It is not so much that. I do not think the World Bank has ever given us assistance on that basis. The argument is put forward in such a way as to prevent the Government from resorting to more than 0.5 per cent inflation. In other words, we never had the problem of anybody cutting off aid on this basis, because the Government at every stage had kept within the limits of the inflation imposed by the World Bank. Incidentally, one of the funny things is that, among the educated levels of the insurgents, one of the demands, and it is rather a strange one you will find in any revolutionary situation for people to come forward and say, "For goodness sake, sever your connections with the World Bank," which just goes to show that the line of thinking I am presenting here is not actually without a certain degree of support in depth.

Q: *What are the insurgents asking for? 5,000-7,000 people are a lot of people to get together?*

A: They have not actually got together in that sense. They consist of small cells of 5 or 10 people in each little area, very well organised. They had managed to rob and collect guns, shot guns, they had manufactured a few rather amateurish grenades out of things like sticks of dynamite stolen from Government Departments.

Q: *Are they students mainly or a wide range of people?*

A: I would say that three-fourths of them are high school students, with a sprinkling of university undergraduates. Many of them are people already in employment, in quite respectable employment in the lower executive grades, who probably hoped to be commissars under a new regime. They claim to be inspired by Mao Tse Tung's thinking and it is rather a blow to them that Chairman Mao himself has disowned them.

Q: *Did you find any evidence of foreign support for the insurgents?*

A: The world press interpreted our actions in regard to North Korea as evidence that the North Koreans were involved in this, but that is not actually right. What actually happened was this. We have discovered no evidence of any foreign weapons or foreign money or any foreign involvement in a direct sense in the insurgent movement at all from any source. Of course people did speculate in the early days whether it could be the hidden hand of the CIA moving in mysterious ways, although we do not think that. The Government did not express its formal attitude on this matter; there were some people who speculated that the Chinese or the Russians were at the back of this, drawing upon their imaginations and parallels in other countries like Mexico and elsewhere – that sort of speculation did take place in Ceylon. I will not say no to that, but the fact is that when you come down to it, our problems with the North Koreans were something else.

The North Koreans have been conducting a diplomatic campaign, or may be a propaganda campaign, in a number of countries all over the world, particularly in Southern Asia, Burma, India and Ceylon. They have been buying newspaper space for advertising at approximately $ 600 a page, and what they did was they published biographical excerpts from the works of their Premier Kim Il Sung, portraying him as the greatest leader, as a man who has done wonders in his country and probably to show that he is greater if not as great as Chairman Mao in China and other Communist leaders. This has been going on for about a year and the Ceylon Government had no objections whatever to anybody buying advertising space in our papers and publishing that, but when the insurgency problem became acute, to have anybody publishing stories of techniques of guerilla warfare appeared somewhat dangerous to us.

Mrs Bandaranaike through her External Affairs Ministry made a request of the Korean Ambassador that he should now desist from this newspaper campaign because, while it may not be directed to that objective, it was being counterproductive to the efforts of Ceylon to meet with the insurgent threat. When this happened we expected that the Ambassador would conform, as most of the Ambassadors do, but this Ambassador took a different line and said, "No, I propose to continue with the campaign". Mrs Bandaranaike promptly declared him *persona non grata* along with the other members of his Mission and asked him to go away which he did. We have not severed diplomatic connections with North Korea. We still continue to recognise the country. There has been no change whatsoever in that, but that is not to say that these people gave any physical assistance or trained any guerillas or had any of these students in their country and taught them what to do and how to do it. In fact, our little insurrection was essentially a sort of do-it-yourself, home-made job.

Q: *You stated earlier that Mr Trudeau had written to Mrs Bandaranaike about giving aid to help reconstruction efforts. Are you going to see him in this connection?*

A: I believe I will be having a meeting with him some time tomorrow but this is largely for personal reasons and not for the purpose of discussing any contributions. A formal request will be made by Ceylon and the items which we are thinking of are things like helping us to repair some of the damage to road networks, culverts, bridges, things requiring steel, and concrete works which had been damaged in the process of the insurgency. I think Canada has in Mr Trudeau's offer dealt with that question and we propose to send him a list.

I am at the moment in charge of those who surrendered and I have got to look after them and see that they are housed and fed and looked after for the moment until we decide what precisely should be done. The rehabilitation programme we have in mind is basically a programme of getting them to work to set right some of the damage they have themselves done in economic terms. That will probably take about 6-8 months. We think work is perhaps the best form of therapy for these young people in this way, but they ultimately have to be sent back to school. They are a useful section of our society and we cannot afford to throw them away. We certainly do not plan to keep them in jails or concentration camps or anything of that sort. We have not asked for assistance from countries that know about concentration camps on how to do that. Really what we propose to do is to work out a programme of rehabilitation but we cannot afford to bend over backwards, to satisfy these people at the expense of those large number of unemployed people in the country who did not take part in any insurgent activity.

I would say that we have got about 500,000-600,000 people unemployed out of a total population of 12 1/2 million. Of them, as I said, at the beginning of May '70 we had 12,000 graduates unemployed and that number has run down to about 3,000.

Q: *How bad has all this hit your tourist trade?*

A: The tourists were coming in spite of the insurgency to start with, but when the insurgent movement started, the Government consciously and deliberately decided that the best would be to warn the tourist agencies that it may be better to cancel the tourist plans that had already been arranged rather than risk the lives of a single tourist. We expect that, probably in the next 2 or 3 months, the situation would be quite normal and everyone would probably revert to tourism in the same way as before. Of course, there are many views on tourism in Ceylon as much as in any other part of the world. We are still relatively unpolluted in the sense in which the word has now become controversial politics in most places, but with compensations, cash-wise, it is a consideration and tourism is good business. A fair volume of tourist traffic comes into Ceylon but, of course, everything depends upon how long it takes and how expensive it is to travel to Ceylon. While we have wonderful beaches, a lot of interesting things in Ceylon, a climate of perpetual summer, and the Government is most interested in the money, we are at the same time looking on this with mixed feelings. The need for foreign exchange is such that if tourism is going to bring foreign exchange, we will have to go after it and get it. Of course problems are there. Every country I suppose must look after itself. We can supply you shirts at one dollar a shirt. You can sell them for 3 or 4 dollars here quite easily but ultimately you have to cut back your quota so as to keep the Quebec textile weavers going. We understand it, but it is a problem.

Somebody asked me at the Ottawa University, when I was talking to them about the rubber-rice pact with China, whether Ceylon is losing on this deal. I have noticed that there seems to be some idea that on barter deal the Chinese are getting the best of the bargain and that Ceylon is getting rid of a useful commodity at a disadvantage to herself. That is not true. The arrangement we have with the Chinese is that we get a price of 2 1/2 pence a ton above the Singapore price which is the world determinant; so we get a premium price on our rubber, while we pay for the rice at the world market price which is the Burmese price. The Rangoon price determines rice whereas rubber is determined by the Singapore price. That is how it goes. That is to say we always get 2 1/2 pence more, and the proof of what I am saying is that this deal was first negotiated by the United National Party Government which was the former Government in office, a more conservative, right-wing oriented government you could not imagine in any underdeveloped country, and they found it profitable, and all governments have found it profitable to continue with it. So it goes to prove my point that it is profitable for the people of Ceylon.

As for speculation that China will get base facilities in Trincomalee, Ceylon does not propose to part with Trincomalee to anybody. We do not like to have any foreign bases on our soil – nobody's bases, Chinese, Russian or American. This story was an internal political canard which came into existence in 1965 just before the general elections. The United National Party suddenly discovered that the terms of the maritime agreement that Ceylon has with Russia and China for commercial shipping and maritime shipping – reciprocal use of ports for shipping cargo, normal commercial trading – they thought it could be interpreted as use of Trincomalee as a naval base and they promptly said "we propose to abrogate this agreement as soon as we come into power" which is a political argument. The UNP came to power in 1965 and, after a few months had elapsed, we promptly shot off the question at question time in the House. "Now that you are in power, are you going to abrogate this commercial treaty for the reciprocal use of ports?" The UNP said, "We don't propose it now. Having read the treaty more carefully and having taken legal advice on it, we now find that the treaty is merely a commercial treaty causing no damage to anybody." That has continued like that ever since.

At this time I categorically state that we do not allow the use of our ports to anybody for the admission of warships without permission, not even for refuelling or bunkering. No ships carrying nuclear weapons, or aircraft carrying nuclear weapons, are permitted to land or to make use of shore facilities in Ceylon. Frankly, we do not know how to recognise nuclear weapons even if we see them face to face. The procedure we adopt, is to ask any country seeking these facilities to declare that they do not carry any. This is the form adopted since 1963 and all ships that have called in Colombo have conformed to this practice. The Americans, the Russians, the Chinese have not sent warships so far, and the ones that have called in Colombo have all conformed to this practice. Pakistan has been following the same practice when she used landing facilities in Colombo; we asked them to sign the same declaration. There are no war-like personnel in transit to any other theatre of war in their own country or elsewhere and the Pakstanis have carefully complied with this and the proof of it is that the Pakistanis and Indians are both helping us with their aircraft and supplies and ferrying transport in the course of our fight against insurgents.

SEVENTEENTH PARLIAMENTARY CONFERENCE – KUALA LUMPUR, MALAYSIA, 1971
Challenges to Parliamentary Democracy
Hon. F. R. D. Bandaranaike, MP, Ceylon
(Minister of Public Administration, Local Government, and Home Affairs, Ceylon, Member of Executive Committee)

Mr Chairman, fellow Delegates, I shall be very brief. I merely wish to suggest that this discussion really falls under two heads. The first one is: Why do these things happen to us in democratic countries? Why do we have military coups and revolutionary movements? Secondly: When they do happen, how shall we deal with them, to preserve parliamentary democracy? Those seem to me to be the two principal questions; and various suggestions have been made in answer to the first question by the distinguished Delegates who have already spoken before me. My honourable colleague from Ceylon, Hon. George Rajapakse, has already suggested economic reasons as perhaps the principal ground. My good friend, Mr S. Radhakrishnan of India, has said perhaps it is because the leadership is not as much in touch with the people as it ought to be.

May I venture, at the outset, to say that I respectfully disagree with Mr Radhakrishnan's diagnosis on this question. I think if you examine the actual historical facts, you will find that there is very little difference between many of the countries where military coups and revolutionary movements have in fact arisen. It required only one lunatic both in India and in Ceylon to perpetuate the greatest political assassinations of our times in either country. I refer to the assassination of Mahatma Gandhi in India and of Solomon Bandaranaike in Ceylon. It is also true that the leaders of both countries are in touch with their people in much the same way. But it has not stopped the Naxalites in India. It has not stopped the trouble in West Bengal. It has not stopped the necessity for presidential rule in four states of India. It has not prevented the rising of an insurrection affecting 12,000 people out of a total population of about 11 1/2 million to 12 million people in Ceylon. That is a sad but true fact. But when minorities, a small group of people, do engage in military coups and revolutionary movements, we are called upon to take stock of the situation and to ask ourselves what precisely has gone wrong. Why do these things have to happen? And when they do happen, how are we going to react to them and how are we going to treat them? I entirely agree with Mr G. Leduc of Quebec when he said, a moment ago, that if it is necessary to deal with minorities who are against law and order, be tough, deal with them hard in order to preserve the fundamental freedoms of the majority. That, I think, is perfectly true, particularly in regard to the second question, which is the method of treatment. That is, in order to preserve parliamentary democracy, it is sometimes necessary to deal with a situation by methods which perhaps do not entirely smack of parliamentary democracy. One cannot deal with such situations by allowing freedom of debate, allowing people to raise questions. Sometimes it is necessary to detain persons for longer periods than one would like without the opportunities to be taken to a court of law and to be tried in the normal forms.

Let us get back to the first question, which, to my mind, is the main question: Why do these things have to happen? In broad economic terms, I would agree with what my colleague, Mr. Rajapakse, has already said, but I would like to add one or two further points. Take the practical case – what happens? Countries become independent in Africa and Asia. Having become independent, we imagine that we are our own masters, capable of ruling our own destiny. We go to the polls; we form into political parties; candidates present their political manifestos to the people and tell the people, "We have a solution to the problems of this country, we can do something for you." In practice it is not that our politicians are out of touch with the people; it is that, in the context of the modern international society, any country of primary producers with limited resources lacks the necessary capacities. Whether in Malaysia, Ceylon, India, or many other countries of Africa, we are unable to do anything practical about our economic situation in order to fulfil the promises and to satisfy the aspirations of the people. This is what happens. Let the other fellow, the fellow fighting the elections against you, come into power. Supposing he comes into power, he is no better either; he cannot do much. It is not that the people are out of touch with their leaders, or the leaders out of touch with the people; it is the other way about. In other words, unless there is a growing realization that parliamentary democracy itself becomes a cherished ideal, something worth protecting, something worth fighting for, something worthy of protection in its own right, however much we follow the forms of parliamentary democracy – rival candidates coming forward with rival sets of promises, hopes, aspirations for the future, let it be nationalization, let it be private enterprise, it makes no difference – if the net result is that the life of the people and the country remain unaltered substantially, then you will find that the seeds of revolutionary movements, of insurrections, and dissatisfactions will become manifest sooner or later. The unrest will not present itself in the shape and form of overthrowing a particular Government which is unpopular; that is not the case. It will become a challenge to parliamentary democracy in itself. It will become the very rationale for saying that this system is no good; we are not making progress this way; let us abandon all the valuable things we have built up through parliamentary democracy.

The fact remains that parliamentary democracy is, by its very nature, a slow system. It is slow so far as economic growth is concerned. We talk and debate and argue about the rights and wrongs of every little thing. In Ceylon, parliamentary democracy has become so entrenched that before we can erect a stand-pipe on a street corner, there is first an argument in the street as to whether it should be at this end of the street corner or that end of the street; and, finally, after a lot of arguments, the stand-pipe will not be erected at either end because, by then, the time has come for the next local elections! I think that sort of democracy is the thing which is making people impatient. One likes to have all the safeguards of parliamentary democracy – independence of the judiciary and such things. One is not complaining. One likes to see legislative processes working in an orderly fashion to achieve results. But, if we want to speed up the process; if parliamentary democracy is to survive not only within the Commonwealth but as an institution worthy of protection throughout the world, I say the responsibility lies not merely on the countries practising parliamentary democracy, but on other countries better placed, more fortunately placed, to accept the responsibility. If a coup happens in some little corner of Africa, if a revolution or a riot occurs in a state in India, in Ceylon, or any other country, the responsibility is really an international one. We are all responsible in one form or another for letting that kind of situation arise. I do not deny that there are cases of the odd military coup arising from the ambition of some particular soldier who perhaps thinks he can do a better job of it than a civilian Prime Minister. I don't deny that; that can happen. But that type of person is easier to deal with. It is no different in any way to the case of the odd lunatic who feels that he is Napoleon Buonaparte! What I am saying is that, in our view, democracy is worth preserving within the Commonwealth. It is something we should cherish and value, and I think that we all have to accept responsibility for its preservation. Thank you.

SEVENTEENTH COMMONWEALTH PARLIAMENTARY CONFERENCE – KUALA LUMPUR, MALAYSIA, 1971
Problems of the Environment
Hon. F. R. D. Bandaranaike, MP, Ceylon
(Minister of Public Administration, Local Government and Home Affairs, Ceylon, Member of Executive Committee)

I am speaking from the wrong place.
Chairman
Are you speaking for Ceylon?
Hon. F. R. D. Bandaranaike, MP, Ceylon
Yes, but I shall not take up your time. I only require one minute.

I was struck by the fact that my friend and colleague from Maharashtra gave us a poem from India on the subject of wildlife. I should like to add a footnote in verse to what Senator Grosart has already said in opening the discussion on the subject of pollution. I should like to give you an imitation calypso written by the American song writer Tom Lehrer. Not being a Commonwealth man, I admit that his calypsos are not of the same quality as those of "Mighty Sparrow" of Jamica, or "Lord Kitchener" of Trinidad & Tobago! Here are the opening words of Tom Lehrer's calypso:

If you visit American City,
You will find it very pretty,
Of just one thing you must beware,
Do not drink the water and do not breathe the air!

SEVENTEENTH COMMONWEALTH PARLIAMENTARY CONFERENCE – KUALA LUMPUR, MALAYSIA
World Security
Hon. F. R. D. Bandaranaike, MP, Ceylon
(Minister of Public Administration, Local Government and Home Affairs, Member of Executive Committee)

Mr Chairman and fellow Delegates, first of all I would like to assure you that I certainly will not require anything like an hour because we have got other engagements this evening – for instance, eating satay with the private sector of Malaysia. We cannot possibly miss that. I shall restrict my remarks to fifteen minutes. I think that is fair enough, and I think I can hear a huge sigh of relief around the hall.

Now, Mr Chairman, I think this debate has been very interesting and of an extraordinarily high standard. It gave us all the opportunity, as Parliamentarians who are accustomed to debating in our own countries, to hear the opinions of Commonwealth Parliamentarians from other parts of the world and to learn the thoughts and feelings which inspire your own Parliament when they sit discussing foreign affairs and other related questions in your own countries. Even though we have not been able on every matter to find agreement among ourselves, I think there is this positive gain from these discussions: as Members of Parliament, not only have we come to know each other socially – in the course of the tours which our gracious Malaysian hosts have arranged for us, but we have been given the opportunity to be able to find out how each of us thinks and works in our own Parliaments, the kind of reasoning which prevails, the emotionally charged feelings that we have on certain subjects. And, of course, we are all talking in the context of our own national interests.

In this debate, three subjects have been set out in three separate sessions, and I think it would be true to say that there is a general area of agreement in regard to all these three subjects. Taken generally, on the topic "South-East Asia and the Indian Ocean: Security and Neutrality," I have not heard a single voice around this hall supporting the point of view that South-East Asia and the Indian Ocean should not be made secure. The ways and means of achieving that security is a matter in regard to which there may be differences. But there are certainly no differences in regard to the need for security; the need for preserving this area as an area of peace; and the need for preserving this area from cold war conflicts and tensions. I think everyone of us in this hall is agreed on that.

If I may highlight the main question which was raised by the Hon. Deputy Prime Minister of Malaysia in his opening remarks as representing one point of view, and if I were to pick a particular Delegate's speech as representing the directly opposite point of view, I would pick Senator Sim's from Australia. Mr Sim made the point that, in the present situation, it would be unrealistic to think in terms of neutralizing the Indian Ocean. He thought that one should look at the question having regard to the interests of the different countries concerned. This is quite true; I respectfully would say that I agree with Mr Sim that we all have interests in the Indian Ocean. This is the case not merely for the countries actually having a seacoast along the Indian Ocean (as, for instance, Australia), but even for countries in the eastern part of Africa, India, Pakistan, Ceylon, Malaysia, with the Straits of Malacca close by. All have interests no doubt. That is quite true. But when we talk of neutralization of neutrality, I don't think that the Deputy Prime Minister of Malaysia meant quite that – that we should remove every warship from the Indian Ocean or have a completely unarmed ocean. I don't think he meant for a single moment that we should not protect our trade routes which are undoubtedly a vital concern to everyone of us representing whatever country we represent in the Commonwealth. Indeed, I don't think that was the argument at all. The argument was simply this: that weapons attract weapons, bases attract bases; and if we once take the position that we should try and keep count of Russian destroyers or submarines that come into the Indian Ocean, and if we try and keep up our own strength at the cheapest possible cost (for I think every country likes to keep their defensive weapons as cheap as possible, and as effective as possible), then we get stuck with a problem. The problem is that the Russians have a right to have their submarines and weapons, and that we also have a right to keep them. Let's try and maintain the balance of power in that way.

I think the whole Malaysian argument was presented very ably, if I may say so, and quite correctly, by the Deputy Prime Minister who took the opposite point of view. This is that, while it may be true that nobody can prevent the incursion of warships, nor limit the freedom of the seas, it would be desirable for us, as a Commonwealth, to work towards the objective of eliminating everybody's weapons from the Indian Ocean – Russian, English, Australian, American, and everybody else's. I appreciate that this is something that cannot happen in the immediate present. No one suggested that it could be done right now. I think that is the very point that Mr Sim was trying to make: that it is not practical politics to think of it.

Actually, this Indian Ocean security question first became an issue at the Singapore Prime Ministers' Conference when Mrs Bandaranaike, the Prime Minister of Ceylon, specifically raised the issue and circulated a paper on the subject. It is one of the only two points, I think, on which there was actual agreement among the Prime Ministers in their final communique. They discussed and considered various matters (that is all in the communique); but one of the only two matters on which they agreed was the need to have the Indian Ocean as an area of peace and security, free from nuclear weapons and the like. Now, the only practical question is: What were they talking about? Were they talking about the freedom of the seas? Were they talking of the need to, shall I say, withdraw all Western forces from the Indian Ocean? Far from it. What they were talking about was Diego Garcia, to use plain and simple language. This was the first time one of the great powers involved in cold war conflicts had acquired a territorial base in the Indian Ocean. They called it a communication centre (supposed not to be a military base at all – could be; we don't know). But the Russians certainly have no territorial bases in the Indian Ocean yet. The Americans have. The simple complaint made by Mrs Bandaranaike was that, in regard to Commonwealth matters, it is highly desirable to have consultation beforehand. These consultations should provide that whatever is done is limited to the specific purposes and objectives, and only after consultation with the countries concerned. That was not done in the case of Diego Garcia in the course of prolonged deliberations between the British and the Americans. That was the simple complaint.

I think that the Ceylon Delegate made that point in the course of his intervention yesterday and, substantially, that is all it amounts to. But I think the need for keeping the Indian Ocean as an area of peace and security is one of general agreement. We may not be capable of achieving it in the sense of suggesting that everybody should withdraw his forces as of now; but certainly we shouldn't welcome the establishment of new bases or the establishment of bases in the hands of foreign powers capable of getting involved in great power conflicts. No one is suggesting that India or Pakistan should not have their own navies; or for that matter, that Ceylon (whose navy I think now consists of one frigate which at the moment is laid up in harbour) should be denied the use of the Indian Ocean. I don't think that is the argument at all.

Now I come to the second matter. We have been debating the issue, very properly raised under the relevant heading in the course of this debate, of Bangladesh. We have been talking about refugees; and we have been talking about the very difficult situation that has arisen in consequence of events in East Bengal. I think the position was very ably summarized, if I may say so, by Mr Arthur Bottomley in his very first intervention on this subject. He stated the facts fairly and objectively, with great sympathy and great understanding, and we in Ceylon are completely in sympathy with that point of view. Also, if I may say so, the rest of the Conference has demonstrated beyond doubt their recognition that the problem of the refugees is not a problem for India alone: it is the problem of the international community – a point of view which I expressed, if you will recall, Mr Chairman, at the very first General Council Meeting of the Commonwealth Parliamentary Association, Seventeenth Conference.

Once having said that this is a problem for the international community, we have to decide, I suppose, the natural consequences that follow from it. Several Indian Members of their Delegation did talk of this. Public opinion should be brought to bear upon this matter, in one form or another, so as to restore conditions in East Pakistan to some kind of normalcy, in which people will not be in a state of being refugees for ever, and in which parliamentary democracy will begin to function once more. There is no question about the fact that the Awami League has won an overwhelming victory at the election in East Pakistan. Whether it was fought on the basis of secession or not, at the time of the elections, certainly, their leadership could command the general respect and confidence of the people of East Pakistan. There can be no question about that. But while one does recognize that the conditions must be restored to normal, the fact remains that this question is still a problem affecting a country whose internal affairs one can do very little about, except for expressing an opinion.

Looked at from that point of view, Mr Arthur Bottomley expressed the view that he had the advantage of having actually visited East Pakistan not long ago – something that I had not been able to do. He said that he has every confidence. Having stated the facts, he said that President Yahya Khan, a military man, no doubt, can in his view, be trusted to restore democracy at the first available opportunity; that he thought that he had made certain mistakes in his handling of the situation; that the appointment of General Tikka Khan was a mistake, and that a more politically perceptive personality might have been able to tackle the situation somewhat better. I do not know; these are Mr Bottomley's views. I do think those views are entitled to respect because they are expressed by a person who had actually studied the problem first hand. I would say the general feeling of the Conference would be that we all hope that conditions will be restored to normalcy in East Bengal; that parliamentary democracy will be restored once more, not merely in East Pakistan but in the whole of Pakistan; and that Pakistan will once again be a full member not merely of the Commonwealth but of the Commonwealth Parliamentary Association in the not-too-distant future.

Then, we have talked about the impact on the Commonwealth of recent events in Southern Africa and the rest of Africa, concentrating largely on two matters – apartheid and the question of arms sales by Britain to the South African Republic. In regard to apartheid, I don't think there are any two views on this point. I think everybody condemns apartheid as a policy and as a philosophy which is rotten to the core, completely contrary to human dignity. I wouldn't think there would be a single representative of the Commonwealth around this hall who holds any opposite point of view.

There are differences of opinion as to whether or not there should be dialogue with South Africa. This is a question, I think, in regard to which different African members of the Commonwealth have expressed different points of view. It seems to me that perhaps the best argument in support of dialogue is one that was presented not long ago by Prime Minister Trudeau of Canada in a different context. When asked why he visited the Soviet Union considering the repression of the Ukranians in that country by the Government of the Soviet Union, he said: "How do you expect me to be able to help the Ukranians in that country except by talking to the Russians, for which purpose I must conduct a dialogue with the Government of the Soviet Union?" This answer he gave in the House of Commons at the time you and I, Mr Chairman, were on the Executive Committee in Prince Edward Island, enjoying the hospitality of the Canadian Government and your personal hospitality. I think Mr Trudeau's words may perhaps reflect the reasoning of some of the African countries who believe that it is better to have a dialogue.

On the other hand, one can understand the point of view of those African countries who do not understand why we are tolerating a country whose policies are so abhorrent to us all, and which we cannot possibly accept. Why are we dealing with these people? Why don't we cut them adrift from the stream of world opinion? Why do we have any transactions with them at all? This is a point of view with which one can sympathize, and with a great deal of understanding.

However, the only practical problem lies in isolation. An economic boycott is ineffective unless the largest countries in the world, the most economically powerful, join in such a course of action. Otherwise it will only be a gesture of individual countries expressing an opinion – saying that they will have nothing to do with South Africa; that they will cut out their rugger teams, their football teams, their tennis teams. (Nowadays, I think it is the fashion, Mr Chairman, to play ping-pong more than any other game!). But whatever the game may be, if you want to take the position that you will be dealing with the problem on the basis of an international boycott, by the cutting away of South Africa from the mainstream of world affairs, I think it can be done, and that it could be effective. It could work, provided there is a concerted international effort on the part of all the remaining countries in the world, representing very important areas of the world (some less important like Ceylon, some more important like Canada) to act together unitedly. A lot depends, Mr Chairman, upon the degree and significance of one's own trade, one's own contacts, the influence one can bring to bear on world affairs. We have many little islands here; Ceylon is one of the smallest, next perhaps to Nauru! I venture to think that the amount of influence that we can bring to bear on a question like this is of minute importance, unless we can interest the major world powers to take such a course of action. I do not really know whether, acting individually, we can bring adequate pressure to bear. We know the sad story of sanctions against Rhodesia. It is a sad but true fact that, whether it is a Conservative Government or a Labour Government in office in the United Kingdom, they are just not going to declare war on Rhodesia. It has not happened; so why pretend? There is going to be no war; they are merely going to be told they are an illegal regime. They say there is to be no independence without majority rule; but the independence is a fact and the majority rule is not a fact. It is not coming, at least not for a long time. So the fact remains that we are dealing with realities; and in reality we are not going to get a war of liberation (or, shall I say, the converse of a war of liberation!). In the case of Rhodesia, what you are really going to find is that the sanctions by themselves are not working because trade considerations are completely overriding political considerations. But nobody in Britain or elsewhere can morally support what is happening in Rhodesia; nor can they morally support the kinds of fascism now developing in Southern Africa, and even in neighbouring territories such as Namibia, and Portuguese-controlled Mozambique. But, we have also got to look, I suppose, with a certain degree of care to see that what we condemn in one place is not, in fact, permitted under any circumstances to come into being within any of our own territories. We in the Commonwealth Parliamentary Association stand for parliamentary democracy. We may not think it is the best form of government in the world, but nobody has yet devised a more satisfactory form.

The debate has concentrated itself entirely upon South Africa, Rhodesia, and the colonial territories of Southern Africa (although the heading reads: "the rest of Africa"). I might say, in passing, that we as a Commonwealth will continue to strive for, and work towards the objective of isolating South Africa. I suppose, in one way or another, we shall try to persuade South Africa to realise, through whatever influence we could bring to bear upon her, the wrongness of her conduct and the impossibility of her position in the international sphere.

The question of arms sales to South Africa was dealt with under the heading of "South-East Asia and the Indian Ocean" by Senator Cameron in his opening remarks yesterday. I think the points he made accurately represent the points of view of many of the African countries and, indeed, many of the Asiatic countries as well: we find it very difficult to believe that British arms sales to South Africa could really be used for external defence, having regard to the context of the Simonstown Agreement. The opposite point of view was put by a Member of the United Kingdom Delegation. Indeed, his argument can be summed up by saying that, as it has been settled in Singapore, we should not take it up; no useful purpose could be served by arguing this matter afresh now. That was the only substantial answer given by him to Senator Cameron. If I may say so, with respect, if he takes that position, the Commonwealth Parliamentary Association may as well fold up because we, as Parliamentarians, cannot say that the power of deciding everything is in the hands of the Cabinets. If that were the case, we might as well remain silent (which will be one of the questions which will be discussed in Committee I tomorrow).

Various discussions were held in Singapore and one of the most important points in that discussion was the setting up of a Study group of eight countries to go into this matter. But the Study Group never met. Indeed, Ceylon was invited to be one of the members of that Study Group and refused because we did not believe that the Study Group served any useful purpose. My colleagues from India will recall that they were one of the countries that did accept to serve on the Study Group. Immediately after arms were actually sold to South Africa, India withdrew and said there was no point in her sitting on the Study Group if she was confronted by a *fait accompli* which cannot be changed. But does it alter the fact that arms sales to South Africa could be used in a repressive manner by a Government bent on repression? It can happen; and it is a point on which the Commonwealth cannot afford to be complacent. We cannot shirk the responsibility of expressing our views. I think the general feeling of this Conference in regard to arms sales to South Africa must be that, while Britain, as a sovereign independent country, is not obliged to subordinate herself to the views of other Commonwealth countries in a matter like this, her decision does not tally with Commonwealth opinion. Indeed, Mr Heath was made aware of this in Singapore.

I have practically reached the end of my fifteen minutes, so, if I may, I shall say a few words in regard to West Asia and the Mediterranean. All I want to say is that Mr Baker summarized the position factually and accurately: at some stage there will have to be a compromise, in regard to the problems in the Middle East, between Israel and the Arab world. I think it would be generally true to say that today we are reaching towards that compromise. Indeed, it is easy for us today, with a certain amount of hindsight, to say that the correct decisions seem to be coming, albeit slowly. Sometimes one wonders whether for the vital security of the Indian Ocean it may not be a good thing if the Suez Canal remains closed for ever. But the fact remains that those of us who trade need the Canal open. It is not merely a question of saying that the Israelis cannot use the Canal. The net result of the whole operation is that nobody gets the Canal; and nobody can use it right now. While I completely agree with every word of what Mr Baker said, I wish he had made some reference to the events of 1957 and helped us to understand how precisely the British intervention helped to avoid the confrontation situation in the Middle-East.

I think we all want to see West Asia (the Middle-East) and the Mediterranean question being solved by agreement. We would like to see countries taking up less inflexible positions. I think it is true to say that, with all the discussions, with all the delays, the best approach to the problems of maintaining security would perhaps be to buy a little more time. That can best be done – as Mr Baker rightly pointed out – by having the ceasefire extended for a longer period.

In conclusion, Mr Chairman, one last word. I think the best feature of our discussions so far has been the avoidance of double standards; that we, speaking as Parliamentarians, have spoken freely and frankly. We have expressed strong views sometimes, emotional views sometimes, and sometimes views which may not have met complete agreement and accord around the room; but we have all spoken with sincerity from the bottom of our hearts. If the little bit of what we said has struck a responsive chord in the hearts and minds of some other Members of Parliament in a more distant and remote area of the Commonwealth, I think we have served our purpose as a Commonwealth Parliamentary Association. I thank you.

Mr F. E. Walker, MP (Canada), Member of Executive Committee was in the Chair.

Chairman:

We thank the distinguished Delegate from Ceylon for his wrap-up. The attention that you received, Mr Delegate, should be gratifying to you. We have had an excellent session today. On behalf of my co-Chairman and myself, and without any condescension at all, I would just like to congratulate all those who participated. I have certainly learnt a lot. The contributions were very effective and very well spoken.

The Conference then adjourned.

EIGHTEENTH PARLIAMENTARY CONFERENCE
(COMMONWEALTH) MALAWI, 1972
Hon. F. R. D. Bandaranaike, MP, Ceylon
(Minister of Public Administration, Local Government and Home Affairs and Minister of Justice, Sri Lanka,
Member of the Executive Committee)

Mr Chairman, I think it was Lady Tweedsmuir this morning who said that, when we talk to one another, we should try as far as possible not to talk to one another as foreigners, but talk to one another as people – not merely ones who speak the same language, but as people with whom we can easily come to an understanding and, more important, communicate that spirit of understanding.

It is in that spirit that I propose to speak now; and only for the purpose of helping this Conference to clear up some of the ideas and thoughts which have already been discussed. I did not intend speaking originally because I didn't know that Asia was going to figure as part of the subject of discussion today. I thought it might come tomorrow; but since it has come up today, I thought I would start there.

Mr Chairman, I observed that two speakers in the course of this afternoon's session referred to the problems pertaining to the Indian Ocean. In the course of their speeches, both of them expressed the view that the peace zone was an idealistic concept; that it was a very desirable thing that the Indian Ocean should be an area of peace, a zone where warships and war-material would be excluded, but that it was not really a practical proposition, having regard to the interests of the different countries concerned in protecting sea-routes, trade routes, essential oil supplies from the Persian Gulf being maintained, things of that sort.

It is almost impossible, they said, to visualize the Indian Ocean actually being made a zone of peace in practical terms. Now, I think that's true; and I think those interests were not forgotten by those of us who ventured to suggest that the Indian Ocean be made a peace zone, perhaps not having lost entirely the idealism with which we are charged. We still think it a desirable thing to do, a desirable thing to have. And when we urge that the Indian Ocean be made a peace zone, please make no mistake; it is not that we have forgotten the essential interests of the countries in the neighbourhood and even the interests of those not in the neighbourhood. Even countries well outside the Indian Ocean region, we concede, have interests to safeguard and protect. It is not a matter of saying that we are like ostriches burying our heads in the sand, disinterested in what happens to the rest of the

Commonwealth or how other countries are going to protect themselves. Rather, it is in the spirit of trying to make our point of view known and understood by others. We appreciate that the problem cannot be worked out by little peoples like people from Sri Lanka or other littoral countries of the Indian Ocean which are certainly not major powers capable of waging war against anybody in effective terms. However, we think that we have a point here which is worthy of consideration, and it is for the purpose of expressing my point of view to our two colleagues who spoke on this subject that I thought I would intervene.

First of all, let it be quite clear that gunboat diplomacy no longer works. It may have been all right in former days, but not now. If I remember my history – and I don't know it very well, unlike His Excellency, the President of Malawi, who was certainly very well acquainted with British history – gunboat diplomacy went out in the days of Lord Palmerston and I think it has never really come back into vogue since then.

I don't really know what sort of weapons one can think of to protect one's trade routes, one's vessels, one's ships, in the Indian Ocean. If you are thinking in terms of regarding the Russians as your natural enemy, as one speaker said, I don't know how you are going to deal with nuclear submarines by means of a couple of conventional destroyers, or flotillas of destroyers, wandering around the Indian Ocean.

I think the position is that all the countries of the world simply have to get together on this one. Dialogue seems possible even among the worst enemies nowadays. You can talk to the Russians, the Americans, the Chinese. Everyone can talk to everyone else – excepting possibly the Russians and the Chinese talking together. It may well be that if everybody with interests in the area were able to agree upon it through the United Nations, then indeed one may be able to treat this as a practical proposition and not merely as a figment of idealism.

There is another small point I would like to make on this same matter and that is in regard to the questions of arms sales to South Africa, which was talked of with reference to the Commonwealth Prime Ministers' Conference in Singapore. Some people seem to regard it as a great victory for Mr Heath personally – that he was able to carry his point of view without breaking up the Commonwealth. Perhaps that's right. But against that, I would also make the point that it would perhaps be a greater victory for the Commonwealth that not one single weapon, not even a piece of small arms, has yet been sold to South Africa in consequence of Commonwealth pressure.

Thank you, Mr Chairman.

TWENTIETH COMMONWEALTH PARLIAMENTARY CONFERENCE, COLOMBO, SRI LANKA, 1973
Hon. Felix R. D. Bandaranaike, MP, Ceylon
(Minister of Public Administration, Local Government & Home Affairs and Minister of Justice, Sri Lanka, Regional Representative – Asia)

Mr Chairman and Delegates, I think the debate in which we have been engaged yesterday and today has been most useful to all of us because it has given us the opportunity to realise that there is a tremendous area of agreement among ourselves in regard to the many policies affecting all our countries.

Yesterday we talked about the Indian Ocean as a Zone of Peace on a proposal presented by my Prime Minister, Mrs Sirimavo R. D. Bandaranaike. I do not think that there is really anyone in this august assembly who disagrees with that view though there were differences of opinion as to how practical the proposal could be and as to how it is actually going to be worked out in practice. I think today's discussion is very much of the same order in the sense that, while we are discussing a wider aspect of the problem, while we highlight particular aspects of the proposal, we are still left with the question of where it is going to take us to. I should like to tell you my point of view.

I really do not know that there is any solution to any of these major international problems unless and until the great powers get together, and the great powers cannot get together until the climate of international public opinion has been created for that. That is where we come into this. The creation of international public opinion is fundamental to the operation. We do not believe that the withdrawal of American forces in Vietnam took place merely because Dr. Kissinger flew on his various missions and won a Peace Prize. We believe it happened because the climate of opinion was created for it within the United States of America itself. We believe that President Johnson did not stand for re-election under the pressure of American public opinion. We believe that President Nixon, in taking the decisions he took, took them also on the basis of public opinion in his own country.

If we want to achieve anything practical I do not know that we can talk of sending delegations around the world to make representations to the great powers. That was tried in Belgrade in 1961. I think delegations did go out of the Soviet Union and did go out of the Western powers. At that time the immediate question was to stop atomic tests. But that is really not the way in which the thing works. The problem is to make sure that when Dr. Kissinger makes his next trip he begins to think about the Indian Ocean as a peace zone, that he begins to think about the problems of South-East Asia and problems of peace and neutrality.

It is fantastic that when the great powers which met at the SALT talks came to grass roots, somehow this whole idea of a territorial area which could become a zone of peace was left out of the reckoning. They talked about many things. Unless international opinion is focussed on this aspect of the matter I do not think we can ever get anywhere, and that is where we come in as ordinary Members of parliament in our respective countries. We can create the climate of opinion for our own questions, and this perhaps establishes something practical. I am not saying that it is going to happen overnight. I am not saying that the Russians or Americans or anybody else are going to give up their natural interests in these matters, but they might be willing to think again if they realize that the climate of international opinion is dead against them. That is why we believe that discussions such as these are useful.

I know my Friend and Colleague, the Hon. Leader of the Opposition in our country, speaking yesterday talked about the impracticability of this. He brought it almost to the level of being a dream – of imagining that we can get a zone of peace unless and until human nature changes and people begin to think differently. That is rather idealistic. You will probably not be able to reach that kind of millennium in the foreseeable future. But does it mean that we should stop trying? Does it mean that any of us should give up and say that this is not a practical thing to do? I take the view that the practicality of it comes in the creation of public opinion.

There is one other matter that I should like to deal with. I refer to the problems of minorities and the problems of international relationship which are exacerbated sometimes in our own region, particularly in South and South-East Asia. We firmly believe that there is only one solution to this and that is the establishment of dialogue and discussion. We believe that there is no problem that will not ultimately resolve itself if, with a spirit of goodwill, we attempt by discussion to solve it. Who would have believed that Pakistan and Bangladesh would be able to resume relations within so short a time? Who would have believed that Sheik Abdul Rahman would have found it possible to visit the Lahore Summit in recent times? Who would have believed that after the horrible situation that existed in the Indian subcontinent not so long ago it would have been possible for India, Bangladesh and Pakistan to come to a state of at least talking to one another? But thanks to the efforts of Sardar Swaran Singh it has been made possible.

We in Sri Lanka have already proved that all our outstanding problems with our neighbours are capable of being resolved, some of them very difficult ones, including that of the repatriation of large numbers of people, by discussion. Perhaps it has not been so successful in our own country. I noticed one of my Colleagues a little while ago talking of the minority problems of the Tamils, on behalf of the Tamil United Front that he represents. Well, all I can say is that our opinion is precisely the same. We are prepared to go to all the corners of our country to talk to them in their own language if we can and try to persuade them. You would imagine that minority problems here are very difficult ones, but I know of no other country in the world where a majority has made it possible for the minority to achieve unheard of economic wealth and to become the most prosperous people in our country through the policies being followed consciously and deliberately by the majority. I should like to urge that even in our own little land dialogue and discussion are fundamental and essential to good relations. Recently I had the privilege of visiting the Northern Province. I tried to speak to the people there in my own faulty Tamil, trying to make contact and to express our point of view. All I can say is that we stretch the hand of friendship and invite our friends of the Tamil United Front to do the same – to come down South and talk to us. It does not matter if they do not know our language. They can talk to us in English or in Tamil. We are prepared to listen. We say that once the dialogue is established, as it can be established – we cannot afford to talk of dialogue in international terms unless we are prepared to do precisely that in our own country – problems can be resoloved.

Thank you.

FELIX ON NON-ALIGNMENT
'Daily News', Monday, 16th August, 1976, Supplement 1 –

Non-Alignment is not something fixed and static, its essential principles have grown over the years. The beginnings of Non-Alignment were seen in the birth of Afro-Asian Solidarity as a concept with the first Afro-Asian Conference in Bandung in 1955. Pancha Seela and other principles of peaceful co-existence of nations and people were enunciated at Bandung. But Bandung was certainly not the beginning of the concept of non-alignment as it is understood today. The countries which were members of military alliances, countries with ideological commitments and countries which do not belong to NAM as it is known today were among the participants at Bandung. Notable examples were the People's Republic of China which is not a member of the NAM.

NAM in its present sense came into being in the 1950's and in the early 1960's when leaders like Prime Minister Nehru of India, President Nasser of the U.A.R. as it was then called, President Tito of Yugoslavia, Prime Minister

Sirimavo Bandaranaike of Sri Lanka and others decided to get together on the basis of principles they had adopted in their respective foreign policies which came to be described as "dynamic neutralism and non-alignment." This was the beginning of an attempt to convert the bans of international relations from the negative to the positive from the mere rejection of the idea of being linked in one form or another to major power blocs, to a search for initiatives and responses which would replace confrontation and conflict with peace and active co-operation.

To understand the implication of this positive aspect of Non-Alignment it will be useful to go back a little further in history to the beginning of the United Nations at San Francisco. At San Francisco with the second world war at an end there was a group of countries which were determined to build a new political order upon the ruins of that war. In that new political order the entire structure was so designed as to give the major share of power to the Big Powers which had the deciding voice within the security council. With their power of veto these major powers held the determining power, the decider on every single issue. In such a situation it was only natural that the other nations of the world should look around for ways of insulating themselves from the preponderant influences of the great powers, for ways in which they too could have a share, in political terms in the determination of the future of the world.

Sri Lanka and many of the other smaller nations which are members of UN today were not at San Francisco. When they were admitted subsequently in the late 50's and early 60's some felt that their safety and security depended very much on military alliances, on taking advantage of political power and patronage of one block or the other which was in their view, geographically or politically important.

On the other hand there were other countries like Sri Lanka which sought their destiny in an independent course, steering clear of the major power blocs and determined to fight for peaceful co-existence, within the framework of a just international order independent of great power conflicts and rivalries – the cold war conflicts which characterised the 1950's and 1960's.

It was the latter group of countries Yugoslavia, India, UAR and Sri Lanka among them which decided that it ought to be desirable for them to find out points of agreement among themselves in the light of their own independent foreign policies, so that within the framework of the UN and its charter they could formulate principles which would give a new meaning and purpose to international politics.

Only 25 countries participated at the first Non-Aligned summit conference in Belgrade in 1961. The movement has since grown beyond the wildest imagination of those who concerned of Non-Alignment as a positive force and positive principles in world politics.

The third world has become a force to be reckoned with which not even the veto power of the great powers in the security council can stifle. It is being called a tyranny of the majority.

Five criteria laid down at Belgrade Non-Alignment.

1. Member countries should have adopted independent policies based on co-existence of status with different political and social systems.

2. Consistently support movements on national independence.

3. Should not be members of multilateral alliances concluded in context of great power conflict.

4. A country with bilateral agreements with great powers or is a member of a regional defence pact – that pact should not have been concluded in context of great power conflict.

5. Any military base to a foreign power should not have been made in great power conflict contexts.

Non-Alignment does not mean mere absence of alignments. The positive concept of non-alignment is peaceful co-existence something much more than merely getting rid of old rivalries. "It is a positive search for a new era of co-operation in place of the confrontation of the past."

N.A.M. is not ideologically tied. It does not have a common ideology as such. Many countries sway in favour of the ideology to another. The desire of nations to pursue independent policies for the good of their own people is fundamental to N.A.M.

It particularly desires co-operation with other countries especially with those struggling for independence. One achievement was the fall of the nation of Portuguese colonialism in Africa.

N.A.M. had many ups and downs. At Belgrade preoccupation was nuclear tests. In Cairo attention had shifted to Middle East problems and tension in Africa. The Lusaka Summit and its delcaration went beyond anything in the past that declaration marked the beginning of economic co-operation and united action by the third world. To ensure that decisions of the General Assembly will benefit all, an economic declaration mapping out areas of co-operation among non N.A.M. emerged for the first time in Lusaka. It meant the essential political will among N.A.M. to co-operate on economic matters. The movement not without problems one of them being the method in lieu of the tyranny of the majority.

What does N.A.M. mean for small countries like Sri Lanka. Their defence and security depend on good relations with other countries. "Good relations with other countries" depend on the degree of understanding between the country concerned and the others – not necessarily the great military power alone but especially its immediate neighbours with whom it must come to terms on the reasonable negotiation.

It is matter of pride that Sri Lanka had achieved this. An example is India with whom problems have been settled through negotiations with complete understanding. Another instance is the 1971 insurrection when Sri Lanka received help from all quarters. This was possible only because of the respect and appreciation the international community had in non-alignment policy and N.A.M. is the greatest single event of nations joined together for a common cause. There Is no other group with such a wide diversity. Yet able to find common ground on questions far apart and by a process of dialogue and understanding arriving at something that goes far beyond *detente* with areas of genuine peaceful co-existence in a spirit of positive co-operation.

THE COMMONWEALTH PRIME MINISTERS' CONFERENCE IN LONDON, 1977

Mr Bandaranaike, Sri Lanka, expressed the regrets of his Prime Minister at not being able to be present because of the forthcoming elections in Sri Lanka.

Mr Bandaranaike thought that the Prime Minister of India had made an excellent point in his opening speech the previous day when he said that he sincerely hoped that this Meeting would carry forward a message of hope to all the people throughout the world and certainly do nothing to add to their misery. Of the 36 Commonwealth countries, 24 were members of the non-aligned movement and two others, Barbados and Grenada, enjoyed observer status. It was perfectly true there were many countries which really had very little choice, because of their geographical situation; the closer a country was to a Super Power the more its actions tended to be viewed by that Super Power from its own point of view, so much so that an independent stance was sometimes taken for opposition. At the same time it should be realised that many of the advances made by insurgencies, by efforts calculated, to overthrow Governments, were not always inspired by foreign Governments from outside. Of course, if there was a dissident group, it could be helped and influenced by outside powers. Sri Lanka had been the subject of attacks of that sort, first in 1962, when there was an attempted police and army coup calculated to overthrow the first Government of Mrs Bandaranaike, and again during the insurrection in 1971, which was led by people who were ideologically trained to think in terms of an ultra-Left movement. A number of Great Powers and friendly countries of differing ideologies had helped the

Sri Lanka Government against the insurgents which showed that the insurgency was not instigated by some Great Power's foreign policy.

It would be wrong to assume that many of these problems arose from anything but the actual conditions prevailing in countries through no fault of anyone, certainly through no fault of the Governments in power. It was right to criticise suppression of human rights in relation to particular things like imprisonment without trial or the denial of fundamental rights for human beings, as was happening in South Africa. Those were horrors of one sort but there was also a fundamental denial of human rights of another sort, the denial of human rights arising from poverty or deprivation. The world recession no doubt created hardships for industrialised countries, but it resulted in acute misery for countries whose forms of trade kept declining over a long period of time, as Sri Lanka's had since 1957-58. It was easy to talk of good financial management, but the reason why Sri Lanka had always been able to come to the surface and to survive was the recognition that human dignity and human work counted for more than simple economics. They had tried to maintain the highest possible standards in health and education, which were expensive, but at the same time necessary if human rights were to be realised in real and practical terms. It was on the economic front that significant advances must be made by both the developed and the developing countries through working together and sharing technology, resources, capital and raw materials.

He looked at the new international economic order not in terms of some minor modifications to the existing order but from the point of view of a new partnership, a new deal, and a new approach. He did not entirely agree with the President of Bangladesh and others that the North-South dialogue had been a complete failure. He was little more hopeful and believed that some progress had been made, though not as much as he would have liked. There was a great deal more to be achieved in future. A beginning had been made in the direction of a common fund and in terms of a special billion dollar fund. The Commonwealth could help in future co-operative efforts.

He agreed with Mr Fraser that there were many aspects where the actions of one nation had consequences for others which it would be too simple to classify into ideological stances. In the field of trade, even after many years of discussion on the question of the effects of British entry into the Common Market, the fact remained that of the Commonwealth countries, those which had really drawn the short straw were the non-associated States in the South-Asian group. He would therefore like to ask the Governments of the UK and others in the Commonwealth to support their case and to help them to get terms of comparative fair entry for their goods into the markets of Europe.

With regard to Vietnam and the dangers which Prime Minister Lee Kuan Yew foresaw, it was true to say that Vietnam, having fought its war, was now turning in a different direction. They were looking for foreign investment. They were passing foreign investment guarantee laws for 10 or 15 years and had joined the International Monetary Fund and the World Bank. It might be unreasonable to assume that Vietnam was necessarily going to become a danger to all others in South or South-East Asia. The far greater dangers that he foresaw were the dangers inherent in the existing systems.

In conclusion, he agreed with the President of Bangladesh that for any just and equitable and final settlement in the Middle-East there would have to be participation of the Palestine Liberation Organisation. He pointed out that in the 1975 Communique there was a reference to the participation of the Palestinian people, though not specifically a reference to the Palestine Liberation Organisation. He suggested that the present Meeting should try a form of words which should include the Palestine Liberation Organisation by name, rather than merely a reference to the Palestinian people.

While reserving his comments on southern Africa, he said that Sri Lanka had always supported the just cause of people on the basis of one man one vote, and black majority rule was inevitable.

With regard to the Indian Ocean, he said that since Mrs. Bandaranaike first raised this question, they had taken the view that this peace zone was extraordinarily important to the area, while recognising that the freedom of the seas must of course be protected and guaranteed. But the question of the freedom of the seas, freedom of navigation and freedom of contacts, were distinct from the question of Great Power competition or Great Power rivalry using the Indian Ocean as a base. He hoped that a stage would come when the Great Powers themselves would be willing to include the Indian Ocean as one of the areas of demilitarisation. He thought that there were some hopeful signs in this regard particularly in view of the attitude of the now American Administration. He also saw hopeful signs in the approach of the Carter Administration with regard to accommodating the aspirations of the Third World. He looked forward to an expanding area of co-operation. Even with regard to nuclear questions, raised by Prime Minister Trudeau, a greater sharing of technology, a way of helping to build a better world, depended upon the willingness to share and co-operate.

He concluded by saying that representatives should bear in mind the need to change the relationships in their own countries by banishing poverty, disease and ignorance, and for this purpose they all required help. The Commonwealth had a record of having settled many problems and of providing such help.

'Mutual understanding and an atmosphere of friendship and goodwill can solve outstanding problems'
HELP BUILD A UNITED SRI LANKA – Felix tells Tamils
By S. G. N. Pushparatnam

I have come to Jaffna not only as a representative of the Government but also as a true friend of the Tamils in the North. I have come here not to ask for your votes, or to canvas for the crossover of your politicians to the Government. I have not come here to talk politics either. The purpose of my visit is to solicit your friendship and co-operation to build a united Sri Lanka where all the people irrespective of the community they belonged to, the language they spoke, or the religion they professed, will be equal and enjoy the same rights.

So said Mr Felix R. Dias Bandaranaike, Minister of Public Administration, Local Government, Home Affairs & Justice, speaking at a public meeting held at the Open Air Theatre, Jaffna on Sunday night.

He said he agreed with those people who said that the Tamils had several of their problems unsolved. Those problems could be solved if the two major communities established a rapport with each other and discussed their problems with a view to solve them.

By having discussions the longstanding problems, including the language question, could be solved easily. By mutual understanding and creating an atmosphere of friendship and goodwill all the problems that confronted both communities could be settled once and for all. Instead of doing this, some politicians in the North were issuing threats on the Government.

He further said a concrete example of solving problems by discussion was the solution that was found to the Indo-Ceylon problems some time back, and recently the settlement reached as regards. The question of the ownership of that tiny island, had now been settled once and for all. He said he was happy to see some of the Tamil politicians including Mr S. J. V. Chelvanayakam who once said that Kachativu belonged to South India had now expressed joy and satisfaction as regards the recent agreement. That agreement was made by the PM not with any political motive, but to help the people of the North, especially the fishermen who used this Island and pilgrims from the North who went there for festivals. The administration of this island would now come under the purview of the Delft local authorities.

Communalism

He further said communalism which once bestrode the Southern and Northern parts of Sri Lanka was now on the way out. The people from both sides of the Elephant Pass had now begun to think as one united nation and as a result communal politicians like Mr K. M. P. Rajaratne and his counterparts in the North had been pushed to the background. He was happy to see the people in Jaffna, too, realised that communal politics would not help them to solve their problems.

FARMERS

Referring to the Jaffna farmers, he said the farmers in the North had proved in recent times that they were superior to their counterparts in the South in all respects.

The Jaffna farmers had now become very rich. The farmers down south had not resented it or accused the government of helping the Jaffna farmers. Instead, they had begun to admire the achievements of the Northern farmers. They had also expressed their willingness to learn from the Tamil farmers to increase production. The Government had been giving all the necessary assistance and encouragement to the Jaffna farmers and would also do so in the future, even though many of them were opposed to the other policies and programmes of the Government.

Referring to the language of the courts, the Minister said he had made Tamil the language of the Courts in the Tamil areas because he felt it would not be fair if the Tamils were forced to conduct the affairs of the courts in a language other than their own. He further said he found that it was fair and necessary to allow the people who came before the courts expecting justice to be done, to be heard in a language that they knew.

Referring to the administration of the Jaffna Municipal Council he said he had not come across a city as clean as Jaffna in recent times. It was mainly due to the untiring efforts and dedicated service of Mr Alfred Duraiyappah, Mayor of Jaffna.

He further said he wished to remind the people of Jaffna that the first person to vote the necessary funds for a water supply scheme for Jaffna was the late Prime Minister Mr S. W. R. D. Bandaranaike. He did so during the height of the 1958 communal riots. It was due to this action of the late PM, that the people of Jaffna were now able to have their own water supply schemes.

GOVERNMENT WILL NOT HARM ANY COMMUNITY: FELIX IN MANDATIVU

"People have greatly benefited by the new judicial reforms introduced recently. The language of the courts is being enforced without causing discrimination to any section of the community," said Mr Felix Dias

Bandaranaike, Minister of Public Administration, Local Government and Home Affairs and Minister of Justice.

Mr Bandaranaike opened the Law Library at the Public Library hall in Jaffna on Sunday. Mr Alfred Duraiyappah, Mayor of Jaffna, presided.

Mr Bandaranaike said he would call a conference of High Court judges as early as possible to discuss the difficulties in implementing the Language of the Courts Act and how to solve problems which may have arisen. It was the Government's intention to rule without harming any community or causing hardships to the people of any particular region in the country.

After the meeting Mr Bandaranaike unveiled a statue of Mahatma Gandhi at the Jaffna Mahatma Gandhi Road. It is one of the statues erected by the Jaffna Municipal Council to mark the council's silver jubilee celebrations which are now on.

The Minister said that the Mahatma did not fight for the independence of India single-handed. The people of Sri Lanka too benefited by the Mahatma's struggle. This country too was able to come out of the grip of its imperialist rulers because of the Mahatma's struggle and the genuine satyagraha campaign launched against the foreign rulers.

Mr Bandaranaike also opened the jubilee hall of the Jaffna Municipal Council. It was constructed to commemorate the Council's silver jubilee. Mr Bandaranaike also visited the Agricultural-Industrial Development Exhibition which is being held to commemorate the council's jubilee.

CHAPTER XV

Felix's Insight into Politics & Economics

The cut & thrust of debate

It started in the Throne Speech Debate. The Member for Dompe, **Mr Felix Dias Bandaranaike,** was discharging with enthusiasm and relish a fusillade of shots at the Government generally when, after nearly two hours of continuous firing, he stopped in his tracks. After a slight pause, during which he shuffled his papers as if to adjust his verbal sights for a direct shot, he said:

"I was hoping that at least in this Throne Speech debate I would be able to say some of our Ministers have realised the error of their ways in making very bad appointments to boards and corporations, but I find that this government will never learn and will never improve.

"The latest example – I will mention it for what it is worth to the Minister of Industries within whose purview the institution falls – is the appointment of a bigamist as cashier-clerk in the National Textile Corporation. Later this bigamist was put in charge of welfare work involving women."

With extracts from the court record and from the prison record, the Member for Dompe sought to substantiate his statement that the man was a bigamist. He then told the house, **"I happen to know this man because at one time he happened to be, strangely enough, working in a government office at Dompe."** It was a piece of information on which the Minister was to weave into his reply a salty witticism.

Mr Bandaranaike then administered his Parthian shot. **"Do not tolerate bigamists" he warned. Do not put them in charge of welfare work involving women. They might want to fall in line with the bigamist in Somerset Maugham's 'Round Dozen.'** It was Mortimer Ellis who, with seven marriages, sighed "It's nothing; It's not even a round dozen." Not many days after his moan, Mortimer Ellis achieved his ambition: he completed a round dozen.

The Minister of Industries **Mr Philip Gunawardena,** had spoken earlier and could not reply to the Member for Dompe in that debate, which concluded the next day. The opportunity presented itself in another debate some days later. The Minister thanked the Member for Dompe for bringing the case of the bigamist to his notice. The matter had been inquired into and the man interdicted. Then, with great gravity, Mr Gunawardena indulged in an irradiant irrelevance:

"I want to say this: This person is from Kurunegala but he committed bigamy in Dompe, I do not know whether it is an offence in Dompe, because the feudal lords there even today exercise the right of PRIMAE NOCTIS over their tenants. I would like the Hon. Member for Dompe to look into the matter and see whether this man's conversion to bigamy took place in the somewhat favourable feudal atmosphere of Dompe."

"PRIMAE NOCTIS? What the hell is that?" asked a backbencher **sotto voce.** After all, everybody is ignorant, only on different subjects. Why, we have had an acting Minister of Finance who once asked, **"What is G.N.P."** – and he wasn't jesting. Mr Felix Dias Bandaranaike later said that he thought that the acting Minister thought it was a dirty word – like UNP.

The right of **PRIMAE NOCTIS,** or as it is referred to in the books, **jus primae noctis** (the right of the first night) was the right of the overlord to go to bed with the bride of any one of his vassals on the first night.

The **ENCYCLOPAEDIA BRITANNICA** states: **"The question is violently controversial and the weight of evidence does point to the existence of such a custom, at an early date, in parts of France and possibly in a few centres in Italy and Germany, BUT CERTAINLY NOT ELSEWHERE."** This note clearly calls for revision. The testimony of the Minister, corroborated by the results of the researches of the Member for Dompe (to which reference will be made presently), make the conclusion inevitable that the feudal lords of Lanka, too, closely observed the custom, either as a demonstration of power (the defloration of a **virgo intacta** being a painful process), or as a source of sensual gratification (though a latter-day Lothario of an overlord would have thought, if he had lived in former times, that the first night was hardly the best night for seduction.)

However, it was no defence or condonation of bigamy or bigamists that the Minister offered by his delectable digression. It was a case of Mr Philip Gunawardena's puckish wit breaking out, and serving to remind his political foes – "toothless lion" and "extinct volcano" are the epithets flung at him recently – that age has not withered the wit of this sexagenarian.

There is in the Government Front Bench a variety of wit: for example, **Mr Dudley Senanayake,** with his bludgeon blows to shock and stun, and

Mr J. R. Jayewardene, with his rapier thrusts delivered with infinite finesse; and there is no doubt that had either chosen, like Mr Philip Gunawardena to take the field, he would have wielded his weapon to good purpose. But the ways of wit are unaccountable and there is no knowing the shape or form of manoeuvre. **Mr Dahanayake** is different. He has wandered so long with Lear over the Great Gromboolian Plain, and with Carroll in Wonderland that it is easy to say that he would have wrapped his wit in a dress of comic or curious verse and from the quirkish reasoning of a rhyme he would have derived an argument pro or con, as the spirit moved him. Surely, he would haved called to aid the young man of Lyme –

Who married three wives at one time,
When asked, Why the third?
He said, One's absurd,
And a bigamy, Sir, is a crime.

Alas! the Doctor no longer meanders along agreeable paths: the cares of office have cramped his style.

Well, when Mr Philip Gunawardena said that the bigamist had been relieved of his appointment and proceeded to delight the House with a dig at Dompe about **jus primae noctis,** it so happened that Mr Felix Dias Bandaranaike was not present. Mr Bandaranaike, however, is one of those Members of Parliament who, having raised a matter in the House, follows it up to see what action has been taken; and in this instance Mr Bandaranaike had presumably looked up Hansard for the Minister's reply.

Can bigamy be regarded as a crime in Dompe?

After all, do not the feudal lords there still exercise **jus primae noctis?** May it not be that such a favourable feudal atmosphere induces even in the virtuous a desire to seek relief from the monotomy of monogamy? Such questions if not expressly raised, were inplicit in the Minister's answer.

The Member for Dompe must have been glad that prompt action had been taken on his complaint. He must also have been glad that the Minister's reply was to afford him an opportunity to indulge in a little bit of devilment, for there is in Mr Felix Dias Bandaranaike an imp that likes to tease and twit. So, in response to the Minister's request that the Member finds out whether the peculiar position prevalent in Dompe was not responsible for the man's conversion to bigamy, Mr Bandaranaike ostensibly undertook some research on the subject.

In the course of a speech a few days later, in which he took a lusty knock at the Minister of Industries, Mr Bandaranaike revealed the results of his research. His eyes twinkling with amusement and mischief, he said:

"My good friend, the Hon. Minister of Industries, referred in the course of a debate to jus primae noctis with reference to the feudal lords

of Dompe. Mr Speaker I do not know very much about this myself. Maybe I was too young. So I took the trouble to gather information from such paternal relations as I was able to locate. My paternal ancestors are no more, but I managed to locate an elderly gentleman among my paternal relations and I asked him. He said, yes, you know, what the Minister of Industries says is not entirely false. Some of the overlords in feudal Dompe may have done things like that – exercised their JUS PRIMAE NOCTIS. But their normal technique was to charter the ferry and cross the river on to Hewagam Korale and there exercise their rights – a matter which the Hon. Minister may be able to verify by consulting perhaps some of his own MATERNAL relations."

Two matters require amplification. Firstly, a part of Hewagam Korale falls within the Avissawella Electorate, which Mr Philip Gunawardena represents. Secondly, according to the authoritative **Encyclopaedia Britannica,** it was open to a serf, on the payment of a certain tax to the overlord, to have **jus primae noctis** waived. But as the overlords of Dompe chartered the ferry to exercise their rights beyond the river, it is unlikely that they would have bartered away this right for filthy lucre. When the ferry failed, they would have swum the river like Lochinvar.

Mr Bandaranaike went on:

"I am grateful to the Hon. Minister that, in spite of this digression on which he knows much better than I do by virtue of his age and experience, for having decided, for whatever reason, that bigamy is not a good thing and that bigamists should be discharged from the performance of their duties in the National Textile Corporation. So it seems to me that, on either side of the river, whether at the receiving end of JUS PRIMAE NOCTIS or the giving end, we hold common views in regard to the undesirability of bigamy. That is established."

Mr Philip Gunawardena sat still and silent.

Thank goodness! the proceedings of Parliament are not always dull.

Felix justifies a Trial at Bar

reasons of justice and fairplay but we have failed to get him to make the necessary amendments in this Bill. Therefore it is that we, who condemn the coup d'etat no less than hon. Members on the other side, are unable to support this Bill. I ask once again that Clause 15 of the Bill be so amended that these persons who are accused of this coup d'etat may be given a right of appeal.

ගරු එච්. ආර්. ඩයස් බණ්ඩාරනායක

(கௌரவ எப். ஆர். டயஸ் பண்டாரநாயக்க)

(The Hon. F. R. Dias Bandaranaike)

Mr. Cháirman—

වෛද්‍යාචාර්ය නාගනාදන්

(டொக்டர் நாகநாதன்)

(Dr. Naganathan)

Do not run away after speaking—

රෝයි රාජපක්ෂ මයා.

(திரு. ரோய் ராஜபக்ஸ)

(Mr. Roy Rajapakse)

You ran away from the Galle Face green without your pants.

වෛද්‍යාචාර්ය නාගනාදන්

(டொக்டர் நாகநாதன்)

(Dr. Naganathan)

I never ran away. I was not, in fact, wearing trousers. I was in a *verti* and a pair of under pants— [*Interruption*]. A hundred rowdies came at me but I did not run away. I am prepared to face a hundred rowdies from over there also— [*Interruption*].

ගරු එච්. ආර්. ඩයස් බණ්ඩාරනායක

(கௌரவ எப். ஆர். டயல் பண்டாரநாயக்க)

(The Hon. F. R. Dias Bandaranaike)

Mr. Chairman, the trousers of the hon. Member for Nallur (Dr. Naganathan) are not relevant to a discussion of Section 15. I suggest that we leave aside all questions of trousers and *verties* and get back to Clause 15.

The question is raised as to why there is no right of appeal to the Court of Criminal Appeal under Section 15. A trial at bar contemplates a trial before three Judges of the Supreme Court. The Court of Criminal Appeal also normally sits in normal circumstances with three Judges of the Supreme Court. Is it suggested that there is any special merit, once three Judges of the Supreme Court have brought their considered mind to bear on a question, in having a right of appeal to another group of three Judges of the Supreme Court on the basis that one group of three Judges might take a view different to that of the Bench of three Judges who have already considered the matter ? In other words, is the merit of a legal decision to depend upon a question of counting of heads or is it to depend on any other principle of determination ? After all, if three Judges have brought their minds to bear on a question of law relevant to the case, what is the argument in saying : Let us have an appeal to a similar tribunal on the basis that they might think differently ?

I can understand it if there is a jury sitting, where there is the possibility of misdirection on law by a judge to the jury or of these other questions arising where jury trials are concerned. We know, for instance, that one of the grounds on which a Court of Criminal Appeal can set aside a judgment or verdict of an Assize Court is on the basis that the verdict of the jury was perverse. There are also matters like non-direction or misdirection by a judge on a material question of law.

But here we have a tribunal consisting of three judges of the Supreme Court to consider a legal question. Having considered and given judgment, the position is taken up that there should be a right of appeal to the Court of Criminal Appeal consisting of another three judges of the Supreme Court.

ඩබ්ලිව්. දහනායක මයා.

(திரு. டப்ளிவ். தகணயக்க)

(Mr. W. Dahanayake)

The procedure you have provided for at the trial at bar is something very novel.

ගරු එෆ්. ආර්. ඩයස් බණ්ඩාරනායක
(கௌரவ எப். ஆர். டயஸ் பண்டாரநாயக்க)
(The Hon. F. R. Dias Bandaranaike)

The procedure that will be followed at the trial at bar will be procedure laid down by the law as approved by Parliament. There is no other law I am aware of that is practised in any Court. It is precisely the law as laid down by Parliament that is enshrined in the Evidence Ordinance, the Criminal Procedure Code and every other statute including this one when it is passed by Parilament. In other words, what is there wrong in saying that the procedure to be followed by a Court is the procedure which is approved by this House, by the Senate and approved by the Governor-General.

වෛද්‍යාචාර්ය නාගනාදන්
(டொக்டர் நாகநாதன்)
(Dr. Naganathan)

By you and your clique.

ගරු එෆ්. ආර්. ඩයස් බණ්ඩාරනායක
(கௌரவ எப். ஆர். டயஸ் பண்டாரநாயக்க)
(The Hon. F. R. Dias Bandaranaike)

Which is Parilament ? In other words, therein lies the argument, the hon. Member for Nallur has pointed it out. They resent the fact that they cannot control Parliament because of a defeat in the elections, because they could not succeed in getting majorities, therefore, Parliament must be deprived of its powers. This is how the defenders of democracy who argue very stoutly in its defence want to practise democracy by saying it is wrong for Parliament, a majority of duly elected representatives of this country, to determine what are the laws in accordance with which justice shall be administered. Now what is the argument ?

වෛද්‍යාචාර්ය නාගනාදන්
(டொக்டர் நாகநாதன்)
(Dr. Naganathan)

Will the Hon. Minister give way ?

ගරු එෆ්. ආර්. ඩයස් බණ්ඩාරනායක
(கௌரவ எப். ஆர். டயஸ் பண்டாரநாயக்க)
(The Hon. F. R. Dias Bandaranaike)
Certainly.

වෛද්‍යාචාර්ය නාගනාදන්
(டொக்டர் நாகநாதன்)
(Dr. Naganathan)

Herr Hitler also utilized the Parliamentary majority to take away all the rights. That is what you are doing.

ගරු එෆ්. ආර්. ඩයස් බණ්ඩාරනායක
(கௌரவ எப். ஆர். டயஸ் பண்டாரநாயக்க)
(The Hon. F. R. Dias Bandaranaike)

Sir, I am not giving way to the hon. Member for Nallur. He can talk a lot as he likes.

වෛද්‍යාචාර්ය නාගනාදන්
(டொக்டர் நாகநாதன்)
(Dr. Naganathan)

We are resenting your Hitlerian methods of utilising the Parliament for totalitarian tactics.

සභාපතිතුමා
(அக்கிராசனர்)
(The Chairman)

Order, please ! If the hon. Member for Nallur keeps on interrupting, I am sorry I will be compelled to ask him to leave the Chamber. Please do not interrupt. You will get your chance of replying to the Hon. Minister.

ගරු එෆ්. ආර්. ඩයස් බණ්ඩාරනායක
(கௌரவ எப். ஆர். டயஸ் பண்டாரநாயக்க)
(The Hon. F. R. Dias Bandaranaike)

I am talking of Clause 15. Under Clause 15 — [Interruption] — Mr. Chairman, we cannot enter into arguments, we have already heard the views of the hon. Member for Nallur expressed by the other side of the House. I cannot enter into arguments of that sort.

Now, Mr. Chairman, where 3 judges of the Supreme Court have brought their considered minds, their considered judgment, to bear on a legal question, is it to be argued

2973   1962 මාර්තු 1   2974

well, if you want to set aside 3 judges, let us have a Court of Criminal Appeal consisting of 5 or consisting of 4 or consisting of 7, anything up to 9 or 11, as the case may be ; let us have a Court of Criminal Appeal consisting of a larger number of judges, which raises the eternal question, is there any merit in counting heads, In other words, does it carry the case any further to arrive at a just result of a case because you have got a larger number of judges ? From 3 let us have an appeal to 4 or 5 or 6 or 7, does that make justice any the more efficacious as far as the people of this country are concerned ? No, Sir.

There is a purpose in having an appeal of a type like that where there is a question of trial by jury consisting of laymen, of lay people, with certain qualifications who are going to be directed or misdirected as the case may be by Supreme Court judges who might make mistakes and where the law has got to be given by the considered verdict of 3 judges. But to say, why stop at 3 judges, you must have another appeal to another 3 judges, is, Sir, a meaningless farce, it would reduce justice to a mockery.

On the other hand, we are told by this section expressly or by implication that nothing is said about the right of appeal to the Privy Council, nothing at all is said about that. I am prepared to state here on the Floor of the House—indeed, I think, many hon. Members of the House might disagree with me and say, " Why are you allowing it ? "—but the fact remains that this Bill nowise takes away what is described as the undisputed right of a subject to appeal to Her Majesty the Queen as stated in the Criminal Procedure Code. Well, it is said so. If you cannot take it away then what are you worrying about , If the right of appeal is there and if you are concerned with the fact that you want the right of appeal and yet you say that it cannot be taken away, it is enshrined in the law already, then

what is your trouble, what is your grievance ? That is the question I am asking you.

In other words, you say there is a denial of justice here. You say there is no right of appeal and you yourself concede that there is undoubtedly a right of appeal to Her Majesty the Queen If that is so what on earth are we arguing about? Is it merely you want to give the accused in the conspiracy case against the State a second bite of the cherry ? In other words, if you fail with 3 judges let · us try our luck and get another 3 judges. So what it amounts to is this: let us keep trying. Why not have three courts of criminal appeal till we exhaust the full number of nine Judges, then have another set of three Judges appointed and see how it goes ? Is that the kind of argument that we are dealing with ?

We are told that, in the fair name of democracy, it is wrong for Parliament to consider the nature of the laws which are to be administered in this country. If that is not what we are going to do, why are we here ? Why did we go before the electors and ask them for their votes ? Why did we come here in order to be the legislators of the country ? We are told, " Oh no ! it is very wrong for you to legislate in order to govern this country. The last thing you must do is legislate. It is undemocratis. " Why ? " Because you have got a majority and you are in a position to get your laws passed. " Therefore, it becomes undemocratic for us to pass laws which are unacceptable to a minority of hon. Members of this House ! But their views are considered. We have been considering them day and night for several days. Indeed, we have been doing nothing else.

In other words, the " anti-democratic " features to which these hon. Members are objecting is ultimately this. It is their objection to the fact that the S. L. F. P. obtained the majority of seats in the last General Election of July, 1960. That is what

[ගරු එෆ්. ආර්. ඩයස් බණ්ඩාරනායක]
is "undemocratic" in their view. If you break up their argument into pieces, you come to that result, pure and simply, and nothing else. I do not think that is an argument which requires a reply. I think that even the hon. Member for Galle (Mr. W. Dahanayake), with this knowledge and experience as a teacher——

ඔබිලිව්. දහනායක මයා.
(திரு. டப்ளியு. தகணயக்க)
(Mr. W. Dahanayake)
I do not agree with you.

ගරු එෆ්. ආර්. ඩයස් බණ්ඩාරනායක
(கௌரவ எப். ஆர். டயஸ் பண்டாரநாயக்க)
(The Hon. F. R. Dias Bandaranaike)
——will accept the point that there is a feature of *reductio ad absurdum* in the whole argument presented on that footing.

Therefore, if you are interested in finding out what the law is and what the law should be, I agree that no person, except Parliament, has the right to determine what the law is and what the law should be. Indeed, Parliament is here seeking to sit in judgment and give an answer to that; and we on this side of the House, say that there is absolutely no purpose served in allowing a right of appeal from a decision of three Judges to another set of three Judges, or to any other set of Judges, counting them by heads. All we say is that there is a right of appeal to the Privy Council, which shows that this Government is not seeking to make any particular judgment final. We are allowing that right of appeal. Indeed, hon. Members on the other side say that we cannot alter it. That is right.

ඔබිලිව්. දහනායක මයා.
(திரு. டப்ளியு. தகணயக்க)
(Mr. W. Dahanayake)
Will the Hon. Minister answer my direct question? When an application is made that the execution of a sentence should be stayed to enable an appeal to be made to the Privy Council, will the Hon. Minister of

Juctice allow such application? That is my straightforward, pointed question.

ගරු එෆ්. ආර්. ඩයස් බණ්ඩාරනායක
(கௌரவ எப். ஆர். டயஸ் பண்டாரநாயக்க)
(The Hon. F. R. Dias Bandaranaike)
May I ask a very simple question? Does the hon. Member for Galle, either during his period or tenure of office, however short it may have been, as Prime Minister, or in the whole course of his experience as a Parliamentarian, know of a single case where sentence was executed pending appeal to the Privy Council? Does he know of a single instance?

ඔබිලිව්. දහනායක මයා.
(திரு. டப்ளியு. தகணயக்க)
(Mr. W. Dahanayake)
That is not an answer to my question.

ගරු එෆ්. ආර්. ඩයස් බණ්ඩාරනායක
(கௌரவ எப். ஆர். டயஸ் பண்டாரநாயக்க)
(The Hon. F. R. Dias Bandaranaike)
Of course, it is.

ඔබිලිව්. දහනායක මයා.
(திரு. டப்ளியு. தகணயக்க)
(Mr. W. Dahanayake)
It is not.

කන්දසියා මයා.
(திரு. கந்தையா)
(Mr. Kandiah)
Oh yes, it is. In other words, the Hon. Minister has told the hon. Member that in no case has it been done, and in no case will it be done in the future.

ගරු එෆ්. ආර්. ඩයස් බණ්ඩාරනායක
(கௌரவ எப். ஆர். டயஸ் பண்டாரநாயக்க)
(The Hon. F. R. Dias Bandaranaike)
Is that the hon. Member for Galle's sense of justice? In other words, that type of thought will occur only to a perverted mind like that of the hon. Member for Galle.

රොයි රාජපක්ෂ මයා. (හක්මන)
(திரு. ரோய் ராஜபக்ஸ—ஹக்மனா)
(Mr. Roy Rajapakse—Hakmana)

His conscience is heavy. His conscience is pricking him !

ගරු එෆ්. ආර්. ඩයස් බණ්ඩාරනායක
(கௌரவ எப். ஆர். டயஸ் பண்டாரநாயக்க)
(The Hon. F. R. Dias Bandaranaike)

We know that the hon. Member for Galle, for the sake of a little cheap trick in Parliament, is willing to say anything. But I must say what I never thought a person who had held the high office of Prime Minister of a country would ever resort to that type of low argument.

ඩබ්ලිව්. දහනායක මයා.
(திரு. டப்ளியு. தகனுயக்க)
(Mr. W. Dahanayake)

Never mind that. Answer my question.

ගරු එෆ්. ආර්. ඩයස් බණ්ඩාරනායක
(கௌரவ எப். ஆர். டயஸ் பண்டாராநாயக்க)
(The Hon. F. R. Dias Bandaranaike)

I do mind it. I mind it very much. I think it is a shame on this country.

ඩබ්ලිව්. දහනායක මයා.
(திரு. டப்ளியு. தகனுயக்க)
(Mr. W. Dahanayake)

I will not make a retort. Answer my question.

ගරු එෆ්. ආර්. ඩයස් බණ්ඩාරනායක
(கௌரவ எப். ஆர். டயஸ் பண்டாராநாயக்க)
(Mr. F. R. Dias Bandaranaike)

I have answered your question. I am grateful to the hon. Member for Kayts (Mr. Kandiah) for rising and drawing attention to a perfectly valid defence which I have indicated. As I have pointed out, it shows the type of low argument to which unscrupulous are prepared to descend.

රොයි රාජපක්ෂ මයා.
(திரு. ரோய் ராஜபக்ஸ)
(Mr. Roy Rajapakse)

His conscience sits heavily on him !

සභාපතිතුමා
(அக்கிராசனர்)
(The Chairman)

Order, please ! If the hon. Member for Hakmana (Mr. Roy Rajapakse) keeps on interrupting. I shall have to ask him to leave the Chamber.

ගරු එෆ්. ආර්. ඩයස් බණ්ඩාරනායක
(கௌரவ எப். ஆர். டயஸ் பண்டாராநாயக்க)
(The Hon. F. R. Dias Bandaranaike)

The right of appeal to the Privy Council is there. It is an undoubted right enshrined in the Criminal Procedure Code in express terms in a Section which, no doubt, the Members of the legal profession present in the House will consider. I refer to the undoubted right of appeal to Her Majesty the Queen in Council. So that if the right of appeal to the Privy Council is there, no one is seeking to create a finality.

But we have gone to three Judges of the Supreme Court by this law. And we say, your request for another right of appeal from their decision to another group of Judges, merely on the chance of giving the accused a second bite of the cherry in case they did not get sufficient from the first bite, is no argument. I do submit that there is no purpose served in seeking to cloud the issue and to try and create an aura that justice is going to be denied to any person, in the course of this case, by virtue of the argument presented on Clause 15.

I have always made it a point to be present on the Floor of the House for the longest possible periods of this for which I think any Minister of a Government is ever able to be present in this House. I have sat through proceedings of this House night after night on innumerable occasions over the period of the last eighteen months, and I think hon. Members will agree with me that no charge can ever be levelled that I am not here when wanted to speak on behalf of the Government and I must say that I have sought within the limits of my ability to do my best to discharge that function.

Tamil Language (Special Provisions) Act Regulations

දෙමළ භාෂා (විශේෂ විධිවිධාන) පනත: නියෝග

our ability not to embarrass the Hon. Prime Minister on whatever steps he may take to solve the minority problem once and for all.

කථානායකතුමා

(சபாநாயகர் அவர்கள்)

(Mr. Speaker)

Order please ! I suspend the Sitting till 4.30 P.M. On resumption the Hon. Deputy Speaker will take the Chair.

ඒඑවිම ඊට අනුකූලව තාවකාලිකව අත්හිටුවන ලදින්, අ. භා. 4.30 ට නියෝජන කථානායක තුන්පත් බි. එස්. ෂර්ලි කොරයා මහතාගේ සභාපතින්වයෙන් නැවත පවත්වන ලදී

இதன்படி அமர்வு பி. ப. 4.30 மணிவரை இடை நிறுத்தப்பட்டு, மீண்டும் ஆரம்பமாயிற்று. உபபா நாயகர் [திரு. சி. எஸ். ஷேர்லி கொறயா] தலைமை தாங்கினர்.

Sitting accordingly suspended till 4.30 P.M. and then resumed, MR. DEPUTY SPEAKER [MR. C. S. SHIRLEY COREA], in the Chair.

එෆ්. ආර්. ඩයස් බණ්ඩාරනායක මයා. (දෙම්පේ)

(திரு. எப். ஆர். டயஸ் பண்டாரநாயக— தொம்பே)

(Mr. F. R. Dias Bandaranaike—Dompe)

It gives me, as usual, a great deal of pleasure to follow upon the first Member of the Federal Party to participate in this discussion. I seem to have found myself periodically in this position in this House in the course of this Parliament. Usually it is my good Friend the hon. Member for Vaddukkoddai (Mr. Amirthalingam) who precedes me. In this instance, I have the pleasure of replying to a former colleague of mine in the university—the hon. Member for Chavakachcheri.

He started off on a very sad note, if I may say so, Mr. Deputy Speaker, while he cheered up in the course of the subsequent remarks he made. He started by telling us that he thought the hon. Fair Member for Uva-Paranagama was concerned with exterminating the minorities. She is not here, I see. But I can assure him that there is one minority that she will never exterminate and that is

the bearded fraternity. So I think he can rest assured that he at least will be safe at the hands of the hon. Fair Member for Uva-Paranagama.

We have had examples one after the other of hon. Members of this House standing up, in the course of this Debate, and telling us about the speeches that others have made in this House on previous occasions, quoting their own statements at them, trying to show the lack of consistency on the part of various hon. Members of this House from time to time. I think—[*Interruption*]. I will come to myself in great detail.

නියෝජන කථානායකතුමා

(உப சபாநாயகர் அவர்கள்)

(Mr. Deputy Speaker)

Even before he starts his speech you are interrupting !

එෆ්. ආර්. ඩයස් බණ්ඩාරනායක මයා. (திரு. எப். ஆர். டயஸ் பண்டாரநாயக)

(Mr. F. R. Dias Bandaranaike)

The Hon. Minister of State in opening the Debate started off very frankly by opening the doors of his cupboard and showing his skeletons. I think the number of skeletons has been increasing in the past few days and they may continue to increase. —[*Interruption*].

නියෝජන කථානායකතුමා

(உப சபாநாயகர் அவர்கள்)

(Mr. Deputy Speaker)

Kindly stop interrupting.

එෆ්. ආර්. ඩයස් බණ්ඩාරනායක මයා. (திரு. எப். ஆர். டயஸ் பண்டாரநாயக)

(Mr. F. R. Dias Bandaranaike)

May I say that, if you start an examination of the language question as a whole, it is probably true to say of most hon. Members of this House who have a history in this Legislature, who have been in this legislature for some time, that practically all of them have from time to time changed their policies on language questions. The hon. Member for Colombo South, Minister of State, tried to prove it.—[*Interruption*].

499   නියෝජිත මන්තුී මණ්ඩලය   500
දෙමළ භාෂා (විශේෂ විධිවිධාන) පනත: නියෝග   දෙමළ භාෂා (විශේෂ විධිවිධාන) පනත: නියෝග

නියෝජ්‍ය කථානායකතුමා
(உப சபாநாயகர் அவர்கள்)
(Mr. Deputy Speaker)

I have warned the hon. Member more than once. I shall ask him to leave the House if he continues to disturb the House. It is not an empty threat. If he continues to interrupt, he will have to leave the House.

එෆ්. ආර්. ඩයස් බණ්ඩාරනායක මයා.
(திரு. எப். ஆர். டயஸ் பண்டாரநாயக்க)
(Mr. F. R. Dias Bandaranaike)

The Hon. Minister of State stated, if I may say so, the history of the language question. He started by telling us of the various Resolutions that have been moved from the days of the State Council soon after he first entered the Legislature in 1943. He told us of Mr. Perera's Resolution. He told us how he himself introduced a Resolution for the introduction of Sinhala as the official language of this country ; how an amendment was introduced which was supported by the late Mr. Bandaranaike ; how the amendment was opposed by Mr. Dudley Senanayake, the present Prime Minister. And, in fact, he gave us even the voting on that particular Resolution. He pointed out there after how the Official Languages Commission was appointed, presided over by a former Chief Justice. It is amazing how former Chief Justices get mixed up with the language question from time to time. But in this instance, Sir Arthur Wijewardene did, if I may say so with respect, an excellent job of work on the Official Languages Commission and produced a document which, the Hon. Minister of State had the grace to state, they were very tardy about implementing. And he admitted his own faults and said that, by 1953, after independence was achieved, after the late Mr. Bandaranaike had left the United National Party, all parties revised their views on the language question.

The late Mr. Bandaranaike within his own party appointed a committee to go into the language question and it is on the findings of that committee that the Sinhala only policy of the Sri Lanka Freedom Party came into existence.

At about the same time, the United National Party also did its own rethinking, and it came to fruition in an entirely different direction when the then Prime Minister, Sir John Kotelawala, went to Kokuvil in 1954, and made a speech in which he declared that the United National Party stood for parity, a parity of status for the Sinhala and Tamil languages.

By 1955 the late Mr. Bandaranaike's Sri Lanka Freedom Party was definitely committed to a policy of Sinhala only.—[Interruption]. I would have spoken in Sinhala but I was requested by hon. Members to speak in English. I did not wish to create any complications and I wished to be understood by every section of the House. That is why I decided to speak in English.—[Interruption].

Mr. Deputy Speaker, the late Mr. Bandaranaike's decision on Sinhala only was followed soon after by the Kelaniya session of the United National Party.—[Interruption]. I do not wish to hurl abuse at anybody. I wish to state the facts correctly. At the Kelaniya session the United National Party deliberately and consciously abandoned their parity policy and decided to adopt Sinhala only. But they decided too late.

Now what does this statement, on which I agree with the Hon. Minister of State, prove ? It proves that throughout the whole course of our legislative history, all the major parliamentarians in this country, persons whose thinking on politics affected the destinies of our nation throughout, have been moving away from parity towards Sinhala only and nothing else. You will find that if you examine the skeletons in the cupboard of the Hon. Minister ; you will find that if you look into the political history of our Prime Minister ; you will find that if you look into the political history of the late Mr. S. W. R. D. Bandaranaike ; you will find that if you look into the political history of practically every single parliamentarian of note in this country who adorns either side of this

501 1966 ජනවාරි 10 502

දෙමළ භාෂා (විශේෂ විධිවිධාන) පනත: නියෝග දෙමළ භාෂා (විශේෂ විධිවිධාන) පනත: නියෝග

House today. You are •throwing taunts at some of my Colleagues in the Lanka Sama Samaja Party and the Communist Party because they once upon a time preached the gospel of parity. All I can say is this. If indeed they have given up parity and turned to Sinhala only they are only doing what practically every politician belonging to the United National Party or the Sri Lanka Freedom Party has at some time or another done.

ගරු ජේ. ආර්. ජයවර්ධන
(கௌரவ ஜே. ஆர். ஜயவர்தன)
(The Hon. J. R. Jayewardene)
They do not say so.

එච්. ආර්. ඩයස් බණ්ඩාරනායක මයා.
(திரு. எப். ஆர். டயஸ். பண்டாரநாயக்க)
(Mr. F. R. Dias Bandaranaike)
I think, they have said so more than once, and their saying so amounts to what you have now described periodically as misleading the people. People are misled to such an extent that curfews and shootings have become necessary in order to avoid the misleading. In other words, is it misleading for a politician to say conscientiously and deliberately, "I am abandoning the wrong political position that I took up in the past. I am throwing it away and taking something new which constitutes the present policy of a political party"? Do you say that that is a wrong thing to do? I ask you Mr. Minister of State. When you started, at the beginning of your speech, to trace the history of the language problem, I for one was very happy because you were proving something which we ourselves know to be the truth.

It is perfectly true, in the early days of the fight for independence for this country when the Members of the State Council were concerned with throwing off the yoke of British imperialism, of trying to get rid of Colonial Governors with veto powers, of trying to establish full sovereignty for the people of our land, that it was only natural that the emphasis should not be on the question of what language we are going to use but rather on the use of any language other than English. In those circumstances, the Minister of State himself was quite prepared to accept amendments transforming his own Sinhala only proposal of those days into the swabasha proposal. The Hon. Prime Minister who those days was a little more far-sighted than the Hon. Minister of State, more far-sighted perhaps than the late Mr. S. W. R. D. Bandaranaike at that time in 1944, thought of Sinhala only then. But he too changed subsequently. He had changed by the time of the Kelaniya Sessions. I do not know whether the Hon. Prime Minister was in that party or not.

ගරු ඩඩ්ලි සේනානායක
(கௌரவ டட்லி சேனுநாயக்க)
(The Hon. Dudley Senanayake)
No.

එච්. ආර්. ඩයස් බණ්ඩාරනායක මයා.
(திரு. எப். ஆர். டயஸ். பண்டாரநாயக்க)
(Mr. F. R. Dias Bandaranaike)
He comes and goes from time to time. We would like him to stay because, at least, so long as he is there we know that the United National Party will find it difficult to run amok. But when your Prime Minister, whether he is there or not, by rejoining the United National Party subsequently with its new changed line——

නියෝජ්‍ය කථානායකතුමා
(உப சபாநாயகர் அவர்கள்)
(Mr. Deputy Speaker)
I think the hon. Member for Dompe might face me.

එච්. ආර්. ඩයස් බණ්ඩාරනායක මයා.
(திரு. எப். ஆர். டயஸ் பண்டாரநாயக்க)
(Mr. F. R. Dias Bandaranaike)
You were also not there those days. I shall certainly address you.

503   නියෝජිත මන්ත්‍රී මණ්ඩලය   504

දෙමළ භාෂා (විශේ ෂ විධිවිධාන) පනත: නියෝග

නියෝජ්‍ය කථානායකතුමා
(உப சபாநாயகர் அவர்கள்)
(Mr. Deputy Speaker)

I am speaking of today. Instead of addressing the crowd behind, you might address the Chair.

එච්. ආර්. ඩයස් බණ්ඩාරනායක මයා.
(திரு. எப். ஆர். டயஸ் பண்டாரநாயக்க)
(Mr. F. R. Dias Bandaranaike)

I would very much wish to address the crowd outside, but I shall address you and, through you, the people, the Sinhalese people of whom you happen to be one.

The Hon. Minister of State has shown only the direction of a political movement, and having shown us this direction he proceeds to justify an attempt by his Government now to turn back the tide of history, to sweep it back in a completely different direction and to try to move this country, by whatever label you call it, in the direction of parity of status. And that, he will find it an extremely difficult thing to do not because the people of a country are being misled but merely because politicians when they change do so in accordance with the wishes of their ultimate masters, the people of this country, to whom they must necessarily be subservient.

For reasons which I cannot understand, the Debate on these Regulations has been argued on the basis that it is an attempt to destroy governments. I can assure you that it is not so. So far as the Sri Lanka Freedom Party is concerned, so far as the Opposition is concerned, the question of destruction or over throw of governments does not arise. You have been elected by the people in the present situation to determine the affairs of this country, they have been committed to you for the next five years, and it is your duty, in accordance with the will of the people, to run their affairs for them. There is no wish for usurpation here. There is no wish to prevent you from governing this country.

දෙමළ භාෂා (විශේ ෂ විධිවිධාන) පනත: නියෝග

But the Opposition, still for all, has a function—a function which the Opposition will perform to the best of its ability. It may not be convenient, it may not be always easy for you to be reminded that public opinion has two facets, and what you like to believe to be the truth is not always the truth as the people may choose to see it. We ourselves have been a government once before. We ourselves have made mistakes. We ourselves have misjudged public opinion. It was not the case with our government only. It is true of some of the greatest politicians of our time. They did make mistakes.

The late Mr. S. W. R. D. Bandaranaike, of whom we in this House speak and of whom you find it convenient to speak from time to time, did, in point of fact, change after he entered into the Bandaranaike-Chelvanayakam Pact. He did not tell the people of this country, "I have entered into a pact. Whatever agreement I have made is perfect. I will not tolerate any person misleading the country or the people of this country into thinking otherwise, into disagreeing with this pact." The late Mr. Bandaranaike, in his conception of democracy, did not demand that there should be no attempt to present any documents to the people or to submit them for examination and close scrutiny by the people. What the late Mr. Bandaranaike did was to place the whole of his document before the country, to submit it to the test of public opinion. He did not say, when the Hon. Minister of State wanted to walk to Kandy— not that he does not have a luxurious car —"I object to your walking to Kandy." He did not say, "I am imposing a curfew to stop you from walking by night". He did not say, "You shall not walk. This is incitement and misleading of the people." Far from it! He said, "It is your point of view. In my view Mr. Bandaranaike-Chelvanayakam Pact is right." But he said, "If you can convince me that public opinion runs in a different direction, I shall act differently". And what happened?

505   1966 ජනවාරි 10   506

දෙමළ භාෂා (විශේෂ විධිවිධාන) පනත: නියෝග

You succeeded. The police did not fire tear gas shells at you. Nobody shot you. The Navy did not turn round and shoot you. The only person who obstructed you was our absent Friend from Gampaha who slept across the road.

ගරු ඩී. පී. ආර්. ගුණවර්ධන
(கௌரவ டி. பி. ஆர். குணவர்தன)
(The Hon. D. P. R. Gunawardena)

The late Mr. Bandaranaike called him "Dahaiyya bonikka".

එෆ්. ආර්. ඩයස් බණ්ඩාරනායක මයා.
(திரு. எப். ஆர். டயஸ் பண்டாரநாயக்க)
(Mr. F. R. Dias Bandaranaike)

He put you to flight on your way to Kandy. It was the "Dahaiyya bonikka" that frightened you. You got scared of a scarecrow.

It was your democratic right to agitate against that pact if you felt that the interests of the Sinhala people were being betrayed by it, as you thought then. You turned round and tried to educate the people, saying that the Bandaranaike-Chelvanayakam Pact constituted a betrayal. The late Prime Minister, in his sincerity, did not think so then but he bowed to public opinion. What was that public opinion? Priests collected. Your stalwarts were broadcasting to us and nearly teaching the dharma day by day in the newspapers—the new dharma according to the U.N.P., about the greatness and the wisdom and the correctness of the course of action being adopted by your Prime Minister. They may be right; they may be wrong. There are always two facets to public opinion, and that is why I say that when these very priests, Amarawansa, Meetiyagoda Gunaratna, Seelawansa—

ගරු මන්තුවරයෙක්
(கௌரவ அங்கத்தவர் ஒருவர்)
(An hon. Member)

Buddharakkhita.

දෙමළ භාෂා (විශේෂ විධිවිධාන) පනත: නියෝග

එෆ්. ආර්. ඩයස් බණ්ඩාරනායක මයා.
(திரு. எப். ஆர். டயஸ் பண்டாரநாயக்க)
(Mr. F. R. Dias Bandaranaike)

Yes, all of them—and I am not drawing any distinction—indeed squatted outside Rosmead Place, they were accorded every protection then. [Interruption].

ගරු ඩී. පී. ආර්. ගුණවර්ධන
(கௌரவ டி. பி. ஆர். குணவர்தன).
(The Hon. D. P. R. Gunawardena)

The jackass from Kotte!

ස්ටැන්ලි තිලකරත්න මයා. (කෝට්ටේ)
(திரு. ஸ்டான்லி திலக்காரத்ன—கோட்டே)
(Mr. Stanley Tillekeratne—Kotte)

You donkey!

නියෝජ්‍ය කථානායකතුමා
(உப சபாநாயகர் அவர்கள்)
(Mr. Deputy Speaker)

Hon. Member for Kotte, please stop that.

ස්ටැන්ලි තිලකරත්න මයා.
(திரு. ஸ்டான்லி திலக்காரத்ன)
(Mr. Stanley Tillekeratne)

He called me a "jackass' and I called him "donkey" in return. I am not going to withdraw that unless you ask him to withdraw what he said.—[Interruption].

නියෝජ්‍ය කථානායකතුමා
(உப சபாநாயகர் அவர்கள்)
(Mr. Deputy Speaker)

Please sit down.

එෆ්. ආර්. ඩයස් බණ්ඩාරනායක මයා.
(திரு. எப். ஆர். டயஸ் பண்டாரநாயக்க)
(Mr. F. R. Dias Bandaranaike)

May I proceed, Mr. Deputy Speaker, if the jackass and the donkey have been silenced.

507   නියෝජිත මන්ත්‍රී මණ්ඩලය   508
දෙමළ භාෂා (විශේෂ විධිවිධාන) පනත: නියෝග   දෙමළ භාෂා (විශේෂ විධිවිධාන) පනත: නියෝග
[එච්. ආර්. ඩයස් බණ්ඩාරනායක මයා.]

In those days Mr. Bandaranaike did not say to himself or to this House, " If necessary I will shoot ". Those were not the days when a Prime Minister shot priests ; those were days when priests shot Prime Ministers. We now live at a time, and at an age, when roles have been reversed, when we find that priests are not permitted on the public highway ; they are not permitted to cross the new Kelani bridge at Peliyagoda.

නියෝජ්‍ය කථානායකතුමා
(உப சபாநாயகர் அவர்கள்)
(Mr. Deputy Speaker)
If you start interrupting—

කෙනමන් මයා.
(திரு. கெனமன்)
(Mr. Keuneman)
I am not interrupting.

නියෝජ්‍ය කථානායකතුමා
(உப சபாநாயகர் அவர்கள்)
(Mr. Deputy Speaker)
We can listen to only one speech at a time and not two.—[*Interruption*]. Order, please !

එච්. ආර්. ඩයස් බණ්ඩාරනායක මයා.
(திரு. எப். ஆர். டயஸ் பண்டாரநாயக்க)
(Mr. F. R. Dias Bandaranaike)
These are days when the Maha Sangha is joining the skeletons in the cupboard. The practice of democracy seems to have changed ; we are told that they are following the policies of Bandaranaike. I think the late Mr. Bandaranaike must be turning in his grave at the thought of how his policies are being perverted in the fair name of democracy by a Government which came into office committed to the protection of democracy, a Government which says to us and to this House—it has been saying so for the last four days—that in their opinion we are misleading the people, that we are raising communal passions, that it is something wrong, something which cannot be permitted or tolerated, and that where it is necessary to shoot, " We shall shoot ".

Yes, Mr. Deputy Speaker, we are not afraid. I am aware that nowadays, under the new dispensation, the only place where one can speak one's mind out on this issue is this House. It is unsafe to do so anywhere else. People are now being taken before the magistrates' courts for the offence of publishing leaflets saying that the present Prime Minister is trying to divide the country. It has now become a crime to say so. We are liable to be remanded by the magistrates for saying that the Prime Minister is going to divide the country. We are not going to say it only here, Mr. Deputy Speaker but if we believe that, in fact, the Prime Minister is going to divide the country, if we believe what the Prime Minister is doing at the moment is in effect destroying the self-respect and the position of the entire Sinhala people of this country, we shall say so without fear. It makes no difference whether we are taken into custody ; it makes no difference if we are locked up immediately after this Debate is concluded, and it makes no difference whether you can use all the powers at your command ; but we in the Opposition are not prepared to keep our mouths shut merely because you choose to express one point of view and say that there is no other point of view but yours. You told us that we were on the road to a dictatorship towards the end of 1964. You told us that we were wrong in wanting to take over the press which were your lackeys at that time. You told us we were wrong. We did not think we were wrong. But the peoples' votes showed that we were wrong and we accepted it. But we did not prejudge the issue ; we left it to the people to decide.

ගරු ඩඩ්ලි සේනානායක
(கௌரவ டட்லி சேனநாயக்க)
(The Hon. Dudley Senanayake)
You brought a Bill.

එච්. ආර්. ඩයස් බණ්ඩාරනායක මයා.
(திரு. எப். ஆர். டயஸ் பண்டாரநாயக்க)
(Mr. F. R. Dias Bandaranaike)
Of course, we did. There was the Throne Speech Debate on which you defeated us.

509   1966 ජනවාරි 10   510

දෙමළ භාෂා (විශේෂ විධිවිධාන) පනත : නියෝග

ගරු ඩඩ්ලි සේනානායක

(கௌரவ டட்லி சேனநாயக்க)

(The Hon. Dudley Senanayake)

So defeat us.

එෆ්. ආර්. ඩයස් බණ්ඩාරනායක මයා.

(திரு. எப். ஆர். டயஸ் பண்டாரநாயக்க)

(Mr. F. R. Dias Bandaranaike)

And ultimately the matter was subjected to public opinion and at the elections you again defeated us.

Would you have done that if you were not free to walk on the road and you had a handkerchief tied in your mouth ? Did anyone shoot you or declare a state of emergency while your priests went round the country telling the people what they thought of us ?

Now the position has changed. There is no other possible view except the view held by the Government.

The view held by the Government is that these Regulations which we are debating are the identical Regulations which the late Mr. Bandaranaike presented on the Floor of this House. That is what they said first of all. They changed and said that they are in accordance with the law which he presented and got passed in the House and are identical with the Regulations which he might have presented had he lived to implement his own statute. I shall come to that in a moment.

I do not propose to enjoy myself quoting back at each of you the different speeches you have made. I have them all. I do not want to remind you of the inconvenient things you have said. I see even the Minister of Education (Hon. I. M. R. A. Iriyagolle) is thinking hard. I have his speeches too.

ගරු ඊරියගොල්ල

(கௌரவ ஈரியகொல்ல)

(The Hon. Iriyagolle)

Quote them all, from beginning to end.

එෆ්. ආර්. ඩයස් බණ්ඩාරනායක මයා.

(திரு. எப். ஆர். டயஸ் பண்டாரநாயக்க)

(Mr. F. R. Dias Bandaranaike)

Does he remember the days of the *Samajawadi Mahajana Peramuna* ? When the Tamil Language (Special Provisions) Act was enacted, do you remember your initial statement ? At the very beginning, on behalf of your party, you indicated precisely what you thought of the late Prime Minister and his laws.—[*Interruption.*] You do. I am glad.

Mr. Deputy Speaker, the late Prime Minister, Mr. Bandaranaike, entered into the Bandaranaike-Chelvanayakam Pact. I am glad that the authorship of that document was admitted by the hon. Second Member for Colombo Central (Mr. Premadasa), if only for the reason that I want to show that it represents the views of the United National Party at that time. Here is the booklet. The cover shows a footprint placed across the map of Ceylon.

The hon. Second Member for Colombo Central read from the Sinhala copy. I have deliberately brought an English copy from which I shall read for the information of all sections of the House.

The Prime Minister told us that in April 1960, when he was Prime Minister, he did not oppose the Bandaranaike-Chelvanayakam Pact on language ; he opposed it on colonization. That is what he told us. But if you read this book you will see a different story altogether.

I am not going to talk about colonization or regional councils. I propose to talk on language which is the subject matter of this discussion. It is on language pure and simple that I shall tell you what the Prime Minister had to say of the Bandaranaike-Chelvanayakam Pact at that time.

511   නියෝජිත මන්ත්‍රී මණ්ඩලය   512

දෙමළ භාෂා (විශේෂ ම විධිවිධාන) පනත: නියෝග   දෙමළ භාෂා (විශේෂ ම විධිවිධාන) පනත: නියෝග

[එච්. කර්. වයස් බණ්ඩාරනායක මහා.]

At page 9 comes the section headed
" Use of Tamil ."

" After discussion it was agreed that
the proposed legislation should obtain
recognition of Tamil as the language of
a national minority of Ceylon and that
the four points mentioned by the
Prime Minister should include provision
that, without infringing on the provisions
of the Official Language Act, the
language of administration in the
Northern and Eastern Provinces should
be Tamil and that any necessary provision be made for the non-Tamil speaking minorities in the Northern and
Eastern Provinces."

That is taken from the text of
Agreement ' A ' printed and published in the " Ceylon Daily News " of
13th August 1957, reproduced in thick
type by the U. N. P. Below that, it is
recorded :

" The   Covenance—The   legislation
proposed to be enacted in pursuance of
this agreement should provide for—

   (a) (i) the recognition of Tamil as
       the language of a national
       minority of Ceylon ;

     (ii) the inclusion of the four
       points mentioned by the
       Prime Minister for the
       special provision that the
       language of administration
       in the Northern and Eastern
       Provinces should be Tamil—

   (b) Such legislation should not
       infringe on the position of
       Sinhala Act.

   (c) Such legislation should contain
       any necessary provision for the
       non-Tamil speaking minorities
       in the Northern and Eastern
       Provinces."

At page 10, the present legal
position is set out.

" The Official Language Act No. 33 of
1956, Section 2 "—

—omitting the formal parts—

" Section 2—Sinhala shall be the one
        official language of Ceylon
        provided that where the
        Minister   considers   it
        impracticable   to   com-
        mence the use of only the
        Sinhala language for any
        official   purpose   imme-
        diately   on   the   coming

into force of this Act, the
language or languages
hitherto used for that
purpose may be continued
to be used until the
necessary change is
effected as early as pos-
sible before the expiry of
the 31st day of December,
1960, and if such change
cannot be effected by
administrative order, regulations may be made
under this Act to effect
such change."

" The resulting position is diagram-
matically illustrated below : "

Now, this is the U.N.P. comment
according to the Sinhala Only Act.
Here, there is a map. According to
the Agreement ' A ' there is another
map. I propose to describe these
two maps. On the first map,
according to the Sinhala Only Act—
I do not know whether you can see
it from this far, Mr. Deputy Speaker
[Interruption]. I think the
Hon. Prime Minister has got a map.
It is marked ; the province divisions
are marked. Across the Eastern
Province is written the word
" Sinhalese "; across the Central and
Uva Provinces is written " Sinha-
lese "; across the Western Province,
Sabaragamuwa Province and the
North-Western Province is written
" Sinhalese "; across the Northern
Province is written " Sinhalese ";
across the Jaffna Peninsula is
written the word " Sinhalese ". On
the right-hand map, according to the
Agreement ' A ', the Northern and
Eastern Provinces are shaded ; and
there is marked " Tamil " against the
Northern Province, " Tamil " against
the Eastern Province, " Tamil "
against the Trincomalee District and
" Tamil " across the Jaffna Peninsula.
On the rest of the map, across the
Central and Uva Provinces is
written the word " Sinhalese ", across
the North-Central Province, Western
Province and a little section of the
Southern Province is also written the
word " Sinhalese ".

Page 11, I am reading further :

" In this context, what meaning can
the words 'without infringing on the
position of the Official Language Act' be
given ? "

This is not quoting from any statute. This is the U.N.P. comment :

" If the Sinhala Act has any meaning, it means that all the nine provinces without exception should be administered in the Sinhala language. By the B-C. Pact, Agreement 'A', two of these provinces have been expressly taken out for administration in the Tamil language. To the meanest intelligence it should be obvious that seven is not equal to nine. "

The arithmetic of the U. N. P. with their *hath hawula* now seems to be getting confused.

ඔරු මන් තිවරයෙක්

(கௌரவ அங்கத்தவர் ஒருவர்)

(An hon. Member)

Haya Hawula.

එෆ්. ආර්. ඩයස් බණ්ඩාරනායක මයා.

(திரு. எப். ஆர். டயஸ் பண்டாரநாயக்க)

(Mr. F. R. Dias Bandaranaike)

—" it should be obvious that seven is not equal to nine. Nine becomes seven only when two are subtracted from it. "—

Just as seven becomes six only when one is subtracted from 7 !

"The phrase 'without infringing on the position of the Official Language Act' is merely eye-wash. If Mr. Bandaranaike thinks that by merely avoiding a verbal alteration or amendment of the Sinhala only Act he can convince the people of Ceylon that he has not violated the integrity of that Act and is not guilty of a grievous infringement of the operation of that Act, then, he is exhibiting a deplorable degree of irrationality. This Pact also concerns the four points 'already conceded by Mr. Bandaranaike in his April 1957 statement in Parliament as concessions for the reasonable use of Tamil.'"

The four points. Now, what are they ?

" (1) Education :

Tamil shall be the medium of education right up to the university ;

(2) Public Service :

For the purpose of entry into the Public Service Tamils shall be permitted to sit for examinations in the medium in which they have been taught, with only this proviso :

That once they are appointed as probationers they will naturally be required to obtain that knowledge of the official language which may be considered necessary for the carrying out of their official duties before the probationary period eventuates in permanent employment.

(3) Transaction of business :

In regard to correspondence and transaction of business with the Government, those who are educated in the Tamil language should have the opportunity of addressing letters, getting replies and so on, in the same language, throughout the Island.

(4) Local Authorities :

In the Northern and Eastern Provinces, the local authorities shall have the option of doing the official part of their work *also* in Tamil if they so wish.

These four concessions will be available to the Tamil community throughout the Island now, in addition to the rights and privileges gifted by the Pact."

And, at page 12, it says :

" Summing up the language concession ...."

I repeat——

" Summing up the language concession given to the Tamils both under the four points and under the Agreement we are entitled to state, that, not only has the Prime Minister recognised Tamil as the language of a national minority but he has also recognised Tamil as an administrative language of a certain portion of the soil of Ceylon, namely, Northern and Eastern Provinces. In other words, Tamil has now become the language not only of a community but also of a considerable territory, which is part and parcel of Ceylon. Indeed, as if to drive home the linguistic annexation of the Northern and Eastern Provinces, the Agreement states ' any necessary provision will be made for the non-Tamil speaking minorities in the Northern and Eastern Provinces.' This means that as far as the Sinhalese in these two Provinces are concerned, because they happen to live in a territory of which the official language is Tamil, provision will be made to safeguard the rights of the Sinhalese residents therein ! Just as under the four points certain concessions have been promised to the Tamils throughout the Island to mitigate the restricted Island-wide effects of the ' Sinhala Only Act,' so certain concessions will be considered for the Sinhalese living in the Northern and Eastern Provinces in order to mitigate the rigours of the Agreement entered into between Mr. Bandaranaike and the Federalists. Clearly, the ' Sinhala Only Act ' will in fact apply only to the seven provinces, the Northern and Eastern Provinces being given another Official Language, namely, Tamil. This position is simply incontestable whatever sophistries are indulged in by the Prime Minister

515 නියෝජිත මන්ත්‍රී මණ්ඩලය 516
පෙම්වල භාෂා (විශේෂ විධිවිධාන) පනත: නියෝග පෙම්වල භාෂා (විශේෂ විධිවිධාන) පනත: නියෝග

[එච්. ආර්. වයස් බණ්ඩාරනායක මයා.]
through the State Radio, the Government
Press, the priviate press or from public
platforms."

I would tell the Hon. Prime
Minister that his own words with
reference to the late Mr. Bandaranaike are equally applicable to him
now. That is, this position is simply
incontestable whatever sophistries
are indulged in by the Prime Minister
through the State Radio, the Government Press, the private press or from
public platforms.

At the end of page 12, it states
further:

"The Agreement in Annexure 'A'
regarding Language proceeds on the false
assumption that the Northern and
Eastern Provinces are the traditional
homelands of the Tamils and that, therefore, now nor at any other time in the
future should the Sinhalese equal or
exceed numerically the Tamils in any
part of these provinces; this condition,
the Prime Minister has secured for the
Tamils by conceding to Federalists the
right to bar the Sinhalese from colonising
these provinces or securing employment
on State assisted schemes in these
provinces."

At the end of that booklet appears
a map which we have all seen—the
coloured map. The hon. Second
Member for Colombo Central
(Mr. Keuneman) asked yesterday,
"What is the relevance of this
map now?" This was the U. N. P.
illustration of the great betrayal
called the Bandaranaike-Chelvanayakam Pact. They are not
having the Bandaranaike-Chelvanayakam Pact, they are now having
the Dudley Senanayake-Chelva-
nayakan Pact. So, he says, you should
produce another and a different illustration because the pact we are now
talking about is not the one they
illustrated.

I can tell you why this is relevant.
Let him read the key to his own map
before he goes any further. May I
read to him a portion of the text
immediately below his map? It
says: "The Tamil Language is accepted as the Official Language in the

two Provinces"—and that is precisely our complaint now, that the effect
of these Regulations, I will show you,
comes to exactly that same conclusion.

Now you will say to yourself, "if
it was good for Mr. Bandaranaike
why is it not good for us now?"
The simple answer is, because the
people of this country rejected it.
When you pointed out to him the
errors, Mr. Bandaranaike had the
courage in response to public opinion
to tear up the Pact, which he should
never have entered into in the first
place. The late Mr. Bandaranaike had
the courage to do that.

What we are asking you, Mr. Prime
Minister, is simply this. Have you
got the courage to face up to public
opinion? Have you got that courage
to face up to public opinion without
having to gag public opinion and
frighten public opinion by terror tactics in order to keep yourself under
the delusion that what you are serving is public opinion? Why are
you scared? Why are you afraid to
allow Buddhist priests to come into
the City of Colombo? Has the Maha
Sangha which came on to the platforms and held Sangha Sabhas in
your favour now frightened you to
that extent? Is it now that the Maha
Sangha constitute a danger? They
are all persons who have been misled, from the Malwatte Maha Nayaka
downwards who now says, at least,
that the Prime Minister should
remember what he said at the time
of the election. The Malwatte Maha
Nayaka certainly did not campaign
on our side. He certainly did not
campaign for the Coalition. He
certainly did not ask anybody to vote
in support of what you have described as Marxists or Socialists or
Coalitionists. The Malwatte Maha
Nayaka called upon all people to protect Buddhism and he thought at that
time that he was protecting Buddhism from Marxism when he told
the people to support you. I think
his problem now is in trying that to
avoid the ditch of Marxism he has
now fallen into the well of the language betrayal of the grossest sort.

517　　　　　　　　　　1966 ජනවාරි 10　　　　　　　518

දෙමළ භාෂා (විශේෂ විධිවිධාන) පනත: නියෝග

So, I should now like to deal with the point of the abrogation of the Bandaranaike-Chelvanayakam Pact and the consequences that followed from it. I should like, first and foremost, to remind you and this House of the circumstances of the abrogation of the Pact and what everybody had to say about the abrogation of the Pact at that time.

I am now reading from the copy of the "Ceylon Daily News" of 10th April, 1958—not the "Aththa" or the "Jana Dina".

It was not proscribed then. Papers were published. In spite of the campaign against it, the late Prime Minister did not find it necessary to silence his critics or silence the Opposition by artificial methods. He was never afraid of public opinion.

First of all, I would like to read to you from the front page on which there is a picture of Mrs. Vimala Wijewardene seated at Rosmead Place with a whole lot of monks. Among those who are recognizable are the Rev. Devamottawe Amarawansa and others.

ගරු ඩී. පී. ආර්. ගුණවර්ධන

(கௌரவ டி. பி. ஆர். குணவர்தன)

(The Hon. D. P. R. Gunawardena)

Is Buddharakkita not there?

එෆ්. ආර්. ඩයස් බණ්ඩාරනායක මයා.

(திரு. எப். ஆர். டயஸ் பண்டாரநாயக்க)

(Mr. F. R. Dias Bandaranaike)

He may be behind Mrs. Vimala Wijewardene. Mrs. Vimala Wijewardene is there.

On this page the first reactions are written at the bottom and let me read to you the first reaction of Mr. Dudley Senanayake quoted in this paper of 10th April:

"Mr. Dudley Senanayake, President of the United National Party, made the following statement to the Daily News last night.

දෙමළ භාෂා (විශේෂ විධිවිධාන) පනත: නියෝග

I am glad, he said, that the Prime Minister, Mr. Bandaranaike, has decided not to proceed with the implementation of the Bandaranaike-Chelvanayakam Pact "—

ගරු ඊරියගොල්ල

(கௌரவ ஈரியகொல்ல)

(The Hon. Iriyagolle)

Even today we are happy it was not implemented.

එෆ්. ආර්. ඩයස් බණ්ඩාරනායක මයා.

(திரு. எப். ஆர். டயஸ் பண்டாரநாயக்க)

(Mr. F. R. Dias Bandaranaike)

—" and the stand that the U. N. P. took at the very outset has been vindicated."—

I read out to you what the stand was on the question of language. This was the stand.

කේ. බී. රත්නායක මයා.

(திரு. கே. பி. ரத்நாயக்க)

(Mr. K. B. Ratnayake)

What stand?

එෆ්. ආර්. ඩයස් බණ්ඩාරනායක මයා.

(திரு. எப். ஆர். டயஸ் பண்டாரநாயக்க)

(Mr. F. R. Dias Bandaranaike)

The stand on the top of the footprint. That is the stand that was vindicated.

—" I always felt that this would be the ultimate fate of this unfortunate agreement. It was not possible to fool all the people all the time. The deception practised on the Sinhalese and Tamil communities could not be carried on much longer. The tension created recently was inevitable."

I suppose if you were Prime Minister at that time you would have told us that the tension created was not inevitable. It was artificial. It has been set up. It has been organized. People have gone round misleading the people. The monks must have been given vehicles and sent there to squat outside Rosmead Place.. They would never have gone there automatically.. Somebody must have worked them up and sent them

519   නියෝජිත මන්ත්‍රී මණ්ඩලය   520
දෙවළු භාෂා (විශේෂ විධිවිධාන) පනත: නියෝග   දෙවළු භාෂා (විශේෂ විධිවිධාන) පනත: නියෝග

[එෆ්. ආර්. ඩයස් බණ්ඩාරනායක මයා.]

there. Of course, he was in the
Opposition then. He was on the
Opposition side. He was not in
Parliament. But what does he say?
He says "The tension created was
inevitable". I agree with you that
the tension created is inevitable
when wrong political settlements
are entered into at the expense of
the people and the people will not
stand for it. That kind of tension
does arise and you will find that
not all the emergencies in the world
are capable of dealing with this
kind of tension.

ගරු ඩී. පී. ආර්. ගුණවර්ධන

(கௌரவ பி. பி. ஆர். குணவர்தன)

(The Hon. D. P. R. Gunawardena)
Speaking from personal experience ?

එෆ්. ආර්. ඩයස් බණ්ඩාරනායක මයා.

(திரு. எப். ஆர். டயஸ் பண்டாரநாயக்க)

(Mr. F. R. Dias Bandaranaike)
You will find that it is so whether
it is in Avissawella or anywhere
else.

ගරු ඩී. පී. ආර්. ගුණවර්ධන

(கௌரவ டி. பி. ஆர். குணவர்தன)

(The Hon. D. P. R. Gunawardena)
I did not speak of Dompe.

එෆ්. ආර්. ඩයස් බණ්ඩාරනායක මයා.

(திரு. எப். ஆர். டயஸ் பண்டாரநாயக்க)

(Mr. F. R. Dias Bandaranaike)
I am not speaking of any other
area. I am now speaking of facts
and of people whom I know and
areas I can speak of with some
knowledge. I am not speaking
generally.

As a matter of fact, the Hon.
Prime Minister. Mr. Dudley Senanayake, at that time, said :

"The tension created recently was
inevitable . . . . ."

Inevitable !

"I foresaw this when I said in
opposing the pact that this so-called solution will be no solution at all, that it
would aggravate communal tension."

If we were to say that now, that
we foresaw that the present action
of the Hon. Prime Minister is
something which could be foreseen
from time to time by entering into
this ill-fated pact with the F.P., that
it would aggravate communal
tension as indeed it will, he will tell
us, "You are inciting the people to
rebellion. You are trying to overthrow the Government." But I can
assure him that we are capable of
foresight just as much as he is
capable of foresight; we are
capable of knowing when tensions
arise just as much as he is capable of
knowing when tensions arise.

On the next day, April 11th, there
is a statement in the "Daily News",
I think, by the hon. Member for
Jaffna (Mr. Ponnambalam) on this
same ill-fated agreement.

ස්ටැන්ලි තිලකරත්න මයා.

(திரு. ஸ்டான்லி திலக்காரத்ன)

(Mr. Stanley Tillekeratne)

False report ?

එෆ්. ආර්. ඩයස් බණ්ඩාරනායක මයා.

(திரு. எப். ஆர். டயஸ் பண்டாரநாயக்க)

(Mr. F. R. Dias Bandaranaike)

It is couched in such beautiful
phraseology that I cannot believe it
is false. The phraseology is such
that I feel that it is indeed the
language of the hon. Member for
Jaffna. In fact, I cannot help
agreeing with some of it myself. The
headline is this :

"TAMILS HAVE NO CAUSE TO MOURN.

The repudiation of the so-called pact
entered into by the Federal Party and
the Government could have come with
far greater self-respect and greater
dignity by the Tamils themselves said
the Tamil Congress leader Mr. G. G.
Ponnambalam, M.P. for Jaffna. 'The
pact was the greatest catastrophe to the
Tamils. The Tamil-speaking people
have no cause whatsoever, I repeat, no
cause at all, to mourn or grieve for what
has happened. It is the best thing that
has happened. It has always been my
view that the so-called pact in express
terms concedes, if anything, less, and
certainly nothing more than what the
Prime Minister decided to incorporate in

දෙමළ භාෂා (විශේෂ විධිවිධාන) පනත: නියෝග

the four-point programme for the reasonable use of Tamil which he published in April 1956 and the regional council scheme even earlier. The Federal Party as a desperate face-saving device accepted what the Tamil-speaking community has rejected and went about perpetrating the fraud that it has extracted some material concessions from an unwilling Prime Minister for the benefit of the Tamil community. It has been my painful duty over a period of five months to expose the hoax and fraud involved. Counterfeit coinage cannot be made to pass indefinitely as genuine currency ".

That last sentence alone convinces me that it is indeed the statement of the hon. Member for Jaffna.

පොන්නම්බලම් මයා.

(திரு. பொன்னம்பலம்)

(Mr. Ponnambalam)

I do not deny any word of it.

එෆ්. ආර්. ඩයස් බණ්ඩාරනායක මයා.

(திரு. எப். ஆர். டயஸ் பண்டாரநாயக்க)

(Mr. F. R. Dias Bandaranaike)

There is a great deal more of his statement but I do not propose to read it. It just shows how different people react.—[Interruption].

පොන්නම්බලම් මයා.

(திரு. பொன்னம்பலம்)

(Mr. Ponnambalam)

I only said that I do not deny one word of it.

එෆ්. ආර්. ඩයස් බණ්ඩාරනායක මයා.

(திரு. எப். ஆர். டயஸ் பண்டாரநாயக்க)

(Mr. F. R. Dias Bandaranaike)

In fact, I quite agree too.

What it comes to is this. The hon. Member for Jaffna was telling us that the Bandaranaike-Chelvanayakam Pact contains nothing new ; it is no achievement for the federalists ; they have got nothing out of it except to pretend that an unwilling Prime Minister has been forced at the point of a sword to make some wonderful concessions. He says that in the interests of the Tamil people it is the best thing in the world that this pact was thrown away but that it would have been better had the Tamils been able to throw it out of

දෙමළ භාෂා (විශේෂ විධිවිධාන) පනත: නියෝග

the window themselves rather than leave it to a Sinhalese leader to tear it up. That is, in fact, what he said.

The Sinhalese people, on the other side, on the previous day led by Buddhist priests staged a protest, and there was the tension that was inevitable and which was foreseen by the Hon. Dudley Senanayake at the moment the ill-fated pact was entered into. He foresaw the communal troubles. Of course, it had nothing to do with the Minister of State trying to walk to Kandy. He was not trying to foment communal trouble. Of course not. Those days he was not a comunalist. That was not racialism. But if people today walk on the streets, if priests seek to give him a memorandum or a statement, that becomes a rousing of communal tensions. If he goes to pray to the gods or sends his Minister of State walking to pray to the gods at the Dalada Maligawa, that is not rousing of communalism.

So you see, Mr. Deputy Speaker, where we are—[Interruption]. The fact remains there was a section of the Tamil-speaking people who thought that the Bandaranaike-Chelvanayakam Pact gave nothing and it was a jolly good thing it was torn up. There was a section of the Sinhalese people headed by no less a person than our Prime Minister who said that the pact is a hoax, a fraud, a useless document, and is something which the Sinhalese people cannot possibly accept. He published his footprint on the document showing the stand he was taking on the language question and, having shown this, he created public opinion which forced Mr. Bandaranaike's hand. You can ask his Colleague, the Minister of Lands, whether what I am saying is not true. He knows all about it.

And so the pact was destroyed. I have no doubt that from the point of view of race relations in this country, if some agreement can be arrived at between the Sinhalese and the Tamil people, it is all to the good. There is no question about it. But it must be an agreement which is considered

523   නියෝජිත මන්ත්‍රී මණ්ඩලය   524

දෙමළ භාෂා (විශේෂ විධිවිධාන) පනත: නියෝග

[එෆ්. ආර්. ඩයස් බණ්ඩාරනායක මයා.]

satisfactory by and large by a large majority of both the Sinhalese and the Tamil-speaking people.

You cannot say that an agreement is satisfactory merely because you have the political plaudits of a section of the people whose support is essential to keep you in office. As far as we are concerned, you can stay in office for the full five years. We have not the slightest objection to that. But do not in the course of that five years take it on yourselves to disregard public opinion.—[Interruption.] Well, you will have another election after that. If you can get elected, fair enough ; we will think about that then. But do not assume it now. We will discuss it then.—[Interruption]. I am talking of what will happen up to the next election. I am not talking of anything beyond the next elections.

So that, as far as we are concerned, you have a mandate to rule. The people of this country have certainly preferred you to us. We accept that and we are not seeking in any way to overthrow your Government though you are extremely worried that that is our intention. It is not. But we are definitely concerned, just as you were concerned then, with the circumstances surrounding what we suspect to be a shoddy deal at the expense of the Sinhalese people of this country, merely for the sake of pleasing a section whose support is undoubtedly necessary for you now. We accept that. We understand your need for their support. I can assure you they have no alternative but to support you anyway. Whether you make a concession or not, we, for our part, are certainly not prepared to make any concession.

ගරු මන්ත්‍රීවරයෙක්

(கௌரவ அங்கத்தவர் ஒருவர்)

(An hon. Member)

You were.

එෆ්. ආර්. ඩයස් බණ්ඩාරනායක මයා.

(திரு. எப். ஆர். டயஸ் பண்டாரநாயக்க)

(Mr. F. R. Dias Bandaranaike)

Therefore, in practical terms, whatever you concede or do not concede

දෙමළ භාෂා (විශේෂ විධිවිධාන) පනත: නියෝග

is a matter of little moment, excepting this. Whatever you concede, please see that it is in the interests of the large majority of the Sinhalese and the Tamil-speaking people, and you cannot assess that by imposing your curfews or your Emergency regulations. If you are not afraid of public opinion, why is it necessary for you to rule by the sword and to talk of shooting when it becomes necessary to shoot ? You will go down in history as the shooting Prime Minister.—[Interruption].

I can assure you we never had any anxiety to threaten to shoot Sinhalese people before they rose on any question.—[Interruption]. No, if the Tamil people chose to go and sit on the Galle Face Green and demonstrate, I think, you will agree, that the only thing that sent them away was the rain. I think, you will agree that anybody can go and sit on the Galle Face Green so long as he does not break the law.

ගරු මන්ත්‍රීවරයෙක්

(கௌரவ அங்கத்தவர் ஒருவர்)

(An hon. Member)

The late Prime Minister shot hundreds of Sinhalese at Padawiya.

නියෝජ්‍ය කථානායකතුමා

(உப சபாநாயகர் அவர்கள்)

(Mr. Deputy Speaker)

If you go on interrupting, some hon. Members will not be here for the voting tomorrow.

එෆ්. ආර්. ඩයස් බණ්ඩාරනායක මයා.

(திரு. எப். ஆர். டயஸ் பண்டாரநாயக்க)

(Mr. F. R. Dias Bandaranaike)

I can assure you that it is not the shooting we are worried about. If the Prime Minister wants to shoot lawbreakers, let him shoot them by all means. He is entitled by law to shoot them. But let him not by threats of shooting seek to intimidate the Sinhalese people of this country and try to keep them in a state of fear by which it would become impossible for the people to express their point of view in a state of terror. We do not mind. If you see us break the law take us into custody and deal with us according to any legal processes you wish. We are aware of that. But that is not the same thing as trying to suppress public opinion because you are afraid of it.

. Let us ask ourselves the question, what is the basic difference between the situation then and now ? I will tell you. The first difference is this. The late Mr. Bandaranaike was not afraid to expose his agreements to the test of public scrutiny ; he showed whatever agreement he entered into. There were no secrets about his agreement, it was published in all the ment 'A' or Agreement 'B', whether you called it the Bandaranaike-Chelvanayakam Pact or any other agreement, it was published in all the newspapers, taken over by you and printed in your yellow booklets, and exposed to the test of public scrutiny.

What is the position about your agreement ? I will tell you what happened to your agreement. First and foremost, on the 21st May 1965, when a Question was asked of you in the House, your Prime Minister gave a strange answer. The question was this. You will find it at column 1676 of HANSARD of the 21st May 1965, Volume 60. The Question was put by me to the Prime Minister. I asked,

" Will he inform this House if after 22.3.65 he has signed any agreement with or given any written undertaking to Mr. S. J. V. Chelvanayakam or the Federal Party ? (b) If so, will he disclose the terms of such agreement or undertaking ? (c) If not, why ? "

This is the answer of the Hon. Dudley Senanayake :

" (a) Mr. Chelvanayakam and I, as leaders of our respective parties, have had discussions at various times on various matters. (b) No. (c) I do not think it is incumbent on me to disclose matters that were discussed between two party leaders.

MR. F. R. DIAS BANDARANAIKE :

Will the Hon. Prime Minister please inform this House whether, apart from discussions, any signed or written undertaking has been drawn up ? This is in fact in answer to (a).

THE HON. DUDLEY SENANAYAKE :

The matters discussed were put in writing.

DR. N. M. PERERA :

Can that document be made available ?

THE HON. DUDLEY SENANAYAKE :

No.

DR. N. M. PERERA :

Why not ? That is not a private document.

THE HON. DUDLEY SENANAYAKE :

It is a private document because it is an agreement that was drawn up before the formation of the National Government.

DR. N. M. PERERA :

It is a document involving the whole country.

THE HON. DUDLEY SENANAYAKE :

The discussions were between two party leaders before the formation of a Government. So, that is not a Government document. Moreover, there is no Ministerial responsibility for me to answer this at all. I could have refused to answer the whole thing. This is not any public or departmental activity under me. I could have refused to answer it. This Question is out of Order. "

Mr. Deputy Speaker, let us analyse this question and answer a little carefully. What were we asking the Hon. Prime Minister ? We were asking him to tell us firstly, whether it is true that after the elections— 22nd March 1965, is the date—he had entered into a written agreement or given a signed or written undertaking to Mr. Chelvanayakam, and the terms of it if he had done so. The Hon. Prime Minister's final or ultimate answer, if I may say so, was, " I am not going to tell you. There is no Ministerial responsibility for it." Technically, under the Standing Orders this is a very good position to take, but politically, it is tantamount to saying, "Whatever I may have done I am not prepared to expose it to the test of public scrutiny." Of course, he is entitled to say that. I am not disputing his interpretation of the Standing Orders, but the fact remains that there is an agreement which he thinks as a party leader he is just not going to disclose. You will notice the initial answer. It starts

527   නියෝජිත මන්තී මණ්ඩලය   528

දෙමළ භාෂ (විශේෂ විධිවිධාන) පනත: නියෝග
[එච්. ආර්. ඩයස් බණ්ඩාරනායක මහා.]

off on a level of really dodging the
question. The question is, " Is there
any signed agreement or written
undertaking ? " He says, " Mr. Chelvanayakam and I, as leaders of our respective parties, have had discussions
at various times on various matters ".
No one asked him about discussions.
There is a world of difference between
asking for tea-time conversations and
asking for solemn documents you
have signed. Our Question was
about signed agreements or undertakings. He says, " I am not prepared to disclose it. There is no duty
cast on me to do so. " Then we
repeated the question, " Can you tell
us please, apart from discussions,
whether there is any agreement that
has been drawn up ? " To this the
Hon. Prime Minister says, " The
matters discussed were put in
writing ". So, it required a supple-
mentary question to come to the
point. Now we have got a piece of
paper. The next question was, " Is it
a private document ? " The Hon.
Prime Minister's reply was, " It is a
private document because it is an
agreement that was drawn up before
the formation of the National
Government ". Now we know that we
have got a document. It started off
as certain matters discussed—discussions at various times on various
matters. Little by little it was established that the thing is in writing
and that the agreement was entered
into before the formation of the
National Government. And this is the
document the text of which the Hon.
Prime Minister still says he is not
prepared to disclose.

It may be that he is not obliged to
disclose it under the Standing Orders.
I am not arguing that question now.
I shall accept, for purposes of argument, that he cannot be forced in
this House by question to answer
these things. But there are situations
in which, if you refuse to answer
certain questions, it is only natural
that the people will draw certain
conclusions. It is a commonsense
thing. Ask the hon. Member for
Jaffna, he will tell you. If there are

දෙමළ භාෂ (විශේෂ විධිවිධාන) පනත: නියෝග
certain facts within a man's
knowledge which in certain circumstances he ought to disclose but does
not disclose, standing upon his legal
rights, I think, it is not unfair to draw
the inference that the answer, if
given, would certanly be unfavourable to the man who refuses to
answer, or at least will contain matters which he considers it dangerous
to disclose. One can certainly understand the Hon. Prime Minister's point
of view. He has entered into a deal.

පොන්නම්බලම් මහා.
(திரு. பொன்னம்பலம்)
(Mr. Ponnambalam)

He does not think it necessary to
disclose.

එච්. ආර්. ඩයස් බණ්ඩාරනායක මහා.
(திரு. எப். ஆர். டயஸ் பண்டாரநாயக்க)
(Mr. F. R Dias Bandaranaike)

I appreciate that. Legal defences
are useful things, but, politically, they
are not always the answer.

පොන්නම්බලම් මහා.
(திரு. பொன்னம்பலம்)
(Mr. Ponnambalam)

I am merely completing your argument.

එච්. ආර්. ඩයස් බණ්ඩාරනායක මහා.
(திரு. எப். ஆர். டயஸ் பண்டாரநாயக்க)
(Mr. F. R. Dias Bandaranaike)

I appreciate that very much. He is
under no legal duty to answer—I myself admitted that. Let us think of
all the possible reasons which the
Hon. Prime Minister could have had.
Let us speculate. I am not going to
by the reports in the " Jana Dina " or
the " Aththa " in regard to these
several arguments. I am looking at
answers given by the Hon. Prime
Minister. He says, " I am not going to
tell you." What earthly reason could
the Prime Minister have for giving
us an answer like that ? I can only
think of one : the answer involves
something which he knows will not,
in his view, be immediately acceptable to the Sinhalese people, and he
wants to gain time to try and convince them, persuade them, with his
personality and his reputed honesty,
that what he had entered into is in
their best interests. He wants time to

529   1966 ජනවාරි 10   530

දෙමළ ශාඛා (විශේෂ විධිවිධාන) පනත: නියෝග

sell them something, sell them a statesmanlike solution, knowing perfectly well that the statement he has refused to make is something which in the immediate present, in the aftermath of the elections, is not capable of disclosure with any degree of safety.

So, the first objective of the Hon. Prime Minister, as I see it, is to gain time. I am not seeking to impute something nasty. I think, it was the Hon. Minister of State who told us to wait nine months. He said that between conception and birth a period of nine months has got to elapse. So, it is possible that the Hon. Prime Minister had his own reasons for not wanting it disclosed. While the hon. Member for Jaffna (Mr. Ponnambalam) was trying to unite the United Nations, you were trying to unite certain other things at home without the dangers of that unity being upset by any, may I say, international forces. So you see Mr. Prime Minister and Mr. Deputy Speaker, we have now got an agreement which could not be disclosed. To this date has it been disclosed? The answer is, "No." What does the Prime Minister tell us about this agreement? On 9th April 1965, at Adjournment time, a question was put on this matter. I think it was the hon. Third Member for Colombo Central who raised it. I have got the HANSARD here with me. I will find it out if you want. Yes, on the 9th April—mind you, before the question had been asked and answered—this was what the Prime Minister said.   It is at Column 221 of the HANSARD of 9th April 1965 :

" THE HON. DUDLEY SENANAYAKE :

Let me assure him that if I enter into an agreement—

MR. KEUNEMAN :

Have you ? "

Hon. Dudley Senanayake daintly answers :—

"—I never let it down. I have been thirty years in public life and I do not think the hon. Member can point to one betrayal.

දෙමළ ශාඛා (විශේෂ විධිවිධාන) පනත: නියෝග

MR. KEUNEMAN :

Will the Hon. Prime Minister—[Interruption].

MR. DEPUTY SPEAKER :

Order !

THE HON. DUDLEY SENANAYAKE :

Mr. Deputy Speaker, if there is an agreement or no agreement, that is a matter between the United National Party and the Federal Party.—[Interruption].

MR. DEPUTY SPEAKER :

Members on both sides, Order !

MR. KEUNEMAN :

Will the Hon. Prime Minister give way ?

MR. DEPUTY SPEAKER :

No

HON. MEMBERS :

Sit down ! Do not interrupt.

MR. KEUNEMAN :

The Coalition had a fourteen-point agreement which they published.

THE HON. DUDLEY SENANAYAKE :

Surely the implementation of any agreement must come before this House. So if there is any agreement, matters of legislation will come up before this House. Then the House will have an opportunity of judging what has happened.

MR. KEUNEMAN :

Why keep it secret ? "

At that stage :

එකල්හි වෙලව අ. හ. 5 වැනි, නියෝජ්‍ය කථානායකතුමා විසින් පුන් ය තෙකිමක මන්ත්‍රී මණ්ඩලය කල් තබන ලදී.

That is how the HANSARD reads. So you see what it amounts to.   At that time when the Prime Minister did not disclose the fact of the agreement before it was forced out of him on 21st May, that is, on the 9th of April, the Prime Minister says : " If I have an agreement or no agreement, that is a matter between me and the Federal Party. If I am going to implement any agreement that I may happen to have, I will bring legislation before the House and you can judge it then "   In other words

531   නියෝජිත මන්ත්‍රී මණ්ඩලය   532

දෙමළ භාෂා (විශේෂ විධිධාන) පනත: නියෝග
[එච්. ආර්. වයස් මණිධරනායක මහ.]

It means : I am not telling you whether there is an agreement or no agreement ; if I have an agreement, it is a matter between me and the Federal Party ; if I have no agreement also it is none of your business ; but, if I have an agreement, then I will bring in legislation so that then you can judge the legislation.

My simple answer to that is that the people of this country cannot be trifled with in that way. It is, of course a good thing for you to say, "I am bringing in legislation". We all know that you cannot pass laws without bringing legislation before Parliament, unless you keep an Emergency going and decide to break records. Assuming that you do not decide to break records—I think you are ; you are the Prime Minister who says that you want to shoot if necessary ; that is a new record ; anyway, leave that as it is—you will have to bring legislation before Parliament, and that is something we all know. Bringing legislation before Parliament is not something new ; it is not something we have never heard of. Of course you must bring legislation before Parliament, but how can we judge your agreement—may I ask Mr. Deputy Speaker—by looking at your items of legislation piecemeal ? How do we know to what extent and what matters you have compromised the interests of the Sinhalese people in this country, and how do you expect the Sinhalese people in this country to have confidence in you when you are not prepared to take them into your confidence and are not prepared to tell them what you have done, or what you are planning to do ? In other words, you tell the country, "I am not going to tell you ; I will bring these things from time to time piecemeal in the form of legislation ; you can then look at them one by one and tell us whether you like it or not". At the moment we have seen the Tamil Language (Special Provisions) Regulations. We know that these Regulations are part of that agreement, because you told us that legislation would be coming.

දෙමළ භාෂා (විශේෂ විධිධාන) පනත: නියෝග

But we certainly know that these Regulations are not the whole of the agreement. We certainly know that the agreement which you entered into with the Federal Party, which you chose not to disclose and which you would not disclose, contains a great deal more.

You expect us to act like a rubber stamp. You want us to set the seal of our approval on each one of the things you do one by one—which is impossible. You cannot expect a contract to receive approval clause by clause. You cannot expect your contract to be approved unless this House has the power and the authority to examine the whole of it and to come to a conclusion as to whether it is in the national interest or not ; and it is precisely because that suspicion exists, it is precisely because that fear exists, that you are finding yourself in the present difficulty of imagining that people are being misled.

It is not a question of people being misled at all. The simple truth of the matter is this, that while we may not be so clever in business matters as our friends from the North, yet when it comes to a question of a contract or agreement of this nature, our people have a native shrewdness and wisdom which makes it impossible for anybody to pull the wool over their eyes. You cannot say, "I am an honest man, please trust me." Your honesty is not in question at all. No one is suggesting that you are inspired by wicked motives. In fact, at the moment, I think, the Hon. Prime Minister feels like a Messiah introducing an era of national unity. It sometimes can be dangerous ; you may find yourself crucified.

May I say this? National unity is a phrase that has different meanings as far as I can see. The Federal Party has once told us that national unity is not possible between the Sinhalese and the Tamils.

ගරු මන්ත්‍රීවරු
(கௌரவ அங்கத்தினர்கள்)
(Hon. Members)
Certainly not !

දෙමළ භාෂා (විශේෂ විධිවිධාන) පනත: නියෝග

ඒ. අමීර්තලිංග් ගම් මයා. (විද්දුක්කො
වෙයි)

(திரு. ஏ. அமிர்தலிங்கம்—வட்டுக்கோட்
டை)

(Mr. A. Amirthalingam—Vaddukkoddai)
Quote !

එච්. ආර්. ඩයස් බණ්ඩාරනායක මයා.
(திரு. எப். ஆர். டயஸ் பண்டாரநாயக்க)
(Mr. F. R. Dias Bandaranaike)
You want the quotation.

ගරු මන්ත්‍රීවරු
(கௌரவ அங்கத்தினர்கள்)
(Hon. Members)
Yes !

එච්. ආර්. ඩයස් බණ්ඩාරනායක මයා.
(திரு. எப். ஆர். டயஸ் பண்டாரநாயக்க)
(Mr. F. R. Dias Bandaranaike)
Mr. Rasamanickam — [Interrup-
tion]. I shall give you the reference
in a few moments.

ගරු මන්ත්‍රීවරු
(கௌரவ அங்கத்தினர்கள்)
(Hon. Members)
Quote or withdraw.

වෛද්‍යාචාර්ය ඊ. එම්. වී. නාගනාදන්
(නල්ලූර්)

(டொக்டர் ஈ. எம். வி. நாகநாதன்—நல்
லூர்)

(Dr. E. M. V. Naganathan—Nallur)
Sir, on a point of Order—
[Interruption].

නියෝජ්‍ය කථානායකතුමා
(உப சபாநாயகர் அவர்கள்)
(Mr. Deputy Speaker)
Let us hear the point of Order.

වෛද්‍යාචාර්ය නාගනාදන්
(டொக்டர் நாகநாதன்)
(Dr. Naganathan)
Yesterday one of their principal
speakers quoted from a document
and he said that he would table the
document today—[Interruption].

ගරු මන්ත්‍රීවරු
(கௌரவ அங்கத்தினர்கள்)
(Hon. Members)
The man is missing.

අමීර්තලිංග් ගම් මයා.
(திரு. அமிர்தலிங்கம்)
(Mr. Amirthalingam)
He has not even turned up.

ගරු මන්ත්‍රීවරයෙක්
(கௌரவ அங்கத்தினர்கள்)
(An hon. Member)
He is hiding.

නියෝජ්‍ය කථානායකතුමා
(உப சபாநாயகர் அவர்கள்)
(Mr Deputy Speaker)
Order, please ! The point of Order
raised by the hon. Member for
Nallur does not arise at the moment.

ගරු මන්ත්‍රීවරයෙක්
(கௌரவ அங்கத்தினர் ஒருவர்)
(An hon. Member)
The other side are unscrupulous—
[Interruption]:

නියෝජ්‍ය කථානායකතුමා
(உப சபாநாயகர் அவர்கள்)
(Mr. Deputy Speaker)
Order please !
One side is talking of donkeys
and the other side of jackasses and
all I hear is braying.

එච්. ආර්. ඩයස් බණ්ඩාරනායක මයා.
(திரு. எப். ஆர். டயஸ் பண்டாரநாயக்க)
(Mr. F. R. Dias Bandaranaike)
Now, Sir, I have got the HANSARD.

රසමානික්කම් මයා.
(திரு. இராசமாணிக்கம்)
(Mr. Rasamanickam)
Please do not quote out of context.

එච්. ආර්. ඩයස් බණ්ඩාරනායක මයා.
(திரு. எப். ஆர். டயஸ் பண்டாரநாயக்க)
(Mr. F. R. Dias Bandaranaike)
Mr. Deputy Speaker, have you
finished with the point of Order ?

535   නියෝජිත මන්ත්‍රී මණ්ඩලය   536

දෙමළ භාෂා (විශේෂ විධිවිධාන) පනත: නියෝග   දෙමළ භාෂා (විශේෂ විධිවිධාන) පනත: නියෝග

නියෝජ්‍ය කථානායකතුමා
(உப சபாநாயகர் அவர்கள்)
(Mr. Deputy Speaker)
Yes.

එෆ්. ආර්. ඩයස් බණ්ඩාරනායක මයා.
(திரு. எப். ஆர். டயஸ் பண்டாரநாயக்க)
(Mr. F. R. Dias Bandaranaike)
I am quoting from the Official Report, Volume 61, column 1928.—[*Interruption*]. I will find the HANSARD and read it to you in a moment.

අමිර්තලිඞ්ගම් මයා.
(திரு. அமிர்தலிங்கம்)
(Mr. Amirthalingam)
He has not found it yet.

එෆ්. ආර්. ඩයස් බණ්ඩාරනායක මයා.
(திரு. எப். ஆர். டயஸ் பண்டாரநாயக்க)
(Mr. F. R. Dias Bandaranaike)
No, I have found the reference and I will give it to you straightaway. The date is 26th August 1965. I am sorry, I was wrong; it is at column 1926 and not 1928. The difference is in the columns between the uncorrected and corrected versions. This is the passage. I made a speech in the course of which this is what happened. I said :
"We believe that this country must have one language as a unifying language permanently enshrined for all time.

MR. S. M. RASAMANICKAM :
Whom are you going to unify ?

MR. F. R. DIAS BANDARANAIKE :
We believe that the people of Ceylon, Tamils and Sinhalese, must be one nation.

MR. RASAMANICKAM :
It can never be."

ගරු මන්ත්‍රීවරු
(கௌரவ அங்கத்தினர்கள்)
(Hon. Members)
Hear ! Hear ! !

රාසමානික්කම් මයා.
(திரு. இராசமாணிக்கம்)
(Mr. Rasamanickam)
rose—

නියෝජ්‍ය කථානායකතුමා
(உப சபாநாயகர் அவர்கள்)
(Mr Deputy Speaker)
Are you on a personal explanation ?

රාසමානික්කම් මයා.
(திரு. இராசமாணிக்கம்)
(Mr. Rasamanickam)
Yes.

නියෝජ්‍ය කථානායකතුමා
(உப சபாநாயகர் அவர்கள்)
(Mr Deputy Speaker)
He is not giving way. Please sit down.—[*Interruption*]. Will those two hon. Members who interrupted please leave the House ? The hon. Members for Kolonne (Mr. (Mathew) and Nivitigala (Mr. Hetti-arachchi), please leave the Chamber. [*Interruption*]. The hon. Member for Kotte (Mr. Stanley Tillekeratne), might have to follow.

රාසමානික්කම් මයා.
(திரு. இராசமாணிக்கம்)
(Mr. Rasamanickam)
I will reply to you.

එෆ්. ආර්. ඩයස් බණ්ඩාරනායක මයා.
(திரு. எப். ஆர். டயஸ் பண்டாரநாயக்க)
(Mr. F. R. Dias Bandaranaike)
Of course, you can do so at the proper time. So, we have the passage in the course of which I said that our objective in this country was to unify the Sinhalese nation and the Tamil nation ; but I was defied by a former President of the Federal Party, Mr. Rasamanickam, who was kind enough to tell us that that can never be.

රාසමානික්කම් මයා.
(திரு. இராசமாணிக்கம்)
(Mr. Rasamanickam)
Under Sinhala only. That is what I said.—[*Interruption*].

එෆ්. ආර්. ඩයස් බණ්ඩාරනායක මයා.
(திரு. எப். ஆர். டயஸ் பண்டாரநாயக்க)
(Mr F. R. Dias Bandaranaike)
Mr. Deputy Speaker, I will do better than that because the hon. Member for Paddiruppu has

also distinguished himself in cold print, with his picture also, and he has printed the presidential address delivered at the Eighth National Convention of the Ilankai Thamil Arasu Kadchi, held at the Ehamparam Arangu, Mannar. This is dated 1.9.62. In the course of this document he has made it quite plain as to what his views are. So there is no question about what he thinks of Sinhala only or anything else. I will read portions of what he said then.—[Interruption.] I have not the time.—[Interruption.] ·I have not the time to read out all the accretions the hon. Member for Paddiruppu wants to have read out. I will read out those portions which I consider relevant to the argument I am presenting here. This is what Mr. Rasamanickam says at page 6 of this publication : " The Presidential Address delivered at the Eight National Convention of the Ilankai Thamil Arasu Kadchi " in Mannar on 1st September 1962.

"As a solution to the communal problem in the country, we put forward a four-point demand at the national convention held at Trincomalee in 1956. Briefly stated, the four demands are :

(1) The replacement of the present unitary constitution by a federal constitution under which the Tamil-speaking people could govern themselves.

(2) Granting Tamil parity of status with Sinhala as an official language of the country.

(3) Granting of citizenship rights to those Tamil-speaking people of Indian origin who have made this country their home.

(4) Stopping of planned colonization by Sinhalese people in the traditional homeland of the Tamil-speaking people.

The above demands of ours formed the basis for all our campaigns since 1956, all negotiations we had and the pacts entered into by us. We had, for the purpose of arriving at some settlement, temporarily relaxed our stand on some points. But there is no gainsaying the fact that if the Tamil-speaking people are to live in terms of equality in this country the four demands must be conceded in toto."

We are extremely pleased today that whatever negotiations entered into were destroyed by the national vigilance of our Prime Minister, who tore up the Bandaranaike-Chelvanayakam Pact.—[Interruption.]

නියෝජ්‍ය කථානායකතුමා
(உப சபாநாயகர் அவர்கள்)
(Mr. Deputy Speaker)

Order, please ! If you continue to interrupt, I will have to ask some other hon. Members also to retire.

එෆ්. ආර්. ඩයස් බණ්ඩාරනායක මයා.
(திரு. எப். ஆர். டயஸ் பண்டாரநாயக்க)
(Mr. F. R. Dias Bandaranaike)

Clearly, the technique of the Federal Party is to speak first and have me to speak afterwards. Now they have the opportunity of having the reverse. Now they are impatient. They cannot wait. The problem is for the Federal Party here to say in plain language, " We have got four points decided by our National Convention in 1956 and we insist on the replacement of the unitary constitution ; we want parity of status for our language ; we insist on citizenship rights for all of Mr. Thondaman's people ; and we want the stoppage of the planned colonization of Sinhalese people in our traditional homeland. "

That is their basic objective, but they let us into a secret. That is : " We had, for the purpose of arriving at some settlement, temporarily relaxed our stand on some points. But there is no gainsaying the fact that if the Tamil-speaking people are to live in terms of equality in this country the four demands must be conceded in toto. " So, there is a temporary relaxation from time to time in order to gain something.

You see, Mr. Prime Minister, why we are so worried, why the Sinhalese people are anxious that you should tell us the whole story of your agreement. It is because the Federal Party has always explained their tactics in very plain language so that the whole country knows what the Federalists

539   නියෝජිත මන්ත්‍රී මණ්ඩලය   540

දෙමළ භාෂා (විශේෂ විධිවිධාන) පනත: නියෝග   දෙමළ භාෂා, (විශේෂ විධිවිධාන) පනත: නියෝග

[එච්. ඇර්. වයස් මණ්ඩාරනායක මැ.]
want, and the Sinhalese people necessarily have certain reservations in
dealing with them.—[*Interruption.*] I
am not referring to you. Please shut
up and wait till your turn comes.—
[*Interruption.*] I am dealing with the
attitude of the Sinhalese people. Why
are you so suspicious ? Your ultimate
objectives are very clear. You are
not prepared to concede anything.
You want to temporarily drop some
little demand and make it appear that
you are willing to accept something
less. But all that is temporary ; all
that is evanescence, very temporary.
They have set their sights on the
ultimate goal. What they want ultimately is clear and that is what is
stated very truthfully by that Gentleman, the hon. Member for Paddiruppu—that national unity can never
be.

Now let me show how different
people react to the Federal Party
when they make demands. Let me
quote to you, for instance, the Hon.
Minister of Industries and Fisheries.
I am not quoting him against himself in any sense. I am not trying to
make a cheap debating point by saying that he said something different
those days. I am not aiming at that
sort of thing. If I do that, all the
HANSARDS in the Library would not be
sufficient. But I am now dealing with
the attitude and approach to an
argument, to a problem. Please do
not regard this as an attempt to
score a cheap gibe. If it is that, I have
got enough material. I have not
even set about approaching the problem that way. I have tried to find an
argument and to present an argument
in a logical way.

This was during the Language of
the Courts Debate in December 1960,
when the Hon. D. P. R. Gunawardene,
the hon. Member for Avissawella,
spoke. I am going to read you something of what he said. There he
criticized the Hon. Leader of the
House, Mr. C. P. de Silva, for compromising on the Standing Orders of
this House relating to the language

of proceedings contrary to the decision of the Standing Orders Committee. The Standing Orders Committee
of which the hon. Member for Avissawella himself was a member had
come to one conclusion in regard to
the language of the proceedings of
this House and as to how the proceedings of this House should be conducted. That was the day before.
Those Standing Orders were brought
before the House, they were debated
and a compromise was effected re-
jecting the Standing Orders Committee's recommendation and modifying
it, and making further concessions,
as he put it, under pressure from the
Communist Party, the L. S. S. P. and
the Federal Party, and even the
U. N. P.

And this is what he said. I am
quoting from HANSARD, Volume 41,
column 4403. The date is 30th December 1960—one but the last day before
the full operation of the Sinhala
Only Act :

"The Leader of the House had no right
whatever to go back on that amendment
without again consulting the Standing
Orders Committee. I say that the entire
procedure adopted was wrong. Simply
because there was pressure on the part
of the L.S.S.P. and the C.P. and the
Federal Party and, later, the U.N.P., you
thought it was necessary to change your
position. You have gone back on what
you promised the country. You have gone
back on the stand you took so far as the
official language is concerned. But let me
tell you this much : You think you can
placate our Federal friends by doing
that. They are like Oliver Twist. They
will ask for more.
You are encouraging Federalism.
Federalism must be got rid of in this
country. We want a unitary Government
in this country, but by encouraging the
Federalists when they ask for certain
things, you are only preventing the consolidation of a strong unitary Government in this country. The people of this
country will never tolerate Federalism.
There is no room for Federalism in
Ceylon. We are too small a place, and
as for our friends, their language is
'sufficiently safeguarded on the other side
of Palk's Strait. It is a language that is
growing daily and getting richer and
richer, and so far as their language in
this country is concerned they do not
need to be afraid of its future."—
[OFFICIAL REPORT, 30th December 1960 ;
Vol. 41, c. 4403.]

541   1966 ජනවාරි 10   542
දෙමළ භාෂා (විශේෂ විධිවිධාන) පනත: නියෝග   දෙමළ භාෂා (විශේෂ විධිවිධාන) පනත: නියෝග

ගරු ඩී. පී. ආර්. ගුණවර්ධන *
(கௌரவ டி. பி. ஆர். குணவர்தன)
(The Hon. D. P. R. Gunawardena)
What is wrong in that ?

එච්. ආර්. ඩයස් බණ්ඩාරනායක මැය.
(திரு. எப். ஆர். டயஸ் பண்டாரநாயக்க)
(Mr F. R. Dias Bandaranaike)
I know. I wiL tell you what is
wrong with it because I was trying to
demonstrate from your speech the
natural instinctive fears that Sinhalese people and you as a good Sinhalese man entertained at that time in
dealing with the Federalists who,
like Oliver Twist, are asking for more
and more, who are determined to
fight for ultimate objectives which
you quite realized the danger of and
which you were not prepared to concede.   You realized instinctively,
whether you had read it or not, the
truth of the matter behind the
strategy stated by the hon. Member
for Paddiruppu (Mr. Rasamanickam),
and so it was not surprising that you
were voicing the views and the fears
of a number of people in Ceylon. You
were not expressing a private thought
of your own. The formulation about
Oliver Twist and Palk's Straight may
be all your own, but not the idea, the
thought, the fears.

And that is precisely why agreements cannot be disclosed, and those
are the things that make people
scared.   If you have an agreement
which is capable of disclosure, and
this present proposal constitutes a
part of it, then let us see the agreement. Let us know what you want
us to approve. But do not ask this
House to come before you blindfolded
for you to place before us piecemeal
statements which you prepare from
time to time, and tell us, " We want
this piece enacted as legislation to
satisfy our Federal friends now ; we
have something else coming a little
while later, and yet another one still
later. "

I am now going to tell you why we
cannot accept this.   May I read to
you a passage which has already been

quoted once before during the Throne
Speech Debate in this House ?   If
you have a look at the " Times of
Ceylon " of Tuesday evening, August
3, 1965, you will find the report of
a speech made by a Federal Party
Member. Then you will realize why
we are frightened and why the Sinhalese people cannot accept this
proposal.   Not that the Sinhalese
people do not know how to settle a
problem ; they do not want to live
with a problem all their lives, but
they cannot agree to this method of
settlement, to this technique of
secret deals, this technique by which
agreements cannot be submitted to
the test of public scrutiny.

I would like to read to you the
report of the speech I referred to.
The headline reads, " In Two Years—
Thiruchelvam gives the Tamil a
pledge. "   Now I would particularly
like to comment on this.   I, in fact,
chose this particular speech merely
because I had the pleasure of being
preceded by my Friend the hon.
Member for Chavakachcheri, he being one of the *dramatis personae*, on
that particular occasion.

I would first of all like to read to
you his speech. This is the speech he
made on the occasion of a visit by the
Hon. Tiruchelvam, Minister of Local
Government, at a reception given at
Uraithivu Community Centre. It has
been quoted by the Leader of the
Opposition once before in Sinhalese
in the course of the Throne Speech
Debate. First of all I am going to read
to you the speech of the hon. Member
for Chavakachcheri who now chooses
to taunt the Lanka Sama Samaja
Party and the Communist Party with
their past history. I am not going to
quote from the " Eela Nadu ", but I
am going to quote from the " Times
of Ceylon "   They would have seen
it.   They cannot say they never saw
it.

Here is the speech made by Mr.
Navaratnam as reported in the
" Times of Ceylon ".

දෙමළ භාෂා (විශේෂ විධිවිධාන) පනත: නියෝග

[එච්. ආර්. ඩයස් බණ්ඩාරනායක මය.]

"Mr. V. Navaratnam, M.P. for Chava-kachcheri, said that Mr. Tiruchelvam was sent to the Cabinet in order to safeguard the language, colonization, and citizen-ship of the Tamil speaking nation.

It was because of the Federal Party that the Tamils now had the chance of welcoming Ministers who in turn were able to see for themselves the actual state of the people of the Northern and Eastern Provinces.

Now, this is the important para-graph :

"Certain politicians were still trying to maintain that the Federal Party had accepted Sinhalese as the Official Language in the Northern and Eastern Provinces. He would categorically state that Tamil would be the only language of administration in the North and East."

This, mind you, is a statement by a Government Member of Parliament Mr. Navaratnam, who today gets up and says "I do not know what you are complaining about."

Who then are the politicians who also have been telling us that Sinhala only is being enshrined by these Regulations in the Northern and Eas-tern Provinces ? Was it not the Hon. Minister of State who in the course of his opening speech told us, " Sinhala only is being enshrined in the Nor-thern and Eastern Provinces. The Sri Lanka Freedom Party did not imple-ment Sinhala only. We are now im-plementing Sinhala only in the Nor-thern and Eastern Provinces. " ?

And what does the hon. Member for Chavakachcheri tell us ? I picked on him deliberately, though others have said the same thing too. I can give you their speeches also if you want. He is not the only one. It has been repeatedly asserted by them.

So we are now going to have a situ-ation where certain politicians are still trying to maintain that the Federal Party had accepted Sinhala as the official language of the Nor-thern and Eastern Provinces. Who are the certain politicians who say so ? In addition to the Hon. the Prime Minister, the Hon. Minister of State and—I do not know if you can

දෙමළ භාෂා (විශේෂ විධිවිධාන) පනත: නියෝග

call him a politician—the Rev. Deva-mottawe Amarawansa. These are the persons who are now trying to tell us that Sinhala only is the official lan-guage in the Northern and Eastern Provinces, and we are expected to swallow this and say, " Well, here you are "—(Interruption). These Regula-tions, if I may say so, were known at this time—[Interruption]. I will tell you why. It is because Mr. Tiruchel-vam said :

"Please wait patiently for the next Sinhalese and Tamil New Year. The Federal Party has given language top priority. The wants of the Tamils come only second."

You are going to get what you are going to get before Thai Pongal ! So that when the hon. Member for Chavakachcheri told the people of Uraithivu, "Don't worry about your drinking water——

නියෝජ්‍ය කථානායකතුමා

(உப சபாநாயகர் அவர்கள்)

(Mr. Deputy Speaker)

Hon. Member for Dompe, I would also like to hear what you say !

එච්. ආර්. ඩයස් බණ්ඩාරනායක මය.

(திரு. எப். ஆர். டயஸ் பண்டாரநாயக்க)

(Mr F. R. Dias Bandaranaike)

I agree, Sir. This is all very alarm-ing. It is so alarming that I think you also should hear this.

The hon. Member for Chavakach-cheri was so worried that, even be-fore it came to the question of dealing with the problem of drinking water for the poor Tamil people of Urai-thivu, the question of language rights—the sole language—must be settled. They could wait for water but the sole language must be established before Thai Pongal before the Sinhalese and Tamil New Year.

අමිර්තලින්ගම් මය.

(திரு. அமிர்தலிங்கம்)

(Mr. Amirthalingam)

It is not the Sinhalese or Tamil New Year.—[Interruption].

545   1966 ජනවාරි 10   546
දෙමළ භාෂා (විශේෂ විධිවිධාන) පනත : නියෝග   දෙමළ භාෂා (විශේෂ විධිවිධාන) පනත: නියෝග

එච්. ආර්. ඩයස් බණ්ඩාරනායක මයා.
(திரு. எப். ஆர். டயஸ் பண்டாரநாயக்க)
(Mr. F. R. Dias Bandaranaike)

It is not, I know.—[*Interruption*]

You are thinking of a different kind of thongal !

May I be permitted to say that when the hon. Member for Chavakachcheri spoke, he spoke his mind ? He told us precisely what they knew was going to happen ; and I shall demonstrate to you when it comes to an analysis of the Regulations that that is precisely what they are getting. The hon. Member was no prophet. I appreciate that all these words, " without prejudice to the Sinhala only Act " are " merely eye-wash " to use the language of the Hon. Prime Minister in describing in the same words which were used in the Bandaranaike-Chelvanayakam Pact when he trampled on the map and took his stand. So when it comes to the question of what is this official language, how are you implementing the official language in the Northern and Eastern Provinces, I shall show you on an analysis, section by section, of what we are going to talk about.

We do not need to wait for the Regulations under the Tamil Language (Special Provisions) Act. I have with me here a form of the Social Services Department. Mr. Minister of Social Services will please pay attention to this. This is one of the printed documents which are given for the preparation of the headman's stock register. The Printer's number on the top is " Form 38 D14 ". It is in regard to food production. November 1965 is the date. It is marked, " 11/65 ". It is printed at the Government Press, and I will give it to you in a moment ; I will table it. The amazing thing is this. Here we have the captions, " Rice ", " Dhal ", " Dried Fish ", " Requisitions ", " Local Orders " and various other things. The curious thing is that you will find the whole document is in English and Tamil only.—[*Interruption*] I do not mind telling you that

this document was obtained far away from the Northern and the Eastern Provinces. I am not going to tell you from which headman this document was obtained because you will promtly sack him. But you can have my word for it that it was not obtained from the Northern and Eastern Provinces ; it was obtained very far away from the Northern and Eastern Provinces. Is this how you are going to enforce Sinhala only ?

Let us assume that it is meant for the Northern and Eastern Provinces. Even then, where is the Sinhala ?

කේ. තුරෙයිරත්නම් මයා. (පේදුරු තුඩුව)
(திரு. கே. துரைரத்னம்—பருத்தித்துறை)
(Mr. K. Thurairatnam—Point Pedro)

This is an act of sabotage !—[*Interruption*]

එච්. ආර්. ඩයස් බණ්ඩාරනායක මයා.
(திரு. எப். ஆர். டயஸ் பண்டாரநாயக்க)
(Mr. F. R. Dias Bandaranaike)

I am tabling this document. I will not request that it be included in HANSARD but I am sending it across to the Hon. Minister of Social Services to look at it and satisfy himself that it is a genuine document. It is not a used document because nobody's hand writing is on it. I would not produce a document like that.

ගරු එන්. එච්. ඒ. එම්. කරුණාරත්න (සමාජ සේවා, ඇමති)
(கௌரவ என். எச். ஏ. எம். கருணாரத்ன—சமூக சேவை அமைச்சர்)
(The Hon. N. H. A. M. Karunaratne—Minister of Social Services)

Is this document printed at the Government Press ?

එච්. ආර්. ඩයස් බණ්ඩාරනායක මයා.
(திரு. எப். ஆர். டயஸ் பண்டாரநாயக்க)
(Mr. F. R. Dias Bandaranaike)

Yes. You can satisfy yourself.

ගරු මන්ත්‍රීවරයෙක්
(கௌரவ அங்கத்தவர் ஒருவர்)
(An hon. Member)

Who gave it to you ?

දෙමළ භාෂ (විශේෂ විධිවිධාන) පනත: නියෝග

එච්. ආර්. ඩයස් බණ්ඩාරනායක මයා.

(திரு. எப். ஆர். டயஸ் பண்டாரநாயக்க)

(Mr. F. R. Dias Bandaranaike)

If I tell you the name you will shoot the man.—[*Interruption*]. You will say it is necessary to shoot such people under an Emergency. And his body will have to be buried by the police who will have to do the *pansakula* rights. I, therefore, prefer not to tell who he is.

ස්ටෑන්ලි තිලෙකරත්න මයා.

(திரு. ஸ்டான்லி திலக்கரத்ன)

(Mr. Stanley Tillekeratne)

Have a secret cremation in the night—[*Interruption*].

එච්. ආර්. ඩයස් බණ්ඩාරනායක මයා.

(திரு. எப். ஆர். டயஸ் பண்டாரநாயக்க)

(Mr. F. R. Dias Bandaranaike)

Your Government talks about Sinhala only in the Northern and the Eastern Province! This form is in use now. You may check up and see whether what I say is correct. It is in use in the Ministry of Social Services. We were not the Government in November 1965. [*Interruption*.]

රාසමාණික්කම් මයා.

(திரு. இராசமாணிக்கம்)

(Mr. Rasamanickam)

This is not a document; it is a form.

එච්. ආර්. ඩයස් බණ්ඩාරනායක මයා.

(திரு. எப். ஆர். டயஸ் பண்டாரநாயக்க)

(Mr. F. R. Dias Bandaranaike)

It is a form. It is only in Paddiruppu that there is a difference between a document and a form. I know the forms that the hon. Member likes are of a different type altogether. I am afraid I cannot supply those forms.

රාසමාණික්කම් මයා.

(திரு. இராசமாணிக்கம்)

(Mr. Rasamanickam)

Not human forms—[*Interruption*].

අමීර්තලිංගම් මයා.

(திரு. அமிர்தலிங்கம்)

(Mr. Amirthalingam)

Similar forms were used by your Government—[*Interruption*].

එච්. ආර්. ඩයස් බණ්ඩාරනායක මයා.

(திரு. எப். ஆர். டயஸ் பண்டாரநாயக்க)

(Mr. F. R. Dias Bandaranaike)

I can assure you that if our Government were having forms they were English ones.

නියෝජ්‍ය කථානායකතුමා

(உப சபாநாயகர் அவர்கள்)

(Mr. Deputy Speaker)

Hon. Members please do not interrupt. If you want to shout please go to the Lobby and start shouting.

එච්. ආර්. ඩයස් බණ්ඩාරනායක මයා.

(திரு. எப். ஆர். டயஸ் பண்டாரநாயக்க)

(Mr. F. R. Dias Bandaranaike)

In fact they are disturbing me. I cannot even think straight. It is impossible to argue a point.

As far as this Government is concerned they have presented us with a set of Regulations and the Hon. Minister of State has been at great pains to try to tell us that what he is doing is, in fact, to implement that which Mr. Bandaranaike did without an enacting Regulation. He tried to tell us first and foremost, " Our U. N. P. Manifesto was a marvellous document. It gives the Federalists much more than what they are asking now. Why, at Kalutara we met one day in 1962 or 1963 and wrote up that manifesto under which the Tamils are entitled to many more things than what we are giving them now. These Regulations are nothing. Look at our U. N. P. Manifesto of 1963. "

I saw in the Distinguished Visitors' Gallery ladies who came to watch the Minister of State. They were, in fact, thrilled. There were Sinhalese ladies also. They thought that this was simply marvellous. [*Interruption*.] Yes, my wife was there. She said it was very interesting. She also told me that she

549   1966 ජනවාරි 10   550

දෙමළ භාෂා (විශේෂ විධිවිධාන) පනුන : නියෝග

realized the U. N. P. were not giving
anything what the Tamil people asked
in this manifesto. My wife told me,
"You are arguing against it. The
U. N. P. have promised them much
more in their manifesto, but see the
little bit they are giving now. How
are you going to meet this
argument ? " So, I thought very hard
about it. I had to somehow or other
convince my wife because I could not
convince anybody else. Life will not
be worth living otherwise, Mr.
Deputy Speaker. So, I had to meet
this argument. I am now trying to
show you how I succeeded. I am
going to show you the very arguments
I used to convince my wife that the
Hon. Minister of State was talking
through his hat.

First of all, we looked at his statement on the manifesto as reproduced
in HANSARD of 8th January 1966. And
I looked into the portion of the manifesto that was put out before the
elections. I discovered a Sinhala
copy of it.

ගරු ජේ. ආර්. ජයවර්ධන
(கௌரவ ஜெ. ஆர். ஜயவர்தன)
(The Hon. J. R. Jayewardene)
It is a summary.

එච්. ආර්. ඩයස් බණ්ඩාරනායක මයා.
(திரு. எப். ஆர். டயஸ் பண்டாரநாயக்க)
(Mr. F. R. Dias Bandaranaike)

It is not a summary. It was also
printed in the Ceylon "Daily News"
and in the other daily papers. I will
show you what they have to say on
"Language". Let us see how he
summarized his Kalutara Manifesto.
Let us see the wording in English
and in Sinhala. This is how the
English one reads—U.N.P. election
pledges taken from the "Daily
News" of 22nd January 1965. I am not
going to read the text of all the false
promises made then, such as the one
which says there will be no persecu-
tion of political opponents. That was
the first whopper. There were heaps
of others, too. I am going to start
with the promise in regard to
language. This is how they
summarized the Kalutara manifesto
—item 17 of the manifesto :

දෙමළ භාෂා (විශේෂ විධිවිධාන) පනුන : නියෝග

"We shall summon a round table conference to discuss ways and means of
unifying the nation within the framework
of Sinhala as the official language of the
State. As Sinhala is spoken by the largest
number of the permanent citizens, it is
natural that this language should be
adopted as the unifying language. Provision will be made for the use of Tamil
so that no harm is caused to any permanent citizen who does not know the
official language."

Fine summary! Where did they
find the round table conference.
From what did they summarize that
round table conference. I can
understand it if there was a long
table which was shortened to make a
round table. There must be some
reference to a table ? You cannot
create a round table in the summary
which did not exist in the original
document after the Kalutara sessions.
Show us where the round table is.

ගරු ජේ. ආර්. ජයවර්ධන
(கௌரவ ஜெ. ஆர். ஜயவர்தன)
(The Hon. J. R. Jayewardene)
Why not ?

එච්. ආර්. ඩයස් බණ්ඩාරනායක මයා.
(திரு. எப். ஆர். டயஸ் பண்டாரநாயக்)
(Mr. F. R. Dias Bandaranaike)

Look at HANSARD and show me,
anywhere in the whole text of what
you read of the Kalutara sessions,
where your round table is.

ගරු ජේ. ආර්. ජයවර්ධන
(கௌரவ ஜெ. ஆர். ஜயவர்தன)
(The Hon. J. R. Jayewardene)
I did not read the whole book.

එච්. ආර්. ඩයස් බණ්ඩාරනායක මයා.
(திரு. எப். ஆர். டயஸ் பண்டாரநாயக்க)
(Mr. F. R. Dias Bandaranaike)

The parts that you read were all
about the Kalutara sessions manifesto. Show me your round table in
the summary. You will find that item
17 is a perfect translation of the
Sinhala text, which I have here. It
reads :

"17. රාජ්‍ය භාෂාව :

රටේ රාජ්‍ය භාෂාව වශයෙන් සිංහල භාෂාව තෝ
වෙනස්ව තබාගෙන ජාතික එකමුතු කිරීම සඳහා
අප පක්ෂය විසින් ඊට වැදි සාකච්ඡාවක්

551   නියෝජිත මන්ත්‍රී මණ්ඩලය   552

දෙමළ භාෂා (විශේෂ විධිවිධාන) පනත: නියෝග   දෙමළ භාෂා (විශේෂ විධිවිධාන) පනත: නියෝග

[එෆ්. ආර්. ඩයස් බණ්ඩාරනායක මහා.]
කැදවනු ඇත.   සිංහල භාෂාව වැඩි ජනතාවගේ
භාෂාව හෙයින් රට ලැබිය යුතු උත්කෘෂ්ට
ස්ථානය ගත වැදයන් මත යන්දයක් නැත.
ඇරඹුවිකට ඇත්තේ දෙමළ භාෂාවත් රාජ්‍ය
භාෂාව වන සිංහල නොදන්නා අය විදිබද ප්‍රශ්න
යන් උළැයි. රාජ්‍ය භාෂාව නොදන්නා කිසිම සිවිර
පදිංචිතාරයකුට අසාධාරණයක් නොවන පරිදි
දෙමළ භාෂාවට යුත්ති ගරුක තැනක් දීමට
ඊහාත වෙමු."

This is by no means a summary of
your Kalutara document. Let us be
fair about this and get one thing
clear. This is part of your former
history. In other words, historically
you have proved that the movement
is always from a position of parity
away towards Sinhala only, and that
is precisely what you did.

ගරු ජේ. ආර්. ජයවර්ධන
(கௌரவ ஜே. ஆர். ஜயவர்தன)
(The Hon. J. R. Jayewardene)
Here it is.

එෆ්. ආර්. ඩයස් බණ්ඩාරනායක මහා.
(திரு. எப். ஆர். டயஸ் பண்டாரநாயக்க)
(Mr. F. R. Dias Bandaranaike)
Those are your old documents. If
you go back further you will find
some more.

ගරු ජේ. ආර්. ජයවර්ධන
(கௌரவ ஜே. ஆர். ஜயவர்தன)
(The Hon. J. R. Jayewardene)
That is not correct.

එෆ්. ආර්. ඩයස් බණ්ඩාරනායක මහා.
(திரு. எப். ஆர். டயஸ் பண்டாரநாயக்க)
(Mr. F. R. Dias Bandaranaike)

Here is your document. This was
issued before the elections. These are
the promises you made to the people
they never read your old books.
They never went into your library
and your archives looking for your
old political history. No one is going
to look into those documents. This is
the document that everybody read.
This is what they say, and they
swallowed it like the *diul gediya*.

Now what has happened? The
Malwatte Mahanayake says in his
most recent statement, "It is true I
asked the people to support the
U.N.P. to save this country from

Marxism, from the horrors of a totalitarian Government, from falling into
a ditch. They held out promises of a
round table conference." The
Malwatte Mahanayake has made
repeated requests of you to put off
this discussion and to ascertain the
views of all sections of the people.
He himself has come to see you. And
what does he say? He says that
when he asks questions he gets
irrelevant replies.

ගරු ඩඩ්ලි සේනානායක
(கௌரவ டட்லி சேனநாயக்க)
(The Hon. Dudley Senanayake)
Who said that?

එෆ්. ආර්. ඩයස් බණ්ඩාරනායක මහා.
(திரு. எப். ஆர். டயஸ் பண்டாரநாயக்க)
(Mr. F. R. Dias Bandaranaike)
The Malwatte Mahanayake.

ගරු ඩඩ්ලි සේනානායක
(கௌரவ டட்லி சேனநாயக்க)
(The Hon. Dudley Senanayake)
When did you ask the question?

එෆ්. ආර්. ඩයස් බණ්ඩාරනායක මහා.
(திரு. எப். ஆர். டயஸ் பண்டாரநாயக்க)
(Mr. F. R. Dias Bandaranaike)
He told us.

ගරු ඩඩ්ලි සේනානායක
(கௌரவ டட்லி சேனநாயக்க)
(The Hon. Dudley Senanayake)
I am shocked! He has still to come.

එෆ්. ආර්. ඩයස් බණ්ඩාරනායක මහා.
(திரு. எப். ஆர். டயஸ் பண்டாரநாயக்க)
(Mr. F. R. Dias Bandaranaike)

He did say that you had refused
to see him several times. He did say
that you gave him irrelevant
answers. All I can say is, you can
read for yourself the statements of the
Malwatte Mahanayake and ascertain
for yourself whether he does or does
not attend meetings and make
speeches. At least the Malwatte
Mahanayake is a known figure. Of
course, I do not suppose he can get
past the Peliyagoda bridge.—
[*Interruption.*]

ගරු ඩඩ්ලි සේනානායක

(கௌரவ டட்லி சேனநாயக்க)

(The Hon. Dudley Senanayake)

I have just checked it up.

එච්. ආර්. ඩයස් බණ්ඩාරනායක මයා.

(திரு. எப். ஆர். டயஸ் பண்டாரநாயக்க)

(Mr. F. R. Dias Bandaranaike)

He can get past the bridge ?

ගරු ඩඩ්ලි සේනානායක

(கௌரவ டட்லி சேனநாயக்க)

(The Hon. Dudley Senanayake)

Not only he.

එච්. ආර්. ඩයස් බණ්ඩාරනායක මයා.

(திரு. எப். ஆர். டயஸ் பண்டாரநாயக்க)

(Mr. F. R. Dias Bandaranaike)

Every one can. There will be one more dead body to be buried. The police will have one more *pansakula* to perform. So the pledge was that we were going to have an arrangement by which the Hon. Prime Minister would seek to ascertain the views of everybody and try to establish the largest measure of accord in a matter of great importance to the nation, the language question, and try to resolve it away from party politics, the controversy of party politics. I can assure you that our approach to this matter is essentially of that order. I had time and again, long before you tabled your Regulations, taken it upon myself, on behalf of the S. L. F. P. and the Opposition, to tell you in plain language just exactly what and how we envisage a solution. You are not obliged to follow us ; you are not obliged to follow the late Mr. Bandaranaike, and you are not obliged to follow, according to you, even the criticisms you then made against the late Mr. Bandaranaike, if you think that the people gave you a mandate. The mandate is true. You are the most popular person in this country, the pin-up boy for your side, but even then you must not take it upon yourself to assume that *janaranjana* qualities are everlasting.

ගරු ඩඩ්ලි සේනානායක

(கௌரவ டட்லி சேனநாயக்க)

(The Hon. Dudley Senanayake)

I know.

එච්. ආර්. ඩයස් බණ්ඩාරනායක මයා.

(திரு. எப். ஆர். டயஸ் பண்டாரநாயக்க)

(Mr. F. R. Dias Bandaranaike)

The best method of doing that is not to destroy your mirrors, but to keep your mirrors ; and one method of keeping the mirrors is not by declaring an emergency and curfew but to let others also join issue.

So, Mr. Deputy Speaker, the Hon. Prime Minister now presents to us a set of Regulations and says, " Here are the Regulations. They are exactly the same thing that you people have been in practice doing. The Minister of State read to us a statement by Mr. N. E. Weerasooriya which was printed by the " Observer " and later reprinted by the Information Department. I think, the hon. Second Member for Colombo Central (Mr. Premadasa) also read that again in Sinhala. Sometimes, the best way of repeating a thing is to get it read by somebody else. Then again, I think, he read also the broadcast speech made by Mr. Sam P. C. Fernando, the then Minister of Justice, in regard to what could be done in the matter under the language legislation of the late Prime Minister. He tried to tell us that what the present Regulations intend doing is merely to give legal sanction to what was, in fact, done already. That is, if I may say so, to say the least a gross misrepresentation of the truth. If indeed we were doing all these things in Jaffna you can ask your friends in the Federal Party. They were complaining that we were doing a lot of things in our time, but certainly implementing the language regulations was not one of them. They told us that we were guilty of proclaiming a state of emergency ; they told us that we were guilty of perpetuating a state of army in the North ; they complained that Major General Udugama was a tyrant and of all manner of things. I am not defending myself. I am a very wicked

[එච්. ආර්. ඩයස් බණ්ඩාරනායක මය.]

man. I am only concerned now with preventing your Prime Minister turning into ways of wickedness.

As far as we are concerned, you have told us of all our sins of omission and commission of those days. The hon. Member for Jaffna (Mr. Ponnambalam) was not here but he probably would have had a lot to say about us at that time. I am not complaining but if you say that you are doing precisely what we did in the Northern and Eastern Provinces it is a damnable falsehood ; it cannot be otherwise, for the simple reason that this is precisely your complaint if you read carefully through the statements of Mr. Sam P. C. Fernando and Mr. N. E. Weerasooriya that you read. I am not going to read them again and waste the time of the House, but I will take point by point to point out what they say. They point out all the things that can be done under the Tamil Language (Special Provisions) Act, the Regulations which can be formulated. Those two gentlemen pointed out what can be done. That is their legal interpretation. I wonder whether the Privy Council will agree or not. But as far as the interpretation of those two laws are concerned. I have no hesitation in accepting the interpretation of the law of these two gentlemen, Mr. Sam P. C. Fernando and Mr. N. E. Weerasooriya, if not their politics.

But what is the difference basically between your Regulations and ours ? We will tell you. The difference is this. If you read the Tamil Language (Special Provisions) Act and read carefully the Debate that took place in that connexion—portions of that Debate were read by the Hon. Minister of State (Hon. J. R. Jayewardena) —you will see that there is a very, very substantial difference.

I want to read two portions of the speech made by Mr. S. W. R. D. Bandaranaike, the Prime Minister, in the course of that Debate. I am going to read those portions which the Minister of State, I think, rather slurred over when he was reading

the same speech, and I want to make it quite plain as to what the Prime Minister, the late Mr. S. W. R. D. Bandaranaike, intended by these laws and regulations that he was contemplating.

You told us by your legal sophistries over the radio, press and everything else, that the word " shall " and the word " may ", in a legal sense, have no difference between them. You were at great pains to tell hon. Members how you interpret these things—that because the enabling statute has the word " may " when you come to prescribe the Regulations you must use the word " shall "

First of all, may I point out to what the author of the Bill himself, the late Mr. Bandaranaike, explained in regard to these clauses ? Dealing with the Public Service he stated this :

" Then I come to the Public Service. There, again, we follow the principle that a person educated in the Tamil language can sit for the examination for admission to the Public Service in the medium of the language in which he has learnt. He cannot answer the papers in Sinhalese. But you will ask me, then, what is the position of the Sinhalese language as the official language ? That person will be only given a probationary appointment and will be required under the Regulations to acquire, within a specified period, the necessary knowledge of the official language. Otherwise, he ceases to be a member of the Public Service. If he knows Sinhalese beforehand, all that process can be cut out by setting one or two papers in Sinhalese in the examination for admission itself. At a point of time in the future when Sinhalese, I trust, will be taught as well as learnt as a second language in Tamil schools, you can do away with this provision of subsequently obtaining a knowledge of Sinhalese by setting one or two papers in Sinhalese in the entrance examination itself. It will take some years to do that, but I am sure that position will normally and naturally be reached. I do not see anything wrong in that."— [OFFICIAL REPORT, 5th August 1958 ; Vol. 31, c. 1969-70.]

That is in regard to the Public Service.

Then, in regard to correspondence, this is what the late Mr. Bandaranaike said.

දෙමළ භාෂා (විශේෂ විධිවිධාන) පනත: නියෝග

ජී. ජී. පොන්නම්බලම් මයා. (යාපනය)

(திரு. ஜீ. ஜீ. பொன்னம்பலம்—யாழ்ப்
பாணம்)

(Mr. G. G. Ponnambalam—Jaffna)

What is the point you are making ?

එච්. ආර්. ඩයස් බණ්ඩාරනායක මයා.

(திரு. எப். ஆர். டயஸ் பண்டாரநாயக்க)

(Mr. F. R. Dias Bandaranaike)

May I explain it after I have read this passage also ? I am not quoting these passages for the fun of reading them. Every single thing I am reading has a point and purpose, and in my own quiet way may I come to it ? I was trying to penetrate the—[Interruption].

පොන්නම්බලම් මයා.

(திரு. பொன்னம்பலம்)

(Mr. Ponnambalam)

With regard to the point you are making ?

එච්. ආර්. ඩයස් බණ්ඩාරනායක මයා.

(திரு. எப். ஆர். டயஸ் பண்டாரநாயக்க)

(Mr. F. R. Dias Bandaranaike)

I am trying to make one point by reading two paragraphs.

" Let us consider how such Regulations may be framed. I am now speaking without prejudice. "—[Interruption.]

There speaks the lawyer !

—" I am speaking in order to give an example with a view to allaying the fears of some of these people. Up to December 1960 under the Official Language Act the status quo can be preserved. No difficulties will arise till then because we have the power to do it. After December 31, 1960, how will we deal with it ? That is a question which has often been asked. Any Tamil gentleman must have the right to correspond in the Tamil language but the position of Sinhalese as the official language must be preserved. He can be sent a reply in the official language, Sinhalese, but for the convenience of the Tamil gentleman who may not know Sinhalese a copy of a Tamil translation or the substance of the reply will be attached to such letter. But as Sinhalese is also taught in the Tamil schools we might quietly be able to drop the Tamil copy. What on earth is wrong with that ? I cannot understand whether anything is wrong with that."—[OFFICIAL REPORT, 5th August 1958 ; Vol. 31, c. 1971.]

That is what the late Prime Minister said. Now, to explain to the hon. Member for Jaffna (Mr. Ponnambalam) why I read these passage, I will tell him why. Surely, it should be plain to any person from a reading of that, that what the late Prime Minister intended was —[Interruption]. I know you like me to emphasize it, and I will do so if you want for the record. You can have it because that is the standpoint of our party. What the late Prime Minister meant was that it was never intended that the Tamil Language (Special Provisions) Act should be permanently enshrined as a parallel official language in the laws of this land.

අ. භා. 6.30

නියෝජ්‍ය කථානායකතුමා

(உப சபாநாயகர் அவர்கள்)

(Mr. Deputy Speaker)

Order, please ! The Hon. Speaker will now take the Chair.

අනතුරුව නියෝජ්‍ය කථානායකතුමා පුටුවෙන් ඉවත් වූයෙන්, කථානායකතුමා පුටුවෙහි වැඩ විය.

அதன்பிறகு உப சபாநாயகர் அவர்கள் அக்கிராசனத்திலிருந்து நீங்கவே, சபாநாயகர் அவர்கள் தலைமை தாங்கினர்.

[Whereupon MR. DEPUTY-SPEAKER left the Chair, and MR. SPEAKER took the Chair.]

එච්. ආර්. ඩයස් බණ්ඩාරනායක මයා.

(திரு. எப். ஆர். டயஸ் பண்டாரநாயக்க)

(Mr. F. R. Dias Bandaranaike)

Mr. Speaker, I was just quoting certain passages from the speech made by the late Prime Minister Mr. S. W. R. D. Bandaranaike, on the 5th August 1958, when he introduced and debated in this House the Tamil Language (Special Provisions) Act. And, in that law he made it quite plain that it was his intention, conception, and idea, that ultimately the Tamil copy could be quietly dropped. He said so in so many words. He said :

" I appreciate that when a government department writes to a person who cannot understand Sinhala, they must send him a Tamil copy. "

559 නියෝජිත මන්ත්‍රී මණ්ඩලය 560

දෙමළ භාෂා (විශේෂ විධිවිධාන) පනත: නියෝග

[එච්. ආර්. වයස් බණ්ඩාරනායක මය.]

Without that he cannot possibly deal with a government department. Look at column 1971 :

"...He can be sent a reply in the official language, Sinhalese, but for the convenience of the Tamil gentleman who may not know Sinhalese a copy of a Tamil translation or the substance of the reply will be attached to such letter. But as Sinhalese is also taught in the Tamil schools we might quietly be able to drop the Tamil copy."

What could be clearer than that ? As far as he was concerned, sending a translation in Tamil was never intended to be a legal duty ; it was never intended that the situations that were created in respect of matters which were prescribed should continue ; it was intended that it should be legally permissible, it should not be unlawful not to do so, because, once the Official Language Act comes into force after the 31st of December 1960, assuming that nothing else is done, it would be impossible, legally, to do anything in the Tamil language or the English language. According to law Sinhala is the only official language in the country. Nothing is capable of being done either in Tamil or in English under the strict legal interpretation of Section 2 of the Official Language Act. Section 2 and the proviso to it make it perfectly plain. Sinhala is declared legally to be the official language from, I think, 1st January 1957, but there is a proviso and the proviso is that you are permitted up to 31st of December 1960, to continue to use whatever languages were, in fact, used prior to 1st January 1957. So that, you could, in fact, carry on in the same languages in which the administration had been carried on, up to the 31st of December 1960. That was the law. So, if a majority of acts in this country were done in English —I think, actually, there was a Gazette notification made by the late Prime Minister—it was in order to avoid any sudden breakdown in the administration by which he permitted everything to be done in the English language which had previously been done in that language ; but the

දෙමළ භාෂා (විශේෂ විධිවිධාන) පනත: නියෝග

deadline is created by law. The deadline is 31st December 1960, and by 31st December 1960, assuming that there is no other law, the only legal language in which official acts can be done is the Sinhala language.

Now, having enacted that, we got the Tamil Language (Special Provisions) Act. The Hon. Prime Minister found it rather difficult some time ago to reconcile these two Statutes without amending one or the other. He did not see how you could, without fooling some of the people all the time, come to these conclusions. The late Prime Minister enacted this law, and what did he say in this law ? He said that the Tamil language may be used for various purposes prescribed by law under the different sections of that law. I will come to those sections one by one in a moment. But in every one of those sections the words used by him—the operative words—are " may be used. " Why ? If he did not use the words " may be used " see what would have happened.

If he said the Tamil language " shall be used " you would have been perfectly right in assuming that there is an amendment to the Sinhala only Act. On the one side, you cannot say Sinhala shall be the official language in the Official Language Act and, on the otherside, say the Tamil language shall be used side by side with it unless you are creating a parity situation.

If the late Prime Minister had used the word " shall ", then certainly he would have created a parity situation and there would have been a necessary conflict because you cannot lay down a legal obligation for an act to be done in both languages. In that case you have to say, it may be done in one or the other of the languages— either is legal, either is equally good and lawful—in which case, you have parity. There is no argument about that at all.

But the late Prime Minister did not say that at all. What he said was that for the purposes prescribed by law, for those purposes within the framework of these sections, the Tamil language may be used.

I am aware, Mr. Speaker, that there is a controversy about this. I have read an article by a friend of a friend of the hon. Member for Uva-Paranagama (Mrs. Kusuma Rajaratna)—I refer to Mr. F. R. Jayasuriya—which states that the Tamil Language (Special Provisions) Act itself is now a dead letter by virtue of Section 7 of the Tamil Language (Special Provisions) Act. It is a possible argument but I am not interested in presenting that argument for the reason that hon. Members in this House have read it already, for one thing, and secondly, I think, it would be, in a sense, an immoral argument, immoral because the late Prime Minister himself definitely intended making use of the Reasonable Use of Tamil Act after December 1960.

He said so in the course of his same speech. That argument weighs with me more than all the legal interpretations contemplated or which can be presented right up to the Privy Council. I am much more interested in what the late Prime Minister intended. After all, we are trying to ascertain the intention of the legislature. Let us be honest about it. It was intended by the late Prime Minister that it should operate. But, what did he intend? Did he intend to entrench this Tamil copy for ever and ever and ever? No. Did he intend to make it a legal obligation that if any single act was done it must be done in Tamil also? No. He made it quite plain that it is not unlawful that the Tamil language may also be used. It is a completely different matter.

In other words, it would have been legal to use the Tamil language after December 1960 unless there was a

Tamil Language (Special Provisions) Act, and he made it plain that there is provision by which the use of Tamil is not outlawed. It was perfectly made permissible. It is a far cry from saying that it shall be in Tamil also. Let us see the consequences of this legislature. What is being sought to be done is to enlarge the enabling Statute.

The Hon. Minister of State says "may" and "shall" mean the same thing. In a given context, in some situations, the words "may" and "shall" may be equal to one another; they may be used as interchangeables depending on the use of words. For example, if I were enacting a law, I do not think you could possibly ever say, "You shall divorce your wife"; you can only say, "You may divorce your wife". It becomes an absurdity. But this is not one of those situations. This is a situation in which the law has been deliberately passed and framed to cover a particular form of words. In other words, all that the law intended was to make it permissible to use the Tamil language for certain purposes after 1960, and the late Prime Minister expressed the hope that as a part of a political settlement it would be honoured notwithstanding the other half to it, the Federal Party, who were languishing in jail at that time. He introduced this law in their absence and he made it quite plain that it was his hope and endeavour not to fix rigid limits but that, with the teaching of Sinhala in Tamil schools, the problem would resolve itself, that, ultimately, we would come to a situation where indeed the people of this country woud be united by the bond of language—the knowledge of a common language.

This is sometimes described by my Federal Friends as genocide. May I say in plain terms that there is no genocide about it at all? No one is suggesting the destruction of the Tamil language. No one is suggesting at any stage that the Tamil language should cease to exist or should not be taught or that the Tamil culture should be destroyed. Indeed, at

563   පාර්ලිමේන්තු මන්තී මණ්ඩලය   564

දෙමළ භාෂා (උච්චේ විධිවිධාන) පනත: නියෝග

[එච්. ආර්. ඩයස් බණ්ඩාරනායක මහා.]

every stage, 1 think, everyone accepts
the point that the language policy of
the late Prime Minister was for it to
be taught as a second language.
Tamil should be the first language for
the people of the Northern and
Eastern Provinces. No one in his
right mind suggested anything else.

ගරු මන්තුවරයෙක්

(கௌரவ அங்கத்தவர் ஒருவர்)

(An hon. Member)

What is the second language of the
Sinhalese?

එච්. ආර්. ඩයස් බණ්ඩාරනායක මහා.

(திரு. எப். ஆர். டயஸ் பண்டாரநாயக்க)

(Mr. F. R. Dias Bandaranaike)

The second language of the Sinhalese could be anything at all. Those
who want to learn Tamil should be
given the opportunity to learn Tamil.
No one is objecting. We are not even
talking of compulsion at this stage.
We are talking of what the late Prime
Minister said. Let us not, under the
cover of following Bandaranaike
policies, try to pervert Bandaranaike
policies in whatever way it is convenient to the Federal Party or
Mr. Dudley Senanayake. Let us be
honest about it.

What have we said at every stage?
We, for the S.L.F.P., have expressed
our mind in no uncertain terms. We
did not even wait for your regulations. I have made at least four
speeches in this Parliament on behalf
of the S. L. F. P. I said so during the
Throne Speech Debate, I said so
during the Budget speech, I said so
during three or four considerations
of the amendments in Committee
stage, are you prepared to send
Sinhala teachers into the schools in
the Northern and Eastern Provinces?
To that question the Hon. Minister
of Education, during the discussion
of the Education Votes. gave an
answer.

ගරු ඊරියගොල්ල

(கௌரவ சரியகொல்ல)

(The Hon. Iriyagolle)

That is my intention.

දෙමළ භාෂා (උච්චේ විධිවිධාන) පනත: නියෝග

එච්. ආර්. ඩයස් බණ්ඩාරනායක මහා.

(திரு. எப். ஆர். டயஸ் பண்டாரநாயக்க)

(Mr. F. R. Dias Bandaranaike)

He said that was his private intention—" පෞද්ගලික අදහසක් ". That
was not in answer to me, but in
answer to the hon. Second Member
for Batticaloa (Mr. Latiff Sinnalebbe). And what did Mr. Latiff
Sinnalebbe tell you? He said, "I
have heard this story before. I made
this request from the Hon. Minister
before. Now he says he will send
teachers, but the truth of the matter
is that he is waiting for the O.K.
signal from the Federal Party".
This is the language of Sinnalebbe.
I will give you the reference. Do
you want me to read HANSARD to
you. I will give you the reference.

ගරු ඊරියගොල්ල

(கௌரவ சரியகொல்ல)

(The Hon. Iriyagolle)

No.

එච්. ආර්. ඩයස් බණ්ඩාරනායක මහා.

(திரு. எப். ஆர். டயஸ் பண்டாரநாயக்க)

(Mr. F. R. Dias Bandaranaike)

Do not imagine that I am inventing
anything. I will give you the actual
words. It is actually in HANSARD,
Volume 62, column 3154—this exchange between Mr. Latiff Sinnalebbe and yourself. He pressed you
to it. You said " පෞද්ගලික
අදහසක් ". Then he asked you, is it
Government policy? Then you
said, "Well to the extent that it is
my intention it is Government
policy". The Minister has very
good intentions but sometimes the
Government, like a steamroller,
moves on regardless.

ගරු ඊරියගොල්ල

(கௌரவ சரியகொல்ல)

(The Hon. Iriyagolle)

No.

එච්. ආර්. ඩයස් බණ්ඩාරනායක මහා.

(திரு. எப். ஆர். டயஸ் பண்டாரநாயக்க)

(Mr. F. R. Dias Bandaranaike)

See even in the matter of school-
books you are in trouble. The
" Dawasa " is gunning for you now.

Felix on Trade Unions

In other words, this is because the newspapers started a canard originally tnat this strike is sponsored by leftist leaders who are trying to overthrow the Government. I can at least vouch for one leftist leader, Dr. N. M. Perera, the Member for Yatiyantota, who was with both of us at Bahamas, and his mind was certainly far away from strikes.

කථානායකතුමා
(சபாநாயகர் அவர்கள்)
(Mr. Speaker)

He was listening to after-dinner speeches.

ඒජ්. ආර්. ඩයස් බණ්ඩාරනායක මහා.
(திரு. எப். ஆர். டயஸ் பண்டாரநாயக்க)
(Mr. F. R. Dias Bandaranaike)

Yes, Sir. At that time his mind was in a totally different direction. He was not even thinking one little bit about strikes.

ගරු ජේ. ආර්. ජයවර්ධන
(கௌரவ ஜெ. ஆர். ஜயவர்தன)
(The Hon. J. R. Jayewardene)

What was he doing?

ඒජ්. ආර්. ඩයස් බණ්ඩාරනායක මහා.
(திரு. எப். ஆர். டயஸ் பண்டாரநாயக்க)
(Mr. F. R. Dias Bandaranaike)

He was performing essential service orders and for which there were no penalties.

So that, the most eessential thing that you have got to remember is not to be misled by your own caucus of newspapers which are determined to fight your battles for you, on any ground. They will fight for you on the baches ven before you are driven to the beaches. The newspapers are determined to finght a last ditch stand in defence of the U. N. P., when the Hon. Prime Minister is fifmly convinced that you all are winning great support throughout the country. He even said that he is in half a mind to dissolve Parliament. I only wish we could persuade him to make up the whole of his mind because then, we will be able really and truly to judge how much the Hon. Prime Minister is a good judge of public opinion. This is rantastic. If he thinks that the present situation is one in which he is immensely popular, if he thinks that all the public servants did not go on strike, if he thinks that all the public servants are going to wait for ever without adequate standards of living compared with the rest of the community who are prospering gloriously, if this is the situation, then, all I can say is we seem to be going in the wrong direction.

I am not entirely unaccustomed to negotiating with trade unions. I too have done my share of this work. The Hon. Prime Minister speaks of these things: of the little questions which are put sometimes, the differnces between trade unions, that one union says, 'We are not interested about the salaries of other officers or technical assistants; you can increase them one hundred per cent we are only interested in our demands."—that is a polite way of saying that they are not going to join issue with their brothers. It is quite understandable. No grade of public servant is going to turn round and sabotage the demands of his neighbour. He will merely remain politely silent and say that it is not his affair. I have received that answer so many times. But does it prove the thesis of what the Hon. Prime Minister is saying, namely, that this is a competitive demand by people trying to set up one against the other?

I do see the Hon. Prime Minister's point of view that he cannot undo the whole effects of devaluation, the cutting of the rice ration and the Foreign Exchange Entitlement Certificate Schemee which was to satisfy the World Bank. To satisfy the World Bank he must withdraw some part of purchasing power from the hands of the vast mass of the people! I think we never did that during the bad old days of the S. L. F. P. Government of Mrs. Sirimavo Bandaranaike and the five Finance Ministers during her time. We hear that too many cooks spoil the broth. In this

421   නියෝජිත මන්තුී මණ්ඩලය   **422**

[එෆ්. ආර්. ඩයස් බණ්ඩාරනායක]

case as least the broth remained un-
spoiled. Not all the five Finance Ministers reduced the purchasing power
of the rupee in the way you have done
to satisfy the American bosses. Your
rupee is still a rupee on paper, but in
its purchasing power terms you can
get practically nothing for it. It is
almost as bad as the Bahamian dollar.

Ultimately when it comes down to
an analysis of looking at the problem,
the Hon. Prime Minister, I think, is a
realist. He knows. Indeed, as soon as
the bugle sounds the departure of the
aeroplane from Ratmalana, the Minister of State mobilizes for war. Maybe he believed it was total war that
was coming. It turned out that all
these preparations were not necessary. He decided to quote Mrs. Bandaranaike to Mrs. Bandaranaike. He
decided—even though portions of her
letter were cut out from the
"Observer"—he must reply to the
other part of her letter. He forgot, for
example, that Mrs. Bandaranaike used
particular regulations, some of which,
I concede, I drafted. One particular
one was a gem.

In June 1961, when Mr. Thondaman decided to call out the
entire plantation workers—the
C. W. C. and the D. W. C.
combined— on strike, paralyzing
the entire State, what was the
strike for ? Was it for a salary
demand ? No. It was a demand that
Dr. Naganathan and his friends
should be given parity of status for
the Tamil language, for which they
were doing satiyagraha outside the
Jaffna Kachcheri in the Jaffna Municipal Council area from which they
have been rejected now. Mr. Thondaman thought he would call out a
strike and there were talks and rum-
bles that emery powder was to be
thrown into tea factory machinery by
the teamakers as a means of getting
parity of status for the Tamil language. At that stage I said that incitement of strikes by leaders will result in the confiscation of property by
Emergency Regulations.

ගරු ජේ. ආර්. ජයවර්ධන
(கௌரவ ஜே. ஆர். ஜயவர்தன)
(The Hon. J. R. Jayewardene)
Any strike ?

ඇෆ්. ආර්. ඩයස් බණ්ඩාරනායක මයා.
(திரு. எப். ஆர். டயஸ் பண்டாரநாயக்க)
(Mr. F. R. Dias Bandaranaike)

Yes. May I say this : Thondaman as
soon as he read that called off the
strike.

ගරු ජේ. ආර්. ජයවර්ධන
(கௌரவ ஜே. ஆர். ஜயவர்தன)
(The Hon. J. R. Jayewardene)

Where is that regulation ?

ඇෆ්. ආර්. ඩයස් බණ්ඩාරනායක මයා.
(திரு. எப். ஆர். டயஸ் பண்டாராநாயக்க)
(Mr. F. R. Dias Bandaranaike)

Why, you were repeating it after
that and were seeking to use it against
the strikers. That is the funniest part
of it. Your regulation has been so
drafted.—[Interruption]. You have
improved upon the original and you
are going to confiscate the property
of strikers who do not have any
property !

ගරු ජේ. ආර්. ජයවර්ධන
(கௌரவ ஜே. ஆர். ஜயவர்தன)
(The Hon J. R. Jayewardene)
No.

ඇෆ්. ආර්. ඩයස් බණ්ඩාරනායක මයා.
(திரு. எப். ஆர். டயஸ் பண்டாராநாயக்க)
(Mr. F. R. Dias Bandaranaike)

Your regulation has been drafted
not to catch the big men ; you are
concerned with catching little men.

ගරු ජේ. ආර්. ජයවර්ධන
(கௌரவ ஜே. ஆர். ஜயவர்தன)
(The Hon. J. R. Jayewardene)

Your one is a good one.

ඇෆ්. ආර්. ඩයස් බණ්ඩාරනායක මහ.
(திரு. எப். ஆர். டயஸ் பண்டாரநாயக்க)
(Mr. F. R. Dias Bandaranaike)

Mine is a fine one. I waved my one in front of Thondaman and it worked beautifully and as far as——

කථානායකතුමා
(சபாநாயகர் அவர்கள்)
(Mr. Speaker)

I think we are all glad that it works somewhere.

මෛත්‍රීපාල සේනානායක මහ.
(திரு. மைத்திரிபால சேனநாயக்க)
(Mr. Maithripala Senanayeke)

Secrets of Bahamas' are coming out.

ඇෆ්. ආර්. ඩයස් බණ්ඩාරනායක මහ.
(திரு. எப். ஆர். டயஸ் பண்டாரநாயக்க)
(Mr. F. R. Dias Bandaranaike)

As for the Hon. Minister of State, he has taken his one, and cut and chopped it in such a way that it no longer functions properly. By altering the regulation in this way it has got wrecked. What is left there? I mean, by draconian laws you are threatening the confiscation of property of clerical servants on strike, the postal officers, and the workers. Have you ever heard of such a thing? Is this democracy? The great defenders of democracy! Their democracy is restricted to the lorry-owners, fleet owners, the Parliamentarians with special privileges, the special leases folk, the coup people on corporation boards. But when it comes down to dealing with the workers, what do they get?

I am the man who refused to implement the Wilmot Perera Salary Commission Report. I was determined like De Gaulle to maintain the value of our currency, and I would have succeeded but for you. I succeeded in holding the line till 1962, and from 1962, thanks to your brilliant efforts, you made it impossible to do so.

Now the Hon. Prime Minister says that the hon. Member for Kolonnawa is irrelevant when he refers to the Public Debt. Mr. Minister of State, you are as good an economist as ever there was in this House—there are none better—so much so that when even Mr. Wanninayake makes a gaffe you remain silent, looking like the Sphinx. But is it not a fact that the future remains so mortgaged that, independent of foreign aid, we are incapable of even making the amortization payments on the obligations you have already incurred during the course of the last three years? In other words, if foreign aid were to stop now you are incapable on your foreign exchange receipts even of meeting the routine repayments of the instalments.

So you think this is a healthy economy? Food production has increased. Yes, indeed, we all hope for a bumper crop next Maha. We hope so indeed, as we hope it will happen in India and in Pakistan as well. We are hoping that you are right; there will be rice equilibrium. If the monsoon works the price of rice must come down. It cannot be otherwise. Whether Mr. Dudley Senanayake takes his camera and walks or not, and whether you sit in your office and smile with a cheshire cap on it will still be all right.

This is the problem: are you seriously telling us that the workers who went on strike, led in the first instance by Mr. Wilfred Perera with whom you have negotiated, should now be separated into two categories, some of whom should be fired from their jobs and some of whom should be kept on an arbitrary line drawn by you? What we can do is to appeal to the Hon. Prime Minister not to be unreasonable about this. I can understand your argument if you say that this is a political strike calculated to subvert the Government, in which event you would have looked upon it as treason. But it is not.

Now that you know the facts, why do you not, even now, at this stage, take a practical view of it and enter

[ඇෆ්. ආර්. ඩයස් බණ්ඩාරනායක මයා.]
into negotiations? Wait till they
come back if you want to, but do not
shut the door in their faces when
they want to come back, and do not
take repressive measures.

Remember the days when you
thought you were subjected to repressive measures. Please remember that governments have a knack
of changing, however much one may
think they are permanent and established for ever. It is seldom like
that.

Mr. Thiruchelvam thought that by
dissolving the Jaffna Municipal
Council the Federal Party was
assured of success. But did it work
like that? He took the matter up
even to the Privy Council. And yet,
when he went to the voters of Jaffna,
both he and Mr. Ponnambalam had
their hopes dashed to the ground by
a relatively unimportant, single individual and his group of friends. And
it looks as if that single individual
and his friends will still outnumber
both the Federal Party and the
Tamil Congress jointly.

Now, you think you are permanent
and you think it will stick merely
because some extraordinary officials
have a knack of giving the same—
pardon me for saying so—damn-
fool advice to successive governments.

කථානායකතුමා
(சபாநாயகர் அவர்கள்)
(Mr. Speaker)
That is unparliamentary.

ඇෆ්. ආර්. ඩයස් බණ්ඩාරනායක මයා.
(திரு. எப். ஆர். டயஸ் பண்டாரநாயக்க)
(Mr. F. R. Dias Bandaranaike)
Sorry, Sir—fool advice. And
sometimes there are Ministers who
tend to take it at its face value. I
do not pretend that we ourselves
have not made mistakes in this matter. But one thing is certain. The
tendency to follow precedents, especially bad precedents, remains a

fact. And you will find your successor Government probably telling you
that what you do now they can do
too.

I think it would be much more
practical to look at this thing in a
broader perspective. I think the
Hon. Prime Minister and his colleagues are all capable of doing that.
This is not a strike in which we are
personally involved. The Sri Lanka
Freedom Party has no involvement
whatever except in so far as the protection of certain fundamental rights,
which we feel everybody must have,
is concerned Mr. S. W. R. D. Bandaranaike did not grant public servants
the right to strike for nothing. He
did not say, "You have the right to
strike," and then say, "It is unpat-
riotic for you to strike."

ගරු ජේ. ආර්. ජයවර්ධන
(கௌரவ ஜே. ஆர். ஜயவர்தன)
(The Hon. J. R. Jayewardene)
He did not give it. We gave it.

ඇෆ්. ආර්. ඩයස් බණ්ඩාරනායක මයා.
(திரு. எப். ஆர். டயஸ் பண்டாரநாயக்க)
(Mr. F. R. Dias Bandaranaike)
Then it is so much the better.
Then why are you complaining when
they strike? Why do you not let
them strike?

ගරු ජේ. ආර්. ජයවර්ධන
(கௌரவ ஜே. ஆர். ஜயவர்தன)
(The Hon. J. R. Jayewardene)
Essential services.

ඇෆ්. ආර්. ඩයස් බණ්ඩාරනායක මයා.
(திரு. எப். ஆர். டயஸ் பண்டாரநாயக்க)
(Mr. F. R. Dias Bandoranaike)
You give them the right to strike
and at the same time tell them, "If
you do strike, the moment we ring
the bell the strike must stop and you
must all go back to school." Now, this
is the funniest part of it. If you concede to them that collective bargaining power, why do you deny them
the right to bargain? And why do
you say the moment they make a
demand, "Well, this is a final demand,

So we are not prepared to bargain. " Now, that is what is completely wrong about it. I do ask you, even now, to consider this problem. You may not be able to grant the Rs. 40 they ask for—I do not know. I sincerely hope I shall never become Finance Minister again to be confronted with that problem. I am content to leave it to experts who know more about it than I, who hope that with hard work and other things it might be capable of achievement in the future.

But so far as you are concerned, you have already decided that the demand is justified in principle. Your Prime Minister's statement that it will be incorporated in the next Budget amounts clearly to a declaration that you can and will to some extent grant an upward revision. The Hon. Finance Minister said in answer to a categorical question that a Salaries Commission was appointed to grant an increase.

Well then, what are you waiting for ? If you can grant the increase and you concede that the present hardships have arisen from your own fiscal measures, how does it help to tell a man, " Please accept a lower standard of living for six months. We shall find you a higher standard of living six months hence. "

" We shall try and give you a higher standard of living six months hence.

What is the meaning of this ? If you once concede that your own action has created the situation, surely, the least you can do, if you accept the fact that it must be ameliorated by the appointment of a commission, is to take some practical action. No one has suggested that you should grant the whole of it now. I think the Prime Minister said that the hon. Member for Yatiyantota took and essentially reasonable attitude in the matter, and he was certain that the hon. Member for Yatiyantota did not give the strikers advice to strike. Well, I know he did not ; he could not have done so because he was with u sin the Bahamas. He has got a perfect alibi this time at least. And I can assure you I did not lead him in

a wrong direction. I would never have done so ; I am not capable of doing so. I do not think he even corrupted me. So, there you are !—[Interruption] Yes, we are completely incorruptible, both of us. I think sometimes he and the hon. Member for Avissawella used to meet and explode occasionally and ignite, but as far as both of us are concerned, neither is combustible materials.

So, really when you come down to it you misjudged the situation, you were led up the garden path by newspapers which were determined to see in this the seeds of a civil war, an insurrection and a determination to overthrow the government. Accordingly, the Minister of State got mobilized for war. He put on his figurative tin hat and his jack boots and got organized for total war, determined to annihilate all sections of the public service before the Big Chief returned from India. And he certainly made his point. He did *satyagraha* in the Parliamentary Group till they applauded him yesterday. He allowed " Rama " and " Sita " to carry the honours abroad, while he played " Hanuman " at home. He set a torch to his tail and went round all the public service unions, one by one, determined to annihilate those which he thought should have essential service orders tagged to them.

What are we asking you to do, Mr. Minister of State ? Please extinguish the light in your tail. There is no need for it now. We ask you, now that Rama has come back to Sita who remained in Ceylon, please accept the situation as it is and do not say : I have declared an Essential Services Order. My prestige is at stake. I am determined to sack somebody. Like Blue Beard, I am determined to slay my wives. Do not do that. I ask you, be practical about it.

You yourself seem to think that the vast majority of public servants are working. If so, well and good. No one has committed any sabotage. The strike has been peaceful you say they are misled. We say the people have been unequally treated in your efforts at economic development, and

429   නියෝජිත මන්තුී මණ්ඩලය   430

[එච්. ආර්. වයස් බණ්ඩාරනායක මහා.]
the wage earning sectors which earn a fixed wage are the hardest hit. You cannot get behind that. You cannot give them Queen's Counselships to make more money. You have not given them Corporation appointments. You have not given them anything. They are still back where they started, with about Rs. 400 million of purchasing power drawn out of their hands by your action in real terms.

The Prime Minister says "The real wages are going up. I can quote from the book, Table 49." All right. What about real expenditure? If your real wages go up a little bit what does it mean? It means that you are comprising the purchasing power of money in rupee terms, in devalued rupee terms. It does not become in re-valued rupees terms. So, your figures do not mean a thing. I mean this kind of a economic argument is too weak even to get past an able man like the Minister of State. He knows it. He is far cleverer than he appears to be, sitting there. He gives the impression that none of this penetrates him, but he knows it all, and he knows it far better than I can ever know it. Even when I am his age I doubt I will understand it so well as he. But, with his understanding, is it necessary to take a hard line on this matter? You think you can score verbal points by saying, "We did it better than you." Have you really done it better than we? Do you really think you are winning a battle against the people of this country? The Prime Minister says" The public servants number only a few hundred thousands. With their families one million." He says, "Make it two million. including unofficial families."

The Prime Minister perhaps knows. I do not know whether it is the Rama and Sita story all over again.

But when you start with this business of saying two million, remember that, after all they are two million or one million of our own people.

Are we here to say to ourselves that we have scored a victory by crushing those people, by crushing their spirit and determination, by crushing their democratic right to ask for a little more?

Now I can understand it if you imposed a wage freeze in a determination to maintain the economic value of the rupee. I can understand it if General de Gaulle in France, after the incidents of the barricades of May, determined to freeze wages now, after his election, and he determined not to devalue. But he is fighting an international currency battle. He is fighting an economic war against the U. S. A. determined to crush his economy. That is a different situation. I can understand a wage freeze policy in that situation.

I can understand the action of Mr. Roy Jenkins in London or of Mr. Callaghan attempting to hold a wage freeze with a determination not to devalue. But what is the situation in England today once devaluation took place? Clerical workers who prior to devaluation were receiving £14 a week in London are now drawing £22.—[Interuption]. I know because I know a few Ceylonese working as clerical servants in London. I got these facts from them. Net of tax the increase amounts to approximately £5 per week per person in employment in London after the decision to devalue was taken. Surely even with English living standards, which today are deplorable compared to what they were ten years ago, if a £5 increase were necessary there, on what basis are you arguing that the devaluation allowance, which you have thrown as a sop in the direction of the workers from whom you knew a demand was coming, has solved the problem?

In the circumstances, that is the purpose of this Debate? The Prime Minister seems to think that the Opposition has identified itself with the strike. Frankly, I do not see that at all. The Opposition is concerned with the fact that a group of workers in this country belonging to the public sector have struck. We have deliberately refrained from involving ourselves in a strike which seems to be of an all-party complexion, including your friends,

431   1968 දෙසැම්බර් 7   **432**

midnight friends, Wilfred Perera and others. They all went on strike. The Opposition remained aloof. We deliberately did not involve ourselves in the argument of the Rs. 40 increase.

But the moment you decided to use repressive measures, determined to use extraordinary degislative powers, to try and crush the working people belonging to our country, we felt we had no choice. We are not going to march the streets with mouth gagged with handkerchiefs. But we do propose to use the legitimate forum of Parliament to voice our grievances and to tell you that this kind of conduct on your part is not going to solve the problem.— [*Interruption*].

Tampoe can have a meeting today. He is your friend. He is going to end up with a Cabinet post in the U. N. P. some day. You can have him. There are so many people like Tampoe. That does not matter. That is not an argument.

But I do say to the Government not to be repressive now. You yourself know what it feels like because you claimed that in the days gone by we acted repressively. I join issue with you on that, because we never did.

We certainly held the line in economic terms up to 1962, and I am afraid we were guilty of back-sliding slowly thereafter due to circumstances beyond our control largely created by your machinations to overthrow the Government. I think we tried to hold the line in economic terms up to 1962 and failed thereafter, thanks to efforts, and finally you carried away the Minister of Irrigation who has not been doing any irrigation ever since. But all this leads you nowhere. Whether with or without technical assistance, do you really believe that Hon. C. P. de Silva can irrigate anything? You might as well pay those technical assistants a little more.

ගරු ජේ. ආර්. ජයවර්ධන
(கௌரவ ஜெ. ஆர். ஜயவர்தன)
(The Hon. J R. Jayewardene)

They are on strike.

එෆ්. ආර්. ඩයස් බණ්ඩාරනායක මය.
(திரு எப். ஆர். டயஸ் பண்டாரநாயக்க)
(Mr. F. R. Dias Bandaranaike)

The Hon. C. P. de Silva has been on strike for the last ten years and is not even on strike for an increased salary. You will find that the amount of water that dribbles through is still negligible either way from the Hon. C. P. de Silva. All this leads you nowhere.

You just cannot afford to fight the people of a country and say to yourself that these people are saboteurs or coup suspects or that these people are guilty of treason. They are not. It is manifestly so. You cannot have a peaceful strike of these dimensions merely because you have got mobilised power. Therefore, I do beg of you, think again, withdraw all these draconian regulations, give these people a chance to come back to work. Governments lose nothing by being generous. My experience has been that it does no good to anybody to create feelings of bitterness.

I frankly do not know that your economic endeavours are going in the right directions. They are lopsided. I think you are helping the wrong people in the hope that they are going to develop the economy. But that is neither here nor there. That is your opinion. You can carry on and help them in any way you like.

But please do not declare war on sectors of your people if the rest of the people feel that it is a capricious act to use anti-democratic powers against them. The danger is that by so doing you can always sow the wind and reap the whirlwind, and specially create wretched precedents for the future Government.

Felix on the Separation of Powers

ගරු f පිලික්ස් ආර්. ඩී. බණ්ඩාරනායක

(கௌரவ பீலிக்ஸ் ஆர். டி. பண்டாரா நாயக்க)

(The Hon. Felix R. D. Bandaranaike)

If they elect a Communist Government all I can say is that people deserve everything they get. As reasonable folk they will be entitled to their choice, and they will no doubt get their deserts.

ගරු මන් ත්‍රිවරයෙක්

(கௌரவ அங்கத்தவர் ஒருவர்)

(An hon. Member)

The people get the government they deserve.

ගරු f පිලික්ස් ආර්. ඩී. බණ්ඩාරනායක

(கௌரவ பீலிக்ஸ் ஆர். டி. பண்டாரா நாயக்க)

(The Hon. Felix R. D. Bandaranaike)

Of course the people get the government they deserve. Only, sometimes one wonders why the people deserve so little. But taken by and large, if sovereignty is to be exercised through somebody and you cannot have direct democracy as in Athens, where you put every question to all the people and ask them, " Now, what do you say, what is your viem ? " ; if you hold a public meeting on every single question according to traditional patterns of ancient city state democracies as in Greece, you have to have it exercised though somebody.

Now, who is to be that sovereign power? Is it to be the National Assembly, the legislative organ of the State or is it to be something else? My hon. Friend argued that you must have this thing with a certain amount of union and a certain amount of separation. All I can say to that is this: if what is good enough as a safeguard in England under the British Constitution is not good enough for you in the United National Party, I should like to ask you why.

Parliaments are sovereign. The House of Commons and the House of Lords and all the rest of it constitute the sovereign legislature in that country. No one talks of the separation of powers in England. No one talks of powers of judicial review, of judges having the power to declare legislation invalid. They have no such power. The only powers they have under the common law are the powers of the writs, which exist under the law and not under the Constitution, to protect individual liberty and everything else. If that is good enough for the people of England from whom the Queen and everybody else you talked about derive their power, if that was good enough to safeguard liberty from the days of the Magna Carta downwards, why is a similar principle not good enough for the new Constitution which we are planning to present through the Constituent Assembly right here and now?

Now, I do know that there is separation of powers in certain Constitutions starting from the time of Montesquieu. This theory has been debated and argued, coming from France. They thought that the experience of the French Revolution proved the case. I do not know. Many Revolutions have come and gone after that and have proved exactly the opposite. But if you ask me the question, " Is there a separation of powers as a necessary ingradient in the British Constitution ? " my answer to you categorically is, there is not. And if the degree of freedom that exists in England is inadequate for you, then all I can say is, you will never be able to find from the experience of modern histories and modern states any country which has a greater degree of freedom within a Constitution then that country.

The British actually did not have a constitution in writing anywhere. Simple powers exist in their Parliaments. And if their Parliament is totally sovereign and their courts do not have the power of declaring their laws invalid, their courts have no constitutional powers declaring acts of Ministers invalid except under the ordinary law, under the common law of England. If then we devise a Constitution under which the new institution corresponding to a Parliament—the National Assembly—is sovereign, without power in the courts to exercise judicial review of the acts of the National Assembly and to declare the laws invalid, and if we provide minor laws under which the equivalent of high prerogative writs can exist, why have these fears.

In Ceylon, under the Courts Ordinance, Section 42, we provide for writs. There is nothing in the Constitution about habeas corpus, quo warranto, mandamus, certiorari, and so on. Evidently, when the Minister of Local Government is taken to court by the other half of the country that does not like his dissolutions of local authorities, it is done under the ordinary law, a very ordinanry law, and not under our Constitution. What is wrong with that ? If we had a Constitution under which such powers are not provided, why are you not content with that, and why are you arguing that you must have the power of judicial review provided in the Constitution for this very purpose ? I do not see the logic or the reason for it.

Now, in our country, the Supreme Court or the Privy Council—I am not certain which—upheld in one or two cases that there is in the present Constitution a separation of powers, which means in practice that the courts have been accorded a right under the Constitution to declare invalid, on various grounds, laws passed by this Parliament of ours which now exists—not on the ground that it does not have a two-thirds majority, not on the ground that it does not have this, that and the other, but on the ground that you cannot pass the law except by certain required procedures.

One such case was the case concerning various tribunals appointed for various purposes by Acts of Parliament. These were declared invalid because they were not appointed by the Judicial Service Commission. Do you want to know why evicted farmers have not been able to get back their lands ? I will tell you.

හමීඩ් මයා.

(ஜனாப் ஹமீது)

(Mr. Hameed)

The hon. Member for Habaraduwa (Mr. Prins Gunasekera) said that, not I. I was giving an answer.

ගරු ෆිලික්ස් ආර්. ඩී. බණ්ඩාරනායක

(கௌரவ பிலிக்ஸ் ஆர். டி. பண்டார நாயக்க)

(The Hon. Felix R. D. Bandaranaike)

You were trying to answer the hon. Member for Habaraduwa, I know, but I will give the answer to that. He was saying it and I think he is right.

In effect what the Supreme Court judge was saying was that Assistant Commissioners of Agrarian Services, to whom is given the power under the Paddy Lands Act to restore evicted tenant farmers, cannot exercise that power because they were not appointed by the Judicial Service Commission. In consequence of that judgement, what followed ? I was Minister of Agriculture when that judgement was given.

I promptly approached the three members of the Judicial Service Commission. They happened to be Mr. Basnayake, Chief Justice, Mr. T. S. Fernando, and one other judge—I cannot remember exactly who it was. It may have been Justice H. N. G. Fernando or Justice Thambiah—one or the other. I contacted these three gentlemen in writing as well as in person and said, " Look, as far as I am concerned this conflict is an imaginary one. The Minister is not anxious to appoint anybody or any person to hear these cases. I do not mind one bit if you make the appointment. But I have no financial provision to make payment of salaries to judges for this very limited purpose of restoring evicted tenants. But I am prepared to let you choose from the entire gamut of the public service suitable persons to function as Assistant Commissioners appointed by you. If there is any particular Assistant Commissioner whom you do not approve of, leave him out. I

1509   1971 ජූනි 12   1510

[ගරු fපිලික්ස් ආර්. ඩී. බණ්ඩාරනායක]
am not prepared to pay them additional emoluments. Please make the
appointments. "

Do you know the answer I was
given ? The then Chief Justice, Mr.
Basnayake said to me, " You see,
your argument is all wrong because
this applies only to paid judicial
officers. There is no special payment
in respect of Assistant Commissioners
of Agrarian Services for the purpose
of restoring evicted tenants. Therefore the power of appointing is
really in the Minister. "

I said, " It is very nice of you to
say that. As far as I am concerned, I
do not give a damn who makes the
appointment. I want the appointments made. I want evicted tenants
restored to possession by the process
of law contained in the Paddy Lands
Act. Your Supreme Court says that
the Minister has no power to appoint.
The Judicial Service Commission
says that the Minister has the power
to appoint. Please settle this among
yourselves. I do not care a damn
which you do, but I want the appointments made. "

And would you believe it ? From
1963 up to 1964, when our Government was defeated by you people
and Mr. C. P. de Silva tried to preserve democracy to live as free men
amongst free people, and for the
next five years when Minister M. D.
Banda was in office, nothing was done
to make any appointments one way
or the other and the matter remained
stuck while all the evicted tenants
remained evicted. These are the
facts.

You are asking me, " Where have
the judges obstructed anybody ? " I
am taking a very practical case about
which I am in a position to give you
the facts. It is all well and good. I
agree with you that independence of
the judiciary is essential. Nobody
wants judges to be stooges, to give
judgments favourable to sides. When
the hon. First Member for Colombo
South was in the Opposition to start

with and we were in the Government,
he quoted sections from Soulbury's
Sessional Paper to show that the
Attorney-General is meant to perform a quasi-judicial office and
should be independent like a judge
and should not be subject to the influence of the Minister of Justice or
of the Government. It is all there in
the Sessional Paper of Lord Soulbury. But when it came to the practising of it, as a Member of the Government my good friend, the Hon.
J. R. Jayewardene, completely
changed his tune. When it came to
prosecuting   Mackie   Ratwatte,
Michael Baas and odd cases like that,
you found the hon. Member singing
a completely different tune.

ජේ. ආර්. ජයවර්ධන මයා.
(திரு. ஜெ. ஆர். ஜயவர்தன)
(Mr. J. R. Jayewardene)
All Ministers do it.

ගරු fපිලික්ස් ආර්. ඩී. බණ්ඩාරනායක
(கௌரவ பீலிக்ஸ் ஆர். டி. பண்டார
நாயக்க)
(The Hon. Felix R. D. Bandaranaike)

He says all Ministers do it. What
can you do with people like this ?
These are the reasonable men sent to
Parliament ! When it happens like
this we find the hon. First Member
for Akurana (Mr. Hameed) in his
innocence thinking in terms of absolute concepts and talking in terms of
judges being independent. Of course,
they must be independent. I would
hate to have a judge who has already
made up his mind, who does not
know how to hear cases, who is incapable of doing justice between man
and man. Nobody wants him. Is it the
suggestion that this Government
wants him ?

Kindly read the Basic Resolutions
already tabled. Kindly read Basic
Resolution 20 which says :

"Save in respect of its powers and privileges, the National Assembly shall
exercise its judicial power only indirectly
through institutions established by its
laws for the administration of justice, for
the making of decisions of a judicial or
quasi-judicial nature and for the adjudication and settlement of disputes. "

Can you think of anything clearer that that ?

In other words, the National Assembly has judicial power in the same sense that the Parliament in England has judicial power, that is, there is no court higher than Parliament capable of throwing out the decisions of Parliament. That does not mean that we cannot under our laws establish institutions and hand over the job of judging disputes to law courts under the law, not under the Constitution. That is what we are arguing for and that is what precisely the Hon. Minister of Constitutional Affairs is seeking to get. We are trying to reject the theory of separation of powers. We are trying to say that nobody should be higher than the elected representatives of the people nor should any person not elected by the people have the right to throw out the decisions of the people elected by the people. Why are you saying that a judge once appointed should have the right to declare that Parliament is wrong ? That you must have judges to do the job of judging is true. We do not want to be judges.

Long ago, in ancient history, there was a procedure by which Parliament used to hear its own election petitions through Select Committees. They said that the courts could not interfere with election petitions. What happened was that Select Committees used to get together and decide election petitions. Well, we know how these Select Committees do work. Governments always have a majority, do they not ? I think the Hon. J. R. Jayawardene established the principle. When he was prosecutor on a Morris Oxford car charge, he said "I must insist on being the Chairman of the Select Committee", and it shows that even though he may not be an excellent legislator he is a very good judge because he proceeded to acquit Mrs. Bandaranaike. He was a very good, independent judge. When functioning as a judge he certainly proved that he was far superior to his own functioning as a parliamentarian. There is no question about it. He is a very fine judge. Now, there is

a case where he did a separation of power in his own mind though there was no separation of power in fact. He continued to be a legislator, he continued to be a prosecutor and became the judge. And all against whom ? Against the Opposition Leader at the time, Mrs. Bandaranaike.

We do not want to hear election petitions among ourselves, do we ? It will be a terribly embarrassing thing if we have to sit in judgment over good Friends like Mr. Gamini Dissanayake and Mr. E. L. Senenayake. How can we ? Who knows, you might have even double-barrelled election petitions in Akurana some day. It might happen. These things are misfortunes. But we do not want to mix up the powers of judging. So we must pass laws and delegate that power to some appropriate body. If we want to delegate that power to an Assistant Commissioner of Agrarian Services, we must have the power to do that. If we want to delegate it to a judge, we must have the power to do so. But we are the supreme people who decide the matter, not judges who can tell us, " We are going to clip your wings ; you can do this and not the other thing. "

Please do not get confused about this matter. No one is talking in terms of distrusting judges. I appreciate that in the early part of his speech the hon. First Member for Akurana was talking of some people saying that judges have an anti-working class bias and all that. I do not think that is quite the way of putting it. I think my good Friend, the hon. First Member for Akurana, carried it to an absurd limit when he said, " This means that you are suggesting that a judge is incapable of giving a judgement in favour of a worker. "—[Interruption]. I am talking now of the argument put forward by the hon. Member. He definitely said that we were suggesting some sort of bias on the part of judges, that judges were incapable of deciding fairly.

හනීඩ් මයා.

(ஜனாப் ஹமீது)

(Mr. Hameed)

That is what the hon. Member for Habaraduwa (Mr. Prins Gunasekera) said.

ගරු f පිලික්ස් ආර්. ඩී. බණ්ඩාරනායක

(கௌரவ பீலிக்ஸ் ஆர். டி. பண்டார நாயக்க)

(The Hon. Felix R. D. Bandaranaike)

Yes, I am telling you the answer to that. There is a world of a difference between what the hon. Member said and saying that there is a class bias in one's actions, depending on the society from which one is drawn, an inarticulte major premise in one's thinking, the ultimate background.

For example, I have come across judges with strange ideas of sociological behaviour. Not that they are unjust or unfair. Please do not misunderstand me. By all the yardsticks in the books they are as honest as one can expect them to be. But their thinking is entirely conditioned by the background they know. They live in a restricted circle. They do not move around in society. By the very nature of their judicial functions they are isolated from society, and some of them have no clue as to what is going on. Let me give you one little illustration.

This is drawn from the experience of a very distinguished old judge of the Supreme Court who is now dead. I do not know whether my good Friend, Mr. J. R. Jayewardene, will agree that he is a distinguished judge, because I think in the past he has expressed disagreement, but let us use the word " distinguished " in the formal sense, for we are not trying to insult anybody. Now, this judge was hearing an election petition. He was Mr. Justice Sri Skandarajah. I was appearing as counsel in the case. It was Mr. Clifford Ratwatte's election petition in respect of the Balangoda seat. Mr. Clifford Ratwatte happened to be giving evidence in the witness-box on that occasion. The merits of the petition are irrelevant, but Mr. Ratwatte said among other things that he did not do any house to house canvassing in the course of that election. The judge promptly sat back and said, " Mr. Ratwatte, why are you lying to me ? It is absolutely impossible for any Member of Parliament to win his seat unless he goes belly-crawling from house to house. " Those were his own words. The judge said, " I have seen it happen in Jaffna times without number. This is absolutely impossible. Why are you telling lies in the witness-box ? "

Mr. Clifford Ratwatte leaned back flabbergasted. He did not know what to do with this judicial storm breaking on his head. So I thought I would try to save the situation, and I interrupted very nicely. " My Lord ", I said, " you know everything depends on the circumstances of each electorate and the situation that prevails there. For example, in my own electorate, which I had won by the second largest majority in the Island, I did not do any house to house canvassing. Having regard to the marginal difference it was not considered necessary. It depends on the circumstances. " Do you know what the judge told me ? He said, " I am sorry, Mr. Bandaranaike, that you have made that statement from the Bar. I have no alternative but to call you also a liar. "

I am not saying that the judge was unfair. He really believed that the conditions that prevailed in Jaffna at the time that he was interested in elections prevailed everywhere else. I am not saying that those conditions prevail there now. Please do not misunderstand me. I am not trying to insult anybody there either of the Tamil Congress or of the Federal Party. That is not my objective. But I do want to say that some judges have queer views.

There are some judges, for example, if you look at their history who have a natural bias against landlords, and

there are some who have a natural
bias against tenants. Please do not
misunderstand. That does not mean
that a judge who is a tenant is in-
capabe of giving judgment for a
landlord or a judge who is a landlord
cannot give judgment for a tenant.
That will be done honestly according
to the evaluation of each particular
case. I have no doubt about that.
But I think there is a world of a
difference from alleging that a judge
cannot be fair and saying that a judge
does not have the built-in prejudices,
the built-in thinking of his whole
social environment. It must happen.

For example, the way a man's mind
works is entirely different, even if he
is educated, depending entirely on the
class backgound from which he
comes. A few people may be so big
that they are able to overcome the
weakness of their class background ;
whether the weakness is drawn from
great economic power or limited
economic power makes no difference.
Some people can. For example
there are the odd moments when my
good Friend the hon. Firist Member
for Colombo South (Mr. J. R. Jayewardene) the Leader of the Opposition can actually bring himself to
think like a worker.

ජේ. ආර්. ජයවර්ධන මයා.
(திரு· ஜெ. ஆர். ஜயவர்தன)
(Mr. J. R. Jayewardene)
I am a worker.

ගරු f පිලික්ස් ආර්. ඩී. බණ්ඩාරනායක
(கௌரவ பிலிக்ஸ் ஆர். டி. பண்டார
நாயக்க)
(The Hon. Felix R. D. Bandaranaike)
How many hours do you work ?

ජේ. ආර්. ජයවර්ධන මයා.
(திரு· ஜெ. ஆர். ஜயவர்தன)
(Mr. J. R. Jayewardene)
Hard work.

ගරු f පිලික්ස් ආර්. ඩී. බණ්ඩාරනායක
(கௌரவ பிலிக்ஸ் ஆர். டி. பண்டார
நாயக்க)
(The Hon. Felix R. D. Bandaranaike)
He says that he works very hard.
I think he has a lot of hard work in
his own party to maintain his position. That is the hardest bit of work
he does.

So I mean quite honestly, these are
problems which confront us all. The
hon. First Member for Akurana himself was saying that hon. J. R. Jayewardene wants the separation of
powers put in plain language. He is
asking for a separation : that the
National Assembly shall be declared
the only repository of legislative
powers ; that the people are good
enough to make laws, but once we
have made the laws some other independent agent must have the power
to declare that those laws are invalid,
and the power of declaring those laws
invalid is something quite different
from what the people want. We say
the people must have that power
through the one and only body which
is elected by the people. Certainly we
have subordinate bodies established
which must be independent, which
must have the power to function.
That is where the controversy lies
in regard to the amendment proposed
by the hon. First Member for Colombo South. It does not mean anything else, and your search for
perfection, to avoid tyranny, is an
exercise, No doubt, that exercised
the minds of men from Socrates to
Plato and others downwards. It has
worried the founders of the famous
Weimar Republic. There are many
authorities over the years who have
examined this problem but who have
found no solution. You can hardly
blame the Hon. Minister of Constitutional Affairs that he has not been
able to think of anything better, and
you have not been able to think of
anything either. So the net result is
we are back to square one in search
of constitutional perfection. When
you are unable to find anything
and the only argument which is
really relevant to this amendment is

1517 ආණ්ඩු ක්‍රම සම්පාදක මණ්ඩලය 1518

[ගරු f පිලික්ස් ආර්. ඩී. බණ්ඩාරනායක]
the question of whether we want a separation of powers in this country or not, my simple answer is, if it is good enough for England to operate without a separation of powers, I do not see why it is necessary for us, merely because the Privy Council has held to the contrary in one or two cases, and obstructed the Government over the years in a very limited number of cases.

In regard to judicial powers exercised by those who are appointed by authorities other than the Judicial Service Commission, I think, in one situation, in the Coup Case judgement, which I have not been able to understand up to date, the judgement in the case Queen vs. Liyanage was limited to the facts of that case only. It is the only judgement I am aware of in the whole history of jurisprudence where the Privy Council has declared the judgement limited to the facts of the case. Normally the Privy Council lays down the principle applicable in one form or another to a class of cases and deals with the principle's general applicability. This is the only case I am aware of in any part of the Commonwealth in which the Privy Council has given a judgement where they themselves declare that the judgement does not constitute a precedent for anything excepting the particular coup trial held in Ceylon.

It is a remarkable situation, but it happened. People have examined this judgement backwards and forwards, politicians have looked at it, lawyers have looked at it, various people have looked at it over the years. Sir Ivor Jennings had considered it and even given advice, before he died, in regard to the validity or not of a piece of legislation, and he had expressed opposite points of view. I think the Secretary of our Constituent Assembly is personally aware of it, having functioned also as one of the counsel advising in the case at that time before the Privy Council. But certainly if you think that the judicial power should exist for the sake of solving an odd problem like that, frankly I think

the Government could have—and I believe it did also—found other ways of communicating its wishes, may be, through the authorities concerned. I believe in Jomo Kenyatta's case the problem was similarly solved before the Privy Council when they heard the appeal in the days gone by. I do not think the courts are there to frustrate governments or to frustrate the will of the people. They are there just as much as other parallel institutions of State power. Possibly, to a farmer, a judge on the bench is less important than the Commissioner of Agrarian Services. But why are we bothered ? The appropriate man must do the job, but it must all be done under and by virtue of the authority of people elected to Parliament by the people.

One last matter : You want to know, what is there to prevent Parliament extending its own life, or the National Assembly extending its own life ? The answer is that there can never be a legal method of stopping that happening so long as you can amend the Constitution, unless you are going to provide a Constitution which is incapable of being amended, where you make a piece of paper the king, unless you are going to provide that the Constitution shall never be amended under any circumstance, in which case the people will amend it by rebellion. It is bound to happen. Equally, if people decide to amend it in an oppressive way, or if we decide to do a secret or dirty deal and we decide to get together and—[Interruption].

හමීඩ් මැ.

(ஜனுப் ஹமீது)

(Mr. Hameed)

That is what I was trying to tell you.

ගරු f පිලික්ස් ආර්. ඩී. බණ්ඩාරනායක

(கௌரவ பீலிக்ஸ் ஆர். டி. பண்டார நாயக்க)

(The Hon. Felix R. D. Bandaranaike)

Could be. But I am telling you that 5,000 policemen or 5,000 soldiers cannot hold at bay 12½ million people. It is principally because the insurgents were not supported by the people that the Government has been able to succeed against them. If the people supported them, by now the Government could not possibly exist. I am dealing with a practical situation. So, please remember when you are talking of insurgency that, if Parliament tries to extend its life in the way that you are saying it, the entire people will rebel against it. And it will not be a question of a few hundred people or a few hundred students trying to peddle Mao's thoughts when the thoughts of Mao have given Rs. 150 million worth of credit to the Bandaranaike Government. That is really the situation. Thank you.

සභාපතිතුමා

(அக்கிராசனர் அவர்கள்)

(Mr. President)

The Sitting is suspended till 2 P.M.

ඒ අනුව රැස්වීම තාවකාලිකව අත්හිටුවන ලදින් අ. භා. 2.00 ට නැවත පවත්වන ලදී.

அதன்படி அமர்வு இடை நிறுத்தப்பட்டு, மீண்டும் பி. ப. 2.00 மணிக்கு ஆரம்பமாயிற்று.

Sitting accordingly suspended till 2 P.M. and then resumed.

ඉස්තාෆා මයා.

(ஜனாப் முஸ்தபா)

(Mr. Mustapha)

Mr. President, we are here not engaged in a theoretical discussion of some abstract constitutional philosophy, but we are engaged in the practical task of framing a Constitution in the interests of good, just, and orderly government for the people of our country. We have promised the people a home-grown Constitution. Therefore, it is well for us, Members of this honourable House, to free our minds or disabuse our minds of the influence of some old political doctrine or constitutional doctrine or legal phraseology or jargon and address our minds to the problems as existing in this country today, the conditions prevailing in the country and the goal that we are aspiring to reach.

Sir, this is not the first time that a Constitution is going to be placed before this country. We have had constitutional government for exactly 40 years. We have had the advantage of having seen the practical working of constitutions and have experienced the working of two constitutions from 1931, that is for the last 40 years.

We are today discussing a basic resolution which even according to the Hon. Minister of Constitutional Affairs is basic to all the basic resolutions. In fact I myself thought that this was the most important basic resolution because it might even be described or defined as the storehouse of all the other resolutions, for it is on the proper construction of Basic Resolution 6 that the quality and condition of all the other basic resolutions would depend in the future. Therefore, even at the expense of taking a little more time, it is necessary for us to go into the question of how the National Assembly of the future should be constituted, what powers and duties must be invested with that institution, so that it would become the effective organ for the exercise of the sovereignty of the people.

A number of speeches have been made yesterday and today on the division of powers and on the doctrine of the division of powers. Our party has introduced an amendment that there should be a separation of powers. That is how the question of the independence of the judiciary has figured very prominently in the course of this debate. It has arisen as a result of our request, as a result of our amendment, that there should be a judicature performing judicial functions.

I said in proceeding to draft a Constitution for our people, it is best that we disabuse our minds of various theories which might have suited a different climate or a different time. As you know, Mr. President, the doctrine of the separation of powers

1521   ආණ්ඩු ක්‍රම සම්පාදක මණ්ඩලය   1522

[මුස්තෆා මයා.]

is an 18th century concept of the British Constitution. In fact, about that time, France was emerging from almost chaos, just after a Revolution, and the French Jurist Montesquieu attributed all the virtues of the British Constitution to this doctrine of the separation of powers. And that was the first time this doctrine was formally formulated.

But we also know that over the years the doctrine of the separation of powers has been found unacceptable to a large number of countries. Not even in the country of its origin, namely England, is it now followed in the spirit of its original concept, not to talk of Europe, so that what we by this amendment are seeking to achieve, Mr. President, is not the supremacy of the judiciary but merely the independence of the judiciary. In fact that, to my mind, is the basic difference on which we are proceeding.

I was very carefully listening to the hon. Member for Habaraduwa. I had a feeling that he was confusing the question of the independence of the judiciary with the supremacy of the judiciary. Nobody in his senses would ever demand supremacy for the judiciary.

ප්‍රින්ස් ගුණසේකර මයා.

(திரு. பிரின்ஸ் குணசேகர)

(Mr. Prins Gunasekera)

මා එහෙම දෙයක් කිව්වේ නෑ.

මුස්තෆා මයා.

(ஜனாப் முஸ்தபா)

(Mr. Mustapha)

I understood it that way. In fact I shall tell you why I drew that conclusion.

We are all agreed, Mr. President, that the sovereignty lies with the people, and that it shall be exercisable, as far as judicial powers are concerned, through the judicature. That is why one of the Resolutions

was to the effect that the judicial power will be indirectly exercised through the judicature.

Sir, in fact our amendment had not been altogether fruitless because we elicited, if I may say so, or we had the benefit of, an assurance not only from the Minister of Constitutional Affairs but also from the Minister of Finance that there will be complete independence for the judiciary even in the future.

In fact, that is an aspect of this matter about which we had certain misgivings, and now that an assurance has been given on the Floor of this House by persons of the calibre of the Minister of Finance and the Minister of Constitutional Affairs, I think we should be satisfied that the independence of the judiciary will remain even under the future Constitution.

Further, Mr. President, I thought that Basic Resolution 33 also has a bearing on the intentions of the Government and of the Minister of Constitutional Affairs. It says :

"Until the National Assembly by law otherwise provides, all laws, written and unwritten, in force immediately before the commencement of the Constitution shall, *mutatis mutandis,* and except as otherwise expressly provided in the Constitution, continue in force."

So, we have a right to expect that, until it is otherwise provided in the Basic Resolutions or in the future Constitution, the laws under which we are now being governed shall continue to be in force, and that, coupled with the assurance of the Minister Constitutional Affairs and the Minister of Finance, dispels the one fear that we had about this problem.

I do not want to speak at length on that aspect of the matter because the whole doctrine of the separation of powers has been thrashed out. However, the best form of government, if we can have it, is government by the people themselves. If all 12 million of us could form a government, that will be an undiluted democratic

316 FDB

form of government. But that is neither possible nor practicable. Therefore it is the duty of this House to devise a scheme by which the people will be enabled to delegate their power or their sovereignty to a suitable number of people for reasonable length of time to perform that function. Naturally, then, we come to the principal of elections.

As I said earlier, we have had two Constitutions before, and I am sure most hon. Members would agree with me that there are very valuable provisions in the Constitution under which we are now functioning and the Constitutions that have gone before it with regard to a number of matters. In fact, it is perhaps for that reason that the Hon. Minister of Constitutional Affairs himself has not thought it necessary to discard some of the very valuable provisions engrained in this Constitution. I sometimes have the feeling that a person from outside can see things in their proper context. We have by trial and error evolved an electoral system which I think is eminently suited both to the conditions in this country and the people living in this country.

I remember listening to the Hon. Minister of Constitutional Affairs when he spoke at a meeting at the Ceylon Moors' Islamic Cultural Home. On that occasion I asked him a question. I remember having read in a paper somewhere that he had said that the vote of one person in one area is sometimes equal to two votes in other areas. What he really meant was that as a result of couplin population and area in the question of delimitation certain electorates got a smaller number of voters than other electorates. In fact, I had the feeling that, if what he felt at that time had been put into the future Constitution, certain areas—for instance, the Eastern Province—would have a proportionately smaller number of seats than they have now. In fact I must express my gratitude to the Hon. Minister

because he proposes to continue that principal in the election of Members, that for every 75,000 people there will be a seat, and an additional seat for every one thousand square miles in that province. Of course, with regard to that matter there are various other amendments to come. I can enlarge on that later on. Suffice it to say that we have to be thankful to the Hon. Minister that a very valuable provision, a well thought out provision, is going to be continued in the future Constitution in the matter electing Members.

As I said earlier, if all the people go to form the proposed National Assembly, then every citizen of this country would have the same right to rule, would have the same say in the Government which they would be setting up. It is because of the impracticability of all the people meeting that we resort to this system of elections. I have no complaint with regard to the manner in which the elections are going to be held. The laws are the same, and we have no complaint against it.

What happens after all these representatives are elected ? In fact, the whole country must shrink into this Chamber, so to say. This must be a true reflection of the conditions outside this House and in the whole country. That means that every elected Member who comes to this House as a representative of the people must have similar rights, the same rights.

With great respect I say that the present Constitution, the British parliamentary system of Government, does not afford those rights at present. I was a little puzzled to note that the Hon. Minister is not seeking to change that system. In fact, as you know, there is a very great demand even in England, the country of its origin, to change this position, to rectify this position. As we know, it is sometimes a great advantage to a Member to be on that side and on this side, to be a back-bencher, to be in the Front Benches there and

1525   ආණ්ඩු ක්‍රම සම්පාදක මණ්ඩලය   1526

[ඉස්තාෆ්ස මහා.]

to be a Front Bencher here. In all humility let me say that I have been sitting as a back-bencher in the Opposition in the second row and for a short time even in the first row in the Government ranks. Except for the short spell when I was a Minister I never felt that I was a participant in the process of administration of this country. I never had that feeling.

In fact, today the power of the people, if you wish to call it that, is concentrated in the Cabinet, in the Prime Minister and her Cabinet. We have even yesterday been waxing eloquent about the supremacy of Parliament, the sovereignty of the people, the will of the people as represented by their representatives. I know we politicians are adept at flattery when it comes to talking to the people. Whether it is in this House on platforms, we are adept at flattering the people who have sent us here. But I ask the Hon Minister, who has had a very long and distinguished career as a Parliamentarian and most of the time in the Opposition, whether that sovereignty of the people is enjoyed in equal measure by every Member who represents the people to rule for and on their behalf in this House ? I say that, except for a fifth of the Members of this House, the others are either back-benchers or sit in the Opposition. We say that the National Assembly—call it Parliament, the House of Representatives or by any other name—shall be the legislative body and that it shall not delegate its power to anybody.

I ask the Hon. Minister whether in practice the back-benchers and the Opposition have any say in the legislation that is brought before this House. No doubt we know that sometimes important proposals are incorporated in a White Paper before they are embodied in a Bill and are discussed at the meetings of the Government Parliamentary Group, but we also know the type of discussion that takes place. No doubt when

the matter comes up before Parliament in the form of a Bill, the Opposition has an opportunity of expressing its views, but more often than not we find that criticism from the Opposition or the expression of views from the back-benchers does not have any effect at all on the Minister concerned or on the Government.

The point I am trying to make is that, to that extent, except for the Cabinet, the other Members of Parliament who are representatives of the people are not brought in as participants in the process of government. In fact what is prevailing today in this country—and that is the basic complaint today in England also—is that there is a complete dictatorship of the Cabinet. What is happening today is this. It is only those elected representatives of the people who have had the good fortune subsequently to be chosen by the Prime Minister, whoever he be or whoever she be, to be Ministers who really perform the functions for which they are elected by the people, and the function for which they have been elected by the people is to rule and participate in government for and on behalf of the people. Today that function is performed only by the Cabinet and by the Cabinet alone.

The others no doubt go to the different Ministers and ministries and see that matters are attended to, but that is not to say that they enjoy equal rights in the performance of the duty delegated to them by the people.

I am not trying to suggest that every person who is returned as a Member of Parliament should be a Minister, but certainly this is a serious problem. It is a problem of paramount importance. In fact, if we are not going to address our minds to a basic problem such as this, there would really be no point in our attempt to caste aside a constitution under which we are functioning and to frame another which would perpetuate the present position.

We have concluded our discussions in respect of five basic resolutions. Most of them, to mind, constitute a re-affirmation of the position which already exists today. For instance, a President is to replace the Governor-General. According to another Basic resolution Buddhism is to be given its rightful place. In fact, it has always enjoyed its rightful place. Other religions are to be respected. That has always been there. Then fundermental rights and freedoms are to be written into the constitution. In fact, people have gone to the courts for the maintenance and preservation of their fundamental rights. Therefore I say that the previous basic resolutions constitute a re-affirmation of the position as it exists today, that is in respect of matters which we are already enjoying.

But today are we satisfied with administrative and governmental machinery as at presently constituted ?

I entirely agree with the Hon. Minister when he said that this Basic Resolution is basic to all other basic resolutions. That is why I discribed this Basic Resolution as the storehouse of all the other resolutions. On the construction of this will depend all the other resolutions. We sometimes find that a person who has been rejected by the people as their representative has greater influence with the Government and that he is brought into participate in the Government while the man who is elected by the people is left out. We see that every day. I ask, is this parliamentary democracy ?

I am speaking on this subject because I am serious about it. In fact, we find a significantly important difference in regard to this matter in the Hon. Leslie Goonewardene and the Hon. T. B. Subasinghe, but there are other Ministers who do not accept that principle. I am prepared to say here that there are others who are prepared to take into their confidence persons who have been rejected by the people and not take into consideration the views of persons who have been elected by the people. We say that sovereignty resides in the people, but where is this democracy ?

In fact I was really thinking, although I did not want to embarrass the Hon. Minister at the stage when we were discussing fundamental rights, that we must have safeguards to protect the right of the elected representative to represent his electorate in the form of fundamental rights. I was contemplating it in the light of the experience we have had over the years.

This is not something new, least of all to the Hon. Minister of Constitutional Affairs. I am not in fact blaming this Government. This may have been perpetrated by the Government that went before it. That is precisely the reason why I say at this stage that this must be changed. After all, it is on an occasion like this that we get the opportunity to suggest these things. It is not every day or every year that an august Assembly like this meets to draft a Constitution or even to amend the Constitution. Now that we have the opportunity of going into these problems, we must see to it that these anomalous situations are completely changed.

In fact, no less a person than the Hon. Minister of Finance said the other day—it was a very significant remark that he made, though is passing, while my hon. Colleague the Member for Kalkudah (Mr. Devanayagam) was speaking—" Why, during your time you had an unofficial Member of Parliament in my electorate ! " Look at the significance of that statement. In fact, it cuts across the entire concept of parliamentary democracy. If such a thing is possible under this system of government, if that is really happening in practice under present system of government, I ask the Hon. Minister, is he going to continue with it ? We have no right to assume that the British parliamentary system of government is the best system of government that we can select.—[Interruption]. I am saying this because I prefaced my remarks by saying that we are preparing a Constitution for Ceylon and that the conditions prevailing in one country are by no means on all fours with conditions prevailing in any other

1529   ආණ්ඩු ක්‍රම සම්පාදක මණ්ඩලය   1530

[උස්තාෆා මහ.]

country. We have to frame a Constitution for the people on the basis of the prevailing conditions here. It may be that people will laugh at us if I say this in another assembly. That is indeed the fact. I am saying that no less a person than the Minister of Finance himself had occasion to give vent to that. If that is the feeling on that side, and if that is the feeling I honestly and sincerely have, well, this is the occasion when we can all get together to change that system.

I do not want to cite instances but I have made my position quite clear. However, I can cite one or two instances which would bring home the point I am trying to make ; but I do not want to do that for obvious reasons. It was even said, " You people did this. So, we are doing this ". I am not annoyed at that sort of thing at all. The fact that that sort of thing takes place may be due to a defect in the system and not due to a defect in the person concerned. I am appealing to the Hon. Minister—he has the maturity, he has the intellect, he has the courage—to bring to bear a fresh mind on this problem, because it is by trying to cast away anomalous things like that that we can give the people a Constitution in keeping with their aspirations. The people who elected us are flung far and wide ; they are not here watching what is happening. The people, after two months of campaigning, select a man who they think is the best man to represent them in this august House, and they are satisfied. They do not know what is happening. So, this sort of vendetta that is going on does not worry them.

In fact, no less a person than the late Mr. S. W. R. D. Bandaranaike had occasion, when he was in the Opposition as well as when he was Prime Minister of this country, to give his mind to this problem. I do not want to cite or read his speeches which are on record, where he says that this system is not all that good, that he is personally aware of the frustration and the disappointment that exists in the back-benchers and the Opposition,

that a system similar to the one we had under the Donoughmore Constitution should be evolved. In fact, it is said that the Donoughmore Constitution was a unique experiment.

That is the frame of mind that we must have in drafting this Constitution. We must put out a Constitution to suit the genius of the people as at present ; we must look at the problem as it is. This Constitution is not being drafted only for the United Front Government. It may be that many of us may not be here when this Constitution comes into force, when it comes to be really implemented. We are framing this Constitution for this Assembly and for several Assemblies yet to come, for many generations yet unborn. So, are we going to bequeath a system under which the pennicious system I referred to would be allowed to continue ?

Just imagine the feeling of an elected representative of the people when his views are not counted for anything but the views of the defeated candidate who may have polled 500 votes are counted as representative of the people's views.

සභාපතිතුමා
(அக்கிராசனர் அவர்கள்)
(Mr. President)
Do you admit that it is due to something wrong in the system ? It is the wrong development of the party system that you have in mind.

උස්තාෆා මහ.
(இறைப் முஸ்தபா)
(Mr. Mustapha)
Even that is not beyond the purview of this Assembly.

සභාපතිතුමා
(அக்கிராசனர் அவர்கள்)
(Mr. President)
Even if you lay it down, what can you do if a party in power recognizes a defeated candidate ? It is a question of political morality.

ඉස්තාෆා මයා.
(ஜனாப் முஸ்தபா)
(Mr. Mustapha)

It may be that I have not made myself clear. It is quite possible while retaining the party system.

සභාපතිතුමා
(அக்கிராசனர் அவர்கள்)
(Mr. President)

You cannot.

ඉස්තාෆා මයා.
(ஜனாப் முஸ்தபா)
(Mr. Mustapha)

Why not ? You can bring in the elected Members as participants in the form of a committee—something like the Executive Committees we had. In that system 7 members from a committee and the head of that committee is the Minister. Of course, the party which has been returned with the largest number of seats would have the largest number of Ministers. But, at the same time every Member of the House would have a part to play, and my position is that they should have a part to play. Sovereignty must rest in the House as a whole, not in a part of the House.—[*Interruption*]. This is not a subject for levity. I must tell my hon. Friend from Hakmana that I am on a very serious and important point. This is not a matter we can play about with. In fact we have a habit of taking the comments of my good Friend, the hon. Member for Hakmana (Mr. Roy Rajapakse) very lightly. He is such a humorous person that even things that are said in seriousness are taken as jokes.

Otherwise this Assembly would be reduced to the status of a voting machine. It would be only a registering organization. It would only be here to keep the government of the day propped up. If that is the only purpose for which the people of this country takes all the trouble to send elected members to Parliament, I am sure we can opt to do much better. That is one thing.

Then in regard to our amendment itself, I was adverting to the fact that I had the feeling that the hon. Member for Habaraduwa (Mr. Prins Gunasekera) was confusing the supremacy of the judicature with the independence of the judicature. We are not trying to question the proposition that the sovereignty must rest in the people and the people alone, and that the sovereignty would encompass the legislature, the executive and the judiciary.

No doubt in the middle or in the early part of the 18th century jurists, merely to set right the conditions of their respective countries at that moment of time—that was 200 years ago—propounded this theory or the doctrine of the separation of powers. As I said earlier, it has now been found unacceptable even in the country of its own origin where the virtues of that division of powers were at one time extolled. In fact, today there is really no separation of powers distributed in the three links. We talk of the legislative, executive and judicial power only to get a clear idea of the functions of a government. The classification of functions is now put under these three heads. Beyond that, I think, the separation of powers is no more tenable.

For that matter even in Ceylon we have a political executive. The Cabinet is the political executive. But the Cabinet is part and parcel of the legislature. So how can we say that there can be this division of powers in watertight compartments ? If that is done the complexities of government are so great that a government would break down. Not only will the process be slowed down but at some stage it will completely break down.

No doubt it is within the power of this National Assembly to set up the judicature, but once it is set up by the National Assembly it is our demand that that creature of the National Assembly shall function independently. I am not trying to say that that must have supremacy over the National Assembly. By no

1533 ආණ්ඩු ක්‍රම සම්පාදක මණ්ඩලය 1534

[උස්තාෆා මය.]
means. But once it is set up as the creature of the National Assembly in the furtherance of the powers that have been delegated to us by the people, we must see to it that provisions are introduced into the Constitution itself to ensure that the persons administering justice as between citizen and citizen and as between the citizen and the State, perform their functions independently and impartially.

I was carefully listening to the speech the hon. Member for Habaraduwa made. In fact he made a speech completely opposed to the speech and the policy that the Hon. Minister and his Colleague the Hon. Minister of Finance gave expression to yesterday. But of course we did not take him seriously. We have every right to go on the speech and on the assurance that was given to us by the Hon. Minister of Constitutional Affairs.

He was almost saying that in the pursuance of this socialist ideal, the judicature must be partial, that they must perform their functions partially, that as between employer and employee the courts must give judgement in favour of the employee —[Interruption.]—That is exactly what he was trying to tell us this morning.—[Interruption.]—

Now, I do not know how to discourage that sort of thing. He was trying to suggest to this august Assembly that courts administering justice must be partial in their decisions when they give decisions. That is exactly what he was trying to say.

සභාපතිතුමා
(அக்கிராசனர் அவர்கள்)
(Mr. President)
I do not think he put it in that form.

උස්තාෆා මය.
(ஜனாப் முஸ்தபா)
(Mr. Mustapha)
That is why I said there was no such conclusion possible except this. And he made some scathing remarks

about the judicature. I will say this. We have maligned the Britishers. We have nothing complimentary to say of them, but when the time comes to write the history of the British occupation of this contry I think we will have a kind word to say at least in respect of one matter, and that is in respect of the English judicial system that was set up in this country. Whatever the hon. Member for Habaraduwa might say or might have said, I take this opportunity for saying that we have in this country a judicature, a system of courts which we have every reason to feel proud of.

සී. අරුලම්පලම් මය. (නල්ලූර්)
(திரு. சி. அருளம்பலம்—நல்லூர்)
(Mr. C. Arulampalam—Nallur)
That was an insult to the system prevailing here then.

උස්තාෆා මය.
(ஜனாப் முஸ்தபா)
(Mr. Mustapha)
In fact the First Member for Colombo South, the Leader of the opposition in the House of Representatives, read instances of a number of cases and at one stage he even said, " Even if certain people had been arraigned at the instance of the Government, the fact that those people had been acquitted by the courts of Ceylon. by the highest tribunal in Ceylon, proves beyond all doubt their impartiality, their independence." All that we are seeking is that salutary provision should be set forth in the Constitution to preserve that spirit of independence.

There are of course other matters that were said, namely, that there is no provision for assuring this in the proposed Constitution. No doubt at this stage we are discussing the basis or the skeleton on which the Constitution is going to be built. At this stage it is not just enough to move an amendment, to have it accepted or rejected and be done with it. It is by expressing our views at this juncture that the Hon. Minister of

Constitutional Affairs would be able to ascertain the thinking of the members of this Assembly, the problems we are faced with as Members of Parliament over a long period of time, so that this expression of views might have the effect of influencing his thinking.

I do not want to take up any more time because certain matters will come up for discussion subsequently under other Basic Resolutions. I reserve my remarks on the other aspects of Basic Resolution 6 until those specific Resolutions are taken up.

අ. භා. 2.45

සි. එක්ස් මාටින් මයා. (යාපනය)

(திரு. சி. எக்ஸ். மாட்டின்—யாழ்ப்பாணம்)

(Mr. C. X. Martyn—Jaffna)

Mr. President, in making my observations I shall not forget at this stage that we are only dealing with Basic Resolutions and not with the Constitution. Much has been said which might be misleading. It has been said that there is no provision for this or the other thing. These are Basic Resolutions intended to convey fundamental concepts, and, if I may say so, I think these Basic Resolutions have been very carefully drafted. Having been a member of the Steering and Subjects Committee, I shall probably be complimenting myself when I say that these Basic Resolutions have been very carefully drafted.

But there are other aspects of this matter which I think merit our attention even at this stage. When the two giants right in front of me, persons who have led heir teams for quite a long time, raised the question of these amendments, I tried to persuade them that the division of powers is not a matter we should worry about at this stage of the development of constitutional matters, but they had their own ideas and I think they did well in bringing up this amendment because, in the process of the discussion that

has ensued as a result of this amendment, we have been able to get the assurance that the independence of the judiciary will be preversed, though no assurance was necessary. That is contained in the Basic Resolution. It is not that assurance that has been helpful ; it is not that assurance which has given us enlightenment ; it is the assurance by both the Minister of Constitutional Affairs and the Minister of Finance, who is himself an authority on constitutions and constitutional matters, that they will not change in any way the present mode of appointment of judges, because if there is any residue left of this so-called theory of the balance of powers or the separation of powers, that is confined purely and simply to the question of the independence of the judiciary.

The Hon. Minister of Finance explained to us very carefully that the Basic Resolutions as they stand at present contan the same, or almost the same, provision in regard to appointments to the highest courts. I shall, if you will permit me, refer to the present provision in order to contrast it with the provsions that are contained in the Basic Resolution.

The present mode of appointment to the Supreme Court is prescribed in Part VI of the Order-in-Council, Section 52. It says:

"The Chief Justice and the Puisne Judges of the Supreme Court and Commissioners of Assize shall be appointed by the Governor-General."

The question arose and the reply to that is very simple.

Section 4, sub-section (2), of the Ceylon (Constitution) Order in Council has this provision:

"(2) All powers, authorities and functions vested in His Majesty or the Governor-General shall, subject to the provisions of this Order and of any other law for the time being in force, be exercised as far as may be in accordance with the constitutional conventions applicable to the exercise of similar powers, authorities and functions in the United Kingdom by His Majesty."

[මාටින් මයා.]

If the constitutional practise is for His Majesty, in issuing Letters Patent to a judge, to act on the advice of the approriate authority, then the appointment of a Puisne Judge or the Chief Justice should be made by the Governor-General on the advice of the appropriate authority, which, in our country, has been the Prime Minister.

Let us see whether in the Basic Resolutions there is any reference to this. I am referring at the moment to Basic Resolution 31:

"The Council of Ministers shall be responsible for appointments in state services and shall be answerable to the National Assembly thereon."

When my Friend, the hon. Leader of the Opposition, made reference to this Basic Resolution 31 (1), my Friend, the Hon. Minister of Constitutional Affairs, and the Hon. Minister of Finance both jumped up and said "answerable" does not mean that they are going to make the appointments. We entirely agree with them. It is absolutely necessary that the Council of Ministers should be answerable because they are the body that is responsible to the legislature and therefore they should be answerable and the appointments need not necessarily be made by them. But let us read sub-section (2) of Basic Resolution 31 :

"The procedure for making such appointments, the delegation of power to appoint and matters relating to state services including the constitution of state services shall be provided by and under laws to be enacted by the National Assembly."

I have not been able to trace anywhere else in these Basic Resolutions any provision specifically made for the appointment of a judge of the highest court. So we will have to have recourse to Basic Resolution 31 (2). In other words, what is now enshrined in the Constitution as the method of appointment has been relegated to an enactment by

the National Assembly. I say that that is a significant difference between the existing position and the position that is contemplated under the new Constitution. I am sorry the Hon. Minister of Constitutional Affairs is not here but his very distinguished Permanent Secretary, who is a Queen's Counsel, is here. I do hope he will make a note of this and if there is any merit of substance in the point I have made, this will be brought up at the time of the enactment of the necessary legislation incorporating these concepts.

Speaking generally on this Resolution, it is a most unexceptionable resolution. It seeks to enshrine in the Constitution of this country the doctrine of the sovereignty of Parliament and the supremacy of Parliament. I do not think any of us who is present here will have any objection to that because we are the representatives of the people. In fact sovereignty ultimately resides in the people from whom or through whom we have derived this sovereignty. So we have absolutely no objection. In fact it is an absolutely necessary provision in any democratic Constitution. But the important thing—now we are speaking particularly on the amendment—is, in what way are we going to preserve the independence of the judiciary in regard to appointments ?

Some may be wondering what is all this fuss that is being made about appointments to the Supreme Court Bench. If you will permit me, I like to quote from a book—it is not a capitalist book nor a chinese document—

සභාපතිතුමා

(அக்கிராசனர் அவர்கள்)

(Mr. President)

It certainly has a significant red cover!

මාටින් මයා.

(திரு. மாட்டின்)

(Mr. Martyn)

Yes. It is " A Grammar of Politics" by that most distinguished professor Laski, the guru of our constitutional pundit, the Hon. Minister of Finance

(Hon. Dr. N. M. Perera). I am reading from page 541. Professor Laski first quotes Henry Sidgwick in " Elements of Politics. "

" 'The importance of the judiciary in political construction,' Henry Sidgwick has written, 'is rather profound than prominent. On the one hand, in popular discussion of forms and changes of Government, the judicial organ often drops out of sight ; on the other hand, in determining a nation's rank in political civilisation, no test is more decisive than the degree in which justice, as defined by the law, is actually realised in its judicial administration, both as between private citizens and members of the government.' "

That is the end of the quotation from Sidgwick. These are Laski's own observations:

" Obviously, therefore, the men who are to make justice in the courts, the way in which they are to perform their function, the methods by which they are to be chosen, the terms upon which thev shall hold power, these, and their related problems, lie at the heart of political philosophy. When we know how a nation-State dispenses justice, we know with some exactness the moral character to which it can pretend. "

You will see therefore how important this amendment is. While we are enshrining the doctrine of the sovereignty of Parliament and the supremacy of Parliament, it is sufficiently important, I will not say as important, that we investigate the manner in which we are going to protect this very important institution, the judicial organ of the government.

I am glad the Hon. Minister of Constitutional Affairs (Hon. Dr. Colvin R. de Silva) has come in. Talking about the independence of the judiciary there is an incident that I would like to relate. When the Soulbury Commissioners came to Ceylon, as a member of the Ceylon Judicial Service I had occasion to join in a delegation to place our views before the Commission. It was during the State Council days. I do not know whether my good Friend, the Hon. Minister was a Member of the State Council at that time. The Hon. Minister saw me coming out of a room where we had given evidence before the Commissioners. The Minister got hold of me and said, " Look here, Cyril, I am sure you have given evidence for the preservation of the independence of the judiciary. Now, you must remember, they may achieve this independence but they will be independent of everybody except the very relevant persons.

I lived through several years after the constitution was drafted and adopted and I cannot say that what the Hon. Minister then said has been altogether without foundation. But the system worked quite well, and I do not know whether any other system would have worked as well. No doubt, every system has its own defects. I mentioned it to him because he might have forgotten it. I distinctly remember it. It is something that I always kept in mind because I have had a great personal respect for the Minister of Constitutional Affairs long before he became the Minister of Constitutional Affairs.— [Interruption]. Yes, that respect is there and it will continue to be there whether he agrees with me or disagrees with me.

Now I wish to deal with the question of the division or the separation of powers. This doctrine which Montesquieu discovered in England was thought to be the reason why the English were fully free. The doctrine of the separation or division of powers and functions had to come because in the olden days the king was the source, the fountain, of all the three powers. He was the legislator, he was the fountain of justice, and he was the chief executive. So, this division had to come at some stage. In various countries it came in various ways, and in England it came in the way of a revolution, the beheading of a king, and the enshrining of the doctrine that a judge holds office during good behaviour.

So, whichever way we look at it, I feel that this doctrine of the institutions should be enshrined in the Constitution in the appropriate way.

1541   ආණ්ඩු ක්‍රම සම්පාදක මණ්ඩලය   1542

[මාටින් මය.]

.I say that the Hon. Minister of Constitutional Affairs has taken great pains to provide for the independence of the judiciary. I remember the opening speech made by the Hon. Minister. He grew rather emotional at a certain stage and said that his motives were misunderstood. I believe he said that he was not using very strong words, but, nevertheless, the idea I got was that malice was attributed to him. I do not think that anybody who knows him well enough will attribute malice to him, although they may not like the fury or the sound of his voice.

One of things we might bear in mind--I happened to discover it among my books—is the address by Lord Justice Denning on the independence of the judges. The first paragraph is rather significant. I do not know why he had started it in that way. It reads thus :

" We regard the judges as standing between the individual and the State, protecting the individual from any interference with his freedom which is not justified by the law. But Soviet Russia regards its tribunals as part of the State machine to carry out State policy. Lenin said that ' the Tribunal is the instrument of the proletariat and the working class ', and this maxim was inscribed in letters of gold in his audience chamber. Soviet Russia rejects altogether the theory of separation between the judicial and the executive power. The judicial power is simply a part of the executive. "

I think whoever made those aspersions might have had this concept in mind, but anybody who makes a critical examination of the Basic Resolutions which have been presented to us will find that it is abundantly clear that the Hon. Minister has not had the concept which has been set out in the address of Lord Justice Denning on the independence of the judges, which I just read out.

There is the question of the separation of functions ; it still exists and it is not quite correct to say that even today there is no separation of functions. Of course, when we take

the British Constitution—in fact, there is no British Constitution as such—a cynic once said that the British Constitution is a logical absurdity : it exists because it has existed, and it will exist because it exists ! But I do not think that we, as responsible men framing a Constitution, can hope that we shall blunder through like the British and arrive at a space landing somewhere. We have to give our thoughts carefully to all the matters that merit our consideration and attention.

Now, it is very significant that in England the Lord Chancellor is an extraordinary figure. He is the President of the House of Lords performing legislative functions. He is the politicl head of the judiciary, all sitting in the House of Lords, in the Privy Council, and so on. He is a member of the Cabinet and the principal constitutional advisor to Cabinet. In other words, he has all three functions rolled into one. That system works satisfactorily nöt because logically it is right—logically it is an absurdity—but because it has worked.

As a matter of fact, after the first World War a committtee was appointed to investigate the position of the Lord Chancellor of England and allied appointments. I believe Lord Haldane, who was an ex-Lord Chancellor, was the chairman of the committtee. After fully examining the position that committee unanimously came to this conclusion :

" However difficult it may be for us to agree with the logicality of the position that exists, this institution is so deeply ingrained in the traditions of this country that we hesitate to disturb the position as it exists. We know that it is an illogical position. "

We have to consider whether we can accept all that is in the British Constitution although we have based our judicial institutions on the British model, and, as the last speaker the hon. Member for Nintavur (Mr. Mustapha) said, when the history of the British occupation of this country comes to be written, it will be recorded that probably one of the main contributions which they made was the judicial system and the rule of law.

Much has been said that there is no separation of powers, and so on. But I think that so far as judicial administration is concerned political thinkers and constitution-makers see the administration of justice as distinct and separate from all other matters.

I shall read to you the observations of Laski. Again, I hope nobody will get annoyed by this red book, but it is a very useful book.

(ගරු ආචාර්ය කොල්වින් ආර්. ද සිල්වා ආණ්ඩු ක්‍රම වැවස්ථා කටයුතු ඇමති)

(கௌரவ கலாநிதி கொல்வின் ஆர். த சில்வா—அரசியலமைப்பு அலுவல்கள் அமைச் சர்)

(The Hon. Dr. Colvin R. de Silva— Minister of Constitutional Affairs)

Is it the little red book ?

මාටින් මයා.

(திரு. மாட்டின்)

(Mr. Martyn)

It is a little red in colour, but it is a big book. I have another book which is not red.

I am now quoting from Harold J. Laski's "A Grammar of Politics". This is what he says at page 129 :

"The second corollary is that the union of the executive and the judicial function is inadmissible. Every citizen needs the amplest protection against the danger that the administrator will himself interpret the meaning of the law that he applies. The concentration of the power to interpret in the same hands as the power to administer has always, historically, been associated with tyranny. It was the characteristic hall-mark of Oriental despotism.... Whatever the solution, the separation and supremacy of the judicial power is integral to the maintenance of rights. For, otherwise, those who serve the State are governed by rules different from those under which their fellow-citizens must live. They are made judges in their own cause ; and however hard they may strive to do justice they cannot hold squarely the balance between themselves and other men."

Now that the Hon. Minister is here I would like to refer him to Basic Resolution 31 (2) because yesterday while we were discussing this question of the appointment of judges both the Hon. Minister and the Hon. Minister of Finance assured us that the present position will not be in any way disturbed ; that is, the appointments should be made in the same way as it is done and the tenure of office will be the same because they will be appointed by the President on the advice of the Prime Minister. Provision is not made for that. I take it, it will be provided for. This is what Basic Resolution 31 (2) says :

"The procedure for making such appointments, the delegation of power to appoint and matters relating to state services including the constitution of state services shall be provided by and under laws to be enacted by the National Assembly."

In other words, at present provision exists for appointments to be made in the Constitution itself, but we have now relegated it to the National Assembly. Therefore, I would submit that that is a vital change, a difference in the existing position. I would earnestly ask the Hon. Minister to reconsider that matter if he thinks there is substance in the point which I have made.

For instance, with regard to the mode of appointment, my good Friend the hon. Leader of the Opposition told you yesterday that I would make some reference to the position in England. We had the tyranny of kings, and once the position was cleared and the doctrine of the separation of functions was assured, then we had the tyranny of the politicians.

In this connection I would like to refer you to a very interesting article by the same author I mentioned earlier. This is not a red book but it is by the same author and it is pretty old. I am citing from this book for certain purposes. I shall read the article out because it is rather significant. Everybody thinks that things were always all right in

[මාවිත් මහ.]
England. It took over a hundred years for them to settle down, and so let us not now start and wait for a hundred years to reach this point at which they are now. I am now reading from Harold J. Laski's Studies in Law and Politics. In this book you get a very interesting Chapter on "The Technique of Judicial Appointment" :

"It is notorious that Lord Halsbury used his position as Lord Chancellor to promote members of his own party ; and it is seldom that an American President has the courage to nominate one of his political opponents."

Talking of Lord Halsbury, one is reminded of a very significant incident which took place in his life. A friend of his approached him once and told him he was interested in candidate 'X' for an appointment to the County Court. Halsbury remembered the name but forgot whether it was in respect of the County Court or the High Court that the request was made, and when an appointment in the High Court was vacant, 'X' was appointed. Of course, he subsequently made good and became a great judge.

I wish to read a few other things which might be interesting. It is from the same page :

"It may be useful to illustrate the working of the system of unfettered executive nomination by an analysis of English experience from 1832 until 1906. Out of the 139 judges appointed in that period, eighty were members of the House of Commons at the time of their nomination ; eleven others had been candidates for Parliament, six of them on more than one occasion. Of the eighty who thus reached the Bench by the avenue of the House of Commons, no less than thirty-three had been either Attorney or Solicitor-General. Excluding these men who became Lords Chancellor in this period, no less than fourteen were made, not merely ordinary judges, but heads of the court to which they were called. It is not, for instance, insignificant that, with one exception, every English Chief Justice for the last sixty years has been an ex-Attorney-General ; and even the exception is explained by the notorious fact—

to which reference was made yesterday—

—"that his successor could not be spared by the Government of the day when the vacancy occurred."

My Hon. Friend, the Minister of Constitutional Affairs, both at the stage of the Steering and Subjects Committee and thereafter, took the view, probably very rightly, that people in high places, when they are called upon to make appointments should be vested with a certain amount of responsibility. We must be satisfied that they will do the right thing. But human nature being what it is, unfettered discretion has always its pitfalls. That is why in England, Professor Laski, who was a great political thinker, suggested this. This is what appears at page 173. I am reading from the same book :

"The best body, I believe, would be a committee of judges selected by themselves for some such term as three or five years. It would necessarily be a small committee, limited, at the outside, to seven members ; and it would probably be necessary to make the Lord Chief Justice, the Master of the Rolls, and the President of the Probate, Divorce, and Admiralty Divisions ex-officio members of it. The responsibility of appointment would still rest with the Lord Chancellor, or the Prime Minister, according to the post to be filled ; but at least we should be certain of a thorough assessment of claims before an appointment was made by men thoroughly competent to assess those claims."

My Friend the Hon. Minister of Constitutional Affairs has recognised this principle in the amendment he has brought with regard to the supporting judiciary. I would strongly recommend to him to consider that there should be some consultation on the part of the person invested with the discretion to make the representation to the President. Now, this consultation principle has been accepted and embodied in the Indian Constitution. The Hon. Minister of Constitutional Affairs told me that consultations can take place and do take place, but why put it into the

Constitution, he asked. I am citing it for that purpose. Section 124 (2) of the Indiain Constitution provides :

"Every judge of the Supreme Court shall be appointed by the President by warrant under his hand and seal after consultation with such of the Judges of the Supreme Court and of the High Courts in the States as the President may deem necessary for the purpose and shall hold office until he attains the age of sixty-five years ; provided that in the case of appointment of a Judge other than the Chief Justice, the Chief Justice of India shall always be consulted. "

and section 217 (1) provides :

"Every Judge of a High Court shall be appointed by the President by warrant under his hand and seal after consultation with the Chief Justice of India, the Governor of the State, and, in the case of appointment of a Judge other than the Chief Justice, the Chief Justice of the High Court, and shall hold office, in the case of an additional or acting Judge,.... "

What I say is that even in the Constitution there is this unfettered exercise of the discretion in order to prevent falling into the pit, as it were, which existed in England for over 100 years. I suggest that some such provision in regard to Ceylon would not be difficult because we have one Chief Justice. When we make a recommendation for appointment consultation can be had with the judges, and in the case of other judges consultation can be had with the Chief Justice. I can see no obnoxious principles involved in such provision for consultation being incorporated in the Constitution.

Now, Sir, it is important for us to remember that, although we do not subscribe to the entirety of this amendment as suggested by the hon. Leader of the Opposition and the former Prime Minister. I thing the former Prime Minister explained to us that his idea of the division of powers arose out of a different concept. We had an idea of a parallel authority. I do not know whether he has given up that idea or not.—[Interruption.] My Friend here says, no. I think he can speak for the ex-Prime Minister more authoritatively than I can.

All that I want to say is this. We are now dealing with Basic Resolution 6, whch enshrines the sovereignty of the legislature and the supremacy of the legislature. Once there is a supreme soveriign legislature you cannot have any other parallel authority : that will so fundamental a change, so fundamental and different a concept from the sovereignty of Parliament. I know it exists in America, and constitutions have been drafted on the American model—in the Philippines, for instance. But I do not think that would suit us at all because it will add to the confusion.

The previous speaker, the hon. Member for Nintavur (Mr. Mustapha), made reference to several grievances he had about the manner in which constitutions and governments work. I do not wish to go into that matter because, although it may be in a very distant way germane to these issues, it is not directly relevant and I do not want to waste time on it. But it is quite clear that once the sovereignty of the legislature is accepted by us, it is difficult to conceive of a parallel authority. If we have a parallel authority, then sovereignty is divided, and to that extent I for one and the party I represent do not and cannot accept that. We accept the position of the sovereignty of the legislature, and that doctrine should be enshrined in our Constitution in the manner suggested by the Basic Resolution, except that we have some amendment in regard to delimitation and so on.

I do not want to take much of the time of hon. Members, but before I conclude I would like again to make reference to the position of judges because it is so important, so fundamental to the achievement of freedom, and because we have so far in this country had a body of judges, a body of men, of whom any country can be proud.

රෝයි රාජපක්ෂ මයා.

(திரு. ரோய் ராஜபக்ஷ)

(Mr. Roy Rajapakse)

Including yourself.

මාටින් මයා.

(திரு. மாட்டின்)

(Mr. Martyn)

I do not speak for any particular person but certainly as a body, and even if I accept to some extent the observations of the hon. Member for Habaraduwa——

සභාපතිතුමා

(அக்கிராசனர் அவர்கள்)

(Mr. President)

Hon. Member for Hakmana.

මාටින් මයා.

(திரு. மாட்டின்)

(Mr. Martyn)

The hon. Member for Hakmana made an interruption but I was thinking of the speech the hon. Member made in the morning . I know him quite well because I was associated with him in journalism for a period of six years, and our associations mere pleasant and even if he has contrary views I have no objection to those. But I cannot say that of the hon. Member for Hakmana because I am new to his jokes and probably I will get used to them in time.

සභාපතිතුමා

(அக்கிராசனர் அவர்கள்)

(Mr. President)

Has he appeared before you ?

මාටින් මයා.

(திரு. மாட்டின்)

(Mr. Martyn)

Unfortunately not. But I am sure if he appeared before me he would have the profoundest respect for judicial administration in this country.

I desire before I conclude, because of the importance of the position of the judges, to read a passage from—

this time it is a capitalist—Sir Winston Churchill reported in HANSARD. It is also found in Lord Denning's book " The Road to Justice ". This book is a little blue. The cover is blue but the inside is green. If it is blue and red I could understand, but blue and green I do not know—whether there is co-operation or anything like that.

ඒ අසිස් මයා.

(ஜனாப் ஏ. அசீஸ்)

(Mr. A. Aziz)

It is a reflection of your mind.

මාටින් මයා.

(திரு. மாட்டின்)

(Mr. Martyn)

You are an expert at knowing reflections of other people's minds, I know. I will read from page 15 of this book without meaning any disrespect to my Friend who knows my mind :

" The principle of the complete independence of the Judiciary from the Executive is the foundation of many things in our island life. It has been widely imitated in varying degrees throughout the free world. It is perhaps one of the deepest gulfs between us and all forms of totalitarian rule. The only subordination which a judge knows in his judicial capacity is that which he owes to the existing body of legal doctrine enunciated in years past by his brethren on the bench, past and present, and upon the laws passed by Parliament which have received the Royal assent. The judge has not only to do justice between man and man. He also—and this is one of his most important functions considered incomprehensible in some large parts of the world—has to do justice between the citizens and the State.... The British judiciary, with its traditions and record, is one of the greatest living assets of our race and people and the independence of the Judiciary is a part of our message to the evergrowing world which is raising so swiftly around us."

We have absorbed some of these ideas, and our institutions have grown in that way, and the Basic Resolutions which have been drafted have been so carefully drafted to preserve the existing indepndence. We are entirely in agreement. We may have disagreement on certain matters in regard to the mode in which these matters have to be

Felix on Finance

සුබසිංහ මහතා

(திரு. சீ. பி. சுபசிங்ஹ)

(Mr. Subasinghe)

We are legally married. We are not for separation.

රාජදුරෙයි මහතා

(திரு. இராஜதுரை)

(Mr. Rajadurai)

சிறுபான்மை மக்களுடைய அபிலாஷைகளீ நீங்கள் தீர்க்கக் கூடுமானால், அது காலகட்டத் திலே இலங்கையின் சரித்திர முக்கியத்துவம் வாய்ந்த ஒரு நிகழ்ச்சியாகவே அமையும்·உங் களுக்கு இருக்கின்ற மூன்றில் இரண்டு பங்கு வாக்குகளைக் கொண்டு நீங்கள் இதைச் செய்ய லாம். இதை மற்றைய எதிர்க்கட்சியினர் எதிர்க்கவோ கண்டிக்கவோ முடியாது. ஏனென்றால், இன்று எதிர்க்கட்சியிலே அதி முக்கியம் வாய்ந்த பங்கை வகிக்கின்ற ஐக்கிய தேசியக் கட்சியினர் சிறுபான்மை மக்களின் அபிலாஷைகளீ ஒரு காலம் ஏற்றுக் கொண்ட வர்கள்; அதை மதித்தவர்கள்; அதற்கான நடவடிக்கைகளீ எடுத்துக்கொள்ள முன்வந் தார்கள்.

සිරිමාවෝ බණ්ඩාරනායක මැතිනිය

(திருமதி சிறிமாவோ பண்டாரநாயக்க)

(Mrs. Sirimavo Bandaranaike)

Then why did they not do it when you were with them ?

රාජදුරෙයි මහතා

(திரு. இராஜதுரை)

(Mr. Rajadurai)

இச் சிறுபான்மை மக்களின் பிரச்சிைகளீ தீர்ப்பதற்கு எங்கள் பக்கத்திலிருந்து எத்த கைய எதிர்ப்பும் வராது என்று கூறி, இந்த வாவு செலவுத் திட்டத்திலே நாட்டின் எல்லா இன மக்களையும் ஒத்துழைப்பையும் இத் தேச வளர்ச்சிக்குப் பெறுவதற்காக நீங்கள் நடவடிக்கை எடுக்க வேண்டும்; இந்நாட் டிலே ஒரு பெரும் பகுதியினராக இருக்கின்ற சிறுபான்மை மக்களீ—ஒரு பெரிய தேசிய இனத்தைத் தொடர்ந்தும் ஒடுக்கி வைத்த அவர்களுடைய அபிலாஷைகளீ—உணர்ச்சி களீப் புறக்கணிக்காமல் ஏற்ற நடவடிக்கை களீ எடுக்க அரசாங்கம் பெருமனதோடு முன்வர வேண்டுமென்றும் எங்கள் முத லமைச்சர்வர்கள் இவ்விடயத்தில் ஜன்னிக் கவனம் செலுத்த வேண்டுமென்றும் கேட்டுக்

கொள்ளுகின்றேன். காலஞ் சென்ற பிரதமர் திரு. எஸ். டபிள்யு. ஆர். டி. பண்டாரநாயக்க அவர்கள் தமது காலத்தில் இச்சிறுபான்மை யின மக்களின் பிரச்சிைகளீக் கொளவமா கத் தீர்க்க முன் வந்தாரென்றால் நீங்கள் ஏன் இப்பிரச்சிைக்குத் தீர்வுகாண முடியாதென்று தான் நான் கேட்கின்றேன். இப்பிரச்சிைக்கு நீங்கள் தீர்வு கண்டால், எபது நாட்டின் சரித் திர வாலாற்றிலே இது மூக்கியமான ஒரு நிகழ்ச்சியாக அமையுமென்பதை நான் மீண் டும் கூறுவதற்குக் கடமைப்பட்டவன் என்ப தைத் தெரிவித்து எனது உரையை முடிக்கின் றேன்.

அ. ஊ. 5.19

f පිලික්ස් ආර්. ඩී. බණ්ඩාරනායක මහතා (රාජ්‍ය පරිපාලන, පළාත් පාලන හා ස්වදේශ කටයුතු ඇමති සහ අධිකරණ ඇමති)

(திரு. பிலிக்ஸ் ஆர். டி. பண்டாரநாயக்க— பொது நிர்வாகம், உள்ளூராட்சி, உள்நாட்டு அலுவல்கள் அமைச்சரும் நீதி அமைச்சர்)

(Mr. Felix R. D. Bandaranaike- Minister of Public Administration, Local Government & Home Affairs and Minister of Justice)

Mr. Speaker, this Budget is the third Budget of our Government. I think all hon. Members of this Assembly will agree that Budgets mean different things to different people. To the Leader of the opposition, the thing that is most important about Budgets is the reality of the expectations stated in financial terms in a Budget Speech. He seems to have doubts about them. I do not propose to anticipate the reply which will be given by the Minister of Finance in his turn on Monday. I shall leave those aspects of the matter to be dealt with by the Minister of Finance. But I should like to ask Members of this Assembly this one question. How many of the expectations in the Budget of the hon. Leader of the Opposition when he was Minister of Finance were actually borne out by facts and circumstances upon examination of the Island's accounts afterwards? Mind you, we have been accustomed to Budgets ever since

Independence, from 1947 onwards, and the first lot of Budgets came from him.

There is actually a preparation of the Island's accounts at the end of the year. He talked a lot about the Budget which gives the expectations of the Finance Minister, but when it comes to the end of the year I do not think there is a single Member of this House who sees the documents containing the actual results, of what the Budget had produced. And you will find that none of the expectations stated by the Finance Minister, myself included and himself included, have really fitted in with the facts and the expectations as stated in Parliament.

If you look at it from that point of view, I think you should be constrained to agree that over the years Budget techniques and Budget have changed from the early days when my old Friend the hon. Leader of the Opposition presented Budgets.   It was then very much of a pure and simple arithmetical exercise. There was no question of policy changes; it was a question of trying to finance a relatively small sum of money. I think the largest amount of revenue which was ever raised in a single year by my Friend the Leader of the Opposition was of the order Rs. 30 million. In those days the totality of the Budget was a negligble figure compared with what we are dealing with today.

I do not propose to talk of his experience. I propose to talk of my own experience. 1962 was the last year in which I presented the Budget —not very successfully I am afraid because I am one of the men who cut the rice ration and went out. I cut it and went with it. I withdrew it and I went home. But I have got no regrets about it.

I should like to say that the total Budget in that year expenditurewise was Rs. 2,200 million. That was the total amount of expenditure provided for in the 1962 Budget. This year you are dealing with a Budget which is more than double that figure. The

expenditure provided for has in fact more than doubled; you will find it is nearly Rs. 5,500 million.

Now, this is something that has happened over the years. Every year there has been an increase.   It happened. whether it was during Mr. Wanninayake's time or Mr. Ilangaratne's time or Dr. N. M. Perera's time.   There has been a progressive increase in the total of Budget expenditure year by year, and every time Governments have come forward and presented ways and means of financing deficits when there were any. The components are there.   A certain amount of that money comes by increasing the National Debt.

The National Debt is increased by means of domestic borrowings. You borrow from various sources within the country, and the amount of the National Debt increases to that extent. Then again, there is the Foreign Aid component, which is really a foreign debt component, also no doubt a charge upon the nation but charged upon and for the benefit of the foreign resources in respect of the Foreign Aid component of the Budget. Then you have got proposals for new taxation and new revenue. Sometimes you leave a portion of the Budget unfinanced, which simply means credit creation or creation of money by inflationary financing.

Well, these are the methods by which Budgets have in fact expanded over the years, and this process continues   It has nothing to do with governments.   There is no political analysis about its finances.   I will not try to say that this is something vicious done by one government or another government. I am merely drawing your attention to something that has happened over the years. Just take the last ten years from 1962 to 1972.   What has happened is that the Budget has expanded from Rs. 2,200 million to Rs. 5,500 million. But that is all. The question that I would like to ask is this. What have you to show for all

1675   ජාතික රාජ්‍ය සභාව   1676

[ෆිලික්ස් ආර්. ඩී. බණ්ඩාරනායක මහතා]
this money? The real question is not
whether you like taxation or whether you do not like taxation. The
reality of a Budget must be judged
in relation to what the country has
gained or lost in that period.

Over the last ten years, for expenditure starting at Rs. 2,200 million
and increasing progressively up to
Rs. 5,500 million, what have we got
to show in real terms? If you
examine the Island's accounts, as
opposed to examining budgets, you
will find that in every year the
revenue expectations have in fact
fallen short of the targets expected,
whether it was during the period
when Mr. U. B. Wanninayake was
Finance Minister or when myself
was Finance Minister or when any
one of my Colleagues was Finance
Minister. It makes no difference. The
real result of the Budget has not
been exactly in the line of what was
expected. We have had budgets in
deficit year after year and progressively budget deficits have accumu-
lated with the result that there has
in fact been inflationary financing
and credit creation over the years. It
was not something deliberately
engineered. It is something that
simply happens.

Now the question is, What is the
feeling of the ordinary man in the
street about this? Does he like it?
Has he got anything to say for it?
Well, if the average man in the
street has something to say for it, if
he is pleased with the results, make
no mistake about it, he will take new
taxation. He will appreciate what the
Government is doing, and I think
there is nothing that people want
but to build a better life for generations to come, for the future. Most
people are concerned about their
children, about the future generations to come, about the kind of life
that is going to be created for people
in the future.

Do not look at this Budget in blinkers but look back and ask yourself the
question, Do you like these revenue
proposals or are you relieved? We

can score over you in a sense. We
can say that our Finance Minister
very successfully fooled you this
time. You thought he had no alternative but to cut the rice ration. You
thought you got your crackers ready
to light from by-election days thinking that our Finance Minister will be
in trouble this time unable to present
the Budget. Well he pooh-poohed
you completely. But does that really
solve the problem ? Have we really
answered the question ? Have we
really solved the problems of the
country ? I would respectfully say
that we have got to think very much
deeper than that to examine the reality of the situation.

The problem is, what have we got ?
I think the answer is that it has
nothing to do with the Finance Minister or the Finance Ministry. This is
an indictment against the entire political system which we are operating
here. If during ten years, with the
changing fortunes of party politics,
with Governments changing at
general elections, all we have got to
show is a static economy or a reced-
ing economy, an economy unable to
move forward, with nothing spectacular happening, with no signs of real
development evident anywhere and
we are here in office governing now—
it may have been you last time and it
may be you the next time ; it makes
no difference—is it a small wonder
that the people look round rather
cynically and say, " Well, on the
Budget we have very little confidence
that the expenditures mean anything.
All we know is that revenue proposals
can involve immediate burdens on us
and to that extent we are opposed to
that ; we are not willing to take burdens, because we have little confidence that those burdens are going to
result in the creation of any new
wealth or real development. " ? This
is the crisis of our times and this is
the real problem we are confronted
with. Some say that the people of our
country are not willing to take burdens, that our people are unwilling to
make sacrifices. I myself do not believe that. I have every confidence
that our people will be quite willing
to make sacrifices, quite willing to

work hard, quite willing to expand and maximize, to bend their energies towards the building up of our country. But this will not happen so long as there is little confidence that the money generated through the new revenue proposals will leave the existing situation pretty much as it was and that at the end of a year no new development will be apparent or will be seen by the people in the mass throughout the country. This is the real problem. It is in a way a vicious circle because without money you cannot have development. The question is, even if you do have the money will development be realized ? This is the real issue and this is something which is not in the hands of the Finance Minister, not even in the hands of the Government. It will be really in the hands of this entire National State Assembly to work together for the common cause of producing that result if we can get their support. If we are going to treat this matter merely as being an issue of party politics in which we say to ourselves, " Why we fooled you this time, we scored a point over you for a debating victory, we have got somewhere with it ", then I really do not know whether we can solve anything.

Now, let us take a practical illustration. If you examine the actual figures over the last three years—and I refer to 1971, 1972 and 1973, the new year to come—you will find the level of capital expenditure in 1971, the real expenditure which was actually spent, was of the order of Rs. 840 million out of the Budget of that year. Take the year 1972—the year is not yet finished and therefore you cannot finalize the accounts,—and the revised estimate for the year leads us to the conclusion that that was the year in which the country remembers that some of the Finance Minister's proposals were sent up in flames by some of us in the National State Assembly. The sugar, flour, cut proposals were withdrawn and the Budget in the National State Assembly itself was distorted to that extent and the expenditures were in fact drastically curtailed. Without that curtailment what was the level of development, the development expenditure, for that year according to the most recent estimates ? It was Rs. 800 million. For the coming year, in the new Budget, what is the level of development expenditure ? It is Rs. 870 million. In other words, whether without taxation proposals or with taxation proposals, what is actually happening is that we are having more or less a constant level of capital expenditure, whether it is Rs. 840 million or Rs. 800 million or Rs. 870 million. It is not all that different. What you are really having is the same level of development expenditure being provided for every year.

In other words, we know what kind of development we had in 1970, 1971 and 1972. If what we are providing for is the same kind of development in the year 1973, that is perhaps the harshest indictment that can be made against our own Budget. I am not presenting it in the form of a criticism ; it is a criticism in a way against myself because if it fails it is nothing but a failure on the part of the administration of this country. It is the framework and the machinery within which we are working and moving which has to be blamed for this situation. I do not know that one can turn round and say that this is a question of financial proposals or financial measures. It is the responsibility of the persons now charged with the task of administering this country in their different fields, let it be in agriculture, let it be in trade and commerce, let it be in the general administration, let it be in local government work. In every single thing, the responsibility is ours. And if we are not able to measure up to producing anything like the requirements that will be necessary, to inspire confidence in people, to make people believe that we are capable of a big breakthrough, of moving into real development, then surely we have believed the very purpose of our existence.

Let us be clear about this. It is not a charged levelled against one particular administration although I took

[ෆිලික්ස් ආර්. ඩී. බණ්ඩාරනායක මහතා]
the last three years into account.
Make no mistake about it. I say,
precisely the same thing occurred
from 1965-70. For all the tall talk of
a Green Revolution, of agrarian
mastery, of hube resources being
piled up in paddy production, there
was a systematic increase of about
six per cent per year, an increase
started by me as Minister of Agriculture in 1963-64. From 35 million
bushels, which was the figure in 1956
when Mr. Philip Gunawardena was
Minister of Agriculture, it increased
to 50 million bushels, a little over 15
million, by 1964, of which 66 per cent
was purchased; about 35 mililon
bushels were in fact purchased at the
guaranteed price. In 1965 paddy production dropped owing to weather
condtions, cyclones and other misfortunes. Then during their time it
went up again to 70 million bushels,
and I am told that the crop this year
might be 80 million bushels.

This 6 per cent increase per year is
what you are maintaining regularly
per year. It happened under the
S. L. F. P., it happened under the
U.N.P., and it happened under the
M. E. P. when Mr. Philip Gunawardena was Minister of Agriculture.
This 6 per cent increase per year has
been a steady increase from 1956
onwards, from the time of the late
Mr Bandaranaike's Government.

Now, the fact is that this 6 per cent
increase per year is just not enough
in relation to the needs of the country. It is a grand achievement in one
sense. The people who are responsible for it are entitled to take pride
in the fact that with new varieties of
paddy, with new techniques, with the
expansion of modern technical know-
how in paddy production, we have
done well. But let us not get any
wrong ideas about it. Let us not
start singing songs over the Sri Lanka
Broadcasting Corporation in paeans
of praise for non-existent economic
victories and fool ourselves into the
belief so much so that when people
cease to hold office suddenly after an
election they are quite surprised and
left wondering how it all happened.

Now, in industrial production we
have a right to be proud of the fact
tht we have certainly made progress
from 1960 onwards in the face of the
bans which we ourselves introduced
upon various types of consumer products, but I am still not happy that
we are producing our industrial products at economic price levels in
adequate quantities. We are making
good progres, but I think a great deal
has got to be done in the improvement of management techniques, in
the methods of costing, in regard to
keeping abreast of our own control of
the situation to make sure that the
administrative machine is working
right.

This once again brings me back to
my point that all these failures are
attributable to the fact that we are
still running the same bureaucratic
structure which existed in the past,
and basically this, in my assessment,
is one of the main causes of this
failure.

The Finance Minister has after all
to provide the fuel. The money provided by the Finance Minister is the
fuel which keeps the machine running. But the question is, if the
machine is not running well, an
injection of fuel is not going to solve
the problem. You will have to consider the question of how to get that
machine operating to the greatest
advantage and to produce the best
results. Sometimes loose connections
in politics are counter-productive.
Loose conections sometimes make it
impossible for a machine to function
properly. The very fact that loose
connections make it impossible for
the administrators to administer the
country properly also tends to create
complications for the country as a
whole, and we must accept that fact.

There is a tendency sometimes for
politicians to feel that for reasons of
political alignment it is necessary to
argue for or to protect a particular
person in the administration even
when they know in their heart of
hearts that that man is guilty of a
breach of discipline that disciplinary
action should be taken against him,
that he does not deserve protection,

that he is inefficient or corrupt. When such things happen and politicians begin to feel that protection must be afforded to such administrators, is it small wonder that the machine does not begin to run properly ?

But that is not the whole story. It is more than that. We have got to examine the entire structure, the institutional machinery, of the Budget, and this is where I personally feel that this Budget has scored its greatest success.

There was an announcement by the Finance Minister in his Budget Speech of a proposal to decentralize capital expenditure on works of a local character in regard to the entirety of the Budget. This, to my mind, is the biggest break-through that we have had in the recent past. In a way—you have heard me speak on this subject before—you know that I have been steadfastly an advocate for the cause of the decentralization of the budgetary allocations. I have been arguing this matter for the last two years. I have mentioned it in Parliament. I have raised it in the Parliamentary Group. I have raised it in the Cabinet and I have informed you on more than one occasion.—[Interruption]. No. It is not a Cabinet secret. It has been announced by the Finance Minister, and you also know that it has been the subject of anxious discussion among Members of Parliament. Now it has been announced as an essential feature of agreed Cabinet policy by everybody, with full authority of the Prime Minister and the entire Government.

The announcement has been made by the Finance Minister of what, I believe, could be the greatest break-through of all time. I do not know how to quantify it ? I do not know how to be able to say how much money is going to be saved, how much enthusiasm is going to be generated and what precise results are going to come in the year that is to follow, namely, 1973. But I believe that the direction is right. I believe that with the co-operation and assistance of every single elected Member of this House to work it, to the extent

that it is worked honestly, with enthusiasm, with deliberate capacities to take decisions to maximise the expenditure of monies and to ensure that every single cent of money produces value for the government and the people of this country—I have every confidence—we are now on the edge of a beak-through, a major break-through, which can lead to elemental consequences in shaping the economy of our country in the years to come.

I do not think I need go into details of the scheme once again, except to tell you briefly what it is all about. Decentralization is a nice word, a word that can mean different things in different contexts. But let us analyse it. What it simply means is this. If I were to ask the hon. First Member for Akurana (Mr. A. C. S. Hameed) or even the hon. Second Member for Akurana (Mr. Hemachandra Sirisena) on our side, how much money was set apart in last year's Budget for the Colombo South Electorate or the Akurana Electorate, I am quite sure that neither of them could answer that. If you were asked the question as to how much money was actually spent in either of these two electorates—I have deliberately chosen two electorates represented both by Government and Opposition in respect of which no one can argue that there has been any discrimination—I think the answer is that you cannot possibly tell me. It is not a surprising thing. If you ask me how much money was set apart for the Dompe Electorate, even I will not be able to tell you that. I can probably tell you how much money has been set apart for health services throughout the country. I can probably tell you how much money was set apart for educational services throughout the country. I can certainly tell you how much money was set apart for local government. The amount set apart for last year was about Rs. 13 million. But if you were to ask me the question as to how much money was set apart for the service of any particular electorate it is impossible to answer that question.

[ගිරික්ස් ආර්. ඩී. බණ්ඩාරනායක මහතා]

If, for example, a road is not built in Akurana within time, there is no guarantee that that money is going to be set apart for any other work in Akurana. It could become a road in Colombo South ; it could become a road in Laggala ; and it could even become a road in Dompe, upon transfer procedures under the virement rules of the Financial Regulations. Well, under the new scheme that is envisaged that cannot happen. The money allocated, on objective criteria depending upon population, territory, backwardness and poverty of an electorate is earmarked for that electorate and the money is transferable from project to project within that year subject to the Central Government having the right of veto upon priorities named and suggested locally through the M. P. of the area, representative, I suppose, of the people of that area, or in co-ordination with such other councils and institutional arrangements as may be devised for that. One cannot, of course, leave it to the M.P. to choose always because the wrong priorities may selected. You can find non-feasible projects recommended ; you can find the entire priorities of the national endeavour being violated. That is not possible. One has to have a rationale to this. The M.P. cannot, for example, say, " I insist on haviing post offices in every village and I do not want any schools ; I do not want any hospitals. " Nor can you have an M.P., culturally minded, saying, " I want to build only temples and vihares in my electorate. I do not want any services for my people in my electorate. " Th Central Government veto must stand.

When the member of Parliament the politician, is involved very closely at the grass-root levels with the choice of priorities and projects and with the implementation of these projects, with the power to supervise and to raise complaints and to draw the attention of the Central Government of inadequacies in performance,

you will see to what extent the money provision can be maximized. Apart from it once the people have confidence that the budgetary allocations are being made at least in respect of a small part of the Budget on this basis—I am not suggesting this for national projects ; I am not suggesting this in regard to recurrent and maintenance expenditure items of the Budget ; I am suggesting this essentially only in regard to capital works of a local character and I can see no problems in this but great advantages —the shramadana efforts of the people can certainly be mobilized to substitute human labour efforts on hard cash which would have to be paid in the form of remuneration using Budget allocations of money. I can see fairly wealthy people within the two thousand rupee ceiling, I suppose, still being willing to contribute. It may be a few hundred rupees occasionally to augment the fund, if it means immediate implementation of a project, which will bring advantages to the local area. In fact, even poor people may be willing to give up their ration of some essential commodities for a limited period of time if they have the certainty and knowledge that the money so saved is going to be used to augment the local fund and to make possible the execution of more work locally with the priority system devised.

These are, to my mind, the principal achievements of this Budget and the greatest victory for the country in terms of the Budget.

Now, I do not see this as being a Budget which rejects the idea of the elimination of subsidies. It has established some very good principles ; it has established a degree of consultation with the Members of Parliament before the formulation of Budget Proposals. The theory of secrecy which goes into these things is, of course, necessary in regard to revenue protection orders, import control notices, and so on and anything which creates windfall profits or shortages cannot obviously be advertized by the Minister of Finance in advance. One

1685 1972 නොවැම්බර් 24 1686

understands that, but certainly the degree of consultation established by 'this Budget is probably something unprecedented in the history of Parliamentary life in this country. I think it has marked a new tradition, and possibly a good tradition, which should be followed and expanded in most spheres of activity because if this happens with regular consultation, I think, we will find ourselves having more of a meeting ground and a common ground in regard to the day to day administration and thus find ourselves less tempted to fall into ways, shall I say, of a bureaucracy whose mind is congealed in fixed paterns and is incapable of accepting changing thoughts and ideas. Now, if this becomes possible, we would certainly be moving far ahead. But is that all ?

Let us take other matters. The Hon. Finance Minister has taken a very courageous step. As to whether it is a popular Budget, I do not think there are any illusions about it. It is popular to the extent that the very immediate dangers that were foreseen by the people have not materialized, namely, the possibility of a change in the rice ration. That, I think, was what the Opposition were counting on. But I think he is right in saying, "Well, I spoofed you this time." He can put out his tongue at them and say, "Well, all your crackers would be damp by the time it comes to exploding." The Budget has belied their expectations and has not produced the results they expected. That is the short-term line on it.

But from a long-term line, he has taken one of the most unpopular decisions, I suppose, and a hard decision in transferring a number of import items on to FEECs and in increasing the FEECs rate. Now, this is not an easy one. No one thinks it is. It involves a direct imposition of price increases upon a wide variety of items. It is hard, and there is no gainsaying the fact. You do not get 360 million rupees out of nothing.

The revenue expectations have to be paid for by somebody, and in the last analysis it is the consumer who is going to pay for all this. It is not anybody else. It must be so. It is no good saying it is a hard Budget. It is a hard Budget. There is no way, for example, as some Finance Minister sought in the past, of extracting the honey without damaging the flower as when the bee sucks honey. Neither do I know of the rhythm of the universe which pulsated around the ears of my good Friend in the years gone by. These are styles of speaking, of attractive phrases. But it does not really mean very much.

The Hon. Minister of Finance has taken a bold decision by this step in selective devaluation. It is selective devaluation because the FEECs system is really taken to avoid the question of a uniform change in money value, to bring about a change in money values at different rates. Monies are being assessed at one valuation for the import of one set of goods and are taken at another valuation for another set of goods. And on the second set of goods there are two results which he will produce thereby, namely, to depress consumption of the items which are on FEECs by limiting and controlling imports, and by reducing the level of dependence upon those items. He has left out naturally the items of mass consumption from this, so that he will not impose hardship upon the poorer sections of society, people who cannot bear those burdens. But of course a variety of items have moved into FEECs, and also the FEECs rate has gone up from 55 per cent to 65 per cent. So, that is an increase and a hard increase no doubt.

I remember at the time that the FEEC scheme was introduced, I myself wondered about the wisdom of it. I did not make a speech in Parliament then though I did, I think, make some rude remarks about Gamini Corea's faeces on that occasion. But apart from making a joke of it, I do not think I got really

[ffපිලික්ස් ආර්. ඩී. බණ්ඩාරනායක මහතා]
involved in a debate on it when the
proposal was presented in the form
of a Bill by the previous Government.

I must say I have always wondered
about this question, whether you
should have selective devaluation of
currency or not. I can certainly
understand a debate continuing on
whether you should have devaluation
or not, but it always seemed to me
that the attractive part of the FEEC
scheme was the way it imposed no
hardship whatsoever on the people
by its application on exports, while
at the same time it would generate
a huge rupee source of funds. The
unfortunate part of it is that the
previous Government applied it to
even non-traditional exports like
cardamoms, cinnamon quills, and a
whole lot of items.

The transferring of exports to
FEECs is painless as far as the vast
majority of the people are concerned.
It can result in the industrialists and
the producers of these items becoming very rich unless you siphon off
a part of the proceeds in the form of
export duty. Now that is a very easy
thing to do. You can take it all back
again if you do not need to allow anybody to get rich quick with profits.
That can be done even if tea, rubber
and coconut products were to be
transferred to the FEECs category. It
does not matter. If the appropriate
duty increases are adjusted you can
make sure that the owners of tea,
rubber and coconut-properties are
not going to enjoy a bonanza through
the transfer of FEECs. What will
happen is, you are getting back an
advantage for the amount of money
you got to spend on importing more
expensive goods from abroad. In
other words you will get back the
rupee surplus.

The Finance Minister has not done
this. But I would like to commend
for his consideration the idea and
suggest to him that, if this is possible,
maybe there will be a much larger
rupee surplus than he anticipates,

much more than the Rs. 370 million
now calculated for purposes of local
works of a capital nature under the
decentralized budget plan. It may
become possible to generate a very
much larger rupee surplus available
for this purpose, which, if it is available, will result in this country really
and truly forging ahead at a far
greater pace than has been possible
in the past. This is something which
might merit his consideration, and I
should like to place it before him to
think about and to contemplate in
the future.

There is no reason why it has to
come with the Budget. These are
things that can be done at any time.
The question is whether it is a good
thing to do or whether it is not a good
thing to do. After all he must evalu-
ate the advantages and disadvantages
of it, and consider it and take his decisions in best interest of us all. I have
no doubt that the Hon. Minister of
Finance will do this.

There are another two matters that
I wish to mention. The first one
relates to local government. In
regard to local government, I should
like to put before this House for its
consideration one major question.
The Budget has provided a very welcome relief to local government by
saying that for the first time new
sources of revenue are actually going
to be added to local bodies. We have
been asking for this from the days
of the Choksy Commission Report, of
the V. C. Jayasuriya Committee
Report and correspondence has been
going on between the Ministry of
Local Government and the Ministry
of Finance from time to time. But
nothing has happened. Up to date
the revenue sources available to local
authorities have remained precisely
where they were.

I do not entirely blame the Ministry
of Finance. Even in spite of the
available financing resources local
authorities hate to impose taxes, and
I suppose the reason why they hate
to impose taxes is precisely the same
reason why the Minister of Finance
hates to impose taxes. We are all
political animals, and I do not think

any political animal enjoys taxing the people who bring him into power. It is an understandable approach, but an approach which is counter-productive when it comes to local government work.

I sometimes wonder why people even bother to get themselves elected to local bodies. Take a village council. After a lot of time and effort — you do not get paid for the service — you stand for election. You go before your voters. I suppose prestige-wise it counts something to get yourself elected and be able to say that you got a reasonable number of votes and got yourself elected to a job. That is fair enough. But what are the powers that these gentlemen have? They have got the power to collect taxes from their voters. The taxes are not even sufficient to pay the salaries of their staffs. Usually the members of the staff are not even from the village. Very often the staff is sent by the L. G. S. C. You collect taxes from your voters to pay the salaries of outsiders, and having paid those salaries you are usually in deficit and you got to ask something from the Central Government to pay the balance salaries, at least the cost of living allowance and the special living allowance. Having done that, you have got to go begging to the Central Government to get money again to undertake some minor development work; even to build a well for each local authority is quite a problem.

In the days of Mr. Tiruchelvam he gave two wells to each place in Jaffna and no wells to the whole of the Western Province. That was his way of doing it as Minister of Local Government. — [Interruption]. Are you suggesting that only people in Jaffna need a bath? I do not know. It seems to me that Mr. Tiruchelvam had a strange idea about the uncleanliness of his own people so that he thought they needed an extra number of wells. That is how he worked it out.

Now, having collected this little bit of money, the local authorities today do not even have the power to get this little work executed on contract by anybody. All they do now is to give it back to the Territorial Civil Engineering Organization for the preparation of estimates for the execution of the work. Sometimes the drawing up of the estimate results in the discovery that money allocated is inadequate. In 1971 this House had the strange experience of seeing that out of Rs. 13 million less than Rs. 3 million had been spent. This year the figures have come showing that the estimates have been prepared in respect of a much larger percentage — about Rs. 8 million out of Rs. 18 million. But when it comes to the actual execution of the work my information is that they are sill at the level of Rs. 2 million out of Rs. 18 million. So, money remains in the Treasury and the Finance Minister will be happy.

I would like to ask the question, why are people standing for local government elections any more and for what purpose if they do not have the power to do anything? In the premier local authority, the Colombo Municipal Council, of which the hon. Second Member for Colombo South (Mr. Bernard Soysa) is a member, the situation is worse. He is an expert on the subject. They have a revenue of Rs. 55 million. It is substantially more than the entire Vote for local government we have in the Ministry. This money is collected from the ratepayers, but for what? Most of the money is spent on routine establishment and maintenance of the staff provided by the L.G.S.C.; for payment of wages and maintenance of the cleansing department staff who do no cleansing; payment of salaries of engineers and the like who draw plans which cannot be executed for lack of funds. Mosquitoes proliferate and filaria is now prevalent in the heart of the city. I am sorry that even the hon. Leader of the Opposition is occasionally awakened in the night by the odd mosquito in his own electorate. This is the Colombo Municipal Council run by the U.N.P. If you find a mosquito buzzing, please remember to ring up the Mayor and

[පිලිප්ස් ආර්. ඩී. බණ්ඩාරනායක මහතා]

ask him why the mosquitoes are buzzing. Since he is a U.N.P. Mayor it must be a green bug at least, if it is not a mosquito.

Now, what is happening? Is it a small wonder that the ratepayers are asking this question? The sewer system in the city—I do not know whether one is bothered to think about it—has to be immediately replaced, within the next five years. The sewers are bursting at the seams from the overflow of raw sewage. Today it is being discharged at the Wellawatte Canal, which is one of the reasons for the stiak, quite apart from the natural pollution and waste matter. Thirty per cent of the city is not sewered. Squatters are being brought into the city and encouraged to squat. Stand-pipes are being put up for them to make life supportable. Having regard to the health conditions prevailing, if this kind of administration is tolerated and permitted, how much longer are we going to survive? I am assure you that the Hon. Minister of Health need not have family planning, for in five years a plague would have reduced the population of Ceylon adequately in this part, Colombo, at any rate, to ensure that family planning techniques will not really be required.

A sum of Rs. 5 million is required immediately as a top priority for a sewage system in the City. Time after time the matter has been raised. Out of the Rs. 55 million available to it as revenue, the municipal council has not found it possible even over the years to make a little saving in order to provide for this type of expenditure. Day by day the City deteriorates in appearance. We are talking of tourism and of park lands, while at the same time cinemas are being put up across street lines by Mayors of the City! Town Planning Ordinances have been enacted, and Housing and Town Improvement Ordinances exist. Why are they not being followed? They cannot be followed because this is one of the pernicious evils of the kind of democracy that is being practised at local levels. I am indebted to my good Friend, Mr. Chandra Gunasekera, the hon. Member for Kottawa, for pointing out to me that when somebody wants to put up a house in an uninhabited area he has only to declare a street line in order that he can get the area passed as a residential area. He says you find street lines in the Dehiwala-Mount Lavinia Municipal Council area proliferating like spiders' webs across houses and across buildings that exist merely because street lines are being drawn on plans to enable the authorities to pass housing plans keeping to the law.

Is that what local government is there for? I should like to raise the question whether local government does not require a good hard look, whether the functions of local government today have been reduced to scavenging in the village councils, and not even scavenging in the City.

Members ask me sometimes why local authorities are being dissolved. Are they suggesting that this type of administration should be tolerated, should be permitted to continue indefinitely? Is it the suggestion that any officer in a local authority today who feels that he has a friend in one council or another who will look after his interests, who will protect him from the consequences of doing no work or of performing inefficiently, should be tolerated?

Last year I directed the Mayor, Mr. Vincent Perera, to actually investigate every work-site in the City of Colombo and satisfy himself that the people who chalked up their names were actually working there. He told me, "No, Sir. It is not necessary. You will not find anything." But ultimately he did do it and he found that two hundred people who had marked their attendance were not at their work-sites. I gave him instructions that they should forthwith be inter-directed and their services terminated. Well, he interdicted sixty but within two weeks they were all back at work again. One or other of the members had interviewed him or the Commis-

1693   1972 නොවැම්බර් 24   1694

sioner and pointed out that some of them had four children, that some had six children, that some had sixteen years' service, and so on. And I am sorry to say that some of the members of the municipal council who had intervened were our own people and not all were U.N.P. people.

These are sad but true facts. But I must ask the question, " Is this what local government is therefor ? " On the other hand, Mr. Speaker, in your electorate there is the Kotte Urban Council which was dissolved, and I have no doubt that, along with the Finance Minister, your Special Commissioner has the unique distinction of having produced a surplus Budget this year.—[Interruption]. He is doing an excellent job. That is what I am saying. Quite apart from the question of fault or no fault, one has to decide the future direction and purpose of local Government.

One last matter. I talked about the bureaucracy. I talked of its inefficiency. I talked of its inadequacies. I talked of the fact that it does not measure up to the requirements of this day and age. May I raise with you one further matter for your consideration ? Is it not time that we reviewed completely the administrative precedures for dealing with people at a diciplinary level ? Can you afford to have co-operative employees upon dismissal going to labour tribunals and getting orders for reinstatement ? If a co-operative society is not able to make charge stick with proof beyond reasonable doubt and they are called upon to reinstate the corrupt official in the co-operative society—and they know that that risk is there—will they ever fire that corrupt man ? How can they do that ? Can a government cooporation run itself efficiently within the industrial sector if after it takes steps to dismiss an inefficient performer in the industrial field that man is liable to be brought back with a bonanza in back-pay and reinstated in the corporation after long, protracted and expensive legal proceedings in which the corporation has

got to spend its resources litigating before the labour courts ? Can this be done ? The line of least resistance for any board or corporation to take will be to say, " We will live with that inefficiency, we will live with that corruption, rather than take the risk of instituting disciplinary proceedings in such cases. "

But is that all ? Even in the public service—I have gone into the statistics of dismissals—there are not many cases. There are generally not more than 50 cases per year on an average. It is a very small number in relation to a total public service exceeding 250,00 people. But the procedures are such under the new Constitution that there are 13 steps to be taken before anybody can be dismissed, and these 13 steps, if properly handled, can be made to drag on for four and a half years approximately.

Now, if this is what is going to happen to us, I think it is high time we thought afresh and decided what changes are necessary. Let us not be too humanitarian about this. Let us look at it from the point of view of giving the vast majority of law-abiding citizens in this country the kind of law, the kind of administration that they deserve and need. Do you believe that any one in this country will object if whipping is made compulsory—I am not referring to small or unimportant offences—in regard to offences like gang rape, throwing of acid, house breaking with violence inflicted upon the inmates, kidnapping of children and things like that ?—[Interruption]. Yes. Throwing of handbombs even in Jaffna !

These are the questions that you have to answer. We are talking of law and order situations. We are talking of good government. I am not talking of anything harsh or hard against law-abiding citizens, but in deciding how to govern the country I think there is a feat of social engineering involved. One has to balance the conflicting interests of both sides, and I think we have to throw our weight on the only side

[fපිලික්ස් ආර්. ඩී. බණ්ඩාරනායක මහතා]
we can throw our weight on—the side
of the people—by giving them an
efficient and good government.

අ. හා. 6.14

ඒ. සි. එස්. හමිඩ් මහතා (අකුරන පළමු
වන)

(இரு. ஏ. சி. எஸ். ஹமீது—அக்குரணை
முதலாம் அங்கத்தவர்)

(Mr. A. C. S. Hameed—First Akurana)
Mr. Speaker, I must confes that the
Hon. Minister of Public Administra-
tion, Local Government & Home
Affairs and Minister of Justice was
very disappointing. His speech lacked
the normal weight, the wisdom, the
fire, the flash, the light and what-not.
I listened to his speech very carefully.
He did not hold a brief for the Budget.
He confessed that it was a hard
Budget. He confessed that the immediate danger of the rice ration being
knocked out was postponed and that
he did not hold a brief for the Foreign
Exchange Entitlement Certificate
Scheme when it was debated in this
House. Of course, now and then, he
made us ponder ; sometimes he took
us closer to Parkinson's Law and at
times he was more or less trying to
advocate the theory of Gunnar
Myrdal. Well, whatever it may be,
certain things flow from his speech.

He said that this was a Budget that
was prepared in consultation with
Members of Parliament, perhaps with
the only Members of Parliament of
the Government Groop.

fපිලික්ස් ආර්. ඩී. බණ්ඩාරනායක මහතා
(திரு. பிலிக்ஸ் ஆர். டி. பண்டாரநாயக்க)
(Mr. Felix R. D. Bandaranaike)
Yes, not you all, but half of Akurana.

හමිඩ් මහතා
(இரு. ஹமீது)
(Mr. Hameed)
I understand that half of Akurana
has participated in it.

Now, the hon. Member for Devinuwara (Mr. R. J. G. de Mel) in his
speech said that an attempt had
been made to stage a coup, similar to
one that was staged against Mr. D.
P. R. Gunawardena in 1958, against
the Minister of Finance. I do not
know that there was a signature
campaign, but I do know that the
young Members of Parliament had
lodged a protest in advance with the
Hon. Pirem Minister that the Budget
should not in any way cast burdens
on the people of the country. I am
just wondering what the hon. Member for Devinuwara said when he
gave expression to the effect that an
attempt was being made to stagt a
coup against the Minister of Finance.
Is there any such thing happening
within the Government ranks ? If
so we would like to know. If it is so
to is a sad thing because in our opinion, perhaps according to the philosophy that the United Front is advocating, the only person who may be
able to interpret that philosophy into economic terms is the present
Minister of Finance. Well, the Prime
Minister said some time ago that the
people of this country are sitting on
a volcano. I fully agree that it is so.

This Government would reach or
graduate itself to three years of
stewardship within the next few
months, but when you look at its
performance during the last three
years you will find a gaping gap between its performance and its promises. Now I am reminded of how
Charles Dickens—I believe it is in
the Tale of Two Cities—described
the environment that existed before
the French Revolution. He said
" Taxes in front, taxes behind, taxes
left, taxes right, taxes here, taxes
there, and taxes every where ; and I
think Dickens also said : " On every
forehead hunger was written." That
is the picture today in this country.

Now, this dissatisfaction is being
generated in the rank and file of the
United Front. The Ceylon Communist Party, (Moscow Wing) which
is a constituent of this Government,
had a following which called for critical support, and it was they whe
were able to seize office during the

Felix on Conflict with the Constitutional Court

[ඉරත් තිනම් මහතා]
" steps are being taken to issue forms
for public use in English, Sinhala
and Tamil. These forms will be soon
made available " ? (b) Will he state
which of these eleven forms are
available in Tamil ? (c) When will
other forms be made available in
Tamil ? (d) Other than those
mentioned in (c) above, what are
the forms in public use not yet
translated into Tamil ? What are
their numbers and when will they
be made available in Tamil ?

කුමාරසූරියර් මහතා

(திரு. குமாரசூரியர்)

(Mr. Kumarasuriar)

(a) Yes. (b) P.O.P. 19, P.O.C. 84
and P.O.N. 65 are available in the
three languages. (c) Of the balance
eight forms, Form P.O.N. 37 is being
translated and Form P.O.N. 10 has
been forwarded to the Legal Draftsman for his approval, after which
these two forms will be sent for
printing. The other six forms which
are in the three languages have
already been sent to the Government
Press for printing. These forms will
be available for use once they are
received from the Government
Printer. (d) All other forms in
public use are available in the three
languages.

කල්තැබීම

ஒத்திப்போடல்

ADJOURNMENT

ආණ්ඩුකුම ව්‍යවස්ථා අධිකරණය සහ ශ්‍රී
ලංකා පුවත්පත් මණ්ඩල පනත්
කෙටුම්පත

அரசியலமைப்பு நீதிமன்றமும் இலங்கைப்
பத்திரிகைப் பேரவைச் சட்டமூலமும்

CONSTITUTIONAL COURT AND THE
SRI LANKA PRESS COUNCIL BILL

දි. මු. ජයරත්න මහතා (ගම්පොල)

(திரு. டி. மு. ஜயரத்ன—கம்பளை)

(Mr. D. M. Jayaratne—Gampola)

කථානායකතුමනි, ආණ්ඩුකුම ව්‍යවස්
ථාව පිළිබඳව මේ ගරු සභාවේ කෙරෙන
පළමු වන විවාදය මෙය වන නිසා අප හැම
දෙනාම බොහොම සන්තෝෂ වෙනවා. ඒ
කතා රාජ්‍ය භාෂාවෙන් කෙරෙනවා නම්.

කථානායකතුමා

(சபாநாயகர் அவர்கள்)

(Mr. Speaker)

අසවල් භාෂාවෙන් කතා කරන්නය ඕ
නියෝගයක් කරන්නට බැහැ. සිංහල,
දෙමළ, ඉංග්‍රීසි යන භාෂා තුනෙන් කැමති
භාෂාවකින් කතා කරන්නට පුළුවන්. මේ
විවාදයේදී ආණ්ඩු පක්ෂයට පැය හතර
කුත්, විරුද්ධ පාර්ශ්වයට පැය හතරහමාර
කුත් වෙන් කර තිබෙනවා. විරුද්ධ
පාර්ශ්වයට වෙන් කර ඇති කාලය පහත
සඳහන් පරිදි බෙද තිබෙනවා :

එක්සත් ජාතික පක්ෂයට පැය 1½ ඕ.
පෙඩරල් පක්ෂයට පැය 1 ඕ. ගාල්ලේ
මන්ත්‍රී ආචාර්ය ඩඩ්ලි දහනායකට
මිනිත්තු 40 ඕ. හබරාදූවේ මන්ත්‍රී වින්ස්
ගුණසේකර මහතාට මිනිත්තු 45 ඕ.
යාපනේ මන්ත්‍රී සි. එක්ස්. මාටින් මහතාට
මිනිත්තු 20 ඕ. නිකවැරටියේ මන්ත්‍රී එම්.
තෙන්නකෝන් මහතාට මිනිත්තු 15 ඕ.
කතා කරන භාෂාව පිළිබඳව කිසිම
බලපෑමක් කරන්නට බැහැ.

මෛතිපාල සේනානායක මහතා (වාරි
මාර්ග, විදුලි බලය හා මහාමාර්ග ඇමති
සහ සභානායක)

(திரு. மைத்திரிபால சேனநாயக்க—நீர்ப்
பாசன, மின்சக்தி, பெருவீதிகள் அமைச்ச
ரும் சபை முதல்வரும்)

(Mr. Maithripala Senanayake—Minister
of Irrigation Power and Highways and
Leader of the House)

As agreed between the Leaders of
Parties, I move,

" That the House do now adjourn. "

ප්‍රශ්නය සභාසම්මුඛ කරන ලදී.

வினா எடுத்தியம்பப்பெற்றது.

Question proposed.

කථානායකතුමා

(சபாநாயகர் அவர்கள்)

(Mr. Speaker)

Before the Debate commences, I
would like to state that the
allocation of time is as follows :

4 hours for the Government

4½ hours for the Opposition, which time will be divided further in the following manner :

U.N.P.	..	1¼ hours
Federal Party	...	1 hour
The Member for Galle	..	40 minutes
The Member for Habaraduwa	..	45 minutes
The Member for Nikaweratiya	..	15 minutes

The allotted times will be strictly adhered to in the course of the Debate.

පූ. භා. 10.10

[පිලික්ස් ආර්. ඩී. බණ්ඩාරනායක මහතා (රාජ්‍ය පරිපාලන, පළාත් පාලන හා ස්වදේශ කටයුතු ඇමති සහ අධිකරණ ඇමති)

(තිරු. පීඑික්ස් ආර්. ඩී. පණ්டாரநாயக்க— பொது நிர்வாகம், உள்ளூராட்சி, உள்நாட்டு அலுவல்கள் அமைச்சரும் நீதி அமைச்சரும்)

(Mr. Felix R. D. Bandaranaike— Minister of Public Administration, Local Government and Home Affairs and Minister of Justice)

කථානායකතුමනි, ගම්පොළ මන්ත්‍රී තුමා (දි. මු. ජයරත්න මහතා) ඉදිරිපත් කළ අදහස මගේ හැඟීමේ හැටියට නුවණට හුරුයි. ආණ්ඩුක්‍රම ව්‍යවස්ථාව පිළිබඳ මේ ගරු සභාවේ සාකච්ඡා කරන පළමු වැනි අවස්ථාවේදී අපේ වාද විවාද රාජ්‍ය භාෂාවෙන් කිරීම නුවණට හුරු වුනත් එක ප්‍රශ්නයක් පමණක් තිබෙනවා. මේ විවාදය ඉතා වැදගත්. අප නීති ප්‍රශ්න පිළිබඳව සාකච්ඡා කරන අවස්ථාවලදී භාෂා දෙකෙන්ම අදහස් ඉදිරිපත් කළොත්=ඉහොඳයි. විශේෂ පැහැදිලිකමක් ඔනෑ කර තිබෙනවා, ජාත්‍යන්තර වශ යෙන්, අප ඉදිරිපත් කරන තර්ක පිළ බඳව. මේ විවාදයේදී අපේ බලාපො රොත්තුව ජාතික රාජ්‍ය සභාවේ ගෞරවය ආරක්ෂා කිරීම පමණක් නොව අපේ අයිතිවාසිකම්, වරප්‍රසාද අංගසම්පූර්ණ විශ යෙන් ලබා ගැනීමට කටයුතු කිරීමයි. එම නිසා එක වචනයක් වරද්දන්නෙත් නැතිව, වැරදි වැටහීම් ඇති නොවන විදි යට අප කටයුතු කළ යුතුව තිබෙනවා. ඒ

නිසා මිස වෙනත් කරුණක් නිසා නො වෙයි, මගේ කතාව භාෂා දෙකෙන්ම කරන්නට මා බලාපොරොත්තු වන්නේ. සිංහල භාෂාව මහහැරීමක් නොවෙයි, ඒ කියමනෙන් ඉදිරිපත් කරන්නේ. ඇත්ත වශයෙන්ම අපට යුතුකමක් තිබෙනවා, ජාතික රාජ්‍ය සභාවේ අයිතිවාසිකම් රැක ගැනීමට.

මෙය ආණ්ඩු පක්ෂයක් විරුද්ධ පාර්ශ වයත් අතර තිබෙන විවාදයක් නොවෙයි. මේ අවස්ථාවේදී අපි කතා කරන්නේ සහෝදර මන්ත්‍රීවරුන් හැටියට අලුත් ආණ්ඩු ක්‍රම ව්‍යවස්ථාව යටතේ අපේ පොදු අයිතිවාසිකම් රැක ගැනීම සම්බන්ධ යෙනුයි. එම අදහස ඉටු කිරීමට මා ගරු සභාවේ සිටින සෑම මන්ත්‍රීවරයෙක්ම අද සහභාගි වෙනවා. අද මේ ඓතිහාසික දින යේදී අප ගත්තා තීන්දුවට මුල් රටටම කියා පෑමට ගත්තා වූ තීන්දුවට විරුද්ධ තාවයක් තිබෙන කිසිම කෙනෙක් සිටී නවා නම්, වචනයක් හෝ ඉදිරිපත් කිරී මෙන් ඒ අදහස=විරුද්ධ විමස හෝ තුව —ඉදිරිත් කිරීමට මා ඉල්ලා සිටි නවා. එසේ නැත්නම් සමහර විට අපට සිදු වන්නේ මේ විවාදයේදී කතා කරන මන්ත්‍රීවරුන්ට පමණක් සීමා වුණ තීන්දු දුවක් ගැනීමටයි. එවැනි තීන්දුවක් ගැනීම නොවෙයි අපේ බලාපොරොත්තුව. ආණ්ඩු පක්ෂයේ හෝ වේවා, ස්වාධීන පක්ෂයේ හෝ වේවා, විරුද්ධ පාර්ශවයේ හෝ වේවා සෑම මන්ත්‍රීවරයෙක්ම පැය අටක මාරක පමණ කාලයක් තිස්සේ කෙරෙන මේ සාකච්ඡාවට සහභාගි වුණත් නැතත් =ම සාකච්ඡාව අවසානයේදී මත දෙකක් නැතිව කවුරුත් එක වගේ කල්පනා කර යම්කිසි තීන්දුවක් ගත් බව මඟ කෙනෙ කුටම, මුළු ලංකාවටම පමණක් නොව මුළු ලෝකයටම—මේ ජාතික රාජ්‍ය සභාව දෙස බලන හැම කෙනෙකුටම—බලා ගැනී මට පුළුවන් වේවිය කියා අපි බලාපො රොත්තු වෙනවා. මේ ජාතික රාජ්‍ය සභා වේ අයිතිවාසිකම් රැක ගැනීමේ ප්‍රශ්න යක් මතු වුණ අවස්ථාවේදී මේ ප්‍රශ්නයට ආණ්ඩු පක්ෂයයි, විරුද්ධ පක්ෂයයි කියා දෙපැත්තක් නැතැයි කියන හැඟීම උඩ මේ සාකච්ඡා ආරම්භ කරන්නයි මා බලාපොරොත්තු වන්නේ.

1339   ජාතික රාජ්‍ය සභාව   1340

[f වි ලික් ස් අර් බි. බණ්ඩරනායක මහතා]
ගරු කථානායකතුමනි, අපේ ආණ්ඩු
ක්‍රම ව‍යවස්ථාවේ පළමුවැනි මූලික අයිති
වාසිකම් පිළිබඳව ඇති වී තිබෙන ප්‍රශ්න
යක් ගැන රජයේ අදහස් පමණක් නොව
ජාතික රාජ්‍ය සභාවේ අදහස් ද ඉදිරිපත්
කිරීමට මා බලාපොරොත්තු වෙනවා. මෙම
ප්‍රශ්නය විසඳා ගැනීම ගැන මුඵ මන්ත්‍රීවර
යෙකුගේ ම අංක සම්පූර්ණ සහයෝගය මා
බලාපොරොත්තු වෙනවා.

Mr. Speaker, as I said a few
moments ago, I think the hon.
Member for Gampola is right in
saying that we should conduct the
deliberations of this Assembly in
the Official Language to the extent
to which we are capable of doing
so, not merely because it is the
first time that the occasion has
arisen to debate a matter of constitutional importance in this
Assembly under the terms of the new
Constitution, but because it is right
and fitting that every Member of this
Assembly must be capable of fully
understanding and participating in
the proceedings on this Debate. While
I shall endeavour to accommodate
that request, I propose to make my
speech in both languages. I spoke a
few moments ago in the Sinhala
langauge, but that is not all I propose
to say in the Sinhala language. I shall
come back to the Sinhala language,
and I shall be continuing my speech
in the Sinhala language in full depth
for the appreciation and understanding of all hon. Members of this
Assembly.

But it is equally important that
when a matter of such importance as
this comes up for debate our voices
from this National State Assembly
should be heard not merely among
ourselves, not merely among our own
people in this country; when we
speak our voices should be heard
internationally. People outside this
country must be in a position to
appreciate our deliberations and be
able to draw conclusions as to the
degree of unanimity of understanding, and the determination of this
National State Assembly to uphold its
own rights and privileges and its
rights under the new Constitution.

Since we are engaging in an important legal discussion I think that every
world should be carefully considered
and that when we speak we should
not speak carelessly or in a spirit of
mere partisan debate where a government and an opposition find them
selves in confrontation with each
other. So far as I know, this is not a
debate where I speak as spokesman
fo rthe Government only. I think our
voices today are the voices of the
entire National State Assembly,
rising up under the terms of the
Constitution to defend and safeguard
the very sovereignty, the very supremacy which has been enshrined in the
new Constitution whcih we are all
bound to safeguard and protect.

The right of unholding the Constitution is not the limited right of any
particular institution created under
the Constitution. It is indeed the function of the National State Assembly,
above all else, as the supreme instrument of State power to protect and
safeguard the Constitution. I look
forward on this occasion to the kind
of non-partisan discussion which indeed the National State Assembly
must engage in from time to time for
the very purpose of safeguarding the
rights and institutions which we as
the National State Asembly set up for
the governance of our own affairs, for
determining our own future under
our own authority and according to
the wishes of our people. This is what
we are here to do ultimately.

Now, Mr. Speaker, although you
have given us long day of about 8½
hours in which to conduct this discussion, it may not be possible for every
single Member of this House to participate in the Debate in a practical way
by making his won contribution, but
I should regard it as unfortunate if
the Debate is considered merely as a
debate among the few persons who
participate in this discussion and that
the views expressed here are merely

the views of a few spokesmen or of a few political parties. l hope that when this Debate comes to be recorded and read any person looking at it will be able to say that the views expressed here are indeed the views of the entire National State Asembly of Sri Lanka. For this purpose, if indeed there be any single Member of this House or any single group who holds different views from the views which I shall express, which my Colleagues here will express, which the Leader of the Opposition will expres, which other Party Leaders will express on behalf of their groups and groupings, if there is a dissentient voice, if there is disagreement. I sincerely hope that it will be expressed here so that at least the persons outside this august Assembly will be able to say to themselves, "We have been able to judge the strength of opinion of this Asembly", notwithstanding the fact that we are not in a position at the conclusion of this Adjournment Debate to put the question to the vote.

I myself have talked privately to many hon. Members on both sides of the Assembly on this very question, and I speak with knowledge and authority of the state of feeling that exists in this Assembly upon the matters open for discussion. Therefore I think I am right in saying that while we may hold different views in regard to the provisions of particular sections of a particular law, whether they are repugnant to the Constitution or not this is a matter in regard to which I think it is true to say there is a difference of opinion on some matters. However there is no difference of opinion on one matter, namely, the supremacy and sovereignty of the National State Assembly.

That, I think, is what is important today, and it is not in regard to the substance or the contents of a Bill that is before the Constitutional Court that I propose to speak today. I do not propose to engage in that discussion. That is a discussion on which, I think, we can say there are several plaintiffs in this Assembly who have invoked the jurisdiction of a court, the most notable plaintiff in this instance being my distinguished Friend and Colleague, the hon. Leader of the Opposition. Fortunately he did not seek to restrain me by injunction. But as a plaintiff, he is well skillel in the art of presentation of his case. He is not the only plaintiff ; there are several. There is also my good Friend and Colleague, the hon. Member for Gale (Dr. W. Dahanayake) who is another plaintiff. We have another in the hon. Member for Habaraduwa (Mr. Prins Gunasekera), and there are others, I think, outside this august Assembly who are also plaintiffs.

In a way, I suppose, Mr. Speaker, I am the virtual defendant on behalf of the Government as the man presenting and taking responsibility for the Bill in association with my Colleague, the Hon. Minister of Information and Broadcasting. We have here a Bill in respect of which, I suppose, he and I—or I suppose I am the first accused and he is the second accused—are the virtual defendants before that tribunal. We all want a decision in regard to a controversial matter. And I must say I as the defendant am just as anxious to have a decision given in regard to the matters in controversy. Let us not imagine that this is a desire felt on the part of the plaintiffs who want relief or redress. The defendant is as much interested in the adjunction and the disposal of the case as anybody else.

But the question arises, are we interested merely in a decision or are we interested in a decision given by a body of people to whom we have assigned the task of giving decisions in accordance with the law and in accordance with the Constitution ? That is the real question that is before us. In other words, are we interested merely in saying, "Let us have a decision which has nothing to do with jurisdiction, nothing to do with

[ගරු ආර් ඩී. බණ්ඩාරනායක මහතා]
validity, nothing to do with the Constitution", and are we proceeding in this way merely because of our interest to have a decision on a matter considered to be of importance by both sides of the Assembly ? Are we going therefore to accede to the position that there is any other institution superior to this National State Assembly and capable of frustrating and avoiding the express terms of the Constitution upon which we have all agreed and which we have adopted on behalf of the very people of Sri Lanka ? That is the question before us.

Now, what is the real problem that has arisen, the real controversy, the deadlock situation that has arisen from the decision of the Constitutional Court ? Under the terms of the Constitution there is no longer a process of judicial review or legislation by any external authority outside this National State Assembly.

The National State Assembly, under Section 5 of the Constiution, is the supreme instrument of State power and becomes the residual source of power and authority under the terms of the Constitution. It will not exercise those powers and authorities directly. It will exercise its legislative power directly, but as far as the executive and judicial powers are concerned, it exercises them through other institutions established under the Constitution. These institutions are not independent of the National State Assembly, and in one way or another their authority flows from it, stems from it. That is the essential and fundamental conception of this new Constitution.

This Constitution nowhere recognizes any theory of separation of powers, nor does it recoknize the fact that any institution under the terms of the Constitution can claim to set itself up as a rival body or a body having paralled authority with the National State Assembly. The National State Assembly alone, collectively—and you are the mouthpiece—has to be the protector of our rights and the guardian of our Constitution. In that sence, the other institutions have to peform functions and make the Constitution work. We cannot work at cross-purposes ; we have to work together. No one suggests that any institution, let it be a court, let it be a labour tribunal, let it be the Cabinet, let it be the Prime Minister or the President, can act countrary to the Constitution. They must act in accordance with the guide lines laid down in the Constitution, and the Constitution is the ultimate authority, the ultimate document, which determines the rights of the National State Assembly, the institutions set up under the Constitution, and their respective relationships.

Now, Section 65 of the Constitution, a section which, I think, many people have lost sight of and not examined in the kind of depth it ought to be, says :

"The decision of the Constitutional Court shall be given within two weeks of the reference together with the reasons. A dissestient member of the Constitutional Court may also state his reasons for his dissent and these shall be forwarded together with the majority decision and reasons."

The question arises : What does this section mean ? Let me read it again.

"The decision of the Constitutional Court shall be given within two weeks of the reference together with the reasons."

When you say, a decision of court shall be given within two weeks, the plain and straighforward meaning appearing on the face of it can only be that you have to conclude your work and come to a conclusion and deliver your judgement within the space of two weeks. It must mean that, and it cannot mean anything else.

There is another Section here—I refer to Section 54 (3)—which says :

"No proceedings shall be had in the National State Assembly in relaton to a Bill referred to the Constitutional Court under sub-section (2) of this section or of section 55 until the decision of the Constitutional Court under sub-section (4) of this section or its opinion under section 55 has been given."

Now, this would say that any Bill, which is the subject of controversy, in respect of which any plaintiff, so to speak, has made a complaint and referred the problem to the Constitutional Court, Through your good offices, Mr. Speaker, must await the decision of the Constitutional Court and should not be taken up for debate untill after the deliberations of the Constitutional Court have been finalized and its decision communicated back to the National State Assembly through you.

These two sections are the ones in respect of which a conflct of interpretation appears to have arisen. Speaking for myself, I should like to express the point of view that if there is a conflct between these two, the conflict only arises in this way. One Section says, the Constitutional Court must give its order within two weeks, and the other Section says, the National State Assembly should not take up a Bill untill the decision of the Constitutional Court has been communicated. It is as simple as that. Does that mean that the National State Assembly should not take up a Bill even if the Constitutional Court has not concluded its decision and communicated its decision within two weeks? Does it mean that we have got to wait for ever, or does it mean a reasonable time? What does it mean?

Now, I do not know whether it is useful for us in a discussion of this type to study Maxwell's Interpretation of Statutes" or to study legal documents and try to interpret the Constitution, to see what precedents there are in regard to other laws, whether this is the correct approach or not. I know only one thing, and that is that if you are called upon to interrupt the Constitution there is only one practical way of interpreting it. One must interpret all the provisions of the Constitution in such a way as to give effect to the Constitution and make it work, rather than to bring that Constitution to a grinding halt. Whatever interpretation is adopted it must be a practical inter-

pretation that gives full force and effect to the Constitution and makes it practicable and capable of being worked as a Constitution. There is no other way. I do not admit for a single moment that one can examine the situation by any other approach or in any other way.

Let us take the extreme interpretations at the two ends of the spectrum and you will see immediately the kind of argument that I am raising. Supposing your interpretation is that the two weeks' rule is mandatory, that the Constitutional Court simply has to give its judgment at the end of two weeks under any circumstances—at the end of two weeks at the stroke of midnight on the 14th day the curtain falls and the work of the Constitutional Court comes to an end and cannot proceed thereafter—you will say to yourself, is this reasonable, can you work the Constitution in this way? You may find yourself asking the question, supposing a judge were to fall ill on the 13th day—he may get a heart attack, or chicken pox which may require him to be in quarantine for more than 14 days or even mumps if he has not already got it—how are we going to work the Constitution? This is one extreme situation that you will have to contemplate. The circumstance of impossibility can arise.

Take the other end of the spectrum. Although the Constitution says the judges must finish their work in 14 days time, this is not binding on the judges and the judges are free to decide for themeslves how long they will take, in the sure and certain knowledge that there is another section of the Constitution which says that the National State Assembly shall not discuss the Bill until such time as the Constitutional Court gives its verdict. You can interpret this to mean that the judges can take three years or four years or six years —as long as they like.

Let us take these two extreme ends of the spectrum and examine them. some people would like to debate this and argue whether a provision in a

[ෆිලික්ස් ආර්. ඩී. බණ්ඩාරනායක මහතා]

Bill is mandatory or directory or peremptory. I find it extremely difficult to tie myself to words. I do not think anything is gained by giving labels to sections. When we enacted legislation we used straightforward words. We said that the Constitutional Court shall finish its work in two weeks' time and the National State Assembly must not take up a controversial Bill until the decision of the Constitutional Court is given. It is as simple as that. We were not concerned with using technical words of legal significance, trying to pitch into legal conflicts. We used words that made sense to us. What the Constitution intended, what we intended, we collectively in this House, as the makers of the Constitution, know better than anybody else. It may be a problem in the future but at the moment we are the same men continuing our same existence, not as the Constituent Assembly but as the National State Assembly, the first Legislature under the new Constitution, I should have thought that either of these two extremes is fraught with danger. On the one side, if you accept the theory that the 14 day limit is absolute it becomes possible, for example in an extreme situation for that section to be made use of in an oppressive fashion either by the Government or by the Opposition. For example, in this case, the plaintiffs are still talking. Some of them have talked for more than 14 days through their lawyers. Still the defence has not been able to say one word before the Constitutional Court through his lawyer. The defence has not yet had a chance to open its mouth. My point of view is still not known ; the representative whom I sent to the Constitutional Court for the first 14 days has had no occasion to open his mouth and make even a little noise. Of course, he has the right to be heard, but he cannot be heard as of right until the Plaintiffs finish their case. So, the plaintiffs are still talking. They have been talking for more than 14 days.

The defence to this date, as a matter of fact has not uttered one little noise. I think it is factually true. The 14 days are over.

Now, take the other case. Supposing the plaintiffs finished within the first day. It will be a horrible thing for the defence through his lawyer to decide to filibuster for 13 days to avoid a decision. That is just as bad. Let us imagine a case : it has not happened here. Supposing the plaintiffs finished saying whatever they had to say in the shortest possible time, the Constitution surely did not intend that the Government—not in this instance ; in some other instance—finding itself embarrassed by the objection taken before the Constitutional Court is able to say to itself, " Let us block the decision by keeping the discussion going for more than 14 days " ? Such a situation I hope will not arise. It certainly is not the intention of the Constitution that the judgement shall be given in 14 days and Government must conform to that judgement, whatever the Government is. We may be the Government today, you may be the Government tomorrow. It does not matter. What is important is that the Constitution is an abiding document of permanent value to this country and we must not make the Constitution unworkable.

Take the opposite extreme. Supposing you start with the assumption that the Court can determine its own time limits and sit for ever notwithstanding the 14 day rule in Section 65, you come equally to an absurd situation. You come to the situation at the other end where you will say to yourself, " The Court can go on sitting and completely disturb the legislative programme of the Government and hold it up for ever and ever, under cover of keeping the matter under discussion ".—[Interruption]Now it will be forse than a partition case. Under the old Constitution the Senate could hold up a Bill for a maximum period of two sessions, and even then not a Money Bill. If this interpretation of the

Constitutional Court become accepted then you will find that we have created a monster, a monster which will be able for three to four years to hold up progress of legislation of a Government or for as long as it likes including Money Bills and Financial Legislation. Please remember that a Government under this Constitution may very well have to function with a hostile Constitutional Court. The Constitutional Court is appointed for a period of four years ; a National State Assembly exists for a period of five years. Supposing a Constitutional Court is appointed by a Government at the end of its term of office, the new Government which is elected, which may well be a different Government, may find itself stuck with a Constitutional Court already in existence which is going to continue for the balance period of four years. In such a situation all that happens is this. If 500 people were to file the identical petition as citizens of this country against any harmless Bill which that Government introduces—let us assume that it is a harmless Bill and let us suppose that each of those 500 petitioners retains a lawyer of his own chioce ; let us suppose the Constitutional Court decides to hear them for three days each. They will have 1500 sitting days with a five-day week. Assuming they are working at that pace everyday—

ජෝජ් රාජපක්ෂ මහතා (ධීවර ඇමති)

(திரு. ஜோர்ஜ் ராஜபக்ஷ—கடற்றொழில் அமைச்சர்)

(Mr. George Rajapaksa—Minister of Fisheries)

And assuming they do not get mumps !

ෆිලික්ස් ආර්. ඩී. බණ්ඩාරනායක මහතා

(திரு. பீலிக்ஸ் ஆர். டி. பண்டாரநாயக்க)

(Mr. Felix R. D. Bandaranaike)

And assuming they do not get mumps, you will find that for 300 weeks that same Bill can be held up, beyond the life of the Natinoal State Assembly, beyond the life of the Constitutional Court itself. I am not saying that is what was intended. I am taking the absurdities of the two extreme positions.

If you want the Constitutional Court to work, I think there is only one way, and that is the practical way. One has to establish practical, healthy conventions to deal with these situations. It is not a confrontation between the Constitutional Court and the National State Assembly. The Court is there to make our tasks easier for us and to give us an independent and impartial judgment upon the constitutionality or otherwise of any particular provision in a Bill. That is what it is there for : to test repugnancy and to give judgment. And both sides, the plaintiffs and the defendants, wanted that judgment. There is no question about it.

I as the sponsor of that Bill, as the defendant, at no stage have asked this Assembly, or shown the slightest anxiety, to take that Bill out of turn or to hurry up the progress of that Bill. I was quite prepared to await a decision legally within the framework of the limits of the Constitution for the enactment of that legislation. Nowhere have I expressed any hurry about it or anxiety to finish that particular piece of legislation in a hurry. I myself, just as much as you want a law which is effective, which is valid and which is constitutional, am not seeking to give validity to laws of an unconstitutional character. We as a Government are just as interested in it.

In fact, at the stage when some objections were taken to the original form of the Bill I took it under my personal charge—I could be right or I could be wrong—and I have endeavoured to make that Bill conform rigidly not merely to the provisions of the Constitution but to the needs of policy and to ensure that that Bill contains the necessary safeguards to make the Bill worthwhile. But let us not debate the Bill. Let us not worry about that. Let us

[ෆිලික්ස් ආර්. ඩී. බණ්ඩාරනායක මහතා]
examine the question as to what
follows from the discussion in regard
to interpretation.

I have pointed out to you, Mr.
Speaker, and to the Members of the
National State Assembly the dangers
that are inherent in adopting fixed
interpretations at extreme positions.
I should therefore like the House to
know the steps that I have taken, the
actions that I have done, so that you
will be in a position to judge for yourselves whether the activities and
actions of Government are right or
not.

Within the period of 14 days I
became aware that there was a grave
danger of an extreme interpretation
being, in fact, adopted. On the very
first day that the Constitutional Court
sat—on the 21st November—it was
brought to my notice that statements
had been made, mainly through the
newspapers. I became aware of the
things that were said in the Constitutional Court which caused a certain
amount of disquiet and worry in my
own mind. The Chairman, Mr. T. S.
Fernando, on the very first day said,
" We are expected to give our decision within 14 days. It would not
be possible for us to comply with that
provision until we have made up our
minds on the matter." On the same
day he said, "The fortnight's time
limit does not deter me. If it is
necessary I will sit for four years. I
am prepared to sit any length of
time, if necessary."

කථානායකතුමා
(சபாநாயகர் அவர்கள்)
(Mr. Speaker)

Are those the observations of the
Chairman of the Court ?

ෆිලික්ස් ආර්. ඩී. බණ්ඩාරනායක මහතා
(திரு. பிலிக்ஸ் ஆர். டி. பண்டாரநாயக்க)
(Mr. Felix R. D. Bandaranaike)

Yes. On the 23rd, in the course of
the discussion, when this matter was
taken up, the Leader of the Opposition was represented by his lawyer,

an eminent and distinguished Queen's
Counsel of our country, who also
happens to be his brother, and an
expert in injunction matters
mainly.

Learned Counsel for the hon.
Leader of the Opposition argued
strenuously that the fourteen day
limit was imperative, that the Court
must finish its work within fourteen
days, and he said, " Look, I completely
disagree with this interpretation.
The only man who is going to suffer
if you do not give your judgment
within fourteen days, is my client,
my brother. He may be restrained by
a permanent injunction of the
Speaker if that were to happen.
Therefore, in the circumstances,
please give your judgment within the
fourteen day period." And I must
say, in fairness to Mr. Jayewardene,
at every stage he has consistently
maintained the position that the duty
of the Court is to give a quick
judgment, a judgment within fourteen days. And he has said, " I am
not interested or concerned with how
long it takes or how long you want to
think about it or the leisurely pace at
which you are prepared to go on. I
want a judgment and I want a valid
judgment, and I want the judgment
within fourteen days."

The question came up on the 23rd
of last month in regard to another
plaintiff, another petitioner, represented by Mr. Nadesan, who I believe
appeared on behalf of the Civil
Rights Movement people. Now, on
the 23rd of November—I should like
to quote from the proceedings—this
is what happened in the Constitutional Court. Mr. Nadesan, Queen's
Counsel, said, "Respectfully, the
question of the Court entertaining a
doubt in respect of any provision is
confined to Section 55 of the Constitution, that is, in the case of urgent
Bills where the Court has to communicate its advice within twenty-four
hours," to which Mr. T. S. Fernando,
the Chairman, has said : " I have
really not been bothered by this
twenty-four hour clause. This Court

1353   1972 දෙසැම්බර් 12   1354

has to consider the matters that come up for decision before it. We are the interpreters of these facts. I think they are directive provisions but that does not mean we are going to flout those provisions in advance and that we will sit and hear arguments till doomsday." Mr. Jayewardene said: "Speaking for my client, I will endeavour to finish in the shortest possible time." The Chairman, Mr. T. S. Fernando, has then said, "I do not want you to rush through this because the issue is very important. I think this kind of issue should have come up before the full Court." Mr. S. Nadesan said: "My client's anxiety is that this Bill might become law if the decision of the Court is not communicated in time." The Chairman said: "It cannot become law until we have communicated our decision."

In other words, the Chairman here indicates quite clearly his interpretation of the matter. His view seems to be, "Look, I do not care what the Constitution says about fourteen days. It is our duty to think about it and to give our full deliberations to this whole matter. I am determined to hear the full arguments. I am not concerned whether we finish within fourteen days or not. I say the Bill cannot become law until we give our judgment. Therefore we can take our time about it—I am not concerned." "Doomsday" was the word used here. "I am prepared to stay any length of time necessary. I will sit if necessary for four years." Now, this was the view expressed by the Chairman.

In the "Sun" newspaper of the 27th of November, he is reported to have said, "We are all in the same boat."

කථානායකතුමා
(சபாநாயகர் அவர்கள்)
(Mr. Speaker)
Who says, "We are all in the same boat"?

ෆිලික්ස් ආර්. ඩී. බණ්ඩාරනායක මහතා
(திரு. பிலிக்ஸ் ஆர். டி. பண்டாரநாயக்க)
(Mr. Felix R. D. Bandaranaiyake)
Mr. T. S. Fernando says, "We are all in the same boat." I shall read what he says: "I may mention that I was one of those who spoke against the concept of a Constitutional Court to examine Bills. I have however been made the Chairman of the Court. The bad boy has been made the monitor of the class."

Well, my point is, Mr. Speaker, if this interpretation is upheld, I foresee and realize the danger that the National State Assembly would be confronted with by precisely this same situation.

On the thirteenth day, in consultation with you and the Minister of Constitutional Affairs, I thought I would express this point of view to the Chairman of the Court and tell him what I thought was perhaps a more reasonable interpretation, and to commend it to him for his consideration. I quite realize that sometimes there may be circumstances in which the Court cannot finish its work in fourteen day's time. With the best will in the world, without adjourning for the Appeal Court to sit, or without adjourning for other tribunals to sit, even sitting non-stop for 24 hours a day, there may be circumstances in which a court might find it difficult to finish it in 24 hours' time. I, therefore, communicated with the members of the Court and suggested to them that, perhaps, as they were not able to finish their work in 14 days, they might on the 14th day communicate with you, Mr. Speaker, inform the National State Assembly that they have not been able to finish their work and ask you to make suitable arrangements for them to be able to continue their work beyond the 14-days limit. I suggested that in that event you, perhaps, would put the matter to the National State Assembly and I would be prepared to move a resolution, seconded by my good Friend,

[පිලික්ස් ආර්. ඩී. බණ්ඩාරනායක මහතා]
the plaintiff, the hon. Leader of
the Opposition, and by joint consent,
with the consent of this whole
Assembly, the ultimate residuary
and authority of power under
Section 5, the National State Assembly could extend the time limit at the
request of the Court.

That was the proposal that I made
to the members of the Constitutional
Court. I made it, in fact, on the 13th
day ; it was last Tuesday. I tried to
get in touch with the three members
and to tell them that that perhaps
was the solution, a practical way
out of it ; the authority of the
National State Assembly if safeguarded, and we can establish a
healthy convention. The Government will not use its power to
prevent the Constitutional Court
from sitting, but the Government
will co-operate to make the work of
the Constitutional Court practical
and possible.

I also discussed this matter with
my Friends, the hon. Leader of the
Opposition. He too thought it was a
reasonable way of approach and he
said he would try to speak to the
Chairman who was his old class-mate
in school. I asked Mr. Dudley Senanayake whether he would co-operate
with me in trying to get the
Chairman of the Court to this point
of view. Mr. Dudley Senanayake
said : "You say that you are the
defendant and J. R. is the plaintiff ;
I say I am the accused on a contempt
charge." Well, I spoke to the members of the Court. Mr. Justice
T. S. Fernando was not at home
when I rang him up. He had gone
for some social engagement. But I
did manage to speak to Mr. Deheragoda and Mr. Joseph Cooray and I
asked them to please communicate
also with Mr. T. S. Fernando and to
let me know. The Cabinet was
meeting on Wednesday, the morning
of the 14th day and I, therefore,
requested that I should like to be
informed what the position was.

I realized that they had not finished
their works. One reason why they had
not finishesd their work was they
adjourned for a whole long week
within these 14 days to proceed with
other cases in the Court of Appeal and
other places. I myself should have
thought that with this provision of 14
days this must get precedence over
everything else. I must express my
gratitude to His Lordship the Chief
Justice for specifically informing me
that he would postpone the C. J. C.
for the whole period of 14 days if
necessary to enable Mr. Justice
Deheragoda to function as a member
of the Constitutional Court, having
regard to the importance of making
the Constitution work.

On the morning of Wednesday I
received a telephone call from Mr.
Justice Deheragoda telling me that
the Judges were not agreed in regard
to my proposal that they should ask
for an extension of time from the
National State Assembly and that I
would guarantee to get it with the
consent and co operation of all hon.
Members of this House and to get it
sponsored with t he plaintiff and the
defendant both asking for the court
to continue beyond the 14 day limit
with the leave of the National State
Assembly.

I was then informed by Mr. Justice
Deheragoda of a matter which I
regretted very much. He informed me
that Mr. T. S. Fernando, if he was
writing a letter, insisted on saying
that he was writing it at the request
of the Minister of Justice. I indicated
at that stage that it was wholly
unsatisfactory. While I was certainly
prepared to take the responsibility of
informing the House and its Members
that I had certainly spoken to the
judges on a matter like this to make
the Constitutional Court work, I did
not want the court to think on a
statement like that, later when a
judgment of the Constitutional Court
comes the judges will equally well
create the impression : " My God, this
demned judgment was written at the
dicatation of the Justice Minister."
This is not what we want. We want

a fair judgment. We want the Constitution to work. But I considered that it was nothing more than an attempt to fix the Minister of Justice, to try to bring him into this operation when all he had tried to do was to make the Constitution work and to be helpful.

That same morning you received a letter, Mr. Speaker, which you are aware of, and the House must know it, where the Registrar of the Court Mr. Sam Wijesinha, behaved a bit like a ventriloquist; he spoke to himself : In his capacity as the Registrar of the Constitutional Court, he spoke to Mr. Sam Wijesinha, Clerk of the National State Assembly. And he communicated to Mr. Sam Wijesinha, Clerk of the National State Assembly, the view of the majority of two members of that court, that they were informing you, without reference to days or references made by you, that they were not in a position to finish their work within 14 days and that they propose to carry on and finish as soon as possible.

කථානායකතුමා
(சபாநாயகர் அவர்கள்)
(Mr. Speaker)

I think it said : "We are continuing". I have sent for the letter.

ෆීලික්ස් ආර්. ඩී. බණ්ඩාරනායක මහතා
(திரு. பிலிக்ஸ் ஆர். டி. பண்டாரநாயக்க)
(Mr. Felix R. D. Bandaranaike)

There was a notification in that Mr. Sam Wijesinha informed himself for the purpose of informing you—[Interruption]. May I have that letter ? I like to read the terms of that. I think the House must know the facts. Let us not get any wrong ideas about it. I am sorry if I take up time. I think you have a right to know the efforts the Government has been making to make the Constitution work. Says Mr. Sam Wijesingha, Registrar of the Constitutional Court of Sri Lanka, addressed to himself :

"I am directed by the majority of the Constitutional Court of Sri Lanka to inform you that the proceedings in respect of the above questions which have been referred to the Constitutional Court are still continuing and that a decision would be given as soon as possible."

It is merely a piece of information. There is no request—[Interruption]. —"majority of the court"—not the court by a majority. A majority of the court, that is two members of the court, had told Mr. Sam Wijesinha something which he has told himself and then told you, that a decision would be given as soon as possible. "As soon as possible" may mean, if necessary, sitting for four years or till doomsday.

In this situation, I should like to say that this is only the view of two members of the court ; it is not even the view of the third member, whoever he may be—I am not getting involved in that now. But that is the fact as it stood on Wednesday morning. The Cabinet met on Wednesday and decided that we have no alternative but to uphold the Constitution, and we decided to uphold the Constitution, quite independent of other persons elsewhere.

කථානායකතුමා
(சபாநாயகர் அவர்கள்)
(Mr. Speaker)

Was it not after you failed in your attempts ?

ෆීලික්ස් ආර්. ඩී. බණ්ඩාරනායක මහතා
(திரு. பிலிக்ஸ் ஆர். டி. பண்டாரநாயக்க)
(Mr. Felix R. D. Bandaranaike)

After this letter came and I failed in my attempts. I was trying hard to persuade the court in some way to making a request. I said, "No use of being abject, no use of using words, no use of using anything. Merely request the Speaker to enable you to continue your sitting." That is all. And I said I would take the responsibility, in co-operation with the hon. Leader of the Opposition, to get that done and get a unanimous agreement from the Assembly.

1359   ජාතික රාජ්‍ය සභාව   1360

[ෆීලික්ස් ආර්. ඩී. බණ්ඩාරනායක මහතා]

We failed, and the Cabinet decided that we must uphold the Constitution. And I think you decided on the following day to make a statement that as you have not received the opinion of the Constitutional Court with its reasons within the 14-day limit, you were directing that the Bill should be proceeded with in accordance with the Standing Orders and Chapter 9 of the Constitution. You were, of course, using the particular words of the Constitution itself, I think, Section 46.

It is quite clear to me that your ruling was on the basis of the same interpretation that I am adopting, that if a request had been made to you within 14 days you would have put it to the House and with the consent of the Assembly an extension might have been possible. But no such request having been made to you, and the 14 days having elapsed, you were not prepared to accept the position, as I understood it, of any person, by his own act, seeking to extent the time limit imposed by the Constitution. I think the position we are taking is not that the 14 days is writ loud and clear like the laws of the Medes and Persians in such a way that it cannot be changed. I think the position you were taking, if we are to make the Constitution work, was that the National State Assembly as the ultimate residum of state power is surely entitled to grant that extension. The question is, Who has that power? Have they the power to arrogate to themselves the right to sit for four years at their will and pleasure or must they subordinate themselves to this Assembly? If it is a question of saying that the Government will use its majority in an oppressive fashion, I can assure you that the Government wants to establish healthy traditions, and I think it has been always clear that in a matter like this we are ready and willing to co-operate between plaintiff and defendant, to subordinate ourselves to the judgment of a court. I think every hon. Member will agree

with this, that this Government has certainly not in any way tried to use its power to prevent the Court from coming to a conclusion. If every one has prevented the Court, the Court has prevented itself.

I would like to tell you this. I think it was last Saturday we made one final effort. Mr. Speaker, your ruling had already we made one final effort. Mr. Speaker, your ruling had already been given on Thursday, but I thought we should not leave it at that, and you and I and the Attorney-General and the Secretary to the Ministry of Justice met at my house at 7 o'clock in the evening of Saturday to review the situation and to try to work out some formula to prevent a situation of deadlock and to find out ways and means even at that point of time to save this country, to help us, out of the embarssment of finding our Constitution brought to naught by an arbitrary opinion expressed by the members of the Constitutional Court. On that occasion, after a discussion, we adjourned, and I think I made a proposal that we should invoke the President of the Republic of Sri Lanka as the ultimate authority to try and help to solve this matter, to try and find a solution which we have not been able to find ourselves and I express my gratitude to the President, His Excellency William Gopallawa, for the efforts he made in this regard. He sent for us all. I think it was 11 o'clock at night when we started our deliberations. He sent for all five members of the Constitutional Court, not merely the three gentlemen who are members of the present Court; he sent for me; he sent for the Minister of Constitutional Affairs; and Mr. Speaker, you were present; the Attorney-General was present, and the Secretary to the Ministry of Justice was present. You will remember what efforts we made to try and point out the situation that was arising, and I remember I expressed the point of view, even though it may not have been one hundred per cent correct in law, that the best solution to this was, even though it may be out of time and outside the fourteen days, if a request is made to the National State Assembly, we can get together and consider the matter of granting an extension of time in such a way as to make the Constitutional Court to continue. I am not even certain that after the fourteen days have elapsed it is within our competence and power to do that in the absence of a request made earlier. This was on Sunday, not on Saturday. We started at 11 o'clock on Sunday night. It was about 4.30 on Monday morning that we concluded our deliberations, but our deliberations concluded in a deadlock. The Chairman of the Court took up the categorical position at that discussion—and I must tell the Assembly that—that they had no difficulty whatsoever. " We are clear in our own minds about the interpretation of this section. We do not admit that anybody has the right to give an extension of time or that we are obliged to ask for time. "

In other words, it becomes simply the question now of what has to determine the manner in which the Constitutional Court shall work. If we once concede to the Constitutional Court the right to determine its own time limit, the right to sit for four years, according to the statement by the Chairman of the Constitutional Court, pleasure remember, every hon. Member of this Assembly, that what you are doing is establishing an institution higher than the National State Assembly and, quite apart from the merits or demerits of the Bill that is being discussed, creating an issue far bigger than that. The entire legislative programme of a Government can be brought to nought by this procedure. It is something which I do not think any single member of this Assembly, whatever political beliefs he holds can possibly accept.

So, this was the situation on Monday morning at 4.30 a.m. when we adjourned. I came to this assembly thereafter. I had no choise, I had to take a difficult decision, but I took it. I decided to withdraw the Attorney-General from the proceedings of the body of people who are now sitting on the third floor. In view of our ruling, in view of the efforts we have been making to get the Constitutional Court to fuction lawfully under the Constitution, I am not prepared to participate is a mock trial. You, Mr. Speaker, may extent courtesies to the Court to enable them to sit on the third floor. You have been so good as to extend these courtesies. I understand your position and I undrstand your reasons. I myself do not wish to be churlish-; I do not wish to be nasty to anybody ; I do not wish to speak in a manner derogatory to any authority ; but I must say this : the people of this country will not understand what you and we are doing.

කථානායකතුමා
(சபாநாயகர் அவர்கள்)
(Mr. Speaker)

I have extended the courtesy to the Constitutional Court set up under Section 54 (1) of the Constitution only.

fෆීලික්ස් ආර්. ඩි. බණ්ඩාරනායක මහතා
(திரு. ஃபிலிக்ஸ் ஆர். டி. பண்டாரநாயக்க)
(Mr. Felix R. D. Bandaranaike)

You, Mr. Speaker, extended that courtesy under Section 54 (1) of the Constitution, but the people who enjoy the benefits of that courtesy are people operating under Section 54 (2). I am well able to understand the logic and the correctness of what you are doing. We are not here to cause pin-pricks on each other. We do not need to be nasty to each other or shut the door in other's faces. We do not need to adopt standards of double conduct. I think we are all gentlemen is this Assembly—and a few ladies, of course !

In these circumstances I think the people of this country will understand the position. If three people sat under a coconut tree and decided to discuss the Constitution ; it is one thing, and the people of this country would know what value to attach to such deliberations ; but if on the other hand, with all the panoply of what was the Constitutional Court on Fri-

1363   ජාතික රාජ්‍ය සභාව   1364

[පිලික්ස් ආර්. ඩී. බණ්ඩාරනායක මහතා]
day, the same three people continue to sit, not as the Constitutional Court but as a mock trial on Monday, the people of this country will not see that distinction and will wonder why the Assembly is in fact stultifying itself.

I agree that the premises we have conceded to the Constitutional Court are not dependent upon the validity or otherwise of this particular tribunal. The Constitutiosal Court, as an institution under Section 54 (1) of the Constitution., has a right to sit there, but the people who are is fact sitting there are sitting under Section 54 (2) of the Constitution. That is the problem. And I think it is clear that one purpose of this discussion and debate must be to shaw the attitude of the Government of Sri Lanka in regard to this matter.

And I think you will appreciate that my withdrawal of the Attorney-General is those circumstances is not in any way an indication of my un-willingness to submit myself to a valid jurisdiction and to have a valid judgment which I expect confidently, as every defendant does, will be in our favour on the merits. Certainly I am not shirking my right and my duty to represent the point of view of the Government of Sri Lanka to a valid tribunal and a valid court. But if the court makes itself invalid by its own action, in spite of every effort that you Mr. Speaker, and I, the President of the Republic, the Minister of Constitutional Affairs, have been making in association with the plaintiff, the other members who are plaintiffs also, and even the accused under a charge of contmpt—if we are unable to do this, what can be done if the court is determined to destroy itself ? And the Court has in fact destroyed itself by its own action.

I am putting this argument forward because I think these are important facts that the House should know. I do not want you to get the impres-sion that here is a situation where the plaintiffs come and say, we have filed the case, we want a judgment. The

Government has done its best, I can assure you, to try and find ways and means. If you ask me whether the Constitution is defective, I would repeat, no, no, and no again. The Constitution is perfectly correct in every line and word of what it says. Merely because you choose to give the Constitution impossible meanings to satisfy the vanity of any one in-dividual who wants to set himself above the Constitution I regret that is not a possible way of testing the validity of the Constitution.

The Constitution does contain provision for, and it certainly con-templated, a judgment being given in 14 days time. You ask me, how can this be done ? I agree, if you decide to give each person a chance to speak for five to six days through his counsel without time limits, if you decide to sit for a few hours only for a day, if you decide to postpone the case every time you decide that you prefer a change of atmosphere in Hulftsdorf or sit in the Court of Appeal, then of course you will never be able to finish your work in 14 days' time. But let us look at the provi-sions of the Constitution itself. What does the Constitution say upon this matter ?

Section 63 lays down the proce-dure, and you will find that under section 63 nobody has the right of audience before the Constitutional Court except the Attorney General. The Attorney-General shall have the right to be heard on all matters before the Constitutional Court. Sub-sec-tion 2 says :

"The Constitutional Court may in its discretion grant to any person such hearing as may appear to the Court to be necessary before dealing with any question referred to it under subsection (2) of Section 540."

Nobody has the right to be heard. This is not something unusual. I may quote and examine situations that have arisen before the Federal Sup-reme Court of the United States of America whose constitutional law and constitutional procedure are well-known to people who are accustomed to these things. I do not know whether you are aware of it and whether hon. Members are aware of it. Every single person presenting his case has to present it in writing : every single argument, every authority. Thereafter they are given only 30 minutes for any individual counsel to appear before the Federal Supreme Court and to explain anything he wishes to explain in clarification of his written submissions to the nine judges of the Court. When this happens he moves up to a lectern where there is a thing like a traffic light with red, yellow and green lights to indicate the time limit. I remember the famous instance when the late Senator Robert Kennedy, then Attorney-General of the United States, of Amedica, had to stop in mind-sentence in the course of his submissions because he had reached the limit of 30 minutes allotted.

If you want to make a thing work, why cannot you make it work ? If you want to make the 14 days rule work, I know of no case which is so complicated in its effects that you cannot come to a conclusion with a time limit, if you decide the adopt suitable procedures and to make it work. The question is, do you want to make it work or do you want to bring it to a grinding halt and create the kind of situation of a confrontation with the National State Assembly, so that the Court can say : we have driven a wedge into the Constitution and created a condition under which the Constitution itself is brought into disrepute ; we have established one fatal blow against the sovereignty of the people through its National State Assembly ? This cannot be done. If you take that view, how are you going to interpret section 55 under which the Constitutional Court is told that the Constitutional Court shall convey its advice to the Speaker as expeditiously as possible, and in any case within 24 hours of the assembly of the court ?

If these gentlemen cannot function within 14 days, how are they going to function within 24 hours ? The Constitution wanted a judgment given by the Constitutional Court within 24 hours. The Constitution says it must be given wihin 24 hours.

The President of the Court told us when we were speaking before the President of Sri Lanka, His Excellency William Gopollawa, that he has assepted office upon the condition that he would not be bound by the 14-day rule. All I can say is, I discussed the matter with the Prime Minister and she is unaware of any condition being attached by any person to the acceptance of office. She is not aware of any condition. I believe the only conditions are contained in the Letters Patent or Appointment. I do not say that those have been varied in the case of any particular appointment or in the case of any particular individual, so far as I know. I do not know whether this is a border line between justice and constitutional affairs but certainly I must most strongly say that there are no conditions upon which any person can accept office under the Constitution except the conditions of the Constitution itself.

Those are the conditions. Those conditions are binding not only upon the Members of the Court, they bind every one of us. They even bind the Member for Uduvil (Mr. Dharmalingam) ! He must obey the Constitution himself even though he boycotted it once. It is now as much his Constitution as it is ours. I know that the Member for Uduvil will respect the Constitution even if the Member of the Constitutional Court find it difficult to do so.

In this situation where do we go from here ? I think the answer to that is something which will have to emerge in the course of this Debate. You and we will have to decide this. We are the National State Assembly. Why should we put in as a proposal or anything else if any of you have any ideas ? I take the view that there is no question of the Constitution

1367   ජාතික රාජ්‍ය සභාව   1368

[f8ලික්ස් ආර්. ඩී. බණ්ඩාරනායක මහතා]
requiring amendment. I think the
Constitution is as plain as a pikestaff.
I think the only convention we
require is the simple question of
making a decision by ourselves if any
situation of extreme types arises.
Where with all the best will in the
world they cannot finish their work
within 14 days it is up to us, as a
matter of convention, to grant them
a reasonable extension and never to
refuse. I do not think the question
of refusal arises. I do not think any
of us are taking that view.

Is there any express provision here
which states what happens if a
Member of the Constitutional Court
dies? There is no provision. You
cannot deal with matters by trying
to find express solutions for each and
every problem as and when it arises
and start amending the Constitution
to suit that purpose. That must never
be done. We must decide among ourselves and I think on this question
every one of us who wants a judgment will find a way. I think the
simple answer is, if the Constitutional Court is not prepared to respect
the wishes of this House there is no
alternative, the Constitutional Court
will have to go.

මන්ත්‍රීවරු
(உறுப்பினர்கள்)
(Members)
Here, here!

f8ලික්ස් ආර්. ඩී. බණ්ඩාරනායක මහතා
(திரு. பிலிக்ஸ் ஆர். டி. பண்டாரநாயக்க)
(Mr. Felix R. D. Bandaranaike)

If a confrontation is arising between
the Constitutional Court and the
Members of this Assembly, in which
we are united and as one, there can
be no other alternative. There is no
question of this House giving way, of
the National State Assembly accepting a verdict out of convenience. If
that happens I can assure you that
the determination and the desire on
the part of the plaintiffs and the
defendants to have the matters in
issue adjudicated upon in the manner

provided for in the Constitution, is
is still our wish just as much as it is
your wish. Nobody wants to force a
decision through leaving the matter
undecided, leaving the question at
issue in the air. Speaking for myself,
I think that is not the view of the
Government and I for one, as the
person responsible for this Sri Lanka
Press Council Bill, can tell you that
I shall not shift an inch in surren-
dering our rights under the Constitution ; nor am I prepared to participate
in a mock trial or to act under any
authority in derogation of the Constitution. Speaking for myself, I shall
certainly respect the wishes of the
House and of any Member of this
House who has raised a challenge to
that Bill by respecting your wishes
to the extent that, until you find a way
to get the adjudication made lawfully and in terms of the Constitution,
I shall not be proceeding with the Bill.
I will give you that assurance.
I have never expressed an anxiety,
but let us get the thing done;
let us do it fast and let us do it
properly. For this purpose I want
the co-operation of every one of you
in this House. I want you to support
us on the principles of what we are
saying. I want you to have an understanding of the efforts that are
being made on your behalf to protect
the interests of this House. I do say
that I cannot agree with the kind of
dialougue that is now going on in
regard to this.

There are two more matters I
should like to mention before I conclude. The first is this. The Constitutional Court, you will observe, is
under a duty to formulate rules of
court and rules of procedure and
practice for itself. So far as I know,
under the Constitution those rules
have to be brought as expeditiously
as possible before the National State
Assembly and we have the right
to approve or disapprove them. To
this day, as far as I am aware, no
rules have come ; no rules have been
gazetted. I am only citing what is
provided in the Constitution. We are
being told pontifically from above

how it should be interpreted. But I do not know up to this day how a court is functioning without having set for itself the rules of procedure that it is required to formulate under the very Constitution under which it claims to function. That has not been done. I have looked up the Gazettes and I have not seen these rules. This House has not had the opportunity to discuss these rules of practice and procedure. What is the practice and procedure, for example, in regard to the 14-day rule? We know that the rules of practice and procedure cannot go against the express terms of the Constitution.

What we have here is a court conducting a dialouge. The newspaper reports are there. Political views are expressed. Legal views and all kinds of other views are expressed. It is quite a different situation that I should have expected. If you have got to do this work within 14 days, give the various persons a time limit of a few days to make their submissions in writing and take time to study them. If you have any questions to ask, send for the people concerned. It is a tragedy when lawyers go on talking for hours and hours. My good Friend, the Member for Galle (Dr. W. Dahanayake), who speaks for hours and hours in this Assembly, I am told, did not survive more than a few minutes before the Constitutional Court.

අවාර්ය ඩබ්ලිව්. දහනායක
(கலாநிதி டபிள்யு. தஹநாயக்க)
(Dr. W. Dahanayake)
I spoke for half an hour.

fපිලික්ස් ආර්. ඩි. බණ්ඩාරනායක මහතා
(திரு. பிலிக்ஸ் ஆர். டி. பண்டாரநாயக்க)
(Mr. Felix R. D. Bandaranaike)
I am sorry. It must have been that the hon. Member for Galle decided to be far more brief and to the point than he is in this Chamber. But the important point is that he kept to the spirit of the Constitution. He realized that the court had to give

its verdict within 14 days and he was determined, therefore, not to go beyond the time limit. I am quite sure of it.

අවාර්ය ඩබ්ලිව්. දහනායක
(கலாநிதி டபிள்யு. தஹநாயக்க)
(Dr. W. Dahanayake)
Otherwise, you would have put the blame on me.

fපිලික්ස් ආර්. ඩි. බණ්ඩාරනායක මහතා
(திரு. பிலிக்ஸ் ஆர். டி. பண்டாரநாயக்க)
(Mr. Felix R. D. Bandaranaike)
I will never put the blame on my good Friend from Galle even where he is to blame on any matter. We always forgive him and we always accept him as an institution in this House.

The same is true of my good Friend the hon. Member for Habaraduwa (Mr. Prins Gunasekera). He too kept within every short limits.

My point is this. Yesterday for the first time we were told that written submissions had again become relevant. Why? Yesterday, subsequent to your declaration, subsequent to the meeting at the President's House what happend? I should like to read to you a few sentences which apparently were uttered from the Bench in the mock trial proceedings that are now going on. This is what was said: "Let us state what we think is the present position. It is the duty of us all, whether we be judges or not, to uphold the Constitution. To uphold the Constitution we as judges must first understand the meaning of the relevant provisions of the Constitution." Very important. "We must understand the meaning of the relevant provisions of the Constitution." I agree. We must make rules, which we have not yet made. We must gazette them. Then we must establish our own practice and procedure. We must not go against any express provision of the Constitution. That is what is meant by, "We must understand the relevant provisions of the Constitution."

[පිලික්ස් ආර්. ඩි. බණ්ඩාරනායක මහතා]

The Chairman goes on :

"For that understanding we have to rely on our own judgment, assisted, if need be, by the opinions of learned counsel. "

They relied on their own judgment on the very first day. That was when the Chairman said : we have the right to continue for four years—until dooms-day. What I object to is this : he states, " .... we have to rely on our own judgment, assisted, if need be, by the opinions of learned counsel. " How many of the learned counsel who appeared in that Court were even consulted on the meaning of the fourteen-day rule ? The Attorney-General has not been heard to this date in regard to the significance of the fourteen-day rule. I would like to ask whether the hon. Member for Habaraduwa (Mr. Prins Gunasekera) was consulted on this matter.

ප්‍රින්ස් ගුණසේකර මහතා (හබරාදූව)

(திரு. பிரின்ஸ் குணசேகர—ஹபராதுவ)

(Mr. Prins Gunasekera—Habaraduwa)

Yes ; but my opinion was rejected.

පිලික්ස් ආර්. ඩි. බණ්ඩාරනායක මහතා

(திரு. பிலிக்ஸ் ஆர். டி. பண்டாரநாயக்க)

(Mr. Felix R. D. Bandaranaike)

Was the hon. Member for Galle heard in regard to this matter ?

ආචාර්ය ඩබ්ලිව්. දහනායක

(கலாநிதி டப்ளியு. தஹநாயக்க)

(Dr. W. Dahanayake)

No. Not on the fourteen-day rule.

පිලික්ස් ආර්. ඩි. බණ්ඩාරනායක මහතා

(திரு. பிலிக்ஸ் ஆர். டி. பண்டாரநாயக்க)

(Mr. Felix R. D. Bandaranaike)

Not on the fourteen-day rule. I believe that Mr. H. W. Jayawardene was consulted. He has maintained that the rule was absolutely manda-tory. He has upheld the right of this House, acting no doubt on the ins-tructions of the Leader of the Oppo-sition. The Attorney-General, my counsel.—no one even bothered about him. Nobody worries about the opi-nion of the client here. Nobody asked me, nobody sought my advice, nobody sought the advice of the counsel re-presenting the State, the Attorney-General, the one person who has got the right of audience.

ඉරත්තිනම් මහතා

(திரு. இரத்தினம்)

(Mr. Ratnam)

He was in the immediate presence of the court.

පිලික්ස් ආර්. ඩි. බණ්ඩාරනායක මහතා

(திரு. பிலிக்ஸ் ஆர். டி. பண்டாரநாயக்க)

(Mr. Felix R. D. Bandaranaike)

Does that mean that you are seek-ing the advice of counsel ? The only two counsel who spoke on this matter were Mr. H. W. Jayawardene and Mr. Nadesan, both of whom said that the provision was mandatory. When Mr. Nadesan tried to argue that it was absolutely mandatory and must be followed, the Judge said it was not. He disagreed and gave his opinion that it was directory. Mr. Nadesan, like the good advocate he is, went home, thought over the position, came back on the following day and said, " I agree that your view is correct. " I have no doubt that he learned that from Dr. Colvin R. de Silva in his day.

ආචාර්ය ඩබ්ලිව්. දහනායක

(கலாநிதி டப்ளியு. தஹநாயக்க)

(Dr. W. Dahanayake)

Why could not the Attorney-Gene-ral exercise the right given to him under Section 63 (1) of the Constitu-tion ? Why did he not take the oppor-tunity and speak ?

පිලික්ස් ආර්. ඩි. බණ්ඩාරනායක මහතා

(திரு. பிலிக்ஸ் ஆர். டி. பண்டாரநாயக்க)

(Mr. Felix R. D. Bandaranaike)

I will tell you why. You will see that the Court determined the order. The last sentence of the statement yesterday states, " We will therefore hear you, the other counsel and the

Attorney-General, in that order."
The Attorney-General is to be heard last. He has a right to be heard but apparently the order of speaking is that. That right does not mean that you can jump into the middle of somebody's argument and interrupt the proceedings. The meaning of saying that the Attorney-General has the right to be heard, the right of audience, is that he has that right subject to the order that has been made.

කේ. ජෙයකොඩි මහතා (උඩුප්'පිඩ්ඩි)
(திரு. கே. ஜெயக்கொடி—உடுப்பிட்டி)
(Mr. K. Jeyakkody—Udupiddy)
When the Chairman of the Court made this ruling about having the right to go on for four years even, the Attorney-General was silent. When both points of view were expressed he was silent.

fපිලික්ස් ආර්. ඩි. බණ්ඩාරනායක මහතා
(திரு. பிலிக்ஸ் ஆர். டி. பண்டாரநாயக்க)
(Mr. Felix R. D. Bandaranaike)
Do you expect the Attorney-General to start an argument in regard to theoretical questions and make the Court a debating society on the first day of the case? The period of fourteen days was not even reached. If it is a preliminary matter the Court can say, "We want your assistance", but the court makes the point here in this observation by saying, "We are not even asking for the advice of counsel. We make up our own minds. We ask counsel if the need be there." So, the court has made up its mind for itself.

Now, is this what we want of a Constitutional Court? Are we prepared to accept a subordination of the position of the National State Assembly?

මන්තීවරු
(உறுப்பினர்கள்)
(Members)
No no!

fපිලික්ස් ආර්. ඩි. බණ්ඩාරනායක මහතා
(திரு. பிலிக்ஸ் ஆர். டி. பண்டாரநாயக்க)
(Mr. Felix R. D. Bandaranaike)
That is the question.

ගරු කථානායකතුමනි, මා මුලින් බලා පොරොත්තු වුණේ සිංහලෙන් සහ ඉංග්‍රීසියෙන් දෙකෙන්ම කථා කරන්නටයි. දැන් මා පැය 1½ක් පමණ කථා කලා. මා ඒ කිව්ව කරුණු නැවත වරක් සිංහලෙන් කියන්නට යාමෙන් සිදු වෙන්නේ කාලය ගත වීම පමණයි. මගේ අදහස් පැහැදිලි ලෙස ගරු සභාවට වැටහෙන්න ඇති. එම නිසා රාජ්‍ය වෙනුවෙන් ජාතික රාජ්‍ය සභාවේ ආරක්ෂාව පිණිස අපේ අදහස් ඉදිරිපත් කරන්නට මට මේ අවස්ථාව ලබා දීම ගැන තමුන්නාන්සේට මගේ කෘතඥතාවය දක්වමින් මගේ කථාව අවසාන කරනවා.

පූ. භා. 11.30

ජේ. ආර්. ජයවර්ධන මහතා (දකුණු කොළඹ පළමුවන)
(திரு. ஜே. ஆர். ஜயவர்தன—கொழும்பு தென்கு முதலாம் அங்கத்தவர்)
(Mr. J. R. Jayewardene—First Colombo South)
ගරු කථානායකතුමනි, මේ විවාදයට මා ඉදිරිපත් වෙන්නේ දකුණු කොළඹ පළමුවන මන්ත්‍රී වශයෙන්, මහජන නියෝජිත යෙකු හැටියටත්, විරුද්ධ පර්ශවයේ නායක හැටියටත්, එක්සත් ජාතික පක්ෂයේ පාර්ලිමේන්තු කණ්ඩායමේ සභාපති හැටියටත් බව මතක් කරන්නට කැමතියි. මේ තුන් ස්වරූපයෙන්ම අදහස් ස්වල්ප යක් ප්‍රකශ කරන්නට මා බලාපොරොත්තු වෙනවා. එක්සත් ජාතික පක්ෂයේ පාර්ලිමේන්තු කණ්ඩායමේ සභාපති හැටියට නොවැම්බර් 14 වෙනිදා මම තමුන්නාන්සේට ඉදිරිපත් කළ, ආණ්ඩු ක්‍රම වයවස්ථාවේ 54 (2) (අ) වගන්තිය යටතේ ලිඛිත නිවේදනයක්, ආණ්ඩු ක්‍රම වයවස්ථා අධිකරණය වෙත යවන්න කියා. මම තමුන්නාන්සේත් මේ සභාවටත් ඉදිරිපත් කරන්නේ ඒ අධිකරණය ඉදිරියේ පැමිණිල්ලක් දමා තිබෙන පුද්ගල යෙකු හැටියට වැදගත් දුක්ගැනවිල්ලක්. මා පමණක්නොව මේ සභාවේ තවත් මන්ත්‍රීන් දෙදෙනෙත් පැමිණිලි දෙකක් ඉදිරිපත් කර තිබෙනවා. මහජනයාත් පැමි

Felix on Plantations

In most countries in the world plantation agriculture is considered perhaps the weakest and rottenest form of agriculture productivity-wise It is good in areas where you have a shortage of labour. Plantation simply means a tree planted in a systematic fashion from which you take the fruit, where you do not harvest the entire plant but you harvest merely the fruit of the plant, and the plant continues to survive and to yield its fruit year by year, season by season.

We are running a plantation economy—let it be tea, rubber or coconut. The basic plantations here are not labour intensive, relatively speaking, nor are they as good in providing returns as the non-plantation type of agriculture with rotation cropping where you harvest the entire plant whatever that plant may be.

Perhaps, to prove what I am saying it is best to take another island race. Take the English. There is hardly a single plantation worthy of the name within the British Isles today. Agriculture is not even a profitable user of land in England any more, within the British Isles. Industry has taken over and made inroads into land user and land requirements. Today you do not have a plantation economy at all.

The proof of what I am saying was demonstrated by the Hon. Dudley Senanayake during his Government from 1965 to 1970 when he argued that cultivating an acre of potatoes or vegetables is ten times more profitable than cultivating an acre of tea. He will not dispute it. It is true. Is it not true that on an acre of paddy field the return is far greater than on a corresponding plantation ? It is true whether it is vegetables, it is true whether it is potatoes, it is true whether it is chillie. We are proving it today, every day. In every area where chillies are under systematic cultivation you will find the truth of what I am saying. You will find the truth of what I am saying. In Jaffna—

ගරු මන් ත්‍රිවරයෙක්
(கௌரவ அங்கத்தவர் ஒருவர்)
(An hon. Member)

Six thousand.

ෆීලික්ස් ආර්. ඩි. බණ්ඩාරනායක මහතා
(திரு. பீலிக்ஸ் ஆர். டி. பண்டாரநாயக்க)
(Mr. Felix R. D. Bandaranaike)

Why not, and sometimes more ? I would like to see it become more. We have no quarrel with that. But the basic argument is intensive agriculture as against extensive plantation agriculture. That is what is needed where you have got a limited quantity of land and a hungry population determined to survive and determined to develop.

Now, what are the arguments brought forward ? " Why are you wrecking our planations ? Why are you spoiling the best plantation lands available in this country ? " Of course, people like my good Friend the hon. Leader of the Opposition will argue anything. What he really wants to say is, " Do not destroy the plantations. Please preserve the wealth of this country. Let them continue to earn the foreign exchange." He does not say so, but says, " Well, why are you cutting it down to fifty acres ? Why do you not cut it down to ten ?" That is the argument he used here. But the real idea at the back of his mind is, " For God's sake, do not wreck the whole thing. Leave it in case the U. N. P. comes to power for us to carry on from there." That is really the argument he is putting forward, in spite of his anxiety to say that he would have liked to have introduced land reform years ago.

The truth of the matter is that this is the first positive attempt made by a Minister of Agriculture and Lands in this country to set about introducing a systematic transformation of an extensive agriculture into an intensive pattern.

For this purpose it is perfectly true that a plantation—any plantation you like, let it be tea, rubber or coconut— during its best period, did not yield profits in relation to the capital

[පුජිත් ස. එ. බණ්ඩාරනායක මහතා]
value. Take the U.N.P. period of 1935
to 1970. if you like. It was the same.
In every estate, including the best-
managed ones—take Palugaswewa of
Baurs for coconuts, or Staratheden of
the Ceylon Tea Plantation Company,
if you like, for tea, or any other cam-
pany—you will see that the returns
they were showing varied between
five and seven-and-a-half per cent
per year. That was the return on
capital invested, according to their
own valuations during their own
Government. But by means of intensive agriculture, according to the
very statistics they have provided in
the days of the Green Revolution and
the Food Drive, they have demonstrated that it is possible to get returns
of 25 to 30 per cent per year.

I do not claim to know very much
about agriculture myself. I learnt
only after I became Minister in 1963,
and I survived only for two years
but during those two years I ventured to learn a little bit about animal
husbandry.

I will tell you from my own knowledge and practical experience. From
a land of ninety acres in Veyangoda
I have been receiving over the years,
depending on prices naturally, varying returns, and I find no embarrassment in talking about it since my
assets are well known and my income
is declared to the Tax Department.
That makes no difference. Most of
my income is professional anyway,
and not from land. The return I get
per month is between Rs. 1,200 at the
least and Rs. 2,000 at the highest, an
average of Rs. 1,700 on the whole
from a land of, say, a hundred acres
for convenience of argument. In 1966
when I was relatively free of the
duties of State and attended Parliament now and then and made a few
speeches in those days, I started a
poultry farm and a dairy. I am interested in telling you that from one
acre of land, which is the space the
poultry farm occupies, the return I
am receiving today is of the order of
Rs. 3,100 a month, as against a varying figure of Rs. 1,200 or Rs. 2,000
from the whole of the hundred acres

of land. Now, this is intensive agriculture, and this is precisely what we
are talking about. It can be done;
and it can be done in different fields:
it can be done in chillies, it can be
done in vegetables, potatoes, onions
and in various things, depending upon your willingness to accept as a
principle the fact that you want the
land to serve to its maximum
productivity.

And you will observe, together
with the Land Reform Bill the Hon.
Minister has introduced a parellel
Bill which must be implemented
along with it, the AgriculturalPro-
ductivity Bill, the aims and objectives of which are to ensure the
maximisation of production by
obtaining maximum yields from the
land so as to benefit the country as
a whole, regardless of the individual.
This is the strategy of action contemplated by the Minister. Now, you
will ask the questions: Why then
has he excluded certain plantations
from this operation? Why has he set
the ceilling at 50 acres? What is the
technique or the method of compensation that will be arrived at? Is it
fair or unfair? These are questions
with which this House has largely
been concerned in the course of this
discussion.

I should like to say this straight-
way. Intensification of argiculture
sounds a very simple operation; but
it is not, really. It is one of the most
difficult things to do. If you look at
the British Agriculture Act of 1947,
amended in 1957, you will find that
these operations in England are far
more sophisticated than in Ceylon
but are extremely difficult to do. The
first requirement is management
skills; the second requirement is
influsion of capital. Without money
it cannot be done, even if you give a
man two or three acres of highland,
with the best motives in the world,
in the Gal Oya Valley, as was done
by the late Mr. D. S. Senanayake, or
in Giritalle, or anywhere else. Look
at those lands. Those highlands, until
recently and most of them even
today, have not been made practical
use of. It is just a waste of land.
Why? Is it that the land cannot be

used? It can be used, but it requires capital resources well out of the reach of the peasantry to whom these lands have been alienated. If alienations are made they have to be coupled with, logically, in every sense of the word, the requirement of capital to make development possible. That is why I should like to sound a warning note in this House: let us not expect the millennium with land reform unless you are prepared to make it part of an overall economic operation, aimed at transforming society. If you simply give two acres of land as a free gift to a man who says he is landless, you are not solving his problems for him, nor are you solving the problems of the country, unless you are prepared, along with the giving of those two acres, to show him what he can do with it, to teach him the correct crops to cultivate, to show him that it could be done, to prove to him by demonstration that that crop is a feasible and worthwhile thing, and to prove, above all, that the financial resources can be made available to him from credit institutions without being dependent upon the perpetual curse of this country, the *mudalali*.

In 1960 our Government was still making the effort to prove that potatoes could become a commercial crop in this country—in the Nuwara Eliya District, in the Dambulla area, in Jaffna, in certain parts of Batticaloa. in conditions where, above an elevation of 5,000 feet, potatoes could be grown free of bacterial disease. We proved it with the assistance of experts from West Germany. We made the crop practical and worthwhile until, I remember, a peasant stopped the Hon. Dudley Senanayake on the road one day when he was Prime Minister and said, "Do not tell the Income Tax but I made Rs. 40,000 from my little plot of potatoes".

Well, if that can be done, what is the logic of retaining tea estates which are producing a maximum return of 5 per cent on the value of an acre? Let us suppose the value of an acre is Rs. 5,000. I do not think it is worth so much today; it might be worth Rs. 3,500; maybe, Rs. 2,500. But if you are getting a return of 5 per cent on that, what is 5 per cent of Rs. 2,500? Work it out for yourself and see. Rs. 125 is the income you are getting on an acre of tea land. This is what we say wrong, and this is what the Hon. Minister is determined to change.

Now, you might ask the question: why has he excluded the company estates? I think the answer is clear. In regard to the company estates there is a special problem: most of them are in areas in the heart of the Kandyan Provinces where you have still got an alien population whose problems should have been settled in 1964 under the terms of the Indo-Ceylon Agreement of that year but which were not settled because a conscious and deliberate decision was taken by the 1965 Government not to make repatriation a condition for the grant of citizenship on the other side but to make it citizenship-for-citizenship. Once that change has been made a practical, immediate, difficult situation arises because labour intensiveness is fundamental to the operation. If you are going to accept the situation of absorbing the entirety of the Indian national population into this country, if that is what you want. I agree it is not impossible to think in terms of intensification of agricultural land. But if you are fixing priorities—here you have an asset that is earning foreign exchange on the one side, and you have an unsettled problem of citizenship on the other side—it may be settled in the future—it is not surprising that where capital resources of a large order have to be injected to make land reform profitable. the Hon. Minister has deliberately left that out in the present law.

Now, the question arises why the ceiling of fifty acres? Why not twenty-five ? Why not ten ? Why not five ? The argument of the Leader of the Opposition (Mr. J. R. Jayewardene) was put on the basis that land reform is a good thing. He thought of

[ෆිලික්ස් ආර්. ඩී. බණ්ඩාරනායක මහතා]

it long ago but just never got down to it. How he managed to contain himself, to restrain himself all these years, is a problem for me ! I should have thought he would have been bubbling over with enthusiasm to introduce land reform, but all these years apparently it just never occurred to him. He says, Why not reduce the acreage ? and he also says that some Members of the Sama Samaja Party have suggested this on our side.

I will tell you what the argument is. If you are going to make an operation you have got to decide in your own mind what the limits of that operation are going to be. If, for example, you set limit at, shall I say, 100 acres, you will probably find that a very small number of persons are affected. If you set it at 50 acres, you will find that a larger number of persons are affected. If you set it at 25 acres, you have a very much larger number of persons who are affected. If you set it at 10 acres, even a much wider set of people are affected. If you set it at 5 acres, practically the whole country is affected. In every electorate you will find five-acre holders. Where are you going to set the limit ? My answer is : according to the needs of the country and the assessment of the extent to which the Government is competent and capable of intensification of agriculture.

One can think in terms of absolutes and say, Why not ? It may probably happen some time in the future. If you think that the fifty-acre ceiling is going to remain fixed for ever under population pressures I think you are wrong. I can see that happening. I am also certain that in time there will be amendments and changes, but I hope those amendments and changes when they come will not be on the basis of destroying our agriculture by the distribution of land but on the basis of a conscious and deliberate attempt to increase productivity along the lines contemplated in the draft law now before this Assembly.

The argument has been taken, Why pay compensation to these people ? Why not confiscate the lands ? The assumption is made here that the lands are wasteful, that they are not put to any practical use. That is not actually true. These lands are of mixed types. There may be some neglected plantations, but you also find excellent plantations by any standard, and the intention is to make these lands much more profitable under intensive agricultural conditions.

If that is so, surely the answer is simple. They want the property expropriated. We have no justification for expropriating one class of property and not all classes of property. If we are a government committed to expropriation, let us tell that to the country ; let us go to the country on that basis. But that is something that we have never done, certainly not the S.L.F.P. Nor did the United Front in its manifesto ever speak of expropriation as one of its objectives or motivations. In fact, I am surprised that the hon. Member for Habaraduwa (Mr. Prins Gunasekera) contested a seat on the United Front ticket as a member of the S.L.F.P. knowing full well that we were not committed to expropriation or indeed to land reform. He now talks as though the Government has gone back on its cherished ideals of socialism. Here is a man whose hypocrisy is such that he thinks nothing of using any argument for his own advantage, for the purpose of sneaking into Parliament on anybody's apron strings. At that stage he was not concerned with land reform. His heart did not then bled for the poor people who were landless and who had nothing to look forward to. He was only concerned with getting into Parliament. If he read the United Front election manifesto as carefully as he reads some of the books he brings here he would have seen that there is not one word in it about the expropriation of property.

I do not see how a government can possibly say, We are going to expropriate certain lands and not expropriate other forms of property. Why do we not expropriate indusrialists ? Why do we not expropriate house property owners ? Why do we not exporpriate persons holding shares ? Why do we not exporpriate every form of property that there is in this country ? Well, the day that the people want expropriation of every form of property probably we shall have reached the state with a completely different type of government in office. But the vast majority of us come from electorates where we have got mixed populations. There are property owners in every electorate, whether represented in the Opposition or in the Government, and I think the answer is, whatever action we take must be within tolerance levels of the people as a whole. I think the Minister has struck a happy compromise in finding that answer.

Then, the levels of compensation— are they generous by any standars ? The hon. Member for Habaraduwa (Mr. Prins Gunasekera) seems to think so. What is provided for ? You get either your valuation in the wealth tax returns or 15 times the average annual profit declared to the income tax over the last five years. That is what is provided for. Now, is that an unfair basis ? Most of the landowners I am aware of have always made their wealth tax valuations at the lowest feasible value that they could get away with because they do not want to keep making a recurrent payment of too high an amount. The wealth tax valuation can never be on the high side, if I may say so. In the income tax declarations also generally the motivation would be to make low declarations or truthful declarations, at the very highest. No one is going to declare a income larger than what he actually received in the hope of being paid compensation. If a 5 per cent return is approximately what is available from a plantation, 15 times the annual profit will only give you 75 per cent of the value of the property. If 75 per cent of the value of the property is what you are

going to get by this yardstick, can it be said that you are being over compensated ?

You may ask me, " Why the higher figure ? " I will give you the answer in plain terms. It is because a landowner who has been scrupulously careful and sought to maintain his assets would probably have replanted it. It may not be producing any income at all. If you look at the income figures the answer may be nil. But the expenses may be high and the land may have been well maintained. And then what is he going to get ? If you say " whichever is lower " he gets nothing. It has to be whichever is higher. But it is not by any means a generous assessment.

The hon. Member for Habaraduwa (Mr. Prins Gunasekera) asks, " Why is 7 per cent interest being paid on 25-year bonds ? " The answer is that the Government today is brrowing money on ten year terms paying 9 per cent at the current rate to finance the service of the Consolidated Fund. The rate was 9 per cent I think in the days of Mr. Wanninayake also I am sure the hon. Member for Senkadagala (Mr. Wimalasena) the Parliamentary Secretary to the then Minister of Finance will confirm that. If this is the current rate at which the Government brrows money from people, if you take property from people in some from other than money what justification have you for taking it on terms which are not even comparable ? These are undoubtedly less generous terms for landowners. I am not suggesting that they should be given ten year terms with 9 per cent interest. But can you offer them a rate of interest of an unrelated character ? Can you offer them 25-year bonds with 1 per cent interest. But can only do it if the Government is not borrowig other forms of property while expropriating one form of property. That surely is not a feasible or a possible thing.

The last question raised by the hon. Member for Habaraduwa under the law as far as I could see was the argument that new rights are con-

[ගරු ආර්. ඩී. බණ්ඩාරනායක මහතා]
ferred on landowners to evict tres-
passers from their lands which are
not available even under the ordinary
law. I am sorry to say I think the
hon. Member for Habaraduwa, as
usual, has not read his law very carefully although he is a lawyer. Even
it he is not arguing for a fee he must
really read his brief.—[*Interruption*].
I am aware of that. He never reads.
I have some hard things to say of
him in a moment.

I should like to tell him that there
is no power given to a landowner to
evict a tenant arbitrarily. All that
exists is the Crown is given the right
to protect property vested in the
State. If you read Clause 15, what is
sought to be protected is property
subject to a statutory lease created
by this Bill. But where the title to
that property is now belonging to
the Government, it is the Government's protection against people like
the Member for Habaraduwa
(Mr. Prins Gunasekera) who would
probably like, for reasons of their
own, for the purpose of causing con-
fusions, to create situations of
squatters hoping that in the event of
trouble they can, perhaps, invite
Lord Avebury and carry his suit case
once more ! No right is given to a
private landowner to make use of
Clause 15 in an arbitrary or oppressive fashion. All that that law gives
you is the right of the Crown to protect the property of the Crown without getting into the situation where
individuals with strongarm methods,
thugs, individuals who are strong
enough to beat the police, would move
in to possession regardless of their
priorities and rights.

But the utilization of this land is
not a thing for individuals to profit
by it. A man does not claim to get
four acres of land to cut down the
coconuts first, cut down the trees
next and have nothing to live on at
the end of it. The purpose of this is
an economic rescue operation which
the Hon. Minister of Agriculture and
Lands is launching right here and
now.

I therefore request every section of
this House to give its total support to
the proposal. It is a good one. Its
implementation can result in difficulties if it is not carefully and properly
handled, and we on behalf of the
Government have every confidence
that there is no better person to give
it the care and attention that it deserves than Mr. Hector Kobbekaduwa,
architect of one of the greatest
changes being brought about in a
society in which you have been
accustomed to talking and talking of
changes but never, never bringing
about changes until we do, and then
the hon. Leader of the Opposition
realizes they thought of it long ago,
but for some reason never got to it.
This happened so often.

They talked of decentralizing the
administration. We are still waiting
to see. They talk of all the things
that they would have liked to have
done ; they always come after we
have proposed the things and when
they are in office we wait and wait
hoping for the changes, but I must
say the changes never seem to happen
under any condition. Even now the
hon. Leader of the Opposition is
learning how to change. We saw
him dance the *baila* last night. We
saw Mr. Dudley Senanayake also
dance the *baila* last night. I can
assure you that we would like you
to come and join the dance, join the
dance so long as you make sure that
you are going forward and not waiting in the same place. What is important is that we should not dance
the twist. But if we concentrate on
going forward together, I think our
country will be a happier place.

In regard to land reform, I do appreciate that it is a sacrifice for
people, for individuals.

ඒ. අසීස් මහතා (පත් කරන ලද
මන්ත්‍රී)

(ஜனாப் ஏ. அஸீஸ்—நியமன அங்கத்தவர்)

(Mr. A. Aziz—Appointed Member)
There is nothing wrong with the
twist.

1653   1972 අගෝස්තු 3   1654

fපිලික්ස් ආර්. ඩී. බණ්ඩාරනායක මහතා
(திரு. பெலிக்ஸ் ஆர். டி. பண்டாரநாயக்க)
(Mr. Felix R. D. Bandaranaike)

Excepting that they always dance in the same place. Sometimes it is a little tortuous also with regard to your approaches.

May I also say that the Member for Habaraduwa (Mr. Prins Gunasekera) talked a lot about laws which he did not understand. But there is one little matter to which I must take grave exception, and that was a reference to me personally, but for which I would probably not have intervened in this Debate at all. He referred to the fact that there is a Minister in the Government who had been childless for 10 years, who had recently adopted a baby. He is wrong. I have been childless for 17 years, and he is perfectly right that I have adopted a baby. I have adopted my wife's sister's daughter who is now about eight months old. I adopted her when she was about ten days old, soon after she was born; that was about the end of November, 1971. She is a perfectly charming child. I wish I could have brought her here. I have no doubt that all of you would have wanted to carry her too if you saw her. She smiles very nicely even with U. N. P. people. There are a lot of uncles and aunts who are U. N. P. people who come and pay visits now and again.

ජේ. ආර්. ජයවර්ධන මහතා
(திரு. ஜே. ஆர். ஜயவர்தன)
(Mr. J. R. Jayewardene)

She is a wise child!

fපිලික්ස් ආර්. ඩී. බණ්ඩාරනායක මහතා
(திரு. பெலிக்ஸ் ஆர். டி. பண்டாரநாயக்க)
(Mr. Felix R. D. Bandaranaike)

She does not discriminate at all. I think she is willing to dance with them too as I hope you are willing to dance with us.

But the hon. Member thought there was something sinister in my action in adopting this infant. He thought that this was in some way a method of either beating the Land Reform Law or creating a right in myself to retain a larger slice of property than I would otherwise have been entitled to under the law. I should like to inform this House that that kind of thinking is unworthy of any hon. Member of this House, and I sincerely hope all of you will agree.

There is no way by which an adoption of an infant could possibly enlarge my legal right. Read the terms of this Bill. It may have been different, for example, if a *mudalituma* down South had adopted the hon. Member for Habaraduwa (Mr. Prins Gunasekera) right now because, being over 18 years of age, that adoption might have entitled the *mudalituma* to hold a slightly larger slice of property. I believe the *mudalituma* did think of that sometime ago but found that it was dangerous to do so since people would have ascribed other motives to the adoption and not the motive of protecting property.

I should like to say straight away that this type of argument is wretchedly unfair, unwarranted and unbecoming of hon. Members of this House. I myself would hate to use personal information and knowledge. The hon. Member for Habaraduwa has been busy hunting up this child's birth certificate. I am quite happy to tell him that her name—she is a girl—is Christine Malkanthi Lakshmie Dias Bandaranaike. She was born to Gamini Wickremanayake, my brother-in-law and his wife Malkanthi, and, as I have said, she is a perfectly charming little child. As soon as she is able to walk I shall bring her round to the tea room and introduce her to every one of you.

Until then I should like to say this: I too have had a look at birth certificates. I would like to tell the hon. Member for Habaraduwa that I have seen his. I have it he e on the table with me. But I am not going to use it because I do not think it is relevant to the argument. And I should like

[පිලික්ස් ආර්. ඩී. බණ්ඩාරනායක මහතා]
to inform the hon. Member that that is the way we believe that Parliamentary affairs are logically to be conducted. Under no circumstances should we resort to that sort of language, that sort of treatment, for purposes of trying to make a feeble point in debate.

I should like to inform all hon. Members of one last fact. I have not known the pleasures of fatherhood. It is something new to me. I am becoming an expert now in regard to the problem of milk foods, for example. I am learning the mysteries of the different types of milk, so much so that the Cabinet now consults me quite often as an expert on the subject.

I have made up my mind that in bringing up this child I shall try to adopt the highest standards. I should like to tell the hon. Member for Habaraduwa that in bringing her up I shall try to see that she retains the common touch, that she does not get attracted by aristocracy whether local or foreign ; that she is never willing to fetch and carry for lords and ladies from distant England even if they come here posing as journalists. I propose to ensure that she is not brought up ever to be a hypocrite and to say the opposite of what she believes.

She may be wrong in anything. She has been baptized as a Christian ; I do not know whether she will continue to be a Christian all her life. That is her choice. I have chosen to remain a Christian in my life, and I have not adopted standards of hypocrisy. I have never followed a leader for the sake of getting elected to the House while being critical in my own mind and thinking different thoughts in regard to the shape of politics, and once having got into Parliament, kicked over the traces and gone in a different direction for the sake of personal ambition' or for reasons of personal frustration. I shall do my best to ensure that little Christine

Malkanthi, when she grows up, fulfils those traditions that I think any young person, being born in Ceylon, is entitled to have as of his right. I hope that the Land Reform Law, which we are enacting today, will inure to her benefit and result in her living in a better society than the society, the unequal society, in which she lives today.

නියෝජ්‍ය කාරක සභාපතිතුමා
(குழுக்களின் பிரதித் தலிசாளர் அவர்கள்)
(Mr. Deputy Chairman of Committees)
Order, please ! I suspend the Sitting for half an hour.

රැස්වීම ඊට අනුකූලව තාවකාලිකව අත්හිටුවන ලදින්, අ. භා. 4.30 ට නැවත පවත්වන ලදි.

இதன்படி அமர்வு பி. ப. 4.30 மணிவரை இடை நிறுத்தப்பட்டு, மீண்டும் ஆரம்பமா யிற்று.

Sitting accordingly suspended till 4.30 P.M. and then resumed.

ඩඩ්ලි සේනානායක මහතා (දෙදිගම)
(திரு. டட்லி சேனநாயக்க—தெதிகம)
(Mr. Dudley Senanayake—Dedigama)
Mr. Chairman, it is unfortunate that the Minister of Public Administraion is not here, but I know that he has to be elsewhere because he is leaving Sri Lanka, I presume. It is also unfortunate that a remark of the Member for Habaraduwa about adopting babies had so irked him, and as he said he would not have taken part in the Debate but for that remark, and we had some very useful retorts by him.

However, during the course of his speech, especially in the remarks pertaining to that particular aspect of the matter, we discovered how anxiously and with what pleasure he seems to be adopting a baby. But I have seen that he has a partiality for more babies than one because I saw the other day that he is adopting a " Baby Austin " ! I was following his car and I can assure you, Sir, that the Baby Austin was more wobbling than any baby he is adopting—and that adoption will have to cease !

Felix on Law Reform

[ජේ. ආර්. ජයවර්ධන මහතා]

The Minister has accepted the Constitutional Court decision and he is deleting these clauses. What I want is this. After the Minister explains the deletion of these clauses let him also explain the result of the deletion of these clauses. Will the judiciary continue to exist or will there be no judiciary? How will the judges be appointed? How will they be transferred? Will there be a Judicial Service Commission? Will there be a Criminal Justice Commission that is now hearing the insurgency trials? I want leave to take up those points before going in depth into the arguments on the Bill itself.

කථානායකතුමා

(சபாநாயகர் அவர்கள்)

(Mr. Speaker)

We can allow it to shape itself in the course of the Debate.

fපිලික්ස් ආර්. ඩී. බණ්ඩාරනායක මහතා

(திரு. பிலிக்ஸ் ஆர். டி. பண்டாரநாயக்க)

(Mr. Felix R. D. Bandaranaike)

I think, Sir, these little problems about whether the judiciary continues or not will probably settle themselves in the mind of the Leader of the Opposition, so that he will be quite safeguarded when injunctions come next time.

කථානායකතුමා

(சபாநாயகர் அவர்கள்)

(Mr. Speaker)

In the course of the Debate we can settle these points.

අ. භා. 2. 36

fපිලික්ස් ආර්. ඩී. බණ්ඩාරනායක මහතා

(திரு. பிலிக்ஸ் ஆர். டி. பண்டாரநாயக்க)

(Mr. Felix R. D. Bandaranaike)

I move,

" That the Bill be now read a Second time."

First of all I should like to inform hon. Members of this House that the three clauses on which the Constitutional Court has made its ruling were the Subject of the petition presented by nobody other than the Attorney-General himself.

ජේ. ආර්. ජයවර්ධන මහතා

(திரு. ஜெ. ஆர். ஜயவர்தன)

(Mr. J. R. Jayewardene)

We kept them in reserve.

fපිලික්ස් ආර්. ඩී. බණ්ඩාරනායක මහතා

(திரு. பிலிக்ஸ் ஆர். டி. பண்டாரநாயக்க)

(Mr. Felix R. D. Bandaranaike)

The Attorney-General presented an argument that in his view these three clauses were inconsistent with the Constitution. The Constitutional Court has upheld all the three points and I have indicated to this House without any hesitation that the Government proposes to follow the Constitution, to express the fullest confidence in the Constitutional Court and to conform to that judgment, and the method of doing that is by the deletion of the offending clauses.

The hon. Leader of the Opposition (Mr. J. R. Jayewardene) asks whether the deletion or the omission of a clause in legislation can have an unconstitutional result. I frankly do not see how that can happen. There is no provision by which legislation which is not introduced can possibly be challenged before the Constitutional Court. If a Government produces a law which is un-workable, then the Government finds itself in the difficulty of having a law which is unworkable. But my respectful submission is that there is nothing unworkable about this law by the omission or the deletion of these three clauses. This law can stand on its own merits or demerits as the case may be. Some people will like it, some people will dislike it, but my respectful submission is that whether a law is perfect, whether a clause should be put into a Bill or should be put into a Bill, is a matter really for Committee Stage discussion, and every Member of this House is quite entitled to express his opinion and to seek to shape the law in the manner best suited to the purposes of this country according to the will of the legislature, and we for the Government will not be unrespective to any suggestion which anybody has to make in regard to this law.

I should like to explain first and foremost, before I come to the actual Bill itself, the effect of these three clauses and so answer some of the problems which are apparently worrying the Leader of the opposition—whether we will have a judiciary to whom he can have recourse in future if and when the need arises, if Cyril Mathew's appointment becomes controversial and so forth.

In regard to things like that all I can say is this. Let us look at Clause 55 first. I put in that clause that every judge who is now functioning on the Supreme Court Bench shall be deemed to be a judge of the new Supreme Court that is to be constituted, that is, without making individual appointments of each of the judgs now functioning on the Bench.

We are all satisfied with the high standards of the judiciary in the country. It will be a tragedy indeed if anything were to happen which would affect their independence. Therefore by statute law a provision was to be made for the immediate and automatic absorption of all the judges now functioning into the new court, subject of course to age limits. Clause 56 makes similar provision in the case of District Judges, Magistrates and Commissioners of Requests; that is, the absorption of all the personnel in the minor judiciary lock, stock and barrel into the new set-up. I did not want anyone to think that one judge is a favourite of somebody and another is out of favour for any reason. The judiciary as a whole must enjoy the confidence of the country. Judges must be an independent group of men capable of giving judgments for or against a Government regardless of extraneous considerations. We thought that the best method of ensuring the independence of the judiciary was by ensuring, apart from future appointments, that the existing persons would be taken over exactly as they stood. That was the simple motivation of Clause 55.

Now, the Attorney-General presented an argument before the Constitutional Court wherein he said that the power to appoint judges is given, in the case of Supreme Court Judges, to the President by the Constitution, and that in the case of the minor judges it is with the Cabinet of Ministers acting on the advice of the Judicial Services Advisory Board. If the legislature usurps that function and says, Judges X, Y and Z, who are already in service, shall be deemed to be judges of the new court, then that is an usurpation of the powers of the President.

That was the argument on which it was held inconsistent. Well, that may be right from a technical point of view. Really it means this : the President is now free, with the abolition of these courts, to make fresh appointments. I can assure you, it is not the intention of the Government to use that power in the wrong way. We propose to use our powers exactly to achieve the objectives here by reappointing the existing judges in same way. But I did not want it to be said that there was even room for executive action. That is why I included Clauses 55 and 56. After all, the President acts on advice. The President could be advised—I am not saying he will be—" Do not appoint " X " or " do not appoint judge 'Y' when you are reconstituting your court. " To prevent even a charge of ing he will be—" Do not appoint judge " X " or " do not appoint judge 'Y' when you are reconstituting your think anybody would object to the preservation of the independence of the judiciary.

But, if on the ruling of the Constitutional Court it is now held that that is illegal, well, the power will now be in the executive to appoint new judges to the new court when the law is brought into force. I can assure

[ෆීලික්ස් ආර්. ඩී. බණ්ඩාරනායක මහතා]
this House that that power will not
be exercised contrary to the intentions expressed in Clauses 55 and 56.
But if it is contrary to the Constitution for any technical reasons, I
accept the point that that can go off.

In regard to the appointment of
judges, in case the hon. Leader of
the Opposition wants to know under
what it is made, the answer is perfectly clear, it is made under the
Constitution. The president is the
person with the power to appoint
judges of the Supreme Court or their
equivalents. And in regard to High
Court Judges, because some of the
judges function as Supreme Court
judges, that power will also be in the
President. In regard to minor judges
functioning in other capacities, it will
be the Cabinet of Ministers acting
on the advice of the Judicial Services
Advisory Board. The provision is
there in the Constitution already.
But the result of all this is that it is
theoretically possible for the Government to nominate any person it likes,
even leaving out the ones there
already and appointing other judges.
It is not the result that I wanted; it
is a result that automatically flowed
from the judgment of the Constitutional Court. My intention is perfectly clear—to preserve the independence of the judiciary in its pristine
from without any changes, and if
these are the results of the decision
of the Constitutional Court I shall
bow to it, and I maintain there are no
consequence flowing from it at all.

Let us take Clause 15 (4). It says
that High Court judges may be transferred by the Judicial Services Advisory Board. The members of the
Constitutional Court have ruled that,
inasmuch as High Court judges perform some of the functions of the
Supreme Court Judges as of now, it
was not contemplated in the Constitution that they were of transferable
office. Well, that in a sense is correct.
We know that Commissioners of
Assize today function from session to
session in individual places to which
they are issued letters patent from
time to time asking them to function.

It is not a transfer in that sense. I
will bow to it and accept it. But the
simple answer will be that the judges
of the High Court will be appointed
by the President. They will hold
office up to the age of 61 years and,
presumably, the President, by an
appropriate form of his letter of
appointment, will be able to give the
them instructions as to where they
should sit within the 16 divisions
from time to time.

ප්‍රේමදාස මහතා
(திரு. பிரேமதாச)
(Mr. Premadasa)
Are you deleting that?

ෆීලික්ස් ආර්. ඩී. බණ්ඩාරනායක මහතා
(திரு. பிலிக்ஸ் ஆர். டி. பண்டாரநாயக்க)
(Mr. Felix R. D. Bandaranaike)
I am deleting that clause. But if
you want to know how you are going
to achieve the objective, it will still
be possible to have the High Court
judges functioning in 16 different
places, which is exactly the intention
we have. There are 16 zones in which
High Court judges will be sitting and
it will be possible for the President
to issue instructions exactly as of now
by means of letters patent. The objective can still be achieved except that
they will not be having the uncertainty of not knowing whether their
letters patent are going to be extended or not. After all, in the case of
Commissioners of Assize, they will
be appointed and they will continue
to hold office up to the age of 61 years
for sure. Now, that is the effect of the
deletion of those three clauses. That
is all it amounts to. That is all the
amendment coming from the Constitutional Court. So I hope we have got
that one out of the way.

ජේ. ආර්. ජයවර්ධන මහතා
(திரு. ஜெ. ஆர். ஜயவர்தன)
(Mr. J. R. Jayewardene)

Would it be convenient if I asked a
question. Once this Bill becomes
law, what is the interval up to the
time of your appointing the new
judges?

ෆිලික්ස් ආර්. ඩී. බණ්ඩාරනායක මහතා
(திரு. பிலிக்ஸ் ஆர். டி. பண்டாரநாயக்க)
(Mr. Felix R. D. Bandaranaike)

There is an appointed date provided for in the Bill. That is, this law, even if passed today or tomorrow, does not come into force immediately ; it has got to be brought into force. And that is one of the reasons why I have put in that Clause. I do not propose that there should be any interregnum or any period of time within which we shall be without law courts. My intention at the moment is to bring this law into force on the 1st of January next year by which time I think it should be possible to have every single thing arranged and and ready to ensure a smooth transition without having a period during which people will cease to hold office. So, even if this law is passed tomorrow the judges as of now do not cease ot hold office automatically. The law has got to be brought into force, and you will find at the very beginning of the Bill a definite provision providing for that. I hope that solves your problem.

ජේ. ආර්. ජයවර්ධන මහතා
(திரு. ஜே. ஆர். ஜயவர்தன)
(Mr. J. R. Jayewardene)

As far as those appointed by the President are concerned. But those appointed by the Cabinet ?

ෆිලික්ස් ආර්. ඩී. බණ්ඩාරනායක මහතා
(திரு. பிலிக்ஸ் ஆர். டி. பண்டாரநாயக்க)
(Mr. Felix R. D. Bandaranaike)

The same position will apply. Until I bring the law into force the old law continues to operate. Unless and until this law is brought into force, even the repealing sections of this law will not be enforced. The law will be on the Statute Book but it does not come into force until it is brought into force in whole or in part in the manner contemplated in the law—if you read the Bill which is now under discussion.

Now I come to the more pleasant part of my duty in introducing the Bill, having got rid of these little doubts and fears and theoretical problems which occur to peoples' minds. We have in this country had a system of courts and laws which can trace their origins back to about 1889, and it has been a long time, for which we should be grateful, that the institutions of justice have commanded respect and won the regard of the whole country for their independence, for their stature and for the great men who served on those courts over the years. But it does not after the sad fact that those laws are hopelessly out of date.; and as far as the ordinary citizen is concerned, about the only confidence he really has is the feeling that the man called upon to give judgment between himself and his fellow-men is independent, honest, a man of integrity and capable of giving a fearless judgment in all the circumstances. That tradition we honour and respect. But when it comes to the question, are we necessarily satisfied with these laws, I think everyone will agree that the feeling has grown throughout these years that these laws are hopelessly out of date that the proceedings are impossible to conform to, that a man who goes into the law courts is never free and has caught a tiger by the tail and ends up in a state worse than if he had given up his legal rights without going into court. These are practical problems, and I think it is with that objective that I should like to review the past and pay a tribute on this occasion to one or two of my predecessors in office.

The only attempt that has ever been made to introduce laws to reform the system was when Sir Lalitha Rajapakse was Minister of Justice in 1947. At that time Sir Lalitha Rajapakse thought that he should try to reform the Mortgage Ordinance and the Partition Ordinance, and on those two things he produced two new Acts in 1949 and 1950. Those laws are still in force, but I think people will agree that even those new laws, with all their checks and balances and safeguards, have still left partition laws and mortgage laws in a state of great complexity. I am hoping stage by stage, with the next package of laws that will come up, to introduce land

ජාතික රාජා සභාව

[ෆිලික්ස් ආර්. ඩී. බණ්ඩාරනායක මහතා]
reform laws dealing with land laws, dealing with the entire gamut of land litigation, settling titles, and things of that sort on which a villager finds himself today in grave trouble. These are things that have to be done, but before that I must take the initial steps, and the initial steps are here enshrined in this law.

The entire Civil Procedure Code was the subject of consideration by Mr. Nagalingam on the Civil Courts Commission. A very fine document was produced but none of the Governments, not even the U. N. P. that appointed it, had sufficient confidence in it to proceed with it or even to pick the wheat from the sheaf and decide how they were going to enact the legislation. No substantial attempt of any form was ever made until Mr. M. W. H. de Silva became the Minister of Justice in 1956. He then introduced the conciliation boards—an attempt to evolve not really a judicial procedure but a form of procedure by which disputes could be amicably settled without considerable expense and delay. It is a good idea and it is still working, but everything depends upon the stature of the men appointed to these conciliation boards. I must say that in many cases the people serving on the conciliation boards have been performing a wonderful job. My Deputy, Mr. Ratnasiri Wickremanayake, is actually exercising a close degree of supervision on their work and I think he will agree with me that it is a matter of considerable pride to us that roughly 50 per cent of the conciliation boards of this country are doing a wonderful job to help litigants to help people with disputes in rural areas and in the villages.

Now, let us come to this Bill. This is the first attempt to really reform the legal system and to ensure changes. What are the changes we the Supreme Court which would conforemost, we are re-fashioning the system of courts. There is at the apex the Supreme Court which would consist of between 12 to 20 judges. These judges alone will be performing appellate functions, and the number of

judges who will be sitting to hear cases will be much the same as now except with this difference : it will be possible to ensure that no cases are disposed of before single judges. I prefer that there should be a minimum of two judges to hear any single case in appeal, so that it is not left to the vagaries of an inividual to determine the fates and fortunes of another individual. I propose as far as possible to ensure that two judges or more should hear an appeal : it could be three in many types of cases.

There is a principle of one appeal only introduced in this Bill. There have been some argument by lawyers and judges and public discussions in the newspapers and so forth in regard to whether this is wise. I should like to inform hon. Members of this House that if they examine the facts they will find that it is not the number of appeals that is a guarantee of the justice that is done to litigants ; it is the degree of consideration received and the number of judges who sit on that bench which guarantees the fairness of a judgement.

One can always argue that there are cases where the Privy Council has set aside particular judgements of the Supreme Court Judges. That is true. All I can say is that there could be such cases even if you had a further Privy Council ahead of the Privy Council, and if you take the total number of judges, you can never guarantee what a praticular judge's judgement is going to be. In any case, how many people in fact have had recourse to this ultimate court of appeal in this country ? Those of you who appear in the law courts, Members of Parliament conducting criminal cases, I have no doubt, will agree that most of the murderers convicted and sentenced in this country have appealed to the Courts of Criminal Appeal, but very few of them have had the time, the money or the resources to have access to a higher tribunal. In practical terms we are not providing theoretical rights for Individuals. We are trying to ensure that justice is done at the highest tribunal which we are capable of providing to ensure justice.

It is perfectly true that when appeals to the Privy Council in London were abolished there were some pending cases before it and it would have been manifestly unfair to take away from people the right which they had of appeal to a further tribunal. We gave them another tribunal in substitution and the Court of Appeal was set up for this express purpose. But in my view there is no case for a further court of appeal today, and I think the ultimate answer is to ensure that cases are heard by the maximum number of judges, with the most careful consideration being given to any particular individual case.

Now, I have made express provision for one thing : that is, for any person to have the right to make an application, and if his case is of any special importance—conflict of decisions or any thing of that sort—he will have an opportunity of having his case heard by a larger number of judges than is normal. If the court decides, it can so happen. That is, for reasons of complexity of the facts of the case or its importance, its public importance, or because there were conflicting authorities which require a final settlement of the problem, to make it possible for the matter to be referred on a special application to a bench consisting of a larger number of judges at the discretion of the court.

Now, I myself would say that this idea of one single appeal in every case has been uniformly adopted and that is the structure. There is one little change that I might want to introduce at the Committee stage, but I would like to discuss this with you and consider your views before I do so. I have provided that the High Court Judges will be functioning in fixed places. They really will be performing functions of Commissioners of Assize as of now, in the disposal of assize cases. These persons will also hear writ applications and an appeal would lie to the Supreme Court from their judgements. I would like to seriously consider, instead of this, the question of handing over original jurisdiction in writ matters

to the Supreme Court as of now without leaving it to the High Court Judges in which case there will be no further appeal from the judgement of the Supreme Court. But, those writ cases I would suggest should be heard by a minimum of three judges in every case—a minimum of three Supreme Court Judges to hear such an application. I am thinking of that. I have not decided. I am trying to find your opinion on that, whether you think it is a good idea or a bad idea. The law as at present drafted provides for writ cases to be heard by the High Court Judges with an appeal to the Supreme Court. That is what is now provided in the present draft form but I am suggesting to you that it may be better to consider the question of writ cases being heard directly by three judges of the Supreme Court without any further right of appeal on the basis that this is an extraordinary remedy and to ensure that the maximum consideration is given to it, in which cases one consequence follows from it. I want to tell you why I am suggesting it. It means that the Supreme Court ceases to perform only appellate jurisdiction ; it gives them also original jurisdiction which means automatcally that the Chief Judge of the highest court of original jurisdiction provided in the Constitution becomes the Chief Justice ; other wise you may find the Chief Judge of the Supreme Court functioning on the Judicial Services Advisory Board and the Disciplinary Board.

ජේ. ආර්. ජයවර්ධන මහතා
(திரு. ஜெ. ஆர். ஜயவர்தன)
(Mr. J. R. Jayewardene)

Which High Court ? There are so many High Courts.

ෆීලික්ස් ආර්. ඩී. බණ්ඩාරනායක මහතා
(திரு. பீலிக்ஸ் ஆர். டி. பண்டாரநாயக்க)
(Mr. Felix R. D. Bandaranaike)

There is a High Court consisting of 16 zones. You can call it one court or each court, depending on how you want to look at it, but the fact is that the High Court consists of that group of judges operating in 16 zones. They will be hearing murder cases and the

[f පිලික්ස් ආර්. ඩී. බණ්ඩාරනායක මහතා]
like rather in the fashion that Commissioners of Azzise are sitting, excepting that they are not appointed *ad hoc* for a session. They will be appointed up to the age of 61 years and will hold office in that way. I think this is an amendment which will avoid the necessity of constitutional amendments at all ; otherwise I may find myself in the difficulty of having to consider seriously a constitutional amendment to make it the Chief Judge of the Appellate Court rather than the original court. I would prefer to conform to the Constitution and in conforming to the Constitution a simple way to do it is to vest the writ jurisdiction directly in the Supreme Court to be heard not less than by three judges in every case. That is the proposal that I like to put forward before you for consideration with regard to that matter.

ජේ. ආර්. ජයවර්ධන මහතා
(තිරු. ජෙ. ආර්. ජයවර්ධන)
(Mr. J. R. Jayewardene)
That is one of the points I wanted to raise.

f පිලික්ස් ආර්. ඩී. බණ්ඩාරනායක මහතා
(තිරු. පිලික්ස් ආර්. ඩී. පණ්ඩාරනායක්ක)
(Mr. Felix R. D. Bandaranaike)
I hope I have already solved it. The Judicial Services Advisory Board should be manned by no one short of the best men we have. The Disciplinary Board was intended to be constituted of the top judges.

ජේ. ආර්. ජයවර්ධන මහතා
(තිරු. ජෙ. ආර්. ජයවර්ධන)
(Mr. J. R. Jayewardene)
Must be the Chief Judge of the Highest Courts—

f පිලික්ස් ආර්. ඩී. බණ්ඩාරනායක මහතා
(තිරු. පිලික්ස් ආර්. ඩී. පණ්ඩාරනායක්ක)
(Mr. Felix R. D. Bandaranaike)
—of original jurisdiction.

ජේ. ආර්. ජයවර්ධන මහතා
(තිරු. ජෙ. ආර්. ජයවර්ධන)
(Mr. J. R. Jayewardene)
Yes. The Supreme Court does not have it.

f පිලික්ස් ආර්. ඩී. බණ්ඩාරනායක මහතා
(තිරු. පිලික්ස් ආර්. ඩී. පණ්ඩාරනායක්ක)
(Mr. Felix R. D. Bandaranaike)
They will have it.

ප්‍රේ මදාස මහතා
(තිරු. ප්‍රේමදාස)
(Mr. Premadasa)
The Supreme Court will also be an original court.

f පිලික්ස් ආර්. ඩී. බණ්ඩාරනායක මහතා
(තිරු. පිලික්ස් ආර්. ඩී. පණ්ඩාරනායක්ක)
(Mr. Felix R. D. Bandaranaike)
It will become the chief original court as well as the chief appeal court, in which case the problem solves itself automatically. So, I want to give this idea to you for your consideration.

ජේ. ආර්. ජයවර්ධන මහතා
(තිරු. ජෙ. ආර්. ජයවර්ධන)
(Mr. J. R. Jayewardene)
Otherwise we cannot appoint judges.

f පිලික්ස් ආර්. ඩී. බණ්ඩාරනායක මහතා
(තිරු. පිලික්ස් ආර්. ඩී. පණ්ඩාරනායක්ක)
(Mr. Felix R. D. Bandaranaike)
I can always appoint judges because there will always be a chief judge of the highest original court. My point is, that is not the intention of the Constitution. The intention of the Constitution is that the highest judge should perform this function, and I want to conform to that. So, I am asking for your co-operation to achieve that object.

ජේ. ආර්. ජයවර්ධන මහතා
(තිරු. ජෙ. ආර්. ජයවර්ධන)
(Mr. J. R. Jayewardene)
Yes, we will give it if you ask

fඑලික්ස් ආර්. ඩි. බණ්ඩාරනායක මහතා
(திரு. பிலிக்ஸ் ஆர். டி.. பண்டாரநாயக்க)
(Mr. Felix R. D. Bandaranaike)
What am I doing but asking ?

කථානායකතුමා
(சபாநாயகர் அவர்கள்)
(Mr. Speaker)
I think it is being given.

fඑලික්ස් ආර්. ඩි. බණ්ඩාරනායක මහතා
(திரு. பிலிக்ஸ் ஆர். டி. பண்டாரநாயக்க)
(Mr. Felix R. D. Bandaranaike)
The hon. Leader of the Opposition wants us to keep on asking, Sir !

The next grade of judges who are contemplated in this Bill are the district judges, performing both criminal and civil jurisdiction functions. The fourth grade of judges are the magistrates, performing also civil and criminal functions. We are not having names like commissioners of requests ; they are being abolished. And in this structure there is no question of assuming of jurisdiction and things of that sort. It is a very simple idea by means of which, without all these complicated schedules, the law sets out a set of principles under which it should be perfectly possible to dispose of cases, and I foresee certain results from the changes in the law. Before long, certainly in criminal cases, there should not be a single case where a man cannot be brought to trial and the trial concluded, with the appeal if necessary, within six months from the date of commission of the offence. That is the target date. A man is entitled to that right, and justice demands that a man should not be kept in jail for one and a half years awaiting trial but that the case should be disposed of early, and if he is innocent he be freed, and if he is guilty he be made to suffer the consequences ordered by court. Now, those are the objectives.

On the civil side, the same results should be possible, but for that a further package of amendments to the civil procedure law and the land laws of this country should be introduced, and this I propose to do later by the addition of another package of a total section, possibly amounting to about another three hundred clauses dealing with these problems. It is now in draft form, and I propose to introduce it as an Administration of Justice (Amendment) Bill to be tagged on at the end of this Bill if and when it becomes law.

On the criminal side, the principles of criminal juris-prudence and procedure have generally been preserved without many changes. But there are a few changes to which I should draw your attention. It may have escaped your notice that women jurors come in under this law so long as they conform to the educational standards laid down and the income requirements of the law. All that is required is that a person should have the S. S. C. qualification with Sinhala or Tamil. I can see the Speaker has doubts as to how it is going to work out, but I think, after all, if ladies can aspire to be Prime Ministers of countries nowadays it does seem to be a little hard if they should be excluded from the function of being jurors.

තේනිවරයෙක්
(அங்கத்தவர் ஒருவர்)
(A Member)
There are lawyers also.

fඑලික්ස් ආර්. ඩි. බණ්ඩාරනායක මහතා
(திரு. பிலிக்ஸ் ஆர். டி. பண்டாரநாயக்க)
(Mr. Felix R. D. Bandaranaike)
Of course, but lawyers are excluded from being jurors ; lady lawyers will not have a chance.

Apart from that, one other change which is introduced, which is a substantial change, is that an accused has lost his right to silence in a way. That does not mean that he should be compelled to give evidence or be harassed in the witness box. It means that he is free not to give evidence if he does not want to ; but if he does not, it is possible for a court to drawn an inference from his silence if the circumstances warrant it, leaving it

[ෆිලික්ස් ආර්. ඩී. බණ්ඩාරනායක මහතා]
entirely to the court. Today, judges
cannot do that, nor can a comment
be made in regard to the failure of
an accused person to give evidence.
But if an explanation is due from an
accused person and the circumstances
of his silence are such that an inference of guilt may be drawn, the judge
is free to take that into account in
coming to a conclusion. That change
is there in the law as now formulated.
I am drawing your attention to some
of the highlights for your information.

In regard to the payment of fines,
a new procedure has been devised
by means of which persons will not
have to hang around the law courts
until their cases are called and to pay
an instalment of Rs. 5 or Rs. 10 on
each day the case is taken up in court.
Instead, a procedure has been devised in association with the banks by
means of which a person sentenced
to pay a fine will be given a set of
vouchers on which he can pay the
fine from time to time over a period
of two or three months, at the end
of which, when the case is called,
either he has paid the fine or he has
not, in which case a default sentence
can be considered in accordance with
the law, or, alternatively, community
service can be exacted from him.
Community service means, you pay
your fine by contributions of labour.
It is a new idea. It has been brought
into force in other countries with
considerable success and satisfaction.

Provisions already enacted by this
House in the form of suspended sentences, in the form of amendments
already made for summary settlement of disputes relating to land and
things of that sort have all been included in the law.

There will be no assuming of
jurisdictions by magistrates in the
future. Magistrate's courts' jurisdictions are separate and distinct, from
the District Court's higher jurisdiction. District Courts and High Courts
will only try cases on indictments,
which means that the Attorney-
general will have to present the case
to court in the Magistrate's Court. I

have not put down a complicated
Schedule as in the old Civil Procedure Code. Instead of that, what I
have done is to provide that any
offence carrying a punishment up to
a certain maximum may be brought
before a Magistrate's Court; but, of
course, the magistrate cannot impose
a punishment up to that maximum.
His limit is 18 months imprisonment
or Rs. 1,500 in the way of a fine. That
is how the provision has been enacted. I want to suggest a change in this.
At the moment the law says three
years' maximum punishment. I think
that is unfortunate. You might have
to increase that maximum and provide that the Magistrate's Court can
take up cases with a higher punishment, five years or seven years as the
case may be, but, of course, subject
still to the maximum punishment of
Rs. 1,500 fine or 18 months imprisonment as the case may be. I am not
suggesting an enlargement of a
magistrate's punitive jurisdiction.
This is because smaller cases like
grievous hurt or those coming under
Section 315 might otherwise find
themselves excluded from Magistrate's Courts under the present
classification, and I therefore propose
that that amendment be made.

There is here a new departure in
the total abolition of non-summary
proceedings. Today, every time a person comes up in a non-summary case,
we know the sad circumstances of
what happens to him. Once in two
weeks the case is called with mono-
tonous regularity; he is remanded;
sections of evidence are heard bit by
bit; he exhausts himself financially
in the process and at the end of the
operation, by the time he reaches the
assize courts, he ends up with assigned counsel to defend him, and that
is the time he needs help most. This
is sad and unfortunate.

The new procedure is like this.
The police conducts the investigations and concludes those investigations. At their conclusion the case is
sent to the Attorney-General direct.
The Attorney-General may or may
not indict him, but if he does the case

goes up. The entire statements constituting the investigations that are relevant will be used and made available to the defence, including the accused's own statement, The accused does not have to defend himself blindfolded, unaware of what is happening. He knows all the facts of the whole story that is there against him. That is what is provided for. That is one of the things that is going to help very considerably in speeding up the procedure which we envisage.

I do not propose to say much more. I can, of course, deal with each and every clause but I merely want to give this House a general idea of what the criminal law changes are going to be.

There is the abolition of testamentary proceedings next. This, I think, is also a very important feature. Today whether there is a dispute or not, the administration of an estate has got to be supervised inch by inch all the way by the district court. This involves a lot of unnecessary delay. Whether there is a dispute or not, it means that whole families including minor children have got to go to court, stand in rows before the court and be identified, have guardians-at-litem appointed—all sorts of stuff of a completely non-controversial character have to be gone through merely because somebody has died leaving an estate which is over Rs. 2,500 or Rs. 5,000 in value. The provision I have made is that the same procedure generally shall be followed but it shall be followed in a public office, in the Department of the Public Trustee who will be responsible for going through the same functions—the same advertisements, the same gazetting of orders nisi and absolute and all that stuff in regard to wills and intestacy and the like—in collaboration with the Commissioner of Estate Duty.

As soon as a dispute arises in regard to heirship, in regard to the genuineness of a will, in regard to whether property belongs to an estate or does not belong to an estate, in regard to whether accounts have been properly submitted to the Public Trustee or not—all the types of disputes that now come up—provision has been made in the sense that as soon as a dispute arises the Public Trustee will refer the dispute compulsorily under the law to the appropriate court for adjudication, because the adjudication of disputes is the work of the courts and not under the supervision of the administration.

The principle advanced is that in transacting business in a government office as distinct from a court, the public can go at their own convenience during office hours to the office of the Public Trustee and have their matters disposed of, while in a court they will have to wait until the case is called up at a particular moment of time and dealt with by the judge sitting on the Bench. This is the principal reason for this—a lot of things can be done privately and without fuss.

I am suggesting an amendment to the provision about estaee duty under this Chapter. This is an important one which I mention now. I have provided that the estate duty people must finish their work within one year and not keep these estates open for ever and ever, but I find that the state Duty Commissioner says that the way that the law has been drafted is unsatisfactory. So in consultation with the Minister of Finance we have evolved a system by which we have provided for a maximum of two years, provided the necessary particulars are furnished to the estate duty authorities, which is apperently the reason for their difficulty. I am grateful to my Colleague the Minister of Finance (Dr. N. M. Perera) for his co-operation and assistance in evolving the shape and form of the necessary amendment to solve this particular difficulty.

Then under appeals procedure there is specific provision in regard to written submissions. Written submissions are not to the exclusion of

[ෆිලික්ස්' ආර්. ඩී. බණ්ඩාරනායක මහතා]
oral submissions, but the oral submissions must follow from the written submissions and solve the problems which the judges may have in either understanding or solving the matters that arise. The Constitutional Court has already established a very useful precedent, and the Court of Appeal in some cases, on a purely voluntary basis without special legal rules, has already started written submissions, and from what I can see the results are eminently satisfactory. Written submissions do not in any way exclude oral submissions if the court decides to hear them but they do provide a simple procedure by means of which the work of the court will move faster.

I should like to tell hon. Members that at the moment there is a backlog of nearly 5,000 appeals not disposed of in the Supreme Court. I am confident that with the enactment of the new procedure and their adoption in our courts we should be down to dealing with current appeals in a matter of eighteen months. The entire backolg will be cleared if this law is passed.

There is provision for the destruction of court records. This is already there in the law. There is provision to ensure that this is done after the necessary safeguards have been taken—the particulars are entered in registers, the relevant deeds and documents are extracted and returned to the parties and so on. There is also provision for the Government Archivist to preserve historical material for posterity and for the service of the Department of Cultural Affairs.

One element in this law which I think has interested people specially in the legal profession relates to what has been described loosely as the unification of the legal professions. I should like to say straight away my approach to this problem. I have had talks both with the Law Society and with the Bar Council at different times, formally and informally, and I suggested to them, as soon as I assumed office, that I would far prefer if the two branches of the profession could, by agreement, evolve some formula which was eminently satisfactory to themselves. The real problem was that many of the young advocates felt that it was a burden on their clients to have to retain two people where they really wanted to retain only one to appear in the case. In the outstations it actually happens in practice, and in the criminal Courts it has now been accepted by the Supreme Court. But the fact remains that this was one of the problems.

The second problem was that the proctors were not very happy about giving up their monopoly in regard to deed work, notarial practice. I suggested the best thing would be to find a formula mutually satisfactory, by discussion.

When I assumed office as Minister of Justice one of the first things I did was to withdraw from the Cabinet a proposal which had been presented by my predecessor. Mr. Jayamanne, proposing the unification of these two branches into one branch, pending a settlement between the two professional bodies. But I found that the two professional bodies, while talking about this, were merely content with the existing *status quo* and were not thinking in terms of any changes at all. No constructive proposals of any sort were really forthcoming. All I have done in this law is to provide for a legal practitioner called an attorney-at-law. Attorneys-at-law can perform all the functions that advocates and proctors now perform. There is no limitation on it. Even in the Criminal Procedure Code today the words 'advocate' and 'proctor' hardly appear. Every one is a pleader, a proctor is a pleader, so is an advocate.

Now what will happen is every advocate and every proctor will become in practice an attorney-at-law. The attorney-at-law is free to perform all these functions. In regard to notarial practice for the future, there will be only one examining body and a person will have to pass papers in conveyancing; for the proctor the problem ceases. But for the past I have provided that a person who practised in a land court for a fixed period of time and who is able to furnish a certificate from a judge of the Supreme Court or from a district judge before whom he has practised will be entitled, without sitting for an examination, to apply to the Registrar-General and obtain a notarial licence. Otherwise, he has to sit for the examination.

This does not mean that every advocate has got to open offices; this does not mean that any compulsion is being placed on a person to change the nature of his practice. Now there are some proctors who will be horrified at the thought of going to court and pleading in court. Their preference is to prepare cases and to retain lawyers to appear for them and their clients. All those safeguards are preserved. There is nothing to prevent any person continuing to practise his profession in the manner and form in which he has been accustomed to do it in the past. No person who does not want to meet his clients is going to be compelled to do so. It is quite possible for one attorney to retain another, to appear with a junior, to have another person instruct him, to be assisted by someone else.

It is equally possible to form permanent associations like partnerships, but none of this is compulsory. No person is being forced into a different form of practice from what he has been engaged in. Total freedoms are there. Every single member of the legal profession who has been of service to the law courts of this country would be able to continue to be of service in precisely the same fashion. But equally, in the present day and age, we have to have regard for the needs of the litigants, for the needs of people, for the needs of persons whose legal rights are going to be adjudicated upon in the courts, and such persons would best be served by being free to make their choice and to ensure that they are able to retain the services of the best person available to them with the least possible expense.

I myself know perfectly well that although I may today be serving this Government in the capacity of a Minister, these things come and go. I am quite accustomed to not holding office, I am quite accustomed to being a Member of the Opposition. But I want to tell you, at all times I have not forgotten that I am a member of the Bar. That is my profession and I am not ashamed of it. I will go back to the law courts as I think all good politicians do ultimately, and when that happens I can assure the Members of this House that I am not afraid of the consequences of the very law that I have enacted. Some people seem to think that the legal profession is being damaged in the process. On the contrary, I take the view that the legal profession will be able to attain new horizons in the service of the community and will be able to win the respect and regard which the legal professsion has always held from time immemorial though in recent times there is a feeling growing that perhaps we have been a little inconsiderate to the very people whom we have to serve.

Those in short are the principal points in the law which I have presented here before this House.— [Interruption]. There is nothing said here about fees. Any person is free to charge what he likes if he can get it. The question is, can he get it ? The economic circumstances of the country are really the limiting factor on fees, as far as I can see. If anybody wants to pay any advocate or proctor anythnig he likes, there is no objection at all. But having regard to the fact that supply and demand in a given economic situation normally determines prices you will find that there is no real danger of any exploitation here, because, after all, the litigant is quite free to choose a person within his means, capable of giving the service he wants and capable of

[පිලික්ස් ආර්. ඩී. බණ්ඩාරනායක මහතා.]

giving that service within the shortest possible time. That is the important point, and that is really what we are seeking to do. I have not sought in any way to regulate the affairs of the profession except to provide that any legal practitioner—[*Interruption*]. The Clerk to the Assembly draws my attention to Clause 36 (3) in Part I. Well, there is a change here of a minor character. I do not think it is likely to cause any problems. It says :

"Every attorney-at-law who renders professional advice or assistance to any person shall have the right to sue for the recovery of any fee due to him and he may also be liable to be sued by his client for professional negligence."

It is not different for auctioneers.

කථානායකතුමා

(சபாநாயகர் அவர்கள்)

(Mr. Speaker)

And doctors.

පිලික්ස් ආර්. ඩී. බණ්ඩාරනායක මහතා

(திரு. பிலிக்ஸ் ஆர். டி. பண்டாரநாயக்க)

(Mr. Felix R. D. Bandaranaike)

But I think, generally, there is a line of decisions that professional negligence means a very high degree of negligence ; and I have no doubt the courts, when called upon to interpret this, will have regard for past precedents. So I do not think anybody need fear that negligence is likely to be taken in a light-hearted sense. I do not think there is any special problem here.

I must also tell you one thing : there is a consequential amendment which I shall have to bring in at the Committee stage. I just mention it now, talking of the legal profession. I shall have to repeal the Incorporated Law Society Ordinance. The reason is that wherever in any enactment the word "proctor" or "advocate" occurs, the word "attorney-at-law" shall now be substituted by an express provision in this Bill which means that all the advocates will become members of the Incorporated Law Society automatically if I do not do that. Therefore, I have no choice but in the list of repeals to include the Incorporated Law Society Ordinance, which I shall be moving to add.

There is nothing to stop the Law Society functioning as an unincorporated body, but the statute under which it functions has to be repealed. There is nothing to stop a group of proctors who are friends forming a club or a law society if they want to, but the Incorporated Law Society Ordinance has to be repealed because otherwise advocates will find themselves compulsorily made into members of the Law Society. The Law Society may not want that and the advocates would not want it either— one does not know. I do not want to force people to associate with one another as freedom of association is enshrined in the Constitution.

Those are broadly the ideas. There are some details I have not dealt with. Please do not treat this as a comprehensive statement on every single clause.

එන්. ඩෙන්සිල් ප්‍රනාන්දු මහතා (ගේලූව)

(திரு. என். டென்சில் பர்ணந்து—நீர் கொழும்பு)

(Mr. N. Denzil Fernando—Negombo)

What about a proxy in a civil case ?

පිලික්ස් ආර්. ඩී. බණ්ඩාරනායක මහතා

(திரு. பிலிக்ஸ் ஆர். டி. பண்டாரநாயக்க)

(Mr. Felix R. D. Bandaranaike)

There will be a second chapter to this whole law later on as an amendment which would include the Civil Procedure Code or its equivalent.— [*Interruption*]. I will ensure that the existing law continues. The Civil Procedure Code is not being repealed by me. In any case, I am hoping before 1st January to have the second package of laws ready. I have been in office as Minister of Justice from the 20th January 1972, I believe. It is not the easiest thing in the world to cover a period of neglect in this field ranging over very nearly a hundred years. I have tried, with the assistance of those in the Ministry who worked with me, to make some impact. It could be that there are errors and mistakes here and there. No one can claim that his work is perfect. If any of you can help me to make it more perfect, I can assure you I shall pay every attention to any suggestions you make. Certainly this law has not been introduced with any sinister motives other than the simple idea that it is our clear and bounden duty to give the people of this country the greatest possible service through the legal institutions.

I should like to thank hon. Members of the House for their total co-operation which I hope I shall receive. I hope the hon. Leader of the Opposition would have had all his doubts cleared, and if he can help me to improve the Bill I am prepared to consider his suggestions and to discuss them with him straight away. It is in that spirit that I am approaching this law. I shall also require your help when it comes to dealing with the next few chapters. Once the main portions of the Legislative Enactments which lawyers have to deal with day to day are settled, it will all appear in one simple book. We are having it in the Sinhala language straight away so that the question of having to translate a large volume of old laws may become unnecessary and it will certainly help the language of the courts. There is a Tamil copy also which has been prepared which will be available to legal practitioners. I am glad to say that the amount of Tamil being used in our courts is increasing. I am very pleased about that. I am happy to say that we are now getting, perhaps, the pressure of the litigants prevailing even over the will of persons who find it more convenient to operate in other languages.

In conclusion, I would like to thank you, Sir, for your patience and for having given me so much time to explain the effect of this law. If there are any difficulties at any stage I shall be available for as much of the time as possible. I may have to leave the House for a little while today between 5 and 6.30 and for a little time tomorrow, United Nations Day. Subject to those two absences, I shall seek to resolve all problems. My Deputy, Mr. Ratnasiri Wickremanayake, will in any case be present.

I should like to pay a tribute to him for the great assistance he has given me and also to all the officers of the Ministry for making this package possible.

අ. භා. 3.31

ජේ. අර්. ජයවර්ධන මහතා

(திரு. ஜெ. ஆர். ஜயவர்தன)

(Mr. J. R. Jayewardene)

Mr. Speaker, this Bill when it becomes law will make very far-reaching changes in the administration of justice in this country. No one can take exception to the general principles mentioned in the caption:

"The provisions of this law are intended and shall be construed to achieve the following objectives:—

(a) simplicity and uniformity in procedure

(b) fairness in administration

(c) the elimination of unjustifiable expense and delay: and

(d) the just determination of every judicial proceeding."

This is Clause 2 of this Bill which is divided into five parts: the first dealing with the judicature, the second with criminal porcedure, the third with testamentary procedure, the fourth with appeals procedure, and the fifth with destruction of court records.

This Bill deals with one of the important limbs of the Constitution, the judicature, the other two being the legislature and the executive, all three based on the will of the people.

The Hon. Minister said that he hoped we would not impute motives for the introduction of this Bill. We certainly do not do so. We think he and his Government are sincere in bringing this Bill, in seeking to provide litigants with easy access to the courts and quick decisions there—the consumation that has been devoutly wished for by the people in this country and the legislators for several

Felix on Independence of the Judiciary

[එ්. ආර්. ජයවර්ධන මහතා]
must be very careful when one is dealing with courts of law unless of course one wants the courts to be completely subordinate to the executive, which I think was not the purpose of the new laws that the Minister brought. He emphasized the independence of the judiciary. He has mentioned that under the Constitution—and we will agree with that—the judiciary must be independent with regard to its decisions. They say that the figure of Justice is blind folded, and we must see that it is so. In fact, when justice is being done, whether it concerns the Minister or the leader of the Opposition or somebody who is not so important justice must be done absolutely fairly, and I feel that in this case, unless the Minister has some proper explanation, he has not called for the record within the terms of the law. So I thought it would be convenient if I raised this question when we are dealing with the rules of court. It is true these rules are drafted by the Supreme Court. Even so it is relevant that at this stage one should really lay down principles that have been accepted in democratic countries in this country, and in this particular case by no less a person than the distinguished father of, if I may say so, a distinguished son.

ගරුතර ආර්. ඩී. ඉණ්ඩාරනායක මහතා
(திரு. பீலிக்ஸ் ஆர். டி. பண்டாரநாயக்க)
(Mr. Felix R. D. Bandaranaike)
Mr. Speaker, I am very grateful for this opportunity which has been afforded to me over this matter, completely outside the rules of court under discussion, to deal with a problem raised by the Leader of the Opposition. It is a pleasure to listen to him on any subject under the sun, even when he is taking in regard to cases in which he himself happens to be a party litigant. In this instance, I should first and foremost like to say that I understand that his complaint relates to District Court case No. 2883/Z in respect of which an

enjoining order has been applied for and obtained by one Mr. A. W. A. Abeygoonesekera of "Abeysiri", Gonawela, Kelaniya as plaintiff, against (1) J. R. Jayewardene, "Braemar", Ward Place, Colombo; (2) U. S. Perera of Pilapitiya, Kelaniya; (3) Andrew Samaratunga of the Office of the Ministry of Public Administration and Local Government and so on.

Now, Sir, it is always interesting of course to find that one cannot resist almost the temptation of saying that in any case in which Mr. J. R. Jayewardene is a party, the affidavit makes wonderful reading. It is almost a foregone conclusion that the affidavits that I have read before, in the past, were interesting. I mean, really you learn facts about people and things which you could have never hoped to learn if you did not read such affidavits. The temptation is almost an overwhelming one for any Minister who wants to read affidavits in any case in which Mr. J. R. Jayewardene is a party. It is almost a foregone conclusion just to say that in any case in which Mr. J. R. Jayewardene is a party, especially where injunctions and affidavits are involved, the case usually ended up with somebody withdrawing the case. I am almost certain that that is exactly what you are going to find in this case.

Now, the hon. Member was kind enough to say that he and the late Mr. Dudley Senanayake had decided to take Mr. Abeyagoonesekera out of Kelaniya and send him to Dompe. I am very greatful because the ones he has so far sent against Dompe had usually ended up as very staunch S.L.F.P. men. It is usually the tradition; it has happened in the past and it may happen again in the future— one never knows. He says, " Now the Minister must be very careful about this man. There is a case pending against him of a criminal character, of cheating or something of that sort. " I must say that this is the first time I am hearing of that one. I did not know, this is the type of candidate you select an dsend up as chairman of Corporations, afterwards to find that they are charged with criminal offences. I usually thought it was the other way round ; I thought you normally appiont as Chairmen of corporations only people who are convicted of criminal offences. That has generally been the tradition of Mr. J. R. Jayewardene in the past. I can think of one or two cases particularly in the Salu Sala and the Hotels Corporation where they distinguished themselves, and the only qualification that one could think of for their appointment was the fact that they had criminal records behind them.

Now, in this instance, I should like to inform the hon. Member who seems to think that I have acted illegally that perhaps it may always be a good thing to think that a man has acted illegally and if you are going to raise it, to inform that man in advance. You can check for yourselves the facts. In this instance, the hon. J. R. Jayewardene has not merely raised it here, but he has already filed an affidavit today in the courts saying that there has been an interference by the Minister with the judiciary in calling for a record. Now, on this matter, I say, I shall have to once again call for th record and I do not propose to make any secret about it. I am issuing the order immediately to call for the record once again to have a look at your new affidavit.

Let us now come to the circumstances under which I called for this record and argue and see whether I am right or not. I have never believed in conducting a secret administration in any of the Ministries I am in charge of ; there is not a single document or file that is secret in any of the Ministries I am in control of. Any hon. Member of this House is entitled to come there and ask for an inspection of any document

that he may care to see and I can assure that all officers of the Ministry have been instructed to without any hesitation make those documents available for total inspection by any one of you if you want to know the facts, the reasons for anything. All that you can find out. Quite apart from having to probe and ask questions in this House you can get that information across the counter. It will be supplied to you. I think all hon. Members, to whatever Party they may belong, will confirm the truth of what I say, that this is the tradition and the principle that has been followed at every stage at least in the Ministries of which I am in control.

The Law that the hon. Member referred to is Act No. 9 of 1958. Under what circumstances is the Minister of Justice empowered to call for records ? Section 2. (1) reads :

"The Minister of Justice may direct any record of any court of justice to be produced for his inspection if he considers such inspection necessary for the performance of his duties."

That is the only limitation that we are talking about. The Minister must act within the framewok of the Law. Certainly, that is, the Minister cannot for example call for the record of a divorce case because he has got a puerile interest in pronography, but if there is a duty to be performed in his capacity as Minister of Justice it becomes really his duty to call for that record.

In this connection I might say that. I read more about Mr. Dudley Senanayake by reading Mr. J. R. Jayewardene's affidavit during the Dedigama by-election and more about Mr. J. R. Jayewardene by reading Mr. Dudley Senanayake's affidavit than Mr. Rukman Senanayake, naw the hon. Member for Dedigama, could have ever imagined when he became the candidate for Dedigama.

641 ජාතික රාජ්‍ය සභාව 642

[fපිලික්ස් ආර්. ඩී. බණ්ඩාරනායක මහතා]
But the interesting thing is not that. Why did I call for this record ? Because I received representations that in my view led me to suppose that I was right in calling for the record. I will read the communication I received in this matter.

"Abeysiri",
Gonawala,
Kelaniya,
1st March, 1974. "

I insisted upon getting this in writing because the representations were originally made to me orally. I was not going to be satisfied with oral representations. I had to act on written representations. The communication was as follows :

" Hon. Felix R. D. Bandaranaike,
The Minister of Justice, Local Government & Public Administration,
Office of the Ministry of Justice,
Hultsdorp, COLOMBO.

Dear Sir,

I am taking this opportunity to place a few facts connected with my case against Mr. J. R. Jayewardene, with a view to seek your intervention against any injustice done.

In order to avoid making this letter too long I am attaching a copy of my resolution to the United National Party against Mr. Jayewardene and a copy of the enjoining order issued on him. I am also attaching copies of my affidavit and petition to Court dated 1.3.74 with a copy of an affidavit of Mr. Jerry Paranahetty, Attorney-at-Law.

The above documents I am sure will give you some idea about the methods adopted in circumventing a Court order.

Mr. D. J. Samaratunga of 'Thusara', Nungamugoda who presided at this meeting at 'Siri Kotha' at 5.30 p.m. on 26.2.74 is a Government teacher by profession who is expected to conduct himself legally in all matters. In spite of his doing so he chaired a meeting which was restrained from holding by Court and furthermore he overruled the objection raised by Mr. Paranahetty whom Mr. Samaratunga knew as an Attorney-at-Law.

Mr. Tudor Dharmadasa who is also an Attorney-at-Law has proposed the resolution which was also restrained by Court even after the objection was brought by another Attorney-at-Law.

Mr. Andrew Samaratunga a party to this case is employed in government service attached to the Ministry of Home Affairs.

Both these gentlemen Mr. D. J. Samaratunga and Andrew Samaratunga, I feel are expected to obey legal orders and conduct legally by virtue of public offices they hold. In this case I believe they have violated this principle and especially Mr. D. J. Samaratunga being a teacher, Ex-School Inspector had participated in an illegal meeting and thereby contravened the ethics of Public Service.

I therefore request you to see that suitable action may be taken against these two public officers and direct other officers concerned to take legal action against Mr. J. R. Jayewardene and Mr. Tudor Dharmadasa for contempt of court.

Thanking you,

Yours faithfully,
Sgd. (A. W. A. Abeyagoonasekera) ".

This is the man whom they are going to send as the candidate for Dompe. He is writing to me.

අවාර්ය කොල්වින් ආර්. ද සිල්වා
(கலாநிதி கொல்வின் ஆர். த. சில்வா)
(Dr. Colvin R. de Silva)

This communication mentions Mr. Abeyagoonasekera's name ?

ƒපිලික්ස් ආර්. ඩී. බණ්ඩාරනායක මහතා
(திரு. பீலிக்ஸ் ஆர். டி. பண்டாரநாயக்க)
(Mr. Felix R. D. Bandaranaike)

I am not saying one word for or against Mr. Abeyagoonasekera. A man makes a complaint here alleging impropriety on the part of two public servants, to say the least of it. He alleges contempt of court or, as one court aratchi once told my Colleague and Friend Mr. Ilangaratne when he was speaking a little too loudly in the court precincts, " කටවහපියව්, නැත්නම් කොටෙන්ට් ඔෆ් කෝට් "

In this instance I am not basically interested in questions of contempt of court. Those are matters for the courts. But if it is brought to my notice that two public servants, at least one of them holding office in a Ministry under my control, are supposed to have violated a court order or done something wrong in respect of a court case I know nothing about, I do not know that it is not within my scope and functions as Minister of Justice to call for the record and find out the facts.

If I receive a complaint I shall act on that complaint. And I do not think that, merely because the hon. Leader of the Opposition chooses to make allegations by affidavit against me alleging that I have no right to call for a record, I am going to be deterred from performing my duty. And I sincerely hope and trust that people will realize.—[Interruption]. I did not bother to communicate with either of them. I merely whispered in the ear of the other Minister.

But, be that as it may, Sir, the net result of all this is that there is apparently some private fight going on as usual within the United National Party. It is not unusual. These

things happen—until they die, of course. There is no doubt that at Mr. Abeyagoonasekera's graveside a different song will be sung in appropriate cantos and with appropriate cadences. But until such time as that happens what stands on the affidavit as sworn testimony will continue to stand.

In this instance the hon. Member says that he was deprived of the opportunity of filing answer. Well, Sir, I do not know about filing answers. That record was called for and returned within 24 hours. It was inspected and read for me—I did not bother to do it—by one of the young men in my Ministry. And this shows how beautifully the young men in my Ministry work. The record was read by a young man called N. V. de Silva. And it is quite clear to me that young N. V. de Silva has not passed on this information even to his father, the Hon. Dr. Colvin R. de Silva, because when the Hon. Minister raised the objection he had not even heard about the case and knew nothing of the contents of the record. It just goes to show how well confidences are maintained and how beautifully the Ministry works to make sure that classified information of any sort simply does not reach unauthorized hands.

In conclusion the hon. Member referred to the case of Agnes Nona. He talked about the independence of the judiciary. So much has been said about the independence of the judiciary that I cannot refrain from speaking a few words about it myself. We have written it into the Constitution. We have ensured that the independence of the judiciary is a cardinal concept of this constitution which has not existed under any previous Constitution. Even the U. N. P. Government never thought of amending the Constitution to incorporate a word about the independence of the judiciary. We have also got the objects of the Administration of Justice Law clearly spelt out in Section 2—fairness in administration, elimination of delays, expense and so forth.

[fපිලික්ස් ආර්. ඩී. බණ්ඩාරනායක මහතා]

What does independence of the judiciary really mean ? Let us get this clear once and for all. I think we are getting a little tired of using words to mean things they do not mean. It simply means that a judge must be free to give his judgment in any given case free of any influences, free of any threats or menaces, free of any influence brought to bear upon him by any outside agency or authority. It does not matter whether it is for or against the State, it does not matter whether it is for or against a private individual, a judge must be free to give his verdict and reasons in any manner he pleases according to the facts of the case and according to law. That is the independence of the judiciary. If it means that judges must be free to proceed at their own pace, to grant dates at their will and pleasure, to be influenced by requests from any particular person, be he an attorney-at-law or not, in regard to the manner in which he does his work or the speed at which he does his work or the times at which he is going to sit or the manner in which he is going to conduct himself or the affairs of his courthouse, then I say that that cannot possibly be the law and it is not the desire of the State to perpetuate such conditions. The Constitution provides for Parliament to legislate or for rules of court to be formulated or for procedures to be laid down to ensure that the courts function in the manner in which the State desires them to function in the common interest of all.

I was asked in my own electorate once what exactly is this independence of the judiciary that people are talking about. I could not think of a way of explaining this to the people in my constituency except to say that this is rather like the way in which you administer the C. T. B. The job of the Ministry is to ensure that the roads are built, that there are buses on the road, that drivers and conductors are appointed to serve these buses and make sure that the people who travel in these buses can really get from point A to point B. There are large buses of the Supreme Court variety, there are medium sized buses of the High Court variety, and there are little ones of the Magistrate's Court and District Court variety. Every one of them has its own driver, and the speed limits are laid down.

ඕ. එක්ස්. මාටින් මහතා
(திரு. சி. எக்ஸ். மாட்டின்)
(Mr. C. X. Martyn)

Can they get old ?

fපිලික්ස් ආර්. ඩී. බණ්ඩාරනායක මහතා
(திரு. பீலிக்ஸ் ஆர். டி. பண்டாரநாயக்க)
(Mr. Felix R. D. Bandaranaike)

I hope they would not. They have been running only for one month. They are still new. It only happens when they get old and end up " kota uda " That is later when they are a little old, but at the moment they are new buses. It is up to the driver to take the people safely to their destinations. There are places where they are not permitted to stop or travel below a certain speed. All those rules are there. But beyond setting the rules and ensuring that the service works, the Minister of Justice is not going to set the destination boards or tell a particular bus driver, " You have got to drive to destination X or to destination Y. " That is not our jobs ; that is the job of the skilled persons whom we put in charge to see that the thing runs.

Agnes Nona's case was cited. I agree with the hon. Leader of the Opposition that the judge who gave that judgment was an independent and fearless judge, even if it be my own father of whom I am speaking. I entirely agree with that assessment and that judgment. But let us take the facts of the case.

The hon. Leader of the Opposition never saw any merit in that judgment till today. When he was in the Government, I like to know, what was their opinion of that particular judge and his judgment ? You can cite and praise anybody you like now when it suits your purpose, but I consider it as being worth as little as either your affidavits or your funeral orations.

What happened in that case? There was a woman called Agnes Nona who was prosecuted for running a disorderly house or something of that sort. She was sentenced to three months' imprisonment by the Magistrate of Colombo South. She apparently was fairly well connected to some people in office at that time. It was not the S.L.F.P. or the United Front Government that was in office. Some suggestion was made to the Minister of Justice, Sir Lalitha Rajapakse, that perhaps it would cause grave hardship if this lady was to serve a term of three months in jail, and perhaps she should be pardoned or some arrangement should be made for lighter punishment. She had appealed to the Supreme Court but her appeal had been dismissed. She had reached the stage when she had actually moved into jail, had started serving her sentence, and a day or two had elapsed.

Upon representations made to Sir Lalitha he took a certain view. I think he had the power to take that view, although personally I am not sure of the wisdom of it; I have never done so up to date excepting for the commutation of a death sentence. I have never taken it on myself to vary the term of imprisonment imposed by any court in this country. If a judge thinks that a sentence of 'X' should be passed, only judges sitting in appeal here got the power to vary that—not Ministers. Sir Lalitha thought differently. Maybe, he had reasons having regard to the Government to which he belonged. He felt that he should impose, instead, an order that this lady be ordered to enter into a recognizance in a sum of Rs. 250 and be released conditionally on an undertaking to be of good behaviour in the future.

The thing that went wrong in Sir Lalitha's case was that instead of communicating his order to the Prison Superintendent he communicated it to the magistrate. He directed the magistrate to call for the record, to order this woman to enter into a recognizance in Rs. 250 to be of good behaviour, and ordered her release. Had he addressed that same identical communication to the Commissioner of Prisons he would have been acting only through the executive; he could have achieved what he wanted. I am not saying it was a desirable order to make. I would never have made that order. But Sir Lalitha did. He had the power to make the order. Only, instead of directing it to the appropriate authority under his control, he addressed it to the magistrate.

Justice Dias called for the record and declared that the act of the Minister in giving the order in that fashion was completely illegal. And I think he was right. But how does it become a great argument for the independence of the judiciary to say that a Minister should not address a communication in that fashion to a judge? All that Justice Dias has said, if you read that judgment carefully, is, "This is the way it should have been done, and not this way" Nowhere does he challenge the power of the Minister to make the order he made; nowhere does he comment upon the wisdom or the unwisdom of a Minister making this kind of order, though I challenge that politically and say that no Minister should do that.

This was the argument on which you people solemnly resisted the Motion of No Confidence introduced by the Member for Yatiyantota at that time, and you said that Justice Dias was merely being very technical about it, technical in regard to the person to whom the order should be addressed. That was the simple issue in the Agnes Nona case.

649   ජාතික රාජ්‍ය සභාව   650

[fපිලික්ස් ආර්. ඩී. බණ්ඩාරනායක මහතා]

If you read further, you will find that Jutice Dias in that order nowhere punished anybody for contempt of court. He took no action against the Minister of Justice for any alleged violation, but having made a pronouncement in regard to the appropriate procedures that should have been followed, he said at the end. "No order". An intelligent and fearless judge has made that pronouncement in that fashion. Are you suggesting that he was ever saying that the Minister should not have made that order? I think the Minister should not have made that order. But Justice Dias did not say so. Justice Dias accepted the fact that a Minister has certainly got the overriding power of exercising prerogative pardons. If I may say so, that is a completely wrong approch to use that power to set aside a sentence in respect of one's friends, politically or otherwise. I have never done so and I never shall.

To this day we hear a lot about the interference with the judiciary. Tell me, have any of you had occasion to feel or to complain that Ministers have in fact interfered with the judiciary? The only person who has made this complaint to my knowledge up-to-date is the hon. Leader of the Opposition in an affidavit filed in D.C. Colombo Case No. 2883/Z. I shall be calling for the record again to see what further action should be taken in this matter.

ප්‍රශ්නය විමසන ලදින්, සභා සම්මත විය.

வினா விடுக்கப்பட்டு. ஏற்றுக்கொள்ளப்பட்டது.

Question put, and agreed to.

තිති අධ්‍යාපන සභා (සංශෝධන) පනත් කෙටුම්පත

சட்டக் கல்விப் பேரவை (திருத்தம்) சட்டமூலம்

COUNCIL OF LEGAL EDUCATION (AMENDMENT) BILL

දෙවන වර කියවීමේ නියෝගය කියවන ලදී.

இரண்டாம் மதிப்பிற்கான கட்டளை வாசிக்கப் பட்டது.

Order for Second Reading read.

අ. භා. 5.7

fපිලික්ස් ආර්. ඩී. බණ්ඩාරනායක මහතා (திரு. பிலிக்ஸ் ஆர். டி. பண்டாரநாயக்க) (Mr. Felix R. D. Bandaranaike) I move,

"That the Bill be now read a second time."

Mr. Speaker, to a large and distinguished audience of Members of Parliament, members of the legal profession and future members of the legal profession I hope, I have pleasure in presenting on this occasion a Law to amend that Council of Legal Education Ordinance :

As far as this Bill is concerned, I think, first and foremost, it is my duty to tell you that in consequence of various representations coming to us from law students, supporting as well as opposing the provisions of this Bill, from discussions I have had with His Lordship the Chief Justice and others, I have given careful thought and consideration to the contents of this Bill and to the ways in which perhaps, the Bill could be amended, perhaps, to make it read a little better and, perhaps, to solve some of the problems and doubts which might arise and occur in the minds of Members of Parliament. I propose to tell you, first and foremost what the amendments are that I propose to introduce at the Committee Stage so that we can conduct our discussion not on the basis of the original wording of the Bill but on

Felix on Interpretation (Amendment) Bill

ජේ. ආර්. ජයවර්ධන මහතා (දකුණු
කොළඹ පළමුවන)

*(திரு. ஜெ. ஆர். ஜயவர்தன—கொழும்பு
தென்கு முதலாம் அங்கத்தவர்)*

(Mr. J. R. Jayewardene—First Colombo
South)

Divide !

ප්‍රේමදාස මහතා

(திரு. பிரேமதாஸ)

(Mr. Premadasa)

By name.

නියෝජ්‍ය කථානායකතුමා

(உப சபாநாயகர் அவர்கள்)

(Mr. Deputy Speaker)

Standing—it is easy to count.

සභාව මතු පළ වන අන්දමට—පක්ෂව 55;
විරුද්ධව 15; යනුවෙන්—බෙදුණේය:

போறவை பிரிந்தது: சார்பாக 55; எதிராக 15.

*The Assembly divided: Ayes 55;
Noes 15.*

සභාවේ රැස්වීම්

போறவை இருக்கைகள்

SITTINGS OF THE ASSEMBLY

මෛත්‍රීපාල සේනානායක මහතා

(திரு. மைத்திரிபால சேனநாயக்க)

(Mr. Maithripala Senanayake)

මෙම යෝජනාව මම ඉදිරිපත් කරනවා :

" අද දින විසිර යැමේදී මෙම සභාව 1974
සැප්තැම්බර් මස 19 වැනි බ්‍රහස්පතින්දා අ. භා.
2 වන තෙක් කල් තැබිය යුතුය. "

ප්‍රශ්නය විමසන ලදින්, සභා සම්මත විය.

வினா விடுக்கப்பட்டு, ஏற்றுக்கொள்ளப்பட்டது.

Question put, and agreed to.

අර්ථ නිරූපණ (සංශෝධන)
පනත් කෙටුම්පත

பொருள் கோடல் (திருத்தம்) சட்டமூலம்

INTERPRETATION (AMENDMENT) BILL

දෙවන වර කියවීමේ නියෝගය කියන ලදි.

*இரண்டாம் மதிப்பிற்கான கட்டளை வாசிக்கப்
பட்டது.*

Order for Second Reading read.

අ. භා. 2.15

fපිලික්ස් ආර්. ඩී. බණ්ඩාරනායක මහතා

(திரு. பிலிக்ஸ் ஆர். டி. பண்டாரநாயக்க)

(Mr. Felix R. D. Bandaranaike)

ගරු නියෝජ්‍ය කථානායකතුමනි, මේ
ගරු සභාවේ අවසරය ඇතුව අර්ථ නිරූපණ
(සංශෝධන) පනත් කෙටුම්පත දෙවන
වර කියවීම සඳහා මම දැන් ඉදිරිපත් කර
නවා.

පළමුකොටම මෙම ගරු සභාව ඉදිරියෙහි
එක'තරා කාරණයක් වෙනුවෙන් මගේ
කනගාටුව ප්‍රකාශ කළයුතුව තිබෙනවා. මේ
අවස්ථාවේදී මෙවැනි සංශෝධනයක් ඉදිරි
පත් කරන්නට අවශ්‍ය වී තිබෙන'නේ
මගේ ඉංග්‍රීසි හැඟීම පැහැදිලි ලදී වීමෙ‍ා්
නිසයි. 1972 මැයි 11 වන දා, ආණ්ඩුක්‍රම
ව්‍යවස්ථාව සම්මත කර ගන්නට පෙර,
මෙම ගරු සභාවට මම අර්ථ නිරූපණ
(සංශෝධන) පනතක් ඉදිරිපත් කළා. එම
අවස්ථාවේදී නීතිය වලංගුව තිබුණේ
ඉංග්‍රීසි භාෂාවෙනුයි. එම නිසා ඉංග්‍රීසි පන
තක් ඉදිරියෙහි—

ප්‍රින්ස් ගුණසේකර මහතා

(திரு. பிரின்ஸ் குணசேகா)

(Mr. Prins Gunasekera)

නැහැ.

fපිලික්ස් ආර්. ඩී. බණ්ඩානායක මහතා

(திரு. பிலிக்ஸ் ஆர். டி. பண்டாரநாயக்க)

(Mr. Felix R. D. Bandaranaike)

දැන් ඒ ගැන තර්ක කරන්නට දුව
මනාවක් නැහැ. එම පනත අපි ඉංග්‍රීසි
භාෂාවෙන් ඉදිරිපත් කළ අවස්ථාවේදී සිං
හල භාෂාවෙනුත් පනත් කෙටුම්පතක්
ඉදිරිපත් කළ එක ඇත්තයි. එහෙත් නීතිය
පෙරලා කියවන්නට සිදු වන විට අර්ථ
නිරූපණය කරන්නට සිදු වන විට එය
කරන්නට සිදු වූණේ සිංහල භාෂාවෙන්
නොව ඉංග්‍රීසි භාෂාවෙන් බව මෙම අවස්
ථාවේදී මතක් කළ යුතුයි. එදා මම ඉදිරි
පත් කළ ඉංග්‍රීසි භාෂාවෙන් මේක තේරුම්
ගන්නට කිසිම අමාරුවක් හිටින‍ේ
නැත කියා එකයි, මගේ අදහස වුණේ.
එදා මේ ගරු සභාවේ රැස්ව සිටි මන්ත්‍රී
වරුන්ට තේරුම් ගන්නට හැකි වන ලෙස
පැහැදිලි ලෙස තොඅනුමනවම අදහස්
ඉදිරිපත් කරන්නට ප්‍රමාණවත් දක්ෂතා

1753   ජාතික රාජ්‍ය සභාව   **1754**

[fපිලික්ස් ආර්. ඩී. බණ්ඩාරනායක මහතා]
වයක් මට තිබුණායයන් නැසි, මගේ අදහස
වුයේ. එ'ත් දැන් මට පෙනී යනවද,
එහෙම දක්ෂතාවක් තිබුණෙන් නැති බව.
ඒ අනුව පෙනී යන්නේ ඉංග්‍රීසි භාෂාවෙන්
ඉදිරිපත් කළ වචන පිළිබඳව අදහස් 2 ක්
තිබී තිබෙන බවයි. ශ්‍රේෂ්ඨාධිකරණයත්
මගේ ඉංග්‍රීසි භාෂාව ප්‍රතික්ෂේප කර මේ
අවස්ථාවේදී තීන්දුවකට බැහැලා නැහැ
නවා. එහැකොට මේ සභාවට ඉදිරිපත් වී
තිබෙන්නේ අප අදහස් කළ දේ' නො
වෙයි. අදහස් කළ දේ' නැතිව වෙනින්
අදහස් මේ ගරු සභා ගර්හයේ තිබී
තිබෙන බවයි ශ්‍රේෂ්ඨාධිකරණය පිළිගන්
නෙ. එහි මුල් වැරද්දකාරයා මළෙයි. ඒ පිළි
බඳ පාපය විඳින්නට මම සුදනම්. ඒ ගැන
ප්‍රශ්නයක් නැහැ. ඒ අනුව මට සිද්ධ
වෙනවා, මේ ගරු සභාවට ඉදිරිපත් වී
තැබූ වර්ක් ඉල්ලීමක් කරන්නට. අපෙ
ස්වෙරි භාවය මේ රටේ සෑම ආයතනයක්
කෙරෙහිම පැහැදිලි ලෙස තොයනුමාන
යොමු දුකාශ කරන්නට සිද්ධ වෙනවා
නම් අප් ඒ කටයුත්ත කරන්නට් සුදනම්
බව මේ අවස්ථාවේදී මම නැවත වර්ක්
ප්‍රකාශ කරනවා.

1972 අප්‍රේල් මාසෙ 20 වෙනිදා පාර්ලි
මේන්තුවේ මම කථා කළ අවස්ථාවේදී මේ
ගරු සභාවේ මත දෙකක් තිබුණාද නැද්ද
කියන ප්‍රශ්නය ගැන මට නම් තේරුම්
ගියේ නැහැ. මට තෝරුම් ගියේ' වෙන්රම්
තුනාකින් යුක්ත ඒ පනත ගැන අප කඩු
රැන් පැහැදිලි ලෙස අදහස් ප්‍රකාශ කල
බවයි. එ'ත් මට දැන් පෙනී යනවා, තත්
වය එසේ නොවන බව. දැන් අවුරුදු
දෙකකට කලින් වෙච්ච ඒ සිද්ධිය අනුව
එදා මෙහි සිටි එකම මන්ත්‍රීවරයෙකුට්වත්
අද කල්පනා කිය එදාවාද තියා ද නැහා,
ගරු ඉඩම් ඇමතිතුමා විරුද්ධව
ඉන්ජන්ක්ෂන් නිකුත් කිරීමට මොනම
හේතුවක්'වත් උඩ ඉඩක් අවකාශයක්
ඉතුරු ඵලාද නැද්ද කියන ප්‍රශ්නය පිළි
බදයි. එටැනි අදහසක් අවකාශයක් අපේ
ගරු පාර්ලිමේන්තුවේ ඉදිරිපත් සැලාද
නැද්ද කියන ප්‍රශ්නය මා සිට කැටටෙක්
හැඟුණාද කියා මට නම් කියන්නට බැහැ.
මට නම් තෝරුම් ගියේ නැහැ එහෙම
එකක්'. එදා සාකච්ඡාවලට අනුව මම හිතු
වේ හරි නේ' වැරදි හෝ පාර්ලිමේන්තුවේ
දී අපි අදහස් කළ දේ' නොහොත් පාර්ලි

මේන්තුවේ අදහස මේ රටේ සෑම දෙනෙක්
ම පිළියෝන තිබුණ බවයි. මම පිළිගන්
නවා, සමහර ඉඩම් හිමියන්ට, රැක දෙන්
නට තන්'කම් ඇති අයට සමහර විට විකක්
රිදෙන බව. නමුත් දැන් ෙෙස් වෙනත්
අදහසක් ඇති වී තිබෙන බව ඇත්තයි.

දි. මු. ජයරත්න මහතා (ගල්පොල)
(திரு. டி. மு. ஜயரத்ன—கம்பளா)
(D. M. Jayaratne—Gampola)
ඒ පර භාෂාවේ වැරද්දයි.

fපිලික්ස් ආර්. ඩී. බණ්ඩාරනායක මහතා
(திரு. பிலிக்ஸ் ஆர். டி. பண்டாரநாயக்க)
(Mr. Felix R. D. Bandaranaike)
ඔව්, මගේ භාෂාවේ.

දි. මු. ජයරත්න මහතා
(திரு. டி. மு. ஜயரத்ன)
(Mr. D. M. Jayaratne)
ඇමතිතුමාගේ සිංහල හොඳයි ඉංග්‍රීසියට
වඩා.

fපිලික්ස් ආර්. ඩී. බණ්ඩාරනායක මහතා
(திரு. பிலிக்ஸ் ஆர். டி. பண்டாரநாயக்க)
(Mr. Felix R. D. Bandaranaike)
මම ඉංග්‍රීසි භාෂාවෙන්ත් මෙහොතකින්
පිළිතුරු දෙන්නම්. තමුන්නාන්සේලාට
තත්ත්වය හොඳින් අවබෝධ කර දෙන්
නයි මම මේ කථා කරන්නේ. ඒ අර්ථ නිරු
පණ පනතින් අර්ථ නිරූපණය කිරීමේ දි
සිද්ධ වී තිබෙන්නේ කුමක්ද? ගරු විජිරි
වයකරතුමන්ලා වැඩි සංඛ්‍යාවක් තීන්දුව
දි තිබෙන්නේ, පාර්ලිමේන්තුවේ අදහස
ඉඩම් ඇමතිතුමාට විරුද්ධව ඉන්ජන්ක්ෂන්
තහනම් නියෝගයක් නිකුත් කිරීමට ඉඩ
අවකාශයක් තිබිය යුතුය කියන අදහසයි.
අපි එදා පාවිච්චි කල වචන අනුව භාවිත
කල භාපාට අනුව ශ්‍රේෂ්ඨාධිකරණයට අව
බෝධ වී තිබෙන්නේ—වැඩි සංඛ්‍යාවකගේ
අදහස වී තිබෙන්නේ—ඉන්ජ්පන්ක්ෂන්
තහනම් නිගෝග නිකුත් කිරීමට ඉඩ අව
කාශ තිබෙන බව යයි දැන් අපට තොර
දී තිබෙනවා.

හැබැයි අපි එකක් හොඳාකාරවම දන්
නවා. ඒ මොකක්ද? එදා අපේ තිබුණ
අදහස මොකක්ද කියා අපි දන්නවා. දැන්
නීතිය කෙසේ අර්ථ නිරූපණය කර තිබු

ණිත් එදා පාර්ලිමේන්තුවේ තිබුණ අදහස මොකක්ද කියා අන් කාටත් වඩා හොඳින් අපි දන්නවා. කෙසේ වෙතත් ශ්‍රේෂ්ඨාධි කරණයට අපහාස වන වචනයන් අපි කියන්නට බලාපොරොත්තු වන්නේ නැහැ. අපි ශ්‍රේෂ්ඨාධිකරණයට හිස නමාගෙන, ශ්‍රේෂ්ඨාධිකරණයට තිබෙන ස්වාධිනත් වය උඩ, නිදහස උඩ එය පිළිගන්න අපි ලෑස්තියි. නමුත් මෙය පැහැදිලි මදි නම්, නොඅනුමාණයෙන්ම තේරුම් ගන්නට බැරි නම් අපි නැවත වරක් ලෑස්තියි අපේ අභිප්‍රාය ඇහැදිලි ලෙස සිංහල භාෂාවෙන් ඉදිරිපත් කරන්නට. ඒකෙන් ශ්‍රේෂ්ඨාධි කරණයේ ස්වාධිනත්වයත් රැකෙනවා.

අපි මෙහිදී ව්‍යවස්ථාදායක අධිකරණයේ මඟ පෙන්වීම පිළිගන්නවා. එපමණක් නොවෙයි, මේ ගරු සභාවේ ස්ටේටි භාව යත් බලයත් අපි මුළු රටටම ඔප්පු කරනවා.

මේ ප්‍රතිපත්ති තුනම ආරක්ෂා වන පිළිවෙලටයි මේ අවස්ථාවේදී අප මේ සංශෝධන පනත් කෙටුම්පත ඉදිරිපත් කරන්නේ. අපේ හැඟීමේ හැටියට පාර්ලි මේන්තුවේ අද කාගේ තිබෙනවා නම් ඕන කමක් තිබෙනවා නම් ශ්‍රේෂ්ඨාධිකරණයට තිබෙන එකම යුතුකම අප භාවිතා කරන වචන දෙස බැලීමයි. පනතක් පිළිබඳව භාවිතා කරන වචන පෙරළා බලා කියවා බලා තේරුම් ගැනීමයි. ඒ හැර වෙනත් විධියක් නැහැ. කණගාටුයි කියන්නට ශ්‍රේෂ්ඨාධිකරණයේ නඩුකාරවරුන් ගෙන් දෙදෙනෙකු පමණයි සිංහල භාෂා වෙන් යුත් කෙටුම්පත දෙස බලවත් තිබෙන්නෙ. කෙසේ වෙතත් වලඟු ඉංග්‍රිසි භාෂාවෙන් තිබෙන පනත තමයි. එය කියවා බලා "සාමාන්‍යයෙන් කෙටුම්පත් පනතේ හාවිතා කරන ලද වචන අනුව අර්ථ නිරූපනය කිරීමයි උසාවියේ යුතුකම; ඒ‍ත අමුතු වචන පටලැවීමෙන් හෝ හැන්සඩ් වර්තා කියවීමෙන් හෝ වටපිට බලා අන්න මනන් ඇසීමෙන් නොවෙයි, පනත් කෙටුම්පතේ භාවිතා කර තිබෙන වචන දෙස බලා තින්දුවකට බැසි මයි ශ්‍රේෂ්ඨාධිකරණයේ යුතුකම" ය කියා අපට කියනවා. ඇමතිවරයකුගේ ක්‍රියාවක් ශ්‍රේෂ්ඨාධිකරණයේ ඉන්ජන්ක්ෂන් තහ නමකින් තහනම් කළ යුතු නැත යන

වචන අප කියා සිටියේ ඒ ඇමතිවරයා යම් පනතක් යටතේ ක්‍රියා කරනවා නම් තමයි. දැන් ශ්‍රේෂ්ඨාධිකරණය අපට කියා සිටිනවා, "හොඳ හිතින් ක්‍රියා කරන්නම්" යන්න ඒකට ඇතුළත් කලයුතුය කියා. නරක චේතනාවෙන් ක්‍රියා කරනවා නම් එහෙම නම් මේ නීතිය වලංගු නැත කිය නවා. ඔය හොඳ චේතනාව නරක චේත නාව කියන වචන පනතේ නැහැ. නරක චේතනාවෙන්—වංක චේතනාවෙන්— කරන දෙයක් වලක්වන්නට නීති හදන්න මා දන්නේ නැහැ. නීතිඥවරයකු හැටියට මා ඒකට අදක්ෂ මදි. තමුන්නාන්සේලා වංක චේතනාවෙන් දෙන තීන්දු මට පිළි ගන්නට බැරිය කියා නඩුකාරවරුන්ට කියන්නට නීති හදන්නට මා දන්නේ නැහැ. එහෙම නීති හදන්නට අප දන්නේ නැහැ.

අප එදා අදහස් කළේ එංගලන්තයේ පවතින නීතිය යටතේ තිබෙන තත්ත්වය සහ අද අපේ රටේ තිබෙන තත්ත්වය සංසන්දනය කර අපේ නීතිය ඒ අනුව මුවා කරන්නටයි. එංගලන්තයේ රජයට විරුද්ධව හෝ ඇමතිවරයකුට විරුද්ධව හෝ ඉන්ජන්ක්ෂන් තහනම නිකුත් කරන්නට බැහැ. ඒ නිසා ම වෙන්නේ ඕනෑ බඩ වෙනුවෙන් ඕනෑ නිලධාරියකු ක්‍රියා අවස්ථා වක එහි ඉන්ජන්ක්ෂන් තහනම නැහැ. 1947 පනවන ලද පනතක් යටතේ උසා වියට එහෙම තහනම් නියෝග දෙන්න බැහැ. ඒ හා සමාන තත්ත්වයක් ඇති කරන්නටයි අර්ථ නිරූපන පනතේ 24 වන වගන්තියෙන් අප උත්සහ කළේ. නමුත් ඒ බලය අවලංගු කලොත් අප රට ඒකාධිපති රටක් වේය කියා එක නඩුකාරවරයෙකු තම නඩු තීන්දුවෙන් කියනවා. මා සිතන්නේ නැහැ ගරු මන්ත්‍රී වරුන් ඒ ගැන බියක් ඇති කර ගන්නට අවශ්‍යයනා කියා. එංගලන්තයේ මෙතෙක් කල් ඉන්ජන්ක්ෂන් තහනම් තොමැතිව ඒ රට ඒකාධිපති රටක් නොවුනා නම් ඇයි අපි මෙවැනි සැක පහල කර ගන්නේ?

අප මේ සංශෝධන පනත් කෙටුම්පත සිංහල භාෂාවෙන් පිළියෙල කළේ බොහොම පරික්ෂාශෙනුයි. මෙය පැහැදිලි මදි නම් තවත් මේක සකස් කරන්නට මේ අවස්ථාවේදී මට ආධාර කරන මෙන්

1757   ජාතික රාජ්‍ය සභාව   **1758**

[fඑලික්ස්. ආර්. ඩී. බණ්ඩාරනායක මහතා]
ගරු මන්ත්‍රීතුමන්'ලාගෙන් ඉල්ලීමක්
කරනවා. පළමුවන වතාවට මෙම පනත
ඉතිහාසගත වන්තේ පනතේ ඉංග්‍රීසි
භාෂාවෙන් අනෙක් සම වගන්තියක්'ම
තිබුණත්, 24 වන වගන්තිය දැන් වැල්ලූ
වන්තේ සිංහල භාෂාවෙන් පමණක්'විම
නිසයි, වෙන භාෂාවක් නැහැ. පසුගිය
වන-වේ, 22 වන වගන්තිය පැහැදිලි කිරීම
පිණිස එංගලන්තයේ උසස්'ම මණ්ඩලය
—ස්'වාමිවරුන්'ගේ සභාවේ "ඊස්'ටේලේ"
සහ "ඇනස්'මිනික්" යන නඩු තින්දු
දෙක ගැන මා කෙටියෙන්', සාරාංශ
වශයෙන්. සඳහන් කළ නිසා, එක් නඩුකාර
තුමකු කියා තිබෙනවා, මේ ගරු සභාවේ
මන්ත්‍රීතුමන්'ලා කවුරුන් ඒ නඩු දෙක
ගැන කල්පනා කර තින්දුවකට පැමිණ,
මේ වවන පාව්ච්චි කර ඇති බව. මා
දන්තේ නැහැ, ඊස්'ටේලෝ සහ ඇනිස්'
මිනික් නඩු තින්දු දෙක ගැන මා සඳහන්
කල කාරණා මතක ඇද්දයි කියන්න. මා
ඒ තින්දු දෙක ගැන සඳහන් කළ බව
ඇත්ත. නමුත් මා දන්තේ නැහැ, අපේ
දුවිධ මන්ත්‍රීතුමන්'ලාට ඒ ගැන මතකයක්
ඇද්දයි කියන්න. ඒ ගැන මතකයක්
ඇද්දයි අපේ සිංහල සහෝදර මන්ත්‍රී
තුමන්'ලාගෙන් එක් මන්ත්‍රීවර
යකු කීවා, ඇනිස්'මිනික් කියන්තේ
බෙහෙත් වර්ගයක් කියා තමන් සිතූ බව.
මේ අනුව කල්පනා කර බලන විට,
වර්තමාන සමාජයේ ජීවත්වන අයවලුන්
හැවයට වටපිටාව, ජනතාව දෙස, සමාජය
දෙස නොබලා නීති පොත දින බලාගෙන
පමණක්, මෙන්න මේ තින්'දුවේ මෙන්'දම
මෙන්න මෙසේ'යයි කියන්නට පුළුවන්
කමක් තිබෙනවාද? ඇත්ත වශයෙන්'ම
බැහැ. එම නිසා අපේ මන්ත්‍රීතුමන්'ලාගෙන්
මෙන්න මේ ඉල්ලීම කරන්න කැමතියි.
අපි අපේ ශ්‍රේෂ්ඨාධිකරණයේ ස්'වාධිනත්
වය රැක ගනිමු. ආණ්ඩු කුම වාවස්'ථා
අධිකරණයේ පහසුව, බලය රැක ගනිමු.
ඒ වාගේ'ම මේ ගරු සභාවේ—ජාතික රාජ්‍ය
සභාවේ—ස්'වෛරීභාවයත් බලයන් අපි
අරක්ෂා කර ගනිමු.

I crave your indulgence on this
occasion to speak a few words, in
introducing this motion, in the
English language as well. I do so
because I appreciate that this law
has been the subject of some controversy, and I think it only fair that
every hon. Member of this House,
whether he is a Tamil-speaking or a
Sinhala-speaking Member, is entitled
to hear from me in plain language,
capable of being understood by him,
what precisely this law is all about.

By the Crown Proceedings Act of
1947, in England, the position in
regard to injunctions against the
Crown was very clearly stated. It is
the law that prevails to this day in
the United Kingdom. There it is
plainly declared in Section 21 of the
Crown Proceedings Act of 1947 that
injunctions do not lie against the
Crown, and the Crown is defined to
include a Minister of the Government; there is also a specific sub-
section which says that no injunctions shall lie against a public officer,
an officer of the Crown, in any situation where the effect of giving an
injunction against such officer would
be to bind the Crown. Now that is
the prevailing English law.

On 11th May 1972, this House, by
an amendment to the Interpretation
Act, decided—I think we decided as
best as we knew—to bring our law
into line with the English Law as
contained in the Crown Proceedings
Act. We were not trying to enact a
new law ; we were not trying to create
new conditions ; we were tying to
equate the law that prevailed in Sri
Lanka with the law that prevailed in
the United Kingdom. Section 24 of
the Interpretation Act was the section
which was to achieve that objective;
we declared it clearly in Parliament.
We did not touch other remedies
that may be available against the
Crown. We have always followed
the 1947 Act of English. Remedies
in tort are available against the
Crown; we have remedies in contract
against the Crown; we had the possibility of getting declaratory orders
against the Crown, but the injunction
remedy was brought exactly in line
with the English Law. That is what
that law was all about.

When we enacted it—I do not think anyone had any doubts about it—it was not a new group of people sitting here; it was the same National State Assembly. I do not think there is a single person present in this House who did not paticipate in that Debate, who did not understand clearly what we were doing If you ask yourselves in all honesty as persons participated in the Debate in this Assembly, did any one of you really entertain any doubt as to what the intention of Parliament was, the reply would be: the intention of Parliament clearly was to bring the law in line with the English Law, with the Crown Proceedings Act of 1947. That was all that there was to it.

Well, their Lordships in the Supreme Court are an independent body. We have striven to preserve that independence; we have guaranteed it in the Constitution under Section 131 in a manner in which it is guaranteed in very few Constitutions. And their Lordships in the exercise of that power have decided, and we respect their judgment, to tell us that according to the language we have used in Parliament we meant something quite different. We intended only to exclude injunctions against the Crown where a Minister has acted *bona fide;* but if the Minister had acted *mala fide,* or it alleged to have acted *mala fide,* Their Lordships of the Supreme Court tell us that the Parliament did not intend to exclude this jurisdiction. Now, no one will ever know whether a Minister acts *bona fide* or *mala fide* until after a long and protracted trial. An allegation of *mala fides* may be there, but a decision on the question of *mala fides* is something that can only be decided at the end of a case, which means, in effect, that the injunction is going to be binding until the final determination is made upon the question of *mala fides.*

Now that is the very question that was before the House on 11th May 1972. That is precisely the matter that the Crown Proceedings Act of

1947 has excluded. You can have all the remedies you like. You can claim damages and you can ask for declarations, but you cannot get injunctions. You cannot restrain the State from moving along the course of development tnat is necessary in this country.

Now, on this question, what was the situation that existed ? You remember my telling you in 1972 that there were pending then about 80 cases in which on the filmsiest evidence, injunctions had been issued by the then Supreme Court against the Minister of Agriculture and Lands, seeking to restrain him from acquiring lands. What were the grounds alleged ? Let us examine them. In every case this is what was alleged : " I am a man who voted for the other side. I am a supporter of the opposite political party. I am a landowner. Here is a clear case of victimization. This Minister is seeking to acquire my lands in order to pauperize me. There are other lands belonging to other people which could easily be taken over. He has not cared to do that. He has taken my land." The allegation is, " My land is being acquired because I voted for the other side." This is the political *mala fides* alleged on which the Supreme Court has issued injunctions. Of those 80 injunctions, which have been pending for years and years, not one to this date has been allowed by the Supreme Court on the ground of *mala fides.* That has never happened during the last ten or twelve years including the period when you were the Government. There has not been one judgment on the ground of *mala fides.* And it would be a wonderful thing to tell the people of a village this : You wanted a piece of land acquired for a cemetery. The owner says that he voted for the U. N. P. and he has got an injunction against the Minister. So for the next so many years you will not get a cemetery and you cannot bury your dead !

In one of the thirteen cases, the subject of the present dispute, the Minister of Lands sought to acquire

[f8ලික්ස් ආර්. ඩී. බණ්ඩාරනායක මහතා]
an extent of 1,200 acres—I read this
in the judgment of His Lordship
Mr. Justice Wilmot Gunasekera—
for village expansion to provide
elbow-room for housing, and one
man, claiming to own one acre out
of the 1,200 acres, went into court
and said, "I am an Indian Tamil. I
voted for the U. N. P. The local
Member of Parliament hates my
guts and therefore he has inspired
the Minister of Lands to take over
this 1,200 acres with the malicious
objective of depriving me of this
one acre." On this the court issued
an injunction restraining the Minister from acquiring the 1,200 acres,
and the people of that village are
expected to wait in perpetuity in the
hope that some day the Supreme
Court will adjudicate on the question
and decide whether the Minister was
inspired as alleged or not. I do not
know, but I suppose in this country
you have got to know what the
intention of Parliament is through
the courts. I ask you, has any of you
the slightest doubt as to what the
intention of Parliament was two
years ago on this particular matter ?
Very learned judgments have been
written both for and against. Much
can be said on both sides, I suppose,
from a purely legal point of view.
But it seems to me that we are
playing round with things which are
really unimportant. One Judge said
that he would be undertaking "a
hazardous voyage sailing on tempes-
tuous seas" if he decided to examine
the HANSARD debates to know what
the intention of Parliament was.
Mr. Justice Malcolm Perera has said
so. I would respectfully agree. He is
the most senior Judge who wrote the
majority order.

I would like to tell you how I look
at it. If I am called upon to find out
the meaning of a statute enacted a
hundred years ago I may find myself
wondering how useful it would be to
read the speeches in HANSARD of the
then Members of Parliament who
may have worn top hats and frocks
coats and cravats, not people dressed
as we are dressed, not people living
in our contemporary environment in
our society. I may be left wondering.
That is quite right. It may not be
very useful to examine those
HANSARDS to find out what people
thought and how they were acting
at that time. There may also be situations in which the Draftsman has
used the words "shall" or "may"
"and" or "or" and where Parliament has not even given thought to
the question of a particular word or
phrase. Reading HANSARD may be
quite unhelpful, but for us that is
quite different from trying to find out
what Parliament enacted yesterday
or last year or the year before. No
person living in Sri Lanka is
unaware, unless he chooses to live in
blinkers, of what the intention of
Parliament is. It is being reported in
the papers. You do not need to read
the HANSARD itself if you live in
contemporary society—the debates
are known and you have not the
slightest doubt about it.

If I may give an illustration from
a source closer home. It may be
unfair but it is an illustration that
comes naturally to me as a Christian.
Suppose it becomes necessary to
know the meaning of a Bible text and
you are trying to understand clearly,
for example, the words of Jesus
Christ in the Gospel, there is a problem here. Today, Churches ranging
from one end of the spectrum to the
other—the Roman Catholic Church,
the Anglican Church, the Episcopa-
lian Church, the Non-Conformists,
the Pentecostalists—give different
interpretatoins based upon texts and
try to tell us what Jesus Christ said.

අචාර්ය ඇන්. ඇම්. පෙරේරා
(கலாநிதி என். எம். பெரேரா)
(Dr. N. M. Perera)
What about Jehovah's Witnesses ?

f8ලික්ස් ආර්. ඩී. බණ්ඩාරනායක මහතා
(திரு. பிலிக்ஸ் ஆர். டி. பண்டாரநாயக்க)
(Mr. Felix R. D. Bandaranaike)
Yes, Jehovah's Witnesses too ! But
I will ask you this question. Would
not the situation have been quite
different in the days of contemporary

society when Christ was still there? In the first 50 years A. D. would the Jewish Christians of those days have required priests or deacons or such persons to interpret the Gospel to tell them the meaning of Christ's message? Would the persons who stood at the foot of the Mount listening to the Sermon on the Mount have had a problem and required people to answer these questions intricately, to put glosses upon the texts, to interpret the texts from pulpits or places of religious worship? I do not know the answer to this. If you live in contemporary society, surely, the situation is different.

When in the Acts of the Apostles those who heard St. Peter speaking in tongues on the day of Pentecost asking the question, "What meaneth this?" in the language of the Bible, they were not asking for an Interpretation Ordinance or an Interpretation Act! They did not have to ask themselves when St. Peter spoke, was he speaking in foreign languages or was he simply making inarticulate noises which nobody could understand claiming to speak in tongues? They heard what St. Peter said and when he said, "What meaneth this?" they were not seeking an interpretation. They were merely marvelling at what they thought they saw and heard. That is all it comes to.

In contemporary society what are we doing? Why are we putting ourselves in blinkers to ask ourselves this question. I am myself a great admirer of Justice Malcolm Perera. I have attended services which he has held as a lay-preacher on many Saturdays. I myself was a great admirer of the way in which he has expounded the text of the Gospel of Jesus Christ. But the situation might have been different if we were looking at it in the contemporary times of Jesus Christ himself. We may need those glosses now. Four hundred years hence if we are called upon to interpret what this Parliament intended and our children and

our grandchildren are called upon to decide these questions, it would be a completely different matter from having to decide it now.

Let us take a few other judgements. You find strange things. I will table all these judgements so that you can read them. I do not know how to summarize 200 pages. I will refer to as much as I can. Justice Ismail has said somewhere that it is accepted as axiomatic that injunctions do lie against the Crown in Sri Lanka and he cites the case in 56 NLR, the case that is popularly known as the Buddadasa case. So I looked at Buddadasa. I find Justice Sansoni there says just the opposite. He says that it is axiomatic that injunctions do not lie against the Crown. Justice Ismail says he proceeds to dissect the law on the basis of that judgement which is the foundation of his entire judgement. Justice Sharvananda has expressed great fears that if an injunction is not made available against the State it is surely going to lead to the establishment of a totalitarian regime. I should like to reassure Justice Sharvananda, and indeed the whole House, that there is no danger of that. In England there has never been an injunction against the Crown and they are pretty far away from a totalitarian state—at least I hope so. We shall no doubt hear more about this as the Commonwealth Parliamentary Association Conference proceeds, starting from tomorrow.

Justice Weeraratne is the only Judge who has dealt with the Principles of State Policy in the Constitution and his approach to it is this: he says unless there is reference in the statute to the Principles of State Policy, it becomes a little difficult to import the Principles of State Policy into the principles of interpretation. Well, all I can say is that I do not know by any stretch of imagination how a law passed before the Constitution was adopted could have referred to Principles of State Policy anyway. He also says that there is no need for this interpretation, and

[ගරු අර්. ඩී. බණ්ඩාරනායක මහතා]
that injunctions have been excluded because the Minister has power under the Administration of Justice law, section 46, to give special jurisdiction to a special court to dispose of land acquisition cases speedily and hurriedly. He may be right, but how on earth could the framers in this Parliament in 1972 take account of a law that was not enacted till 1974—the Administration of Justice Law?

All I say is that it does not matter whether we agree with the judgement or not. Is it possible for me to legislate on the basis that people are going to do exactly the opposite of what the law expects them to do? I do not know how to legislate on the basis of *mala fides*. How do I legislate, for example, for an independent judiciary if I start with the assumption that every single judge is dishonest or politically coloured? It cannot be done. All my legislation is built on the assumption that the different public functionaries who have been given work to do in their respective fields are going to do that work honestly, ably, and well within the limits of their capacities. There is no other way. That is the only way in which laws can be drafted. I cannot start on the assumption that every time I use a word —an adjective, a noun or a verb—I have got to interpolate the words *bona fide* or *mala fide*. Some judges have solemnly said that if I want to exclude *mala fide* I must indicate it : that every time a Minister acts, *bona fide* or *mala fide*, an injunction shall not lie. I think it would be completely contrary to the intention of Parliament to start on the assumption that anybody acts *mala fide*. If anybody does act *mala fide* the law must operate against him. That is a different thing. Remedies must be found. But was it the intention of this House that the remedy lay in the courts? The answer is, no.

A great deal of the arguments has gone on the basis of the judgment of Lord Reid in what is known as the Anisminic case. Now, the Anisminic case is a most interesting case. It arose from the disposal of the compensation money which was acquired by the British Government by freezing Egyptian assets soon after the closure of the Suez Canal and its nationalisation in 1956. And in this matter the questions that further arose are whether the jurisdiction of the courts should be excluded and also the extent to which the courts are entitled, on the ground of nullity, to declare the ouster clause unaffected by the doctrine of *ultra vires*.

Justice Vaithialingam says, " all Members of this House must have known all about the East Elloe and the Anisminic case. " I read bits and pieces of it during the course of the debate. I checked on this by asking one of our Sinhalese-speaking Members of this House as to what he thought of the Anisminic case and he said he thought that it was a patent medicine! I have not checked how my Friends in the Federal Party stand on the matter. I really do not know what they think. Certainly, some of our Sinhalese-speaking Members said that it was a patent medicine. They have thought that it was an insecticide for agricultural purposes!

Anyway, the important point is, taking into account all these judgements, I am certain that if Lord Reid really sat down—as the hon. Member for Nuwara Eliya (Mr. Gamani Dissanayake) is trying to do—to read the nine judgements—he will be most surprised—[*Interruption*]. Well, I have no doubt in my mind. I have read all the judgements, including the judgements of Justice Pathirana and of Justice Wilmot Gunasekera, and I would like to say that I wish to pay them a compliment.

Let us examine the situation. Some judges seem to have been rather guided by the theory that there is

1974 සැප්තැම්බර් 5

basically in this country the protectional right of the citizen to his property. I think it is about time we all threw away the shackles of the past and came to realize that the whole attitude to property has undergone a fundamental change in recent times and in recent years. We have rights to property in this country—we respect them—but it is only in so far as they are recognized by law. There is no fundamental right to property in the Constitution. We respect property—we like it—so far as it is protected by the law. But if you ask me myself personally, " Felix, to what extent do you feel you are a property owner today? ", I would say, " Only to the extent that the State does not need my property and does not ask me for it, and if the State wants it then I am afraid all I have is the right to compensation. " That is the law.—[*Interruption*] Thirty acres. The hon. Member for Walapane tells me that I might find myself entitled to thirty acres, which is where I stood when I started politics. He is right.

I will say this. Today the Principles of State Policy are enacted in law in the Constitution. We established fundamental rights—to freedom, liberty and many other things. But at no stage is there entrenched in our Constitution a right to property. It must be subject to the overriding needs of the State and its requirements.

Does this mean that Ministers should have complete freedom to act arbitrarily, to act in a vicious fashion, to be made use of as instruments to wield injustice or to cause problems? My answer is, no The Government of Sri Lanka is not interested in perpetuating an injustice just as much as the Government of the United Kingdom in excluding injunctions against the Crown has not perpetuated any injustice. The remedies are administrative. The remedies lie within the framework of executive and legislative government.

Do you really think that if I, as a Minister, were to act oppressively, any of you in this Assembly is going to let me get away with it? You will pursue me with questions, you will purrsue me with Motions of No Confidence. you will hound me around this Assembly, even if we have got the numbers, so much so that the situation will become so embarrassing that the Prime Minister will probably call for my resignation. That is one side of it. It that all ? There is more than that. If I act oppressively you can still make representations to my Colleagues in the Cabinet, to the Prime Minister, so that the Prime Minister herself will call me to ask. It is bound to happen.

She herself has asked me to announce to this Assembly that if it helps to really allay your fears she proposes to appoint an administrative body of three persons which will be required to report to her within 10 days on any alleged oppressive acquisition, so that any person can make representations if he says he is unfairly treated. There will be no need of injunctions. She will be advised by an independent body of three persons nominated by her. If any person makes representations that he has been unfairly treated his case will be examined, but weighed against the larger interests of society.

We cannot on a frivolous allegation that somebody is an Indian Tamil owning one acre, hold up the acquisition of 1,250 acres needed for a public purpose. I am not prepared to tell people any longer to bury their dead in water-logged soil for lack of cemeteries. I am not prepared to act on the assumption that the construction of a roadway can be laid by for perpetuity because one little owner in the middle says he voted for the other side and alleges political *mala fides*.

This not possible in a country in crying need of development. Such a country cannot stand and look on while this type of legislation is being interpreted restrictively, in strange ways, to mean the exact opposite of

[පිළිස්ස් අ.ඩී. ඩී. බණ්ඩාරනායක මහතා]
what Parliament intended. If I was wrong in using the wrong words I have already told you in Sinhala that I owe an apology to this Assembly. This whole mess arose from my inadequacy in the English language. This Law was enacted in English on 11th May 1972. I thought that the words I used were so plain and clear that nobody could fail to get the message right. It seems that I was wrong. I should have thought that every one of you understood what I said whether I was talking in English or Sinhala. But it seems to me— perhaps it is good for my vanity to know it—that my knowledge of English is not as good as I thought it was.

Never mind. You are a very forgiving lot of people I know. I am sure you will make excuses for my inadequacies. And this time I have tried to draft the Bill in the Sinhala language. I have checked every word of it and I have satisfied myself that this time not only is the Law going to be enacted in Sinhala but it is going to be interpreted in Sinhala and will not have an English version with it at all.

It becomes necessary for us to speed up the process if we find that we are living in two different worlds, if we find ourselves living in contemporary society on the one side in this Assembly, and on the other, in an imaginary society in other environments in Sri Lanka. The message has to be got across. And if there is no other way of doing it, I think we shall have to take the step of speeding up the process of transition by which we move into the administration of the law courts in our own language.

I have already had representations from Members of Parliament who passed a unanimous resolution in the Government Parliamentary Group demanding this. I have begged and pleaded with them to just let me attend to this at my own pace and not to force me to sacrifice law for language; to let the process be orderly so that the transition can take place without complication.

I am certain that all Members of this Assembly will pay heed to what I say even if I am wrong in the use of the language, because I know they love and respect me, and that is the more important thing. I do not know that anyone of you personally dislikes me even if I may be wrong on something or disagrees sharply on various matters.

What is important is trust and confidence, that I will not let you down, that I shall see to it that your intentions are accurately translated into action. That is what is important. I give you that promise on this occasion. I would like to tell you that there is no problem at all if we make our meaning clear. We bow to the decision of the courts by accepting the judgment. We accept the fact that the words we used were not clear in their meaning because the courts have told us that.

having accepted that what have we proceeded to do? We have demonstrated to the whole world the efficacy of our Constitutional Court provisions in regard to the speed and the efficiency with which we have obtained the pronouncement that the Bill before the House does not violate one tittle of the Constitution.

We have established, perhaps, the most important principle of all, the sovereignty of Parliament, and that sovereignty is something which we shall jealously guard. Nobody is going to invade that sovereignty by telling us that Parliament intended something other than what it really intended to. That is what this Debate is all about. I have already tabled the judgments for those who would like to read them. They are very long. I can only add one word on that. The judicial system in this country can only go by convention. One of the conventions I had hoped could grow up in this country is that judges would not merely listen to arguments and write judgments based on them but would consult with each other and bring their collective mind to bear on cases, think together on those things, and come to common conclusions. I am left with a feeling, after reading these nine judgments—each of it runs into 40 pages—that this is very much the efforts of nine individual judges, quite honestly made according to their best capacities and judgments, conclusions upon the argument placed before them. But there has been very little consultation, comparison, because I do not see, for example, how Justice Ismail and Justice Vaitilingam who both supported the majority view could have said exactly opposite things in their judgments in regard to what 56 N. L. R. said in the case of Buddhadasa. A thing like that simply could not have happened. There has been just no consultation here. When we create a final court of appeal and entrust the work to three judges, it is extremely important that the three judges meet and consult. It may be they will disagree sharply. That is their privilege. But it cannot be done on the basis of writing separate judgments without showing them to each other and keeping them as closely guarded secrets until the date of their release in technicolour. Consultation is extremely important.

If this is not understood and if conventions do not develop on these lines, perhaps we shall have to legislate ; perhaps the Interpretation Ordinance will have to grow a little longer so that the things which we thought would develop automatically, good, healthy traditions, would automatically grow. Perhaps if we have got to tell the judges that, in interpreting statutes, they should know how to get the message of Parliament across, it may be we have to think of other ways; it may be we shall have to adopt systems by which the interpretation as to what Parliament intended can actually be referred to Parliament itself. A standing committee of lawyer members, perhaps,

would be able to advise the judges that they are out of tune and cannot get the right wave-length.

රෝයි රාජපක්ෂ මහතා (හක්මන)
(திரு. ரோய் ராஜபக்ஷ—ஹக்மீன)
(Mr. Roy Rajapakse—Hakmana)
Sir, on a point of Order, some man is sitting in my seat.

නියෝජ්‍ය කථානායකතුමා
(உப சபாநாயகர் அவர்கள்)
(Mr. Deputy Speaker)
Order please, he has got up now.

f පීලික්ස් ආර්. ඩී. බණ්ඩාරනායක මහතා
(திரு. ' பீலிக்ஸ் ஆர். டி. பண்டாரநாயக்க)
(Mr. Felix R. D. Bandaranaike)
Now that we have finished the little interlude of Goldilocks and the three bears, may I suggest we get back to the Interpretation Ordinance ?

ගරු මන්ත්‍රීවරයෙක්
(கௌரவ அங்கத்தவர் ஒருவர்)
(A Member)
Make him a judge !•

f පීලික්ස් ආර්. ඩී. බණ්ඩාරනායක මහතා
(திரு. பீலிக்ஸ் ஆர். டி. பண்டாரநாயக்க)
(Mr. Felix R. D. Bandaranaike)
I was going to say that it becomes extremely important to evolve new conventions and new laws. If in bringing about a transformation we have to legislate on many matters on which I thought we should not have to legislate, on matters on which I assumed the intentions of Parliament, the intentions of contemporary society and the intentions of a changing world in Sri Lanka were clear, then maybe we shall have to move faster both in language, in our institutional framework and in regard to other things.

I myself have been trying to make sure that we do not live in a little, inward-looking world, like frogs in a pool, not being aware of what is going on in the wide world

1773   ජාතික රාජ්‍ය සභාව   1774

`[fපිලික්ස් ආර්. ඩී. බණ්ඩාරනායක මහතා]
around us. Some people seem to
imagine that if the matter of granting injunctions against the State is
withdrawn our little world will
cave in and the roof will fall
in upon us and we shall become a
one-party State and major disasters
will come upon us. It has not
happened elsewhere, and I think the
best answer to this is to create more
opportunities for our judges to
travel. I have already sent the Chief
Justice on a tour of West Germany,
and I am hoping very soon, by the
end of next month, to arrange a
tour for two of our judges, of the
Soviet Union, and I hope that then
a lot of the theoretical fears that they
entertain about many things
will disappear. There is justice even
in a one-party State though we may
not want to copy—[Interruption].

ජේ. ආර්. ජයවර්ධන මහතා
(திரு. ஜெ. ஆர். ஜயவர்தன)
(Mr. J. R. Jayewardene)
What about the author
Solzhenitsyn ?`

fපිලික්ස් ආර්. ඩී. බණ්ඩාරනායක මහතා
(திரு. பிலிக்ஸ் ஆர். டி. பண்டாரநாயக்க)
(Mr. Felix R. D. Bandaranaike)
Yes, he is a wonderful guy. He
wrote a good book. Have you read
it ?

I would like to say this in
conclusion. When nine judges sit
together we want their collective
wisdom, as I said, and not their
individual efforts. Think for yourselves what would have happened in
the United States of America if the
nine judges, who had to decide on the
question as to whether the Watergate
tapes should be realeased, thought
separately and wrote separate judgements.

රෝයි රාජපක්ෂ මහතා
(திரு. ரோய் ராஜபக்ஷ)
(Mr. Roy Rajapakse)
The United States is different from
Sri Lanka.

fපිලික්ස් ආර්. ඩී. බණ්ඩාරනායක මහතා
(திரு. பிலிக்ஸ் ஆர். டி. பண்டாரநாயக்க)
(Mr. Felix R. D. Bandaranaike)
Maybe President Nixon would still
be there—[Interruption].

I can see that the hon. Member for
Hakmana (Mr. Roy Rajapakse)
obviously entertains strong feelings
about the Interpretation law. Now
that it is being amended I am sure he
will quieten down in due course.

Thank you very much.

අ. හා. 3·11

ගාමිණී දිසානායක මහතා (නුවරඑළිය)
(திரு. காமினி திசாநாயக்க—நுவரெலியா)
(Mr. Gamini Dissanayake—Nuwara
Eliya)
ගරු නියෝජ්‍ය කථානායකතුමනි, අර්ථ
නිරූපණ පනත 1972 මැයි මාසයේ 11
වැනිදා මෙම ගරු සභාවට ඉදිරිපත්
බවත්, එය සිංහල භාෂාවෙන් ඉදිරිපත්
කළා නම් මේ විධියට අඩුපාඩුවක් ඇති වී
ශ්‍රේෂ්ඨාධිකරණයට යන්න වුවමනාවත්
නැති බවත් ගරු අධිකරණ ඇමතිතුමා
ප්‍රකාශ කළා. මොන අඩුපාඩුව නිසා මෙම
පනත සංශෝධනය කරන්නට සිදු වුවත්
fපිලික්ස් ආර්. ඩයස් බණ්ඩාරනායක ඇමති
තුමාට තිබෙන ඉංග්‍රීසි භාෂාව පිළිබඳ
දැනුමේ අඩුපාඩුව නිසා වරදක් සිදු වී
ඇතැයි කියන තර්කය නම් මා පිළිගන්නේ
නැහැ. ලංකාව තුළ පමණක් නොව, පොදු
රාජ්‍ය මණ්ඩලය තුළද ඉංග්‍රීසි භාෂාව පිළිබඳ
විශිෂ්ඨ දැනුම ඇති පුද්ගලයන් අතර
fපිලික්ස් ආර්. ඩී. බණ්ඩාරනායක මහතා
එක් කෙනෙක්. ආචාර්‍ය කොල්වින් ආර්.
ද සිල්වා මහතා තව කෙනෙක්. ආචාර්‍ය
එන්. එම්. පෙරේරා මහතා තව කෙනෙක්.
විරුද්ධ පාර්ශ්වයේ නායක ජේ. ආර්.
ජයවර්ධන මහතා තව කෙනෙක්. [බාධා
කිරීමක්]

රෝයි රාජපක්ෂ මහතා (හක්මන)
(திரு. ரோய் ராஜபக்ஷ—ஹக்கமீன)
(Mr. Roy Rajapakse—Hakmana)
ඇයි මං ?

Felix on the Emergency

එතැක්. ඔහුටත් කොන්දේසි මාලාවක්
දමා තිබෙනවා, කිසිම පොදු රැස්වීමකට
සහභාගි වෙන්න බැරිය,, විශ්ව විද්‍යාල
මණ්ඩපවලට ඇතුළුවීම තහනම්ය කියා.
එතුමා මට පෙන්නුවා ඒ කොන්දේසි
මාලාව. එම නිසා මම කරුණාකර ඉල්ලා
සිටිනවා, මෙසේ නිදහස් වී ඇති සැක
කරුවන්ට එවැනි කොන්දේසි දැම්ම
අසාධාරණයක් නිසා ඒ කොන්දේසි
ඉවත් කර, ඔවුන්ට විශ්ව විද්‍යාලවලට
ඇතුළු වීමට, පොදු රැස්වීම්වලට සහභාගි
වීමට හැකිවන පරිදි මානුෂික නිදහස
ලබාදෙන්නය කියා.

f පිලික්ස් ආර්. ඩී. බණ්ඩාරනායක මහතා
(திரு. பீலிக்ஸ் ஆர். டி. பண்டாரநாயக்க)
(Mr. Felix R. D. Bandaranaike)
Mr. Chairman, I have not requested
for permission to intervene in this
Debate, but because of one or two
matters that have been raised on the
Votes of the Hon. Prime Minister
I request leave of hon. Members
to give way to me, for a few minutes.
I do not propose to take much time—
on matters on which, although not
pertaining strictly to the subject of
Defence and Foreign Affairs, come
within a discussion on the Hon.
Prime Minister's Votes.

I would like to deal with the question of the Emergency, in regard to
which many hon. Members made
various comments. One such
comment was addressed to me when
I was not in the Assembly by the
hon. Member for Agalawatta
(Dr. Colvin R. d Silva) who raised
many matters pertaining to the need
for the Emergency.

I quite understand that an Emergency should not be the order of the
day or a matter of routine when it
comes to the conducting of
the affairs of the country,
and I myself am one of those
people who hold the view that
emergency powers must also be used
with restraint, moderation and
within the limits of what is necessary
at any given moment. As far as I
can see I do not see any disagreement on the general principle of it.
But having said that, when it comes
to the application of it, I do see that
there is a certain amount of controversy and contradiction in the
attitudes of hon. Members of the
Assembly depending on which side
of the Assembly they are at any
given moment. And if I draw attention to it I do so not in a spirit of
wanting to be nasty to anybody or
with any personal motivation but
merely to draw attention to what is
factually true.

For example, let us start with 1971
and the circumstances in which the
State of Emergency occurred and in
which it was certainly necessary to
declare a State of Emergency at that
time. I do not think anyone will
disagree with that. The members of
the L.S.S.P. were members of the
Government at that time. Indeed,
the hon. Member for Agalawatta
(Dr. Colvin R. de Silva) in his
observations conceded that there was
a case for the declaration of a state
of Emergency. So let us not argue
about that. Let us not argue whether
there was a mistaken notion that
these people were revolutionaries or
C.I.A. inspired or how it all happened.
The fact is that there were circumstances prevailing at that moment
which everybody, myself included,
the hon. Member for Yatiyantota
(Dr. N. M. Perera) included, the
hon. Member for Agalawatta
included, the Hon. Prime Minister
included and the other Cabinet
Ministers included, jointly took the
view that there was a case for the
declaration of a state of Emergency.
That is factually so.

Now the hon. Member for Agalawatta says this, and I think he is
buttressed by the hon. Member for
Panadura (Mr. Leslie Goonewardene) : " You know while we were
members of the Government we did

175   ජාතික රාජ්‍ය සභාව   176

[ළිපික්ස් ආර්. ඩී. බණ්ඩාරනායක මහතා]

not like to say some things that might hurt the feelings of the Hon. Prime Minister, for reasons of solidarity." That was put forward as an argument at some stage. "I have always said what I have had to say, whether anyone likes it or not, members of the L.S.S.P. or anyone else. Certainly, even at Cabinet meetings if ever I disagreed on any matter I never kept it secret or unknown. The fact that it might hurt somebody was not a reason for not saying it. Whatever had to be said was said, certainly on my part. I never adopted the policy that because it might hurt somebody's feelings I should keep my mouth shut. I have never done that, and I do not believe that any other Minister in our Cabinet at that time did that either."

On the Emergency, what happened ? The Emergency has been used for a number of purposes, let us face it, and is my assessment every one of those purposes is justified. The last occasion was an occasiin when I was not even in Ceylon, but I know about it because I was told about it soon afterwards and even spoke to the Hon. Prime Minister at one time. I discussed the matter over the telephone from London where I happened to be at that time for some personal reasons of my own. That was in April 1974 when the United National Party decided to hold a series of meetings, 150 meetings, all over the country. On that occasion I believe there was very careful consultation among the Cabinet Ministers who were in Ceylon. I was not among them. The discussions were on this basis : Would it be possible to control a security situation without recourse to an Emergency ? To what extent were the army and the police capable of dealing with this situation under the ordinary law ? To what extent was the situation capable of being tackled under the ordinary law ?

I believe the Hon. Ministers, including the members of the L.S.S.P., were strongly of the view that Emergency powers should be used to deal with that situation which cropped up at that time, and also to seal the Dawasa Group newspapers. That was part of the same deal.

We also used the Emergency for the purpose of passing on wage benefits of employees. Mr. Dudley Senanayake did that on one occasion at least when he was Prime Minister. We have also made use of the Emergency recently for the purpose of dealing with synthetic textiles. There are many situations in which we have made use of the Emergency in the rehabilitation process.

There are a hundred people today who are reporting to the authorities under no other rule of law than the Emergency Laws. They are today at liberty. Out of the 18,000 people who were taken into custody at one stage, they are today released from custody and reporting to the various authorities under no other sanction of the law. There is no other law requiring them to report to the D. R. O. or the grama sevaka or to anybody else. The entire supervision is under the Emergency Laws. I am sorry I was wrong. It is not a hundred people who are in custody. There are 300 persons in custody awaiting trial in C.J.C. (1) right how before two panels of judges appointed recently by the President. Of them there are 200 in respect of whom I am considering recommending for bail. I have made a recommendation for bail. That is how I came to the figure 100. I must apologize to the House if my figures are not accurate. It is as usual a small matter of arithmetic ! The hon. Member for Yatiyantota (Dr. N. M. Perera) will appreciate that it is not my strong point.

කේ. බී. රත්නායක මහතා
(திரு. கே. பி. ரத்நாயக்க)
(Mr. K. B. Ratnayake)
New maths !

ෆිලික්ස් ආර්. ඩි. බණ්ඩාරනායක මහතා
(திரு. பிபிக்ஸ் ஆர். டி. பண்டாரநாயக்க)
(Mr. Felix R. D. Bandaranaike)
I will not go so far as to say that.
Maybe I have not used my little
pocket calculator properly. But anyway the result is the same. There
are a hundred people also held in
custody today under the sanction
and authority of the Emergency
Laws. My simple question to hon.
Members is ; is it your view today
that the "Dawasa" newspaper
should be released immediately from
its present restraint and restored to
publication ? Is it your position that
the United National Party should
now be permitted to hold 150 meetings simultaneously ? Because when
the question arose in exactly the
same fashion in April, 1974 you yourself took up the position that they
should not be allowed to do so. I think
we are agreed that the common
enemy is the United National Party
whose only representative at the
moment here is the ubiquitous
Member for Hiriyala (Mr. S. B.
Herat), who is studiously reading
something and avoiding listening to
my speech ! These are the questions
which do occur to any person
listening with any degree of attention.

If we take the view that Emergency
Laws are bad and we are perfectly
satisfied that every single element in
this country is proceeding on democratic procedures and democratic
lines under which it becomes unnecessary to have restraints, I myself would take the same view. More
recently the hon. Member for Kankesanturai (Mr. S. J. V. Chelvanayakam) made what is tantamount to a
declaration of war. I do not know
how seriously you would take his
declaration of war, but I do not
under-estimate the dangers of a
declaration of war. The hon. Member
for Kankesanturai is a very honourable person whom I have respected
from the time I was a small boy, and
I am happy to have him back in the
House. I am not prepared to start
with the assumption that merely because the hon. Member for Kankesanturai says a thing like that, I am
not prepared to give it due weight
and attention. We have seen, for
example, how extremist elements act.
We had seen a political assassination
recently in Jaffna and it may be that
there are two sides to the case.
Sometimes one thinks that there are
reasons for an assassination, which
may be political or may be not. I do
not want to involve myself in such
arguments. I am only saying that
when a political personality is wiped
out, obviously by an act of assassination, one cannot be blind to these
things. One cannot be blind to acts
of sabotage and so on which are in
fact happening. Hon. Members who
make a request for the preservation
of democratic principles must stop
and think and ask straight questions
to which we must come up with the
right answers. You cannot turn
round and tell the Government, "So
long as we were with you we liked
it ; when we are not with you we do
not like it and ask you to remove
it. "

When you were in the Government
you took the view that some of the
things that were done in that Emergency were not in your interest. I am
particularly thinking of the occasion
of the CFL rally on which you told us
in no uncertain terms that you felt
it was unjust and unreasonable use
of power against what you considered a perfectly justifiable procession
and demonstration on the occasion
of the C.F.L. rally. I appreciate your
point of view. There were occasions
when you argued against it in respect of that particular case. I am only
asking you now, please do not look

179   ජාතික රාජ්‍ය සභාව   180

[fපිලික්ස් ආර්. ඩී. බණ්ඩාරනායක මහතා]

at it from a narrow point of view, unless you are prepared to go the whole distance and think of every single illustration I gave you, including the "Dawasa" newspaper and the U.N.P's approach to holding a series of meetings on a single day which was stopped by the declaration of a curfew, when I think the hon. Leader of the Opposition held a little meeting outside his house at Ward Place. These are things which I cannot ignore and, furthermore, I would like to conclude on the subject of emergency by asking the hon. Member for Kankesanturai one little question, which I hope will not embarrass him. I ask him, do you feel that the Emergency prevailing in India is justified?

I am merely wondering whether it is a view of your Party, because India I think is an example that you often look to, whether you approve or not of the declaration of a state of Emergency in India.—[Interruption]. You do not like to talk about India because it embarrasses you. I am asking this question because very often you cite India as the best illustration of how democracy functions, and I would like to ask you a straight question. Since you have asked us, having declared war, why we are abusing democratic processes, am I not entitled to ask you, considering the close ties you have and the fact that you look to India always for precedent, to what extent do you support the declaration of an Emergency in India by the Prime Minister, Mrs. Indira Gandhi? I think I am entitled to ask that question. I am not asking that question –in a dirty fashion. I am asking you a straight political question because I think I am entitled to know your views on this matter on behalf of the people of this country.

ඩී. එන්. නවරත්නම් මහතා
(திரு. வி. என். நவரத்தினம்)
(Mr. V. N. Navaratnam)

They have Emergencies for limited periods for limited purposes.

fපිලික්ස් ආර්. ඩී. බණ්ඩාරනායක මහතා
(திரு. பிலிக்ஸ் ஆர். டி. பண்டாரநாயக்க)
(Mr. Felix R. D. Bandaranaike)

Is that your answer or Mr. Chelvanayakam's—[Interruption].

I would love to have it on record as coming from Mr. Chelvanayakam. It will be so valuable to us to have that on record once and for all. If you approve of all the things that have been done in India, then I think our Prime Minister is entitled to point to anything that happened there as a precedent and to give you that as an answer.—[Interruption]. I do not want a character certificate. I want you to give a character certificate to the Prime Minister of India, whom you always look up to when you search for a precedent. I think I am entitled to say that.

There is one last matter I wish to refer to. I understand that a certain amount of the Debate in this House has been in respect of a gentleman who is not a member of this House, Mr. Anura Bandaranaike. A number of matters were raised particularly when I was present. I happened to walk in at the time—I was not able to be here throughout the Debate—when the hon. Member for Panadura (Mr. Leslie Goonewardene) was raising a question pertaining to the exact status of Mr. Anura Bandaranaike in the framework of the Government of Sri Lanka. I think he was asking that question with reference to a limited matter in relation to a visit to the Maldives. I believe that was how he put it. I would prefer to take the question in a more general form rather than limit it to that one instance. I shall come back to that single incident also.

He asked what status Mr. Anura Bandaranaike enjoyed in the Government of Sri Lanka. So far as I know, the facts are these. There was a question of his being appointed at one stage as an adviser in the planning Ministry with reference to, I think,

Felix extends his hand to the Tamils

සි. එක්ස් මාටින් මහතා (යාපනය)

(திரு. சி. எக்ஸ் மார்டின்—யாழ்ப்பாணம்)

(Mr. C. X. Martyn—Jaffna)

Mr. Speaker, the matter I wish to mention relates to the visit of the Hon. Minister of Public Administration, Local Government & Home Affairs and Minister of Justice to Jaffna, which I must say was a very successful visit. It has generated a feeling of fellowship and confidence in the Government of which the Hon. Minister is a member.

I mentioned a small matter to the Hon. Minister and he said that it would be but fair that I make a reference to it on the Floor of the House. I was not present at the particular meeting but the Hon. Minister is alleged to have said, as it is reported in some Tamil newspaper " Ealanadu ", a local paper with some circulation, that the Member for Jaffna requested the Minister to dissolve the Municipal Council of Jaffna, that the Minister resisted it, and that I had a motive for making that request.

What I asked the Hon. Minister was that the peccant and errant mayors who have not paid the surcharge be removed from office. The Minister has written to me on two occasions that he is taking action. On the last occasion he said that the matter was before the Cabinet for consideration. It is in HANSARD. I wish to state clearly that I am not interested in dissolution. I asked the Hon. Minister with his customary capacity for investigation to have a watchful eye in view of the many complaints which have been received about the Jaffna Municipal Council.

fෆිලික්ස් ආර්. ඩී. බණ්ඩාරනායක මහතා

(திரு. பிலிக்ஸ் ஆர். டி. பண்டாரநாயக்க)

(Mr. Felix R. D. Bandaranaike)

I am very grateful to my good Friend the hon. Member for Uduvil (Mr. Dharmalingam) for giving me the opportunity to say something which I have already said in Jaffna, for the information of those who chose to stay away and who invited their supporters to stay away from us at Jaffna, so that ultimately, unfortunately, the only point of view which the supporters of the Federal Party had of the position of the Government of Sri Lanka and of the Ministers of the Government of Sri Lanka was at second hand in the way it was reported to them by the leadership of the Federal Party.

By staying away from people you cannot really come to understand what their views are, what your reactions to them are. In the kind of democracy we run in this country the people are the ultimate judges, and, in the last analysis, it is the people who have got to decide who is right, what is right and what is wrong. I am not saying that what a Minister utters on a public platform should be accepted as gospel truth or that it should be accepted uncritically or without comment. If what we say makes sense we expect the people to listen to it and to decide in their own minds what part of what we say makes sense to them and what part of it does not make sense to them, what part should be accepted and what part should be rejected. We do not go there to make converts, and certainly I should like to say on the Floor of this House that when I visited Jaffna recently I did not go there to speak to our party supporters or our party organization. I did not go there to make contact with them. I went there deliberately to try and make contact with those who are critical of us, who do not approve of the Government of Sri Lanka, who have their own reservations towards us, their own doubts and fears, after twenty years of hostility generated by communal politics ; I tried to bring about some degree of understanding at least as a groundwork for the future, and I did try in all goodwill. nad I meant it quite sincerely when I spoke there.

1037   ජාතික රාජ්‍ය සභාව   1038

[ෆිලික්ස් ආර්. ඩී. බණ්ඩාරනායක මහතා]

I tried to speak in Tamil, but I know perfectly well that my Tamil has its limitations. It was only of gesture value. I can state a proposition after careful preparation in Tamil but I really cannot argue a point in Tamil. I do not have that capacity. There are many members of the Federal Party who cannot argue a case in Tamil. In fact I think I did better than Mr. Tiruchelvam who I think has not yet addressed a single audience in Jaffna in Tamil."

ධර්මලිංගම් මහතා

(திரு. தர்மலிங்கம்)

(Mr. Dharmalingam)

He has.

ෆිලික්ස් ආර්. ඩී. බණ්ඩාරනායක මහතා

(திரு. பிலிக்ஸ் ஆர். டி. பண்டாரநாயக்க)

(Mr. Felix R. D. Bandaranaike)

He has, has he ? Well, I am glad to hear it. Somebody told me that he has not. I would not know. But I must say this. What is important here is not so much the gesture. Somebody told me, "You know, it is a pity you Ministers do not come here more often. You come once in so many years." I said, "I entirely agree. It is our fault, and if there is a criticism in this regard I am sorry for it." I only wish there are more Members of the Federal Party and its leaders who would also come down south and present their point of view to our people. It is not a question of saying that you have not convinced the leaders on this side. It is not a matter of dealings between leaders. That is my whole premise, that is my whole case. This business of doing shoddy little deals between leaders of parties—secret deals, secret arrangements—and then telling the people, "look, now we have got an agreement signed, sealed and delivered. Please have trust and confidence in the United National Party ; let us trust Dudley because he has made promises to us " or," let us trust Mrs. Bandaranaike because we think she might make promises to us", is not going to take you anywhere.

Even in the matter of the agreement on Kachchaitivu, it is not Mrs. Bandaranaike and Mrs. Gandhi who made the agreement ; it is the ratification by the people of Sri Lanka and India that gives force and validity to that agreement. To this day, have the people of Jaffna been told what the terms of that agreement between the Federal Party and the United National Party were ? No. That is my point. Let us face the fact : communalism is dead in this part of the world. There was a time when Mr. R. G. Senanayake and Mr. K. M. P. Rajaratne bestrode this place in a fashion that even a non-communal Sinhalese party could not afford to ignore. The pressure of public opinion arising from people like that was such that they had to take account of it. Fortunately, such a situation no longer exists—not in that form. There is not a single person here who would deny that communalism in that unadulterated fashion has gone out of vogue.

That was the message I carried to Jaffna. The Sinhalese people are not unreasonable people. Show me any other country in the world where a communal majority supposed to be oppressing the minority, according to you, had created by its very policies conditions which have made the Tamils the richest community in the country in agriculture—not through pensions, public service payments. Show me any other country in the world where such conditions exist. When the fences are broken down and replaced by concrete walls, when your city becomes one of the cleanest in the Island, when there is a rush of building activity in every main road— this is the kind of prosperity that is seen—is there one single Sinhalese person who has expressed a sense of jealousy ? In fact, they are lost in admiration of what your people in Jaffna are doing by sheer hard work.

There is no question of resentment, no communal feelings. I am telling you this because you did not come for those meetings. If you did, you would have learnt a few things and seen that the dent has occurred among your own major, established people. I did not go there to meet the Federal Party Member. I went there to meet groups of men who would normally not come for these things. They came to a public dinner ; they paid for the privilege, Rs. 12.50 a person.' Make no mistake. The people who mould public opinion in Jaffna, big business people, professionals, men who are behind your Tamil United Front, the real thinking people who constitute the establishment of the Federal Party, were there. I can assure you that I did my best to convey my message to them. I am not saying I convinced them ; but I think there is a dent made in the fortress you are trying to build around your communal politics.

Let us take this particular case. May I ask you, what is the objection to your presenting your point of view to our people ? Do you think that our people are incapable of understanding sympathetically the point of view of other people ? Are you serious in saying that if I go back to your people I am doing the wrong thing, or that I must restrict my talking to Mr. Chelvanayakam and Mr. Dharmalingam and a few others ? I never accept that position. The rulers of this country are not the elected representatives alone ; it is the people of the country.

Why should not the Sinhala people be entitled to know what the Tamil leaders are thinking and saying ? We are asking you to drop communalism where vestiges still remain.

ධර්මලිංගම් මහතා
(திரு. தர்மலிங்கம்)
(Mr. Dharmalingam)
You remove the ban on the press.

ෆීලික්ස් ආර්. ඩී. බණ්ඩාරනායක මහතා
(திரு. பீலிக்ஸ் ஆர். டி. பண்டாரநாயக்க)
(Mr. Felix R. D. Bandaranaike)
I am telling you that there is no ban on press. " Ealanadu " is publishing every day stuff favourable, the

stuff which you would not probably like ; it is publishing the speeches and statements I made, if you will read them in Tamil.

What is your objection now ? Let us come to your point : letters in Tamil. You asked me under what law that is being done. Now, may I ask you this in counter-point : under what law should anybody reply to your letters at all ? Supposing somebody sends a letter to a public servant, to a Government department, where is the law that says that it has to be replied at all ? What is there to stop a public servant taking that letter, tearing it up and putting it into a waste-paper basket ? There is no law about it ; it is an order of the Minister. It is the discipline in an office which demands that. If any public servant of mine is found receiving a letter from Mr. Dharmalingam and not treating that with the respect that it deserves, he will get the sack. And why does he get the sack ? He gets the sack not because there is a law which says he must reply a letter ; he gets the sack because he is not fulfilling my orders. It is as simple as that.

Now, if a man is not obliged by law to answer a letter, how can you say there must be a law to regulate the language in which he ought to reply. Is it wrong then for me also to issue an order saying that if you have to reply a letter which you receive from a Tamil man in this country, for goodness' sake please reply in a language he can understand ? Is it wrong for me to do that ? Are you telling me that I am acting against the interests of the Tamil people in directing public servants to do that ? How can you say this ?

You are talking of laws. How can you have a law which compels any person to reply a letter ? How can you say that any person who invites you to a wedding is entitled to a reply ? How can you talk of public servants ?

ධර්මලින් ගම් මහතා
(திரு. தர்மலிங்கம்)
(Mr. Dharmalingam)

I was talking about Tamil.

ෆිලික්ස් ආර්. ඩී. බණ්ඩාරනායක මහතා
(திரு. பிலிக்ஸ் ஆர். டி. பண்டாரநாயக்க)
(Mr. Felix R. D. Bandaranaike)

I am talking about the question of replying letters. That was your question. You were asking me, under what law ? I will tell yuo there is never a law under which any person is obliged to reply letters. It is administration, good administration, the order of the Minister, which ensures that letters are replied to. [*Interruption*]. If you do not want it in Tamil it is your business, but I think it is reasonable that a man who receives a letter must receive a letter that he can understand. If you do not think so, explain it to the Federal Party, explain it to your people in Jaffna, explain it in any language you like, but if you tell me that I have done wrong, that I am not treating you fairly, all I can say is that your politics completely passes my comprehension. I do not understand whether you are trying to argue for your people or against your people. You are talking of laws in regard to a matter where laws do not operate. Where does all this take you ?

You raised with me a question about a statement that I am supposed to have made somewhere about your people not coming down to the South. It is not a question of whether you convinced me or did not convince me. There are many matters in regard to which you will find it very difficult to talk to me on the bargaining table because I bargain hard. But, I will also tell you this much : look at it from the point of view of ordinary human sympathy. I would recommend for your reading sometime, even though you are not a Christian, Chapter 13, verses 4-7, of the First Epistle to the Corinthians. If you read that you will find the definition of charity, of love and what love means. If you read it you will realise

that that definition, in practical terms, is a kind of relationship which we are trying to build up between the Sinhala and Tamil communities in this country. It may end up with the complete destruction of communal politics here. But that is your misfortune ; it is not ours. We believe there is no room for communal politics and we welcome this as a united country. Unlike Mr. Dudley Senanayake we do not turn round and say, " We are grateful to a Divine Providence for having given us inadequate seats because it has helped us to bring about national unity. " We put it the other way. With an absolute majority in our hands—that does not matter— we do not need to buy the support of anybody, but we are very glad when, regardless of communal considerations, members of other parties, seeing the light, decide to abandon those parties and come over and join the mainstream of national development.

You talk in terms of my issuing a circular to people to put up the Buddhist flag on Wesak day. I do not know in what language you got that. But I think you have misunderstood the circular. Nobody in Chunnakam was instructed that he had to fly a Buddhist flag. I am telling you it was not done. All that that circular said was in general terms, that there was no objection to the flying of the Buddhist flag by any local authority in the Island if it wanted to. No one here wanted to compel them to fly it. We do not force people to fly flags or pull down flags. I have never flown a pillow-case in my life. I have never gone in for black flags nor have I asked any person to close shops or to open shops or to fly black flags on any occasion. Those are things you know about.

ආරියදාස මහතා
(திரு. ஆரியதாச)
(Mr. Ariyadasa)

Not even to fly a kite.

fපිලික්ස් ආර්. ඩී. බණ්ඩාරනායක මහතා
(திரு. பிலிக்ஸ் ஆர். டி. பண்டாரநாயக்க)
(Mr. Felix R. D. Bandaranaike)

But I have certainly told the local authorities generally ; and I do not see any reason why I should draw distinctions when local authorities are issued circulars. It will be issued to every single local authority in Jaffna just as much as anywhere else. Those instructions will never be issued by me, which applicable to one part of the country and not to others. I will not compel people to fly flags, and I wish he would also give up compelling people to do things to flags. One way or the other I hope you will learn to respect the National Flag above all others and come to join us with love and affection in your heart towards all people, whether they be Sinhalese or Tamils, and without adopting standards which vary from place to place.

If I may be permitted to deal with one or two other little matters, I would like to tell the Member for Jaffna plainly and categorically that there has been a misunderstanding somewhere. I do not think "Eela Nadu" deliberately intended to mis-represent anything I said. But I think what happened was this. At the Jaffna Municipal Council meeting I did say that sometimes I am con-fronted with this situation that there are Members of Parliament who find that a municipal council in their own electorates held different political views to their own. And when that happens, it does sometimes happen that I am called upon by those Mem-bers of Parliament to consider whether I should or should not dis-solve those municipal councils on the basis of various allegations. I cited a few examples, for instance, the cele-brated case of the Member for Galle who is also asking me to dissolve the Galle Municipal Council. I gave that by way of illustration. I made no reference to Mr. Martyn by name or as the Member for Jaffna. But I did say that that kind of situation is there, I understand it and it can happen ; that I am not willing to accept allegations simpliciter, but if

there is cause, not even my best friend will protected, and added by way of a joke this : judging by the records of the bribery department all I can say is the paucity of the com-plaints I have received in Jaffna leads me to one of two conclusions, either the Jaffna bribe-giver is a long-suffering and patient man in this country or your officials are the most honest individuals you can hope to find throughout the length and breadth of the land. I do not know which. I did say that. But beyond that I can assure you I made no reference and I certainly do not wish to be understood as saying that Mr. Martyn has ever asked me to dissolve the Municipal Council of Jaffna or made any request to that effect. Wherever there is a fault, it is my job to set it right. I do not think as Minister of Local Government I am here to des-troy local government institutions ; I am here to preserve them and to make them work well. If I have to dissolve councils in the manner in which my friend Mr. Tiruchelvam dissolved the Urban Council of Point Pedro for political reasons, I should consider I have failed in my task as Minister of Local Government. That is not going to happen with me. But wherever there is a fault I shall do my best to set it right and to work with councils regardless of whether they belong to political associations hostile to my own.

In regard to the Member for Haba-raduwa (Mr. Prins Gunasekera) and his references to the problems arising in Galle on the Judicial Medical Officer's front in relation to the police, I should like to tell him I have already taken action on the matter he brought to my notice on an earlier occasion and the result is that we have come to an arrangement which will be under review for the next two months. If it is not working satisfactorily I can assure the hon. Member that we have in mind the next steps that are necessary.

But here you are dealing with officials of a very high order, and I think that the question involved are not of such difficulty or complexity

1045   ජාතික රාජ්‍ය සභාව   1046

[ෆිලික්ස් ආර්. ඩී. බණ්ඩාරනායක මහතා]
that they cannot be solved. What is important is that the different arms of the Government must work in co-operation and co-ordintaion one with the other

I believe that the steps I have taken, which have been fairly reported in the newspapers, constitute an adequate effort in that direction. I believe so and I would like to try it. I do not know that one can make judgments about individuals officers and start bandying these things here. Really, there are faults on both sides. It may be, for example, that there are wrong interpretations, wrong assumptions. What is important is mutual goodwill and a detrmination to make it work. I am confident that it will work. But if it does not, make no mistake about it, we shall take the necessary steps. But I do not think that that is likely to arise. I have confidence that everybody understood what they are expected to do and that the thing will work well.

In regard to the complaint about police assaults, these things happen, unfortunately. I do not deny it. But I do not know that there is a special increase in the number of complaints. I have checked up with the Ministry of Defence and I am told it is not so.

Bue even a single incident of assault, to my mind, is bad enough. If even one such incident occurs, it is something that should not occur and action has got to be taken against it. The only thing we can do is to honestly endeavour to investigate each case as it arises and see that justice is done in a deterrent form. And those steps are being taken. I think I can say that the matter is being pursued with vigour and energy and not in a spirit of light heartedness, of assuming that these complaints should be trifled with. That is all I wish to say on that matter, and I think I have covered the ground.

ප්‍රශ්නය විමසන ලදින්, සභාසම්මත විය.
Question put, and agreed to.

ජාතික රාජ්‍ය සභාව ඊට අනුකූලව අ. හා. 5.07 ට, අද දින සභා සම්මතිය අනුව, 1974 ජූලි 23 වන අඟහරුවාදා අ. හා. 2 වන තෙක් කල් තිබේ ය.

Adjourned accordingly at 5.07 P.M. until 2 P.M. on Tuesday, 23rd July, 1974, pursuant to the Resolution of the Assembly this Day.

THE CHARGE OF THE SLFP BRIGADE

NOW THAT THE OPPOSITION IS DEAD SET ON OUTVOTING THE UNP GOVERNMENT, LET
US EXAMINE THE ALTERNATIVE CABINET, THEY INTEND TO OFFER US, FOR A PROGRESSIVE LANKA:—

THE HON. MR. T.B. ILLANGARATNE,
MINISTER FOR HOUSING
AND SOCIAL UPLIFT,
BEGINNING WITH
HIMSELF

THE HON. MR CAS MARIKKAR,
MINISTER FOR THE ERADICATION
OF BRIBERY AND CORRUPTION

THE HON. MR. J.P.OBEYSEREPA MINISTER FOR
UPHOLDING FAMILY HONOUR, OLD SCHOOL TIE ET·
AND SEEING THAT R.G DOESN'T OUST C.P
BEFORE HE DOES!

THE HON. MR. R.F.DIAS,
MINISTER FOR
CONTESTING
J.P.O's CLAIMS

ON STRIKE

THE HON. DR N.M.PERERA,
MINISTER FOR STRIKES,
AND HOPES OF BEING
P.M SOMEDAY.

THE HON. MR JIM
MUNASINHA, MINISTER
FOR RIGHT-WING POLICY
AND KEEPING AN EYE
ON PHILIP.

THE HON MR R.G. SENANAYAKE
MINISTER FOR INTERNAL INSECURITY,
INSUBORDINATION AND WAITING FOR
A CHANCE TO GRAB THE P.M's CHAIR!

THE HON. MR. C.P. de SILVA,
PRIME MINISTER (TEMPORARY
AND UNPENSIONABLE)

THE HON. MR PHILIP GUNAWARDENE,
MINISTER FOR LEFT-NING POLICY, ANTI-
CATHOLICISM AND COMMUNAL HATRED

UNDER·THE·TABLE MANNERS

THE LONE RANGER

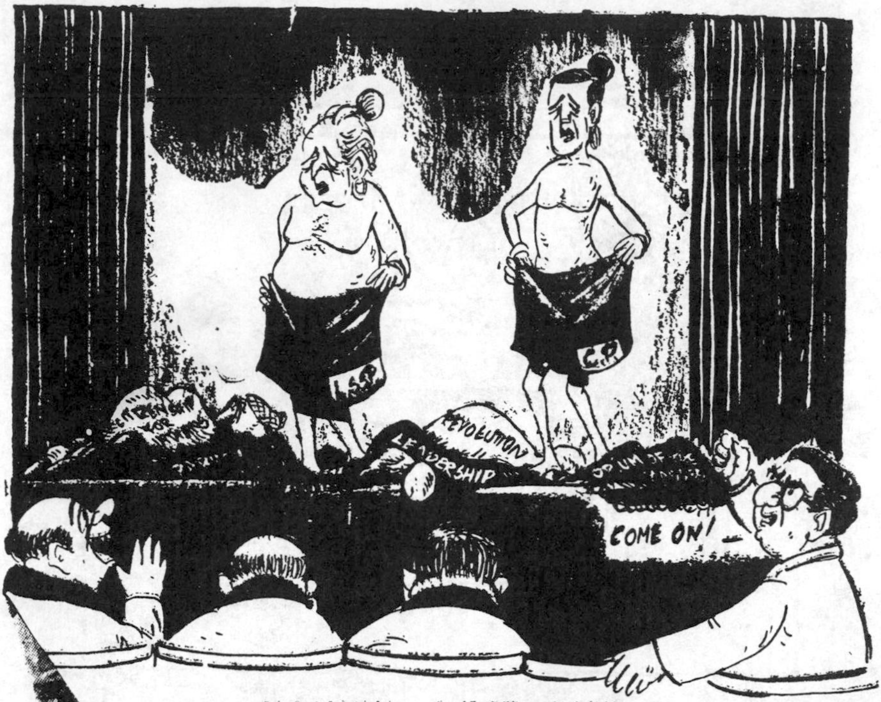

POLITICAL STRIP-TEASE

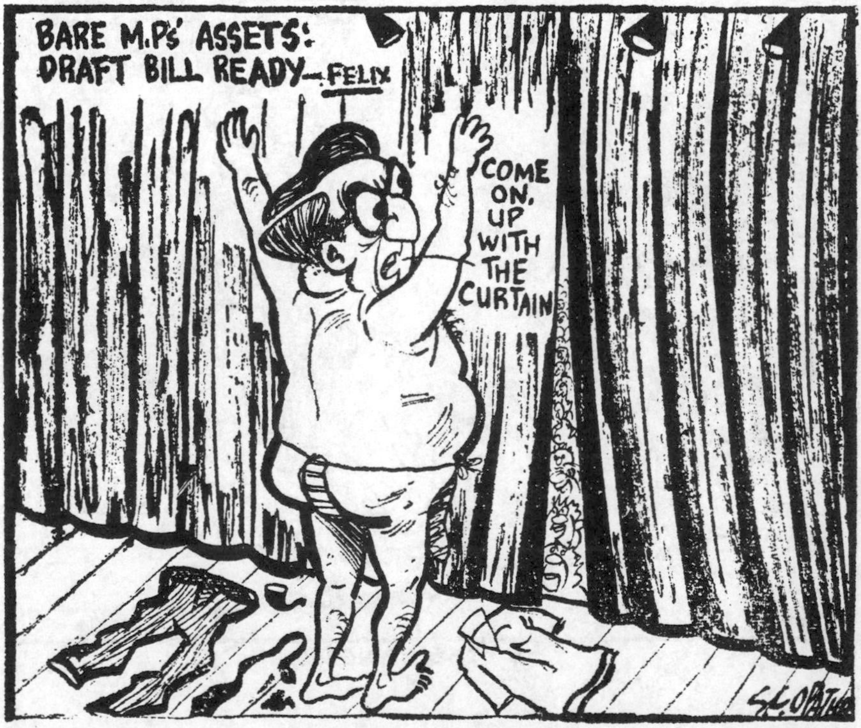

BARE M.Ps' ASSETS: DRAFT BILL READY—FELIX

COME ON, UP WITH THE CURTAIN

CHAPTER XVI

In Memoriam

VOTE OF CONDOLENCE: FELIX R. D. BANDARANAIKE

M. Vincent Perera – Minister of Parliamentary Affairs and Sports

Mr Speaker, I rise with a keen sense of the loss this country has sustained by the untimely death of Mr Felix Reginald Dias Bandaranaike, Bachelor of Laws, Attorney-at-Law and Cabinet Minister who represented the constituency of Dompe in the Legislature for nearly 17 years. He passed away on the 26th of June, 1985, at the age of 54 years.

Mr. Bandaranaike hailed from a distinguished legal family. His father was a Puisne Justice and his grandfather was Additional District Judge of Colombo. Born on 5th November, 1930, Mr Felix Dias Bandaranaike was educated at Royal College, Colombo, from where he entered the Ceylon University and obtained the Degree of Bachelor of Arts. Thereafter he entered the Law College and passed out as an Advocate. He led the University Debating team for 3 years and won medals for oratory both at the University and the Law College.

Mr Felix Dias Bandaranaike entered the arena of national politics unexpectedly after the assassination of Mr S. W. R. D. Bandaranaike in 1959. He contested the Dompe seat as a candidate of the Sri Lanka Freedom Party at the General Elections held in March and July 1960 and was returned as Member for Dompe by large majorities at both elections. He was appointed Minister of Finance in July 1960 at the age of 29 years and was the youngest to hold a Cabinet Portfolio. He was also Parliamentary Secretary to the Minister of Defence and External Affairs and to the Prime Minister. He was the official spokesman for the Prime Minister in the House since Mrs Sirima Bandaranaike was then in the Senate. In July 1962 Mr Bandaranaike in presenting the third Budget of the Sirima Bandaranaike Government, proposed a reduction of the rice ration. That proved to be an unpopular measure and in view of protests within his own ranks he resigned from the office of the Minister of Finance in August 1962. Though at this stage there was some uncertainty about his political future, he rejoined the Cabinet on his 32nd birthday and was appointed Minister without Portfolio. In early 1963 he once again took over as Parliamentary Secretary to the Minister of Defence and External Affairs.

With the formation of the second Cabinet of Mrs Bandaranaike in May 1963, Mr Bandaranaike was appointed Minister of Agriculture, Food and Co-operatives. He held this Portfolio until 1965 when the Government fell. From 1965 to 1970 he played an active role as a prominent member of the Opposition.

Mr Felix Dias Bandaranaike, who contested again from the Dompe constituency, had the honour of being returned with the largest majority at the General Election of 1970. His majority was 22,373, polling 31,515 out of the 40,687 votes that were polled. In the United Front Coalition Government which followed he was appointed to the Portfolio of Public Administration, Local Government and Home Affairs. When Mrs Bandaranaike formed her second Cabinet in 1975 he was given the Portfolios of both Finance and Justice.

However, in the 1977 General Election Mr. Bandaranaike lost the Dompe seat which he had held through four General Elections since its creation in 1960.

During his eventful political career of 25 years, he helped in shaping the foreign policy of Sri Lanka, particularly in relation to the Non-Aligned Movement. He represented Sri Lanka at conferences of Finance and Justice Ministers. He also attended several conferences of the Inter-Parliamentary Union and the Commonwealth Parliamentary Association.

He was present at the Commonwealth Prime Ministers' Conference held in London in March 1961 with Prime Minister Mrs Sirima Bandaranaike, and in September he, with Mrs Bandaranaike, attended the Non-Aligned Summit Talks at Belgrade from where he proceeded to New York to participate in the U.N. General Assembly Sessions.

He accompanied Mrs Sirima Bandaranaike to the Non-Aligned Summit Conferences held in Lusaka in September 1970 and Algiers in September 1973 and to the Commonwealth Prime Ministers' Conference in Singapore in 1971.

He played a vital role in the Non-Aligned Summit Conference in Colombo in August 1976 and was elected Chairman of the Non-Aligned Foreign Ministers' Meeting when he succeeded Abdel Aziz Bouteflika, the Minister of Foreign Affairs of Algeria. In this capacity he presided at the meetings of the Non-Aligned Co-ordinating Bureau in September 1973 and to propose the Vote of Thanks to Queen Elizabeth the Second was one of the highlights of his parliamentary career. The London press acclaimed his speech as a historic one which brought sustained applause from parliamentarians assembled at Westminster Hall.

Mr Bandaranaike represented the Prime Minister at the Commonwealth Prime Ministers' Conference in June 1977 as head of the Sri Lanka delegation.

Mr Felix Dias Bandaranaike has made a lasting contribution in the spheres of Agriculture, Finance, Co-operative Development, Local and Provincial Administration, Administration of Justice, and International Relations which at various times came under his purview. Both friend and foe have paid tribute to his tireless capacity for work, his fearless approach to problems and his outstanding intellectual gifts. He possessed supreme self-confidence with a lot of dash and dynamism. He remained totally loyal to his leader in triumph and adversity.

In his last days F.D.B. the politician turned evangelist and gave the same fervour and dedication he gave to statecraft to the Christian religious activities in which he participated.

F.D.B. shone in every field of activity he chose to participate in. With his death Sri Lanka has lost one of her worthy sons. May he rest in peace.

Mr Speaker, I propose that the condolence of this House be conveyed to the Members of the bereaved family.

Anura Bandaranaike – Leader of the Opposition

Mr Speaker, It is indeed with a very heavy heart that I wish to associate myself on the Condolence Vote moved by the Hon. Minister of Parliamentary Affairs on the death of Mr Felix Dias Bandaranaike, and I wish to associate myself along with the Opposition, in particular the Sri Lanka Freedom Party and the Sri Lanka Freedom Party voters in the Dompe electorate on this very sad ocasion when we pay a tribute to one of Sri Lanka's greatest political figures.

As you are aware, Mr Speaker, it was one of the last wishes of Mr Felix Dias Bandaranaike that there should not be a Condolence Vote moved in this House after his death, and as requested by him, I conveyed to you that these were his last sentiments. But at your request yesterday we both discussed this matter, and thereupon I discussed this matter with his wife and decided, I think wisely, that we should in fact move a Vote of Condolence.

Mr Speaker, I had known Mr Felix Dias Bandaranaike both politically and personally for a period of well over 25 years. I associated with him very closely, admired him as a politician, and respected his numerous talents and skills, so ably described by the Hon. Minister of Parliamentary Affairs and Sports.

There were times, Sir, that I agreed with Mr Bandaranaike and there were times that I disagreed with him, but at all times we remained very close personal friends.

Mr Felix Dias Bandaranaike hails from a brilliant intellectual family. His father, Mr R. F. Dias Bandaranaike, was a distinguished and learned judge. His brother, Professor Michael Dias Bandaranaike, held the Chair of Jurisprudence in the University of Cambridge for well over 25 years and is today the Final authority on the subject of Jurisprudence in the University of Cambridge.

As a student of Royal College Felix excelled himself, so much so that on the marble tablets that adorned the assembly Hall at Royal College the name of Felix Dias Bandaranaike stands in a number of places. At the University and at the Law College, where he continued his brilliant academic career, he carried away many prizes for his oratorical and debating skills. I think many of those on either side of the House will agree with me that his was one of the most incisive and brilliant brains in recent Sri Lankan politics. More than anything else, Mr Speaker, he had discipline in him in that he was able to easily sift the relevant from the irrelevant. He was able to see through cobwebs that many of us would not have been able to see through. Therefore, Sir, I think the Hon. Minister of Parliamentary Affairs and Sports was quite accurate when he stated that he was indeed a brilliant politician.

Sir, Felix Dias Bandaranaike was a student to his death. Whether it was in studying law, studying politics or studying theology, which he turned to after 1977, he did it with a unique sense of dedication and skill, so much so, Mr Speaker, that when he was afflicted with an incurable cancer, in that short period in which he suffered from this disease I think he learned more about the illness than many of the cancer experts in Sri Lanka. When he and I were flying back from London in March this year when he was returning from his medical treatment three months before he died, he gave me a long discourse on the subject of cancer which has made me a mini expert myself. On that occasion Mr Bandaranaike in fact requested me to do whatever I could to obtain a cancer scanning machine, which we do not have in Sri Lanka. I think in his own case, as in the case of many less fortunate than himself, if cancer is detected at an early stage various treatments are possible. But in his case, as in a number of other cases, a wrong diagnosis was made. The only way in which one can circumvent this is by having a scanning machine, however costly it might be. That, sir, was one of the last requests he made of me.

Mr Speaker, to Mr Felix Dias Bandaranaike politics came quite suddenly. After the death of Prime Minister S. W. R. D. Bandaranaike, when the then Attanagalla constituency was divided into two, a part of it was called Dompe and it came into existence in March 1960. At the insistence of the Sri Lanka

Freedom Party and Mrs Sirimavo Bandaranaike he came into politics quite reluctantly. The first time he contested he won with a record majority of 12,000 votes. In the July 1960 General Election he was returned with an increased majority of 14,000 votes. In 1965, when the Sri Lanka Freedom Party was defeated, he was returned to Dompe with another record majority of 16,000 votes. In 1970 he had the largest majority in the General Election being returned with a majority of 22,328 votes.

I accompanied him on a number of occasions to functions, religious, social and political, in the Dompe Electorate. It was a unique thing that he remembered the names, I may say without exaggeration, of most of his supporters. He knew their background, their families, the jobs they were doing. He virtually knew their ages. It was a computer-like brain that he had, which I think drew him very close to the electors of Dompe. It was this remarkable ability which I think endured him through four General Elections with such large majorities in the Dompe Electorate.

He was a remarkable politician. One may have agreed with him, one may have disagreed with him, sometimes quite violently, but none will deny the fact that like a colossus he strode the political scene in Sri Lanka for 17 years when he was active in politics. As the Hon. Minister of Parliamentary Affairs quite rightly mentioned, perhaps he was one of the youngest Ministers of Finance in the world, holding that very important portfolio at the age of 29. He thereafter held the offices of Minister without Portfolio, Deputy Minister of Defence and Foreign Affairs, and Minister of Agriculture, Food and Co-operatives; and in 1970 he held three Ministries – the Ministries of Home Affairs, Public Administration and Local Government. Thereafter he once again held the office of Minister of Justice for a number of years. He left an indelible impression in the minds of those he worked with as well as those he was opposed to, and no one can deny that he stamped his remarkable skill on all the Ministries that he had undertaken.

Not only was he a remarkable politician in Sri Lanka, his talents and skills extended across the international stage. In 1961 he accompanied the then Hon. Prime Minister, Mrs Sirimavo R. D. Bandaranaike, to the Commonwealth Prime Ministers' Conference. Thereafter at each Non-Aligned Summit, whether it was in Belgrade or in Lusaka or in Cairo, or in Colombo where he chaired the Conference of the Foreign Ministers before the main Non-Aligned Conference began at each of these international forums he left his brilliant stamp. I was quite taken by surprise when I visited the Prime Minister of England, Mrs Margaret Thatcher, at Downing Street last year. In a virtually hour-long conversation she spent more than fifteen minutes asking me about Mr Felix Dias Bandaranaike. It was then I knew that he had such a wide range of international friends. Not only the Prime

Minister of England but even the former Prime Minister of India, the late Mrs Indira Gandhi, Marshal Tito, President of Yugoslavia, and Gamal Abdel Nasser, President of Egypt, were all his personal friends. He knew them personally and he kept in touch with them.

Mr Speaker, another aspect of his illustrious political career was his remarkable skill as a Parliamentary debater. I think Hon. Members of Parliament and the staff of Parliament will agree with me that he was one of the finest speakers that this Parliament has ever produced. Whether it was in defending a Bill or attacking a Bill, whether he was presenting a Budget or demolishing a Budget, he did it with a skill which was unique and remarkable. Mr Speaker, I remember as a young man sitting enthralled and mesmerised in the Gallery at the talents of Mr Bandaranaike. The way he demolished with absolute brilliance the arguments of his opponents was something which I think all those who heard him in Parliament and all those who sat in the same Parliament would remember for a very long time.

Mr Speaker, Mr Felix Dias Bandaranaike was a man of principles, honour, courage, faith and dedication. I have selected these words not merely to adorn him with praise. I have selected these words with care, because I know that every one of these descriptions would apply to him. His courage and faith enabled him to virtually conduct single-handed the government investigations into the attempted military coup d'etat of 1962, which I think was the first occasion on which this nation as a whole admired him and his brilliant political abilities. Then again in 1971, when the insurgency occurred, he played a principal and key role in restoring democracy and faith once again in this country.

Mr Speaker, he fought for what he believed was right. Others may not have agreed with him, but he always fought with courage and faith for what he believed was right. He did something which was very unique for politicians in Sri Lanka. When he presented the Budget in 1962, a controversial Budget, there was an uproar in the Government Parliamentary ranks. Without any compunction he resigned and sat as a beck-bencher for nearly three months. Sir, such principles are rare in Sri Lankan politics. Once again, when he was summoned before the Presidential Commission – I do not wish to say anything controversial at a time like this – he faced it, even though he knew it was a hopeless battle from the start. He went through it, he faced it with courage, and whatever the judgement may have been he came out of it unscathed.

Then, Sir, his courage and faith enabled him to fight cancer, a cancer which was virtually incurable. He fought it with fortitude and he fought it with magnanimity. When he knew he was dying of cancer he never lost his sense of humour, he never became depressed, which I think most of us would have become if we were in his position. He faced it with the same bonhomie with which he faced all his political debacles.

Another lesson from his political life to all of us is that those who climb the dizzy heights of politics, those who exercise power, at the judgement of the voters must learn to face defeat. It was a lesson that all in power must learn some time.

Sir, in his moment of sorrow and solitude he turned to religion. He was always religious-minded, and he turned to it with fervour because in it he found the kind of mental peace and solace which probably he needed at this hour. I can say that towards his end he harboured no ill-will towards anybody. He was ridiculed. Even films were made to humiliate him and ridicule him. He fought them courageously. He took them to court. But he never harboured any thoughts of revenge against those who humiliated him and ridiculed him. That, I think, Sir, is one of the greatest tributes we can pay him on this sad ocasion.

As the Hon. Minister of Parliamentary Affairs and Sports quite correctly mentioned, another remarkable quality in his life was the fierce loyalty with which he served his leader and his party throughout his career not only as a parliamentarian, not only as a super-Minister of the Sri Lanka Freedom Party, but also in defeat. In defeat he exercised the same loyalty and the same dedication. Mr Speaker, this sometimes has been misinterpreted as sycophancy. It has been misunderstood as blind loyalty. No, it is not that, Sir. As you yourself have been a devoted loyalist of your party, you will admit that loyalty cannot turn into sycophancy. Loyalty is always loyalty if properly exercised.

In conclusion, Mr. Speaker, I wish to say that Mr Felix Dias Bandaranaike, to whom we pay tribute today, will not easily be forgotten, in the sense that whoever he met, whatever he did, whoever he disagreed with or fought with, he left a lasting impression in their minds. It is not easy, particularaly to those who knew him closely, to imagine that Felix Dias Bandaranaike is dead. His memory will live not for years but for decades, and with the passage of time, when historians and his associates can distance themselves away from the events which are far too close to them and wipe away the cobwebs, even his most fervent opponent will admit that he bestrode the political stage of Sri Lanka more as a colossus than as a politician.

On behalf of the Sri Lanka Freedom Party and on behalf of the voters of the Sri Lanka Freedom Party in the Dompe constituency, I wish to associate myself and my party with this Vote of Condolence on the death of Mr Felix Dias Bandaranaike.

Thank you.

Dr. Nissanka Wijeyeratne – Minister of Justice

At the outset, I would like to comment on a point made by the Hon. Leader of the Opposition and also referred to by the Hon. Member for Dompe (Mr Saratchandra Rajakaruna), namely, the fact that discussion had taken place in regard to a Vote of condolence. A few days ago, in conveying my sympathies to Mrs Felix Dias Bandaranaike, I said that it was only appropriate that this House follows its traditional practice of expressing its sympathies on the demise of one who had been a Member of this House. She said that it had been her late husband's wish that sentiments offered in the House were not what Mr Felix Dias Bandaranaike expected. Perhaps he may have had deep feelings about the loss of his civic rights. In my view that might have been at the back of his mind. But I did express the view afterwards to a number of Members of Parliament that the right and obligation of referring to any Member of the House is not only an exclusive privilege of the House but on the passing away of a Member, is also the bounden duty of the House. Therefore, I feel that all of us who participate today, those speaking on this Vote of Condolence as well as those who are here, are following the great tradition of honouring those who in their lifetime adorned with their membership the House of which we too are Members.

Mr Felix Dias Bandaranaike, Mr Speaker, truly adorned this House. The duty of a Member, if he is on the Government side, is to support the motions that are conceived by the Government for the benefit of the country, and it is the bounden duty of the Opposition to dissect those measures and point out, in the interests of the country, those which they feel are likely to be prejudicial to the interests of the nation. That is why, Mr Speaker, both as a member of the Government and as a member of the Opposition, Felix Dias Bandaranaike fulfilled the highest traditions of Parliamentary government.

Mr Speaker, Mr Felix Dias Bandaranaike had many advantages. He was born to a social position, a position that came by a measure of wealth and by achievements of his father, his grandfather and other distinguished members of his family. In a great measure Mr Felix Dias Bandaranaike could claim to belong to one of the great legal families of Sri Lanka from the time Sir Harry Dias was brought in as a Puisne Justice and subsequently adorned the position of acting Chief Justice of Sri Lanka. And that tradition was continued by his nephew, Mr F. R. Dias, and by Mr. Felix Dias' father, Mr Reginald Bandaranaike, and by Mr Felix Dias Bandaranaike in the courts of law. They have established themselves in a learned profession in a much more significant way than members of their family achieved as officials under the Government of the British in Sri Lanka.

Mr Felix Dias Bandaranaike had, however, a right to claim connection with ancestry not because ancestry conferred upon him a position but because he too conferred upon lineage the proud achievements of intellect and of service.

Quite often it is said, Mr Speaker, that those who refer to their ancestors only speak of the achievements of others, but here was a case of one who, by his academic record in school, his carreer at the Bar and the distinction he gave to politics by his participation, claims a niche in the history of our country.

I remember him in school. Even when he was young there was not merely a sense of *noblesse oblige* but a bubble of effervescence that sometimes bordered on what some masters thought was insolence. It is because he was not intimidated by form or authority.

Dignity and achievement and capacity in others won from him respect, but he would have been the first to prick the bubble of arrogance. This he showed as Minister of Finance when many of my brother Civil servants were at the receiving end of his caustic tongue – and many of them deserved it.

He expected a dedication to work, a thorough grasp of facts and an intelligent presentation of them. He did not suffer fools gladly, and to many he was therefore abrasive. But, Mr Speaker, it is not what an individual leaves by way of impression in others that ultimately matters in the life of a politician. It is the solid record of work.

In the case of Mr Felix Dias Bandaranaike I consider one of his great achievements was the solid support and the analytical work he did for his leader in helping towards the solution at that time in the Sirima-Shastri Pact. Both, the then ambassador in Delhi, the late Mr Shirley Amerasinghe, and the Permanent Secretary of the Ministry of Foreign Affairs, the late Mr N. Q. Dias, on many occasions told me that were it not for Mr Felix Dias Bandaranaike much of that achievement would never have been realised.

I remember too, Mr Speaker, how with a far-seeing vision he supported a demand made by me when I was Government Agent of Anuradhapura and subsequently when I worked as a Permanent Secretary, the first for the extension of the land administration from Anuradhapura into Kadukulampattu in Trincomalee, a one-time Sinhala area, which was less than a century ago administered under the British by the RM of the area, the uncle or grand-uncle of the Hon. Member for Medawachchiya. Mr Felix Dias Bandaranaike realised that some day there would be an attempt by intransigent elements to link up the North and the East and protection was necessary for Trincomalee if it was to serve the entirety of the nation. And I also remember, as a government servant in a higher capacity, when I presented to Mr Felix Dias Bandaranaike the need to link Panamapattu with the Siyambaladuwa AGA's division, he readily accepted that proposal when he was Minister of Home Affairs and Public Administration.

Mr Speaker, he was not an easy man to approach but he was a fine listener if he felt that there was sense in what you said. There was also an essential kindness in the man. To the weak and the fallen he was sympathetic. There may have been times when he liked to assume and arrogate to himself powers. That, Mr Speaker, is a disease that all of us who hold power suffer from, and it is something which we have to always remember. And if at times he forgot it sometimes, we who have power should remember that we too are capable of forgetting it.

Mr Speaker, as Minister of Justice I pay here a tribute to the significant changes he made in the system of law in this country. Some may have been too radical and too hasty, but some, like the joining together of the two professions, the simplification of procedures and the search for quick and effective justice, have left behind in the Ministry an ideal which we will not easily forget and which will serve to inspire us in the work we do.

Mr Speaker, the Hon. Member for Maharagama referred to the bridge at Hanwella. It was a dream of his heart. Siyane Korale and Hewagam Korale have many things in common. The family of Mr Bandaranaike itself came originally from the Hewagam Korale, but that link was not a link of families or people. There was something more. It was an economic link, a necessary link. But there was also something more significant, for in that attempt to join the electorate of Dompe with that of Avissawella, Mr Felix Dias Bandaranaike sought to present to the country something which the UNP Government of 1965 learnt, that socialism of the Avissawella brand, which did not forget its national heritage, was something that could with advantage serve a great party. If the SLFP missed that opportunity, Mr Speaker, the dream of Mr Felix Dias Bandaranaike was realised by ours.

Mr Speaker, the last years of his life were unhappy, but as every speaker pointed out, with fortitude and infinite courage he faced the tragedy that nature had chosen to impose upon him. Long before he left Sri Lanka on his divinity studies I met him and had the occasion to discuss many things, for with him, though I had disagreed politically, I maintained a close friendship, and for him I had a warmth of affection. When he returned a sick man, I was grieved. Both in hospital and a few days before he died and before I had left Sri Lanka I sat with him in his house for a long time talking with a sick and dying man but someone who revealed in his suffering a warmth of feeling for his friends, a concern for his country and above all that forgiveness which he learnt, in the course of his early life and his studies in divinity and which is associated with the master whom he followed in his faith.

Mr Speaker, may I take this opportunity of requesting you, in forwarding the sympathies of this House, to associate my own deep sympathies to Mrs Lakshmi Dias Bandaranaike on the sorrow she has sustained.

Desamanya Dr. P. R. Anthonis,
Consultant Surgeon D.Fc., F.R.C.S. (Eng.), F.I.C.S., F.S.C.S.
Chancellor of the University of Colombo

Though I cannot recall when first I met Felix Dias Bandaranaike, imperishable is my memory of this great man. Our early professional relationship developed into a friendship of mutual trust and understanding. The more we met the more I realised his honesty, sincerity, and his brilliant legal mind. In July 1960 in an epic victory in "a miracle in leadership rarely seen in any country" Mrs Bandaranaike became the first lady Prime Minister the world had known; she filled the vast void created by the tragic loss of her husband, late revered S. W. R. D. Bandaranaike. It was at this difficult period that Felix Dias Bandaranaike supplied the necessary brains, discipline, and the analytical mind acquired by his law studies and also inherited from his father and grandfather – legal giants of their time. With these inborn and inherited talents the contribution made by him was recognised both in Sri Lanka and the outside world as of very high quality.

While he was Hon. Minister for Public Administration none could go past him by hoodwinking or with made-up cases. He studied every file and knew the details of a particular case.

Once on a request by a friend of mine, father-in-law of a civil servant transferred out of Colombo, I interviewed him with the story given to me, the Hon. Minister rattled off all the details of the story which was quite different to the one given, and later the Hon. Minister's version proved to be correct.

All disciplined men of analytical minds and of great efficiency with quick judgement and action appear cold and hard and often to be feared. Yet it was our privilege, late Dr. Medonza and myself, his physician and surgeon respectively, to know this great personage very intimately. He was very tender, sympathetic and lovable to the poor who had no "voice." I often recalled in my mind Charles Lamb's sentence "The Precision of the lawyer was united to the tenderness of a friend" applied well to Felix. His sincerity was very deep, honesty of very high quality, his brilliant analytical mind together with an unparalleled gift of retentive memory made him a very rare man. Once he addressed an important world assembly (one hour's address) without a single note!

Time cannot delete the memory of this great man when Guy Fawkes Day November 5th comes on and I yet feel very sad: the dinner, and open house, and the lawn with Guy Fawke's effigy and all his intimate friends and close family relatives gathered to celebrate his birthday. If ever Dr. Medonza and myself visited unannounced any time close to lunch or dinner an improvised dinner or lunch was a *'sine qua non'* and he never accepted a "no" for an answer. Even when out of political power, he was undaunted and accepted it with stoic equanimity. His manner never changed. He was yet simple, honest and lovable with his childlike simplicity. Such men are rare.

Felix talented and clever
Joe Sigera – Daily News – 1985

Brilliant people do not often suffer fools in silence. The late Jawaharlal Nehru was one who belonged to that category, not to mention, Sir Winston Churchill. It could be said that those who belong to this category are also many a time eccentric and also come down heavily on their lesser intellectual fraternity.

Felix Reginald Dias Bandaranaike who died comparatively young at the age of fifty four after bravely bearing an agonising illness, was one of the most talented, if not cleverest man this country produced. Coming from a distinguished blue-blooded family in Siyane Korale, Felix was the son of the late Mr Justice Reginald Felix Dias Bandaranaike, perhaps the most outspoken judge this country has ever had.

When Rukmani Devi and Eddie Jayamanne were brought before him at the Colombo District Court by an enraged father of Rukmani (Daisy Daniels) for the offence of eloping without parental consent, Mr. Justice Dias Bandaranaike made the now famous pronouncement, "Go to the nearest registrar's office and get married. You (Eddie) the Charlie Chaplin of Ceylon and you (Rukmani) is the nightingale of Ceylon."

To go back to Felix Dias Bandaranaike it could be said that his brightness flashed like a star while still a student at Royal College. Dickie Attygalle, one of the finest teachers of English in this country discovered his talent in class and is said to have advised him on the lessons of life.

Siyane Korale which comprises the Gampaha district, has been for generations the home of the Bandaranaikes. Sir Solomon Dias Bandaranaike lived in splendour there like an English nobleman. So, when Felix contested the Dompe seat in March, 1960, later in July the same year and in 1970, it was plain sailing for him. In 1970, Felix won Dompe with the largest majority, to be precise, 22,373 votes.

He first entered parliament in 1960 at the age of twenty nine. Although there were many seniors in the Party at the time, it was to Felix that Prime Minister, Mrs Sirima Bandaranaike looked up to. The shrewd lady knew how to use the talents from the young man from Mahanuge Gardens. Over the years until the SLFP's debacle in 1977, Felix Dias Bandaranaike was Mrs Bandaranaike's super Minister, in short he was the man for all seasons.

Since the dawn of Independence no man, has held as many portfolios as Felix, he was Minister of Finance, Justice, Public Administration and also was Deputy Minister for Defence and External Affairs.

A Barrister-at-law of the Inner Temple, Felix Dias Bandaranaike had a lucrative practice in Colombo and the provinces, mainly Kurunegala where his friend, Jaya Pathirana helped him before he took to the uncertain world of politics.

This much misunderstood man who was respected by some and spurned by others, is a political figure that cannot be forgotten. When he had to do a job he did it relentlessly in the manner of Joseph MaCarthy pursuing the Communists in the fifties. This straight man got the Bribery Department to work overtime and many were netted in. Some of his officials later let him down, but his intentions were genuine.

Power sometimes goes into the head, I do not have to quote Lord Acton for that. But Felix at the height of his power spoke about "a little bit of totalitarianism." These are the kind of statements which men in power could be forgiven for in the height of their power.

In the death of Felix Dias Bandaranaike this country lost a man of superior intellect and outstanding ability.

Never such a controversial figure
History will have much to say of FDB
H. B. W. Abeynaike

It was only a few Sundays ago that I saw Felix Dias Bandaranaike for the last time at his parish church of St. Michael and All Angels, Polwatte, (Kollupitiya) where he and his father the late (Justice R. F. Dias) were regular worshippers.

He appeared quite fit and alert. But on June 26, the hand of death moved against him as he succumbed to cancer, which came to him unexpectedly and took him away from the scenes of his triumphs then as an undisputed leader, and later from the miseries to which he fell since his defeat after 1977.

Felix Dias Bandaranaike was born on November 5, 1930, and after his education at Royal College Colombo, he proceeded to the University of Ceylon and obtained the degree of Bachelor of Laws. He next joined the Colombo Law College and passed out as an Advocate. He won medals for Oratory both at the University and the Law College.

Politics came to him unexpectedly consequent on the assassination of Prime Minister Bandaranaike when he found himself nominated for Dompe in the March 1960 general election. He was re-nominated for the July elections to the 5th Parliament, and the then Premier, Mrs Bandaranaike made him Minister of Finance.

On July 26, 1962, Felix Dias Bandaranaike in his Budget speech made a proposal for the reduction of the rice ration. It was a time when rice was politics in this country. He said he was not making anybody to pay a higher price for a measure of rice.

It may have been a good move from his government's point of view, but it proved an unpopular move and resulted in a hue and cry against the Finance Minister.

Felix Dias Bandaranaike on this issue turned out to be a man of honour and resigned his portfolio of Finance in August that year.

Although there were some doubts about the future of Bandaranaike at this stage, such fears were abandoned early, when just over two months, on his birthday, he was appointed Minister without Portfolio. His rise on the political map of Sri Lanka commenced again.

When Mrs Bandaranaike formed her second Cabinet, in May 1963, Felix Dias Bandaranaike was made Minister of Agriculture, Food and Co-operatives. After his period in the Opposition from 1965-1970 when the UNP under Premier Dudley Senanayake was in power, Felix was again at the helm with Mrs Bandaranaike's return as Premier.

He became Minister of Public Administration, of Local Government and Home Affairs and Justice. Later he took over Finance when Dr. N. M. Perera quit the government.

In the last days of his parliamentary life, Felix Dias Bandaranaike held a record number of portfolios. He was Minister of Finance, of Justice, of Home Affairs, of Public Administration, of Local Government, and of Agriculture, Food and Co-operatives.

In addition he was Deputy Minister of Defence.

Felix was a violent opponent of bribery and bribe-givers.

Religion

He then turned to religion earnestly. He studied Divinity in the United States and continued his interest in religion till death called him to his rest.

History will have much to say about the life of Felix Dias Bandaranaike and history alone can decide on his acts of omission and commission.

All that this article can wish for him is that the God in whom his faith was reposed will rest his soul.

CHAPTER XVII

Personal Notes

Prime Minister's House
24 Sussex Street

June 26, 1971

Ottawa

Dear Felix and Lakshmi,

Pierre and I were so pleased that we were able to see you, if only briefly, during your visit to Canada. It was a great pleasure for me to meet you both, Pierre had spoken to me about your great kindness to him in Ceylon.

I also want to thank you so very much for the beautiful gift you gave me. Amethysts are such dear stones to me, I had a pendant made for my wedding with an amethyst in the centre. The ring will be greatly cherished by me, thank you both so much.

431

Pierre is just finishing the last days of the session, what a joy it will be for him to be free of the House for two months. He will be working on planning and policy all during July, then August will find us without a care as we take our vacation.

I have now moved up to our country residence, a beautiful, solitary lake not far from Ottawa. Pierre commutes each day, but it is such a pleasant drive he does not mind. To be away from the city, amongst the flowers and the deer, is just too much joy for me.

I do hope you are enjoying better times politically in Ceylon now, and that you are not too tired after your long journey.

With Pierre's warmest regards and my admiration,

Margaret Trudeau.

PRIME MINISTER

New Delhi,
February 11, 1980

Dear Mr. Bandaranaike,

Thank you for your message of congratulations
and good wishes, which I value greatly.

The election was tough but the real difficulties
begin now. Our opponents, the so-called saviours of
democracy, are in no mood to accept the verdict of
the people and are doing all kinds of things to
obstruct us.

My thoughts are constantly with Mrs. Bandaranaike
and her family.

Yours sincerely,

(Indira Gandhi)

Mr. Felix Dias Bandaranaike,
Colombo (Sri Lanka).

Lakshmi Dias Bandaranaike LLB
ATTORNEY-AT-LAW

Tel: 27343

No. 3, Mahanuge Gardens,
Colpetty,
Colombo 3.
16th September, 1985

The Hon'ble Margaret Thatcher
Prime Minister,
No. 10, Downing Street
London
England

Dear Mrs Thatcher,
Thank you very much for your sympathetic letter on the death of
my husband Felix, and for the very kind sentiments expressed.
This letter has been a source of great consolation to me.
I am well aware of the regard Felix had for you over the years.
It may interest you to know that Felix graduated in Theology in
1984 in the States. On his return to Sri Lanka he fell ill and it
was unfortunate that his case was misdiagnosed due to lack of
diagnostic facilities in this country. Eventually it was found
that he was suffering from a lung cancer, which Dr. Brechen,
Professor of Oncology at Addenbrookes hospital in Cambridge
(England) stated could have been operable had it detected in time
by means of a CAT Scan machine.
It was Felix's great wish to try and secure a CAT Scan Machine
(for a start a body SCAN) for the premier Cancer treatment Centre
in Sri Lanka. He was exploring the possibilities of obtaining
such equipment to serve the people of Sri Lanka under its free
health service policy, so that even the poorest individual would
stand to benefit.
Since his death it is my intention to implement his wish.
It has been decided to form a memorial trust for the purpose of
securing CAT scan equipment.
Would it be presumptious of me to ask whether you could help us
to obtain such equipment which would be more than deeply
appreciated.
Once again may I express my gratitude to you for writing.
With kind regards.

Yours sincerely,

Lakshmi Dias Bandaranaike

From LORD HOME OF THE HIRSEL K.T.

October 18th.1985.

Dear Mrs Bandaranaike

Thank you for your letter.
I am sorry to hear that Felix
has died. I send you my sympathy
and understanding.

May I make some enquiries about
a possible source of funds and let
you know.

Yours sincerely

Home

Mrs. Lekshmi L.Bandaranaike.
3 Mahanuge Gardens.
Colpetty.
Colombo 3. Sri Lanka.

THE RT. HON. JOHN E. SILKIN, M.P.

HOUSE OF COMMONS
LONDON SWIA OAA

21 October, 1985

Mrs. Lakshmi D. Bandaranaike,
No. 3 Matanuge Gardens,
Colpetty,
Colombo 3,
Sri Lanka

Dear Lakshmi,

Thank you for your letter of 18 September. It
was lovely to hear from you and I very much
approve of the idea of a memorial to Felix
hich would take the practical form of a scan
machine.   The only thing that worries me
is whether there would be sufficient expertise
in Sri Lanka at the moment to operate it
correctly.   However, I am examining the
situation and will write to you again in due
course.

Yours ever,

John

1O DOWNING STREET

THE PRIME MINISTER   11 December 1985

Dear Mrs. Bandaranaike

    Thank you so much for your letter of 16 September about
your plan to establish a memorial trust with the aim of buying
cancer scanning equipment.

    We would be glad to help as far as we can in establishing
a fitting memorial to your late husband. But it is not easy for
us to judge what will best fit Sri Lanka's needs. That is why
we make it a rule to discuss priorities for the use of the aid
funds with the Sri Lankan Government. We are already doing a
good deal in the medical fields: for example, we have recently
helped to provide a British medical aid team, and we also assist
with Sri Lanka's anti-malarial programme.

    You will I am sure be discussing your ideas with the
Sri Lankan Government. If they decided that they should give
priority to CT scanning equipment we would certainly consider
what contribution we could make from our aid programme. In the
first place we could help with technical advice.

    Meanwhile we can help with the training of staff to work
in cancer treatment and diagnostic units. I have therefore asked
our aid officials in Colombo to discuss this question with the
Sri Lankan Government and to examine the possibility of our
offering training in radiology and other related areas to
Sri Lankan medical staff. I do hope this will be of initial
help to your project.

                            Yours sincerely

                            Margaret Thatcher

Mrs Lakshmi Bandaranaike

March 31, 1988

Mrs. Lakshmi Dias Bandaranaike
No. 3, Mahanuge Gardens
Colpetty
Colombo 3, Sri Lanka 10-3-88

Dear Lakshmi:

I was pleased to receive your letter and to learn something of what you are doing and that Christine has been on a trip to Australia and to the States. We trust that the Lord will guide her and encourage her heart as she pursues her education and ultimately, career.

I was interested to learn that you have in mind writing something about Felix's life and service to his country. You mentioned his coming to Multnomah, and I thought it would be of interest to have some of the official papers which tell about his studies and stay here at the school. So we are enclosing Xeroxed copies of these documents.

I considered it a real privilege and honor to have your dear husband in my class. He showed his keen intellect and his deep love for the Lord and it was an encouragement to me to realize that I was investing a part of my life in encouraging such a choice servant of God.

We did thank God that He led Felix up to a place of service to his country and service to the kingdom of God. We know that you continue to miss him and we join you in wondering why God removed him from this scene so soon after he had finished his work here at Multnomah.

Thank you for your invitation to visit. The possibilities of our getting into that part of the country are remote at the present time, but should we do so, we would count it a delight and an honor to accept your invitation.

May the Lord bless you abundantly and encourage you in your project of writing something about Felix's life. If we can be of more specific help, please let us know.

Sincerely yours in Christ,

Willard M. Aldrich

WMA:ho
Enc.

Appendices

LETTER FROM PROFESSOR S. A. DE SMITH

1. I have already expressed the opinion that if the SLFP were to win a majority at the General Election it would not be constitutionally improper for the Governor-General to appoint as Prime Minister an elected member of the SLFP who accepted office on the understanding that he would resign in favour of Mrs Bandaranaike once she had obtained a seat in Parliament. I adhere to this opinion despite the fact that there appears to be no United Kingdom precedent for such conduct. To this extent I am in accord with local opinion. Nevertheless, I regard this as a clumsy expedient which, if resorted to, is hardly calculated to enhance respect for the Constitution or the dignity of the Prime Minister's Office. It may, however, be necessary to resort to this circuitous device if (a) no Member of Parliament who is able to form a government is willing to do so except on these terms and 9b) it is unconstitutional to appoint as Prime Minister a person who is not a Member of Parliament.

2. Where I seem to differ from a significant body of opinion in Ceylon is in the answer that I give to the question implicit in (b) The question is a difficult one which admits of reasonable differences of opinion. I am unable to agree that either the letter of the Ceylon Constitution or the writings of commentators in the United Kingdom point irresistibly to the conclusion arrived at by some authorities in Ceylon.

3. Neither the structure nor the practical working of the Ceylon Constitution follows exactly the pattern of the United Kingdom. It is not to be expected, therefore, that the constitutional conventions of Ceylon will be exactly the same as those of the United Kingdom. Indeed, section 4 (2) of the Ceylon Constitution recognises that there may be differences, for it provides that the Governor-General's powers shall be exercised as far as may be in accordance with the conventions applicable to the exercise of similar powers by the Queen in the United Kingdom. In the circumstances my cautious observation that "the constitutional conventions of Ceylon are not necessarily to be regarded as a carbon copy of those followed in Britain" appears in retrospect almost platitudinous.

4. In particular, the status of the Opposition differs in the two countries. In the United Kingdom the office of Leader of the Opposition is now recognised by statute. The Ministries of the Crown Act, 1937, prescribes rules of strict law for determining who is the Leader of the Opposition, and the rules provide that he must be a member of the House of Commons. Who was the Leader of the Opposition in Ceylon's last parliament? In the third edition of his Cabinet Government (at p. 32) Sir Ivor Jennings

states that the convention in the United Kingdom is that on the defeat and resignation of the Government the Queen should first send for the Leader of the Opposition. The reasons behind this convention are that the Queen must demonstrate her impartiality and that the accepted leader of the main party that was in opposition to the former government is *prima facie* better equipped than any other person to form a new government and should therefore be given the first opportunity of so doing. But if, as I believe, there was no generally accepted Leader of the Opposition in Ceylon's last Parliament, it is impossible to see how the United Kingdom convention could be exactly applied in the event of an SLFP victory at the polls. Once this point is conceded, it follows that the Governor-General has a wider discretion than the Queen has in the United Kingdom in choosing a Prime Minister. It would clearly be proper for the Governor-General to invite one of the leading parliamentary figures in the S L FP to form a government, even though the appointee is avowedly acting in the capacity of a caretaker. But if none of these parliamentary figures was the 'Leader of the Opposition,' if none of them is the acknowledged leader of his party, if the leader of the party is in fact a person who has as yet no seat in Parliament, and if none of the parliamentary figures is able and willing to form a government except as a caretaker, it seems to me reasonable and qually proper for the Governor-General to invite the acknowledged leader of the party to form a government – unless he is absolutely precluded by constitutional convention from following such a course.

5. The problem resolves itself into two questions. Firstly, is there a convention in the U.K. that in no circumstances whatsoever can a Prime Minister ever be appointed from outside Parliament? Secondly, assuming that the answer to this question is in the affirmative, does this convention automatically apply in Ceylon? I have already given reasons for my opinion that United Kingdom conventions are not of necessity automatically applicable in Ceylon. And it is well to bear in mind two other passages from Sir Ivor Jennings' works: "Neither precedents nor dicta are conclusive"....."it is necessary to justify a constitutional convention not merely by precedents but also by reason" (The Law and the Constitution) (5th ed.), p. 136; Cabinet Government (1st ed.) p. 9. If it becomes more reasonable – reasonable, that is to say, in terms of the efficient working of a modern Constitution – for the Governor-General or the queen not to follow a series of constitutional precedents than to follow them, I do not regard the Governor-General or the queen as being constitutionally obliged to follow the more unreasonable course of action. The capacity of conventions to evolve is a manifestation of the flexibility of the United Kingdom and Ceylon constitutions. And conventions evolve and atrophy imperceptibly over the years. Moreover, even an apparently rigid convention may contain within itself concealed elements of flexibility. Let us suppose that at the next United Kingdom General Elections the Liberal Party win as many seats as the Conservatives have now, but that the acknowledged leader of the Liberal Party (who was not, of course, Leader of the Opposition before the Election) is for one reason or another, unable to obtain a seat at the Election. The Government resigns. Would any constitutional writer of repute suggest that the Queen would thereupon be obliged to send for the former Leader of the Opposition? Would all constitutional authorities unanimously declare that the queen could not properly invite the leader of the Liberal party to form a Government,

even though it was known that he would immediately obtain a safe seat? The fact is that general statements by British commentators are invariably based on situations that have arisen in Britain or are likely to arise in Britain in the foreseeable future. In relation to situations that have not arisen and have not been foreseen they carry no greater weight than the broad *obiter dicta* that judges often propound. If Britain had had a fluid multi-party system in recent years, in which extraordinary problems of party leadership had arisen, I have no doubt that some of the leading commentators would have used more carefully guarded language in expressing the conventions relating to the choice of a Prime Minister. And I should have sided with those who declined to lay down rigid rules designed to cover every conceivable contingency.

6. Consequently I do not accept the view that in no circumstances whatsoever can the Prime Minister in the United Kingdom be appointed from outside Parliament; and even if I were compelled to bow to an overwhelming weight of opinion on this matter (which I am not) I should still be prepared do deny that such a convention was automatically applicable to Ceylon with the present characteristics of its party system.

7. The case of Southern Rhodesia is, I think, of some persuasive authority. Naturally it is not a binding precedent, but I have yet to see any published argument that the action taken by the Governor was constitutionally improper, and I think it likely that expert constitutional advice was taken before he decided to appoint Sir Edgar Whitehead. In any event, what actually happened in a situation comparable with that which may shortly arise in Ceylon seems to be at least as relevant as general statements made by British writers who had almost certainly not addressed their minds to the possibility that such a situation might arise in Britain.

ELECTORAL AGREEMENT BETWEEN THE SRI LANKA FREEDOM PARTY AND THE LANKA SAMA SAMAJA PARTY

The Sri Lanka Freedom Party in order to form an independent and stable government with an absolute majority in Parliament, and the Lanka Sama Samaja Party have entered into the following electoral agreement for purposes of the forthcoming general election to be held on the 20th of July, 1960:–

1. That this agreement is in the nature of an electoral agreement only, and does not signify a change of principles or policy on the part of either party.

2. That the LSSP will not nominate candidates for election in the electorates enumerated in the First Schedule to this agreement, and that the LSSP will further request its supporters in these electorates to support the candidates of the SLFP.

3. That the SLFP will not nominate candidates for election in the electorates enumerated in the Second Schedule to this agreement, and that the SLFP will further request its supporters in these electorates to support the candidates of the LSSP.

FIRST SCHEDULE

Borella	Laggala	Maskeliya
Wattala	Matale	Balapitiya
Negombo	Rattota	Bentara-Elpitiya
Divulapitiya	Wattegama	Hiniduma
Mirigama	Akurana	Ratgama
Minuwangoda	Galagedera	Akmeemana
Attanagalla	Yatinuwara	Galle
Gampaha	Udunuwara	Habaraduwa
Jaela	Kandy	Weligama
Mahara	Senkadagala	Deniyaya
Dompe	Kundasale	Hakmana
Kelaniya	Teldeniya	Matara
Kolonnawa	Minipe	Devinuwara
Kottawa	Walapane	Beliatta
Homagama	Hanguranketa	Mulkirigala
Avissawella	Hewaheta	Tissamaharama
Horana	Gampola	Trincomalee
Bandaragama	Nawalapitiya	Muttur
Beruwala	Kotmale	Amparai
Matugama	Nuwara Eliya	Puttalam
Dambulla	Medawachchiya	Dedigama
Nikaweratiya	Horowapotana	Galigamuwa
Yapahuwa	Kalawewa	Kegalle
Hriyala	Kekirewa	Rambukkana
Wariyapola	Minneriya	Mawanella
Bingiriya	Polonnaruwa	Ratnapura
Chilaw	Mahiyangana	Pelmadulla
Nattandiya	Bibile	Balangoda

Wennappuwa	Passara	Rakwana
Kuliyapitiya	Badulla	Nivitigala
Dambadeniya	Soranatota	Kalawana
Polgahawela	Bandarawela	
Kurunegala	Haputale	
Mawatagama	Monaragala	
Anuradhapura		

SECOND SCHEDULE

Colombo North	Kalutara	Dehiowita
Colombo South**	Agalawatta	Kiriella
Katana	Ambalangoda	Kollonne*
Dehiwala-Mt. Lavinia	Baddegama	Bulathsinhala
Moratuwa	Mihintale	
Kesbewa	Yatiyantota	
Panadura	Ruwanewlla	

* The question of adjustment regarding the two seats Nivitigala and Kolonne to be left over for decision upon a basis mutually satisfactory to both parties.

** The question of whether the SLFP should contest this seat either with an SLFP candidate or with an independent candidate, to be left over for decision upon a basis mutually satisfactory to both parties.

Secretary, SLFP
17th May, 1960

Secretary, LSSP
17th May, 1960

PRESS RELEASE

The Sri Lanka Freedom Party in order to form an independent and stable government with an absolute majority in Parliament, and the Lanka Sama Samaja Party have entered into an electoral agreement for purposes of the forthcoming general election. This agreement, which will eliminate contests between these two parties in all seats, was signed this morning. The agreement is an electoral agreement only, and does not signify a change of principles or policy on the part of either party.

17th May, 1960

Secretary, SLFP

Secretary, LSSP

NO-CONTEST PACT WITH COMMUNIST PARTY

The Sri Lanka Freedom Party, in order to form an independent and stable government with an absolute majority, and the Ceylon Communist Party have held discussions with a view to avoiding mutual contests in the forthcoming general election and have reached agreement.

While both parties retain their independent principles and policies, the avoidance of contests under the agreement will permit the widest mobilisation of forces in order to defeat the UNP.

Both parties expressed their belief that the no-contest arrangements made between various anti-UNP parties will contribute substantially towards inflicting on the UNP a defeat similar to that which it experienced in 1956.

The first signs of the effectiveness of such arrangements can be seen in the fact that Mr J. R. Jayewardene has recognised at long last that the voters of Kelaniya need a change.

Felix R Dias Bandaranaike
....
(Secretary, Sri Lanka Freedom Party)

Pieter Keuneman
....
(General Secretary, Ceylon Communist Party)

WHY THE TAMILS SUPPORTED THE SLFP
Chelvanayakam explains, Daily News 28.5.60

The leader of the Federal Party Mr S. J. V. Chelvanayakam declined to give a point by point answer to a series of questions put to him regarding the Federal Party and the SLFP on the grounds that he did not wish to involve himself: "in an issue which has arisen at the moment between the UNP and the SLFP" he said he would prefer to make a general statement on the question raised.

Questions were as follows:

1. Did the Federal Party put forward its 4 points demand to the SLFP or did it not?
2. If it did not do so, why?
3. Is it true that the SLFP did not agree to any of the demands of the Federal Party offer to support an alternative Government formed by the SLFP as stated in the joint opposition letter of protest to the Governor-General following the dissolution of Parliament?
4. Did not the Federal party thereby draw a distinction between the UNP and the SLFP.

The statement

Mr. Chelvanayakam's statement is as follows:

"The position taken up by the SLFP was that they would not enter into any agreement with us and that they were not asking for our support on the basis of any agreement. Their position was that if they were called to form a Government they would make a policy statement covering among others the issues in which the Federal Party was interested and it would open then to our party to support the SLFP government or vote against it according to our view of that policy statement whether the same was acceptable to us or not.

In these circumstances the Federal Party was prepared to support the SLFP to form a government.

It is a mistake to think that we drew a distinction between the UNP and SLFP. The issue before the House on April 22 was whether we were to support the then Government when it had failed to come to any agreement on understanding with us on our Four Point proposals, that Government had rejected our proposal IN TOTO and hence from our point of view, it is interesting to note what the four points were:

1. Change of the official language policy
2. No colonisation by Sinhalese in certain Tamil areas
3. Enfranchisement of some 1,000,000 Indians and
4. Four nominated MP's appointed on the advice of Mr Thondaman.

FOREIGN AFFAIRS

The Prime Minister, Mrs Sirimavo Bandaranaike, making a statement in the Senate regarding the Commonwealth Prime Ministers' Conference in U.K., which she attended, said that it was her personal belief that the Commonwealth remained a stronger and more cohesive unit than ever before and a factor of influence in world affairs.

The following is the text of her statement:-

"You are aware that I left Ceylon on 4th March to attend the Commonwealth Prime Ministers' Conference and I think it is my duty to inform this House as to what happened at that Conference. I wish to make a short statement now and I might also mention that a similar statement will be made on my behalf by the leader of the House in the House of Representatives.

"The meetings of the Commonwealth Prime Ministers started on 8th March and continued till the 17th of March. The countries participating in the Conference, besides Ceylon, were the United Kingdom, Canada, Australia, South Africa, New Zealand, India, Pakistan, Ghana, Malaya, Southern Rhodesia and Cyprus. The last named country was a new admission to the Commonwealth, after her recent attainment of independence, and was only able to come into the Conference two days before it concluded.

"At past meetings of the Prime Ministers the practice had usually been to exchange views on the world political and economic situation in a general way. On this occasion, however, it had been agreed that the Prime Ministers should concentrate their attention on a few specific problems which were of concern to them all. These problems were disarmament, South Africa, structure of the United Nations, Congo and Laos.

"It was generally agreed that disarmament was the most important problem facing the world today and that, in the absence of a satisfactory and speedy solution to this problem, not merely was world peace endangered but the very survival of the human race was in jeopardy. While it would be correct to say that little progress could be made on this matter without a working understanding between the two major powers U.S.A. and U.S.S.R., it was, however, felt that worthwhile contribution could be made by the other powers as well, particularly the neutralist and the non-aligned ones. It was in this belief that a considerable amount of the time of the Conference was spent in discussing ways and means of promoting an agreement for worldwide disarmament, subject to effective inspection and control. I believe that as a result of these discussions, what might be described as a Commonwealth approach to disarmament, has emerged, which might well constitute a useful contribution to the forthcoming negotiations on the subject of disarmament.

South Africa. "The next most important subject which engaged the attention of the Prime Ministers, and which was in reality a challenge to the very existence of the Commonwealth, was the question of South Africa. As you are aware, consequent on a plebiscite held in October, 1960, South Africa decided to change from a monarchical to a republican form of government. The constitutional measures to implement this decision will be effected by 31st May this year. The South African government made a request to be permitted to continue membership of the Commonwealth after attaining republican status on May 31st this year. Ordinarily, this would have been agreed to by the other Commonwealth Prime Ministers as a matter of course, as happened when India, Pakistan and Ghana became Republics. But, in view of the special circumstances pertaining to South Africa, it was felt that this could not be dealt with as purely a procedural matter.

"It has long been a tradition at this conference not to discuss the internal affairs of a member country except with the consent of the Prime Minister of that country. On this occasion with the consent of the Prime Minister of South Africa, a full and frank discussion did take place. The views expressed in the course of this discussion made it clear that the racialist policies pursued by South Africa were incompatible with membership of a multiracial body such as the Commonwealth and, accordingly, the Prime Minister of South Africa withdrew his request to remain in the Commonwealth after becoming a Republic on 31st May.

United Nations. "As regards the structure of the United Nations, various proposals have recently been put forward for changes. The present structure of the United Nations is as it was settled in 1945 when the total membership was limited to some 51 nations. Since then, the membership has greatly increased and the present number is 99 nations. Nearly all the additions subsequent to 1948 were newly independent nations from Asia and Africa. Obviously, the structure and constitution of an organisation determined for meeting the needs of an association consisting of 51 nations drawn predominantly from the European and American continents, would be found grossly inadequate to meet a situation where there are 99 nations drawn from every continent of the world. There was a full discussion of various proposals put forward for dealing with the present situation. It was recognized, however, that no changes could be made without general consent of the members of the United Nations Organisation and that whatever adjustments were made, it was vitally important to uphold the purposes and principles of the United Nations Charter and to preserve the international and independent character of the Secretariat.

Congo. "The explosive character and the threat to world peace inherent in the Congo were recognized. In the light of this, the Prime Ministers reaffirmed the support of their governments to the efforts of the United Nations to restore order in the Congo, to secure its independence and integrity and to shut out any intervention in Congolese affairs other than through the United Nations. It was agreed that the security Council resolution of 21st February should be fully implemented and that, for this purpose, the United Nations forces in the Congo should be strengthened.

Laos. "Laos appears to have become a cockpit for the Big Powers jockeying for position in that part of the world, to the grave detriment and suffering of the Laotian people. The Prime Ministers noted this situation with concern and expressed the hope that the parties would be able to reconcile their differences, that intervention from outside would cease and that Laos would be able to enjoy an independent neutral and peaceful existence. As cessation of the fighting that is now going on was a prerequistie to peace in Laos, it was agreed that urgent steps should be taken to set up some form of international control machinery to stop the fighting and prevent intervention in Laotian affairs by interested parties from outside. I might add in this connection that after my return from London I addressed a personal message to Mr Kennedy and to Mr Khrushchev conveying to them the anxieties of my

Government on the dangerous situation in Laos and soliciting their good offices in effecting a peaceful solution to the problem without resorting to military action.

"In conclusion, I would wish to say that this Conference has been extremely useful, and I was happy to have been able to attend it. The frank, and sometimes divergent, expression of views on various matters, and the full discussion that ensured, have the practical advantage of a broader appreciation of controversial issues, and consequently assist in the formulation of one's own policy on particular questions, quite apart from the advantage of the mutual understanding and the personal contacts which these meetings of Prime Ministers provide. It is my personal belief that the Commonwealth remains a stronger and more cohesive unit than ever before, and a factor of influence in world affairs."

THE PIED PIPER OF CEYLON POLITICS
By P. A. Ediriweera

In March 1960, a young man in his thirties left the hallowed halls of Hulftsdorp for a swim in a stormy political sea.

The wigged wallahas took off their funny looking ornaments and wiped the sweat off their bald heads. It was all nonsense, they exclaimed. A brilliant lawyer with a more brilliant future was courting disaster. Some others with lesser intellect in their gowns were happy.

This adventurous young man was none other than Mr Felix Dias Bandaranaike, who was born on November 5, 1930.

Nobody burns his effigies though the day he was born is associated with Guy Fawkes Day. But he loves fireworks, especially in the National State Assembly where he has up to now placed on record in Hansard more than the 2.8 million words written by Leo Tolstoi.

Mr Felix Dias Bandaranaike hails from an illustrious family of lawyers. He himself is an LLB (Ceylon) and an Advocate who has always advocated the cause of the poor man in the dispensation of justice.

He was the youngest to hold the portfolio of Finance in 1960 and later Minister of Agriculture and Food.

When Mrs Sirimavo Bandaranaike formed her first Cabinet as the world's first lady Prime Minister the British newspapers described Mr Bandaranaike as the "Power Behind the Throne." No wonder that eminent journalists by the dozen streamed into Ceylon to see what was happening.

I met one of them. His summing up of the political situation at that time was that the Prime Minister if she wanted to, could sack the entire Cabinet and give Mr Felix Dias Bandaranaike seven telephones of different colours and that he could run the country.

"Would you cable this to your paper?" I asked him what for? It would be as ridiculous as cabling description of the Taj Mahal which was so perfect. No one could find a flaw and without a flaw there is no news."

Despite the gloomy forecasts of our political pundits, the Pied Piper of Ceylon politics drew the voters to the polling booths with his chanting political tune.

He is a man of conviction. When he found that the country's economy could not be salvaged without reducing the rice subsidy he did not hesitate to introduce it out in rice ration in 1964.

His budgetary proposal raised a hornet's nest not only within the Cabinet of the day but also among his parliamentary colleagues in the Sri Lanka Freedom Party.

Some party Members of Parliament shed a tear. There were others who cried. And from the Opposition rows there were key left leaders breathing fire and brimstone and virtually saying. "Woe be unto you, What happened to Dudley in 1951 will be your fate too."

Undaunted by these pressures, intimidation and political boycotts he embodied the proposal in his Budget and took the consequences gallantly, but not without a show of strength.

For the first time, Colombo witnessed a procession wending its way from Victoria Bridge to the Galle Face green supporting a cut in the rice ration. Prominent among the processionists and speakers in support of the rice cut were Mr Alvai Moulana and another MP at the time who now is elevated to an exalted position in the judiciary.

Felix would have no doubt realised that statesmanship does not pay in a mug's game like politics.

But today, Mr Felix R. D. Bandaranaike stands vindicated. Those very people who vehemently opposed his then budgetary proposal are at the moment crying: "To hell with subsidies."

He quit the Cabinet saying that he would not come back even to plant grass. But destiny had thought otherwise and he did come back to grow rice and there is no doubt that as Minister of Agriculture he was a great success.

The biggest tribute to him as Minister of Agriculture came from the late Mr M. D. Banda who after taking over the same portfolio indicated on the floor of the House of Representatives that he was merely following the agricultural plan mapped out by his predecessor Mr Felix R. D. Bandaranaike.

This is not all. Whenever entrusted with a job he did it magnificently turning a deaf ear not only to his critics but also to his flatterers.

The significant role he played in crushing the Coup of 1962 is now recorded history.

Here too, he was not worried about those who made allegations of "a coup within the coup" but proceeded with the investigations with such minute care which eventually led to a prosecution of the coup suspects.

Mr Bandaranaike is forthright. He does not mince his words. This is the key to his success whether it be in the North Western Province organising an election campaign or introducing legal reforms in the teeth of opposition from vested interests.

Mr Felix Dias Bandaranaike has his conscience where other people have their purses! This explains why he resigned his portfolio in 1962 when his budget proposals came before the firing line.

In a brief but meaningful speech he said: "Conscience is my guide, I do not see a distant dawn."

Frank and outspoken Mr Bandaranaike does not mix his metaphors. The development of a developing country he once said needed a little bit of totalitarianism.

He, however assured his supporters that he was not a follower of Marxism, nor would he become a Marxist. His only ambition was to implement the policies laid down by the late Mr S. W. R. D. Bandaranaike and create a socialist Lanka.

To achieve this he added, it was essential to see that reactionary elements were wiped out from the political field.

May be he is having another tune up his pipe!

MISSION TO THE SOVIET UNION

THE Following article by N. Sitnikow relates to the visit of the Finance Minister, Mr Felix R. Dias Bandaranaike, to the U.S.S.R.

The Soviet public justly appraised the visit of Mr Felix R. Dias Bandaranaike to the U.S.S.R. as a new step in strengthening U.S.S.R.-Ceylon friendship. The Ceylonese guest was cordially welcomed in various cities. The meeting arranged at the Moscow Friendship House was a manifestation of these friendly feelings towards the Ceylonese people. And now when Mr Bandaranaike's visit to the Soviet Union has ended I should like to tell the Ceylonese readers in detail about the friendly meeting I witnessed which mirrors the feelings the Soviet people entertain towards the people of Ceylon.

People in high spirits filled the cosy halls of the Friendship House that evening. These representatives of the public came to meet the envoys of Lanka, Mr F. R. Dias Bandaranaike and his wife, and Mr S. Amarasinghe.

The distinguished guests who arrived together with Mr G. P. Malalasekera, Ambassador of Ceylon to the U.S.S.R., were met by V. Garbuzov, Minister of Finances of the U.S.S.R., V. Gorshkow and T. Zuyeva, Vice Chairmen of the Presidium of the Union of Friendship Societies, and Professor V. Aboltin, President of the U.S.S.R.-Ceylon Friendship Society. The meeting was attended by prominent Soviet scientists, artists, writers and public figures, Academician Oparin, famous aircraft designer Tupolev, Vice Chairman of the State Committee on Cultural Relations with Foreign Countries of the U.S.S.R. Council of Ministers, V. Kochemasov, former U.S.S.R. Ambassador to Ceylon V. Yakovlev, and others.

V. Gorshkow, cordially greeted the Ceylonese guests on behalf of the members of the U.S.S.R.-Ceylon Friendship Society and on behalf of everybody present.

The Soviet people, he said, highly valued the successes achieved by the industrious and talented Ceylonese people, and admired their achievements in the struggle for their freedom and sovereignty, for the happiness and prosperity of Ceylon. The sympathies of the Soviet people are entirely with the Ceylonese people because the Soviet people have themselves traversed a difficult path in overcoming their age-old backwardness and scored outstanding successes in this direction.

The relations between the Soviet Union and Ceylon have never been marred by anything because they are based on principles of mutual respect and equality, and because they are united by community of views on the basic issues of the present international situation.

We soviet women, said T. Zuyeva, are happy of the occasion to convey through the guests most hearty greetings to Madame Sirimavo Bandaranaike, Prime Minister of Ceylon. We are particularly happy to greet her because, for the first time in the history of Ceylon its government is headed by a woman. We wish the Ceylonese people successes in their struggle for prosperity, for the happiness of their country.

These words called forth enthusiastic applause.

In his reply speech Felix R. D. Bandaranaike, Minister of Finance, Parliamentary Secretary of the Foreign Ministry and Defence Ministry, said that he came to the U.S.S.R. in order to further strengthen the friendly relations existing between the two countries.

Your hospitality and cordiality, he said, are unsurpassed. During the tour of the Soviet Union I was asked whether I felt homesick. I replied that I came to your country from London, where occasionally I did feel somewhat homesick. But here in the U.S.S.R. where your people surrounded us with friendship and hospitality, we did not have that feeling at all. I have met many prominent statesmen of the Soviet Union. We were received by Mr Khrushchev. Our conversation was exceptionally friendly and although we spoke different languages we understood one another perfectly because our common language was the language of sincere friendship and all the peoples of the world should speak with one another in this language.

We were delighted with everything we saw in your country, your successes since 1917 are tremendous. The people in all parts of the world are striving to raise their living standards and your country is the best example of how this should be done. You have achieved not only unprecedented economic and scientific development. You have trained your people in a new spirit. A state should be primarily responsible to its people, and we have become convinced that your state is coping with this responsibility excellently.

Mr Bandaranaike made his concluding part of the speech in Russian. He said that he admired the achievements of the Soviet people, that neither Ceylon nor the Soviet Union want war, and that by common effort countries could accomplish a great deal not only in economic co-operation but also in the field of general disarmament and establishment of peace on earth.

Mr Felix Bandaranaike's speech was listened to with keen interest and attention. The loud applause with which the concluding words of the distinguished Ceylonese guest were met furnished best evidence that these words met with a ready response among everybody present.

The visitors did not leave the Friendship House for a long time that evening. And it seemed that our peoples have become still closer friends.

THE PRIME MINISTER IN BELGRADE

The Prime Minister, Mrs Sirimavo Bandaranaike, headed the Ceylon Delegation to the 25-nation conference of non-aligned countries held in Belgrade, from 1st to 6th September.

The other members of the delegation were the Parliamentary Secretary to the Minister of External Affairs, Mr Felix R. Dias Bandaranaike, the Permanent Secretary, Mr N. Q. Dias, an Assistant Secretary, Mr Y. Duraiswamy and the Private Secretary to the Prime Minister, Dr. M. Ratwatte.

Mr M. M. Maharoof, Ceylon's Ambassador to Yugoslavia and Mr D. A. de Silva, Charge-d'affaires in Paris, joined the delegation in Belgrade.

The Prime Minister addressed the Conference, on September 3rd. The following is the full text of her speech:

Mr Chairman and friends: I consider it a great honour to represent my country at this Conference which could prove to be of historic significance in the cause of world peace. I am happy to attend this great assembly not only as a representative of my country but also as a woman and a mother who can understand the thoughts and feelings of those millions of women, the mothers of this world, who are deeply concerened with the preservation of the human race. I am also happy that we have chosen to hold the Conference in this beautiful city of Belgrade not only because of the warmth and hospitality of the Yugoslav people of which there is so much evidence but also because in holding it in a European city we have demonstrated to the world that the ideals and hopes which we all share are not confined to a continent or region but reflect an awareness on the part of human beings, wherever they may be, of the urgent need for international peace and security.

We in Ceylon count ourselves fortunate that the people of our land were spared the horrors of two world wars and that we were able to throw off the shackles of colonial power without strife or bloodshed. But it was not until eight years after the attainment of independence, when my late husband was elected Prime Minister, that the foreign bases were taken over and definite and positive policy of non-alignment with power blocs adopted in foreign affairs.

The experience of many countries represented around this conference table has not been so fortunate. Some countries like Yugoslavia, have had to see their homelands made into battle-grounds; others, like Cuba and Algeria, have had to sacrifice their sons and daughters in order to be free; and some others, like Tunisia, are yet striving to exercise sovereign power over the bases situated within their territory.

Common Decisions

This Conference at Belgrade has not been convened, however, for the consideration of specific problems peculiar to individual nations; we are gathered here in the firm belief that the positive policy of non-alignment with power blocs followed by each of our several countries and that our common dedication to the cause of peace and peaceful co-existence gives us the right to raise our voices in common decisions and declarations in a world divided into power blocs and moving rapidly towards the brink of a nuclear war.

Many of the Heads of States and Heads of Governments who addressed this Conference in plenary session have emphasized the point that our group of nations do not propose to become a third bloc or a third force. None of us can really disagree with that view, for that would be inconsistent with the very idea of non-alignment. But it is important to remember that in our anxiety to avoid becoming a third force we must not allow our spirit of unity and purpose which has been so evident at this Conference to disintegrate and fall apart. We should endeavour to maximise the influence of non-aligned thinking in world affairs. We cannot, in my view, rely on the haphazard form of consultation which we regret to note, however, that no satisfactory solution acceptable to all the parties concerned has yet been found. Fears and prejudices, some real and others imaginary, have stood in the way of a solution. A spirit of compromise and conciliation should therefore be adopted by the parties directly concerned in order to arrive at a settlement of this question. We believe that the situation in Germany today should not be regarded as a testing-ground for courage and will in the military sense, but as a practical challenge to the politics and strength of the forces of universal progress and of total peace.

Peaceful Negotiation

It is our view that as a first step towards creating international confidence the great powers should firmly resolve and make it known to the world that they will not resort to military engagements and will depend solely on peaceful negotiations to arrive at a solution. The great powers must also agree to the withdrawal of all foreign armed forces from their respective sectors in Germany and to the demilitarization of Germany. The great powers must immediately get down to the task of reopening direct East-West negotiations designed to achieve a final settlement by peaceful means. For the success of such negotiations it would be essential for the two Germanies to participate in the discussions, since the future of Germany must be determined not in accordance with the cold-war strategy to suit either of the great powers but in order to establish a unified state, insulated as far as possible from the cold war and unaligned with either of the existing power blocs. No lasting solution of the German problem can be found on the basis of unilateral abrogation of rights and obligations. Likewise a rigid attachment to positions formulated by mere legal technicalities cannot pave the way towards an abiding settlement. The great powers must recognise that whatever rights and obligations they hold must be regarded as capable of modification in the face of existing realities.

We feel that a settlement on these lines would permit the reunification of Germany on conditions acceptable not only to the German people but also to those countries who, with good reason, have cause to fear a revival of German militarism. The world has been devastated by two major wars in the first half of this century and we cannot allow a third one to destroy mankind and all that we cherish in our civilization. A satisfactory solution must be found. That solution must reconcile the conflicting interests of the various nations concerned if we are to move away from tensions and war towards a lasting and abiding peace.

Colonialism

Ceylon has consistently advocated the eradication of colonialism in all its forms and manifestations. We share the view expressed at this Conference that colonialism is morally unjust and politically out of date. Though many of the countries of Asia and Africa have emerged as full-fledged sovereign states in the past, nonetheless a few colonial powers today doggedly cling to their colonial positions on various pretexts, claiming peaceful motives but in practice resorting to rough and ruthless methods to retain them. The refusal of these powers to read the writing on the wall only causes human suffering and creates bitterness and hatred – a state of affairs which is not conducive to peaceful co-existence and which constitutes a threat to peace.

The United Nations General Assembly at its fifteenth session made a significant declaration on the granting of independence to colonial countries and peoples. That resolution called for immediate action to be taken to end the colonial issue in all dependent territories but did not specify a date line. One of the matters which this Conference may have to consider will be the desirability of translating that resolution into practical terms.

Disarmament is a crucial question of our times. An early settlement of this question will be of paramount importance in building confidence among nations and in decreasing the dangers of war. It would also be an important milestone in the improvement of relations between nations and would mark the end of two power blocs with all that it portends for the future peace and security of the world. Vast sums of money that are expended in manufacturing these weapons of destruction could usefully be spent on economic and social development in various countries of the world.

Unfortunately, no tangible results have followed. The mutual fear and suspicion of the powers concerned have prevented even a start being made in disarmament. We accept the need for an immediate treaty for general and complete disarmament, and this should be achieved in rapid stages. Every stage or phase should be established by having an effective method of inspection and control over its operation and maintenance. In this connection I would commend to this Conference the statement on disarmament referred to in the final communique of the Commonwealth Prime Ministers' Conference held in March of this year. Cyprus, Ghana and India, together with Ceylon, who are represented at this Conference, were parties to this statement. We felt at that time that an effective international agreement could be concluded on the lines indicated in that statement. The Commonwealth Premiers statement on disarmament urged the reopening of disarmament negotiations at the earliest possible moment with the aim of completely eliminating all means of waging war. This document was later circulated to other members of the United Nations for their information. Unfortunately disarmament negotiations, regarding both nuclear tests and general disarmament, have come to a standstill. *Reproduced from "Ceylon Today" published by the Ceylon Government Information Department.*

CONFERENCE OF SIX AFRO-ASIAN NON-ALIGNED COUNTRIES

Colombo, which was the venue of the Colombo Foreign Ministers' Conference in 1950, and the Colombo Powers' Conference in 1954, was again the scene of another historic conference in December this year.

Six Afro-Asian non-aligned countries – Burma, Cambodia, Ceylon, Ghana, Indonesia and the United Arab Republic – met in the Senate Building, Colombo, on December 10th, 11th and 12th, to discuss the possibility of these countries making a joint approach to the Governments of India and China with a view to preventing a deterioration in the serious situation which had developed on the Sino-Indian border.

This conference was convened by the Prime Minister of Ceylon, Mrs Sirimavo Bandaranaike.

A communique issued at the end of the deliberations said that the six countries reached unanimity in regard to the suggestions which they propose to make to the Governments of India and the People's Republic of China in their attempt to bring these two countries together for negotiations to consolidate the ceasefire and to settle the boundary dispute between them. The conference decided not to publish the text of their conclusions which are to be communicated to the Governments of India and the People's Republic of China lest premature disclosures prejudice their endeavours.

It was the wish of the Conference that the Prime Minister of Ceylon Mrs Sirimavo Bandaranaike, should visit New Delhi and Peking, in order to convey the results of the deliberations.

The Conference decided that their efforts in seeking to bring about negotiations between India and the People's Republic of China should not end with this meeting in Colombo, but should continue until the final settlement of this problem can be negotiated directly between the Governments of the two countries concerned.

The Conference commenced its proceedings with opening statements by the leaders of delegations. The leaders of delegations expressed concern over the developments which have occurred as a result of the boundary dispute between the two countries – especially as regards the implications of these developments for the future of peace not only in Asia and Africa but also in the world at large. They were of the view that these developments were a threat to Afro-Asian solidarity and the policy of non-alignment. They expressed the hope that their deliberations would help the two countries to arrive at a peaceful settlement of the border dispute.

A communique issued at the end of the first day's proceedings said the conference decided that its purpose was not to consider the merits and demerits of the dispute but to provide for an exchange of views in order to assist the two countries to resume direct negotiations with a view to arriving at a peaceful settlement.

Documents supplied by the Government of India and the Government of People's Republic of China were placed before the conference.

The various delegations were led by the following:- Cambodia by Prince Norodom Sihanouk; Burma by General Ne Win, Chairman of the Revolutionary Council; United Arab Republic by Mr. Aly Sabry, Chairman of the Executive Council; Indonesia by Dr. Subandrio, Deputy First Minister and Minister for Foreign affairs and Foreign Economic Relations; Ghana by Mr K. K. Ofori Atta, M.P., Minister of Justice; and Ceylon by Mrs Sirimavo Bandaranaike, Prime Minister and Minister of Defence and External Affairs.

The delegations started arriving in Ceylon two days before the Conference commenced.

MISSION OF PEACE TO THE PEOPLE'S REPUBLIC OF CHINA AND INDIA

At the request of the Conference of six Non-Aligned Afro-Asian nations which met at Colombo in December, 1962 the Prime Minister of Ceylon, the Hon. Sirimavo R. D. Bandaranaike, conveyed the proposals of the Conference to the Prime Ministers of China and India. The purpose of her Mission, as she stated in her Message to the Nation on her return, was to explain the unanimous proposals of the Conference to the two Prime Ministers and to request them to accept these proposals as the basis of direct negotiations between their Governments for the settlement of the Sino-Indian Border Dispute. She was assisted in her task by Dr. Subandrio, the Foreign Minister of Indonesia in the People's Republic of China and by Mr Aly Sabry, Chairman of the Executive Council of the U.A.R., and Mr K. A. Ofori Atta, Minister of Justice of Ghana, during her talks with the Indian Prime Minister. In addition, the Prime Minister took the opportunity of her visit to China and India to have informal discussions with the two Prime Ministers on several matters of common interest and to strengthen still further the strong and enduring ties of friendship that exist between Ceylon and these two countries. It was also therefore a Mission of Friendship and Goodwill.

The Prime Minister's historic journey, perhaps unexampled in the annals of what has come to be called Personal Diplomacy, evoked great interest and received wide coverage in the World Press. The following account is an eye-witness description of the less-publicised aspects of the Prime Minister's visit to China and India.

After brief stops en route in Kuala Lumpur and Hong Kong, the Prime Minister, accompanied by the Hon. Felix R. D. Bandaranaike, Minister without Portfolio, and the rest of her delegation, entrained from Kowloon in the colony of Hong Kong for Canton on 30th December. At Samchun, where a little iron bridge marks the frontier between the People's Republic of China and the new territory leased to Hong Kong on the mainland, the Prime Minister was received by the Vice-Governor of Kwangtung Province and Chinese Protocol officials. His Excellency Hsieh Ke-Hsi, Chinese Ambassador in Ceylon, also accompanied the Party from there on in the special train to Canton. After a 3 hour train journey through a countryside strikingly similar to rural Ceylon, with its paddy fields and irrigation channels, Canton was reached. At the Railway Station a Reception had been organized and the Prime Minister was formally welcomed to the city by the Provincial Governor of Kwangtung. Long lines of children carrying the flags of Ceylon and China cheered the Prime Minister shouting "Long Live Friendship between China and Ceylon." Outside, in the Station square, several thousands of people, dancers in traditional Lion costumes, and bands playing Chinese music greeted the delegation. After inspecting an impressive Army Guard-of-Honour and reviewing the March-past, the Prime Minister, was formally welcomed to the People's Republic of China by the Governor of Kwantung, who referred to the friendly relations that bound the peoples of the two countries together and to the common desire of the people of China and Ceylon for Peace.

In recent Chinese history Canton has been the centre of revolutionary ferment. It is here that the Opium war had its beginnings, the revolution which ushered in Dr. Sun Yat Sen's Proclamation of a Chinese Republic took place, and where in the early 1920's the Communist Movement gained ground. That afternoon, the Prime Minister visited the site of the Peasant Movement Institute.

FELIX R. DIAS BANDARANAIKE MEMORIAL TRUST

THIS INDENTURE and declaration of TRUST is made this 21st day of October, nineteen hundred and eighty five between ELIZABETH MUTHULAKSHMI DIAS BANDARANAIKE also known as Lakshmi Dias Bandaranaike of No. 3, Mahanuge Gardens, Colombo 3 (hereinafter called "the settlor") of the one part AND 1. ELIZABETH MUTHULAKSHMI DIAS BANDARANAIKE, 2. JAYA PATHIRANA, 3. BARNES SHELTON CARLYLE RATWATTE, 4. HERMAN LEONARD DE SILVA President's Counsel, 5. BALAKUMARA MAHADEVA, 6. HITAKAMI CHIDRUPA PEIRIS, 7. PERIN CAPTAIN, 8. SIVAGAMI OBEYESEKERE, 9. WILLIAM STANLEY DE ALWIS, 10. ASITHA PERERA, 11. DOCTOR OLIVER ROBERT MEDONZA, 12. PRINS GUNASEKARA, 13. DOCTOR UPALI MENDIS, 14. HARRIS WICKREMATUNGA, 15. HALEEM ISHAK, Member of Parliament, 16. ASKER MOOSAJEE, 17. FELIX PREMACHANDRA DE ALWIS, 18. MABULA BANDUSENA ABEYWARDENE, 19. CYRIL GARDINER, 20. VIJAYA COREA, 21. MALKANTHI WIKRAMANAYAKE, 22. DINESH GUNAWARDENE M.P. all of Colombo (hereinafter called "The Trustees", which term as herein used shall where the context so requires or admits mean and include the Trustees for the time being appointed under the provisions hereinafter contained of this instrument of Trust) of the other part.

WHEREAS it was the earnest wish and desire of the late Felix R. Dias Bandaranaike to provide a facility for the early detection and diagnosis of cancer that would be accessible to all people in Sri Lanka, in all stations of life without distinction and for that purpose to purchase or otherwise obtain a scanning machine for the computerised axial tomography of the human body, usually called a C.A.T. Scanner, and since it is the common intention of the settlor and the Trustees and numerous other friends of the late Felix R. Dias Bandaranaike to create an institution and establish a charitable Trust in his memory for the fulfilment of the aforesaid purpose.

AND WHEREAS the settlor and the Trustees being desirous of making a settlement for the charitable objects hereinafter mentioned and the settlor having paid to the Trustees a sum of Rupees One hundred thousand (Rs. 100,000/-) of lawful money, and further contemplates paying from time to time to the credit of the said trust, including other monies received by the Trustees from members of the public or which the settlor or other persons, including the Trustees themselves or any of them, may at their, his or her discretion pay, or gift or transfer or make over or by last will give devise and bequeath unto the Trustees, to the intent and purpose that the Trustees may hold the said sum and such other monies and other properties and income therefrom upon trust for purposes and subject to the conditions and powers hereinafter declared.

NOW THIS INDENTURE WITNESSETH as follows:

1. The Trust constituted by this settlement shall be called "THE FELIX R. DIAS BANDARANAIKE MEMORIAL TRUST."

2. The objects of the Trust shall be –

(a) to finance the purchase of a scanning machine for the computerised axial tomography of the human body, (also described as a C.A.T. Scanner) or any other equipment of an equivalent nature and effectiveness as to function, as a means of or as an aid to the early detection and diagnosis of all diseases and in particular cancers in the human body, which would be beneficial to all people in Sri Lanka in all stations of life without distinction; and

(b) for the more effectual realisation of the said object and the maximum utilisation of available resources in Sri Lanka, in co-ordination with the health care services provided by the State, to donate, grant and make over the funds of the Trust and contributions made thereto by members of the public, institutions and organizations to the National Health Development Fund established by the State under the provisions of Act No. 13 of 1981, as amended, of the Democratic Socialist Republic of Sri Lanka, in order to finance the purchase of such machine and ancillary equipment and provide for its establishment and maintenance, including the training of personnel necessary for its operation, as contemplated by Section 7(c) of the said Act and with the object of securing the exemptions and benefits provided under the said Act which are as follows:

(1) exemption from the payment of any income tax in respect of the total value of any donation to the Fund which shall be deemed to be an approved expenditure for the purposes of the Inland Revenue Act No. 28 of 1979;

(ii) gift tax payable under the Inland Revenue Act No. 28 of 1979 to the extent of the total value of the gift;

(iii) any customs duty on any goods imported by the Fund;

(c) to provide from time to time such assistance, financial or otherwise, in services or material, as may be required or conducive to the efficient functioning of the aforesaid project and its proper administration;

(d) to promote a better appreciation and understanding of cancer in all its aspects, the study and undertaking of research in the incidence of carcinoma in Sri Lanka including its causes, diagnosis, treatment, the avoidance and prevention of cancer and the general amelioration of the conditions of persons afflicted by such disease;

(e) to receive contributions and donations of money or other property movable or immovable from members of the public, institutions or organizations, whether in Sri Lanka or abroad interested in or concerned in the achievement of all or any of the aforesaid objects and to carry out the same.

3. In order to facilitate the realisation of the objects of the trust by the Trustees and for their guidance in the administration of the trust the Trustees may invite not more than 7 persons to be the Patrons of the Trust. The First Patrons of the Trust who have accepted the invitation of the Trustees are the following:

    (1) Ven. Galaboda Gnanissara There
    (2) Ven. Wanaluwa Pagnasiri Thero
    (3) Rev. Lionel Pieris
    (4) Rev. Fr. Mervyn Fernando
    (5) Mrs Sirimavo Bandaranaike
    (6) Dr. Ranjith Atapattu
    (7) Dr. Nissanka Wijeyeratne

4. In this settlement where the context so requires or admits the term "the trust property" shall mean and include the following:

    (a) the said sum of Rupees One hundred Thousand (Rs. 100,000/-) of Lawful money aforesaid paid by the settlor to the Trustees as the nucleus for the fund and which the Trustees hereby acknowledge having received;

    (b) any further monies and other property which the settlor may from time to time hereafter at her discretion gift or transfer or set over or convey or make over or cause to be gifted or transferred or conveyed or made over to the Trustees or which the settlor may by Last Will give, devise or bequeath unto the Trustees to be held by them upon trust and with every one of the powers granted by this settlement;

    (c) any money or property which the Trustees may from time to time hereinafter shall and at his or her or their discretion pay or gift or transfer or make over or cause to be paid or gifted or transferred or made over to themselves as Trustees or which any other person or persons or body of persons may pay or gift or transfer or make over or cause to be paid or gifted or made over to the Trustees or which he or she or they may by Last Will give devise and bequeath to the Felix R. Dias Bandaranaike Memorial Trust to be held upon the Trust and subject to the powers in this settlement declared;

    (d) all monies, property and investments as may be made from time to time representing the proceeds of sale of the same or any part thereof and;

    (e) whatever income that may accrue from the aforesaid monies and investments.

5. The Trustees shall stand possessed of the Trust property upon trust at their discretion either to permit the same to remain in the form in which the same shall respectively be received or transferred or acquired by them or at any time or times at their discretion to sell and convert into money the same or any part

thereof to apply or invest that part of the Trust property which shall constitute of money and the nett proceeds of such sale and conversion for any of the purposes or in or upon any other sums of investment authorised by this settlement.

6. The Trustees shall stand possessed of the Trust property referred to in this settlement upon trust for the charitable purposes set out in clause 2 hereof until the same or any part thereof is paid or made over to the National Health Development Fund.

7. Monies required to be invested under the Trust of this settlement may be invested in the names and under the legal control of the Trustees in or upon any of the forms of investment hereinafter mentioned i.e.

   (a) in the purchase (whether for occupation income or other purpose) or land or immovable property in Sri Lanka either freehold or leasehold;

   (b) in or upon any of the public stock or funds or government securities including Treasury Bills of Sri Lanka;

   (c) upon temporary or Fixed Deposit with any Bank or Banks in Sri Lanka;

   (d) in or upon any of the forms of investment authorised by the laws of Sri Lanka for the time being for the investment of trust Funds;

   (e) in the repayment of monies borrowed for the purpose of purchasing immovable or movable property or for fulfilling the objects of the Trust.

8. In addition to such powers as may be necessary for the fulfilment of the objects of the Trust the Trustees shall have the following powers:-

   (a) to organise the collection and receipt of funds on a national basis from any persons whomsoever either in Sri Lanka or abroad for the objects of the Trust;

   (b) to receive gifts of property movable and immovable and convert the same into cash if not required for any of the objects of the Trust;

   (c) to appoint any Bank or Banks or other public institution and to delegate and to such Bank or Banks or other institution the power to collect monies funds or contributions for the fulfilment of the objects of the trust and to remit or deposit the same from time to time as directed by the Trustees;

   (d) to determine what monies are to be considered as capital and what as income;

   (e) to determine what expenses, costs and outgoings are properly payable out of the capital or income respectively;

   (f) to determine all matters of doubt and questions arising in the execution of the Trust and the exercise of the power herein contained with liberty however to obtain the advice of Counsel thereon and/or to apply to Court for the determination thereof and every such determination whether expressed or implied shall be conclusive and binding on all persons who are or hereinafter become interested under or in the Trust;

(g) to vary from time to time the powers and functions of the Trustees by a simple majority of the Trustees present other than for the benefit of the Trustees;

(h) to vary or transpose any investment into or for any other or others of any nature hereinbefore authorised and to vary or agree to a variation of the terms of any property comprised of any security;

(i) to apply for any money in the erection improvement or structural repairs of any buildings on any land forming part of the Trust property and in the repayment of monies borrowed under Clause (j) whereof for the purpose of purchasing immovable or movable property;

(j) to raise any money by negotiating or charging as a primary or secondary mortgage the Trust property or any part thereof for the purchase of as an investment for the Trust of any property whether immovable or movable including plant and machinery or any Trust property or the erection or construction of any building in the Trust property or any part thereof for any other purpose of the Trust as shall in the opinion of the Trustees be necessary and the cost of and incidental to the mortgage thereof shall be charged upon and out of the Trust income;

(k) to sell or give on lease for such period or periods for and on behalf of the Trust or purchase or take on lease for such period at the discretion of the Trustees any land buildings residential or agricultural properties and movables without any restrictions whatsoever and all such sales leases or purchases shall be at a market value;

(l) to lease any Trust property for such period or periods and to take on lease property which may be offered as an investment at the sole discretion of the Trustees;

(m) to make endorse and issue cheques promissory notes bills of exchange bills of lading and all other negotiable instruments;

(n) to sign seal execute and deliver all documents deeds conveyances transfers agreements leases receipts releases or other instruments and writings whatsoever as shall be required or as the Trustees may think necessary or desirable for giving effect and validity to any sale or other disposition lease assignment transfer or any other transactions or matter whatsoever affecting the Trust property and the Trust herein created;

(o) to open keep operate and maintain in such Bank Accounts in the name of and for the purpose of the Felix R. Dias Bandaranaike Memorial Trust as the Trustees shall and in their discretion deem fit with power to operate thereon as hereinafter contained.

9. The Settlor and Trustees hereby declare that:-

   (a) There shall not be more than 25 and not less than 7 trustees;

   (b) the Trustees hereinbefore named shall be the First Trustees and shall vacate office in the event of resignation, death or other legal incapacity or their failing to attend three consecutive meetings without reasonable cause;

   (c) the Trustees shall nominate a suitable person or persons to fill such vacancy or vacancies after obtaining the consent of such person or persons to serve as such Trustee or Trustees;

   (d) there shall be elected a person to be the Chairman of the Board of Trustees. The Chairman of the Board shall have the power to summon meetings as often as shall be deemed necessary. The Chairman shall on a written requisition of not less than five members summon a meeting. In making any such requisition for a meeting such members shall state in writing the matters to be discussed at such meeting. The quorum for any meeting shall not be less than seven. The Chairman shall preside at all meetings of the Trustees. In the absence of the Chairman the members present shall elect a Chairman pro tem for that meeting;

   (e) the decision of the majority of the Trustees shall be deemed to be the decision of all and shall be final conclusive and binding upon all persons benefiting under the Trust of this settlement and every act decision or other matter relating to or in the exercise of the Trust powers and authorities of this settlement which may be required to be done by all the Trustees may be made done or performed by the majority of them.

10. All documents in connection with the Trust of a contractual nature shall bear the signature of any two Trustees as shall be authorised by the Chairman of the Trust in writing. A certified copy of the resolution under the hand of the Chairman shall be binding and effectual against the Trustees.

11. Unless otherwise found desirable the financial year of the Trust shall commence on the First day of April in one year and expire on Thirty first day of March in the following year. Within three months of the expiry of any financial year the Treasurer shall submit an audited statement of accounts.

IN WITNESS WHEREOF the settlor and Trustees have set their respective hands hereunto and to two others of the same tenor and date aforementioned.

Settlor.

Contributors

JOHN DE SARAM – Formerly Director, Office of the Legal Counsel, United Nations, presently member of the United Nations International Law Commission. Represented Sri Lanka in 1948 Olympic Games.

HARIS HULUGALLE, LLB – One time Chairman of the Times of Ceylon and founder of the Sunday Leader.

CHRISTINE WICKRAMASINGHE – is a graduate of the Ceylon University. She has got a diploma in Ceylon History and is interested in free-lance writing.

JUSTICE A. C. ALLES – Law Officer of the Crown, Solicitor-General, Judge of the Supreme Court, and author of "The Famous Criminal Cases" and "The JVP of 1959-1989."

SAM WIJESINHA – Attorney-at-Law, Crown Counsel and later Secretary-General of Parliament. Ombudsman and now Chairman of the Human Rights Task Force.

VERNON MENDIS – Former High Commissioner for Sri Lanka in UK, Canada and Ambassador in Paris. Representative of UNESCO for the Arab Countries. He is a Peace Fellow of the US Institute of Peace, Washington DC.

DESAMANYA B. MAHADEVA – was Permanent Secretary in several ministries which Felix Dias Bandaranaike held, including Agriculture, and Public Administration. He was also a senior Official of the United Nations and was Director of the UN Asian Pacific Development Administration Centre. Mahadeva was also Chairman of the Development Finance Corporation and the National Development Bank.

H. S. WANASINGHE – a member of the former Ceylon Civil Service, served the Government as a Government Agent, Commissioner of Co-operative Development, Director of SLIDA and Director-General of Public Administration. He also served for a long period as a senior official of ESCAP. He has headed many Government Boards and Commissions, including the Administrative Reforms Committee and the Presidential Commission on Privatisation.

C. A. COOREY – was the Secretary to the Treasury and later Executive Director, Asian Development Bank, Manila. At present he is Chairman of the Development Finance Corporation of Sri Lanka.

P. H. SIRIWARDENA – Deputy Controller of Exchange and Director Planning. Secretary, Ministry of Public Administration, Local Government and Home Affairs and later Deputy Executive Secretary ESCAP.

H. L. DE SILVA, PC – One of Sri Lanka's foremost Civil Lawyers. Appeared for Mrs Bandaranaike and Felix Dias Bandaranaike before the Presidential Commission in 1980. Permanent Representative for Sri Lanka at the United Nations 1995.

ELMO DE JACOLYN SENEVIRATNE – Foreign Service Officer, High Commissioner for Sri Lanka in Australia 1995.